GESTURES O

M E R I D I A N

Crossing Aesthetics

Werner Hamacher

Editor

Stanford
University
Press

Stanford
California
2005

GESTURES OF ETHICAL LIFE

Reading Hölderlin's Question
of Measure After Heidegger

David Michael Kleinberg-Levin

Stanford University Press
Stanford, California

Printed in the United States of America on acid-free,
archival-quality paper.

Library of Congress Cataloging-in-Publication Data
Kleinberg-Levin, David Michael, date–
    Gestures of ethical life : reading Hölderlin's question of
measure after Heidegger / David Michael Kleinberg-Levin.
        p.   cm.—(Meridian)
    Includes bibliographical references and index.
    ISBN 0-8047-5087-4 (cloth : alk. paper)—
    ISBN 0-8047-5088-2 (pbk. : alk. paper)
        1. Ethical relativism.   2. Ethics—Methodology.
3. Body language.   4. Gesture.   5. Hölderlin, Friedrich,
1770–1843.   6. Heidegger, Martin, 1889–1976.   I. Title.
II. Series: Meridian (Stanford, Calif.)
BJ37.K575 2005
170—dc22   2005010902

Original Printing 2005

Last figure below indicates year of this printing:
14   13   12   11   10   09   08   07   06   05

Typeset by G & S Typesetters, Inc. in 10.9/13 Adobe
Garamond

It is by the gestures that touch and move us—
and by the gestures that we, in timely response,
are moved to make—
that we must be, will be, measured
and called for the second time.

Contents

x   *Contents*

Acknowledgments

For permission to reproduce their image of the Attic sarcophagus bas-relief showing the life of Achilles, I am grateful to the Archivio Fotografico dei Musei Capitolini. The work itself is in the Musei Capitolini, Rome.

For permission to reproduce an image of the Attic bas-relief showing Hermes, Eurydice, and Orpheus, I am grateful to the Museo Archeologico Nazionale, Naples, where the work is on display.

For permission to publish a revised version of "What Measure Now? A Survivor's Reflections on the Holocaust," I am grateful to *Philosophy Today*, which published the earlier version in vol. 45, nos. 2/4, Summer 2001.

For permission to publish a revised version of "The Invisible Hands of Capital and Labour," I am grateful to *Philosophy and Social Criticism* and to SAGE Publications, Ltd., publisher of that journal.

Is there on earth a measure?
There is none.

—Friedrich Hölderlin,
  "In lovely blueness . . . "

And if there is an indubitable good within one's reach,
one stretches out one's hand.

> —Iris Murdoch,
> *The Nice and the Good*

The disproportion between the reach of our sight and
that of our hand gives rise to phantasms and provokes
great disillusionments.

> —Vitaliano Brancati,
> "Trampolini encounters a lady on the
> threshold of the garden"

We must be human.
Yet we need eternity, because it alone grants space to our gestures;
But we also know that we dwell in a cramped finality.

> —Rainer Maria Rilke,
> *Diaries from the Early Years*

A strange measure . . . , certainly not a palpable stick or rod but,
in truth, simpler to handle than they, provided our hands do
not abruptly grasp but are guided by gestures befitting the measure.

> —Martin Heidegger,
> " . . . Poetically Man Dwells . . . "

Preface

In the truest sense, doing philosophy is—a caress [*Liebkosen*].
It bears witness to the deepest love of reflection [*Nachdenken*],
to absolute delight in wisdom.

> —Novalis [Friedrich von Hardenberg],
> "Logological Fragments"[1]

In his "Remarks on *Antigone*," Friedrich Hölderlin wrote, "Sophocles is right. . . . The infinite, like the spirit of states and of the world, cannot be grasped other than from an awkward perspective [*aus linkischen Gesichtspunkt*]."[2] Or say, as Benjamin does, that the condition of the world might be indicated most suggestively with the left hand.[3]

I, too, like to reflect on things from oblique angles. Who is to say that such angles are any less revealing, any less instructive? But I must also admit, here at the beginning, that in a certain sense I have, like Benjamin, "lost every measuring rod for this work."[4] This may simply be another way of saying that the present book, concerned as it is with the question of measure, can only, if it is to remain philosophically responsible, leave it, in the final analysis, an open question. A question to be reflected upon—or, say, handled—from as many different angles as possible. And in such a way that we are, in our lives, kept open to its questioning. "Writing," as Blanchot observed, "is opening oneself to measurelessness."[5]

The writing of this book was provoked by the question about measure that figures in a late poetic text attributed to Hölderlin—a question that brought forth from Heidegger some meditations of importance for the understanding of our time. But while reading Rilke's *Duino Elegies* in the midst of my own brooding on the question of measure, I suddenly found myself confronted by the invocation of measure in Rilke's figuration of gesture, specifically, a gesture of touching. I then realized that the question of measure could be—and indeed needs to be—thought out, or, say, worked through, in terms of our gestures. And this led me into a broader field of inquiry: what I would like to call the "physiognomies of ethical

xvii

life." Taking up for thought texts by Rilke, Hölderlin, Plato, Benjamin, Adorno, Heidegger, Merleau-Ponty, Levinas, Primo Levi, and others, this book accordingly interrogates a constellation formed around two principal ideas: measure and gesture. Through the prism of "measure," we will be concerned with values, norms, and ideals. But in their embodiment as gesture, these forms of measure can appear in different ways, different physiognomies: as meter, rhythm, restraint and excess, violence and tenderness of touch, different modes of tactility, and social practices of tact, the polite manners of social existence. Thus, in conversation with poetical and philosophical texts illuminating the ethical questions that gestural physiognomies of measure raise, the book explores how our gestures, especially those in which we use our hands, "bear" the values, norms, and ideals constitutive of measure.

One might therefore most profitably read the chapters of this book— each one devoted to a different philosopher, a different body of thought —as so many odd-shaped constructions of experience, pieces of a puzzle that have been missing, or have perhaps merely lain unnoticed. For, as Wittgenstein pointed out, "The aspects of things that are most important for us are [often] hidden because of their simplicity and familiarity. . . . And this means: we fail to be struck by what, once seen, is most striking and most powerful."[6] Such as, for example, the way our gestures are touched and moved by their sense of measure. Moved, perhaps, in compliance, perhaps in defiance, or moved as a medium of disclosiveness, manifesting the measure by reference to which they are moved, bringing that measure to light, handing it down, questioning it, resisting it, preserving it, altering it.

Instigated by Hölderlin's poetic and philosophical works, and by lines from one of Rilke's Duino Elegies that I read while in the grip of certain questions raised by Heidegger, my main text begins with an epitaph written for the handshake; a brief meditation on those lines of verse (Chapter 1); and a brief reflection on gestures and measures in Plato's dialogues on ethical education, civility, and the art of politics (Chapter 2). What follows are lengthy chapters on Hölderlin and Primo Levi, a short chapter on Marxism (Chapter 5), and further lengthy chapters on Adorno, Benjamin and Nietzsche, Heidegger, Merleau-Ponty, and Levinas. These chapters all pursue the vexing question of measure and its intricate relation to the ethical character of our gestures.

As I conceive this book, the chapters are like prisms, obliquely refracting possibilities about our gestural physiognomies and the sense of measure they embody. More specifically, the chapters in their different ways all seek to bring out the ethical dimension of the gestural "contingencies" that are involved in the forms of our social life.

Thus we will be undertaking a project of thought already in some ways suggested by Heidegger, who said, in one of his rare references to ethics: "If the name 'ethics,' in keeping with the basic meaning of the word *ethos*, should now say that ethics ponders the abode of the human being, then that thinking which thinks the truth of being as the primordial [*anfänglich*] element of the human being, as the one who exists, is in itself originary [*ursprüngliche*] ethics."[7] Whence the importance, for the design of this project, of Heidegger's phrase "gestures befitting the measure" (*Gebärde die dem Maß entsprechen*). Taking over this richly evocative phrase from Heidegger's 1951 lecture ". . . Poetically Man Dwells . . . ," I will here give thought to the intricate relation between our gestures and our ethical life. How are ethical values, norms, and ideals embodied? How do they constitute the very substance of our bodies—its sense and sensibility, its touch, its tact, its rhythms, impulses, metrics? How do they motivate and move our gestures? Reading texts by poets and philosophers, I will reflect phenomenologically on our lived experience with gesture, in order to gain—despite a certain Cartesian dualism that still, even today, holds us spellbound with its demonic mechanization of the body—some understanding of how our gestures gestate and bear the moral order, receiving it, bringing it into the spaces and times of disclosiveness, maintaining it, handing it down, expressing it, disputing it, resisting it, neglecting and forgetting it. How are the values, norms, and ideals of our lifeworld—what in this work the word "measure" will gather into its aporetic convocation—present or operative in our gestures, in the ways of our hands? And how might we think further about these gestures, these ways of the hand, if we understand them as *physiognomies* of ethical life?

Reflecting on Benjamin, Giorgio Agamben, in his "Notes on Gesture," quotes from Varro's *De Lingua Latina*, according to which the expression *res gerere* is used to mean carrying something out, in the sense of taking charge and taking it upon oneself, assuming total responsibility for it. To which Agamben wants to comment: "What characterizes gesture is that in it there is neither production nor enactment, but undertaking and supporting. In other words, gesture opens the sphere of *ethos* as the most fitting sphere of the human."[8] I cannot agree that in gestures there is neither production nor enactment; but I like his recognition, following Hannah Arendt, that undertaking and supporting are essential to the ethical substance of our gestures. Agamben then poses some questions: "But in what way is an action undertaken and supported? In what way does a *res* become *res gesta*, a simple fact become an event?" And, we must add, in what way can even the simplest gesture become, and be interpreted as, a historically disruptive event? We should keep these questions in mind as we continue our reflections in the present study.

In our engagements with philosophers whose thinking has touched on the relation between gesture and measure, we will enter a realm of textuality where, in spite of numerous deflections, a memory borne by the body of felt experience, a memory touching—however impossibly—on the preoriginary, is to be awakened through the questions and provocations that emerge from its interaction with the inheritance of ethical life in forms of individual and cultural memory.

Lamenting, in his essay "Education," our neglect of nature's gifts—especially its gift of a moral compass, Emerson wrote: "We do not teach them [our children] to aspire to be all they can. We do not give them a training as if we believed in their noble nature. We scarce educate their bodies. We do not train the eye and the hand. . . . The great object of Education should be commensurate with the object of life. It should be a moral one . . . touching his [the child's] own nature."[9] Perhaps our reflections here can help return to our cultural memory what, in "The Songs of the Icebergs," W. S. Merwin was inspired to call "hands extended in gestures out of the dreams of men."[10] The words of the poet remind us that much more is in question here, much more at stake here: nothing less than the recollection and recuperation of gestures whose character and motivation—or, say, sense and sensibility—ultimately draw on a body of experience the dimensions of which, in many ways, our prevailing cultural discourses have seldom recognized—or seldom understood in sufficient depth.

I want to think of this book as a work of memory. And, although I also think of it in relation to the present and future, this way of understanding it strikes me as absolutely crucial, for, as I will attempt to show, our ethical life depends on gestures that, in social practices and practices of the self, have remembered their immeasurable gift of freedom—a freedom, however, that the immeasurable holds open to the risks of excess, the consequences of transgression. It will be, then, by the second and third of Kant's critical questions that this work of memory finds itself most deeply stirred: "What is my moral responsibility?" and "For what may I reasonably hope?"

But, as human history has compelled us in suffering to acknowledge, no work of memory can reduce the contingencies that inevitably disturb it. My reflections here on the physiognomies of ethical life will accordingly recognize in the resistance of these contingencies another question that calls for thought. This is what it means, though, to come to terms with our present in a time indebted to its still unredeemed future—"a future," in Nietzsche's words, "alive with anticipation"—by virtue of its indebtedness to an ethically charged art of memory that can never avoid a haunting suspicion: that memory is nothing but a belated work of invention or fabulation, for the "past" that it would rescue and redeem from its mortification in historicism is a past that has not yet been present.[11]

Introduction

I. Gestures Befitting the Measure: Modernity in Crisis

> Ah, if only the right measure [*das rechte Maß*] could be encountered!
> What remains for me now . . . to hope for in calm presence [*in stiller
> Gegenwart*] from the future!
>
> —Johann Wolfgang von Goethe,
>   "Delimitation"[1]

For the philosophers and poets of antiquity, and for many of those living
in the centuries that followed, the question of measure—of right or fitting
measure—lay at the very heart of their reflections and arguments concerning the values, norms, and ideals that should inform the conduct of
ethical life. Taking the measure of the just and the good, they touched
upon the golden mean. Weighing pleasures and pains, favoring one desire
over another, giving one obligation precedence over another, they took it
for granted that the scales must somehow always balance, that avoiding
both deficiency and excess is the only way to bring what is good and just
within our reach.

In his *Satires*, Horace (65–8 B.C.E.) repeatedly recommends a certain
relation to measure in our ethical life: "There is measure in all things," he
declares. "There are fixed bounds, beyond and short of which right can
find no place."[2] His self-assurance, his absolute confidence in settled nor-
mativities, would belong to the same cultural spirit that brought forth the
carefully argued ethical works of Plato and Aristotle—except, perhaps,
that, reflecting on the corruption of his time, he felt even more strongly
than they the threat hidden within moral relativism. Goethe, however,

poet of the Age of Enlightenment, writing in the early years of modernity, could not escape the conflict of convictions that defined that revolutionary historical moment: he confronted his time, troubled by doubts but still full of hope, believing—or trying to believe—that there is, after all, a "right measure" to be known. But we of today—we can have no such confidence, no reassuring authority, no secure ground, no eternally reliable point of reference.

Is Horace's assertion a counsel of wisdom or of prudence? If the former, would the counsel not be beyond straightforward calculation—beyond measure at least in that sense? And what about the proposition *nihil est sine ratione*, the *principium rationis* for which Leibniz argued so elegantly? Commonly understood as asserting that nothing is without (a) reason, without a ground that reason can know and affirm, it might also be taken to assert that nothing is without measure. But could this mean, or grant the possibility, that nothing is without *its own* measure, a measure inherent in its own "essence"? Or would this principle always require an exterior measure, a measure absolutely independent, or transcendent—unconditioned and unconditional? Must the ground or measure in question here be an ultimate, absolutely unconditioned ground or measure—and, if so, must it not be—as Hölderlin, Novalis, and Schelling insisted against Fichte's transcendental egology—a ground or measure absolutely beyond the reach of the subject's reflective comprehension, a ground or measure impossible for any "intellectual intuition" to grasp? Would it not, then, be a ground or measure accessible, if at all, only by way of purely subjective feeling, an inwardness that could never be, however, above rational suspicion? What authority, what legitimacy, could such a ground or measure possibly provide?

Theodor Adorno took such questions to be symptomatic of a crisis condition that is definitive of the modern age. "No measure remains," he declares, "for the measure of all things."[3] It can remain now only as a cipher, reminding us to think about what we have lost thereby and what, in the course of rational disenchantment, we may have gained. Hannah Arendt argues a similar point in *The Origins of Totalitarianism*. In struggling to overcome the forces of evil, she says, we find ourselves compelled to worry that "we actually have nothing to fall back on in order to understand a phenomenon that nevertheless confronts us with its overpowering reality and breaks down all standards we know."[4] Having won our freedom from the "natural law" and the authority of tradition, we who are responsible for this modernity increasingly find ourselves compelled to question this freedom, which threatens to destroy the sense of measure on whose normativity it depends for its very possibility.

It cannot be denied that we of today must learn to live without any ultimate, absolutely unconditioned measure, universally valid and universally recognized as such. But this is a situation of our own making: a consequence of the "enlightenment" processes—the disenchantments demanded by the public use of critical reason, freedoms gained through persistent political struggles, major adjustments in the institutions of justice—processes that have irrevocably transformed the modern lifeworld. But if we experience our situation as in certain ways fraught with danger—as a "crisis" in this sense—we also experience it as a period of recognized needs and rights, realized potentials for social justice, and emerging opportunities for participatory democracy. In "Understanding and Politics," Arendt therefore finds in the reflective accomplishments of modernity an occasion for measured hope: "Even though we have lost yardsticks by which to measure, and rules under which to subsume the particular, a being whose essence is beginnings may have enough of origin within himself to understand without preconceived categories and to judge without the set of customary rules which is morality."[5]

The question of measure, broadly conceived, is more than merely "bound up" with the antinomies of a modernity that is increasingly self-reflective, self-critical, doubt-ridden, anxious, and insecure. Indeed, the question of measure—of measure as a question—constitutes the very core of this modernity, its problematic both an urgency that cannot be ignored and an opportunity that must not be missed. What is at issue can be registered in terms of a number of different two-sided conflicts in which both positions must be taken seriously and in which the two positions, while contradicting each other, also depend on each other—indeed, require each other. Each of these conflicts, therefore, presents, in effect, a double bind, a bind or antinomy that is, moreover, not simply synchronic, because the bind is always constituted in a diachrony that is stretched between the responsibility that comes from a preoriginary time and the responsibility emergent from the exigencies of the actual situation.

The double bind has many dimensions, some of which I would like to mention here:

1. the conflict between the moral claims of the universal and the moral claims of the particular, the singular that resists the violations inherent in subsumption and subordination even as it requires the protection and justice of the universal;

2. the conflict between the pragmatics of the relative and the dogmatics of the absolute;

3. the conflict between the inevitably compromised claims of the situationally conditioned and the uncompromising claims of the absolutely unconditioned;

4. the conflict between the finite and the infinite, or, say, the limited and the excessive;

5. the conflict between the subjective and the objective;

6. the conflict between the immediate pressures of the real and the transcendent imperatives of the ideal;

7. the conflict between the nature of the body, with its drives and desires, and the commandments of the moral law, which requires the suppression of drives and desires while nevertheless depending for motivation on their faithful activation; and

8. the conflict between a naturalism incapable of acknowledging that our corporeal nature is always encountered as already mediated by an immemorial history of cultural constructions and a social constructionism that refuses to acknowledge a corporeal nature to some extent independent and irreducible, capable of being stubbornly resistant to the socially organized will.

Measure itself, measure as such, is accordingly entangled in a double bind. On the one hand, measure loses its imperative moral authority, its title as moral law, unless it is recognized as of immeasurable, incalculable value. On the other hand, the immeasurable can lose its incalculable moral authority by being too tightly entangled in, and thus compromised by, the always debatable measures and calculations of social practices; but the immeasurable can also lose its moral authority by being totally disconnected from these measures and calculations.

As a poet who freely submitted his freedom of thought to the laws of rhythm and meter, Hölderlin was keenly aware of the aporetic logic, the double bind, into which we are always thrown by the nature of our freedom and the questions concerning measure that this freedom compels us to confront. What he calls the "laws of spirit" in his essay "On Religion" can only make the relations and measures constitutive of our ethical life possible: they are not, he says, these relations and measures themselves. Thus, while recognizing the worthlessness of spiritual laws that remain mere objects of desire and thought, mere abstractions detached from life, Hölderlin also perceived that, in the course of their necessary mediations in concrete life, spiritual laws are subject to tragic corruptions, sometimes reduced to nothing more than "vain etiquette" or "stale rule[s] of taste," forms of tact passing themselves off as forms of enlightenment finally liberated from their dependence on obsolete metaphysical legitimation.

Even if there are spiritual laws relating mortals to the infinite and the divine, Hölderlin insists that, because of the corruptions which never cease to threaten in the realm of life—the realm of the singular—those laws

> are insufficient to the extent that they are understood and represented only by themselves and not in life, . . . because the law, even if it were universal for civilized people [*gesittete Menschen*], could never be conceived of without a particular case unless one were to take away from it its distinction [*Eigentümlichkeit*], its intimate relation with the sphere in which it is enacted. And even then, the laws of that infinite relation [to the divine] in which man exists with his sphere are always only the conditions which make that relation possible, and not the relation itself.[6]

It is not enough for this "higher relation" to exist merely in the realm of thought. "Thus," Hölderlin continues, expressing a critique of society that is echoed in Adorno's "dialectic of tact,"

> one can speak of the duty of hospitality, of the duty to be generous to one's enemies, one can speak of what is and what is not appropriate [*schicke . . . nicht schicke*] for this or that way of life [*Lebensweise*], for this or that rank [*Stand*], for this or that generation [*Alter*] or gender [*Geschlecht*], but we have in fact partially turned those more refined and infinite relations into an arrogant morality [*arrogante Moral*], and partially into a vain etiquette [*eitle Etikette*] or a stale rule of taste [*schale Bestimmungsmaßregel*] and consider ourselves thereby more enlightened . . . than the ancients, who regarded those tender relations as religious ones, that is, as relations which one had to look at not in and of themselves but rather from [the viewpoint of] the spirit that ruled the sphere in which those relations existed.

A barely concealed anger lurks in these words—but also a recognition of changing times. Thus they are also a reflection on the passing of something, a departure that Hölderlin feels as a terrible loss. A loss that no mourning can measure.

If modernity suffers a "crisis," that is because these conflicting claims, these conflicting demands, each one simultaneously opposing and requiring the other, permit no easy, ready-made resolutions, and because, however we resolve these demands, we know that we can no longer lay claim to any ultimately reassuring grounds, putting an end to uncertainties, to questions and anxieties. In *The Philosophical Discourse of Modernity*, Jürgen Habermas gives this interpretation a lucid summary formulation— and draws from it a lesson that faintly echoes Nietzsche: "Modernity can and will no longer borrow the criteria by which it takes its orientation from the models supplied by another epoch; it has to create its normativity out of itself." [7] Thus, with regard to the claims of values, norms, and ideals, the situation of modernity may accordingly be defined, as Arendt was perhaps the first to argue, as requiring of individuals and social collectivities what Kant called "reflective judgment": a form of judgment in which the particular is given and the appropriate universal, the fitting law or measure, needs to be found.

For the individual, this means the development of what Aristotle called *phronesis*: in the absence of any formula to prescribe the bearing of universal principles on particular situations, *phronesis* is the capacity to determine the measure that most befits what the concrete situations in which one finds oneself require and to make, accordingly, the most appropriate action-oriented judgments. For communities, this necessitates free and open dialogue, gathering all the concerned parties into a conversation grounded in the hope that, through this public use of reason, they might find appropriate principles or measures to which they could all consent.

With penetrating foresight, Friedrich Nietzsche, adopting a word introduced by Friedrich Jacobi, announced the experience of "nihilism," proclaiming the devaluation of all values. The traditional sources of moral authority, Nietzsche observed, have dried up. Abandoned by God, no longer bound by the traditional forms of social relation, we must now rely on our own resources of spirit. He welcomed this turn of events but also, despite himself, feared it. We are no longer reassured by the old consolations, no longer content with the metaphysics that once supported us, encouraging us with its teleologies, its theodicies, its grand narratives of progress and redemption. But we also cannot rest in unyielding skepticism, with its threat of excessive relativism.

In passages of the *Nicomachean Ethics* (for example, 5.10.1137b10–20), Aristotle clearly recognized that the law, if it is to be just, must declare itself in abstract and universal terms, yet it can never address particular circumstances without the mediation of a supplementary judgment affirming the existence of a "fit" between law and situation. But for him, neither the possibility of such a "fit" nor confidence in that judgment were in any way problematic. Measure becomes an issue for modernity, then, because what is fitting, what is required of us, can no longer be taken for granted. We have no recourse to the hidden hand of Providence inscribing its indisputable wisdom in the Book of Nature or in the books of History. No legible measure, no tangible measure is to be found in the very nature of things. Nor can any calculus, any algorithm, help us determine what is good or right by pleasure and pain, happiness and unhappiness, origins and finalities. Whatever measures we affirm are always understood as open to critical questioning, continuing interpretation, reasonable controversy. Perhaps modernity could accordingly be defined as the staging of a permanent crisis—of authority, legitimacy, rationality, judgment. But how, then, could a thinking compelled to relinquish its moorings in traditional forms of life nevertheless preserve and transform them?

In the aporetic experience of freedom that defines modernity, the problematic logic of measure shows itself with inescapable determination. Individuality requires a certain freedom from conditions, from subsumption under the law of the universal; yet this law in its universality is the guarantor of freedom, the condition necessary for its very possibility. The dialectic of freedom—freedom understood as the capacity to give oneself one's own laws—must simultaneously posit a measure and exceed it: for the very act of positing is itself, as such, always already excessive. But this excess is not necessarily total disorder, anarchy, chaos; for precisely in our moment of exceeding, we can take the measure with us, giving it new conditions, new interpretive life. Such is the nature of freedom! Freedom is the gift of measure, in both the subjective and objective senses of the genitive. On the one hand, freedom is a gift given by measure: freedom always derives from a given measure, a measure that freedom in the very act of applying it always exceeds. On the other hand, measure is a gift that freedom gives: freedom is the only way for the measure to be enacted and consequently realized. Human freedom by nature always harbors a secret longing to transgress all measure; but at the same time, this temptation is restrained by the limits and conditions that only transgressiveness can disclose. "There is nothing," writes Maurice Merleau-Ponty, "that can set limits to freedom, except those limits that freedom itself has set in the form of its various initiatives. . . . It is freedom which brings into being the obstacles to freedom, so that the latter can be set over against it as its bounds." [8]

As Jacques Derrida argues in *Voyous: Deux essais sur la raison* (Rogues: Two essays on reason), a recently published work, freedom and equality simultaneously require one another and negate one another. [9] Freedom by nature resists reduction to measure, tolerates no imposed limitation, while equality of course insists on an order of measure and calculation. And yet, in spite of this ineliminable opposition, each simultaneously requires the other: where there is no equality, there can be no freedom; where there is no freedom, there can be no equality. So the incalculable requires "anchorage" in calculation and the calculable must be supported, backed up, by the incalculable. In Derrida's (translated) words, "equality tends to introduce measure and calculation (therefore conditionality) there where freedom [*liberté*] is as a matter of essence unconditional, indivisible, heterogeneous in relation to calculation and measure." But, as an intrinsic dimension of freedom, equality can no longer be straightforwardly calculable: "It is an equality as such [*en elle-même*] incalculable and incommensurable; it is the unconditional condition of freedom [*liberté*]." Perhaps Derrida had Maurice Blanchot in mind here. Addressing that same question in *The Infinite Conversation*, Blanchot had argued that "there is neither measure nor limit" in human relations—nothing to prevent human beings from entering the realm of the monstrous. "But," he added, "it may be that I cannot give the measure of equality its true sense unless I maintain the absence of common measure [*commune mesure*] that is my relation to the other." [10]

Of course, there is also, correlatively, an aporetic experience of Reason—of Reason as measure. For the value of Reason lies not only in its degree of abstractness, its unconditionality, its independence or transcendence of conditions, but also in its intricate pragmatic entanglements in the concrete conditions of life. Thus, once Reason, as measure, is abstracted from the actual conditions of life and, for the sake of a sovereign power of judgment, insists on maintaining its purity, its innocence, it loses the authority to which it aspires. Its power to grasp what is at stake in the reality we are living is a power that requires entanglements in the world that constantly compromise that same power. The "rational meaning" of our experience, situated as we are in the lifeworld, is therefore perpetually threatened, repeatedly unsettled, frequently undecidable. Whence the modern crisis of confidence, the impossibility of a self-assurance that, once upon a time, could be taken for granted. The auratic experience of measure, of Reason, is granted no more.

When ethical life must simultaneously submit to the unconditional demands of the law of Reason and yet preserve its freedom from compulsion, only irony can save it from the two extremes of nihilism and dogmatism. Similarly, when Reason is thoroughly instrumentalized, posited in a firm calculus, so reifying it that it can serve as measure only for what is no longer a living freedom, irony alone can rescue it from such mortifying gravity. It is precisely in recognizing the limits of Reason, its vulnerabilities—even its exposure to the death that is part of life—that we maintain it as life-affirming measure.

In his *Phenomenology of Spirit*, Hegel tells us, "the life of Spirit is not the life that shrinks from death and keeps itself untouched by devastation, but rather the life that endures it and maintains itself within death." [11] And if, as Hegel says, "by the little that now satisfies spirit, we can measure the extent of its loss," [12] then perhaps by the loss that spirit endures with highest awareness, we have just as much to gain, just as much to learn. But only if we affirm that spirit in its power of determinate negation, questioning the prevailing measure, resisting it, and even, at times, subjecting it to the most extreme call to arms. For, as Adorno says, "only what does not fit into this world is true" [13]—or is good and just, for that matter. The true trial of a law—its only true measure—lies in the measure of resistance and transgression that it safeguards within itself.

Blanchot is right: "We untiringly construct the world in order that the hidden dissolution, the universal corruption that governs what 'is,' should be forgotten in favor of a clear and defined coherence of notions and objects, relations and forms—the work of tranquil man." [14] However, in an important sense, philosophical thought is not merely destructive, not merely negative. For its negative moment, revealing limitations, can bring into the lifeworld an irrepressible sense of the immeasurable. In this way, while "doing violence to the object of its syntheses, our thinking," as Adorno points out, "heeds a potential that waits in the object, unconsciously obeying the idea of making amends to the fragments for the damage done to them." [15]

But what will be the destiny of this "potential" as long as our "think-ing" is under the spell of a paradigm that worships calculation? In one of Heidegger's numerous commentaries on Aristotle's assertion that the hu-man being is the animal endowed with *logos*, or as Heidegger puts it, "the living being endowed with reason" (*das mit Vernunft begabte Lebewesen*), Heidegger interprets this endowment in terms of measure and unfolds some of the implications suggested by this interpretation.[16] If philosophy has from its inception been determined by the belief that we differ from the other animals in having a measure (*ratio*) to live by, and in having thereby a *maßgebende* capacity, an ability to give or manifest measure, then, for Heidegger, the urgent question for our time concerns the fateful reduction of this measure to calculation, *Rechenschaft*, a measure totally determined by an economy in which technologization and commodifi-cation must prevail.

Because of the triumphs of science and technology, objectivity has be-come the prevailing paradigm, the dominant measure, of knowledge, truth, and reality. But this has brought about a certain atrophy, delegiti-mation, and derealization of experience. And the phenomenology that Husserl introduced as a method to rescue experience from this destruction has, in the final analysis, betrayed it, rendering it so subjective and so tran-scendental as to amount to nothing more than a philosopher's dream. The word "experience" derives from the Latin *experiri*, meaning "to undergo." And the radical, here, is *periri*, as in *periculum*, referring to peril, or dan-ger. The corresponding word in German is *Erfahrung*, which comes from the old High German *fara*, meaning "dangerous journey." To experience thus involves a willingness to experiment, to venture, to risk, to welcome uncertainty, exposing oneself to the unknown in a way that lets something new emerge from its immeasurable reserve. Ultimately, to experience is to measure oneself against the immeasurable.

However, as Hölderlin astutely remarks, "one can *fall* upward just as easily as downward."[17] Thus, although he wholeheartedly asserts that every life worth living depends on a certain degree of "enthusiasm," of *Begeisterung*,—for this is, after all, the very spirit of freedom—he also in-sists that one must use wisely "the measure of enthusiasm which is given to every individual," restraining or modulating this high spirit with fitting "tenderness, sincerity, and clarity" (*Zartheit, Richtigkeit und Klarheit*). When the spirit of freedom soars too high, its enthusiasm will bring it down in a tragic fall; when it plunges into the abyss, its enthusiasm can lift it to the heights of dangerous power. Freedom requires acceptance of our measured, earthbound conditions, requires a "temperate presence of mind," a spirit *im nüchternen Besinnung,* so that the individual "surpasses himself [*sich selber übertrifft*] only to the degree and in the way that the situation requires [*in dem Maße und in der Art, wie es die Sache erfordert*]." [18] This requires, however, a consciousness of "higher destiny" that can be retrieved (*wiederholt*) neither by mere thought (*bloße Gedanken*) nor by the normal powers of memory (*Gedächtnis*), because thought, however noble, cannot produce concepts up to the task, while those powers of memory cannot retrieve a relation that does not originate in the ordinary order of time. For Hölderlin, freedom must, with wisely measured gestures— gestures befitting the measure—take perilous risks, reaching for the immeasurable.

Tied to principles of conceptual intelligibility, to measures that fit the concepts that intelligibility can readily produce, thought may be tempted to avoid such risks—risks that, in the realm of thought, appear in the guise of inevitable aporias. But in "Slow Obsequies," one of the chapters in his book *Friendship,* Blanchot urges those committed to freedom of thought to risk the fall against which Hölderlin warns us:

> It is clear that, when philosophy lays claim to its end, it is to a measureless end [*une fin démesurée*] that it lays claim and in order to reintroduce, through the measurelessness of the end, the exigency in it for a new measure beyond all measure. In this way, measurelessness [*la démesure*] would be the last word of a philosophy ready to be silent but still continuing to say to us: Measurelessness is the measure of all philosophical wisdom. [19]

Because of its relation to this imperative, the present book inevitably becomes a work of memory—of remembrance and recollection—but no less an attempt to think toward another future that remains unrecognizable, beyond the temporal order within which suffering can neither have nor imagine its end.

II. Physiognomies of Ethical Life

> The spirit is to intuit itself within the animated matter. And yet, the spirit itself is distinguished only by its inwardness. . . . Hence, at any given moment this body must be the faithful copy of its inner condition. . . . The body must imitate and portray every inward movement. Hence, man is the only being to have a physiognomy. . . .

If the body is the faithful copy of the soul, then both will coincide in one intuition.

> —F. W. J. von Schelling, "Treatise Explicatory of the
> Idealism in the Science of Knowledge"[20]

A new view of physiognomy: as a prosody [*Metrik*] of the Inner, and of its relations.

> —Novalis, "The Encyclopedia"[21]

The more spiritual [*geistvoller*] and cultured [*gebildeter*] a man is, the more personal [*persönlicher*] are his limbs—for instance, his hands, his eyes, his fingers. . . . The relevance [*Anwendung*] of antiquity, of physiognomy, of the singular realization [*sonderbare Meinung*]: that each member must give its specific contribution to the invention [*Zeugung*] of a man.

> —Novalis, "The Encyclopedia"[22]

Meaning is a physiognomy.

> —Ludwig Wittgenstein, *Philosophical Investigations*[23]

Cultural criticism must become social physiognomy.

> —Theodor W. Adorno, "Cultural Criticism and Society"[24]

Every form of the reality principle must be embodied in a system of social institutions and relations, laws and values which transmit and enforce the required modification of the instincts. This "body" of the reality principle is different at different stages of civilization.

> —Herbert Marcuse, *Eros and Civilization*[25]

Urban spaces take form largely from the ways people experience their own bodies. For people in a multi-cultural city to care about one another, I believe we have to change the understanding we have of our own bodies. . . . The modern master image of the individual, detached body has hardly ended in triumph. It has ended in passivity [i.e., docile bodies acquiescent in domination].

> —Richard Sennett, *Flesh and Stone:*
> *The Body and the City in Western Civilization*[26]

For many years, I have been occupied with a philosophical project of research and thought that I eventually named "The Emerging Body of Understanding." At the heart of this project has been the attempt to recognize in Martin Heidegger's formulation of the "preontological" the first embodied stirrings of an originary ethics, and, correspondingly, to bring out in his formulation of the "ontological" the formal indication of an ethics, an *ethos*, a way of dwelling, radically at odds with the ethics promoted by the spirit of modernity. What prevails in modernity is an ethics of self-centered individualism that puts freedom ahead of responsibility, that values the logic or rationality of essentialized identity over that of plurality and difference, that abandons its inheritance of an originary past to live in the immediacy of the present, that is perpetually distracted by a phantasmagoric future of the ever-new (which is ever-the-same), and that reduces the being of all beings—trees, animals, and even human beings—to the commodified condition of mere objects, things always either ready-to-hand or fixed in a state of permanent presence.

But my project could not be confined within the limitations of Heidegger's own discourse. Deeply indebted to Maurice Merleau-Ponty, for example, I have also been attempting to think the relation between our ethical values, norms, and ideals and the nature of our embodiment—our "human nature." It has, however, gradually become clear to me that this endeavor requires breaking away from the metaphysical picture of the body as substance that has dominated Western thought at least since Plato.[27] Whence my preference for the term "embodiment," with which I displace wherever possible the more misleading term "body," which perpetuates that false picture. This terminological substitution enables us to concentrate on the body as a unified and unifying system of processes and capacities,[28] the medium for the first stage of the function that Kant called "the transcendental unity of apperception." And this, in turn, calls attention to the potential for developing those capacities—what Stanley Cavell might refer to as the question of "perfectionism." Needless to say, Merleau-Ponty would become a major source of inspiration for this undertaking. But also, of course, Aristotle, Hegel, and perhaps even more so, Hegel's friend Schelling, whose philosophical reflections on nature were of considerable importance for Merleau-Ponty's phenomenology, especially regarding developmental phases and dimensions in our embodiment.[29] Schelling's poetic reflections invoke the emergence, from the depths of nature, of a spirit that, even in its earliest phases of incarnation, summons the sensuous nature of the body to its divinely assigned historical task.[30]

In writings along the way to the present work, I have explored this question of the ethical-moral development, or *Bildung*, of our capacities as embodied beings, specifying the phases and dimensions of this development in terms of our vision, our hearing, our entrance into language, and our gestures. The more I reflect on this question in the context of Heidegger's

thought, the more I am convinced that a certain "meta-ethical" normativity is implicit, first of all, in his very conception of phenomenology as
letting the phenomenon show itself from out of itself; secondly, in his
reading of the history of philosophy as a history of the forgetfulness to
which the question of being has been abandoned; and thirdly, in his critique of modernity as the age of nihilism, a will to power ruling over being. But should we not then try to understand how this normativity appropriates and summons our life—the life, for example, of our gestures?
In this book, I want to pursue Heidegger's occasional remarks—hints I
find intriguing—in regard to the question of an "originary ethics." By
"originary ethics," Heidegger seems to mean an ontological understanding of human being concerned with how, in our way of building, dwelling,
and thinking, we might correspond to the claim on our comportment that
comes from the dimensions within which the concealment and unconcealment of being takes place. Taking *Da-sein* ("being-exposed") as the appropriate measure, "originary ethics" thus casts our ethical life into an
openness that makes human freedom responsible for its life in response to
a world that, as Schelling had argued, is without ultimate grounding in
reason, opening onto the immeasurable, the abyssal dimension of being.

The values, norms, and ideals constitutive of ethical life can exist only
if somehow affirmed, somehow maintained, received, and handed down
—for instance, by deeds of example, by gestures that, in accordance with
their character, their disposition, in one way or another carry them forward, inevitably submitting them to the critical potential inherent in
every situation.

If, as Wittgenstein said, "the human body [*Körper*] is the best picture of
the human soul," then should we not suppose that the body is the first
medium for the realization of measure?[31] No practical measure is without
its gesture—and no gesture without its operative measure, be it conscious
or unconscious, willed or unwilled, benevolent or not. There are rhythms
and measures imposed by the pulse; measures operative in the intensities
of the corporeal tensions that eventuate in intentionalities of desire and
disposition; measures singing in the rhythms of easy movement; measures
prescribing for the realm of the tactile the character of touching and of all
other pragmatic engagements of the hands; measures determining the
spacing and timing of contact; measures controlling the social displace-
ments of contact in conventions of tact, the essence of polite manners and
civility; and measures at work in the discipline of writing. Not even the

most ordinary, most quotidian of gestures—for example, bringing a cup of tea to one's lips and setting it down again on the saucer—can take place without the functioning of measure.

In "Fate and Character," Walter Benjamin justly ridicules what he calls "modern physiognomics," remarking its connection with the old mantic art:

> Physiognomic signs, like other mantic symbols, served the ancients primarily as means for exploring fate, in accordance with the dominance of the pagan belief in guilt. The study of physiognomy, like comedy, was a manifestation of the new age of genius. Modern physiognomics reveals its connection with the old art of divination in the unfruitful, morally evaluative accent of its concepts, as well as in the striving for analytic complexity. In precisely this respect the ancient and mediaeval physiognomists saw things more clearly, recognizing that character can be grasped only through a small number of morally indifferent basic concepts, such as those that the doctrine of temperaments tried to identify.[32]

I would certainly not want the "physiognomies" of ethical life that this book examines to be burdened with such doctrines of fate and character. But Benjamin himself turned to the ancient art of "reading" physiognomies, showing a more responsible way to practice it. The etymological history of the term takes us back to antiquity. "Physio-" derives from the Greek words φύσις, meaning "living nature," and φύω, meaning a constellation of things regarding this nature, including "to grow," "to gestate," "to bear," "to bring forth," "to bring out," "to give rise to," "to arise," "to show itself," "to let emerge," and "to emerge." And "-gnomies" comes from another etymological gathering of Greek words: γιγνώσκω, meaning to "perceive" or "know" with the wisdom that comes from practicing the art of hermeneutics; γνώμη, meaning a "law of nature" or a "deep truth"; and γνωμονικός, meaning "fit to give insightful judgment." It is also related to γνωμολογία, naming a collection of rules or maxims, and to γνωμοσύνη, invoking a prudence in judgment that takes its bearings from the insight of practical maxims. Philo Judaeus of Alexandria (30 B.C.–45 A.D.) introduced the term φυσιογνωμονεῖν to describe his practice of dream interpretation, a hermeneutic art. As this brief etymological history shows, the term "physiognomy" can refer equally to an art or practice and to the object or product of that art or practice. More specifically, it was a *hermeneutic* art or practice, using what our embodiment reveals to formulate inferences about an "inward" disposition of the mind or soul. In the context of an inquiry into the question of an "originary ethics," what I am calling "physiognomy" will be concerned with the modes of disclosiveness (*legein*) through which our gestural embodiment could express and exercise a proto-moral disposition that derives its orientation from a preontological attunement by and to our relation to being.

Despite his ridicule of physiognomy as a charlatan art, however, Benjamin gathered this constellation of meanings into a usage he introduced into his critical praxis, asserting that even a sentence has a "face," a "physiognomy," and that what is required of criticism is therefore a "physiognomic reading." The "highest traditional physiognomy" must be a practice that can "read what was never written."[33]

Merleau-Ponty also, I would claim, practiced such a reading—but he did so in the context of a material phenomenology of embodiment. In his essay "Indirect Language and the Voices of Silence," Merleau-Ponty argued that "the body's gesture towards the world introduces it into an order of relations about which pure physiology and biology do not have the slightest inkling." Taking this point further, he calls our attention to the fact that "despite the diversity of its parts, which makes it fragile and vulnerable, the body is capable of gathering itself into a gesture which for a time dominates their dispersion [in the unity of a certain style]."[34] In his earlier work, *Phenomenology of Perception*, Merleau-Ponty had already introduced the word "physiognomy" to refer to this organically coherent structure of meaning experienced in its sensuous integrity and syncretic richness. Describing the world of a soldier who suffers from major injury to the brain, he writes: "The world in its entirety no longer suggests any meaning to him, and conversely, the meanings which occur to him are not embodied any longer in the given world. We shall say, in a word, that the world no longer has any *physiognomy* for him." The interpretation continues:

> The translation of perception into movement is effected [in this patient] by way of the express meanings of language, whereas the normal subject penetrates into the object of perception, assimilating its structure into his substance, and through this body the object *directly regulates* his movements. This subject-object dialogue, this drawing together, by the subject, of the meaning diffused through the object, and, by the object, of the subject's intentions—a process which is physiognomic perception—arranges around the subject a world which speaks to him of himself, and gives his own thoughts their place in the world.[35]

These two passages suggest, moreover, that measure or law is always at work, always tangibly functioning, in the physiognomies that emerge through the "subject-object dialogue." From the very beginning, our gestures anticipate the order of ethical life, since physiognomic regulation, measure, *nomos*, a "melodic arc" of intentionality, already operates in their autonomy, their freedom of movement, and, as Merleau-Ponty says about painters, a "norm" or "law" is always secretly at work in every gestural style.[36] Aristotle's notion of an ἀρχὴ τῆς κινήσεως articulates the deepest law of freedom at work within our gestures: a law that could, if retrieved by phenomenologically thoughtful gestures, become what Merleau-Ponty has felicitously termed—perhaps with Aristotle's "arche-principle" of movement in mind—a "melodic arc." Thus, in the context of our inquiry, "physiognomy" refers to the gestural configurations and dispositions through which the character and style of our relation to the ethical—whatever that relation may be—is made manifest.

Perhaps Merleau-Ponty's most directly pertinent invocation of physiognomy is to be found in "The Child's Relations with Others," where he observes, "I live in the physiognomic expressions [*expressions de physiognomie*] of the other as I feel him living in mine."[37] Here the philosopher indicates that such physiognomies can play a crucial role in the formation of ethical experience, constituting a moment of self-recognition for which the physiognomic presence of the other is absolutely essential.

In the present work, "physiognomies," fittingly disenchanted, will name the investment in gestural shapes that the measures constitutive of ethical life can assume. It will also name that gestural embodiment, that "nature" of the ethical, which, as the responsibility of inward spirit, is in pre-originary touch with a sense of the immeasurable—and would bring this sense forth, to bear on the question of measure that, through numerous mediations, always confronts the judgments and actions in which our gestures take part. I will accordingly evoke an embodiment of gestures that brings a physiognomic sense of the immeasurable to bear on this ethical question of measure, to show how that sense can enable us in various ways to get our ethical bearings in the many situations into which we may be cast. Might that make it possible to detect, in the gestures thus bearing the values, norms, and ideals of our ethical life, hints of what Nietzsche, in *Daybreak*, characterized as "virtues of the future"?[38]

According to Richard Sennett, St. Francis of Assisi "taught that in our bodies we contain the ethical yardstick for judging rules, rights and privi-

xl   Introduction

leges in society."[39] From this Sennett concludes, "the more these cause pain, the more our bodies know they are unjust." I cannot say whether he is right about St. Francis, but I am convinced that the substance of these thoughts harbors a critical truth. As a reading of Aristotle will remind us, there is already, in the human capacity for self-initiated movement, the enduring beginning of *autonomy*, an experience of freedom in its self-generated normativity or lawfulness.

Before we leave these questions, we must reckon with what Benjamin argues in his *Trauerspiel* study: "The allegorical physiognomy of nature's history, brought to the stage by tragedy, is really present as a ruin."[40] Taking this observation to be, greatly to our misfortune, no less true of the ethical or allegorical character of the physiognomies enacted in the gestures of our own time, I suggest that what needs to occur, as the authors of *The Dialectic of Enlightenment* recognized, is "the remembrance of nature in the subject."[41] Such a remembrance, escaping both rationalism and empiricism, could attempt to retrieve from the "ruins" of today's corporeal nature what might be called the gift of a "moral compass"—an inquiry that I assume to be worthwhile, even if that compass proves to be nothing more than the most rudimentary and precarious sense of measure.

Can morality be entrusted to nature—to the nature of the body? As Hölderlin points out, it seems that the "law of freedom," the "moral law," "rules without regard for the help of nature."[42] Although he acknowledges, in a crucial if qualified concession, that "Nature may or may not be conducive to its [the moral law's] enactment," he also observes that this law "presupposes a resistance of nature, for otherwise it would not rule." So it should come as no surprise, he thinks, that "the first time that the law of freedom discloses itself to us, it appears as punishing." Moreover, "the legality that could be engendered by mere nature would be a very uncertain thing, changeable according to time and circumstance." "Thus," he concludes, "morality can never be entrusted to nature."

Our nature does resist morality—and this is not entirely a bad thing. But even if the moral law in its *first appearance* assumes the form of a guilty, self-punishing conscience, arguably this does not preclude the possibility that a rudimentary moral sense already operates in the nature of the body, a sense with which moral education could work in harmony, eliciting a capacity for feeling that could truly come to constitute the body's realization of the moral law as its "second nature." As creatures conscious of the moral law, yet by nature embodied, how can we deny that morality is somehow entrusted to nature? Where could this law come from, if not from a rudimentary moral order already attuning our corporeal nature? Assuming the necessity of moral education, how can we deny that the moral law depends on the informed nature of sense and sensibility? Ethical life is manifest nowhere else but in its distinctive physiognomies.

Should we not attempt, breaking out of prevailing preconceptions, to learn whether our gestures carry a felt sense of measure, a sense that is situationally affected and capable of setting in motion the gestures constitutive of ethical life? How, for example, are we to understand the confessional gestures of a guilty conscience? Do they not suggest the presence of a partially repressed capacity to feel, and in this sense to recognize, the wrongness of cruelty? Do they not suggest a moral predisposition, a moral sense and sensibility that the body would always in some way bear? The studies in this book argue for the presence of such an endowment, carried by the body, inscribed in its very flesh. But they also argue that we can have no guarantee that its guidance will be heeded. Even if we feel the presence of such a moral compass, such an inwrought sense of measure, that knowledge cannot reassure or console us. For what that moral sense indicates may always be ignored or even defied. And the compass itself—the body's situational attunement, its felt sense of the appropriate measure—can be damaged in many ways. Moreover, even if we grant a compass intact and in good condition, there still is no true north, no absolutely independent point of reference, no metaphysically unconditioned measure, about which we can be certain. The threat of undecidability can never, it seems, be entirely excluded.

Further, as Nietzsche understood, even if these matters could be settled, other urgent questions for our time would remain. How is our moral compass to be brought into consciousness—and into the forms of ethical life? Is it, as a "first nature," to be educed by social processes that would perpetuate a history of repression and reification? If so, that would invariably keep the sense of measure motivating our gestures inscribed within the prevailing degenerate conventions—a mere semblance of the enlightened ethical moment presumed to emerge in "second nature." Could our gestures break the spell of a violent history? Could the *res gestae* of the future interrupt the *historia rerum gestarum*, a narrative woven of terrible cruelty and suffering?[43] The irrefutable truth of history is that whatever inwrought sense of measure we might be endowed with can never be enough for ethical life.

Pertinent here is a deeply thoughtful comment by Italo Calvino, which I would like to quote at some length. "My hands grew up," he writes, "in an epoch of transition, habituated to wait for the realization by other hands of the gestures [*gesti*] indispensable to survival." The thought continues, culminating in a social critique:

> That this state of affairs could not be permanent I always knew—at least in theory. In theory, my hands await nothing other than reacquiring their [ancestral] ability to accomplish all the manual tasks of human beings. Whereas, in archaic times, a hostile nature surrounded human beings armed with only their hands, today we are surrounded by a mechanical world, certainly more at ease in the manipulation of brute nature: a world in which, henceforth, the hands of each one of us will have to return to doing things for ourselves, without being able to ask of the hands of others the mechanical work on which the life of every day depends.[44]

Our gestures are literally the allegorical metaphors of social existence. They are its medium of continuation and innovation—as in transcription and translation—but they are also its medium of transgression and transcendence. In other words, words borrowed without permission from Nietzsche, the sublime truth about our gestures is that they are, in effect, a mobile constellation of metaphors.[45] Entrusted to their physiognomies, to their potential for communicative disclosiveness, the character of our ethical life runs its course.

But what ethical course may we expect? What hope for a community more hospitable to the realization of our humanity lies already in our hands? In the final analysis, even our finest gestures—or rather, perhaps, especially these—are always, like works of art, persistently enigmatic, the physiognomies of an "objective spirit" that, as Adorno observes, "is never transparent to itself in the moment in which it appears."[46] And never is this absence of measure more tangible than in the act of writing. But, when one follows the question of measure obliquely, through some of its more marginalized permutations in the realm of modern thought, this question draws one, as we shall see, into numerous unsuspected abysses of intangibility, there where the measure supposed to prevail is irremediably broken, interrupted by hesitations and uncertainties, even, at times, impossible to determine.

Because of the decisive role of writing in every victory for the cause of freedom, justice, and peace, I would like, before concluding, to consider the writing of the hand. In this gesture, a gesture in the very nature of which I always become myself-for-the-other, I am irrevocably dispossessed. But without self-possession, I am also, in a certain sense, without identity. I am exposed to the claims of the others. Committing my hand, moved as it is by an experience of measure, to the task of writing, I put myself in their hands. The gesture of writing is always, in this sense, already burdened with a moral commitment, a responsibility to others. Writing, therefore, is an act that belongs not only to a future of the imagination but to remembrance and recollection: it is a discipline secretly measured by the reach of its concern for the social redemption of gestures—the intangible potential that still awaits recognition in the physiognomies of ethical life and ethical culture. As Spinoza said long ago, but without any sense of what he could be taken to mean: "No-one has yet determined what [a] Body can do." [47] According to Louis Althusser, Spinoza believed

> that one can liberate and recompose one's own body, formerly fragmented and dead in the service of an imaginary and, therefore, slavelike subjectivity, and take from this the means to think liberation freely and strongly, therefore, to think properly with one's own body, in one's own body, by one's own body— or better: that to live within the thought of the conatus of one's own body— was quite simply to think within the freedom and the power of thought. [48]

III. Hope in Our Hands: Beyond Ontologies of Violence

> When will humanity begin to remember itself [*sich selbst zu besinnen*]?
> —Novalis, "Pollen" [49]

> Since ancient times, it has been a custom to have the sacred fire of philosophy preserved by pure hands.
> —F. W. J. von Schelling, "Treatise Explicatory of the Idealism in the Science of Knowledge," [50]

Continuing a poetry of remembrance, Paul Celan invokes, in "Chymisch," the "charred hands," hands "cooked like gold," hands that, if only by their absence, can still bear witness to the genocidal exterminations that took place during the Shoah. [51] But despite the holocausts, too many even by one, despite our abandonment by and of the sacred, a spirit of hope persists. This spirit, however, does not come without its dialectical negation, for only by nurturing this hope might we begin to grasp the immeasurable suffering that has left our civilization with so many haunting reminders of the brutality of which we mortals remain capable. In "Atemkristall," another poetic testament, its title inevitably recalling the holocaustic terror of Kristallnacht, Celan puts hope in our hands—but perhaps only its most minimal measure:

> Paths in the shadow-rock
> Of your hand. . . .
> Out of the four-finger-furrow
> I grub for myself the
> Petrified blessing.[52]

No blessing from the hand of God, from the hand that, as it is said, created this world, is to be found in the rock. Yet a measure of hope survives, its blessing revealed, pulsing still, through the dreadful rhythms of our grubbing. But are there—could there be—any gestures befitting such a measure? Perhaps a time will come when this hope in our hands can enable our gestures to bring forth an ontology beyond the reach of violence.

It would be comforting to believe that the modern world is after all, in Schlegel's memorable phrasing, "a chaos that awaits but the touch of love to unfold into a harmonious world."[53] But our world is also a chaos that with intensifying despair demands social justice. And there can be no redemption by the gestures of love without the peace that comes from justice. Can empty hands be reconciled?

Epitaph for the Handshake

We are at one with a man's personality in his handshake.

> —G. W. F. Hegel, *Aesthetics: Lectures on Fine Art*[1]

My body . . . discovers in that other body a miraculous prolongation of my own intentions, a familiar way of dealing with the world. Henceforth, as the parts of my body together comprise a system, so my body and the other person's are one whole, two sides of one and the same phenomenon, and the anonymous existence of which my body is the ever-renewed trace henceforth inhabits both bodies simultaneously.

> —Maurice Merleau-Ponty, *Phenomenology of Perception*[2]

By the end of the nineteenth century, the gestures of the Western bourgeoisie were irretrievably lost. . . . In the cinema, a society that has lost its gestures seeks to reappropriate what it has lost while simultaneously recording that loss.

> —Giorgio Agamben, "Notes on Gesture"[3]

Undamaged experience is produced only in memory, far beyond immediacy. . . . Total remembrance is the response to total transience, and hope lies only in the strength to become aware of transience and preserve it in writing.

> —Theodor W. Adorno, "On Proust"[4]

In 1979, the two legislative bodies of the State of Connecticut passed into law, without much public attention, a historically decisive initiative. They called it the Home Improvement Act. This act requires all "major" home improvements involving work in return for wages to be preceded by a legally valid contract in some written form. The argument behind the act is compelling: with so many "gentlemen's agreements" broken, so many misunderstandings and abuses, so many cases for litigation, it is entirely reasonable, indeed imperative, that the state insist on the written contract. Its time has come. But the significance of this historical moment should not be missed: it registers the degenerating condition of the body politic— and the passing away of old customs, old traditions, bonds forged out of mutual trust and respect, bonds strengthening this trust and respect. For generations of industrious Connecticut Yankees, the neighborly handshake sealed all verbal agreements, and its traditional interweaving of hands was always thought sufficient to bind all those who took part in the conversation that preceded it. Already too much dishonored, this once beautiful handshake, acknowledging a certain equality, is now still further betrayed, this time by a legislative act that consigns it to the ruins of the past. Felt contact can no longer bind. The time of the verbal contract and its concluding gestures has passed forever. A coldly formal contract has now replaced the warmth of personal contact. Only a few old-timers skilled in the crafts of a passing generation, and a few of their younger apprentices, feel the sadness of this moment and give their politically unheeded voices to the elegy that now needs to be sung.

In Levinas's "In Memory of Alphonse de Waelhens," in which he disagrees with Merleau-Ponty's phenomenological representation of touching hands, the author contemplates the ethical meaning of the handshake, connecting that gesture with a shared experience of trust, and consequently of peace. Essential to the gesture is the "fact" that it involves giving one's hand to the other. Thus Levinas asks: "Is the handshake not, then, an attuning [*un s'accorder*] of oneself to the other, a giving of oneself?" "The handshake," he says, "is not simply the acknowledgment of an agreement, but, before that confirmation, the extra-ordinary event of peace."[5] Perhaps it will always, therefore, prophetically intimate—without the two parties even knowing it—a certain utopian or messianic dimension of the future.

We need, as Jacques Derrida says in *Specters of Marx*, "a politics of memory, inheritance, and generation."[6] This book has been written in remembrance of that vanished handshake, a once great gesture that participated in the moral order as an embodiment of trust and respect. It exists now as little more than a polite greeting, its morally binding function displaced by the legally binding written contract, an instrument of mistrust and coercion.

Is there any hope for what Merleau-Ponty once dreamed of: "an ideal community of embodied subjects, an intercorporeality"?[7] Is there not at work, in the historical memory our gestures never entirely cease to maintain, what Heidegger, in a beautiful phrase, called "the quiet force of the possible"?[8]

GESTURES OF ETHICAL LIFE

§ 1 A Gesture Most Tactful

Rilke's Second Duino Elegy

On January 10, 1912, while working on the second of his Duino Elegies, Rilke wrote to Lou Andreas-Salomé:

> Once in Naples, I believe, in front of some ancient grave-stone, it flashed through me that I ought never to touch people with stronger gestures than were there depicted. And I really believe that I sometimes get so far as to express the whole impulse of my heart, without loss and fatality, in gently laying my hand on a shoulder. Would not this, Lou, would not this be the only progress conceivable within that "discretion" you bid me remember? [1]

The work that made such a deep and lasting impression on him was a bas-relief of extraordinary poignancy showing Orpheus and Eurydice about to leave the underworld, petrified in the instant immediately after Orpheus, breaking his vow, has turned back to assure himself that his beloved is right behind him. The work captures that fateful, heartbreaking moment of parting when Hermes, taking hold of Eurydice's arm, firmly begins to restrain her, separating her from Orpheus, on whose shoulder she gently and with immeasurable sadness lays her hand. In 1904, two years after his visit to the Museo Archeologico Nazionale, Rilke composed a poem commemorating this mythic story. It bears the title "Orpheus, Eurydice, Hermes." Allegorically interpreted, the story imparts the realization that the singer must in the end renounce the dream of making the origin of his song present in the song itself—although, as a reward from the gods for this submission, he is granted the privilege of finding, in the sadness of memory, the words that will nevertheless let fading echoes of the origin resonate and sing.

In the Second Duino Elegy, the poet redeems his experience in the museum, quite transforming it through the alchemy of his imagination, writing—with his hand—of ancient hands and their gestures. Lines 66–73:

> On Attic steles, did not the circumspection
> of human gesture amaze you? Were not love and farewell
> so lightly laid upon shoulders, they seemed to be made
> of other stuff than with us? Remember the hands,
> how they rest without pressure, though power is there in the torsos.
> The wisdom of those self-masters was this: we have got so far;
> ours is to touch one another like this; the gods
> may press more strongly upon us. But that is the gods' affair.[2]

In this translation, "circumspection" is used to render poet's word *Vorsicht.* This of course preserves the German association with vision; but other English words must be heard: "discretion," "tact," "heedfulness," and "prudence," alternative translations of the German—and also "restraint," which the English translators have used to interpret the poet's phrase *in denen es größer sich mäßigt* (line 79). In another work, "Early Spring" ("Vorfrühling"), Rilke writes of the "reserved gestures" (*wartende Gebärde*) he used when quenching his thirst on a walk in the country, letting water that had gathered in the hollow of a tree trunk gently run over his wrists. With this memory in mind, he addresses his beloved, promising to use "only a light touch of my hands" (*nur ein leichtes Anruhn meiner Hände*) in satisfying his desire. And here, as in the Second Elegy, he speaks of touching the shoulder with a gentle restraint.

But the gesture is rendered in its absence, a moment now to be wrought only by felt memory. Is it not significant that the gesture reveals something of its essence within the mood of an elegiac measure? Does the poet believe that, in our time, the possibility of a gesture like the one he attributes to the figure on the stele has been almost irretrievably lost? We cannot say. But it seems that the stele he describes is a work of the poet's purest imagination, the gesture a trace of the poet's vision, gently touched by the ancient powers of the dream—"desires [that] are the memories from our future."[3]

In a letter written in 1915 to Princess Marie von Thurn und Taxis-Hohenlohe, the poet reflects:

> It is certain that the divinest consolation is contained in humanity itself—we would not be able to do much with the consolation of a god; only that our eye would have to be a trace more seeing, our ear more receptive, the taste of

a fruit would have to penetrate us more completely, we would have to endure more odor, and in touching and being touched be more aware and less forgetful—: in order promptly to absorb out of our immediate experiences consolations that would be more convincing, more preponderant, more true than all the suffering that can ever shake us to our very depths.[4]

In the touch that connects one life with another, there is so much pain to be felt, so much suffering to be redeemed—so much to bring to remembrance. What consolation must we, could we, offer to others? And for the sake of this consolation—with what self-restraint?

FIGURE 2.1   Attic bas-relief of Hermes, Eurydice, and Orpheus. Courtesy of
the Museo Archeologico Nazionale, Naples.

§ 2 Measure in παιδεία and πολιτεία

Learning a Gentle Restraint

ἀλλ' ἀεὶ τὴν ἐν τῷ σώματι ἁρμονίαν τῆς ἐν τῇ ψυχῇ ἕνεκα
ξυμφωνίας ἁρμοττόμενος φανεῖται.
—Plato, *Republic* 9.591d[1]

τίς οὖν δὴ πρᾶξις φίλη καὶ ἀκόλουθος θεῷ; [. . .] ὅτι τῷ μὲν
ὁμοίῳ τὸ ὅμοιον ὄντι μετρίῳ φίλον ἂν εἴη, τὰ δ' ἄμετρα οὔτε
ἀλλήλοις οὔτε τοῖς ἐμμέτροις. Ὁ δὴ θεὸς ἡμῖν πάντων
χρημάτων μέτρον ἂν εἴη μάλιστα, καὶ πολὺ μᾶλλον ἤ πού τις,
ὥς φασιν, ἄνθρωπος.
—Plato, *Laws* 4.716c1–6[2]

I. Measure

Aristotle defined the human being as ζῷον λόγον ἔχον, a definition commonly translated today as "the animal capable of reason or speech," or, as
we might say without venturing far from this interpretation: "the animal
capable of giving a reflectively rational account of itself."[3] The Romans
translated λόγος by the word *ratio*, thereby setting in motion the reading
that still prevails today. But *ratio* suggests a certain measure or proportion
as well as ratiocination. So it could be said, I think, that we are beings of
measure, not only in the sense that we are capable of measuring things, but
also in the sense that we belong to measure, or, say, dwell in measure—
dwell in the reception of what it gives, and of how, in guiding our judgment, it can enrich our lives. For, as Socrates argues against the Sophists
(*Protagoras* 351b–358e), "virtue" is the art of measuring—measuring, first
and foremost, pleasures and pains. But this means, in turn, that we are to
be measured by the character of the life we choose to live.

Bearing this in mind, we might turn to Plato's *Statesman* (Πολιτικός),
a late dialogue on the art (τέχνη) of statesmanship, containing an important discussion of measure in the realm of politics (283c–285c).[4] The
question of measure—in the initial discussion, a question of μετρητική,
the art of measurement—arises because the interlocutors, young Socrates
and "a Stranger," are attempting to understand "the whole nature of excess [ὑπερβολὴν] and defect [ἔλλειψιν]," since only such understanding

would enable them to praise and blame κατὰ λόγον, that is to say, on rational grounds. Very quickly, therefore, the dialogue moves on to the role of measure in ethical life. The Stranger initiates the shift: "Well, but is there not also something exceeding and exceeded by the principle of the mean, both in speech and action, and is not this a reality, and the chief mark of difference between good and bad men?" "We must then suppose," he continues, introducing the thought of an ideal standard, "that the great and the small exist and are discerned in both these ways, and not, as we were saying before, only relatively to one another, but there must also be another comparison of them with the mean or ideal standard [τὸ μέτριον]." He then argues that, without the possibility of comparing the less and the more, the deficient and the excessive, not merely with one another but with the absolute mean, and consequently without that ideal standard to guide them, "all the arts [τέχνας] and their works [τἄργα]" would fall into the realm of shadows, where everything is merely relative. Thus, he says, all the arts—above all, that of the statesman—must be "on the watch against excess and defect, not as unrealities, but as real evils," for "the excellence of beauty in every work of art is due only to this observance of measure."

While recognizing that it may not at first seem easy to demonstrate the need for an ideal standard, a concept of the mean, the Stranger, observing that "the art of measurement is universal" and that "all things which come within the province of art certainly partake in some way of measure," expects to convince Socrates that the very existence of the arts is sufficient to prove his argument. "For if there are arts," he says, laying out the first step of the argument, "there is a standard of measure, and if there is a standard of measure, there are arts; but if either is missing, there is neither." The next step involves dividing the art of measurement into two categories: in the one, the arts of number, length, depth, breadth, and swiftness would be measured merely in relation to their opposites, whereas in the other, these arts would be measured by reference to the mean. Seeing the truth in this division is essential, he says, if reason, and not a delusion lost among images and shadows, is to prevail in the art of statesmanship. But what kind of reason?

In "Understanding and Politics," a major essay, Hannah Arendt addresses the current "crisis in authority": "Even though we have lost yardsticks by which to measure, and rules under which to subsume the particular, a being whose essence is beginning [the capacity to initiate, to inaugurate] may have enough of origin within himself to understand without preconceived categories and to judge without the set of customary rules which is morality."[5] The metaphysics that once supported our moral order is now "under erasure," its inherited wisdom no longer compelling. But Arendt sees in this crisis a potentially liberating experience, for it makes us rely on our capacity for what Kant calls "reflective judgment": the ability to draw on our imagination and disclose—or perhaps invent—the general principle that best illuminates how we should act in our particular situation.

Completing his argument (at 299e), the Stranger warns that the arts will "utterly perish" if they are made in blind obedience to inherited laws, principles, and standards, rather than in accord with achieved insight—an immediate knowledge of the ideal and a practical sense of the particular.[6] But since statecraft is, for Plato, one of the arts, the statesman can rely on no decision procedure, no ready-made standards and answers, no traditional formulae: he must turn to his φρόνησις, a reflective capacity for sensitive discrimination and good judgment. In a certain crucial way, this capacity cannot be grounded in any absolute standard entirely outside the rational vision of right proportion that the statesman has nevertheless learned to cultivate. This means that for Plato the statesman's craft is an art in something like Kant's sense. In his *Critique of Judgment*, Kant says: "Only that which a man, even if thoroughly knowledgeable about it, does not thereby immediately have the skill to accomplish belongs to that extent to art."[7] Moreover, it means that the statesman's art is an exemplary type of freedom—indeed, a "demonstration" of freedom.

This surprising turn in Plato's argument suggests that, as one of the arts—in truth the highest art—yet also as a type of πρᾶξις, or action, statecraft must ultimately repudiate the tradition of μίμησις, renouncing ποίησις, the teleology of production, all types of making in conformity to a prior ideal or grounding principle, as its paradigm for judgment. But statecraft must also free itself from the logic of identity and repetition that it has repeatedly imposed on πρᾶξις, on possibilities for inceptive and inaugural action. Thus, in the realm of politics, the realm, namely, of action, πρᾶξις, it is necessary that the art of judgment (φρόνησις) resist reduction or subordination both to instrumentalism, that is, the terms of production, and to rationalism, the terms of deduction.

This perhaps brings us to the threshold of the enigmatic, paradoxical, and aporetical character of human freedom that Maurice Blanchot adumbrates when, in *The Infinite Conversation,* he asks, "As men of measure [*hommes de mesure*] through knowledge of the lack of measure [*démesure*] that was close to them, did they [the Greeks of antiquity] not recommend that Proteus be held firmly and bound in order that he should agree to declare himself truthfully in the most simple form?"[8]

Thus, at the end of the day, there is a sense in which, despite what Plato says he thinks, it is not the universal, not the absolute, but rather the contingent and the particular that triumph. Or, if the universal triumphs, it does so only through a dialectic that leaves its marks on the claim. Consequently, despite the philosopher's confident claims, shadows of uncertainty and even—dare one say it?—an unmasterable undecidability reign in the halls of state. Perhaps, despite the Stranger's words, it will always be the statesman's judgment about τὸ πρέπον, "what is fitting" (286c), more art than science, that brings the absolute measure, the ideals of the Good and the Just, down to earth—right here, among us mortals, where the political properly requires that statecraft be a matter of vigorous public debate, διάλεκτος, talking things through, with well-reasoned hypotheses regarding the Good as our only available measure.

II. Corporeal Schema

According to the dominant interpretation, Plato regarded the human body (σῶμα) with unqualified contempt, calling it the prison-house or tomb (σῆμα) of the soul. (It is possible that Plato could still hear in the word σῶμα its Homeric meaning—"corpse," in contrast to δέμας, a living body.) A reading of the texts (e.g., *Phaedo* 64–68) can easily confirm this interpretation, pointing to the many passages declaring the body to be the site of pleasures and pains that disturb and distract the soul, and to be the source of appetites that can lead the soul only into error, corruption, immorality, and impiety. But, although this interpretation correctly reads what might be called Plato's systematic thought, it overlooks his philosophical reflections on moral education. When we turn our attention to these reflections, we find that, far from representing the body in wholly negative terms and denying it any positive role in moral education, Plato instead follows and appropriates the doctrines embodied in the cultural practices—the disciplinary regimes—of his time. These practices not only recognized the fundamental importance of the body in moral education but counseled that the forming and informing of the body—the body of the infant and the child—be given the greatest possible thought and care. Yet he never seems to have perceived any tension or contradiction between the attitude articulated in his systematic thought and the attitude implicit in his discussions on moral education. Something quite similar could, I think, be said of Aristotle, whose theory of education, drawing as it does from the same cultural sources, is not much different from Plato's, although it is certainly formulated in terms of a more intricate, more exactingly crafted conceptual framework.[9]

It is difficult to deny the importance of the body for Plato's moral theory, since the soul's recollection of virtue must be awakened through the body that it will for a time inhabit. Moreover, during its sojourn on earth, the body, as outward expression, appearance, and shape (σχῆμα) of the soul, is, as Wittgenstein argued, the "best picture" of the soul we could possibly get. Even more crucially for present purposes, the body's attitudes—its balance, its uprightness, its bearing, its poise and gracefulness of gesture, its ways of touching, grasping, handling, and holding—really matter to the virtuous life. For it is not enough that the soul remembers and knows the essence of virtue; what it knows in its inwardness must operate in the world, determining and attuning one's gestures and bearing, one's judgment and action. Virtue is not just the theoretical knowledge contained in the soul—it is also, necessarily, embodied in comportment. The embodiment of virtue matters so much, in fact, that Plato cannot imagine how a man whose soul is regulated by a true knowledge of the Good could nevertheless make no effort to embody the virtuous life.

In book 3 of the *Republic*, Plato argues that *mimesis*, showing children by example, is the best way to begin imparting moral concepts and the capacity for moral judgment. Mimesis can communicate immediately with the young, undisciplined body, directly reproducing proper forms of comportment, teaching even without resort to language—even without the mediation of consciousness. "Did you never observe," Socrates asks Adeimantus, "how imitations, beginning in early youth and continuing far into life, eventually settle into habits [καθίστανται εἰς ἤθη] and become a second nature [φύσιν καθίστανται], affecting body, voice and mind [κατὰ σῶμα καὶ φωνὰς καὶ κατὰ τὴν διάνοιαν]?" (*Republic* 3.395d). Imitation thus lies at the very heart of moral education in ancient Greece, informing the interior life of the child by shaping the child's exterior life, teaching morality as bodily bearing and gesture, κατὰ σχῆμα (3.393d, 397a). Plato accordingly has Socrates say, "When there is a coincidence

[ξυμπίπτη] between a beautiful disposition [καλὰ ἤθη] and corresponding [ὁμολογοῦντα] and harmonious beauties of the same type in the bodily form [ἐν τ' εἴδει], this is most worthy of contemplating [θεᾶσθαι]"
(3.402d). Mimesis is the best way to achieve this coincidence between the
inner and the outer. Of course, children should imitate only those people
whose character, bearing, and actions are eminently worthy of being imi-
tated. Further, since children are easily influenced and easily overcome
by the silent power of mimesis, it follows that they should be exposed as
little as possible to people of bad character—whether in real life or in the
theater.

According to Plato (*Republic* 9.583e), it is as a "kind of motion" (κίνησις)
that pleasure and pain, which first affect the body, correspondingly disturb
the soul. For this reason, Plato wants the children and even the adults in
his republic to be protected from all motions of an extreme nature, for
their own good and for the common good. And, inasmuch as emotionally
charged words—mean words, violent words, ill-mannered words, words
arousing strong desires—can cause the body to be overcome by strong
motions, Plato wants to control children's exposure to speech: "Ugliness
[ἀσχημοσύνη] and discordant rhythm [ἀρρυθμία] and inharmonious
motion [ἀναρμοστία] are closely connected to ill words and ill nature, as
grace and harmony are the twin sisters of goodness and virtue and bear
their likeness" (*Republic* 3.401a). The arts of gymnastics, wrestling, dance,
music, and poetry are therefore especially useful means for teaching the
life of virtue, because they submit the body to a discipline of rhythms, meters, and harmonies that can awaken the soul to a mimetic recollection
(ἀνάμνησις) of the harmony, balance, and measure proper to its exercise of reason. In particular, Socrates argues that "musical training is a
more potent instrument than any other, because rhythm and harmony
find their way into the innermost places of the soul [ὅτι μάλιστα κατα-
δύεται εἰς τὸ ἐντὸς τῆς ψυχῆς ὅ τε ῥυθμὸς καὶ ἁρμονία]" (*Republic*
3.401d). Through the arts, especially music and dance, the "brutish part"
(θηριῶδες) of the soul can be lulled and tamed and the "gentle part"
(ἥμερον) "liberated" (ἐλευθεροῦται), so that the necessary habits of tem-
perance (σωφροσύνη), righteousness (δικαιοσύνη), and practical wisdom
(φρόνησις) can be nurtured (*Republic* 9.591b) and the soul's several faculties brought into internal harmony (ἐμμελής) (*Laws* 7.816).

Justice is always a question of measure, of division, apportionment, set-
tling what is due: in praise and blame, in benefits and penalties, in prop-

erties and attributes. Since, for the Greeks of antiquity, music and dance were social activities in which a vital sense of measure, of rhythm and meter, would take shape, they were esteemed as ways of introducing the bodies of the young to a felt sense of justice—and were even recognized as ways of maintaining a connection to this vital sense in the rest of the community. In that bodily felt sense of measure, of harmony, lay an experience that could support the belief that goodness and justice are values inherent in, and constitutive of, the "natural order."

Books 2 and 7 of Plato's *Laws*, a much later work of thought, are especially useful for understanding his theoretical vision of moral education, an education that would best prepare citizens of the city to participate in its political life.[10] In book 2, Plato's "Athenian" says:

> I call "education" the initial acquisition [τὴν παραγιγνομένην πρῶτον] of virtue [ἀρετήν] by the child, when the feelings of pleasure and affection, pain and hatred that well up in his soul are [already] channeled in the right courses [ὀρθῶς] even before he can understand the reason why [μήπω δυναμένων λόγον λαμβάνειν]. Then, when his understanding has been awakened [λαβόντων δὲ τὸν λόγον], his reason and his emotions are in accord [συμφωνήσωσι] in telling him that he has been properly trained by the inculcation of appropriate habits [προσηκόντων ἐθῶν]. Virtue [ἀρετή] is this general concord of reason and emotion. But there is one element you could isolate in any account you give, and this is the correct formation of our feelings of pleasure and pain. (*Laws*, 2.653b)

It is essential that these feelings be "correctly disciplined." In the culture of Plato's time, this meant, first of all, subjecting the bodies of the young to appropriate disciplinary regimes, teaching them to keep their bodies still and their tongues quiet. Choral singing and dancing were especially important in this regard, because they introduced the young bodies to certain experiences of rhythm and harmony that would enable them to develop, in time, a sense of order and disorder: "Whereas animals have no sense of order and disorder in movement [οὐκ ἔχειν αἴσθησιν τῶν ἐν ταῖς κινήσεσιν τάξεων οὐδὲ ἀταξιῶν]—'rhythm' and 'harmony' we call it—we human beings have been made sensitive to both and can enjoy them. This is the gift of the gods" (*Laws* 2.653e). Thus, we note that— quite contrary to the unequivocal rejection of the sensuous that we are accustomed to reading into Platonism—the Athenian gives a certain virtue-making role to the sensuous nature of the voice: "When the sound of the voice penetrates the soul, we took that to be an education in virtue" (*Laws* 2.673a).

Although the superior citizen is ultimately required not only to live a virtuous life but to form a clear "intellectual conception" (διανοεῖσθαι) of virtue (*Laws* 2.654d),[11] the first step in this formation will always be the child's *embodiment* of rhythm and harmony. For it is through measured, choreographed movements of voice and body (*Laws* 2.659d–660a), through an immediate, bodily felt sense of rhythm and harmony, that the child begins to acquire an understanding of the fundamental elements of virtue. Thus, before becoming an articulate conception, this understanding emerges as a corporeal schema, the body's initial schematism of virtuous movement, bearing, gesture, and voice—the outward appearance or form (σχῆμα) of virtue. The Athenian draws the conclusion very clearly: "So if the three of us could discern what 'goodness' is in singing and dancing [τὸ καλὸν ᾠδῆς τε καὶ ὀρχήσεως], we would also have a sound criterion [πέρι γιγνώσκομεν] for distinguishing the educated man from the uneducated" (*Laws* 2.654d). How does this "discernment" happen? In the best of circumstances, the ceremonial roles assigned in singing and dancing—which require the performers to embody, in a mimesis of voice (φωνή), song (μέλος, ᾠδή), dance (ὄρχησις), and gesture (σχῆμα), the representations of character that the roles involve—appeal to their "natural character" (κατὰ φύσιν) and "acquired habits" (κατὰ ἔθος), and accordingly take hold in a particularly effective and beautiful way (*Laws* 2.654c, 654e, 655b, 655e). As he says (*Laws* 7.792e), it is in the early years of a child's life that, "in the most decisive way [κυριώτατον], a character [ἦθος] for the whole of life can be implanted and cultivated [ἐμφύεται] by the formation of proper habits [διὰ ἔθος]."

In *Love's Knowledge*, Martha Nussbaum argues that, in the cultural world known by Plato and Aristotle, the ethical was a matter of "perception": "perception" in the sense of *phronesis*, the ability to achieve a "perceptive equilibrium . . . in which concrete perceptions 'hang beautifully together' both with one another and with the agent's general principles; an equilibrium that is always ready to reconstitute itself in response to the new."[12] Thus, the ethical was essentially a matter of judging the mean, the proper measure, called forth by each situation, judging what would most likely bring about a good "attunement" between the situation and our principles and between ourselves and the values of the community. This conception of ethical life in ancient Greece conflicts with the still predominant picture of that life—a picture filtered through Cartesian and Kantian rationalism. But the merit of Nussbaum's conception is that it presents the Greeks in an ethical culture that renders them believably human—much more so than the rule-following characters in the morality plays of rationalism, who always seem like the mere projections of an argument. Perhaps what restores the Greeks' humanity for us is Nussbaum's emphasis on perceptivity and sensibility—bodily experiences—in matters ethical.

Aristotle argues that, in a life of virtue, the Good is the ultimate principle, the ultimate cause, of movement. But what is involved in one's being "motivated" and "moved" by the Good? How could the Good bring about this movement without there being a bodily predisposition to respond to the idea of the Good? Is it not necessary to recognize an orientation to the Good—or, say, a capacity to be affected and moved by its solicitations—already operative, already schematized, in the form of the body?

The child's body is a disorder that is, however, already an order—a disorder that is capable of and open to the discipline of a moral order. The Athenian remarks:

> All young things, being fiery and mettlesome by nature, are unable to keep their bodies or their tongues still—they are always making uncoordinated noises and jumping about. No other animal, we said, ever develops a sense of order [τάξεως δ' αἴσθησιν] in either respect; man alone has a natural ability to do this. Order in movement is called "rhythm" [τῇ δὴ τῆς κινήσεως τάχει ῥυθμὸς ὄνομα εἴη], and order in the vocal sounds—the combination of high and low notes—is called "harmony"; and the union of the two is called "a performance by a chorus." (*Laws* 2.664e–665a)

We might say, then, that the community's efforts at moral education are designed to turn a wild first nature into a well-trained second nature. But, as we shall see, this can be attempted in many ways; and how the training is undertaken can make all the difference: in particular, the difference between a life of virtue and a life of vice, intemperance and brutality.

Because mimesis is so "natural," so "spellbinding" and "seductive," especially for children, the child must be shielded from bad exemplars, both in real life and in staged performances:

> The soul of the child has to be prevented from getting into the habit of feeling pleasure and pain in ways not sanctioned by the law [τῷ νόμῳ] and those

who have been persuaded to obey it; he should follow in their footsteps and find pleasure and pain in the same things as the old. That is why we have what we call songs [ᾠδὰς], which are really "charms" [ἐπῳδαί] for the soul. These are in fact extremely serious devices for producing this concord [συμφωνίαν] we are talking about. (*Laws* 2.659d)

The discussion of moral education in book 7 of the *Laws* is in many ways the most fascinating. Here Plato expounds his theory of child-rearing practices in remarkable detail, even insisting that moral education begins with proper nourishment for mother and child while the child is still in the womb (*Laws* 7.789a–c). (Once again, we see Plato taking into his theory δόξαι, "common beliefs," seemingly at odds with many of his "doctrines" but current in the culture of his time. Not surprisingly, Aristotle makes the same argument; see his *Politics*, bk. 7, chap. 14.) Convinced that the character of young children can be shaped by the same methods used to shape their bodies (*Laws* 7.790c), the Athenian draws on ancient cultural practices (ἐπιτηδεύματα) to formulate instructions—policies and rules, in fact—for handling the newly born infant, arguing, "All bodies find it helpful and invigorating to be shaken by movements of all kinds [ὑπὸ τῶν σεισμῶν τε καὶ κινήσεων]" (*Laws* 7.789d):

> All young children, and especially very tiny infants, benefit both physically and mentally from being nursed and kept in motion [κίνησιν], as far as practicable, throughout the day and night; indeed, if only it could be managed, they ought be kept gently rocked, living as though they were permanently on board ship [οἷον ἀεὶ πλέοντας]. But, as that is impossible, we must aim to provide our new-born infants with the closest possible approximation to this ideal. (*Laws* 7.790c)

The Athenian continues, introducing now, in a turn surprising for Plato, the empirical evidence for this counsel:

> Here's some further evidence, from which the same conclusions should be drawn: the fact that young children's nurses, and the women who cure Corybantic conditions, have learnt this treatment from experience [ἐξ ἐμπειρίας] and have come to recognize its value. And I suppose you know what a mother does when she wants to get a wakeful child to sleep. Far from keeping him still, she takes care to move him about, rocking him constantly in her arms, not silently, but humming a kind of tune [μελῳδίαν]. The cure consists of movement [κίνησιν], to the rhythms of [certain forms of] dance and song. (*Laws* 7.790d)

"So we can affirm," he concludes, "that exercising very young children by keeping them in motion [ἐν ταῖς κινήσεσιν] contributes a great deal towards the perfection of one aspect of the soul's virtue" (*Laws* 7.791c). For certain types of movements, coming from the outside, can teach the child how to master (κρατεῖν) the soul's internal movements of fear and frenzy and thereby induce (φαίνεσθαι) in the infant's soul a feeling of calm and peace (*Laws* 7.789d, 791a). But only certain types of movement will produce an effect of this nature: only gentle yet vigorous and invigorating movements stimulate the body's senses and powers in a way that awakens the traumatized soul from its slumber, bringing it, so to speak, into life. Violent movements, producing extremes of pleasure or pain—or fear and frenzy—are to be avoided, for their agitation of the body disturbs the equilibrium and moderation of the soul.

In later life, the properly educated child, the Athenian maintains, should prepare for the community's ceremonial dances, undergoing rigorous instruction in the appropriate movements. Speaking of the youth who takes part in the "dances of peace," he observes:

> The greater his pleasure, the brisker his body's movements; more modest pleasures make his actions correspondingly less brisk. Likewise, the more composed the man's temperament, and the tougher he has been trained to be, the more deliberate are his movements; on the other hand, if he's a coward and has not been trained to show restraint, his actions are wilder and his postures change more violently. (*Laws* 7.815d–816a)

Violent motions are bad. Movements and gestures that are violent (βίαιοι) not only express an already intemperate soul—a soul without balance, harmony, and a proper sense of order—but also agitate and disturb the soul, causing it to become even more disordered (Plato, *Laws* 7.816a; Aristotle, *Politics* 7.1335b10 and 8.1338b42, 1342b3–5). The ancient Greeks understood the mimetic impulse: in our comportment toward others, we tend to reproduce how others comported themselves toward us when we were small. Whether as children we are handled gently and tactfully or with rough, violent gestures, we learn to respond in kind, for we generate our gestures toward others from within our bodily felt sense of those early experiences.

According to similar reasoning, requiring the youth of the community—especially those born of the nobility—to participate in ceremonial dances was regarded as one very good way to teach the community's cultural ideals and values and its social norms and codes. For in these ritual-ized performances, the dancers directly embodied those ideals, values, and norms in movements—movements that, if internalized, would create in the soul the harmony that is of the essence in all the virtues. (In *Nico-machean Ethics* 10.6.1177a11, Aristotle speaks of "activities in accord with virtue": κατ' ἀρετὴν ἐνεργείαις.) It thus stands to reason that Plato's Athenian and his interlocutors must disapprove of the ceremonies that, according to Cleinas, commonly take place in many cities and villages: "In dancing and all the other arts, one novelty follows another; the changes are made not by law but are prompted by wildly changing fancies that are very far from being permanent and stable, like the Egyptian tastes you're ex-plaining" (*Laws* 2.660b). At stake, as the Athenian reminds us, is not only the ethical character of the individual's life, but also the political life of the entire community: it is important, he asserts, "to ensure that as far as possible the entire community [συνοικία] preserves in its songs [ᾠδαῖς] and stories [μύθοις] and doctrines [λόγοις] a lifelong unanimity" (*Laws* 2.664a). For this reason, the Athenian does not hesitate to call for very spe-cific, strict rules and policies regarding child-rearing and education: "The state's general code of laws will never rest on a firm foundation as long as private life is badly regulated" (*Laws* 7.790b). He also comments on the sacred origin of these conventional, man-made laws and policies in ances-tral customs:

> All the rules we are now working through are what people generally call "un-written customs" [ἄγραφα νόμιμα], and all this sort of thing is precisely what they mean when they speak of "ancestral law" [πατρίους νόμους]. Not only that, but the conclusion to which we were driven a moment ago was the right one: that although "laws" is the wrong word for these things, we can't afford to say *nothing* about them, because they are the bonds of the entire social fab-ric [δεσμοὶ γὰρ οὗτοι πάσης εἰσὶν πολιτείας], linking all written and es-tablished laws with those yet to be passed. They act in the same way as ances-tral customs [ἀρχαῖα νόμιμα] dating from time immemorial. (*Laws* 7.793b)

Recognizing an essential difference between "natural abilities" (τὰς φύ-σεις) and "acquired habits" (τοῖς ἔθεσιν), both of which, as equally nec-essary for the formation of good character, must be the concern of moral education, the Athenian emphasizes that neither the acquired habits nor the ways in which they are taught should go "against nature" (παρὰ φύ-σιν), ruining (ἀποθλάπτωσι) nature's endowment of moral predisposi-tions (*Laws* 7.795a, 795d). (See Aristotle's *Ethics* 10.1179b30–31, where he claims that character, τὸ ἦθος, which has at the outset, προσ-υπάρχειν, a "natural affinity" for what is fitting or proper, οἰκεῖον, must be secured, by means that draw on the body's predisposition, διακεῖσθαι, toward this end.) In other words—words suggested by Heidegger's discussions of ἀληθεύειν—it is of the utmost importance that the teaching of ideals, norms, and values should work *in harmony with* this natural endowment, bringing it out, letting it show itself (φαίνεσθαι) from out of itself. The souls of the young can be brought into internal and external harmony only if the culture's ways of teaching and communicating virtue can make them grow (φύειν) naturally, being themselves in harmony with nature.

Because children love to play games, and because games are rule-governed activities, the Athenian recommends traditional games as a major way of teaching children to obey and respect the community's rules and norms. "I maintain," he says,

> that no-one in any state has really grasped that children's games affect legislation so crucially as to determine whether the laws that are passed will survive or not. If you control the way children play, and the same children always play the same games under the same rules and in the same conditions, and get pleasure from the same toys, you'll find that the conventions of adult life too are left in peace without alteration. (*Laws* 7.797b–d)

But he is distressed by what he sees:

> But in fact, games are always being changed and constantly modified and new ones invented, and the younger generation never enthuses over the same thing for two days running. They have no permanent agreed standard [ὁμολο-γουμένως] of what is becoming and unbecoming [εὔσχημον καὶ ἄσχημον] either in comportment or in their possessions in general; they worship anyone who is always introducing some novelty or doing something unconventional to shapes and colors and all that sort of thing. In fact, it is no exaggeration to say that nothing could ruin a state more profoundly, because it quietly changes the character of the young by making them despise old things and value novelty. (Ibid.)

The young are not learning constancy, continuity, and the social significance of norms; they are not being properly trained (ἀγύμναστος) in the practice of self-restraint; they are not being taught to obey rules, to respect tradition, to value the Forms, to comport themselves in harmony (ἐμμε-λῶς) with a moral order that is permanent and unchanging, to become temperate in their reactions (γεγονὼς πρὸς τὸ σωφρονεῖν), to follow a life of moderation (μέσον δέ τινα τέμνειν ἀεί), to move and gesture in a well-tempered way (κοσμιώτερος), with composure and grace. Instead the young are being allowed a dangerous form of freedom. They are allowed to become ever more unruly (μείζους) and violent (σφοδροτέρας) in their behavior (*Laws* 7.793a, 815e, 816a). Therefore, Plato makes a plea for a process of education that would prepare the young—above all, the children of noble birth, destined to serve as rulers (ἀρχομένων) in the new republic—for a life befitting their nobility (μεγαλοπρεπές), a life of virtue and good citizenship (*Laws* 7.795e). The Athenian accordingly recommends that, an early age, the child must above all be taught self-mastery and self-restraint in bearing, movement, and gesture. For this is the basis of φρόνησις, the very embodiment, of rational judgment—a practical and prudent wisdom.

For Plato, both rationality and justice are essentially questions of proportion, the just or right measure, the just or right *ratio*: τὸ μέτρον. (In *Nicomachean Ethics* 5.3.1131b4–5 and 5.6.1134a23, Aristotle makes a similar point, referring to τὸ ἀνάλογον τὸ δίκαιον. At 5.3.1133b31, he argues that just conduct, δικαιοπραγία, is a mean or mediation, μέσον, between doing injustice, ἀδικεῖν, and suffering injustice, ἀδικεῖσθαι. In other words, it is a third alternative, the golden mean, avoiding both these extremes.) This "right measure" is the key to understanding the emphasis on an education in certain forms of poetry, music, dance—forms of bodily bearing, gesture, and expression, in which, through exemplary experiences of balance, rhythm, meter, and harmony, the child learns, if only in a rudimentary way, the essential meaning of rationality and justice. He learns what these are, what they mean, simply by virtue of his experience of embodiment. The task of education must accordingly be understood, after Heidegger, as an ἀληθεύειν, a process of bringing out the truth of (in) our embodiment—that indwelling λόγος, that innermost sense of reason, of right measure and justice, which we already carry within the very nature (φύσις) of our ensouled bodies, and which we need to cultivate until virtue becomes habit, character, second nature, and comes of itself to beautiful appearance (φαίνεσθαι) in our private and civic life.[13]

III. The Body Politic

It is of the gestures distinctive of friendship—or more exactly, those of the male citizens of the city, gestures of mutual recognition and respect among equals within the ruling class—that Plato and Aristotle seem principally to be thinking when they characterize the classical ideal of the gesture. The essence of the virtuous gesture is not to be seen in the caresses of lovers, nor in the act of writing, in skillfulness in the arts and crafts, or in the gestures required by war. The ideal gesture, embodying virtue in a way that exemplifies virtue's beauty, would be a gesture of friendship moved not by passions but by love for the Good: a gesture harmonizing with the Ideas of Δίκη and 'Αλήθεια; a gesture spirited and wholehearted but also graceful and tactful, always showing an exquisite awareness in the manner of its approach, its sense of spacing and timing, contact and pressure, of just the right measure; a gesture touching only lightly, with restrained intimacy, the expression of a mastered impulse. Such a gesture, beautiful in the lucid demonstration of its character, would be achieved only through the most demanding practice of self-discipline. Although nothing excludes the possibility that such a refined gesture could be found among warriors, merchants, laborers, women, and slaves, one gets the impression that, for Plato and Aristotle, such a gesture could never represent the essential virtue of their class or kind.

This fact obliges us to submit this ideal gesture to some critical questioning. First of all, it presupposes a system of education designed to establish and maintain certain fixed class and gender divisions based on the assignment of essential functions and responsibilities within the order of the state. Secondly, moreover, as the discussion of children's games shows very clearly, the ideal gesture represents the harmony of virtue—and teaches it—with an emphasis on repetition and sameness, preserving the traditional forms of virtue, the outward shapes in which it has appeared, through a mimetic pressure to conform. Even if virtue is a universal, always and everywhere the same, we can see that it does not necessarily assume, always and everywhere, the same cultural forms. Thus Plato does not merely assert an absolute difference between the supersensible realm of the Forms and the realm of sensuous appearances; rather, he goes beyond this difference when formulating a program for the teaching of virtue, arguing for the virtue in tradition, in a conformity to the particular forms that would preserve the familiar past and ensure a sameness that exceeds what the ideal universality of virtue requires.

This emphasis on harmony—and, accordingly, on gestures of gentle restraint and exquisite tact—points, finally, to a third problem, namely, the exclusion of gestures of protest, resistance, and defiance, gestures moved by the injustice of suffering and oppression, gestures sometimes compelled even to violence in defense of truth, virtue, and justice. Plato's republic idealizes and immortalizes the gestures that would preserve it from change, from challenges to its political divisions and investments. In his study of Baudelaire for the Arcades Project, Walter Benjamin remarked, "The concepts of the ruling class have in every age been the mirrors that enabled an image of 'order' to prevail." [14] There can be little doubt that the gestures Plato admires and wants to see taught are expressions, reflections, and reproductions of the ruling order that claimed his own loyalty.

But shall we imagine that, when Socrates was teaching the young, in the agora, in the symposium, his gestures were always gentle and tactful? Are we to suppose that the gestures of this man, whom Athens accused of subversion and put to death, always conformed to the appearance of right measure, beautifully reserved and restrained? Are we to imagine that they were always in perfect harmony with the traditional conventions of the state?

As long as the utopian republic does not exist and the injustices of an unreconciled society prevail, our conception of the most virtuous gestures must surely include gestures of protest, resistance, and defiance. It is much too soon for us to teach the idealized gestures of virtue that Plato and Aristotle advocate without also encouraging—teaching—gestures that question a false social harmony. But by writing down, for future generations, his luminous evocations of Socrates' life and death, perhaps Plato nevertheless handed down, after all, the exemplary gestures of a most eloquent resistance—quite unwittingly, and despite himself.

§ 3 Freedom in Right Measure

Hölderlin's Anguished Question

Πολλῷ τὸ φρονεῖν εὐδαιμονίας/ πρῶτον ὑπάρχει. Χρὴ δὲ τά γ᾿
εἰς θεοὺς/ μηδὲν ἀσεπτεῖν. μεγάλοι δὲ λόγοι/ μεγάλας πληγὰς
τῶν ὑπεραύχων/ ἀποτείσαντες. . . .

[Wisdom is the supreme part of happiness; and reverence toward
the gods must be inviolate. But great words of prideful men are ever
punished with great blows.]

> —Sophocles, *Antigone*[1]

Those who question have set aside all [mere] curiosity; their seeking
loves the abyss, in which they recognize the oldest ground.

> —Martin Heidegger, *Contributions to Philosophy*[2]

The age for which the ground fails to come hangs in the abyss.

> —Martin Heidegger, "What Are Poets For?"[3]

To the spiritual *restitutio in integrum* . . . corresponds a worldly
restitution that leads to the eternity of downfall; and the *rhythm* of
this eternally transient worldly existence, transient in its totality, . . .
the *rhythm* of Messianic nature, is happiness. For nature is Messianic
by reason of its eternal and total passing away. To strive after such
passing . . . is the task of world politics, whose method must be called
nihilism.

> —Walter Benjamin, "Theologico-Political Fragment"[4]

I

"Giebt es auf Erden ein Maaß? Es giebt keines." At a certain point in "In
lovely blueness . . . " ("In lieblicher Bläue . . . "), a textual fragment attributed to Friedrich Hölderlin, the poet, overcome in the last period of
his life by an awareness of the great suffering endured by his people, is
moved to ask: "Is there on earth a measure?" Immediately, without apparent hesitation, he gives the answer he cannot deny: "There is none."[5]

"There is none" means, for the poet, that the people are living in a time
of banishment, abandoned by the gods. But if it also means, as his writings clearly tell us, that the people are living in a time of unbearable hard-
ship, inexcusable injustice, and extreme forms of political oppression, one

could perhaps speak of a "state of exception" (*Ausnahmezustand*), understanding this word—which, for a very different political objective, Walter
Benjamin takes from Carl Schmitt—as indicating a crisis that opens up
an exceptional time for something new to emerge. This is the sense it bears
in the eighth proposition of Benjamin's "Theses on the Philosophy of History": "The tradition of the oppressed teaches us that the 'state of emergency' [*Ausnahmezustand*] in which we live is not the exception but the
rule." Consequently, he says: "We must arrive at a conception of history
that is in keeping with this fact. Then we shall clearly realize that it is
our task to bring about a real state of emergency."[6] Bringing about such
an emergency means recognizing and realizing, as the very word implies,
an emerging potentiality. It is in the light of this analysis and the defiant
thought to which Benjamin carries it that we will be attempting here to
interpret Hölderlin's poetic works.

Living as he did through the end of the eighteenth century and the very
beginning of the nineteenth, Hölderlin experienced in the keenest way the
crisis of freedom and measure that was challenging the world of his time.
For, encouraged by the arguments and incitements of the Enlightenment
and romanticism, cries for freedom were ringing out, coming from people
whose voices had never before been heard; but at the same time, and precisely in keeping with this new awakening to freedom, the old, traditional
sources of moral authority were losing their auratic, spell-binding power.
The theological beliefs that had for so long given an absolutely unquestionable grounding to the moral law were increasingly losing their hold,
their authority. Thus, the new experience of freedom found itself without
the security of an absolute point of reference—a measure setting limits to
the exercise of freedom. This was the crisis, the dilemma, into which
Hölderlin saw the world of his time thrown. With the shouts and shots of
the French Revolution still echoing in his ears, the poet contemplates the
possibility that only the most radical, most absolute break in the fateful
continuum of history could offer hope of relief—an end to political oppression, an end to poverty and destitution. Or, as the poet says in "Patmos," it may be only when the greatest conceivable danger is threatening
to overwhelm that the way of hope, the way of rescue, is revealed. If, on
the one hand, every moment has become exceptional, exposing fundamental norms and values to the danger of groundlessness, on the other
hand, at any moment the next gods may come, indicating a way out. But
how could the poet serve the cause of freedom? In "Bread and Wine,"

Hölderlin asks, "What are poets for in a time of need?"[7] As if in answer to this question, the poet wrote a letter to his brother. It bears the date January 1, 1799: "If the forces of darkness invade with violent means, we cast the quill under the table and go in God's name where the need is greatest and where we are most needed."[8] But in "As when on holiday . . . ," Hölderlin addressed the other poets of his land with a more hopeful spirit, saying:

> Yet, fellow poets, us it behooves to stand
> Bareheaded beneath God's thunderstorms,
> To grasp the Father's rays, no less, with our own two hands,
> And, wrapping in song the heavenly gift,
> To offer it to the people.
> For if only we are pure in heart,
> Like children, and our hands are guiltless,
> The Father's ray, the pure, will not sear [*versenken*] our hearts.[9]

This mood, this faith, however, does not always stay with him.

Poets bear a singular responsibility, for their vocation is a calling to find in their words, and with their words, the right rhythm and meter for the expression of poetic freedom. While departing from *what is* for the sake of the possible and the impossible, they must nevertheless hear in their work the measure that both grants and binds their poetic freedom. It is out of that experience that Hölderlin will ask: Is there any moral law, be it of divine or of human origin, by reference to which we mortals can judge and act? For him, this question cannot be separated from the "jurisdiction" of poetry—and therefore from his own poetic practice, serving a "higher" dictation.

Some of the later poems express, in painfully broken lines—especially in the abysses of silence between the words, where language has withdrawn its gift—the poet's inconsolable despair:

> O were it possible
> To spare [*schonen*] my native land . . .
> Yet not be too timid,
> I would . . . rather
> Give my own life, against all
> Measure [*Unschiklich*], to the Erinyes,
> For powerful forces
> Wander the earth,

> Whose destiny [*Schiksal*] is grasped
> By those who witness it [*zusieht*] and suffer,
> Grasping [*ergreifft*] the people in their heart.[10]

Yet even here, precisely in the depth of pain, in the few pieces or parts (*Teilen*) of language he can assemble, the poet's words impart (*mitteilen*) a readiness to act, to battle against these forces of evil, even to sacrifice his life, if needs be, for the sake of his dream for his native land.[11]

For the poet, it is a question of how to take part (*teilnehmen*) in the struggle for freedom, justice, and peace.[12] Thus, as Heidegger remarks in his commentary on the poet's assertion "Es giebt keines," denying any measure on earth: although it "sounds like a token of hopelessness and despair," it should rather be read as an intense way of calling his contemporaries to take part in the struggle for their own destiny, taking to heart the question of the right measure for building and dwelling in a poetic way on the holy earth. For the gods have not directly given us human beings this measure, plainly putting it in our hands; nor is the measure something *zuhanden*, already present in our world, immediately ready to hand, simply awaiting our recognition and use. There may well be signs of a measure to be recognized in the heavens; but here on earth, there is none to be found, none already given, merely awaiting adoption. Instead, what the gods have given us is the announcement of a fateful task. Thus we are called upon to realize the fitting measure in the way we build and dwell, mindful of the earth and the sky.

"In lovely blueness . . . ," words a friend claimed to have written down, lends itself to more than one interpretation. And if there is any seemingly unresolvable conflict of interpretations, perhaps this is because the poetic meditation is compelled to register a certain deep equivocation. For when the poet says that there is on earth no measure, he opens up an abyss of uncertainty—an instability of meaning—because even if, in one sense of "given," it may be said that the gods have already given us the fitting measure, in another sense, it must be conceded that the measure will not have been "given" until the time of an appropriate reception and response—that is, until we take that measure to make an indeclinable claim on our freedom and to appropriate our responsibility for its essential role in the course of our destiny. Thus, he concludes that only if we can learn to imitate (*nachahmen*) the "kindliness" (*Freundlichkeit*) of the divinities, taking *that* as our example of measure, our ethical compass, might we realize that we have "found" and "received" the "proper" measure for joyful living.

Before expressing his despair over the absence of any measure to be readily wrought—or easily found—here on earth, the poet says:

> But the gods,
> Ever kind in all things,
> Are rich in virtue and joy.
> Which man may imitate.

Consequently, there is a question to be answered:

> May a man look up
> From the utter hardship of his life
> And say: Let me also be
> Like these?

"Yes," the poet says:

> As long as kindness lasts,
> Pure, within his heart, he may gladly measure himself
> Against the divine.

Then, not willing to fall into doubt, he asks: "Is God unknown? Is he manifest as the sky?" To which he answers: "This I tend / To believe. Such is man's measure." This might seem to settle the matter; but less than two lines of verse separate this assertion from the shadow of doubt that then crosses his mind, as if in undisguised argument with Kant:

> But the shadow
> Of the starry night is no more pure, if I may say so,
> Than man, said to be the image of God.

Does this begin to challenge the authority of the divine measure, the measure dictated, bringing it down to earth—or does it exalt the highest measure that can be wrought here on earth? Immediately following those three lines of equivocation, of undecidability, we stumble upon the question, "Is there measure on earth?" and confront the poet's answer: "There is / None."

But if, in these dark times, the gods have abandoned us, if their spirit will no longer inhabit our hearts, then it seems that the hope expressed elsewhere is here utterly shattered. In many writings, the poet leaves little doubt that he can see nothing but a tragic freedom of will, and misery spreading across the land—land once favored, and now abandoned, by the gods.

We must leave for another time the difficult questions to be asked about the poet's intricately metaphorical relation to what he here calls "my native land." For now, what most urgently calls for thought is the poet's commitment to fight the forces of evil hostile to the right measure. But would it not be a misprision to hear, in the occasionally resolute tone of Hölderlin's words, the confidence of one convinced that he *knows* what the proper measure is? May we assume, from the words written to his brother, that his commitment posits good and evil as opposites that absolutely exclude one another? And may we assume, from the circumstances of its expression, that this commitment initially takes place "outside" the "jurisdiction" of poetry? If so, would this commitment in any way compromise, or be compromised by, the freedom of his poetic practice? [13] Or would it ultimately, in fact, within the very measures that solicit his poetic words, take him closer to the abyss—there where the logic of identity is suspended and the absolute separation of good and evil, grounding measure and groundless abyss, is no longer secured, closer to the proper land of the poets, that place of origin, that unnameable source, always beyond the return of the poet's words, where poetic freedom receives its song? Must the poet not risk exposing his art, and most of all the measure that sets it in motion, to the dangerous proximity of evil, the abyss that cannot be measured, letting it enter into his writing, letting it interrupt and affect his writing, the very meter and rhythm of his words? Isn't it precisely this exposure of the measure, the moral law all too easily taken for granted, that defines the exceptional responsibility, the vocation, of poetic writing? Do the poet's later works suggest that his seemingly untroubled confidence in the measure—the impassioned confidence of 1799—was subsequently shaken, even, perhaps, overwhelmed by despair? Not, I believe, necessarily. For I think he allowed himself to hope that, in the very language of his poetry, at least in this realm, he was already bringing back from the depths of memory intimations of a fitting measure for poetic building and dwelling.

And yet, in the poet's writings, we seem to encounter a certain oscillation between hope and despair, conviction and doubt, confidence and anxiety—as if the question of the relationship between the right measure and what exceeds all measure, or even the very presence and identity of a grounding measure, must remain forever undecidable. As if, in spite of all his efforts, the poet's commitment to care for the gift of measure and see to its transmission could be realized only by admitting the destructiveness of the abyssal into the very structure of the poetic work. As if it were the condition of mortals that they be granted the possibility of right measure only through an acknowledgment that its order, coming from the immeasurable, is ultimately beyond grounding. (In *Contributions to Philosophy* [*Beiträge zur Philosophie*], Heidegger confronts this very question—the question of a certain "undecidability.")[14]

II

In a draft fragment for "The Death of Empedocles," Hölderlin has the hero brazenly boast:

> I know everything, I can master everything;
> I recognize it as entirely the work of my own hands, and direct,
> as I want,
> a lord of spirits, the living.
> The world is mine, and submissive [*untertan*] and useful
> are all powers to me.[15]

Hölderlin sees in Empedocles' defiance of measure, in his claim to dominate, a subject for sustained questioning. For the poet, we human beings, cast into a realm between the animals and the gods, must recognize in ourselves the mortality of our condition—and we must take this mortality as the measure of our lives and the sentence of our fate. But, precisely as human beings, we are free to defy this measure, even free, for example, to choose certain death for the sake of a cause we hold dearer than life itself. And it is in this heroism of principle, this moral affirmation of freedom, grounding it in the just measure, that we mortals experience the enigmatic essence of tragedy, wherein it is our very lucidity, our very power of insight, that ultimately blinds us, and leads us, in the name of our submission to the justice of a measure we recognize, to exceed most dangerously what due measure requires. Inherent in mortality, the measure of finitude allotted to us, is a freedom for transcendence that is drawn toward the abyss of possibilities—and into a course of action where not even knowledge of the just measure—a moment of insight—and a will of noble intentions can avert the unfolding justice of a tragic fate. On both poetic and philosophical grounds, Hölderlin accordingly found himself deeply, intensely provoked into a thoughtful meditation on the essence of the experience of fateful freedom represented in its purest form by the art of Greek tragedy.

If any thinker exists for whom the question of "right measure" was of the utmost concern, any thinker for whom, in this question, nothing other than first and last things were at stake, it is without doubt Friedrich Hölderlin. Traversing his poetic writings, although appearing explicitly only from time to time, is an intense meditation on the question of measure. Do we, upon whom the gods have bestowed the gift of freedom, know the right measure for mortals to live by? Can we even be sure that there is, in the realm of the metaphysical, if not here where mortals dwell, any absolutely authoritative measure?

In "Hyperion's Youth," Hölderlin seems to credit the conviction that, although measure imposes no limits, or perhaps precisely because it imposes none, we mortals can and should voluntarily impose our own limits and our highest ideals on the exercise of our freedom:

> The full measure . . . against which
> The noble spirit of man measures the things,
> Is without limits, and so it must be and remain;
> The Ideal of everything that appears,
> That, pure and holy, we must preserve.[16]

Hölderlin's representation of the right measure is considerably more complicated than it might seem at first. In fact he feels deep conflict, not only in regard to the question of measure—whether there is any measure at all, and if so, what it is—but also, correspondingly, in regard to the proper use of our freedom in its appropriation. For, although the divine gift of a measure for living imposes conditions limiting our freedom, the no less divine gift of freedom seems to imply actions exceeding the measure, actions heroically—if also tragically—defiant of the measure, the moral law we believe to be imparted and commanded by God.

For Hölderlin, human beings, mortals assigned a place of dwelling between the realm of the animals and the realm of the spirit and the gods, are torn between, on one hand, the estrangements of freedom, independence, and self-assertion, a life exceeding the measure, and, on the other hand, the powerful attraction of belonging, integration, shelter in the unity of Being, a life befitting the measure, at home in the world. In "The Rhine," the poet hopes for a certain measured balance:

> Men and gods then celebrate their marriage,
> Every living thing rejoices,

> And for a while
> Fate [*Schiksaal*] achieves a balance.[17]

This thought, perhaps nothing but a heartfelt hope, may also be what Hölderlin wants to hear in Ignatius Loyola's epitaph, which he puts at the head of his novel, *Hyperion*: "Non coerceri maximo, contineri minimo, divinum est" ("Not to be confined by the greatest, yet to be contained within the smallest, is divine"). We approximate the divine by not being limited in our aspirations, but also in being humble and modest, mortals sensible of our finitude.

At stake for the philosophers of German romanticism is, to take a phrase from Heidegger's "Metaphysics as History of Being," the question whether and how man's "assurance of himself and of his effectiveness" will determine the conditions of truth and reality.[18] According to Heidegger, the metaphysics that defined the modern age affirmed that "the creator god as first cause [*Ursache*] is what primarily effects [*das erstlich Wirkende*], and . . . his effects [*sein Gewirktes*] are the world, and within the world, the true effector [*Wirker*], is Man,"[19] working with God's gift of freedom. If that is true, then German romanticism, Hölderlin and Novalis in particular, must be read as deeply ambivalent about this metaphysical representation of "Man"—far more ambivalent—and far more prescient—than the philosophers of the Enlightenment, who were less disposed to look back toward the past in elegiac mourning over what was sacrificed for the sake of a rational progress in freedom, far less visionary in their dreams for the future, and much too confident in the benevolence of reason to seize the opportunities for critical action in the present. The spirit of romanticism harbors an inconsolable longing and striving for the fulfillment of a paradisiacal past that has never been present—a lost past in that sense. But precisely because of this experience of loss, the romantics are passionate in their affirmation of freedom, committed beyond reason to the possibility of a radically new future. This melancholy hope is haunted, however, by irrepressible anxieties, a keen, almost tragic sense of the temptations and dangers that—for the sake of their utopian dream, for the sake of their divine entrustment—they know that they must risk confronting.

Though longing for an absolute unity of being in a world they experienced as increasingly fragmented, a world their fragmented prose reflected, the romantics would not be consoled by any false or unmediated unity. Hölderlin's powerful fragment "Judgment and Being" helps one to discern this integrity in the writings that belong to the spirit of romanticism, arguing with sublime lucidity that the very logic of judgment, a power to synthesize which cannot avoid positing a prior differentiation, makes impossible the metaphysical attempt to reach, through judgment, a primordial, originary unity untouched by division. If there is a unity of thought and being, Hölderlin's fragment asserts that it is not a unity that thinking can ever grasp. The ground that can be grasped is not the ground. Against the pretensions of an idealism that refuses to avow the temporal conditions determining its possibility, the fragment argues for the finitude of the individual subject—and thus for limits to the sovereignty of reason. (I read Heidegger's lecture course, published with the title *The Principle of Reason,* as attempting to think with differently attuned ears toward a postmetaphysical notion of reason that would be in harmony with being as its ground. Is it possible to hear the claims of reason without commitment to an ontologically deaf measure?)

In his 1794 preface to the "Hyperion" fragment published in *Neuer Thalia,* Schiller's review, Hölderlin—perhaps with the story of Empedocles in mind—recognizes "the all-desiring, all-subjugating dangerous side of man [*die alles begehrende, alles unterjochende gefährliche Seite des Menschen*] as well as the highest and most beautiful condition [*Zustand*] he can achieve." [20] Thus, granted our freedom, our capacity—and our temptation—to exceed all measure, the question for Hölderlin must be not only whether there is on earth any measure, but also what our relationship to measure, as the finite beings we are, should be. Are we, must we be, as Hölderlin says in "Hyperion's Song of Fate," "fated to fall downward for years into the unknowable [*ins Ungewisse*]"? [21] The poet's word *Ungewisse* also means "the uncertain," "the undecidable." Its mood may also be translated by "abyss."

Unlike the philosophers of the Enlightenment, and long before the heirs to the Enlightenment project, the representatives of German romanticism—above all, perhaps, Hölderlin—anticipated the anguishing dilemma that eventually compelled philosophers of the twentieth century to attempt to overcome or deconstruct the history of metaphysics. For German romanticism, and for Hölderlin in particular, the "flight" of the gods—their withdrawal and our abandonment, leaving us to resolve on our own authority the moral conflicts in social life that freedom inevitably creates—called into question, indeed threatened to negate, the very possibility of a just measure, a normative universality, with the power to gather and unify without coercion or violence. How can we use our gift of freedom wisely in a time of absent gods, in a time, therefore, denied the guidance and restraint of an absolute measure commanded by the gods? For, unlike the Enlightenment, with its unshakable faith in the progress of a normative universal Reason, its innerworldly substitute for the absent God, romanticism recognized in the logic of our freedom the transcendence of all limitation, the questionability of all law, and glimpsed, beyond the jurisdiction of the just measure, the abyssal vortex into which, bereft of the signs of divine presence, bereft of their commanding restraint, mortals were in danger of falling. Indeed, Hölderlin saw all too clearly that the very desire for the Absolute, the unity of Being, could draw us into a use of freedom that would cast the just measure into an abyssal suspension. But, limited by the peculiar blindness of his very lucidity, he was not able to see the possibility of any postmetaphysical resolution to the moral and spiritual crisis that was already beginning to make itself felt in his time.

In "Hyperion," Hölderlin, a poet become stranger in his own land, in exile even from the customary syntax of his native language, acknowledges that no homecoming, no return to the original unity and wholeness of Being, is possible once we have chosen to live in the freedom of reflection. For critical reflection inherently creates a crisis, dividing the unity. Thus, although we may be favored with certain "intimations" (*Ahnungen*) of a unity and wholeness belonging to a prereflective past beyond the reach of memory, we cannot avoid recognizing the impossibility of a return. We live in a world of diremptions and estrangements. This means that we are thrown into a rhythmic oscillation, now celebrating the sublime transcendence achieved by the exercise of our freedom and our capacity for reflection, now disturbed by the uncanniness, even the monstrosity, of this very transcendence. If any peace of mind can be attained, it would have to come from a certain reflectively achieved understanding and acceptance of our dependence on the ground of Being—a dependence, however, which only our incessant struggle for freedom from all metaphysical grounds will show us that we can master neither in thought nor in deed. Our dependence cannot be overcome, yet the struggle for freedom reveals the ground of being to have no bottom. Freedom thus reveals its release—but also its danger, its risk. For Hölderlin, it is poetry, its freedom both bound and released by measure, that best registers this morally essential rhythm of life, for the philosophical thought of his time recognized no metaphysical measure, no ground beyond reason, but only the *ratio* that a rationality severed from sense and sensibility is able to posit out of itself.

Ralph Waldo Emerson, in a journal entry dated February 1854, reflects on poetic metrics, on measure. In keeping with the transcendental spirit of romanticism, he expresses his longing for a rhythm, a measure, that would ground the harmony of nations and peoples:

> Meters. I amuse myself often, as I walk, with humming the rhythm of the decasyllabic quatrain, or of the octosyllabic with alternate sexsyllabic or other rhythms, and believe these meters to be organic, or derived from our human pulse, and to be therefore not proper to one nation, but to mankind. . . . [If only] one could fill these small measures with words approaching to the power of these beats.[22]

This prereflective rhythm, manifesting the unity of Being in its normative universality, is what, in our needful times, the poet is called upon to bring to words as a measure for life. But what can we hope for? Like Hölderlin, Emerson sees a world that "lacks unity, and lies broken and in heaps . . . because man is disunited with himself."[23] How can we be confident that in the exercise of our freedom we have affirmed as our measure what Emerson calls "action proportioned to nature," when, as he himself avers, coming close to experiencing the alienation of the poet, it cannot be denied that "we are as much strangers in nature, as we are aliens from God"?[24]

In another late poem fragment bearing the title "Vom Abgrund nemlich . . . " ("Setting out from the abyss . . . "), Hölderlin, letting us know at once that what he has to say has been drawn "from the abyss," suggests that, when thinking of human being, it is necessary

> to speak of man
> By [reference to] nature's stamp [*Abdruck*] upon
> The human shape [*Gestalt*].[25]

But what has this "stamp," this "sign," inscribed, what has it assigned? Can we say? Is it legible — or, if legible, is its meaning decidable? In "Bread and Wine," the poet must finally ask:

> Why no more does a god imprint on the brow of a mortal
> Struck, as by lightning, the mark [*den Stempel*], brand him, as once he
>   would do?
> Otherwise he would come to himself, assuming a shape [*Gestalt*] that
>   was human.[26]

As if in answer to this question, in "The Titans" the poet says, "The divine does not approach those who do not partake [*Göttliches trift Untheilnehmende nicht*]." [27] In the second version of "Mnemosyne," the poet can say only that, though we may once have received a sign, or measure, and became thus ourselves a sign embodying the divine measure, we have since that immemorial time lost the language that would connect us to what it signifies. This is intriguingly reminiscent of Pelagianism, the doctrine that the gift of grace has been so deeply inscribed in our nature that it is unknowable and unappropriable:

> A sign are we, without meaning
> Without pain are we and have nearly
> Lost our language in foreign lands. [28]

If the stamp assigns the capacity to obey the divine gift of measure, it also assigns, perhaps precisely because we have been deprived of its meaning, freedom—the capacity to forget it, to betray it, to transgress and exceed it. Deprived of the key to its meaning, without a connection to its origin, we are—or seem to be—truly abandoned, released to our freedom. Thus the poet reminds himself, in the first version of "The Only One":

> Never, much though I wish to, can I find [*Nie treff ich, wie ich wünsche,*]
> The right measure [*Das Maas*]. But a god,
> If he comes [*wenn kommt*], knows what I wish, the best. [29]

"If he comes"! In effect, it seems that we are given a historical task that we cannot possibly realize, a task that must fail: an assignment the signs of which Maurice Blanchot might describe as "effaced before being written," causing "the anxious search for what was never written in the present, but in a past still to come." [30]

At this point, a letter that Gershom Scholem wrote to Benjamin regarding Franz Kafka's conception of law might shed some light on Hölderlin's words "a sign without meaning." Scholem suggested that it would be worth thinking of "a stage in which revelation does not signify [*bedeutet*], yet still affirms itself by the very fact that it is in force." [31] Being in force without recognition, validity without meaning (*Geltung ohne Bedeutung*), is for Scholem, as Giorgio Agamben astutely observes, "the correct definition of the [exceptional] state of law in Kafka's novel." [32]

When we read a short text Hölderlin wrote on the question of freedom, a further dimension of the problem comes to light. Hölderlin says:

> The law of freedom *commands* [*gebietet*], however, without any consideration for nature's help. Whether or not nature supports the exercise of the law, the law commands. Rather, it presupposes a resistance [*Widerstand*] in nature; otherwise it would not need to *command.* The first time that the law of freedom showed itself to us [*sich an uns äußert*], it appeared as punishing. . . . Morality can therefore never be entrusted to [mere] nature.[33]

Many are the propositions in this passage that call for thought, beginning with what Scholem's insight would suggest: a question, namely, regarding the commandment. What exactly is being commanded by this law of freedom? As the announcement of a law of freedom, is it not—in fact must it not be—a commandment that commands nothing? Is it not communicated by a sign signifying nothing, a sign without an assignment—so that all meanings, all interpretations, are granted as potentially realizable?

If it is true that, on the one hand, morality can never be entrusted to nature, that it therefore requires the intervention or supervenience of divine law and social judgment, it is also true, on the other hand, that the very possibility of morality presupposes freedom—and perhaps also that, although this freedom is a freedom to betray the moral law, a predisposition for guilt and expiation has also been inscribed in our nature. What would it mean, then, to suppose that morality (*Sittlichkeit*) has been entrusted to the sensibility (*Sinnlichkeit*) of human nature? Would it not, according to the poet, have been entrusted already to the sense and sensibility of human nature—if only in the form of a mere potentiality—a potentiality that can always also not be actualized? Might it not be a question, therefore, of an endowment that requires the most careful cultivation—and not, or not only, the interventions of a punishing *Ur-teil,* a punishing judgment? Are transgression, guilt, and punishment necessary for our awareness of the moral law, as the poet suggests in the short essay "On the Concept of Punishment"?[34] If so, then it seems that the moral law must indeed command a freedom that transgresses its commandment.

Is it certain that, for the poet, in spite of expressions of an intense desire for the evidence of measure, the excesses of freedom are in every instance—even when they do not bring misfortune and do not teach inevitable tragedy—deeds we must disavow? Could there be, as the poet once rashly suggested, "a morality of instinct [*eine Moralität des Instinkts*]"?[35] Does this even make sense? Would a god, if it came, make the moral impulses of our nature known to us, revealing the true human physiognomy in "nature's stamp"?

III

"Is there a measure on earth?" In other fragments of "In lovely blueness
. . . ," the poet seems to express a less despairing answer to that question,
for he speaks of "the serenity of virtue" (*der Tugend Heiterkeit*) in a way
that suggests he regards it as an ideal measure that mortals may perhaps
be presumed capable of realizing, at least to some extent. So he writes,
"As long as kindliness, which is pure, remains in his heart, a man may
measure himself [*misset*] not unhappily in relation to the divinity." Is this
because the appropriate measure has been given, has been embodied, and
is after all, for those not blinded by the historical forces in egoism, unquestionably manifest? Hölderlin follows his questions with an affirmation of belief that generates more questions than answers, its evasiveness
concentrated in the *ist's*, an abridgement that seems to conceal something
essential about the measure: "Is God unknown? Is He manifest as the
sky? This rather [*eher*] I believe. / It is the measure of man [*Des Menschen
Maaß ist's*]." This *ist's* is an abbreviation that cannot be ignored: What is
withdrawing, withholding itself from the poet's powers of expression? Is it
the *origin* of the measure? Does the measure belong to man? Or does man
belong to measure? In that poetic elision or collision, what is vouchsafed
its absence, its concealment? Why is the poet's language here so sparing,
schonend?

"Homecoming" is another late poem in which the poet imagines the
revelation of measure: the god's "measureless, tireless workshop [*die uner-
meßliche Werkstatt*], busy sending out gifts [*Gaaben versendend*] day and
night." Thus:

> Silent he dwells, alone, and bright shines his countenance,
> He, the aethereal one, seems disposed to give life,
> To generate joy, with us [mortals], as often when, making known the
>   measure [*kundig des Maases*],
> Acknowledging those who draw breath [*Kundig der Athmenden*], hesi-
>   tant, restrained and sparing [*schonend*], the God
> Sends well-allotted fortune [*Wohlgediegenes Glück*] to the cities and
>   houses.[36]

In the final version of his "Celebration of Peace," also a late work, Hölderlin once again connects a sparing gesture and the granting of measure,
observing:

> For sparingly [*schonend*], at all times announcing the measure [*des Maßes*
>   *allzeit kundig*]
> Only for a moment [*Nur einen Augenblik*] a god will touch [*rührt . . . an*]
>   the dwellings
> Of men, foreseen by none, and no-one knows when.[37]

Although the measure is announced "at all times," this version says that it
is "only for a moment" if at all, that we may actually be touched and
moved by the presence of the divine in the world of our dwelling. However, in the first version, the poet distinctly emphasizes the peculiar temporality of this moment: imagining a future past, he sees this moment as
a belated experience of the divine presence, an experience belonging to the
"has been" (*gewesen*) of a redemptive time already coming from the future. The *Augenblik*, if it happens, is the moment after, when the god's
having ever so briefly passed and touched will have been felt at last. Everything ultimately hinges on the moment of belated recognition:

> only an *Augenblik*
> And they do not know it, yet long
> Do they ponder it [*Gedenken sie des*], and ask who it was [*wer es ge-*
>   *wesen*],
> But when a time has passed, they recognize it [*Wenn aber eine Zeit vorbei*
>   *ist, kennen sie es*].[38]

Here the poet evokes the "passing by" (*Vorbeigang*) of the last god and, at
the same time, our responsibility as mortals to maintain a vigilant, guardian awareness—what Heidegger refers to, in *Contributions to Philosophy*, as
the *Wächterschaft des Menschen*.[39] The ecstatic temporality of the *Augen-*
blick—that moment, impossible within the customary order of time,
when the presence of divinity enters into our lives and enables us to realize
the fitting measure for our dwelling on earth—cannot come to pass unless, with what Heidegger will call "resolute anticipatory openness" (*vor-*
laufende Entschlossenheit), we fittingly prepare ourselves for its coming, its
presence. We must learn to wait with patience in anticipatory preparedness; but only the heavenly ones—or, say, the coming of another era—can
determine the whether, the when, and the where of this moment.

But since the poet is singularly called upon to seek and impart the
fitting measure, Hölderlin sings of this preparedness, this anticipatory vigilance,[40] in "Bread and Wine," anticipating with images of joy the return
of the gods and the beginning of another history. With bread and wine,

he says, we would bethink and give thanks to the heavenly ones, "who once [*die sonst*] / were there [*Da gewesen*], and who will return at the right time [*die kehren in richtiger Zeit*]."⁴¹ However, the poet's joy is mixed with sorrow, for he knows that, even when the divine has come again, we may remain blind and unaware: the human being, he says with feeling, "fails to see it and recognize it" (*kennet und sieht er es nicht*).⁴²

The divine touch (*Berührung*) comes near and—in part because of the *Nachträglichkeit*, the belatedness of the experience—touches without touching. Different from this gently passing touch, the poet remarks, are the gestures of *das Wilde*, the "daimonic" one, the one "excluded" (according to my radical translations of the German), who therefore represents the innocent, prehistoric, pre-ethical condition of humanity.⁴³ *Das Wilde* is the one who "must come" to the "holy place" from the remote ends of the earth and who,

> roughly fingering [*übt rauhbetastend*] , works through his daimonic
>   madness [*den Wahn*],
> So fulfilling a fate [*ein Schicksal*] .⁴⁴

Working through this daimonic madness, fulfilling a fate, he leaves behind its ancient mythic spell, its enchantment. And this makes possible his exposure to the prophesies of redemption. Although, according to the poet, "thanks will never follow at once the god-sent gift [*gottgegebnen Geschenke*]."⁴⁵ The primordial allotment or measure that comes in this gift is also a primordial or originary judgment, or assignment, a task constitutive of our very existence as mortals: an *Ur-teil* in both of these senses. Yet the gift can be—perhaps must be—forgotten, even defied. In earlier drafts of this poem, the god is described as touching the dwellings of men "with a sparing hand" (*mit schonender Hand*) , while the wild and "daimonic" one, deprived of moral self-knowledge, is said to be "blindly fingering" (*blindbetastend*), as he "works through [the delusion of] his daimonic madness and fulfills a fate."⁴⁶

The touch of the gods is "sparing," "transitory," "only for a moment," restrained in its measure, a passing "nearing," touching without touching. This is one of the poet's ways of resisting an experience of time and history that, bound as it is to the "metaphysics of presence," can produce only an endless repetition of its injustice, reducing the fitting measure to the ready-to-hand. The uncanny time in which the heavenly ones come to "presence" has, of course, its own measure. Correspondingly, the "pres-

entness" proper to the poetic dwelling of mortals will belong not to a succession of now-present moments but to our timely whiling in the openness of a receptive vigilance, preparing to make divine presence at home
in our way of dwelling, if and when we are granted that possibility: *in der
Gegenwart . . . eine Weile zeitig zu stehen.*[47] The time of this whiling is of
necessity measured. For "only at times [*Nur zu Zeiten*] can human beings
bear [*erträgt*] divine fullness."[48] Inevitably, this difficulty has been reflected in our metaphysics. And only with the greatest difficulty has the
fateful closure ruling in the "fullness" of that metaphysics been perceived
and breached.

Thus, for example, in *Speech and Phenomenon*, Jacques Derrida has undertaken a powerful critique of the metaphysical representation of how
the present of time presents itself, an account that has made it absolutely
impossible for philosophers to conceive the peculiar "present" (*Gegenwart*) of poetic dwelling:

> Within the metaphysics of presence . . . we believe, quite simply and quite lit-
> erally, in absolute knowledge as the closure if not the end of history. And we
> believe that such a closure has taken place. The history of being as presence,
> as self-presence in absolute knowledge, as consciousness of self in the infinity
> of the *parousia*—this history is closed. The history of presence is closed, for
> "history" has never meant anything but the presentation (*Gegenwärtigung*) of
> being, the production and recollection of beings in presence, as knowledge
> and mastery.[49]

But when the poet renounces knowledge and mastery for the sake of a last
hope, must he not be prepared to renounce a vision of the very measure
on which his hope depends? Does not the renunciation of metaphysical
presence, the totally present, necessary for another beginning, necessary
for the coming of other gods or other ways for beings to presence, also at
the same time compel the poet to leave the presencing, the *es gibt*, of the
measure in a time of suspense? And would not this renunciation take effect first of all in the poet's writing, in a certain irreconcilable tension—
or strife—between sound and sense, meter and meaning, rhythm and
signification?[50] Would there not be, destructive to the temporality of predictable succession, untimely grammatical interruptions and postpone-
ments of sense—emissary traces of a higher dictation?

In "Bread and Wine," Hölderlin warns us that "what is heavenly arrives
as profound disruption [*tiefschütternd*] / Down from the shadows arrives
for humans their day."[51]

IV

"Bread and Wine" recognizes a singularity that cannot be measured or subsumed under universal law; but at the same time, it also affirms unequivocally the "presence" of an authoritative measure, presumably transcendent, or transcendental, a measure or judgment (*Urteil*) that, in poetic terms, may be referred to a divine origin:

> One thing remains firm [*bleibt fest*]: whether it be early or late, always a
>   measure endures [*bestehet*],
> Common [*gemein*] to all, though to each one his own [measure] is also
>   allotted [*beschieden*],
> Each of us goes towards and comes to whatever place he can.[52]

Can the measure "common to all" secure a balance between the claims of individual freedom and those of a justice for all? The claim that there is a measure common to all is difficult to interpret. Thus, it may be asked whether "common" here means a "normative universal" or "universal norm." Perhaps not. But what is implied by a recognition of the difference? And how are we to understand the apparent implication that there is another measure, another law, one unique to each individual? Besides the one measure common to all, are there many other measures—as many measures as there are individuals? Or is there only one measure, common to all, which different lives appropriate in different ways? Perhaps it can at least be said that the measure supposed "proper" to each individual, though signifying its belonging to a singularity, does not *originate* in the freedom of our egoism but is experienced as something divine, a freedom, therefore, allotted and assigned. As such, it is a freedom that enjoins a solemn and sober responsibility. But, for the poet, if this means that each one's measure is not—or not merely—empirical, natural, it will also mean, in the final analysis, that it is not to be left hostage to metaphysical interpretations. For the measure in question both is and is not something immediately present in the present, both is and is not our own, both is and is not the achievement of our freedom, both is and is not the ground of our freedom.

Thus it is in the dimensions of this ambiguous relationship between human freedom and the ground of the moral law that the paradoxes confronting the people of Hölderlin's time—the paradoxes elicited by Scholem's reading of Kafka—begin to emerge as symptomatic of much more than a "crisis of legitimation" in the body politic. Loss of confidence in the narrative of origin from which the institutions of state claim to derive their authority is but one indication of the groundlessness recognized by the poet in the experience of modernity. For as an *Ur-teil*, the measure constitutive of our humanity is an allotment or assignment that divides up, that separates. Where there is *Ur-teil*, there is *Ent-scheidung*. In other words, at the same time that mortals are *given* the proper measure for living, they are also separated from it—banned, left in abandonment, left without measure to find their own way to redemption. Perhaps this is why, in *Totality and Infinity*, Emmanuel Levinas maintains that the will "essentially harbors betrayal in its own essence" and that it "thus moves between its betrayal and its fidelity, which, simultaneous, describe the very originality of its power."[53]

When we read Hölderlin's great river poem, "The Rhine," we again find him assuming a measure, or law, "proper" to each of us. But here we must understand that not everyone realizes the character of this, "his own" measure; for the poet voices his conviction that those who do are singularly blessed: "Hence happy is he who has found / A fate to his proportion [*wohlbeschiedenes Schiksaal*]."[54] But is this fate a true or false measure of happiness? Would our answer not depend on the nature of this "proportion"—whether it merely serves the purposes of self-preservation or instead exposes us to the powers of prophecy and redemption? In question, for the poet, is that "rhythm of Messianic nature" within which Benjamin attempts, in the passage from his "Theologico-Political Fragment" that we read at the beginning, to hear intimations of a happiness that cannot be owned. Thus the poet, deeply attuned to rhythm and meter, asks us to imagine a time of true happiness, a time when men and gods could celebrate their reconciliation or "marriage," so that "for a while" fate achieves a balance, and even

> the unreconciled [*die Unversöhnten*] are transformed [*umgewandelt*],
> Rushing to take each other's hands
> Before the benevolent light
> Descends into night.[55]

As Heidegger reads this, the night is a figure for the time of the going-under (*Untergang*), preparing or beginning a time of transition (*Übergang*) as we await the promised coming of another god, the beginning of a time bringing peace and goodwill at long last.[56] "The Rhine" continues, forming a new stanza, again seeming to recognize not only that there is a measure "common to all" and that there is a measure uniquely appropriate for each individual, but also that, if the *one* measure "common to all" vouchsafes the existence of a measure "proper" to each singularity, it can accomplish this only by suffering its own radical dissemination—a separation (*Ent-scheidung*) from itself so extreme that it brings mortals, *with* their measure, to the very edge of the abyss, where no measure can ever protect them. The poet's night is a night without order (*ordnungslos*), a bewildering "primeval Chaos" (*uralte Verwirrung*).[57] Everything fateful (*geschicklich*) hinges on what the word *doch*—twice intoned, exceedingly insistent, and, though little, not at all inconsequential—does not let us forget:

> For some, however [*doch*], all this
> Quickly passes, others
> Have a longer hold.
> The eternal gods are full of life
> At all times; but [*doch*] a man
> Can also keep the best in mind
> Even unto death,
> Thus experiencing the Highest.
> Yet to each his measure.
> For misfortune is heavy
> To bear, and fortune weighs yet more.

This theme recurs in "The Wanderer," where we read, in an echo, perhaps, of Heracleitus: "here also there are gods, and they reign; / Great is their measure, yet man still too readily measures [instead] with his own span [*doch es mißt gern mit der Spanne der Mensch*]."[58] Going "under," the poet undertakes to question and make way for the possibility of a redemptive future; but he must also, as Heidegger points out, warn against *das Unbedingten zu vergötzen*, "idolizing as the unconditioned [the absolute ground and measure] what are only [the contingent] conditions for its existence."[59]

V

So we should not be surprised when, in the first version of "The Only One," speaking, perhaps, in his own voice, the poet laments:

Much though I wish to, never
Do I achieve the right measure. But a god knows
When he comes, what I wish for, the best.[60]

This wish also figures in the first stanza of "The Ister," as always connecting fate and fitting measure: "long we / Have sought what is fitting [*Das Schikliche wir gesucht*]."[61] But who is intended by this "we"? The poets? Mortals? The Germans? Whatever the answer, it is crucial for the poet that such longing and striving occurs, just as it was crucial for Kant that an irrepressible "enthusiasm" for justice welled up in the very throes of the French Revolution, despite its errancy, despite the eventual Reign of Terror.[62] Although the uprising that gathered strength in Tiananmen Square in April 1989 failed to overthrow the government, it nevertheless gives heartening testimony to the irrepressible longing for freedom. Thus, the last two poetic passages cited above should be read together with some lines from "The Rhine." Here the poet likens us to the gods, who of course "are full of life at all times": "Even into death [*bis in den Tod*] a mortal, too, can keep / Stored in memory the best [*Im Gedächtniß doch das Beste behalten*]."[63] "But," the poem continues, "each of us has his own measure." This small line provokes some large questions. Is the poet denying that there is one measure for all? Or is there just one measure for all, which we each realize in our own most fitting way? Or must we recognize both a universal measure and also many different particular measures, among which only one is proper to each individual? Whatever we conclude from this line, the poet, in his second version of "The Only One," clearly envisions the coming of a time when we mortals would choose to find our dwelling on the path of life, protecting "the measure" that protects us. He describes this time of his imagination thus:

With discernment [*Fein*] human beings see, that they
Do not take the path of death but protect the measure [*hütet das Maas*],
    that each
Is something independent [*für sich*], the *Augenblick*,
The destiny [*Geschik*] of a time also great.
Fearing its fire, they meet it, and where
An other goes their way, also there they see
Where a destiny may be [*sei*], but make it
Something secure, resembling human beings or laws [*Menschen gleichend
    oder Gesetzen*].[64]

The poem seems to leave us confronting in our freedom a decision between two paths of destiny—indeed confronting, if we pursue this reading of the last line, a question for our powers of vision, our sense of what it might take to build and dwell on this ever-patient earth according to the most fitting measure.

In another poem, "Reticence" ("Blödigkeit"), the effort to do what is fitting, what accords with one's singular fate, one's singular endowment, is now recognized as a task the measure of which is embodied in gesture, a task for the hands:

> Someone, some way, we too serve, are of use, are sent [*geschikt*]
> When we come, with our art, and of the heavenly powers
> Bring one with us. But fitting,
> Skillful hands [*schikliche Hände*] we ourselves provide.[65]

"As when on holiday . . . " says more regarding such well-endowed hands, such gestures:

> And hence it is that without danger now
> The sons of Earth drink heavenly fire.
> Yet, fellow poets, us it behooves to stand
> Bare-headed beneath God's thunderstorms,
> To grasp the Father's ray, no less, with our own hands
> And, wrapping in song the heavenly gift,
> To offer it to the people.
> For if only we are pure of heart,
> Like children, and our hands are guiltless [*schuldlos*],
> The Father's ray, the pure, will not sear our hearts.[66]

Moreover, this task is given not just to our hands but also to our feet, for the god invoked in the third and still incomplete version of "Greece" limits "unmeasured paces" (*Ungemessene Schritte/ Begränzt er aber*), giving even our feet their proper measure:

> To travelers, though,
> To him whose feet, from love of life,
> Measuring all along [*messend immerhin*], obey him [*gehorchen*],
> More beautifully blossom the roads, where the land—[67]

So our paces are being measured; they embody an assigned measure, whether we know it or not. But a deeper, more *reflexive* understanding of this assignment would make all the difference, were its acknowledgment of the higher law reflexively embodied in, and as, the very measure of our stride. For we are mortals, and our days and nights are numbered.

VI

Returning now to "The Only One," but this time to the second version, we find the poet evoking the danger—the "death wish" of the peoples (*Todeslust der Völker*)—which the gift of measure might enable mankind to avoid: "Well men can see now, so that / They do not go the way of death and keep the measure [*hüten das Maas*]."[68] But the poet, whose art requires the keeping of appropriate meter, will insist that, despite the divine gift of a measure by which to live, there are times when mortals are "immoderately boundless" (*unmäßig gränzlos*), unruly, unable to control themselves,

> so that the hands of men
> Assault (*Anficht*) the living, even more than is fitting [*schiket*] for
> A demigod, the design [*Entwurf*] transgresses beyond
> What is divinely ordained [*heilgesetzes übergeht*].

According to the poet, this transgression can be heard in the registers of a long history, a history that must not be told without the recognition of unbearable suffering, and the need for a vigilance compelled by mourning; for mortals are able only with great difficulty to "keep the measure."

But the poet's compassion exceeds his capacity to speak from the heart within the traditional measures of poetic form. And through his exposure to what interrupts and unbinds his measure, breaking it open so words can listen to the immeasurable suffering of humanity, he knows that the violence unleashed by the unbound in the world they attempt to dominate must be judged with severity.[69] The poet says:

> For since an evil spirit [*böser Geist*]
> Has taken possession of happy antiquity, unendingly
> Long now one power has prevailed, hostile to song, without resonance,
> That within measures transgresses [*In Maasen vergeht*], the violence of
> the mind [*des Sinnes gewaltsames*]. But God hates
> The unbound [*Ungebundenes*].

Here, the "unbound" are those mortals who are without fitting measure: as the *Untheilnahmende*,[70] obedient only to the excesses of their own blind egoism, they transgress the moral boundaries assigned them by divine allotment (*Ur-teil*), breaking into irreconcilable parts (*Teile*) the world supposedly lived, once upon a time, in the keeping and imparting of a unifying common good. As primordial *Ur-teil*, the very judgment that inaugurates the law and commands right measure also, at the same time, establishes the conditions for a freedom that radically *separates* human beings not only from the past, from the repetition of a history that legitimates barbarism, but also from the force of the enlightenment potential in the moral law.

Thus, if the poet is addressing the unbound here, he evidently does so in the belief that, unless they mend their ways, they are bound to meet a fate much worse than death.

But are not transgressions of measure committed by those who are moved by the good as well as by those moved by evil? More radically, does not the moral law, as a "law of freedom" or "law of being," require—and, in effect, command—an immeasurable potential for transgression? Must we not concede that, if freedom is essential to the law, then what is most "proper" to the law will be the potential in freedom for acts of transgression? According to Maurice Blanchot, "Transgression does not transgress the law; rather, it carries it away with it."[71] In his essay "On Potentiality," Giorgio Agamben remarks:

> Every human power is *adynamia*, impotentiality; every human potentiality is in relation to its own privation. This is the origin (and the abyss) of human power, which is so violent and limitless with respect to other living beings. *Other beings are capable only of their specific potentiality; they can only do this or that. But human beings are the animals who are capable of their own impotentiality. The greatness of human potentiality is to be measured by the abyss of human impotentiality.* Here it is possible to see how the root of freedom is to be found in the abyss of potentiality. . . . This is why freedom is freedom for both good and evil.[72]

Thus, with the thought of the abyssal never out of his mind, Hölderlin's poet is unable to rest, unable to keep within the measure. For the abyss is the poet's figure for the perpetual suspension of the right measure or law—that crisis, that "state of exception" in which, sent on our way by the gods, we are—for the time being—destined to live. So if, in this time of destitution, abandoned by the gods, there are any heroes, their transgressions must ultimately be rethought, placed in a certain precarious and dangerous suspension.

Is it possible, as Hölderlin's essays on the law of freedom and on punishment suggest, that the commandments of the moral law, and thus their
prophecy of redemption, could, paradoxically, be fulfilled only by being
transgressed, abandoned to a groundlessness and measurelessness that call
into question the very measure that makes freedom possible? The poet
now seems to have thought his way to the very boundaries of ethical life—
and to the time and place of our banishment and greatest danger, where,
as he says in "Patmos," a "saving power" might nevertheless somehow
appear:

> Near and
> Hard to grasp, the god.
> Yet where danger lies,
> Grows that which saves.[73]

Where the danger is greatest, the god comes near. The god nears, but since
we mortals are not sufficiently prepared, his caring touch cannot yet become tangibly present. Blanchot expresses this well: "A hand that extends
itself, that refuses itself, that we cannot take hold of in any way."[74] Returning to Hölderlin after reading Heidegger's *Contributions to Philosophy*
brings to light a hitherto unnoticed significance in the poet's frequent use
of the word *Nähe*, a frequency suggesting that it functions as an allegorical cipher, withdrawing the coming god of the new beginning from *parousia*, the metaphysics of plenary presence.

The poet's words point to a message of hope concealed within the time
of danger. If the condition of modernity is an emergency, exposing us to
the gravest danger, it is also the right time for an emerging understanding
of the redemptive potential concealed by the chain of events we call "history." But how should we of today think the boundaries, the edge of the
abyss, to which, as mortals, we have, according to the poet, been banished?
Have we not been thrown into an inescapable groundlessness where we
must somehow, nevertheless, recognize in advance a difference between
the excesses that will bring only evil and the excesses that could perhaps
make a better world? Can we ever be certain that, in the excesses of well-
meaning mortals, a justice is at work beyond the logic of equivalence, a
generosity beyond duty, the gift of a courageous deed, a sacrifice, beyond
the reach of reciprocating gratitude? Hölderlin would undoubtedly agree
with Novalis, who wrote that "a transcendental perspective on this life still
awaits us."[75]

In "The Titans," while recognizing that "The time [of the new gods, or of redemption] has not yet come" and lamenting the fact that "we lack song to set the spirit loose," the poet attempts nevertheless to sing of daily life, enriching it with memories of history and legends, reminding those who would listen of a world that mortals, feeling the presence of something higher, have built so that the gods might return and feel at home:

> But when the day's
> Business is kindled
> And the lightning
> Chains sparkle
> With dawn's
> Heavenly dew,
> Even mortals must feel
> The presence of something higher.
> Which is why they build houses and run workshops
> And send ships across the sea.
> And men offer their hands
> To one another in barter; pensive it is
> On earth, and not for nothing
> Are eyes fixed on the ground.[76]

Here the poet speaks of a humility and gratitude bound to the grounding measure laid down for mortal life by the earth. "Eyes fixed on the ground" are eyes that, in a certain way, serve it as the support and the grounding of life. But while he celebrates and honors this attitude, these gestures, he also calls attention, though not without an audibly anxious admiration, to the archaic time of the Titans, legendary figures who conceived the necessity for deeds not bound by their obedience to law and measure, acts of heroic transgression:

> Something of them has faithfully
> Survived in writing,
> And something in the legends of the time.

Thus the poet must also celebrate the Titans, "thinking of the dead":

> Yet you also feel
> A presence of a different kind.
> For under the firm measure [*unter dem Maße*]
> Crudity, coarseness [*Des Rohen*] exist, useful,
> That the pure may know itself [*sich erkenne*].[77]

Heidegger points out that the "usefulness" in question here makes for "difficult thinking." For if the poet does not "affirm" the crude, neither does he reject it: We are not dealing "with a gross justification of the crude, taken by itself, nor does the crude appear merely in the role of a catalyst to bring forth purity, by itself. For, 'under the firm measure,' there exists neither the splendid self-sovereignty of the pure nor the self-willed power of the crude, each cut off from its counterpart, which it uses."[78]

Measure, in fact, requires even more: it demands of mortals a certain mindfulness of the abyssal. "The Titans" continues:

> And down into the depth
> To make it come to life,
> Reaches he who shakes all things,
> They believe the Heavenly comes
> Down to the dead, and mightily
> In the unbounded abyss [*ungebundenen Abgrund*],
> The all-perceiving, light breaks.

Like the thinker, but in a different register, the poet is called upon to remind us no less of the abyssal, the boundless depths, than of the earthen ground, which grants us the blessings of its measure:

> For from the abyss we
> Began and have walked
> Like the lion.[79]

In *Contributions to Philosophy*, a work so profoundly influenced by Hölderlin that it could be read as an effort to extend the poet's meditations, Heidegger interprets the poet's experience of modernity (*die Neuzeit*) in relation to the urgent questions that constitute the first task of thinking: What would it mean for a history dominated by the metaphysics of presence to end, and what would it mean for us to prepare for the possibility of another beginning? Recalling the poet's reference to "nature's stamp" in "From the Abyss" and his question in "Bread and Wine" about the mark imprinted on the brow of mortals, Heidegger observes, "This is . . . the mark [*Auszeichnung*] of Da-sein: to stand unsupported and unprotected downward into the abyss [*Ab-grund*] and therein to surpass the gods."[80] Explaining what he means by this "surpassing," he says, "The surpassing [*Übertreffung*] of the gods is the going-under [*Unter-gang*] into the guardianship [*Gründerschaft*] of the truth of beyng [*Seyn*]." This may also be read, I think, as an interpretation of the poet's words in "Mnemo-syne." This poem not only invokes the guardian deity of memory but also, becoming itself an act of memory, recalls our nearness to the edge of groundlessness:

> Not everything
> Is in the power of the gods. Mortals would rather [*eh'*]
> Reach toward the abyss.[81]

Thus, is it not also in relation to the abyssal, the incommensurable—in our capacity for deeds that exceed the boundaries of mortality laid down for us, in our capacity as mortals to build a world *without* foundations, a world *without* any fully effective revelation of meaning, a world hovering over the abyss—that we must become who we are, realizing and fulfil-ling, through our radical transformation,[82] the uncertain promise assigned to our nature? For Heidegger, we are the ones destined to undertake a grounding of our world order, its ground now threatened by the abyss it covers over.[83] But precisely here begins the tragic history of our transgres-sion—and yet also the need from which may somehow emerge the vision of another god, another epoch of being in the destiny of mankind, per-haps another revolution—the most radical—in the transformation of mortal dwelling.

VII

But what if we turn away from the "essential decision," the breach (*Ent-scheidung*) in the world order, that would open up for us such a perspec-tive? What if, at the very moment when we are most in need of a sense of measure, we renounce the struggle for appropriate measures? In his *Con-tributions to Philosophy*, Heidegger describes our time as "the time of re-nunciation in the struggle for measures" (*die Zeit des Verzichts auf den Kampf um Maßstäbe*).[84] What hope, then, do we have?

Heidegger gives no answer to that question. But his *Contributions to Philosophy*—written while he was reading Schelling's *Philosophical Inves-tigations into the Essence of Human Freedom* and while Hölderlin's *Dich-tung* was very much on his mind—attempts at least to illuminate the question of measure, taking up for thought (*Besinnung*) the poet's always sparing intimations. It will be useful, therefore, to work through these re-marks in *Contributions*, if only briefly and in a preliminary way.

Contemplating the nihilism fatefully determining the contemporary world order, Heidegger uses a word, *ver-rückt*, which portends not only a frightening estrangement but also the possibility of derangement and madness:

> Dis-placed [*Ver-rückt*] *out of* that situation [*Lage*] in which we find ourselves, namely, the gigantic emptiness and desolation [*Leere und Verödung*], without measures [*ohne Maßstäbe*] and above all without the will to inquire into measures, driven into taking possession of a transmission that has become unrecognizable [*eingezwängt in das als solches unerkennbar gewordene Überkommene*]. But desolation [*Öde*] is the hidden abandonment by being [*Seinsverlassenheit*].[85]

We must therefore undertake a "denial of all history" (*Verleugnung aller Geschichte*) to prepare ourselves for the possibility of a new beginning and the "recasting of the hitherto existing human" (*Umwerfung des bisherigen Menschen*) (*B*, §130, 248/175). According to Heidegger, the daunting task for us involves nothing less than "standing in the midst of the clearing of self-sheltering-concealing [*inmitten der Lichtung des Sichverbergenden*] and drawing from that clearing the ground and strength to create our humanness [*daraus Grund und Kraft des Menschentums zu schöpfen*]" (B, §234, 363/254). For Heidegger, this fateful task calls into question our ability to ground our humanness in *Da-sein* (§213, 338/237). Nothing less than "a transformation of the human being who understands" (*eine Verwendung des verstehenden Menschen*) is at stake, he says, "with *Da-sein* as measure" (*da-seinsmäßig*) (§5, 14/10). This measure, *Da-sein*, invoked again and again, assumes a singular meaning in Heidegger's thought. But in spite of his struggle to understand its significance, it resists and remains enigmatic. Above all, however, it must not be identified with the actual existence of human beings. Nor does it refer to what the metaphysical tradition has understood as a human nature or human essence: "In the hitherto and still customary usage, *Dasein* means the same as being extant here and there [*hier und dort vorhanden*]" (§173, 298/210). But Heidegger, hearing in the gift of the "*Da-*" the ancient memory of an opening to the openness of beyng, brings out a radically new meaning carried by the word: "*Da-sein* is something totally non-ordinary [*einvöllig Ungewohntes*]; it is *destined far in advance* [*vorausgeschickt*] of all knowledge of man" (§198, 322/226). Thus, "In the sense of the other beginning, *Da-sein* is still completely strange to us" (§173, 297/210). But it is, he says, "that clearing of beyng

[*Seyn*] in which future man must place himself in order to hold it [the interplay of concealment and unconcealment] open" (Ibid.). In other words, in the word *Da-sein*, Heidegger would have us hear a reminder concerning the contingent "givenness [*Grund*] of the possibility of a future humanness" (§173, 297/209). Thus, in our relation to *Da-sein*, we find ourselves thrown into a "crisis," torn "between the first and the other beginning" (§173, 295/208).

Since Hölderlin's *Dichtung* brings together evocations of the gods of pagan antiquity and of the God of Christianity, Heidegger will interpret *Da-sein* both in relation to the divine and in relation to the truth of beyng. In relation to the divine, he describes *Da-sein* as charging us with the task of becoming "the preserver of the site for the moment of the fleeing and arrival of gods" (*der Wahrer der Augenblicksstätte der Flucht und Ankunft der Götter*) (*B*, §143, 264/186). It is, he says, "out of *Da-sein*" (*aus dem Da-sein*) that the world of human dwelling could be transformed (*verwandelt*) into a place for the guardianship (*Wächterschaft*) of the gods (§271, 488/344). Shifting from theological language into the language of beyng, Heidegger represents our historical task as a question of our responsibility for "grounding our humanness in *Da-sein*" as the site (*Stätte*) for the grounding (*Gründung*) and preserving (*wahren*) of the truth [i.e., the interplay of concealment and unconcealment] of beyng (§44, 90/63; §176, 300/212; §213, 338/237). The guardianship of the "truth" of beyng thus means "groundership" (*Gründerschaft*), a responsibility for "grounding" or "preserving" in care the interplay (§173, §271) in the midst of the strife between earth and world (§9, 29/21; §198, 322/226).

At stake, then, is the "grounding" of the human in *Da-sein* and the "grounding" or "staking" of *Da-sein* "in" the human (*B*, §214, 340/238). These gestures require that we learn what it would mean to live "with *Da-sein* as the measure"—that we realize the historical course, the possible destiny, given to us as a task by way of our *Da-sein*, determining our humanity accordingly. But for Heidegger, this *Überantwortung*, this condition of being claimed for the task of protecting the ground of uncon-cealments (*Wahrerschaft*) and maintaining a vigilance open to epochal eventualities (*Wächterschaft*), could not be more distant from what the metaphysics of humanism has taken to be the "humanizing" (*Vermen-schung*) responsibility of man (§271, 490/345). Heidegger emphasizes the frightening dimensions of this distance by writing of a *Ver-rückung des Menschenseins*, a "dis-placing" of our humanness, the madness of a radical overturning of our accustomed place (*Stellung*) among beings, a transformation so extreme, so uncanny, that in the time of transition, of crisis and the need for commitment, we would be like absolute strangers to ourselves, without our familiar home, without the customary assurance of a festive homecoming (§213, 338/237). For to live with *Da-sein* as the measure is to live in the most absolute, frightening exposure within the openness of beyng.

This provokes Heidegger to ask: "Why is *Da-sein* the ground and abyss [*Abgrund*] for historical mankind? Why . . . should mankind not continue to be the way it is? . . . What appraisal [*Schätzung*] according to what measures [*nach welchen Maßstäben*]?" (*B*, §194, 317/222). It is of the utmost importance, for Heidegger, that we of today attempt "to find the measure [*das Maß*] for Da-sein" (§256, 412/290). But the path of his thinking only brings him to the edge of an abyss, for *Da-sein* is our exposedness (*Ausgesetztheit*), our standing-out (*Hinaus-stehen*) into the openness (*Offenheit*) of the clearing (*Lichtung*). It is ultimately this opening, beyng presencing as the open, that has, despite a history of reductions, totalizations, and reifications, continued to set the measure (*maßgebend blieb*) for *Da-sein*, calling upon us to assume responsibility for our ability to respond to the claim this openness makes (§178, 302/213; §193, 316/222; §214, 338/237ff.). Thus it is a question of our readiness (*Fügsamkeit*) to put ourselves at the disposal (*Verfügung*) of the most extreme interruption (*Ereignis*) of the familiar, metaphysically determined history of being, letting ourselves be open to appropriation (*ereignet*) by whatever may thereby be conferred (§§181–84, §189). But what could be conferred, he says, are the possibilities of a moment (*Augenblick*) for decisive commitment (*Entscheidung*) to a breaching (*Ent-scheidung*) of the historical continuum that is beyond all measure (*unermeßlich*) (§189, 309/217).

Thus, when the question of grounding is no longer framed by the assumptions and categories of metaphysics, it eventually compels us to confront the immeasurable, the abyssal—and, as Heidegger's reflections on the tragedies of Sophocles call to our attention, to recognize, "with *Da-sein* as measure" (§271), the daimonic estrangement—the repressed monstrosity—of the human dis-position.

As a thinker, therefore, Heidegger must respond to the poet's *Dichtung* by endeavoring to overcome the history of metaphysics, which cannot acknowledge that our fall into the abyssal is "grounded" in, is "owing" to, an abyssal dimension constitutive of the measure itself. In other words, the thinker is compelled to ask: What if there were something "older" than the ground posited by metaphysics, something radically other than a rational measure within the very sway (*Wesung*) of measure—a separation from measure within measure itself? What if the guardianship of beyng, a task requiring extreme vigilance, and preparedness to recognize and respond to new ontological eventualities, is ultimately our responsibility for a measure that can be drawn only from the chaos of the abyss? Must we first enter, or rather fall, into the abyss? Could any measure we might derive from this experience avoid corruption, avoid complicity in evil?

Although both Hölderlin and Heidegger take us toward the uncanny, the abyss, a realm of danger far from the realm of familiar experience, these questions ultimately open up for their thinking very different interpretations of destiny. If Hölderlin's conception of the "coming return of the gods," of "new gods," imagines a time of peace and justice and evokes a poetizing way of dwelling on the earth, by contrast, Heidegger's conception of the *Ereignis*, an abrupt interruption of the historical continuum that intimates the possible inception of an absolutely different epoch in the way that the being of beings presences, is ultimately without any promise of the good. In the *Ereignis*, it seems, nothing is vouchsafed. But there is hope, nonetheless—in preparatory thinking, anticipating the opening up of new possibilities for a world threatened by nihilism.

VIII

"The Ister," written in remembrance of the ancient spirit that the great river ceaselessly brings to life, begins with the words:

> Now come, Fire!
> We are impatient [*Begierig*]
> To see the day.[86]

Is the poet playing with fire? Is he welcoming catastrophe, receiving whatever it ordains—and obliterates—into the very interstices of the poem's grammatical form? In his *Contributions to Philosophy*, Heidegger interprets this fire:

> At times, those founders of the abyss [*jene Gründer des Abgrundes*] must be consumed by the fire of what is deeply sheltered [*im Feuer des Verwahrten verzehrt werden*], so that *Da-sein* [as the "site" for the gathering of the Fourfold and the grounding of the "truth" or "unconcealment" of beyng] becomes

possible for humans [*Menschen*] and thus steadfastness in the midst of beings [*Seienden*] is rescued [*gerettet*]—so that in the open of the strife between earth and world beings themselves [*das Seiende selbst*] would undergo an experience of restoration [*die Wiederbringung erfahre*].[87]

Is, then, the fire invoked by the poet the visible manifestation of the coming gods, the next gods to come? In his extraordinary novel, *Heinrich von Ofterdingen*, Novalis, after Hölderlin the greatest poet of German romanticism, has his character say, "I would almost [*fast*] say that in every poetizing work [*in jeder Dichtung*] the presence of Chaos must shimmer through the regular veil [*Flor*] of order."[88] Doesn't this fit the effect of Hölderlin's poetic work?[89] Doesn't the holy fire appear in the poet's verse as the shimmering of Chaos? Hölderlin's *Dichtung*, his poetic strategies, his style, has received considerable commentary—some of it indispensable, such as Theodor Adorno's essay "Parataxis: On Hölderlin's Late Poetry." I cannot even begin here an adequate meditation on the poet's style. But I would like to take up, if only briefly, an observation that Adorno makes in that essay:

> Hölderlin's aesthetic *coups de main*, from the quasi-quantitative stanzaic divisions of the great elegies to the triadic constructions, are witnesses to an impossibility at the very core. Because the Hölderlinian utopia is not substantial in the Hegelian sense, not a concrete potential of reality in the objective spirit of the era, Hölderlin has to impose it through the stylistic principle.[90]

Adorno is right to call critical attention to the poet's use of parataxis and other poetic devices. These devices, interrupting the flow of the text, creating rhythmic tensions and abrupt alterations of tonality, show that he is also right to observe that the poet's "utopia" is not to be read as cipher of the last phase of progress in a historical continuum determined by teleological law. What Adorno calls poetic "style" is the effect on the writing of an act of writing that has let itself be wholly exposed to the madness of the world, wholly vulnerable to its violence. Hölderlin's poetic strategies and devices have been imposed not by the poet but by the material conditions of an act of writing that, in order to receive and transmit the redemptive message, submits to the sacrifice of its measure, even though this means opening itself to the experience of a possible groundlessness, the very absence of measure. Is it not precisely through its broken measure that his poetry most purely imparts the redemptive hope?

But how are we to know what the right measure for living is, when no measure is to be found, given in the order of nature, given to be "read" in the very nature of things? (The task in this question recalls the task that Kant, in his *Critique of Judgment*, assigns to "reflective judgment," namely, to find the appropriate universal principle, or measure, when only the particular, only the singular, is given.) In "Celebration of Peace," the poet's use of the caesura suggests the possibility of an answer:

> For sparingly, at all times knowing the measure,
> A god touches only for a moment the dwellings of men,
> By none foreseen, and no one knows it, when?
> And over it then all insolence may pass
> And to the holy place must come the savage
> From ends remote, and crudely handling, work out his delusion,
> And befalls thus a fate, but thanks [*aber Dank*],
> This never follows at once upon the god-sent gift.

Caesurae *open* the poetic meditation to an extreme experience of freedom. But this opening is not only the source of the work's deepest originality; it is also the condition of its vulnerability to danger: to the catastrophic forces of destruction—and most of all to the seductions of a freedom that can be violent in ways we cannot even begin to imagine. But, although the counterrhythmic interruption (*gegenrhythmische Unterbrechung*)[91] effected by the caesura of the "but" (*aber*), interrupting the very statement of the "law of fate," is already a gesture, an enactment of freedom, this freedom takes the form of thanksgiving for a gift from God that, precisely because it is neither simply given nor immediately grasped, breaks through the spell imposed by the ancient causality of fate. The pause of the caesura—its temporal interruption—accordingly sets in motion a double movement, simultaneously abrogating the sentence of fate and inaugurating a moment of restrained, modulated, carefully balanced freedom: the "sobriety," as Hölderlin will later say, of a freedom characterized by its extraordinary receptiveness to what, in the meantime, in a prophetic interval of silence, might possibly be granted.

"The silent god of time" (*Der stille Gott der Zeit*) named in the final version of "Celebration of Peace" is, in the poet's "Remarks on *Oedipus*," "nothing other than time."[92] Poetry is an art that requires that the poet be willing to listen deeply into the rhythms of language, rhythms that grant a sense of divine presence—but also impart, in a measure of time, in the "meanwhile" of the *Augenblik*, a knowledge of the "path of death." This is a path we mortals cannot avoid, no matter how great our achieved independence. For, as we must not forget, "the god is present [*gegenwärtig*] in the form [*Gestalt*] of death."[93] As the mortals we are, we live out our lives measured by the rhythms of life and death. Knowing this, we learn how to dwell "poetically," appropriated by the saving measure.

The poet's rhythms, meters, parataxes, caesurae, and even, in some cases, his broken and unfinished lines are the strategic poetic correlates of the wish for an end to the historical temporality that has brought us destitution, oppression, and injustice.[94] In effect, the devices constitute a deconstructive force, a medium for invoking the destructive forces that are contained—in both senses of that word—in the thought of redemption.[95] In meter and rhythm, the poet is working *against* an experience of homogeneous time—against an order of time that, while seeming to progress toward utopia *within* history, in fact makes redemption impossible—for redemption must be redemption *from* the narrative of history. Thus, in their parataxes, interruptions, and breaks—precisely there where words leave off—the poet's words open up moments of silence, spaces of exposure, sites where an "involuntary memory of redeemed humanity"[96] could suddenly take place, bringing with it, if only in the briefest of flashes, what Benjamin calls "dialectical images." The poet's silences, those places where his words break off, give us much to hear.

In his *Contributions to Philosophy*, Heidegger is moved to ask: "Do we who are to come have an ear for the resonance of the echo [*Ob wir Künftigen das Ohr haben für den Klang des Anklangs*], which must be made to resonate in preparation for the other beginning?" (*B*, §52, 112/78). Perhaps he has suggested an answer when he reflects that "if a history is still to be granted to us, i.e., a style [*Stil*] of *Da-sein*, then this can be only the *sheltered history of deep stillness* [*die verborgene Geschichte der großen Stille*], in and as which the mastery [*Herrschaft*] of the last god opens and shapes beings" (§13, 34/25). If ever the true "voice of the people," the voice heard in the poet's dreams, is to come into language, radically transforming its usage, that would be possible only insofar as we learn how to listen with a guardian awareness to the deep silence that the poet's words preserve and into which their fading echoes draw us.

In his third preliminary draft of "Celebration of Peace," the poet wrote these words:

> Much has humankind experienced [*erfahren*]. Have called by their
> names many of the Heavenly ones,

> Since we have been a conversation
> And able to hear from one another.[97]

The final version is somewhat different:

> Much, from the morning onwards,
> Since we have been a conversation and hear from one another,
> has humankind learnt [*erfahren*];
> but soon we shall be song.[98]

The breakings off of words, the empty spaces of silence where we must "read what was never written,"[99] are not always "citations" of pain and loss. They can also be occasions for our sharing with one another silent feelings of joy: the "singing" of a joy mixed, to be sure, with disappointment, pain, and mourning, but arising from a remembrance (*Gedächtnis*) granted hints of the prophetic message of hope—the revolutionary utopian promise—somehow kept alive in the forgetfulness of a memory registering a past that has never yet been present.[100]

One of Hölderlin's epigrams from the terrible years concluding the eighteenth century, just two lines, in homage to the poet Sophocles, reads:

> Many have tried, but in vain, with joy to express the most joyful
>   [*das Freudigste*];
> Here at last, in grave sadness [*in der Trauer*], wholly I find it
>   expressed.[101]

In *Minima Moralia*, Adorno asks, "What would happiness be that was not measured by the immeasurable grief at what is?"[102] In the very grammar of Hölderlin's verse, we are taken into the depths of a joy measured by sadness, a hope measured by mourning; and if we are reminded of the gift of a measure befitting our condition, we are also left exposed to the unsettling traces and echoes of an unfathomable abyss, deeper than even our deepest pain can know. Perhaps it is ultimately in our response to this loss of grounding that we as mortals are being measured, and that the very future of mankind—the possibility of another inception, a time for the coming of another god—is already being decided.[103]

In the final section (§281) of *Contributions to Philosophy*, Heidegger returns to the question of language: "When gods call the earth and a world resonates in the call, and thus the call echoes [*der Ruf anklingt*] as the *Dasein* ["guardian awareness," *Wächterschaft*] of man, then language is as historical, as history-grounding word." (§281, 509–10/358–59) It is in language—especially a poetizing "use" of language—that the authentically historical is kept in remembrance. For it is in the memory of language, the language of poetizing thinking, that the ancient strife between earth and world is most eloquently and appropriately revealed—revealed in a way that protects the strife as enigma, preserving its withdrawal from constant and total presence into self-concealment. Withdrawing from a memory sunk into deepest forgetfulness, the experience of this strife is returned to a radically different forgetfulness—a forgetfulness that, for safekeeping, *sustains* the strife in all its fateful significance within the recesses of our remembrance. The language of thinking and poetizing assumes its historical, history-grounding mission to the extent that it lets this strife come to speech in all its uncanniness, all its disquieting, even terrifying echoes and reverberations.

Heidegger's thinking continues there, calling attention to the presencing of the strife between earth and world in—and also as—the force field of our affective and conative perceptiveness: "*Language and enowning* [*Ereignis*]. Fleeting shimmer of earth, resonance of world [*Aufklang der Erde, Widerklang der Welt*]. *Strife.* The originary sheltering [*die ursprüngliche Bergung*] of the cleavage [*Zerklüftung*], because the innermost rift [*der innigste Riß*]. The *open place* [*offene Stelle*]" (§281, 510/359). "Language, whether spoken or held in silence," he says there, is commonly taken to ensure "the primary and broadest humanization [*Vermenschlichung*] of beings." Or so it seems. For, paradoxically, language can also cause the most originary dehumanization (*Entmenschung*) of the human. Precisely in its grounding of *Da-sein*, language exposes the human being to the "innermost" repercussions of strife: the potential for monstrous dehumanization.[104] Within its poetic precincts, language calls us away from the familiar, the commonplace, making strange and dreadful what had always been familiar, bearing us inevitably into the proximity of evil. Under the spell of the uncanny and the monstrous, the language of poetizing transposes us to the very edge of that abyss of dehumanization which is always also our living potentiality. Our freedom—for better and for worse. Likely with Hölderlin in mind, listening intently to the caesurae, parataxes, breakings off of words at the edge of forgotten memory, Heidegger writes:

> Language is grounded in silence. Silence is the most sheltered measure-holding [*das verborgenste Maß-halten*]. It *holds* the measure [*das Maß*], in that it first sets up measures [*Maßstäbe*]. And so language is measure-setting [*Maß-*

setzung] in the most intimate and widest sense. . . . But insofar as language [is] the ground of *Da-sein*, the measuring lies in this [grounding of *Dasein*] and indeed as the ground of the strife of world and earth. (Ibid.)

Silence preserves the measure that appropriates the language of the poet. But the silence from which language comes and into which it fades and perishes also shelters the immeasurable. Hölderlin's grammar listens into the immeasurable, waiting for the gift of measure: listens to and obeys it, hoping to keep the measure most of all in the dreadful reserve of silences and echoes that befall it, there where its compliant form surmises what the measure requires.

Indeed, in "Ground for Empedocles," where Hölderlin calls attention to the inner transformation that Empedocles underwent in his relentless drive to know, the poet says that Empedocles began to feel "vulnerable" to the very things he had always dominated and learned accordingly that this measure requires him to become "more infinitely receptive" (*unendlicher empfänglich*).[105] Echoes of this beautiful phrase, which is possibly the most fitting way to translate or interpret Heidegger's term *Gelassenheit*, eventually found their way into Rilke's thought. In a letter written in 1915 to Princess Marie von Thurn und Taxis-Hohenlohe, Rilke reflects:

It is certain that the divinest consolation is contained in humanity itself—we would not be able to do much with the consolation of a god; only that our eye would have to be a trace more seeing, our ear more receptive, the taste of a fruit would have to penetrate us more completely, we would have to en-dure more odor, and in touching and being touched be more aware and less forgetful.[106]

Perhaps, then, Hölderlin is asking us to acknowledge a certain awareness of the intimate connection to the veiled abyssal dimension shimmering and reverberating around every gesture—an awareness essential to the understanding of our mortality—when, inspired by a "lovely blueness," he sings of our "poetic" (*dichterisch*) way of dwelling on this earth. And perhaps a "holy" chaos is shimmering not only through Hölderlin's words but also through the profane, worldly life that he names with the word *dichterisch*: "Full of merit, but poetically, man dwells on this earth" (*Voll Verdienst, doch dichterisch, wohnet der Mensch auf dieser Erde*).[107] But this is a dream. We must bear in mind that, despite our great achievements, we mortals have seldom if ever dwelled on this earth in a thoughtful, poetic way. So we might say with him:

> long have we
> Sought what is fitting.
> (*lange haben*
> Das Schikliche wir gesucht.) [108]

What, then, is the measure that calls upon us through the nature of the human being? In these lines from "The Ister," the poet suggests that we can discern this measure only in the restless spirit of our seeking, the passion of our questioning. The river poems are about this journey. A journey that sometimes seems to be bringing us close to home and sometimes seems to have no end.

This journey is also a quest for measure. Protagoras is supposed to have said πάντων μέτρον ἄνθρωπος. But is it true—and if so, in what sense true—that "of everything, man is the measure"? Wisdom—for example, the wisdom that Oedipus gained only as his tragic fate unfolded—is the capacity to discern and live within limitations. Cleverness, the cunning ingenuity of Odysseus—the prototype, in many ways, of the "self-made" bourgeois subject that emerged during the Industrial Revolution—is desire constantly struggling to overcome all limitations. But if a great imbalance prevails between wisdom and cleverness—that is, between self-restraint and self-affirmation—we may find ourselves exposed to the terror of a tragic freedom. For even when a limit is posited, in that very moment it is already overreached. According to Kant, freedom is the capacity to give oneself one's own law. Thus the sovereign subject becomes the measure, and its freedom exceeds the law. Nevertheless, since the law in question, for Kant, is the moral law, law in its unconditioned universality, right and just for all, the subject's freedom is, and must be, subordinate to the law. Consequently, the Kantian subject seems to be protected from the terror of a tragic freedom.

In his translations of Sophocles, Hölderlin found a poetic device to call attention to the danger of excess that is absent in Kant: using the caesura as a "counterrhythmic interruption," he attempted to balance the freedom of poetic expression against the necessity for restraint.[109] Similarly, in the poet's Schellingian characterization of Hyperion, the protagonist's gestures express a certain measured rhythm: the rhythmic interplay of hindrance and striving. According to Schelling, "Everything about man has the character of freedom. Fundamentally, man is a being that inanimate nature has released from its guardianship and thereby entrusted to the fortunes of his own (internally conflicting) forces." With this independence come unforeseeable dangers, occasions for errancy, temptations to fall into evil—but also exposure, precisely where the danger is greatest, to the "saving power": "His fundamental continuity is one of a danger, forever recurring and forever to be mastered anew, a danger that man seeks by his own impulse, and from which he saves himself anew." [110] Perhaps the question of human freedom is, therefore, the question of how finite gestures and actions can be made possible by an openness, a receptiveness, that actualizes itself through restraints on the exercise of freedom. Hölderlin accordingly showed a way to give to the "measure" at stake in Protagoras's saying a much deeper meaning than the Enlightenment wanted to recognize: a meaning that contests its reduction to anthropocentrism. Thus it would be a question of exercising the gift of freedom bound not by any dictated measure but by a remembrance that gives thanks. Do we know such a freedom, born not of insolence and reckless will but instead of thanks—in the poet's own words, cited earlier: *aber Dank* ("Celebrations of Peace," final version)?

But we must not forget that the poet offers, in "The Rhine," a crucial supplement to his thought of the most fitting, which seemed to imply a universal measure, one for all. Always affirming the essential law of human freedom, however tragic its blindness, the poet says:

> The eternal gods are full of life
> At all times; but a man
> Can also keep the best in mind
> Even unto death
> Thus experiencing [*erlebt*] the Highest.
> But we each have our own measure [*Nur hat jeder sein Maas*].[111]

Perhaps, then, whenever we are on the verge of despair, or are about to break through all restraints, we need to be reminded that, as the poet says in "In lovely blueness . . . ," "To desire more than this is beyond the nature of human measure." [112]

§ 4 What Measure Now?

A Survivor's Reflections on the Holocaust

The general possibility of evil . . . consists in the fact that, instead of keeping his selfhood [*Selbstheit*] merely as the grounding potentiality [*Basis*] or the instrument [*Organ*], man can strive to elevate it to be the ruling and universal will [*zum Herrschenden und zum Allwillen zu erheben*], and, correspondingly, try to make what is spiritual in him into a means.

—F. W. J. von Schelling, *Of Human Freedom* [1]

Evil [*Das Böse*] is derived not from finitude in itself [*an sich*], but from a finitude that has been exalted to independent being [*aus der zum Selbstseyn erhobenen Endlichkeit*].

—F. W. J. von Schelling, *Of Human Freedom* [2]

Evil is derived not from the principle of finitude in itself [*für sich*], but only from the dark and selfish [*selbstischen*] principle that has been brought into intimacy [*Intimität*] with the center. And just as there is an enthusiasm [*Enthusiasmus*] for the good, there is also an enchantment [*Begeisterung*] with evil.

—F. W. J. von Schelling, *Of Human Freedom* [3]

The entire tradition has understood evil as ego-ism, and egoism as the fury that by itself determines the undetermined absolute, finitizing the infinite and infinitizing the finite.

—Jean-Luc Nancy, *The Experience of Freedom* [4]

What the Germans have done withdraws [*entzieht sich*] from understanding, particularly by psychology, just as, indeed, their horrors [*die Greuel*] seem to have been committed rather as measures of blind planning and alienated terrorization [*planvoll und entfremdete Schreckmaßnahmen*] than for spontaneous gratification. According to eye-witness reports, the torturing and murdering was often done without pleasure [*lustlos*], and perhaps for that reason so utterly without measure [*über alles Maß hinaus*]. Nevertheless, a consciousness that wishes to withstand the unspeakable finds itself again and again thrown back on the attempt to understand, if it is not to succumb subjectively to the madness that prevails objectively. The thought obtrudes [*sich drängt*] that the German horror [*das deutsche Grauen*] is a kind of anticipatory revenge [*vorweggenommene Rache*]. Germany's position in the competition between imperialist powers was, in terms

of the available raw materials and of her industrial potential, hopeless
in peace and war. . . . To commit Germany to the final struggle in this
competition was to leap into the abyss [*in den Abgrund springen*], so
the others were pushed into it first, in the belief that Germany might
thereby be spared.

—Theodor W. Adorno, *Minima Moralia*[5]

I. More Questions Than Answers

At the end of *The Drowned and the Saved*, Primo Levi reflects on some of
the letters he received following the publication, in Germany, of a translation of his book *Survival in Auschwitz* (*Se questo è un uomo*).[6] His reflections on these letters resumes the discussion in "Useless Violence," an earlier chapter in *The Drowned and the Saved*, in which, as an Italian Jew who
survived the hell-realm of Auschwitz, he attempts to comprehend why and
how the evil of the Shoah took place. In this chapter, he asks: "Were we
witnessing the rational development of an inhuman plan or a manifestation (unique in history and still unsatisfactorily explained) of collective
madness? Logic intent on evil or the absence of logic?"[7] And he observes,
"As so often happens in human affairs, the two alternatives coexisted."[8] He
then ventures the thought that any explanation of the Shoah must examine certain features of what he takes to be the German mentality—in
particular, a certain "arrogance and radicalism, hubris and *Gründlichkeit*
(thoroughness); insolent logic, not insanity."[9]

Levi's suggestion that there may be two different evil mentalities at
work—a logic and an insanity—is intriguing. For it may be argued that
the Holocaust would not have been possible if complacency and indifference—the banal evil manifested in administrative hierarchies, plans, and
routines that enabled a large number of people to avoid recognizing what
they were doing—had not collaborated with willful brutality—the evil of
some terrifyingly twisted minds.

One of the Germans with whom Levi reports engaging in an extensive
correspondence is H.L., a young student from Bavaria. In her first letter
to Levi, H.L. wrote that she was not sure "that one day the lack of measure that is typical of Germans will not explode again, in a different guise,
and directed at other goals."[10] A second letter arrived soon thereafter, following what the young woman described as "exhaustive" research. This
letter, responding to Levi's request for "more precise information about

the situation in the Germany of that time [the Adenauer period]," was very long, in effect, he says, "a masters thesis, compiled thanks to a frenzied work of interviews carried out by phone and letter." [11] But despite the young woman's enormous effort to honor his request and perhaps also, in some sense, to make amends, Levi judges her severely. Sneering at the "comical sincerity" of her apology for having rushed her research, he comments, "This nice girl, too, even though for a good end, had a propensity [*propensa*] for *Masslosigkeit*, that same lack of measure [*mancanza di misura*] she herself had denounced." [12] Levi remarks pointedly that he, for one, is not "without measure" (*masslos*): his experience of Auschwitz taught him, he says,[13] how to "take the measure of people" (*misurare gli uomini*).

What does H.L. mean when she refers to "the Germans" as "a people without measure"? And in what way does this girl herself show a propensity for *Masslosigkeit*? Are these two conditions really the same? And what does Levi mean when he says that, unlike the young woman, he for one is *not* without measure? What is the measure? What is the moral significance of its absence? On what does he ground the certainty and fairness of that judgment? How does the assumption that "the Germans" are without measure explain the monstrosity of the Shoah? What is the connection between the absence of measure and the hell of Auschwitz? What is the connection between *Masslosigkeit* and radical evil? Can it be shown that the Germans' supposed *Gründlichkeit*—a thoroughness that will at all costs get to the bottom of things, seizing and laying claim to the absolute ground of things—is related in an essential if seemingly paradoxical way to their presumed *Masslosigkeit*, and also, therefore, to their readiness to tolerate or take part in the work of evil?

Levi does not answer these questions. But we may surmise that, for him, they are not questions that compel one to challenge the essence of morality. Even if, in our time, theological doctrines are no longer convincing, no longer serve as a secure ground for the fight against nihilism, Levi is quite secure in the belief that, with his deeply felt sense of measure, he knows what is good, right, and just, and that, with this moral knowledge, he can avoid falling into the groundlessness or measurelessness of evil. But how?

II. Between Measure and Abyss

Although Levi avoids elaborate metaphysical arguments, he nevertheless casts his thought in the familiar but problematic language of German metaphysics. It is of course possible that the resources of this metaphysics are nothing but exquisitely contrived abstractions, empty words, turning on the phenomenon of evil only the mere semblance of illumination. However, since we are concentrating here on Levi's construction of the problematic, we must take the terms for our discussion from the metaphysics of measure and abyss and examine the question of evil only within the conceptual configurations—and limitations—of that discourse.

Within the categorial force field of this metaphysics, Levi's reflections on the Holocaust suggest that those who have confronted the ultimate groundlessness or measurelessness of the moral and political are immediately exposed to a dangerous temptation: the temptation, namely, to turn the fascination and horror of this groundlessness into a false grounding, a false measure, a totality that the finite will could appropriate for its own ends. The proper response to that horror, Levi suggests, is instead to affirm courageously as our binding moral measure the immeasurable dignity of the human, while acknowledging the fragility and precariousness of this measure—and the inherent uncertainties challenging all judgment.

But what about the Nazi's supposed *Gründlichkeit*? Could this also, contrary to first appearances, be—in a way that Kant and Schelling darkly anticipate—a form of groundlessness, a response to the loss of a felt sense of measure? How might we understand that? After all, is this *Gründlichkeit* not precisely a determinate grounding? It is, of course, a grounding. But what kind of grounding? Is it not an anxiety-driven attempt to take possession of the ground, to grasp the totality? This interpretation may seem to be correct. But this typical *Grundlichkeit* actually does not preclude the possibility that the Nazis and their supporters were groundless and without measure, hence prone to be spellbound by the inhabited everydayness—the very "banality"—of an administrative and therefore impersonally executed evil. For in fact, paradoxically, the contrary interpretation, might after all be correct: that it could be precisely this relentless *Gründlichkeit*, this arrogant attempt to possess and dominate the immeasurableness of the moral ground, to make the groundlessness of the ground into a mobilized totality, that constitutes the Nazi's fall into a groundlessness, a lack of regulatory measure, leaving them vulnerable to the temptations of a "thoughtless" and "guiltless" evil.

Being and Time contains a statement that can shed light on this problematic, suggesting, as it does, the ontological dimension of these temptations. Heidegger observes there that *Dasein*, "which as such has to lay the ground for itself, can *never* gain power over that ground, and yet it has, in its existence, to take upon itself the ground [*Grundsein*] that it is. To be the ground into which it has been thrown is the possibility of existence [*Seinkönnen*] about which care must be concerned."[14] What this passage says is that we are responsible for how we relate, in the conduct of our lives, to this requirement of self-grounding. Our very existence poses the question, How will we take upon ourselves this grounding—a grounding that, since it is left to us to achieve it, although we can never gain power over it, ultimately reveals itself to be the very condition of our groundlessness? Will we attempt to dominate the abyss in order to deny it? Will we use our ultimate powerlessness, hence our ultimate groundlessness, as the justification for an existence abandoned to evil? Or will we instead take that limitation, that finitude, that impotence to be the assignment of our due measure?

At a certain moment in his meditations on Nietzsche's "will to power," Heidegger finds himself compelled to confront the question of hate. What is hate? To what extent can hate explain the Nazi embrace of racism—its fall into the groundlessness of evil? Heidegger writes:

Hate cannot be produced by a decision; it seems [instead] to overtake us—in a way similar to that when we are seized by anger. Nevertheless, the manner in which it comes over us is essentially different. Hate can explode suddenly in an action or exclamation, but only because it has already overtaken us, only because it has been growing within us for a long time, and, as we say, has been nurtured in us. But something can be nurtured only if it is already there and is alive. In contrast, we do not say and never believe that anger is nurtured. Because hate lurks much more deeply in the origins of our being it has a cohesive power; like love, hate brings an original cohesion and perdurance to our essential being. . . . Hate does not "blow over." Once it germinates it grows and solidifies, eating its way inward and consuming our very being. But the permanent cohesion that comes to human existence through hate does not close it off and blind it. Rather, it grants it vision and premeditation. The angry man loses the power of reflection. But he who hates intensifies reflection and rumination to the point of "hardboiled" malice. Hate is never blind; it is perspicacious. Only anger is blind. . . . To passion belongs a reaching out and opening up of oneself. Such reaching out occurs even in hate, since the hated one is pursued everywhere relentlessly. But such reaching out in passion does not simply lift us up and away beyond ourselves. It gathers our essential being to its proper ground, it exposes our ground for the first time in so gathering, so that the passion is that through which and in which we take hold of ourselves and achieve lucid mastery over the beings around us and within us. [Hate, as a kind of passion, is] the lucidly gathering grip on beings.[15]

According to Heidegger, then, the question of grounding has a deep connection to the question of hate—a connection that could be fateful. For hate is an expression of the will to power, and, as such, it exposes the groundlessness of our ground and drives us to struggle, come what may, for an absolutely secure domination over all beings.

We tend to think of evil as the work of hate; Heidegger also sees this connection, but gives it an ontological or metaphysical interpretation. However, as Hannah Arendt's research made us realize, evil can also result from a certain indifference, when the work of evil is accomplished by administrative operations that not only permit but encourage extreme emotional detachment in its agents. Thus, in the case of the Nazis, the administrative structures and procedures made it possible for the people who carried out the dark work of evil to be immediately motivated less by conscious and avowed ethnic hatred than by a keen sense of patriotic duty, habits of obedience, or simply pride in operational efficiency. Those structures and procedures also allowed many people—accomplices and bystanders in the routinized work of the "final solution"—to take refuge in a certain "thoughtlessness."

If a terrible evil can take root in the indifference of such an everydayness, as Hannah Arendt proposes in *Eichmann in Jerusalem*, that is because a will to power lies concealed within this myopic absorption in routines of everydayness, a will to power bent on the domination of a totality, a will to power that refuses to heed the only measure that counts: the immeasurable dignity of the neighbor, whose singularity is a life beyond the reach of all measures but that very one. Such heedlessness can find no good grounding, no just measure, no home, in the immeasurable. Thus it leads to a spiritual disintegration at the very center of the subject—and to the groundlessness of evil, a turning to extremes of brutality in order to destroy a human presence whose otherness is at once all too close, all too kindred, and yet infinitely beyond reach—unbearably threatening. The "banality" of evil is the avenging destructiveness that comes all too serenely from a monstrous emotional detachment. As Lawrence Hatab says, returning our thought to the citation from Jean-Luc Nancy that opens and frames our present reflections, "a finite being cannot take command of the full being of another being without disowning its own finitude."[16]

What could compel a nation of finite beings to attempt this command, this power over life and death, this rule of totality—and the "ethnic cleansing" its logic of identity requires? Perhaps it is necessary to consider what happens when many people are gathered into solidarity through their experience of extreme physical and spiritual deprivation—or are gathered into a political movement because of conditions that expose them to acute insecurity and normative confusion. Could it be that the experience stalking them in these conditions is a despair in their finitude—and a haunting dread of this finitude? If so, it could be precisely this despair and dread that, paradoxically, drive them to cling to the compensatory security of a finitude based on the absolutes of unity, identity, and totality. And yet, as I would like to argue, this leads to a second paradox, for it is this very clinging to the finite—essentially a desperate seizure of the finite, and a desperate assertion of the totality that the people have unified for the sake of their own massive unity—which ultimately exposes them to the immeasurable abyss. For the ground that *can* be grasped is not the ground. Thus the finitude—the finite measure—to which they turn in fear and despair is a false finitude, a false measure, a totality of sheer violence; and the reduction of the immeasurable to that finitude, that measure, that totality, seemingly so readily within reach of their will to power, inevitably abandons them, instead, to the abyss—a groundlessness infinitely more terrible, infinitely more dangerous, than the finitude they feared and tried to possess.

But must we think about evil in a narrative intelligible within metaphysics? Only if we can begin to think about it in a narrative that, in the final analysis, will breach the categorial framework of metaphysics. But perhaps there is still much to be learned from an interrogation that begins, as in this case it must, from the reserve of concepts immanent within that framework.

Does evil come from a collective fantasy of omnipotence, and consequently from the madness inherent in the dread of finitude, the dread of being finite? Or does it come from an excessive attachment to the finite, and consequently from the madness inherent in a dread of the infinite, the immeasurable? Perhaps evil involves both; perhaps, in fact, these two sources are inextricably implicated; perhaps they are even, paradoxically, one and the same. For of course the infinite, the immeasurable, transcends and limits the human will to power, threatening fantasies of omnipotence. So an overweening attachment to finitude must harbor a dread of the infinite, a dread of the immeasurable. But there must be at work within this attachment not only a dread of the infinite and the immeasurable, but also a certain dread of the finite, for attachment is always threatened by loss, by conditions that impose its negation. The fantasy of a "Thousand Year Reich" dominating the finite world is a fantasy of omnipotence; but the stronger this fantasy seems to grow, the weaker it actually becomes, since it becomes increasingly vulnerable to the uncontrollable vicissitudes of the finite—the indeterminacies and unpredictabilities of a finitude that cannot, in spite of all efforts, be denied. An overweening attachment to finitude can easily turn into dread of finitude. At the same time, far from canceling dread of the infinite and the immeasurable, this twist of fate only intensifies it. Such, I suspect, is the vortex of madness that turns into evil.

Evil takes hold when human beings fall into *unmediated* groundlessness and have lost their way in relation to the measure appropriate for mortals, turning this very condition of groundlessness—this nihilism—into their regulatory Ground. This is a condition, a fate, that can come about only from denying, for the sake of a finite regime—and the apparent security of a finite totality—all sense, all traces and intimations, of the immeasurable. In other words, if the *immediate denial* of the immeasurable abandons us to the potential for evil self-assertion, so will an *immediate appropriation* of the immeasurable, whereby the immeasurable is totalized and reduced for the grasp of finite ends, and so will an *immediate leap* into the abyss, whereby we lose contact with all sense of measure, all sense of the appropriate, making our ultimate groundlessness into an excuse for malevolence. For the immeasurable, manifest before the eyes of an agent bent on evil as the singular dignity of another human being, cannot by itself confront that agent's will—that is, the immeasurable cannot confront that will without the mediation of the right measure, the moral law, which the sensibility of the human body, however errant, and often despite itself, nevertheless innately knows. The will not only must acknowledge its own ultimate groundlessness but must also submit its sense of the immeasurable and its sense of measure to the dialectic of a critical mediation.

We must, therefore, acknowledge a much deeper wisdom than has commonly been recognized in Kant's frequently cited observation:

> Two things fill the mind with ever new and increasing admiration and awe, the oftener and more steadily we reflect on them: the starry heaven above me and the moral law within me. I do not merely conjecture them and seek them

as though obscured in darkness or in the transcendent region beyond my horizon: I see them before me, and I associate them directly with the consciousness of my own existence.[17]

For Kant, an essential connection holds between the moral law and the star-filled sky of the night: not only are they both given as immeasurable measures; they implicate one another in a critical, dialectical mediation. The immeasurable openness of the star-filled sky, overwhelming in its vastness, offers the possibility of a critical perspective by which we mortals can measure and judge the moral worthiness of our intentions and actions. The sky grants such a measure not in spite of its abyssal transcendence but precisely because of it. Thus, it is through our experience of the immeasurable magnitude of the nighttime sky that we are rendered susceptible to the moral law, whose measure, inscribed in the very nature of our flesh, we bear within us, whether we know it or not.

Recognition of the immeasurable does not necessarily lead to moral groundlessness; nor does it necessarily abrogate the finite authority of a measure. Indeed, Kant's evocation of the stars suggests, on the contrary, that our moral life requires the two to affirm one another in mutually critical mediation. Kant's passage also suggests that, if there is a sense in which the immeasurable checks and restrains us, there is also a sense in which a willful self-assertion that pushes *beyond* all measure crushes critical self-examination and self-restraint.

Is the immeasurable as such a groundlessness that inevitably makes all possibilities—including the evil of genocide—absolutely permissible? If, on the one hand, the benevolent can derive from the sublimity of the immeasurable a moral law or measure that preserves and protects its immeasurability, disclosing it *as* the immeasurable, as that against which all their finite measures must be judged, so that, even though the immeasurable withholds itself from their apprehension as ultimate metaphysical ground, they are nevertheless granted a measure of grounding, not in spite of their recognition of the immeasurable but precisely *because* of it, then the malevolent, on the other hand, reduce the immeasurable to the totality, the measure posited by their finite will, and lose the moral measure, falling precisely thereby into an immeasurable abyss of groundlessness. There is, in this fall into the abyss, a logic that fits their perversion of normative reason, according to which nothing exists to check the madness of their impulses, fantasies, and convictions.

Understanding the finitude of freedom, Primo Levi believes that he has carefully maintained a concrete relation to the appropriate measure, a lucid sense of the good, the right, and the just, the human and the humane—a strong sense of measure that can come only from a recognition of the immeasurable, that worldly presence of life that cannot ever be measured, cannot ever be reduced to or grounded in a controlled, calculable totality.

It is evident from his writings that Levi's measure, the ground of his morality, is not only a code of moral principles but also a moral sensibility put to the test during his time in the Lager. His guiding measure is not the consequence of calculations of self-regarding interest or advantage, not a mechanical obedience to laws and rules, not a way of conforming to social expectations. Rather, it is a situational ethics of fitting discernment, appropriate response and judgment: an ethics appropriated by the other, for whose welfare he is able to feel an immediate concern and an indeclinable responsibility. Others, for him, have an immeasurable "value." But, significantly, this "value" is groundless; it cannot be grounded in any finite measure. Nor, of course, can this measure, this "value," defend itself simply by claiming some kind of a grounding in the immeasurable, since the immeasurable exceeds the grasp of the strictly rational. And yet, though Levi's empathy for others, his deep sense of responsibility for their welfare, is in this sense groundless, reaching into the abyss, still it is not often shaken—not even, it seems, in the brutal conditions of the Lager. If, despite the most extreme adversity, his gestures are nevertheless morally fitting, that is because he has let them be appropriated by the right circumstantial measure.

But how can the "measure" by which Levi is guided keep him under the sign of the immeasurable? Perhaps, as a first conjecture, we might suppose that Levi's measure is immeasurable in the Kantian sense that, as a moral compass or principle, a categorical imperative, it absolutely forbids questions of moral judgment to be determined in accordance with pragmatic measures, calculations of utility, happiness, and pleasure. (We must recall Kant's distinction, in his *Critique of Judgment*, between the mathematical experience of the sublime and the dynamic experience of the sublime.) Levi's measure would thus be an absolute law that could not itself be subordinated to any measurement: a measure that resists measure, a measure without measure. Something, namely, immeasurable, putting us in touch with the sublime, infinite, and absolutely untouchable nature of the other human being, keeping us open to the experience of others, so that we may be touched and moved by their very untouchability, the withdrawal of their humanity from objectifiable presence.

But insofar as this ethical measure is, or manifests, the immeasurable, would it not therefore be—at least for all intents and purposes—ultimately groundless? And yet, precisely insofar as it is finite and conditional, would it not also resist and reject every possible grounding that might be claimed for it? If so, how could it ever denounce evil as evil and finally triumph over its spell? And insofar as it is a measure that concerns the allotments of justice, how could it remain pure, avoiding any "contamination" by calculations of utility, interest, and happiness?

If the immeasurable at the heart of Levi's measure is the absolute inviolability—or, say, the otherness—of the other person, it must also, at the same time, recognize in the other a shared humanity. In other words: the ethical relation is normatively constitutive for the intertwining of identities and differences, whereby I recognize the other as truly different, as a singular individual not reducible to my elective identity, yet also as undeniably the same, as another human being with whom I share the hope of a moral community. But the evil in racism—and the nationalism to which it gives rise—constitutes a totally different logic, imposing two ethnic and racial identities, each constructed to be so absolutely fixed, so essentialized, and so irrevocably different that no mutual recognition remains as a possibility. Nor can the evil acknowledge any contact with the phenomenological ground of this recognition in a bodily felt sense of the identity in difference and difference in identity constitutive of an open community. For evil on the one hand requires that the feared and hated other demonstrate a pure, unquestionable identity, and on the other hand imposes on this other the sentence of an absolute, intolerable difference—an exclusion so extreme that its logic can even require murder and extermination. It is a twisted logic that Heidegger, notwithstanding his complicity in Nazi efforts to exclude Jews from German life and obliterate all traces of Jewish contributions to German culture, seems to have understood with exceptional lucidity: "In all hatred, there lies concealed the abysmal dependence [*die abgründigste Abhängigkeit*] upon that from which hatred at bottom [*im Grunde*] always desires to make itself independent [i.e., desires to get rid of]—but never can, and can all the less the more it hates."[18]

Adorno's dialectical formulation of the matter is also useful: "The racial difference is raised to an absolute so that it can be abolished absolutely, if only in the sense that nothing that is different survives. An emancipated society, on the other hand, would not be a unitary state, but the realization of universality in the reconciliation of differences." [19] The violent histories of racism and nationalism are tragic demonstrations of the monstrous evil in this logic—a logic against which Hölderlin warned his people in an epigram from 1799 bearing the title "The Root of All Evil" ("Wurzel alles Übels"): "Being at one is god-like and good; but whence, then, the mania among men which insists there is only the One?" [20] Evil triumphs, we might say, when freedom is transformed into something totally subjective, a subjectivity represented as the stern necessity of fate, as manifest destiny, as natural law—a freely enacted denial of freedom, reducing it to what is claimed to be an absolute ground. But this is an absolute that nevertheless, in point of fact, is really nothing but a measure determined by nation, race, nativity, a common substance grounding an inalterable essence. For Schelling, evil gains its positivity and radicality when the evil will, in view of the groundlessness of existence, can freely posit itself as its own ground. Precisely this is the arrogance, the excess of the evil will—which, as Emmanuel Levinas says, "harbors betrayal in its own essence." [21] Thus, in "Transcendence and Evil," Levinas asserts:

> In evil's malignancy, it is excess. Though the notion of excess evokes from the first the quantitative idea of intensity—by its degree surpassing all measure—evil is excess in its very quiddity. . . . The rupture with the normal and the normative, with order, with synthesis, with the world, already constitutes its qualitative essence. . . . The "quality" of evil is this *non-integratableness* itself, if we may use such a term. [22]

For the Nazis, the immeasurable became a groundlessness that permitted arbitrarily reducing the immeasurable to a violent measure based on domination and totality—a measure such as the law that criminalized being a Jew in Germany For Primo Levi, on the other hand, we might say that it is precisely the measure—the just, humane, civilized treatment of other human beings—that is immeasurably precious. To state the matter even more paradoxically, we might say that Levi has a measure to guide and ground his comportment toward others because what he heeds as his measure is precisely the immeasurable: the infinite dignity of the other, the other person as a measure beyond all means, beyond all measure—a measure beyond being. Levi's measure—a respectful solicitude for the

concerns of others, a deep sense of responsibility for their well-being—
serves even in its fragility as a mighty refuge for the immeasurable moral
worth of the other. But also, conversely, by virtue of this measure, the immeasurable becomes a refuge for his measure, defending it against abuses
of power, against closure.

The Nazis, however, drawn to the beauty and the horror of the abyss—
the possibility of total war, of mobilizing mythic fantasies of world-
dominating nationalism, of unleashing the deepest hatreds in racism, and
evoking ancient fears about purity of blood—were dangerously devoid of
guiding measure. They were so because they seized control of the immeasurable, the infinite preciousness of the other and reduced it to the
measured calculations of their "master plan," and because to be grounded
in such a measure, in a biopolitics of identity that refuses to recognize the
irreducibility of the other, is to be without ethical grounding—without
what Levi refers to as "measure." In fine, the hellish world of Nazism produced moral groundlessness in three different ways: (1) by annulment, directly abrogating all the traditional normative grounds constitutive of the
moral order, (2) by reduction, making these grounds in their absolute normative immeasurability into a ground that could be totalized and measured
with arbitrary standards, and (3) by inflation, establishing their code, their
law, as the absolute ground, the final source of judgment.

III. Amendments: Is Metaphysics Beyond Mending?

Amendment 1. It is of the utmost importance that we do not interpret in
a merely psychological way the "selfhood" (*Selbstheit*) of Schelling's
propositions cited at the start of this chapter. For the "egoism" at stake in
these statements refers to the transcendental subject, the structural "position" of the subject, which is manifest not only in the form of an individual psyche but no less in the form of a people, a nation, a culture—a collective, social subject. In every instance of evil, this egoism manifests itself
as the will to power—a power that, regardless of the suffering it imposes,
insists on a unity and totality that it has determined. It is accordingly a
power that makes a mockery of Enlightenment reason, reducing it to its
most instrumental, most calculative, and most exclusionary—and indeed
most violent—employment. It reduces the spiritual to a means and reduces the ground to a figure it can appropriate in measure and use. Evil,

then, is the exaltation of this power, its assumption of an absolute determination: as Nancy phrases it, "finitizing the infinite and infinitizing the
finite." Evil is a freedom that recognizes no limits to its power of judgment
over life and death. But how are we to understand evil following the end
of metaphysics? What is left of the metaphysical subject? Is there not, in
the very metaphysics that must eventually be overcome, in the historical
influence of its categories and its logic, an insight—a lesson—still to be
educed?

Amendment 2. In our citation from Adorno's *Minima Moralia,* the
question of measure appears at first to draw us into a paradox. But in fact
it points toward the same logic that Schelling attempted to reveal. Measures of blind planning and terrorization—measures detached from personal responsibility, detached from the experience of pleasure and pain—
easily become excessive, "utterly beyond measure." They do so because
they submerge all sense of finitude, all signs of alterity, under an absolute
will that knows no limiting measure, no satisfaction, but only its instru-
mentality for the sake of a unified totality. In subordinating the immeasurable to a calculus of means, the measures adopted eliminate the only
thing that could resist their fall into the abyss of monstrous, measureless
excess.

In some lectures on metaphysics that he gave in 1965, Adorno remarked
that the attempt to obtain direct intuitive or affective access to the absolute,
access without the mediation of reflective judgment, fetishizes the absolute
as a measure and leads inexorably into the immeasurable brutality of fascism.[23] This observation strikes me as profoundly right. Thus, when in
Eichmann in Jerusalem Hannah Arendt speaks of the "banality of evil" and
characterizes it as a certain kind of "thoughtlessness," one must take this
"thoughtlessness" to call attention to a phenomenon that can no longer be
interpreted within metaphysical discourses that resort to the language of
depth. This "thoughtlessness" is therefore an evil that Kant's "noumenol-
ogy" fails to explain. It is a complacent, dogmatic certainty regarding the
immediacy of one's relation to the normative absolute that is at stake. It is
the immediacy of this relation that constitutes the fall into evil.

The reflections on measure and its absence that we find in Adorno and
Levi certainly converge, suggesting thereby the power of those concepts to
interpret the Holocaust. But I think it begs the most difficult questions
to explain the Holocaust, as Adorno does at the end of "Measure for

Unmeasure," in *Minima Moralia*, as the effect of a *Vernichtungsdrang*, a "destructive drive." What can this really explain? Does it perhaps merely repeat, in the guise of an explanation, precisely what cries out for explanation? Moreover, as the influence of Freud's psychoanalytic speculations wanes, we are encouraged to question whether there really is such a drive—whether positing such a drive explains anything at all.

Amendment 3. It is imperative that we attempt to understand the Holocaust, the Shoah, in all its dimensions. What this implies, I think, is that we must not posit the Holocaust as a metaphysically unique event, however distinctive it may be in the history of civilization, even though understanding it in this way is an attempt to honor the victims. But is it possible to renounce the claim of metaphysical uniqueness without abandoning the conceptual configuration of measure and abyss?

Amendment 4. Primo Levi writes eloquently about the Nazis' frequent resort to a gratuitous violence (*violenza inutile*) that challenges the reports of the witnesses whom Adorno cites. According to those reports, very few camp inmates endured forms of brutality motivated primarily by sadistic or vengeful pleasure. This lends support to Arendt's argument about the banality of evil. But isn't every form of essentialism an unnecessary violence? If so, then what are we to think of Levi's characterization of the German mentality? Are "arrogance and radicalism, *hubris* and *Gründlichkeit*" typically, characteristically, or essentially German? Is racism somehow more "naturally" a trait of the German character than it is a trait of the French, the Japanese, the Russian? Is the "essence" of the German character more swayed by evil intent than that of, say, the American? We heirs to the American fortune must not forget the history of slavery and the popular efforts, supported by national policy, to slaughter and exterminate the native tribal populations. Can we not avoid the violence in essentialism without abandoning the effort to explain and understand—and without renouncing the possibility of moral judgment? And is there not a mystifying silence in Levi's reflections regarding the Holocaust—an essentialism that locates evil in the German character and in German nationalism, rather than in the history of ethnic hatred and racism? This displacement, concealing the roots of the problem, is not unrelated to his own unexamined essentialism.

Amendment 5. Levi thinks that the "exhaustive" research efforts of H.L., the German student, betray a "comical sincerity" and *Masslosigkeit*, "that same lack of measure she herself had denounced." But where is the comedy in her sincerity, in her earnest endeavor to learn, to understand, and to respond to Levi's request? And where, in truth, is the *Masslosigkeit*? Is it not, rather, Levi's harsh interpretation of her effort that is excessive? Worse, does he not trivialize the *Masslosigkeit* of the Nazis by drawing a comparison between the girl's zeal and theirs? Is there not an extreme disproportion here that precludes such measure-taking? Isn't the Nazi *Masslosigkeit* beyond such comparison? And is there not in the very making of that comparison a disturbing *mancanza di misura*, an absence of measure, that is not easily explained away?

Amendment 6. What is, according to Levi, the right or proper measure? What is his *sense* of measure? There is unquestionably something disturbing about Levi's moral certitude. He is so sure that he possesses the right measure, so confident in his moral judgment. Does he think that his experience of Auschwitz renders his moral judgment unimpeachable? Moral certitude all too easily becomes dogmatism, intolerance, closure—a denial of finitude.

Levi's serene confidence in his sense of measure, a confidence he never examines or defends, is also disturbing because, as we know, other individuals and communities have felt an equal confidence in measures that, unlike his, construct invisible walls of exclusion, call for a justice of revenge, incite violence nursed in ethnic hatred, and perpetuate systems of enslavement. Confronted with a measure so inimical to his, what could Levi have said on behalf of the measure that guided his life? Perhaps nothing! Perhaps a time arrives when justification comes to an end—a time when words must break off. There can be no answer to someone who demands an argument to show why it is necessary to be moral, for such a demand can represent only a position outside the moral community.

Amendment 7. What about justice? If there cannot be a politics, a justice, without measure; if justice requires, as it surely does, a measure of calculation; if political life requires the rationality of a justice that weighs claims, balances the scales, assigns equal rights, distributes equal goods, then, it seems to me, the measure by which Levi is guided can resist recourse to calculation only within the face-to-face of the ethical relation. Once it becomes a question of the political, of relations of power, of justice, calculation would seem inevitable. In the final analysis, therefore, it is difficult not to conclude that, insofar as Levi claims to be guided by a sense or a knowledge of incalculable measure, a measure that forbids me to make the welfare of others a means to my ends, his reflections on the

Holocaust remain within the realm of ethical relations. Yet his attempt to explain what took place in Auschwitz in terms of the Nazis' relation to measure and ground manifestly draws him into the realm of the political. It is precisely here, of course, in the crossing of the ethical and the political, that the problematic of measure comes most urgently to light. For the difference between good and evil is not the difference between the use of measure and the renunciation of measure, but rather the difference between a relation in which the measure and the immeasurable vouchsafe one another, each serving as a refuge for the other, and a relation in which the immeasurable is reduced to a measure that is without the immeasurable to delimit it, to mark its finitude, call it into question, make it tremble, make it bend under the weight of an inconsolable grief over the suffering of the other—a relation in which the immeasurable, the spirit of humanity, the moral claim proper to every human being is reduced to a measure that can only turn violent and self-destructive.

Amendment 8. Finally, we must return to our questioning of the authority of metaphysics. What are we doing when, resorting to the discourse of metaphysics, we theorize and speculate about the origin and nature of evil? To what extent can such a discourse constitute a refuge, a way of avoiding any real confrontation with the concrete actuality of evil? What does metaphysical thought accomplish? What could it possibly accomplish? What thought could the philosopher contribute? How could a metaphysical understanding of evil challenge and diminish its dominion? Could the philosopher even hope to offer words of consolation? What service could the philosopher's words render? We cannot conclude our reflections here without giving voice to these haunting questions—all our hesitations, suspicions, misgivings, reservations. The metaphysical is still a powerful temptation, and perhaps must remain so, inasmuch as evil, as distinct from the bad, compels us to take our bearings on the uncertain boundary that has traditionally attempted to separate the moral from the theological. To what extent is this separation a deferment of the onto-theological interpretation?

And with what are we philosophers left when we abandon onto-theology, thereby finding ourselves banned from the metaphysical, abandoned by its consolation—abandoned, also, by its gift of lamentation? Are we left without any relation to the immeasurable? Are we left without any way to experience this finitude and take it to heart? Are we refused all sense of a groundlessness that would ground us in our moral finitude? Are we abandoned to a blind empiricism, a positivism that denies the life of the spirit, a political economy driven by profit, by a standard of measurement that cannot give us any measure for justice, nor any way to measure moral height? Where are we philosophers to turn, when called upon, at the end of metaphysics, to think the Holocaust? What are we to say? What meaningful thing *could* we say?

In *Allegory and Derisions* (*Allegoria e derisione*), Vasco Pratolini (like Levi an Italian, but unlike him, an Italian attracted in his youth to fascism) remarks, "Either we will again find a measure of man [*ritroviamo una misura dell'uomo*] made manifest by the skeletons of Buchenwald and Hiroshima, or we will have to acknowledge once more our moral failure."[24] Levi's affirmation of measure constructs a connection to the metaphysics of ground and groundlessness, a metaphysics of good and evil. But do we require such a metaphysics in order to recognize the evil in the massacre of innocent women, old men, and children at My Lai, Vietnam? How do the discursive resources of metaphysics—how could they—shed any light on the tribal massacres in Rwanda, or on the violence of ancient ethnic hatreds in Northern Ireland? Not only does the metaphysical interpretation of evil, working in terms of grounding measure and abyss, seem unable to explain these events, but further—and even worse—the failure of these events to fit the metaphysical interpretation might even tempt us to refrain from calling these massacres evil.

Is metaphysics, then, beyond mending? Could it be amended in a way that would enable it to mend a world in anguished strife? More questions than answers. But despite the concerns expressed in this section, what cannot be denied is that, with the gestures of a writer, Primo Levi has left on paper the instructive traces of a moral consciousness that has seen the Gorgon face of evil and somehow survived—survived, perhaps, only in order to bear witness to the unimaginable horrors of Auschwitz and turn our thoughts toward a measure for ethical life, a measure that, in the final analysis, is and must be beyond all measure. A paradoxical and uncanny measure, this! Properly used only with hesitation, only with anguish, only with courage. And only with gestures that are moved by the dream of a world free not only of fear and hate but also of cowardice, complacency, and indifference.[25]

Isn't the only truly *ethical* measure of evil the immeasurable suffering of its victims?

§ 5 The Invisible Hands of Capital and Labor

Using Merleau-Ponty's Phenomenology to Understand
Alienation in Marx's Theory of Manual Labor

I walk among humans as among the fragments and the limbs of
human beings. . . . And when my eyes flee from now to the past,
they always find the same: fragments and limbs and dreadful
accidents—but no human beings.
> —Friedrich Nietzsche, *Thus Spoke Zarathustra* [1]

Capitalism circulates, as it were, through the body of the laborer as
variable capital and thereby turns the laborer into a mere appendage
of the circulation of capital itself.
> —David Harvey, *The Limits to Capital* [2]

Everything is to be at the service of the hand that grasps it, but the
grasping hand regresses to the repetition of what is available, which
is not actually that at all.
> —Theodor W. Adorno, *Aesthetic Theory* [3]

"Poverty disgraces no man." Yes. But *They* disgrace the poor man. . . .
When there was work that fed a man, there was also poverty that
did not disgrace him, if it arose from deformity or other misfortune.
But this deprivation, into which millions are born and hundreds of
thousands are dragged by impoverishment, does indeed disgrace. Filth
and misery grow up around them like walls, the work of invisible
hands.
> —Walter Benjamin, *One-Way Street* [4]

I

In one of his fragmentary aphorisms, Novalis sings rhapsodically of "an
attitude of the beautiful, rhythmic soul . . . movement in the land of
beauty—everywhere the faint trace [*leise Spur*] of the fingers of humanity—free regulation—victory over raw nature in every word . . . humanization—enlightenment—rhythm." [5] A poet's poetic utopia, wherein we,
having become human beings at last, would have learned how to dwell poetically. But of course, in today's world, such enraptured enthusiasm can
only be dismissed as *Schwärmerei*, the ravings of a dreamer. Do we dwell

today in a world more humanized, more enlightened than that of our ancestors? What have our fingers wrought? Has their touch, their work, left traces that attest to an enlightened realization of humanity?

For Denis Diderot, a society based on the labor of slaves differs fundamentally from a society based on freedom: "Among enslaved people, everything becomes degraded. One must debase oneself in tone and gesture, in order to deprive the truth of its weight and its offence."[6] But even the tactfulness of the bourgeoisie often seems to him no more than empty forms of slavish conventionality—the historical, merely contingent forms of rationalization and normalization by which the newly emergent bourgeoisie has constituted and regulated class-structured social relations. But, although he dreams of a society of emancipated individuals—people whose gestures would have the qualities of a certain "poetic" spontaneity—Diderot, like Jean-Jacques Rousseau, laments the bourgeoisie's "civilized" alternative to barbarism and the manners of the court: "The more a people is civilized, the less its ways [*moeurs*] are poetic."[7]

II

But can the manual labor essential to the political economy established by the bourgeoisie realize this poetry in its gestures? Can capitalism preserve in some new modality the marvelous poetry that inhabited, once upon a time, the skilled gestures of the master craftsman, the gestures that worked with a disciplined love, a form of labor belonging to earlier historical times?

Before attending to these questions, I would like to evoke memories of the gestures constitutive of an earlier form of labor.

George Sturt, wheelwright, in memoirs published in 1923, laments the devastating sacrifice of the fir woods required by the First World War. That loss figured for him nothing less than "the death of Old England." The trees might grow again. "But what would never be recovered," he says, "because in fact War had found it already all but dead, was the earlier English understanding of timber, the local knowledge of it, the patriarchal traditions of handling it."[8] Anxiously, Sturt bears witness to these traditions, to ensure the handing down, if not of the skills he inherited, at least of a record and a celebration of a way of life the passing of which he regards with immeasurable sadness. He writes:

> I have known old-fashioned workmen refuse to use likely-looking timber be-
> cause they held it to be unfit for the job. . . . Under the plane (it is little used
> now) or under the axe (it is all but obsolete) timber disclosed qualities hardly
> to be found otherwise. My own eyes know because my own hands have felt,
> but I cannot teach an outsider, the difference between ash that is "tough as a
> whip cord" and ash that is "frow as a carrot" or "doaty" or "biscuity." (*WS*, 24)

(The reference here to a process of disclosure deserves further thought; we will return to this matter in the chapter on Heidegger.)

Referring to an old wheelwright he once knew, Sturt says, "He knew, not by theory, but more delicately, in his eyes and fingers" (*WS*, 54). The old wheelwrights knew what they knew because of what Sturt describes as a certain "intimacy" with their materials and tools: they "were friends, as only a craftsman can be, with timber and iron. The grain of the wood told secrets to them" (*WS*, 55). Such was the nature of the wheelwright's marvelous transpersonal wisdom, a wisdom transcending the identity of its subjects, handed down in and by their hands from one generation to the next:

> In farm-yard, in tap-room, at market, the details were discussed over and over
> again; they were gathered together for remembrance in village workshops;
> carters, smiths, farmers, wheel-makers, in thousands handed on each his own
> little bit of understanding, passing it to his son or to the wheelwright of the
> day, linking up the centuries. But for the most part, the details were but dimly
> understood; the whole body of knowledge was a mystery. (*WS*, 74)

Sturt describes how a man "skillful with his draw-shave" would cut a butterfly design into wood destined for an axle-bed or strutlock: "Quite useless, it refreshed the workman's temper. Can you not imagine a little," he asks, "the joyous sensation running up his wrists and calming his nerves as he feels the hard wood softly yielding to his wishes, taking the fine, clean-edged shape under the faithful tool?" (*WS*, 82). The old-timers "knew," he says, "better than any other may do, the answer of the elm when the keen blade goes searching between its molecules." Then, with modesty and self-effacement, he adds, "This was, this is, forever out of my reach" (*WS*, 101).

Today, Sturt declares, the craftsman has become nothing but "a cog in the industrial machine," a worker-employee struggling to make ends meet within an economy driven by capital and market demands. "But," he states, "no higher wage, no income, will buy for men that satisfaction which of old—until machinery made drudges of them—streamed into their muscles all day long from close contact with iron, timber, clay, wind and wave, horse-strength. It tingled up in the niceties of touch, sight, scent. . . . But these intimacies are over" (*WS*, 202). The men who once "grew friendly with the grain of timber and with sharp tools" are no longer present among us (ibid.).

Other old-timers share the wheelwright's sentiments. Horry Rose, saddler, remarks in an interview: "You don't make much money if you work with your hands. You can't make the turnover. But I have no regrets working so slowly. I began in a world without time."[9] Likewise touching on an experience transcending subjective identity and outside the conventional order of time, Gregory Gladwell, blacksmith, observes: "I have a lot of my grandfather's features, although I'm not as tall as he was. I have his hands. Hands last a long time, you know. A village sees the same hands century after century."[10] "My wife," he recalls,

> went round [the village], keeping her eye open for bolts, latches, handles, grates; drawing them and finding out their dates, and I made more of them as exactly as you're not likely to tell the difference. Mind you, it took time. It took hours. But it was a fine thing for me to have something lying on the bench before me, made by one of the old men, and my hands doing again what his had done.[11]

Old hands. Hands belonging to the time of a timeless tradition. Old hands graced with memory, handing themselves down, handing down their inwrought wisdom. Young hands receiving what the old hands know. But the old-timers speak in elegiac tones, tones that mourn the end not only of a work of the hands but of an entire way of life, which they, with still keen memories, would rejoice to see continued.

Although the society in which the old-timers lived tolerated extremes of inequality, injustice, even destitution and degradation, it also provided at least some laborers with work that deeply fulfilled the sensibility and imparted an enduring sense of personal accomplishment.

A world of difference lies between the handmade objects of the craftsman, made with care and beautiful even when their primary value consists in their utility, and the mass-produced objects of the factory assembly line, useful but without expressive beauty. Likewise, a world of difference lies between the older and newer modes of production and between the older and newer experiences of the productive gesture. Only in the older mode of production is this gesture experienced as a soliciting, as a poetic bring-ing-forth-into-the-light, as what Heidegger would call an "unconceal-ment," translating the Greek *aletheuein*.

Artist Ilya Kabakov, reflecting on his experience as a painter work-ing at his art despite the repressive regimes of Soviet communism, re-marked: "The person inside me didn't have any contact with my hands, with what was produced by these hands." In this alienated condition, his hands conformed, making objects that would pass the brutal laws of cen-sorship, while his true art remained safe but unborn in an inner semblance of freedom.[12]

III

According to Aristotle (*Politics* 1253a18–23), a hand physically severed from the human body is a hand in name only. He holds this view because he defines the hand in terms of its function as part of the body as a whole.

But a hand can also be spiritually severed—for example, in conditions of alienated labor. Here, too, we may observe, the hand is a hand in name only, for it is separated from its subjective interiority, its function in mean-ingful gesture, its part in a meaningful whole, bodily felt to be such. More-over, it is severed from the objective materials upon which it works, sev-ered from the tools it uses, severed from the process of production, and severed from the surplus value enjoyed by the representatives of capital. The more the required patterns of social labor sedimented or inscribed in the gesture are objectified within a capitalist economy, the more the ges-ture becomes alien to itself, as if possessed by an invisible, demonic force.

In André Breton's *Nadja*, Breton's companion, after whom the narrative is named, evokes Gérard de Nerval's tale "The Haunted Hand" ("La Main enchantée"). The hand is haunted by the Reign of Terror, which has be-trayed the utopian dreams of the Revolution. What prompts Nadja to bring back this tale, constructed around a demonic, dismembered hand? Sensing the return of the repressed, Breton insists on the need to make ex-plicit the connection between this fictional demonic hand and the real de-monic hands working on factory assembly lines, hands suffering not only alienation but also serious injury, sometimes even the horror of physical severance. He says to her: "I know that at a factory furnace, or in front of one of those inexorable machines which all day long, at a few seconds' in-terval, impose the repetition of the same gesture, . . . or [even] before a firing squad, one can still feel free, but it is not the martyrdom one undergoes which creates this freedom." [13]

The repetitions of the factory impose a material order of identity that secretly obliterates the workers' subjective identity, alienating them from themselves, from one another, and from their sense of a universal humanity. Severed from its spiritual nature, the hand is reduced to a demonic, destructive materiality, already close to death. Behind the worker's alienated—or, say, severed—hand lurks the invisible hand of corporate capital, a hand of demonic powers concealed behind the spellbinding phantasmagoria that the system is designed to produce.

These alienations are reflected in the discourse of philosophy, which is not only a reflection *on* the world of its time but also very much—even when it attempts to resist—a reflection *of* this world, a reflection in thought that inevitably mirrors and repeats the world. In "The Spatiality of One's Own Body and Motility," a chapter in his *Phenomenology of Perception,* Maurice Merleau-Ponty critiques the way in which the two major systems of modern thought have attempted to understand our gestures. On one hand, naturalism, or empiricism, represents our body as if it were nothing but a material object, so that our gestures, the movements of our hands, can be fully understood with the concepts of a neurophysiological mechanics. On the other hand, intellectualism, or idealism, represents our body as if it were a mere projection or phantasm of the mind, so that our gestures and movements are, as it were, predetermined according to an a priori concept of the world. Naturalism cannot account for the event in which, as we would normally say, I raise my arm to perform some symbolic or meaningful action, whereas intellectualism cannot account for the event in which, as we would normally say, my arm is a material object being raised by independent causes outside the body, or for our gestures' unavoidable accommodations to the resistance of facticity.

Arguing first against the representations of naturalism, Merleau-Ponty asserts that the "parts" of the human body "are inter-related in a peculiar way":

> They are not spread out side by side, but [organically] enveloped in each other. Thus, for example, my hand is not a collection of points. . . . The various points on the left hand are transferred to the right as relevant to a total organ, a hand without parts. . . . Hence they form a system and the space of my hand is not a mosaic of spatial values. Similarly, my whole body for me is not an assemblage of organs juxtaposed in space. [14]

But am I really, then, as Merleau-Ponty says next, assuming he is faithfully describing our experience as we actually live it, "in undivided possession" of my body, my arms, my hands? To what extent might the philosophical representations that he is attempting to refute by appealing to our lived experience actually be the all too accurate reflections of our experience with gesture in a world that, organized according to the exigencies of capitalism, increasingly objectifies, commodifies, alienates, fragments, and calculatingly measures our gestures? Is it only in cases where someone is suffering damage to the brain that the gesture loses its "melodic character"—an "intentional arc" in which "each instant of the movement embraces its whole span"—and "becomes manifestly a collection of partial movements strung laboriously together" (*PP*, 105, 136, 140)? Is it only in the science of "pathologies" that movement appears comprehensible as "a collection of sensible qualities," and not as "a certain way of giving form or structure [sc., meaning] to our environment" (*PP*, 115)?

Significantly, what is missing most of all from the accounts of naturalism is the recognition that our gestures are not "tied to actuality," not confined to the punctate now-present, to the temporal order posited as our irrevocable reality in accordance with the metaphysics of presence, but take place, rather, "in the realm of the potential" (*PP*, 109, 135). Thus Merleau-Ponty argues, "The normal function which makes abstract movement possible is one of [anticipatory] 'projection,' whereby the subject of movement keeps in front of him an area of free space in which what does not . . . exist may take on a semblance of existence" (*PP*, 111). The world as naturalism represents it is ultimately, for Merleau-Ponty, not very different from the world of some brain-damaged patients. "For these patients," he says, "the world exists only as one ready-made or congealed" (*PP*, 112). Their "practical field" has been severely reduced to the concretely actual, to the concrete presence of what is immediately present (*PP*, 116). The space of the gesture is therefore oppressively restricted, without contingency, without freedom. Yet is there not a certain truth in this representation—a truth that neither the naturalism Merleau-Ponty rejects nor the phenomenology he advocates will acknowledge? If the pathologies of gesture that Merleau-Ponty describes bear a striking resemblance to the character of gesture under the conditions of contemporary capitalism, to what extent is the supposedly "normal" experience of gesture in the name of which Merleau-Ponty argues against the representations of naturalism not, in truth, the still-unfulfilled dream of a redeemed humanity—that other humanity envisioned, perhaps, in Marx's early manuscripts?

In spelling out his argument against naturalism, Merleau-Ponty emphasizes the limits of causal explanation:

> Insofar as behavior is a form in which "visual" and "tactile contents," sensibility, and motility appear only as inseparable moments, it remains *inaccessible to causal thought* and is capable of being apprehended only by another kind of thought: that which grasps its object as it comes into being and as it appears to the person experiencing it . . . and which tries to [represent] the subject's whole being. (*PP*, 126; italics added)

Is it not precisely for "the subject's whole being"—for what naturalism cannot recognize—that Marx is fighting in his *Economic and Philosophical Manuscripts*? Is he not attempting, like Merleau-Ponty, to reclaim this wholeness for philosophical thought?

In his discussion of the insurmountable difficulties encountered by science in its effort to understand the distinction between grasping (*Greifen*) and pointing (*Zeigen*), or between concrete and abstract gestures, Merleau-Ponty concludes that these distinctions will never be understood as long as gestures are "reduced to the condition of an object" in a discourse of causalities, a discourse that admits explanations only in terms of neurological stimuli, muscular contractions, and innervations. In this discourse, both "gestures and movements, employing as they do the same organ-objects, the same nerve-objects, must be given their place on the map of interiorless processes inserted into the compactly woven stuff of 'physiological conditions' (*PP*, 122–23). Symbolic gestures, meaningful gestures and movements, can be understood only when the discourse of naturalism is supplemented—and in a sense deconstructed—by a phenomenology that takes first-person experience into account.

But if naturalism cannot succeed, can intellectualism come to the rescue? Since phenomenology may seem to be nothing but the latest avatar of idealism, Merleau-Ponty emphasizes that understanding meaningful gestures solely in terms of a theory of consciousness is equally impossible: "If we relate the act of pointing to consciousness; if once the stimulus can cease to be the cause of the reaction and can become [internalized by consciousness as] its intentional object, it becomes inconceivable that [consciousness] should ever function as a pure cause or that the movement should ever be blind" (*PP*, 123). "Consciousness," he insists, "is in the first place not a matter [as it is for Descartes] of an 'I think that,' but rather of an 'I can.' . . . Movement is not thought about movement, and bodily space is not space thought or represented" (*PP*, 138). Thus, for example, "in the action of the hand which is raised towards an object is contained a [meaningful] reference to the object, not as an object represented, but as that highly specific thing towards which we [bodily] project ourselves, near which we are, in anticipation, and which we haunt" (*PP*, 139). Intellectualism makes meaning an entirely interior object, an object withdrawn from the body that constantly accompanies it; and it therefore claims to be in possession of a meaning completely formed prior to its gestural "expression." But if intellectualism is unable to recognize and account for the role of the gestural event, not only in the communication of meaning but in its very formation, then it cannot claim to understand what gesture is. In the final analysis, therefore, since neither naturalism nor intellectualism can understand meaning, neither can give an adequate account of the gestural event.

According to Merleau-Ponty, the analysis of gesture offered by intellectualism is, however,

> less false than abstract. It is true that the "symbolic function" or the "representative function" underlies our movements; but it is not a final term for analysis. . . . The mistake of intellectualism is to make it self-subsistent, to remove it from the stuff in which it is realized, and to suppose in us, as if we were non-derivative beings, an undistanced presence in the world. For, using this consciousness, an entirely transparent consciousness, this intentionality which admits of no degrees of more or less as a starting-point, everything that separates us from the real world—error, sickness, madness, in short, incarnation—is reduced to the status of mere appearance. (*PP*, 124)

"Admittedly," he says, "intellectualism does not bring consciousness into being independently of its material." But, on the other hand, he says, it is equally clear that "if consciousness is placed outside being, the latter cannot breach it; and then the empirical variety of consciousnesses . . . cannot be taken seriously; there is nothing to be known or understood, and one thing alone makes sense: the pure essence of consciousness" (*PP*, 125). In sum, then, even if intellectualism does not "bring consciousness into being independently of its material," it clearly avoids the *dialectics* of materialism. In effect, this deprives our gestures of any real meaning—and of the power to change the world:

> Critical philosophy [e.g., the philosophies of Descartes, Kant, and Husserl] duplicates the empirical operations of thought with a transcendental activity which has the task of bringing about all those syntheses for which empirical thought provides the elements. . . . When I move about in my house, I know

without thinking about it that walking towards the bedroom means passing near the study, that looking at the window means having the fireplace on my left, and in this small world each gesture, each perception, is immediately located in relation to a great number of possible co-ordinates. (*PP*, 129)

In effect, intellectualism must reduce the critical potentiality essential to the very meaningfulness of our gestures to the actuality or facticity registered within the abstract logic of our present concepts. Thus we see that intellectualism is as incapable as naturalism of recognizing potentiality and illuminating its meaningful role in our lives.

IV

Reflecting on the peculiar nature of the commodity, Marx observes that intriguing similarities obtain between the way commodities enchant and take possession of our world and the way the gods of religion bind the world to their spiritual powers:

> In that world [posited by religion], the productions of the human brain appear as independent beings endowed with life, and as entering into relation both with one another and with the human race. So it is in the world of commodities, with the products of [human] hands. This I call "fetishism": that which attaches itself to the products of labor, so soon as they are produced as commodities, and which is therefore inseparable from the very production of those commodities.[15]

The modern capital economy does indeed, therefore, appear to be guided by the invisible hand. But there is more than one invisible hand. Certainly the "cunning" of an instrumental, technologized Reason may be traced back to the invisible hand of capital, to a political economy that systematically mystifies what it is doing, calling it fate and concealing its dark work from the manual laborers it employs. But the workers' suffering hands are also invisible: every possible trace of their objective role in the economy to which they have been sacrificed is obliterated. (The invisible hand of capital could thus be regarded as the heir to Leibniz's preestablished harmony.) For the time being, the hands of the capitalist, pulling the strings above his puppet workers, yet protected from revolt by his concealed position behind the political theater he has established, are invisible—but also, because of that invisibility, all the more powerful in their domination.[16] Therefore, until this domination can be ended, the hands "proper" to a redeemed society, one in which the social and political con-traditions would finally be reconciled, will also remain invisible (although in a redeemed society, the word "proper" would of course undergo a certain displacement).

V

It is in Marx's early writings—in the *Economic and Philosophical Manuscripts* of 1844, for example—that he most forcefully elaborates his radicalization of Enlightenment anthropology, a humanism consistent not only with dialectical materialism but also with a critical social theory. In these "utopian" manuscripts, Marx boldly envisions the eventual reconciliation of the ancient conflict between Man and Nature, and accordingly proposes a new interpretation of naturalism that would also represent a new interpretation of Enlightenment humanism. In this spirit, he calls for the "emancipation of all human senses."[17] Marx saw with remarkable lucidity that all our senses and bodily capacities have fallen under the spell of capital, of self-interest, property, possession, a system that can survive only through the domination and exploitation of Man and Nature. "The human being," he writes, "had to be reduced to this absolute poverty in order that he might yield his inner wealth to the outer world" (*EPM*, 139). In a crucial formulation of his vision, intricately reminiscent of Friedrich Schiller's *Letters on the Aesthetic Education of Man*, Marx says:

> Only through the objectively unfolded richness of man's essential being is the richness of subjective *human* sensibility (a musical ear, an eye for beauty of form,—in short, *senses* capable of human gratification, senses affirming themselves as essential powers of *Man*) either cultivated or brought into being. For not only the five senses, but also the so-called mental senses . . . —in a word, *human* sensibility—the human nature of the senses—comes to be by virtue of its object, by virtue of a *humanized* nature. The forming of the five senses is a labor of the entire history of the world down to the present. (*EPM*, 141)

Thus, the reconciled society would be a society that could "produce Man in this entire richness of his being—produce a human being richly and profoundly endowed with all the senses—as its enduring reality" (ibid.). In such a society, labor would no longer be estranged from itself; and *a fortiori*, the productive gestures of arm and hand thereby engaged would no longer be effectively severed from the worker's body of experience, deprived of all meaning and all inherent value. If manufacturing, once meaningfully connected to the hand's labor, has bound the hand to the nerve-

damaging movements of the factory assembly line, in the redeemed society everyone would recognize that "his own sensuousness first exists as human sensuousness for himself only through the other person" (*EPM*, 143);
the domination and exploitation of some by others would be abolished;
and the wholeness of gestural meaning would be returned to the hand.

Friedrich Schlegel eloquently expressed a vision that I would like to believe Marx and Merleau-Ponty shared in:

> Many people have spirit or feeling or imagination. But because singly these
> qualities can only manifest themselves as fleeting, airy shapes, nature has taken
> care to bond them chemically to some common earthly matter. To discover
> this bond is the unremitting task of those who have the greatest capacity for
> sympathy, but it requires a great deal of practice in intellectual chemistry as
> well. The man who could discover an infallible reagent for every beautiful
> quality in human nature would reveal to us a new world. As in the vision of
> the prophet, the endless field of broken and dismembered humanity would
> suddenly spring into life.[18]

Merleau-Ponty's description of gestural motility contributes not only to
the account of reification and alienation that Marx proposes in his writings on manual labor, but also to the reflections, at once critical and
utopian, that Marx set out in *Economic and Philosophical Manuscripts*,
evoking in terms of praxis the realization and fulfillment of our sensuous
nature as active, embodied beings. Moreover, recognizing that philosophical thought is never merely a reflection *on* our world but also always a
reflection *of* it, inescapably influenced by the dominant paradigm of reality, Merleau-Ponty shows in his critique of the accounts of gesture formulated by intellectualism and empiricism that, in spite of their evident
differences, both philosophies are ideological systems of thought that uncritically reflect, and consequently reproduce, the alienations and reifications to which Marx called attention in his critique of capitalism. Thus,
as long as the invisible hand of capital rules, the damaged hands of the
worker—and indeed the fully realized hands of which Marx in his early
years dared to dream—will remain invisible.

VI

This brings us to the final theme we shall consider, continuing Marx's radicalization of Enlightenment anthropology. Since we have already given
some thought to the question of alienated labor, in particular the way in

which alienated labor is manifested in and as gestures of the hand, we need now to reflect, if only briefly, on Marx's version of humanism and his conception of human being and human nature.

Marx radicalizes the humanism of the Enlightenment and its understanding of human nature in some crucial ways. First of all, Marx finds it essential for a dialectical, material humanism to consider the material conditions of our embodiment and the contemporary possibilities for transforming these conditions in order to realize our potential, not so much as individuals than as members of a species[19]—in other words, to realize a richer, more intricate sensibility, a deeper, more subtle satisfaction of the senses, and a more immediate sensuous awareness. This vision of an aesthetic sensibility, reminiscent, as I said, of Schiller's *Letters on the Aesthetic Education of Man*, draws on both the rationalism of the Enlightenment and the aestheticism of German romanticism to formulate a conception of the human in terms of a critical, dialectical materialism. This conception envisions, for the first time in history, not only that the very nature of the human body is in some measure a social construction, a product of social power, but also that this body is in its very nature always already social. It envisions, further, that the body's experience of labor and of the material conditions of labor play a major role in the process of social construction, and that the body's enlightened social nature—what Marx calls its species being—would be fulfilled not just in the rationality of labor but also in the realization of our aesthetic presence: our sensibility and our capacity for perceptive awareness.

But while Marx writes at length about the body's felt need for sensuous satisfaction, he may seem to have little to say about the body's communicative gestures, its social and cultural activities. His emphasis on the aesthetic, however, is always accompanied by a critical analysis of the pragmatic and its material conditions—an analysis that cannot avoid the temptation to imagine, to dream of, to hope for, a radically better world. And he almost says that the body's gestures carry a felt sense of the good, the right, and the just—that for conceiving a critical theory of society and putting it into practice, there is a more immediate material source of critical judgment than the rationalism of the Enlightenment was willing to acknowledge.

But in a short poem called "The Hand," Rilke returns us to reality with a reminder and, perhaps, a warning:

> Ah, so confusing a hand is
> even when out to save.

> In the most helpful of hands
> there is death enough still
> and there has been money.[20]

When will we grasp for what it is the invisible hand of capitalism hidden within the machines of the factory, directing the worker's every gesture, a hand hidden also within the financial, political, and cultural institutions that govern our lives? When will we refuse the death it secretly hands out and require that a more humane life be handed down?

We must not conclude our reflections without observing that there is another invisible hand: that hand whose nature, character, and potential have not yet been realized, a hand that has not yet fulfilled its promise. If, bearing in mind all the works of art wrought since time immemorial by the human hand, we may still speak of the "origin" of the hand, we might recognize in its gestures an uncanny power: the power to bring things forth from nonbeing into being. On the walls of the caves at Lascaux, the miraculous gestures of this passage are recorded for all time. But we cannot yet see clearly enough the grace of a hand whose movement would be beyond availability, productivity, efficiency, calculation—a hand beyond use value. This hand remains mostly hidden, suppressed by the practices and institutions of an economy organized around the exigencies of capital.

In a fragment of a sketch for a poem never finished, Rilke wrote:

> When from the merchant's hand
> the balance passes over
> to that Angel who, in the heavens,
> stills it, appeases it by the equalizing of space . . . [21]

Why was this poem never completed? Perhaps it is not, must not be, in the poet's power to give it an ending. Perhaps the poem must remain without an ending, so that "that Angel," the one coming "when the balance passes over," can announce the ending of a history of greed and the beginning of a new order of time—an order ruled, at long last, by justice. The angel's hand is not yet visible, not yet tangible. How much longer must we—should we—wait?

§ 6 Keeping Up Appearances

The Dialectic of Tact in Adorno

> There is no outward sign of politeness that does not have a deep basis in morality. A proper education would convey both the sign and that basis together.
>
> —Johann Wolfgang von Goethe, *Elective Affinities*[1]

> We show elegance when our coarsenesses have been rubbed away. We scrape and polish one another until we fit satisfactorily. Thus arises tact, which manifests a refinement in our power of judging what is pleasing and displeasing to others.
>
> —Immanuel Kant, *Lectures on Ethics*[2]

> Manners are characteristic edges.
>
> —Friedrich Schlegel, *Philosophical Fragments*[3]

> Have you ever been able to touch the whole extent of another person, including all his rough spots, without causing him pain? Then both of you need furnish no further proof of being cultivated human beings.
>
> —Friedrich Schleiermacher, "Athenaeum Fragments"[4]

I. Gestural Mimesis: Social and Cultural Formation

In the course of formulating a conception of the *habitus*, enabling social theory to appropriate for its own use the ancient Greek sense of ἦθος, Pierre Bourdieu observes: "Social institutions *depend* for stability and efficacy on certain norms being accepted as natural and this acceptance in turn depends on people's being socialized into a sense of the appropriateness of certain styles of comportment. Our sense of what is appropriate sets up the power relations which, in turn, give institutions the powers codified as rights and obligations."[5] Moreover, as Bourdieu showed, "the sense [of appropriate comportment that has been] objectified in institutions" is continually "reactivate[d]" by a prelinguistic body of understanding, a corporeal "habitus," which arises through a mimesis of power, a "contagion," that reaches even into "the imperceptible cues of body hexis."[6]

Our gestures, our postures, and even our gaits attest to the subtle normative operations of power, shaping the body, forming and informing the character of its social presence. For example, with regard to standing the appropriate distance from others, Bourdieu observes:

> A child learns such a social norm from her parents without the parents even sensing they are inducting her into the practice. Simply, if the child stands too close or too far away, the parent feels a tension and corrects the impropriety by moving closer or backing away. The child then ends up feeling comfortable in each specific situation only when standing the culturally appropriate distance.

The "appropriateness" of this comportment is not a manifestation of some natural norm—a norm inherent in human nature. Rather, it arises through processes of socialization, which in different cultures involves different norms and accordingly different body schemata. "Human nature" seems to lack an essence. Yet when one compares cultural proprieties, bearing in mind their meaning, their function and purpose, one can discern some remarkable similarities and affinities—contingent universals. For although the body is a social formation, there are limits imposed, in effect, by nature on what is tolerable for that culture and what is not. If a culture were to attempt imposing on itself normative body schemata that are too extreme—too repressive, too painful and, in this sense, "contrary to nature"—it would not long survive. Perhaps we must say, then, that "human nature" is nothing other than an indeterminate but always further determinable delimitation of our possibilities.

In any case, however, the formation of the appropriate "habitus" is also a way for each culture to define for itself its relation to animality and to embody accordingly the "humanity" constitutive of its self-understanding. Every distinct culture has distinctive, normatively constituted body schemata, registering the way in which the culture both repudiates and perpetuates the affinities that recall its emergence within the realm of the animal. Avoidance of the animal always betrays proximity. And the rituals of negation always reiterate the abhorrent identity. Moreover, history demonstrates that the denial of animality can issue in another animality—an animality much more brutal than anything to be seen among the animals from whose existence we suppose ourselves removed.

II. Freud on Tact and Taboo

> The bestial . . . may in a flash, like a disappearing express messenger, suggest premonitions of what dwells within—just as the glance or

> gesture of the insane in a moment shorter than the shortest moment parodies, ridicules, and jeers at the rational, self-possessed and clever man with whom he is talking.
>
> —Søren Kierkegaard, *The Concept of Dread* [7]

Walter Benjamin related the emergence of a code of tact to an inhibition or prohibition of contact, and explained this restraint as a decisive affirmation of the difference between human beings and animals. The institution of codes of tact would thus be a way for us, as human beings, to overcome our sense of shame in the face of our resemblance to animals. But Freud proposed what seems, at first, a very different genealogical narrative:

> At the root of the prohibition [taboo against contact] there is invariably a hostile impulse. . . . This impulse is repressed by a prohibition. . . . In the [cultural] taboo, the prohibited touching is obviously not to be understood in an exclusively sexual sense, but rather in the more general sense of attacking, of getting control, and of asserting oneself. If there is a prohibition against touching a chief [king or priest], or anything that has been in contact with him, this means that an inhibition is to be laid on the same impulse which expresses itself on other occasions in keeping a suspicious watch upon the chief. . . . The attitude of primitive peoples to their chiefs, kings, and priests is governed by two basic principles which seem to be complementary rather than contradictory. A ruler "must not only be guarded, he must also be guarded against." . . . Both of these ends are secured by innumerable taboo observances. We know already why it is that rulers must be guarded against. It is because they are vehicles of the mysterious and dangerous magical power which is transmitted by contact like an electric charge and which brings ruin and death to anyone not protected by a similar charge. Any immediate or indirect contact with this dangerous sacred entity is therefore avoided; and if it cannot be avoided, some ceremonial is devised to avert the dreaded consequences. . . . Here we are met by the remarkable fact that contact with the king is a remedy and protection against the dangers provoked by contact with the king. No doubt, however, there is a contrast to be drawn between the remedial power of a touch made deliberately by the king and the danger which arises if he is touched—a contrast between a passive and an active relation to the king. [8]

For Freud, then, the prohibition originates in our anxieties about aggression. Through codes of tact we are required to inhibit our "natural" impulses, which often dispose us to acts of self-interest and self-aggrandizement that are shadowed by violence—or the threat of violence. The essence of civilization, for Freud, consists, first, in the recognition of our instinctual urges—a recognition of what Kant, in his "Idea for a Univer-

sal History with a Cosmopolitan Intent," called our "unsociable sociability"—and, second, in the renunciation of these aggressive urges, impulses,
desires: the renunciation, in effect, of a monstrous animality whose naked
competitive egoism is supposed to be still lurking just beneath the surface
of our socially imposed sociability.

For Theodor Adorno, however, the two interpretations—Freud's and
Benjamin's—are not incompatible. Indeed, Adorno's penetrating optics,
uncompromisingly ruthless, shows how the two come together in a dialectical analysis of the gestures and manners of the modern bourgeoisie.
In both interpretations, what is submitted to question is the passage from
the animal to the human: the passage from nature to culture as it takes
place in the lifeworld of the bourgeoisie. In the lifeworld of this class, the
passage involves the inhibition and mastery of the instinctual urges of our
animal nature, their binding in forms of profitable work, and their sublimation into symbolic gestures of social tact. But the tact that supposedly
disproves our kinship with animal nature inhibits our urges only to give
them the freedom of a "social nature" that uses tact to disguise their continuation of this kinship in the brute egoism and competitiveness of a
capital-driven economy. In the lifeworld imposed by the present form of
capitalism, the "second nature" that bourgeois society produces can be
just as brutal as the first—the same, only more "refined," and more resistant to unmasking.

Although there is a conceptual distinction to be made between "nature"
and "culture," "first nature" and "second nature," it is difficult, if not impossible, to draw their boundaries without inviting legitimate questions
and challenges. For we cannot leave our culture for some neutral terrain
in order to draw the boundaries. As Merleau-Ponty puts it: "It is impossible to superimpose on man a lower layer of behavior which one chooses
to call 'natural,' followed by a manufactured cultural or spiritual world.
Everything in the human is both constructed and natural. . . . Thus it is
no more natural, and no less conventional, to shout in anger or to kiss in
love than to call a table 'a table.'"[9] Many questions regarding the distinction between the natural and the conventional need to be addressed, questions that it would have been wrong not to acknowledge; but further
exploration of the conceptual intricacies would take us too far off our present course. Suffice it to say that what is at stake for Adorno and company
is the moral character of the "second nature" that Western culture has constructed within the force field of late capitalism.

Reflecting, in his *Theory of the Novel,* on the question of "first nature"

and "second nature," Georg Lukács asserts that what the bourgeois novel
shows us is a socially constructed "second nature" that is nothing but
"a complex of meanings that are petrified and estranged, and that are
no longer able to awaken [a sense of] inwardness; it is a charnelhouse of
rotted interiorities [*ein erstarrter, fremdgewordener, die Innerlichkeit nicht
mehr erweckender Sinneskomplex; sie ist eine Schädelstätte vermoderter Inner-
lichkeiten*]."[10] This originally Hegelian figure of the charnel house, or
house of skulls, calls for attention.[11] For Emmanuel Levinas, in his commentary on the Talmudic distinction between the "future world" and the
"messianic era," notes that according to an important rabbinical scholar,
the messianic era is "a charnel house [*charnier*] between two eras rather
than an end to History": a time in which the "promise of a delivered and
better humanity" is not yet fulfilled, but is in the process of being fulfilled.[12] The figure of the "charnel house" accordingly carries here, as is so
often the case in Talmudic texts, a provocative double meaning. On the
one hand, as in the passage from Lukács, the figure describes our present
time as a time ruled by moral decay; on the other hand, it names the site
that separates the dead from the living, the place where the purifying fires
of redemption are already at work destroying all that is corrupt and evil.
Hence the figure signifies the promise of a world, a time to come, no longer
ruled by moral decay, injustice, violence, and death.

   With the figure of the charnel house, Lukács cleverly disenchants the
socially constructed conventions that bourgeois ideological mystification
claims to be "natural," "first nature" shaped into a "second nature." This
claim, supposed to strengthen and legitimate the conventions' authority,
Lukács sharply turns against the conventions, thereby dispelling the spell
of their inevitability by recognizing the transience and decay that is fated
for all that belongs to the realm of nature. Even if bourgeois conventions
were "second nature," transience would still be their fate, for they participate in the "nature" of the historical.[13] As Adorno remarks, commenting
on Lukács: "For radical natural-historical thought, . . . everything existing
transforms itself into ruins and fragments, into just such a charnelhouse."[14] For Lukács, we can see in "second nature"—in the gestures of
bourgeois tact, the rhythm and measure attuning bourgeois life—the
ethics of a world experienced as abandoned by God and dying in spirit.[15]
In its historical condition as reified and estranged, this "second nature" ex-
erts over us a spell-binding power, which we can neither easily nor completely understand and master. Thus, according to Lukács, the "laws of
tact and taste," which "belong wholly to the sphere of mere life" (*der*

bloßen Lebenssphäre angehören) and which conflict with the moral requirements for a truly human world, have become the only way for bourgeois subjectivity to maintain itself with some degree of intactness: a minimal integrity.[16]

Amplifying Nietzsche's genealogical critique, Adorno argues that our experience of bourgeois tact is nothing but a "lie," an ideological myth, which so blinds us that we do not see the "shadow of terror" (*den Schatten des Entsetzens*), the "horror" (*Grauen*), just beneath the surface of our manners—our "civility."[17] Indeed, "sociability [*Umgänglichkeit*] itself connives at injustice by pretending that in this chill world we can still talk to each other" (*MM*, §5, 26/25–26). Tact is often no more than the illusion of solicitude and respect—and a fastidious avoidance of contact (§118, 206–7/183–84).

"Thou shalt not murder!" The first of the Ten Commandments. According to Levinas, the face of the other expresses this commandment, subjecting the "I" to the moral law. It is commonly said that the "humanity" within us is sacred: that even evil people bear within them, in spite of their monstrosity, a moral disposition whose "humanity" is still intact and sacred. A debatable conviction. In this regard, it is telling that two opposite meanings are at stake in the Latin word *sacer*: it refers on the one hand to what is sacred or blessed, and on the other hand to what is unclean, accursed, dangerous. The two meanings of this word reflect, perhaps, the ambiguity—one might even say the duplicity—of the passage from animal nature to human culture, a passage in which the violence of nature is not transcended but reproduced in the successive historical forms of social life. We see this legacy of violence in the will to power of a naked competitive egoism that our ritualized forms of social interaction cannot easily conceal—and that, in fact, the social mediations under capitalism perpetuate in a semblance of "social progress." Beneath the surface of middle-class manners, the ego's "sublimated rage" (*sublimierte Wut*) against constraints on its will to power can barely be contained (*MM*, §72, 121/109). Sociability thus "masks a tacit acceptance [*Akzeptieren*] of inhumanity" (§5, 27/26). That is its violence, its persistent kinship with the animal nature supposedly left behind by the progressive rationalization, enlightenment, and humanization of society. Adorno's use of the word *Akzeptieren* is a subtle reminder of this kinship, making the point that the animal (*Tier*) is still present, even if concealed, in a society that still tolerates inhumanity.

The sacred—our humanity—is in one sense blessed and thus ap-

proachable, yet in another sense accursed, so that it must not, indeed
cannot, be touched. For the natural immediacy of touch—an immediacy
that does not recognize the other's withdrawal from nature and thus does
not respect the other's "sacred" humanity—the mediations of cultural
forms substitute ritualized gestures and manners of tact. But does it matter whether we refrain from touching the sacred out of tact or dread or
love? In any event, Freud, Benjamin, and Adorno agree in regard to the
social practices of tact, alike insisting that the animal desire to make contact—to touch, perhaps, with violence—however transformed by its passage through the symbolic, cultural mediations of the past, has not been
totally repressed and in every trace obliterated.

The tact of manners is, at the extreme limit, then, an inhibition of violent impulses: an inhibition of nature, of a "dreadful violence" (*verhäng-
nisvolle Gewalt*) that cultural forms can by sublimation only partially alter
or conceal (*MM*, §13, 35/33). In the bourgeois society ruled by late capitalism, neither the sublimation nor the concealment of the violence inherent in the "blind self-interest" (§13, 36/34) of our animal nature can
ever be complete. The task for a critical social theory must therefore be to
unmask the social practices and institutions that perpetuate this violence
even as they sublimate and conceal it through a code of tact. Adorno wor-
ries about "the savage spread of the social under the mask of universal
nature" (§100, 176/156). The task is to unmask the brutality of human nature under capitalism that ideological systems continue to conceal. Scattered throughout *Minima Moralia* are notes in which Adorno submits familiar gestures to critical-theoretical analysis. Not even the most "esoteric
gesture" (*esoterische Gestus*) can be allowed to escape the attention of this
critical disenchantment (§13, 35/34).

III. Touched by the Other

Adorno has little to say about touch and contact in human relations, but
his *Aesthetic Theory* does contain an "Excursus" in which he describes an
experience he takes as decisive for the formation of subjectivity—for our
sense of ourselves as human beings:

> Ultimately, aesthetic comportment is to be defined as the capacity to shud-
> der. . . . What later came to be called subjectivity, freeing itself from the blind
> anxiety of the shudder, is at the same time the shudder's own development; life
> in the subject is nothing but what shudders. . . . Consciousness without shud-

der is reified consciousness. That shudder in which subjectivity stirs without yet being subjectivity is the act of being touched by the other.[18]

For Adorno, aesthetic experience is the preeminent realm in which this intersubjectivity, this connection between myself and the other, can take place. But the main point is that there are certain experiences that almost compel me to recognize myself in the other and the other in myself—yet without in any way reducing the other to a duplicate of myself, without in any way diminishing the differences constitutive of our singularity. Mutual recognition begins prior to consciousness, in a shudder of the body responsive to being touched at a distance by the presence of the other. Touched without being touched: touched by the presence of a certain absence. But isn't the shudder an ambiguous testimony? Is it not also the body's manifestation of its anxiety, its skepticism, not yet confident that the other's first nature—or, for that matter, one's own—has been sufficiently mastered?

IV. Courtly Manners: Second Nature in Kant's Enlightenment Anthropology

> All human virtue in circulation is mere vile coppers. . . . Anyone who takes it for real gold is a child.
>
> —Immanuel Kant, *Anthropology from a Pragmatic Point of View*[19]

In a lecture on ethics, Kant emphasized the social importance of a tact, a "sense of decency" that requires keeping certain matters to oneself. How one handles these matters is of fundamental concern to society, for the very concept of the human is at stake. Thus he says that one's sense of decency "must be observed and weaknesses therein restrained so that humanity is not injured thereby. Even to one's best friend one must not reveal oneself as one naturally is and knows oneself to be, as that would be disgusting."[20] He is obviously referring here to the tactful concealment of one's bodily urges and functions. Manners must remove us from the embarrassing vestiges of our animal nature: an embodiment that he can only regard as "disgusting."

But manners not only separate us from the most basic conditions of our animal nature; they also modulate the egocentric nature of our desires. While acknowledging, in his 1784 "Idea for a Universal History with a

Cosmopolitan Intent," [21] that we are basically motivated by self-love, a certain "unsociable sociability," Kant argues that this disposition, far from impeding the progress of enlightenment, actually serves to bring us to our senses, so that, after suffering the consequences of such "unsociability," we become more receptive to the motivations of moral life—and may find awakened in our hearts that "love of humanity" which, he thinks, is the deeper spring of human action.

In the first three of the "Theses" that Kant sets out in "Idea for a Universal History with a Cosmopolitan Intent," he voices the speculative assumptions at work in his approach to the narrative of history:

First Thesis: "All of a creature's natural capacities are destined to develop completely and in conformity with their end."

Second Thesis: "In man (as the sole rational animal on earth) those natural capacities directed towards the use of his reason will be completely developed only in the species, not in the individual."

Third Thesis: "Nature has willed that man, entirely by himself, produce everything that goes beyond the mechanical organization of his animal existence and partake of no other happiness or perfection than what he himself, independently of instinct, can secure through his own reason."

The next thesis introduces the ground of his confidence in this progress of social rationality:

Fourth Thesis: "The means that nature uses to bring about the development of man's capacities is the antagonism among them in society, as far as in the end this antagonism is the cause of law-governed order in society."

But, disagreeing with Rousseau, Kant holds that, in consequence of our living in society with others, "man feels himself to be more than man, i.e., feels himself to be more than the [mere] development of his natural capacities." Kant, however, agrees with Rousseau that there are, in social existence, many corrupting influences and conditions. Thus, in his *Anthropology from a Pragmatic Point of View*, he attempts to look with the analytical detachment of an ethnographer at the social relations of his time and place. As the title of this work tells us, what he wanted to think about was the normal "pragmatism" (*Klugheit*) prevailing in the social practices and institutions that attracted his attention.[22] Kant realizes in these writings that "pure" moral theory must come to terms with the realities of life—the weaknesses, corruptions, confusions and vagaries of will that all too often determine our judgments, our actions, our institutions. But his faith in the progress of reason separates his "pragmatic" anthropology from earlier discourses on manners—the cynical "pragmatics," for example, of La Rochefoucauld's *Maxims*, which perversely delight in describing the decadence of social relations in the life of the court.

Should we be surprised that the intrigues of the court are so well-suited to representation by the stylized, theatrical gestures of marionettes? In "On Permissible Moral Semblance," section 14 of the *Anthropology*, Kant observes:

> Men are, one and all, actors—the more so the more civilized they are. They put on a show of affection, respect for others, modesty and disinterest without deceiving anyone, since it is generally understood that they are not sincere about it. And it is a very good thing that this happens in the world. For if men keep on playing these roles, the real virtues whose semblance they have merely been affecting for a long time are gradually aroused and pass into their attitude of will.—But to deceive the deceiver within ourselves, [in other words, to deceive] inclination, is to return to obeying the law of virtue; it is not a deception, but an innocent illusion of ourselves.[23]

In Kant's "pure" moral theory, there can be no exceptions permitting untruth. But here, separated by an abyss that his pure ethics absolutely forbids him to span or close, he makes a "pragmatic" argument for mimesis, "impure" moral theory, taking as its starting point human beings just as they are—and what they may reasonably be expected to become. Unlike Plato, Kant is not disturbed by the mediation of "semblance." At least not here, in his "anthropology," where the philosopher notorious for his extreme, uncompromising defense of the absolute principle of truth-telling is willing to "tolerate" the weaknesses of human nature and make something of an "apology" for them. But he is, in effect, counting on the "cunning of reason" (*List der Vernunft*) to exploit whatever materials it is given to work on. Thus, in his *Anthropology*, he expresses faith in moral progress even from such dubious beginnings: "Even the *appearance* of goodness in others must be worth something to us, because out of this play with pretence—which earns respect without perhaps meriting it—moral worth that is meant in earnest might well arise."[24] Benjamin seems to concur with this assessment, arguing that fine manners (*Höflichkeit*) constitute "the true mediation" (*das wahrhafte Mittlere*) between maxims of self-preservation or self-interest and maxims affirming ethical principles.[25] Given the state of human nature, this betweenness would seem to be, all things considered, just the right measure. And while, on the one hand, manners are nothing but beautiful forms of semblance, on the other hand they do preserve, within the inevitable social conflicts, a certain acknowledgment or presupposition of the claims that ethical principles make on us—an acknowledgment or "practical postulate" maintained beneath the surface of our social conventions.

But what happens when—as in our present time, according to Adorno—the reflective capacity of subjectivity has atrophied almost completely? What happens when interiority has shrunk to a surface—nothing but outward behavior? Would the "semblance," our manners, not become an empty form without moral substance? Kant can permit "moral semblance" only because—unlike La Rochefoucauld and Machiavelli—he assumes that, behind the masks, behind the theater of manners, there is actually a deep, transcendentally constituted subjectivity capable of grounding its will in the absolutism of universal reason and acting out of "real virtue." But if no such subjectivity exists, then morality as Kant defines it—a reflective capacity for acting not only in accordance with the moral law but out of respect for it—becomes impossible. Moreover, knowing only the semblance, only what mimesis solicits, people would be exceedingly vulnerable to malevolent social influences, especially the authoritarian pressures at work in totalizing regimes of power. Mimetic semblance would not prepare people to understand and respect the "law of virtue" but would instead habituate them to blind obedience or seduce them into habits of moral compromise and moral complacency—perhaps even into a morally corrosive cynicism.

Kant's reflections on this social "use" of dissimulation continue, showing him to be so much under the spell of Enlightenment optimism that he occasionally seems to forget the danger he elsewhere explicitly realizes is courted by such dissimulation. "In order to preserve virtue," he says, "or at least lead us to it,"

> nature has wisely implanted in us a tendency to give ourselves over readily to illusion. A *dignified bearing* is an outward show that instills *respect* in others, keeping them from being too familiar. [Thus] *modesty* (*pudicitia*), a self-constraint that conceals passion, is still most salutary as an illusion that keeps

the sexes sufficiently far apart so that one is not degraded into a mere tool for the other's enjoyment.—In general, all that we call *propriety, decorum*, is this sort of thing—simply a handsome show.

Thus:

> *Courtesy, politesse*, is a semblance of graciousness that inspires love. *Manifestations of deference*, compliments, and the whole of *courtly* gallantry, along with the warmest verbal protestations of friendship, are not always the *truth* ("My dear friends: there is no such thing as a friend." Aristotle); but this still does not make them *deception*, because everyone knows how to take them, and especially because these tokens of benevolence and respect, though empty at first, gradually lead to real attitudes of this kind.[26]

Perhaps. Perhaps tact—how we are supposed to show respect for the other in gesture, word, and bearing—could be, or could become, the way that the moral law comes to appearance in our embodiment. But what if semblance were to become the norm, the "pragmatic supplement" that takes the place of the moral law within us? What if the mimetic practices Kant recommends gradually dissolved the very distinction between semblance and moral truth—and reinforced a political regime that depends on the obliteration of this distinction? What if this "semblance" compromised and corrupted the social "construction" of "second nature," so that the distinction between morality and egoism, morality and "first nature," would immediately be jeopardized?

Kant recognizes a commendable, if not entirely admirable, form of "semblance": a *Spiel mit Verstellungen*, a certain conscious "playing with pretences," playfully dissimulating thoughts and feelings, as well as intimate facts about one's "natural life."[27] But he also sees a pernicious "use" of "semblance," as when it becomes a mere *Scheinwissen*, an excuse to evade moral self-improvement: "The [mere] semblance of good *in ourselves* we [must] ruthlessly wipe away: we must tear off the veil with which self-love covers our moral defects. For if we delude ourselves that our debt is concealed by what has no intrinsic moral content, or reject even this and persuade ourselves that we are not guilty, the semblance *deceives* us."[28] Kant's "pragmatic" anthropology seems, at first, to be an innocent appropriation of the common sense grounding our social practices. But further reflection brings out, I think, the dialectical ambiguity—an ambiguity that reflects the very duality, or duplicity, afflicting human nature. We are not given to live as *res integrae.* "So," he says, "it already belongs to the basic composition of a human creature and to the concept of his species to explore the thoughts of others but to withhold one's own—a nice quality that does not fail to progress gradually from *dissimulation* to *deception* and finally to *lying*."[29] Tact is a form of "semblance" in the sense that it is human nature refashioned as an appearance of spirit. But it is also "semblance" in the sense that it is the bourgeois subject's "beautiful illusion" of a "natural" morality, the display of a false reconciliation in ethical life between the categorical moral imperatives of reason and the egoism of an animal nature that the subject has simultaneously disavowed and persistently tried to satisfy.

Keeping up the semblance of respect for the humanity of the other, tact nevertheless keeps alive the dream of a *sensus communis* as the standard or measure for a sociability and culture befitting our humanity. But tact can do this only by simultaneously perpetuating and legitimating the very conditions of egoism, of "unsocial sociability," that forever betray this dream and accordingly require tactful semblance as a compromise reconciliation. Here tact becomes a cynical and corrupt substitute for that "universal feeling of sympathy" and "ability to engage universally in very intimate conversation" the cultivation of which would constitute, as Kant says in *Critique of Judgment,* "the sociability that befits [our] humanity and distinguishes it from the limitation [characteristic] of animals."[30]

Socially encouraged forms of semblance that conceal the truth can all too easily become hypocrisy: a cynical perversion or displacement (*Verstellung*) of the imperative moral obligation to live by the truth—to accept truth as the sole *measure* of one's moral standing. In his *Anthropology,* Kant provides no absolutely clear, absolutely fixed delineation of the difference between the moral and the immoral. The lines between right and wrong—lines that, in his "pure" ethics, are laid down with clarity and finality, tolerating no question of their reference, no breaching, no transgression—here begin, under the pressure of a certain "pragmatism," to tremble and buckle. In the social world of tactful manners, our sense of the difference between right and wrong is no longer reliable. That method by which, in the works of pure formal ethics, we are to take the measure of our intentions has become more difficult to discern. We are left without certitude, without any guarantees.

In our time, we cannot ignore the dialectical corruption in such semblance. It can be observed in the tact of the moral cynic, who consciously uses it for his own conceits; in the tact of those who, weak in the will to virtue, blindly "go along" with the majority; in the tact of the obsequious gestures of the scheming subordinate; and in the tact of the faceless servant of total power who hides his complicity in violence under the administrative mask.

But if tactful semblance encourages a self-centered form of individualism—an egoism still bound to the brutal laws of the animal realm and to the immediacies of that realm's instrumental rationality—the absolute rigorism of Kant's "pure ethics," attributing moral reflection and judgment to the transcendental will of a monadological subjectivity, imposes a violence all its own, sacrificing the claims of singularity to the cold instrumentalism inherent in an abstract universalism.

What becomes of the moral order, once the social practices constitutive of ethical life can no longer claim the authority of a metaphysical "naturalism" and are consequently experienced as conventional? Does this make them arbitrary constraints, arbitrary impositions? Is there no longer any difference between rules of etiquette and moral principles? Or, in the absence of any other point of reference, any measure outside majority opinion, does the moral imperative reduce to the calculus of self-interest, capital mask of self-preservation?

Centuries ago, in a society very different from our own, Laotse recognized this fateful dialectic and articulated with compelling insight what Adorno would surely call its "logic of disintegration":

> When Tao is lost, the doctrine of goodness appears.
> When goodness is lost, the doctrine of philanthropy appears.
> When philanthropy is lost, the doctrine of justice appears.
> When justice is lost, only social rituals, rules of courtesy and manners
>   are left.
> When this is lost, social chaos begins.[31]

The "semblance of virtue" that Kant proposes in his *Anthropology* creates a temptation to benefit from hypocrisy—the corruption of moral consciousness and the social order it demands. But he hopes that it will ultimately inculcate the practice and habit of moral virtue and civility. Semblance, however, which is nonidentity hiding behind the appearance of identity, creates a space of freedom, of nonidentity and contingency, an indeterminate space in which either the nonidentity that hypocrisy masks will destroy the very fabric of social virtues, its subtle corruptions leaving noth-

ing in their wake but calculated self-interest, or else these virtues will gradually succumb to the critical pressures in the negative dialectic of nonidentity, making room for new and perhaps more humane conventionalities.

Kant's "pragmatic anthropology" thus seems ultimately committed to a
purely speculative hope: the same hope, perhaps, to which Adorno gave
uncompromisingly paradoxical expression when he asserted, in *Negative
Dialectics*, that "semblance is [at least] a promise of non-semblance." But
as Adorno well knew, semblance can betray this promise. For if the promise—in essence an indication of the moral utopia—depends on the immanence of semblance, suspended in that mediation, one cannot exclude
the possibility that it is nothing but a mirage.[32]

V. Keeping Up Appearances: Measure à la Mode

In the society that came into existence with bourgeois capitalism, social relations were still a question of keeping up appearances. Keeping up appearances is still socially important, and still means conforming to the expectations of one's social *milieu*: modulating the rhythm of one's gestures,
for example, so that they keep to the appropriate time and timing, the appropriate measure—the measure (*modus*) of tact à la mode. Our gestures
are still regarded as tactful to the extent that they demonstrate a certain
modicum, or measure, of modesty: not only a restraint befitting the intricate social meanings of the situation but a delicacy in one's comportment
exquisitely attuned to the perceptions and sensibilities of others. Such tact
is needed when it is not possible to depend on the implicitly recognized
rules and principles taken for granted in certain social practices, and when
even the established rituals constitutive of "good manners" fail to provide
sufficient guidance. Tact is thus the intuitive ability—more like a talent
or knack—to negotiate social situations that are potentially embarrassing,
offensive, or disruptive, with some delicacy and skill, and without benefit
of ready-to-hand conventions or rules. ("Talent" derives from the Greek
talanton, meaning "that which is weighed out or apportioned to one."
Thus tact, the talent for determining the fitting measure, is itself something measured out.)

But often, and more deeply, tact serves to reinforce the illusions of ideology that hide and preserve what is really going on: a brutal social reality.
And all too often, gestures that appear to be tactful are nothing but the
shrewd tactics of a ruthless, self-preserving egoism. Taking the words in

this sense, "keeping up appearances" can only arouse Adorno's unmitigated contempt. The secret complicity between these appearances and prevailing social reality must be overcome. Adorno formulates very precisely what is at stake: "Essence [*Wesen*] is what must be covered up, according to the mischief-making law of [pragmatic] non-essentiality; to deny that there is an essence [truth of the matter] means to side with appearance, with the total ideology which existence has become."[33] Keeping up appearances functions in the context of social relations just as identity thinking functions in the metaphysics that reflects those relations: for all its disarming "charm," blunting our sensitivity to the brutalities of social reality, keeping up appearances is an instrument of class domination that puts into practice the logic of identity at work in the systematic reproduction of capitalism. "Appearances" create the illusion of an absolutely reasonable social order: an order concealing all traces of the inassimilable Other. Keeping up appearances thus becomes, in effect, a "rationalized rage" against an Other that can be neither denied nor disguised by the repressive immanence of the marketplace. Moreover, the pressure to keep up appearances is a pressure that, little by little, almost imperceptibly, destroys subjectivity, causing it to disintegrate from within.

But there is another way of thinking about the keeping up of appearances, according to which Adorno would see in the characteristic social gestures that sustain those appearances a certain potential for disruptive play. For the irony or parody in the *play* of appearances, in the theatricality of manners, could deny to the compulsions, alienations, and reifications constitutive of prevailing social reality some of their apparent fatalism. For, after all, appearances are only appearances! Thus, just when we may feel trapped in a suffocating social immanence, with no possibility of critical transcendence, semblance—keeping up appearances—could give the lie to the "logic of identity," introducing into the social force field a potentially disruptive caesura, a moment of uncertainty, a moment of dialectical nonidentity. Thus, Adorno also needs to redeem the concept of appearances. He needs this concept for the morally imperative work of critique, where he assumes a quasi-Kantian transcendental standpoint in order to distinguish appearances from "noumenal" truth and to reveal, through these "appearances," this "semblance" of social reality in which modern bourgeois manners are invested, the harsh reality that those "appearances," denying their semblance character, charmingly conceal. He also needs the concept of appearances in order to imagine the possibility of a future "reconciliation," a time when a radically different social order would no longer require the binding of appearances to tactics of deception, gestures of manipulation, conventions of hypocrisy. In this time of reconciliation, the social function of appearances would differ radically from what it is now, when appearances are kept up in the service of an oppressive ontology of identity, a social order that Adorno relentlessly attacks.

Thus if the concept of "appearances" is treated as a dialectical image, its duplicity must also be seen from the perspective of a process of social reconciliation. In "Veblen's Attack on Culture," Adorno confronts the virtually irremediable ethical corruption in social relations. His argument there suggests that he thinks, like Kant, but without Kant's Enlightenment optimism, that appearances must be kept up to preserve the possibility of a moral transformation of society—a possibility that we cannot, and must not, entirely abandon: "As a reflection of truth, appearances are dialectical; to reject all appearance is to fall completely under its sway, since truth is abandoned together with the rubble without which it cannot appear [at all]."[34]

We need to keep the concept of appearances so that, despite the charm of appearances, we can think the possibility of a different social reality. In *Being and Time*, Heidegger suggests a similar critical strategy, although his intention could not be more divergent. Arguing that what his hermeneutical phenomenology has uncovered is still nevertheless "disguised" (*verstellt*), showing itself, "but in the mode of semblance," he writes:

> It is therefore essential that Dasein should explicitly appropriate what has already been uncovered, defend it *against* semblance and disguise [*Schein und Verstellung*], and assure itself of its uncoveredness again and again. The unconcealment of anything new is never done on the basis of having something completely hidden, but takes its departure, rather, from unconcealment in the mode of semblance.

From this he concludes that "truth (unconcealment) is something that must always first be wrested [*abgerungen*] from entities. Entities get snatched out of their hiddenness. The factical uncoveredness of anything is always, as it were, a kind of *robbery*."[35]

Could there be a "weak messianic power" surviving even in the moral corruption of social relations, a remnant of some original commitment to humanity still faintly discernible, in spite of its damaged condition, its disguise, within the very decadence of appearances? Could a time come when tactful manners would measure the remaining task of social and political reconstruction—our distance from the realization of truly humane social relations? Could a time come when tactful manners, in their own way keeping up appearances, would make manifest and thereby keep up, keep intact, intimations—and evidence—of that sense of redeemed humanity, that sense of the moral and the just, by which we are in the end to be measured? It would thus be a question of attempting to maintain, however inadequately, appearances of a humanity still to come. And although Adorno, despite his struggle to preserve transcendence within the realm of his materialism, would remain committed to a certain skepticism, one might suppose that what is required of us is to try to let the regulative Idea of a redeemed society appear through the measured tact of our gestures—in the hope that that prospect of eternal goodness might shine through the very impossibility of our tactful mediations.

In his book *Negative Dialectics*, in a section within the "Meditations on Metaphysics" that the translator perceptively entitled "The Semblance of Otherness," Adorno asserts,

> However void every trace of otherness [*Spuren des Anderen*] in it [the world], however much all happiness is marred by revocability: in the breaks that belie identity, entity is still pervaded by the ever-broken pledges of that otherness [*das Seiende wird doch in den Brüchen, welche die Identität Lügen strafen, durchsetzt von den stets wieder gebrochenen Versprechungen des Anderen*].

Later in that section, he reflects on semblance (*Schein*) in the work of art, concluding with a sentence on which we have already commented:

> Art is semblance even at its highest peaks; but its semblance, the irresistible part of it, is given to it by what is not semblance. . . . No light falls on men and things without reflecting transcendence [*Kein Licht ist auf den Menschen und Dingen, in dem nicht Transzendenz widerschiene*]. Semblance is a promise of nonsemblance [*Im Schein verspricht sich das Scheinlose*].[36]

Bourgeois tact is reified social reality captured in the lie of commodified appearances. If a time comes when society is no longer repressive, the persistent complicity between semblance and social reality might finally be sublated: where appearances once concealed the reality of violated human dignity, they would now give rise to a redeemed reality.

But semblance harbors a dialectical ambiguity that, for Adorno, cannot be overcome, because, as he says in another connection, we must recognize in the ritual gestures of social convention "the vanity of [an] immanence [that] secretly liquidates transcendence as well, for transcendence feeds on nothing but the experiences we have in immanence." [37]

In "Final Serenity," a note in *Minima Moralia*, Adorno comments that the bourgeois "is tolerant." That is to say, "his love of people as they are stems from his hatred of what they might be [*Haß gegen den richtigen Menschen*]" (*MM*, §5, 26/25). Bourgeois tact is thus like "a gravitational force that pulls everything downwards." The artifices and conceits of tact often require that social interactions become superficial, reducing possibilities for meaningful experience to empty conventions bereft of human warmth (§118, 206–7/ 183–84). Reducing and distorting our sense of what, as human beings, we could become, "the misdemeanors [*Bosheiten*] of the upper classes—now in any case being irresistibly democratized—reveal in all its crassness what has long been true of society: that life has become the ideology of its own absence" (§121, 214/190). The tactfulness of bourgeois manners thus alienates us from ourselves:

> Because the formalization of life becomes a task requiring the adherence to rules, the artificial preservation of a style, the maintenance of a delicate balance between correctness [*Korrektheit*] and independence, existence itself appears endowed with meaning. . . . The constant injunction to do and say what exactly befits one's status and situation [*dem Status und der Situation Angemessene*] demands a kind of moral effort. By making it difficult to be the person one is, one gains the feeling of living up to a patriarchal *noblesse oblige*. At the same time, the displacement of culture from its objective manifestations to immediate life dispels the risk of one's immediacy being shaken by critical thought. The latter is spurned as a disruption of aplomb, a want of good taste. . . . But for all its aristocratic trappings, ritual falls into the late-bourgeois habit of hypostatizing a performance [*Vollzug*] in itself meaningless as meaning, of degrading mind to the duplication of what is there in any case. The norm followed is fictitious; its social preconditions, like its model, court ceremony, have ceased to exist, and it is acknowledged not because it is felt as binding, but in order to legitimize an order advantageously illegitimate. (MM, §121, 213–14/189)

In another note, Adorno expresses his skepticism about the "spirit of practicality" behind Hume's argument that "delicate sentiment" (*zarte Gefühl* in Adorno's translation) plays an essential role in our moral life. In our time, Adorno observes, the "spirit of practicality" has subordinated all social relations under the rule of "a proficient estimate of the ratio of forces" (*rechten Einschätzung von Kräfteverhältnissen*),[38] a calculative, instrumental rationality that makes profitability the measure of all value:

> The practical orders of life, while purporting to benefit man, serve in a profit economy to stunt human qualities, and the further they spread, the more they sever everything tender. For tenderness [*Zartheit*] between people is nothing other than awareness of the possibility of relations without purpose, a solace still glimpsed by those embroiled in purposes; a legacy of old privileges promising a privilege-free condition. The abolition of privilege by bourgeois reason [*bürgerliche ratio*] finally abolishes this promise too. If time is money, it seems moral to save time, above all one's own, and such parsimony is excused by "consideration for others." (MM, §20, 44–45/40–41)

This supposed "consideration" takes on a calculative and manipulative character: one is calculatingly and deceptively "straightforward [*geradezu*]." Bourgeois tact is becoming nothing but a refinement of the instrumental rationality that now prevails, even determining the character of most social relations. Thus, for example, according to Adorno, gestures are increasingly subjected to the calculus of time as money. Friendly contact is a casualty: "That, instead of raising their hats, they greet each other with the hallos of familiar indifference; that, instead of letters, they send each other inter-office communications without address or signature, are random symptoms of a sickness of contact [*beliebige Symptome einer Erkrankung des Kontakts*]" (*MM*, §20, 45/41). The aphorism continues, arguing for a distinction between two forms of proximity, two forms of distance: "Estrangement shows itself precisely in the elimination of distance between people. For only as long as they abstain from importuning one another with giving and taking, discussion and implementation, control and function, is there space enough between them for the delicate connecting filigree of external forms [forms of tact] in which alone the internal could crystallize." Barely concealing his contempt, Adorno concludes the note with a scathing indictment of the hypocrisy inherent in bourgeois manners, almost betraying a nostalgic preference for the conventions of an earlier time that those more "modern," more "modest" manners swept away:

> Behind the pseudo-democratic dismantling of ceremony, of old-fashioned courtesy [*altmodischer Höflichkeit*], of the useless conversation suspected, not even unjustly, of being idle gossip, behind the seeming clarification and transparency of human relations that no longer admit anything undefined, naked

brutality [*nakte Roheit*] is ushered in. The direct statement without divaga-
tions, hesitations, or reflections, that gives the other the facts full in the face,
already has the form and timbre of the command issued under Fascism by the
dumb to the silent. Matter-of-factness [*Sachlichkeit*] between people, doing
away with all ideological ornamentation between them, has already itself become an ideology for treating people as things [*als Sachen*]. (MM, §20, 46/42)

We may not regret the vanishing of the courtly ceremonies; but in the
present decay of the more "democratic" forms of tact, of politeness and civility, that the bourgeoisie instituted in their wake, there is a reification of
the other that is more akin to the brutality of fascism than we have been
willing to recognize. Such is the historical "progress" of bourgeois tact, its
characteristic gestures observed with an eye to unmasking its current subjection to the dialectical "logic of disintegration." [39]

VI. The Extinction of Delicacy

"What is more delicate than the extinction of delicacy?" [40] Posed by Henry
James in a letter reflecting on the death of Walter Pater, this question,
which would be provocative in any case, is made even more challenging
for interpretation by a context that leaves it not only unanswered but unexplained. James gives no clue as to what he had in mind. We are consequently left to construct our own interpretation.

Perhaps the most compelling interpretation would identify the truest
form of delicacy—or tact—as that which "comes naturally," without effort, artifice, or show. One could accordingly speak of the extinction of
delicacy when, by virtue of the alembications of a consciousness finely attuned to its social milieus, the situationally appropriate comportment has
become "second nature"—a culturally mediated *semblance* of nature. Just
as, according to Valéry, "the essence of prose is to vanish," so, we might
say, the essence of delicacy, of tact, is to vanish as the conventionally constituted artifice that it is and to reappear as if it were simply "natural." Like
the beauty that Kant attributes to the products of art and craft, the artifice
of tact virtually perishes through a semblance of nature.

Without necessarily contesting James's remark, Adorno would surely
want to remind us that, because of its peculiar subjectivity, such delicacy
always risks extinction by the very dialectic it sets in motion. When, for
example, I speak with the delicacy required by "political correctness," I am
exceedingly careful in referring to people of certain ethnicities, choosing

my words with an exquisite sense of tact, while continuing to support the institutions that oppress them. We must also recognize that hypocrisy and even malice can cause terrible damage when adorned, with consummate delicacy, in the fair semblance of good will.

VII. The Dialectic of Tact

In aphorism 16 of *Minima Moralia*, Adorno provides an exemplary instance of what, with his characteristically ironic wit, he names his "micrological myopia": a critical reflection on the historical emergence and dialectical fate of the social practices we call tact. The dialectical history of tact that he narrates takes up the commitment described succinctly in *Dialectic of Enlightenment*: "The task to be accomplished is not the conservation of the past, but the redemption of the hopes of the past."[41]

In the story that Adorno wants to tell, the dialectic of tact begins with the historical period of courtly manners, manners experienced by the aristocracy as fitting into the natural order of things, and consequently as inherently meaningful social forms. The narrative then takes us through the disintegration and disappearance of these practices of politeness and civility, in a time when the power of the aristocracy was yielding to that of the increasingly demanding bourgeoisie. The "historical moment of tact" accordingly begins in the Enlightenment when the more artificial conventions of bourgeois manners replace courtly manners. But although it was the emergence of the bourgeoisie that made the Enlightenment possible, the calculating rationality that this class introduced into its conventions of tact subverted the moral principles underlying these conventions and betrayed the spirit of the Enlightenment. Thus, this moment, dialectically unstable, gave way to a third, more contemporary stage, in which, with the celebration of individualism, freedom took the form of an unapologetic egoism, and the conventions of the earlier bourgeois tact, conventions manifesting a moral authority originally taken for granted, began to appear more and more as *mere* conventions, arbitrary forms emptied of all metaphysical and moral meaning. This made the bourgeois conventions vulnerable to corrosion by subjective reflexivity, with its acids of irony and cynicism. But how does this narrative in aphorism 16 continue? Contrary to what one might expect, Adorno seems not to consider the possibility that tact might carry with it a utopian impulse or sensibility, a felt awareness of the other's own sensibility. However, in other aphorisms from

Minima Moralia, his "melancholy science" is compelled to recognize in tact more promising dialectical potentialities.

An unstable precipitate of the metaphysics of respect, bourgeois tact emerged, he claims, as a culture of virtue in response to the disappearance of courtly manners. However, because the bourgeoisie increasingly submitted tact to the motivations of a calculative rationality, its practices gradually weakened the authority of the ethical principles that, in the Enlightenment this new class inaugurated, it had invoked to replace the ethics of the courtly code: principles purporting universality, a more inclusive sense of humanity than earlier social practices had recognized. In the absence of compelling authoritative conventions, tact must increasingly depend on the fine attunement of the individual's social perceptiveness and on a sensibility capable of intricate subtleties of experience. But in today's world, a time "out of joint," when social life no longer fits into the older forms and when self-interest has corrupted the metaphysics of respect, the uneasy compromise that tact may briefly have accomplished, at once drawing on and sublating empty, ritualized conventions and naked self-interest, has lost even the remnants of its auratic authority. If modernity always finds an arbitrariness, and thus a trace of violence, in empty conventions and in individual choices unconcerned with respect, the emergence of tact in the eighteenth century can be seen as an attempt to reverse the superficiality and hypocrisy of courtly manners and restore experiential meaning. In the filtering of egoism's intrigues required for delicacy and discretion, the tact of bourgeois Enlightenment did at least justify its gestures by reference to recognition of the moral dignity of others. For, despite its failings, tact has always been a recognitive social practice, acknowledging the feelings of others and showing them due respect in situations where no settled rules exist to regulate social life. Bourgeois tact was a fitting development, because it continued the older, established forms, but without their formalism, thereby leaving rational judgment and action to the individual's exercise of freedom. This, however, encouraged unruly tendencies in the increasingly assertive and self-centered individualism of the bourgeoisie, which in any case had no use for forms it perceived as emptied of higher meaning and more or less arbitrary in their constraints.

The formation of inner life that the conventions of bourgeois tact have created—an inner life in many ways rotten, in many ways complicit in the oppressive conditions of outer life—has been accompanied by the progressive recognition in objective reality of human and civil rights. Such duplicity is the discreet charm secretly trading, secretly working its will, on the dialectical character of tact. Recognizing this, we moderns must weigh on the scales of justice that inner life against the objective rights that formed in its wake.

At the same time that Adorno attacks the manners through which bourgeois morality emerged—attacks, from a perspective beyond their ken, the tactlessness of their tact—he also, with a faintly audible tone of regret, calls attention to the decay of fine manners. But in this wearing-away of adornments, the ugly truth begins to show itself in all its nakedness. Tact, perhaps the most prized of bourgeois virtues, a virtue cultivated in the marketplace and perfected in the social life that takes place between the hours of business, has functioned as a morally compromised "accommodation" with the prevailing social system. But by protecting the fabric of mutual expectations that maintains this system, tact has also functioned as an instrument of ideology, masking and thereby perpetuating the inhumanity of social relations in an economy organized by and for the reproduction of capital. Adorno wants to show us that tact keeps up the appearances that do their best to conceal the truth about the world we live in—and that in many ways, life in our world is still, for all our progress, for all our enlightenment, for all our culture and refinement, nasty, brutish, and short. (Henry James, writing in 1895 to Edmund Gosse, laments the rudeness of social relations and expresses his gratitude for the protection granted by every remaining measure of tact: "These are days in which one's modesty is, in every direction, much exposed, and one should be thankful for every veil that one can hastily snatch up or that a friendly hand precipitously muffles one withal.")[42]

Tact becomes such a necessary tactic in this economy only because, as Kant already perceived with great acuity, in the name of freedom we have been encouraged to become self-centered, self-interested egos, egos estranged from one another by competition and motivated only by the terms of an unsociable sociability. Consequently, conflict is what now determines relations among individuals—a turn to "fate," to the right of the powerful, that is inevitably promoted by a social system based on domination and exploitation, and the privileges of power. We should bear in mind here one of the aphorisms quoted at the beginning: Schlegel's keen observation that "manners are characteristic edges." Tact alleviates the system-threatening edge of the antagonisms, but only by leaving intact the underlying inhumanity of the system.

But has the hour that will decide the future of bourgeois tact finally arrived? Adorno discerns in the conventions of the present historical moment not only a "logic of disintegration" but also a dialectic between, on the one hand, the efforts of the bourgeoisie to break free of the constraining manners inherited from an earlier generation and, on the other hand, the need to embrace these manners and keep up the appearances that maintain the smooth functioning of the system.

In the "modern" gestures of tact—and in the "ethical substance" these gestures have simultaneously betrayed and preserved, Adorno sees the bourgeois subject inventing the terms of its emancipation: an "enlightened" way out of the premodern forms of sociality—the forms of the feudal order, which are now morally distasteful, and the early-modern forms, in which manners embodied an ethics of virtue. In these earlier forms, social relations between and within the different classes were intricately regulated by preestablished conventions, social practices taken for granted and assumed to manifest a rationality inherent—quite simply—in the very "nature" of things. Once emancipated from these conventions, the bourgeois subject would supposedly be free to act according to the disposition of his or her own ethically informed intuitions. The individual's "inwardness," a certain sense and sensibility, a certain intuitive sense of the fitting measure, could thus be substituted for the prescribed forms. But without these ready-to-hand forms, each situation required its own singular interpretation, its own intuitively grounded judgment—what we might describe, borrowing from Kant's third *Critique*, as a capacity for "reflective judgment."

Yet vestiges of the earlier, traditional forms have lingered on, radiating some of their original charm even in their decay, their faded "after-life"— if only, perhaps, in a mimetic parody, compelled to "quote," but without real conviction, the older, hollowed-out forms.

But doesn't the freedom we have wrested from these conventional forms grant us a measure of hope, and a possibility of drawing upon our own social and moral intuitions, our own bodily felt sense of what is fitting and proper for each of the situations in which we find ourselves? Is there not hope in the possibility that, from the struggle to gain this freedom, we could learn a social tact and contact grounded not in violence but in finely tuned sensitivities, exposing us in all our vulnerability to the experience of others? The aphorism with which Adorno concludes his *Minima Moralia* certainly attempts to contemplate this possibility, referring us to the character of our "felt contact" with things. But this assumes that we can make contact with—and retrieve—our bodily felt sense of peaceful contact. And it assumes that this bodily felt sense of our humanity remains intact despite the brutality of a capitalism of technologies—that the body's capacity to register by sense and sensibility what is good and right has not been destroyed.

Adorno attempts to think this possibility in terms of our capacity to remember, with and in our bodies, the promise of redemption that has been given to our bodies. To accomplish this, we must somehow recollect the potential for peaceful contact that is immanent in the very nature of tact. The dialectical logic of Adorno's critique compels him not only to reflect on the gestures that embody tact—the afterlife of old rituals, rituals of greeting and hospitality and farewell, the egalitarian handshake that replaced kissing the hand—but also to reflect on the new gestures of solidarity and conflict used by today's disaffected youth. In *Negative Dialectics*, however, Adorno also turns his attention to the body as such, as the medium in which the moral law is first inscribed.[43] For even while the gestures of tact retain the charm that conceals society's ugliness, they also preserve, for possible retrieval by memory—by the conscience remaining in memory—a trace of our recognition that we bear moral responsibility for the welfare of other human beings, beings in whom, "without willfulness," we have always already felt, if only in the obscurity of unacknowledged impulses, the kinship of a common humanity. Here it is worth noting Adorno's exact words in the final aphorism of *Minima Moralia*: "To gain such perspectives [perspectives that reveal the world in a 'messianic light'] *without willfulness or violence* [*ohne Willkür und Gewalt*], entirely from *felt contact* with its objects—this alone is the task of thought" (§153, 281/247). There is still, intact in our gestures of tact, a long-forgotten dream of peaceful contact. There is still, inscribed in our very gestures, inscribed as their rhythm and measure, a sensible relation to the moral law, a long-repressed sense of our shared humanity, which an act of memory could, though only with difficulty, bring into deeply felt awareness.

For Adorno, gestures of tact are important enough to warrant lengthy reflection. Aphorism 16, in *Minima Moralia*, begins with an assertion regarding Goethe: "Goethe, acutely aware of the threatening impossibility of all human relationships in emergent industrial society, tried . . . to present tact as the saving accommodation [*rettende Auskunft*] between alienated human beings." The poet recognized, in tact, an ethically motivated effort to find a balance among unruly individualism, conventions emptied of meaning, and the authority of a certain "naturalism." But Goethe could not avoid penetrating the appearance of mannerly forms to perceive, behind the charm of tact's disguises, some terrible compromises: "This accommodation seemed to him inseparable from renunciation, the relinquishment of total contact, passion and unalloyed happiness [*Diese Auskunft schien ihm eins mit der Entsagung, mit Verzicht auf ungeschmälerte Nähe, Leidenschaft und ungebrochenes Glück*]."

But should we believe that only our renunciation of warm human contact—the body's utopian dream—could possibly salvage the happiness that the bourgeois subject had hoped for in its emancipation from the manners of the old regime? The reflection continues: "The human [*Das Humane*] consisted for him in a self-limitation which affirmatively espoused as its own cause the ineluctable course of history, the inhumanity of progress, the withering of the subject." But the historical hour for even this minimal resistance has passed:

> But what has happened since makes Goethean renunciation look like fulfillment. Tact and humanity [*Takt und Humanität*]—for him the same thing—have in the meantime gone exactly the way from which, as he believed, they were to save us. For tact, as we now know, has its precise historical hour. It was the hour when the bourgeois individual rid himself of absolutist compulsion. Free and solitary, he answers for himself, while the forms of hierarchical respect and consideration [*hierarchischer Achtung und Rücksicht*] developed by absolutism, divested of their economic basis and their menacing power, are still just sufficiently present to make living together within privileged groups bearable.

"There is a sense," he declares, "in which . . . Kant's deduction of scholastic categories from the unity of consciousness [may be regarded as] eminently 'tactful' [*taktvoll*]." That is because there is, in this gesture, a "seemingly paradoxical interchange between absolutism and liberality": "liberalism" in the boldness of a "subjective reconstruction" to assure reason of the legitimacy of the categories, "absolutism" in affirmation of their origin. Kant's "pragmatic" account of tact mirrors this paradoxical character of the deduction, counting rather too uncritically on the liberalization permitted in semblance to return subjective motivation to the authority of the moral absolute.

Continuing his argument concerning the dialectical history of tact, Adorno observes:

The precondition of tact [*Voraussetzung des Takts*] is convention no longer intact yet still present [*in sich gebrochene und doch noch gegenwärtige*]. Now fallen into irreparable ruin, it lives on only in the parody of forms, an arbitrarily devised or recollected etiquette for the ignorant, . . . while the basis of agreement [*das Einverständnis*] that carried those conventions in their human hour [*zu ihrer humanen Stunde*] has given way to the blind conformity of car-owners and radio-listeners.

Now it stands to reason that, as he says, "the demise [*Absterben*] of the ceremonial moment" would "seem at first to benefit tact." Indeed, "one might expect that, emancipated from all that was heteronomous and harmfully external, tactful behavior [*taktvolles Verhalten*] would be guided solely by the specific nature of each human situation." In other words, one might expect that the bourgeois individual would finally be free to judge and act for himself, returning in self-reliance to a faculty of intuition capable of discerning, in each situation, what gesture, what action, what words would be most fitting. If the ceremonial gestures common in premodern European society, gestures perceived as the "natural" expression of one's proper station and role, correspond to the historical condition of heteronomy, the gestures of tact that replaced them would correspond to that historical moment in which the ideal of autonomy beckoned, promising new possibilities for social relations and individuation. "Such emancipated tact [*emancipierte Takt*], however, meets with the difficulties that confront nominalism in all contexts." For, as Adorno says,

> tact meant not simply subordination to ceremonial convention: it was precisely the latter that all later humanists unceasingly ironized. Rather, the exercise [*Leistung*] of tact was as paradoxical as its historical location. It demanded the reconciliation [*Versöhnung*]—actually impossible—between the unauthorized claims [*Anspruch*] of convention and the unruly ones [*dem ungebärdigen*] of the individual. Other than convention, there was nothing by which tact could be measured [*gar nicht sich messen*].

Again a question of fitting measure. Tact as an intuitive ability could not, in the moment of practice, be relied upon; but the conventions by which the appropriateness of its promptings could be measured were no longer compelling, or no longer available.

And yet, "convention [still] represented, in however etiolated a form, the universal which made up the very substance of the individual claim." Now this, according to Adorno, takes us into the very center of the aporia:

"Tact is the discrimination of differences [*eine Differenzbestimmung*]. It consists in conscious [and freely chosen] deviations. Yet when, emancipated, it confronts the individual as an absolute, without anything universal from which to be differentiated, it fails to engage the individual and finally wrongs him." Thus, for example, "the question as to someone's health, no longer required and expected by upbringing, becomes inquisitive or injurious, [and] silence on sensitive subjects [becomes] empty indifference, as soon as there is no rule [*keine Regel*] to indicate what is and what is not to be discussed." These delicate matters, when left up to the individual, suddenly acquire a significance, an intentionality, that in earlier times they did not possess. Bereft of the protection—the concealment—of an impersonal convention, the subjectivity of the individual is threatened, risks being left utterly exposed. Demonstrating the operation of a dialectical logic, virtue in tact is eventually twisted defensively into its aggressive opposite. "Thus," Adorno says,

> individuals begin, not without reason, to react antagonistically to tact: a certain kind of politeness [*Höflichkeit*], for example, gives them less the feeling of being addressed as human beings, than an inkling [*Ahnung*] of their inhuman conditions, and the polite run the risk of seeming impolite by continuing to exercise politeness, as a superseded privilege [*Vorrecht*]. In the end, emancipated, purely individual tact becomes mere lying.

To be sure, Adorno acknowledges that "[tact's] true principle in the individual today is what it earnestly keeps silent, the actual and still more the potential power [*Macht*] embodied [*verkörpert*] by each person." But, looking at social life with the optics of a "melancholy science," he does not recognize here any redeemed or redeeming role for the gestures of tact and contact. Our embodiment seems to be, as Foucault would say some years later, "totally imprinted by history." Adorno writes: "Beneath the demand that the individual be confronted as such, without preamble, absolutely as befits [*angemessen*] him, lies a covetous eagerness to 'place' him and his chances, through the tacit admissions contained in each of his words, in the ever more rigid hierarchy that encompasses everyone." "The nominalism of tact," he says, turning signs of hope into an argument for despair, "helps what is most universal, naked external power [*der nakten Verfügungsgewalt*], to triumph even in the most intimate constellations." Hence the dialectical aporia: "To write off convention as an outdated, useless and extraneous ornament is only to confirm . . . a life of direct domination."

As if driven by the Furies toward an inexorable fate, the dialectic of the Enlightenment project thus draws the gestures of tact into complicity with the material conditions that keep us estranged from one another in a state never far from the state of nature: "That the abolition [*Fortfall*] of even this caricature of tact in the rib-digging *camaraderie* of our time, a mockery of freedom, nevertheless makes existence still more unbearable, is merely a further indication of how impossible it has become for people to co-exist under present conditions." Without the old conventions, long ago obsolete, tact now all too easily declines into the tactics of a utilitarian calculus, the prudence of a calculative rationality that permits us to use others—without shame, without hesitation—as means to our ends.

But must we consent to Adorno's dialectical despair? Must we follow him into a dialectical dead end? Could gestures of tact ever be moved as if by a "purposiveness without purpose" (*Zweckmäßigkeit ohne Zweck*): moved, that is, with only the other in mind?

When Adorno states that tact demanded an impossible reconciliation "between the claims of convention and the unruly ones of the individual" and that, other than convention, "there was nothing by which tact could be measured," is he not making some doubtful assumptions? He seems unable to move beyond the very metaphysics he accuses of oppression, because he can recognize in the absence of socially imposed convention only one possibility: an unruly nature, a body moved only by its egoism. For him, either the body is nothing but a social construction, totally exposed to the forces of oppression and the conventions of a brutal society, or it escapes all forms of subjection, but thereby attains only the monstrous freedom of an absolutely unruly nature, deprived of any felt sense of shared humanity. In the final analysis, then, despite many dialectical turns and twists, Adorno proves unable to imagine a fulfillment not "damaged" beyond repair by renunciation. Goethe's compromise construction of tact cannot after all, it seems, be sublated.

Adorno avers that, with our abandonment of the traditional sources of moral authority and the traditional conventions determining social relations, tact has lost its proper rhythm and measure—its necessary moral compass. But he does not conceive the possibility of a fitting measure grounded in, but equally also maintaining, a post-conventional moral order: an order such as the one envisioned in Jürgen Habermas's theory of communicative action, his most significant contribution to critical social theory. We cannot unfold the implications of this possibility now. However, perhaps it will suffice for present purposes to say that the theory imagines a situation in which dialogue, listening, and the gestures of tact that accompany them would be mutually experienced as appropriate, good, and right. Thus if we can imagine, with Habermas, the character of a post-conventional morality, can we not imagine the possibility of correspondingly post-conventional gestures of tact—gestures in touch with a sensibility still somewhat intact and moved by a sense of shared humanity—despite the corruption of ethical life?

If it is true that the nature of the human body is not reducible to the ontology of a currently fashionable social constructionism, it may be argued that we are in need of a morality in touch with its embodiment. We are in need of a morality, and a capacity for tact, in touch with the body's own felt sense, still intact, however faintly, of the fitting measure: a sense of the social universal not totally bound to the conventional. In his final aphorism, 153, Adorno does point toward gestures without ego-driven willfulness and violence, gestures of touch and tact in felt contact with that sense of humanity, which, if only as a ghostly trace, is still intact within us and to which Kant's "Doctrine of Virtue" directs our attention.[44] This recognition of felt contact is an extremely promising moment in his critique of contemporary life. Nonetheless, note 16 in "The Dialectic of Tact" suggests that Adorno lost touch with this felt sense, the embodiment of the moral law from which the fitting measure for tact might be drawn. But it must in fairness be said that this was for Adorno—is still for us—a most instructive failure.

VIII. Resisting Fascism: The Categorical Imperative in the Body's Violated Flesh

In a lecture Adorno gave in 1965, he declared, "The true basis of morality is to be found in bodily feeling: in identification with unbearable pain."[45] It is a statement I wholeheartedly welcome. But he carries this forward in a problematic way when he states: "Hitler has placed a new imperative on us: that, quite simply, Auschwitz should not be repeated and that nothing like it should ever exist again."[46] Because this "new imperative" is first "recognized" by the body that Enlightenment rationalism stripped of its aura and reduced to mute primordial impulses, and because "the sphere of right action does not coincide with mere rationality," this "new imperative" has become, as he explains, a mere "supplement" or "addendum."

The following year, Adorno introduced this thought into his *Negative Dialectics*: "A new categorical imperative has been imposed by Hitler upon unfree mankind: to arrange their thoughts and actions so that Auschwitz will not repeat itself, so that nothing similar will ever happen."[47] There is an important, even urgent, moral truth here. The Holocaust shattered many illusions about moral and spiritual progress. But we must nevertheless interject a caution: saying that this imperative was "imposed" risks denying that the body can be, as one of his 1965 lectures in moral philosophy asserts, a source of moral reason—and a crucible for the syntheses of its judgments. The text continues:

> When we want to find reasons for it, this imperative is as refractory [*widerspenstig*] as was the one in Kant once upon a time. Dealing discursively with it would be an outrage [*Frevel*], for the new imperative gives us a bodily sensation of the moral supplement [*an ihm läßt leibhaft das Moment des Hinzutretenden am Sittlichen sich fühlen*]—bodily [*leibhaft*], because it is now [a question of] the practical abhorrence [*Abscheu*] of the unbearable physical agony to which individuals are exposed.

Adorno here suggests that the only possible moral response to the horror of the Holocaust is a response that takes over the very flesh of the body, imposing a consecration that commits us to ensuring that such horror never happens again. Not afraid to exaggerate, he laments, "It is only in the unvarnished materialistic motive that morality survives." But he also argues that it is the "course of history" that "forces materialism upon metaphysics, traditionally the direct antithesis of materialism." He states this more concretely as follows: "The somatic, unmeaningful stratum of life [*Die somatische, sinnferne Schicht des Lebendigen*] is the stage of suffering, of the suffering which, in the camps, without any consolation, burned every soothing feature out of the mind, and out of culture, the mind's objectification." These reflections on morality and metaphysics after Auschwitz are certainly right to insist on the monstrously agonizing character of the Holocaust—and to recognize, moreover, that this agony, strictly moral in its essence, cannot be dissolved into the substance of reflective judgment. It is ethical reason embodied, inscribed in the very nature of the flesh: reason in its most immediate exigency and urgency, reason that, before thought, makes its judgment bodily felt. Felt, for example, in the shudder of horror and revulsion that engulfs us when we see the face of barbarism.

Adorno's reflections are not, however, without certain questionable assumptions: metaphysical assumptions that, because of their moral and cultural implications, must be challenged. For the body that could cry out in moral agony is not a merely "biological" body submerged in instinctual life, a life of preconscious impulses and sensations bereft of meaning and voice. Such a body could never experience the moral significance of a brutality attempting to reduce its humanity to the condition of "mere life" (*bloßes Leben*). Nor could it assume the responsibility that this new historical form of the categorical imperative requires.

In spite of his thoughtful observation of gesture, in spite of his considered use of the words *Leib* ("body") and *leibhaft* ("bodily"), and in spite of his efforts to overcome the spell of metaphysics still captivating his own thinking, Adorno seems to think of the body only in a way that objectifies it, reproducing the very thing he denounces: a repression of the body that has been its fate since the beginning of civilization. His pessimism regarding morality thus derives in part from an unrecognized reification of the lived body, the body-subject. This reification is difficult to avoid without a very clear-minded overcoming of the logic of a metaphysical dualism that separates "mind" and "body" into two distinct substances. Adorno's *Leib* is, in the final analysis, a mute body, a mindless body, reduced to mere "sensations" and "archaic impulses," a "somatic stratum" incapable of forming constellations of meaning, unable to make sense of its "impulses" and "sensations." It is a body that can suffer pain but cannot *make sense* of its experience; nor, *a fortiori*, can it speak to us coherently and directly from out of this sense of pain. In Adorno's thought, the oppressed body is therefore condemned to a cruel silence—a silence more silent than silence.

Adorno invokes the body's "impulses" and "sensations," implying that they could be, as they are for Benjamin, a potential source of critical-emancipatory energy; yet he assumes that they are inherently irrational—and he completely ignores the body's more differentiated, more discriminating phases of sense and sensibility. Moreover, whereas in his critique of gesture in *Minima Moralia* he seemed to presuppose that the body is a crucible of meaningful experience, here, in *Negative Dialectics*, he once again inscribes the body in a materialism that reifies its experience. The body is the victim of a crude materialism—that same dialectically unmediated materialism upon which the philosopher elsewhere heaps his scorn. Thus, at the same time that he laments the reduction of the moral to the cold, positive "materialism" of the bourgeoisie, he perpetuates a way of thinking about the body that prohibits a philosophical understanding of how the body bears the moral law and brings it forth into the light of expression and deed—into the negative dialectics of a very different materialism.

He has also forgotten his own recognition, earlier in *Negative Dialectics,* of the body's dreams and fantasies—those anarchic "impulses" that precede the formation of the ego, a formation that conforms to the processes of socialization to which the ego is subjected. To the extent that these recollected "impulses" remain intact, they preserve a deep connection to the *promesse de bonheur* at the heart of the Enlightenment project—and by way of this connection, their unbound energy could be appropriated by the moral law for its most radical judgment on the human condition. Asserting their freedom prior to the ego, these "impulses" can never be suppressed or obliterated. And the desires, the dreams, the fantasies that represent them never cease to talk back to regimes of power that try to control or deny them. They are, in effect, the bearers of the body's rudimentary sense of justice. They have always, since time immemorial, registered the body's resistance to brutality—its involuntary shudder in the presence of evil.

But the disenchantment set in motion by the Enlightenment destroyed the remaining auratic vestments of the body. That is why Adorno suggests that the claims of moral reason live on, today, only as a mere corporeal "addendum" or "supplement" to conscious understanding, and why he has attempted to rescue the auratic body from destruction by philosophical thought, pointing to the normal body's visceral reactions when confronted with the cruel suffering of others. What makes Adorno's argument so timely is that it responds to the moral outrage we feel when we realize that no "rational grounding" of ethical life in formal universal principles of disinterested reflective procedures and calculi could have prevented the horrors of the twentieth century—and that such rationalism, far from challenging what Nietzsche called "the devaluation of values," actually contributed to the destruction of the aura that had once been constitutive in our moral perception of an intangible attribute—the humanity of the other.

In "The Concept of Enlightenment," which Adorno wrote in collaboration with Max Horkheimer, the authors assert: "The regression of the masses today is their inability to . . . touch the unapprehended with their own hands [*Unergriffenes mit eigenen Händen tasten zu können*]—the new form of delusion which deposes every conquered mythic form."[48] There

is an important critical insight here; but urging the touching of the "unapprehended" is not without its dangers. For the willful touching of what
cannot—and must not—be touched is arguably one of the greatest evils
of fascism.

Fascism imposed on social relations a regime opposed to the "refined"
conventions of the bourgeoisie. It attempted to abolish the conventions of
tact achieved by this class. But it was by virtue of these conventions that
the distinctive "inner life" of modern experience came into being—and
in the process articulated anew the essential moral difference between
human and beast. By destroying these conventions, fascism violently as-
saulted the untouchable inwardness that tact, for all its superficiality and
duplicity—indeed, paradoxically, by virtue of these very traits—protects.
Bourgeois tact is obsessed with superficialities, with keeping up appearances; and yet, ironically, and indeed paradoxically, precisely because of
this concern for "exterior life," it fashions an inner life—a private dimension of the individual that it constitutes as absolutely untouchable and in-
destructible. Tact thus becomes a demonstration of respect for the other's
inwardness, an inwardness that cannot, and must not, be touched: observing the conventions of distance, tact becomes a way of touching the
untouchable "being" of the other without touching it, without violating
its untouchability.

In book 8 of the *Odyssey*, Homer tells how Odysseus, while listening to
the minstrel's song as a guest in the palace of the Phaeacian king, covered
his head and wept, concealing himself from those present. Calling attention to this scene in an essay on Heracleitus, Heidegger remarks, "Concealment here defines the way in which a man should be present among
others."[49] Such self-concealment, however, would not be possible without
the participation of the other guests: for Odysseus to remain present in
concealment, they must turn away, must avert their gaze, must let a certain "aura," what Levinas might describe as a certain "curvature" of existential space, take shape around him. His concealment results at least as
much from their turning away as from his own gestures. For his is not a
physical but a psychological concealment, a form of privacy, a respect for
his ownmost dignity. The guests turn away, letting him be with himself,
as if completely alone: present, yet concealed in their very midst. This is a
lovely example of archaic gestures of tact, a code of tact befitting their nobility. A tact that respects the man's withdrawal into inwardness, a tact that
shows how deeply touched they were by his emotional response—and
how careful to create between them a certain auratic distance, a "clearing"

through which they could nevertheless remain in felt contact, touching him only with their concern to shelter his innermost untouchability.

Fascism takes the metaphysics of totalized presence to its ultimate extreme of violence and brutality. To substitute for the bourgeois tact that it sweeps away, it returns us to the immediacy of touch and a directness that cuts through the outward appearances, the social masks, behind which the self could withdraw into its private concealment. In the name of what we can regard only as a fetishized, monumentalized "naturalness," in the name, therefore, of what we recognize as a false immediacy, a false directness and candor, fascism attempts to vanquish the decadent and hypocritical tact of bourgeois "decency"; but what it institutes instead is a reign of violence and terror. Its "return to nature" is not a more humanized sense of nature but a more brutalized sense of humanity. Although the tact of the bourgeoisie keeps up appearances that conceal the brutal conditions of social reality, the immediacy that fascism imposes is the return of a brutalized nature bereft of even a minimal sense of humanity.

On the second day of June 2001, after a young Palestinian freedom fighter detonated an explosive device that ended his own life along with the lives of nineteen innocent Israeli youths, a spokesman for the prime minister of Israel said: "Even when the blood boils and the heart is torn, we must be measured [in our response]." In its multiple voices, the last word calls for thought, suggesting more than what was immediately intended. For it is saying that we must always be "measured": not only in the sense that we must respond with gestures of self-restraint but also in the sense that our gestures must be submitted to moral judgment. But restrained and judged by what measure? I take the question to be whether our gestures are capable of interrupting the prevailing system of measure: whether we are moved, or willing to be moved, not by the "justice" of equivalence, an archaic "justice" measured out in acts of revenge and retaliation, but by a radically different justice, a justice that can be measured only by the quality of our offering of forgiveness and the success of our work for peace and reconciliation.

IX. Redemption: Only a Parable?

But are the gestures of tact *Schein* only in the sense of mere "semblance"? If "semblance is a promise of nonsemblance," as Adorno says in the passage from *Negative Dialectics* quoted earlier,[50] will not the *Schein* constitutive of tact also be the appearance of the universal? Will tact not also be

Schein in that other sense, whereby tact, despite itself, preserves a sense of what human beings could be even while obliterating that sense? In *Negative Dialectics*, first published in 1966, Adorno says: "That the universal is not merely a hood [*ein bloß Übergestüptes*] pulled over individuality, that it is its inner substance, this . . . fact ought to be tracked down [*aufzuspuren*] in the center of individual modes of conduct [*Verhaltensweisen*], notably in human character."[51] But aphorism 39 of *Minima Moralia*, Adorno's earlier contribution to a "melancholy science," asserts, "No measure remains for the measure of all things." The passage from *Negative Dialectics*, a work published fifteen years later, suggests that a universal measure could perhaps be "traced back" to the "inner substance," the ethical impulse, of our gestures: a measure operative even when its motivating impulse fails to determine the gesture—even when the gesture's fidelity to its "inner ethical substance" is badly damaged, badly compromised by its participation in the cruelties of a theater of semblance. Perhaps, though, keeping up appearances *in the ironic consciousness that they are only that* may be, for the time being, our only hope. A minimal hope, perhaps— but hope none the less. But if the promise of nonsemblance must itself partake of semblance, how could the measure of hope it seems to offer be anything but a mirage?

Yet even such minimal hope, even a hope negated from within, must hold onto every shred of evidence it is aware of that might indicate an uncompromising measure of responsibility, a measure of maximum ethical conscience—for, as he says in the later work, reflecting on ethical life "after Auschwitz": "If thought is not measured by the extremity that eludes the concept, it is from the outset in the nature of the musical accompaniments with which the SS liked to drown out the screams of their victims."[52] A passage of the utmost importance. But what is the "extremity" that eludes the concept? Adorno's word lends itself to two absolutely opposite but dialectically intertwined readings, both of which require of thought the recognition of that for which its conceptual inheritance is utterly unprepared. On one reading, "extremity" refers to the unimaginable evil of the Holocaust, an evil the monstrosity of which no concept can adequately indicate or demonstrate. On the other reading, it refers to "the standpoint of redemption," registering, beyond what any concept can rationally grasp, our feeble hope for an end to the history of barbarism, a desperate faith in the possibility of a social existence realizing our humanity.

After the Shoah, practical reason is compelled to take account of—and remain accountable to—a social reality and a history that challenge its claim to autonomy, transcendence, a morally authoritative voice. Unless it does, it will preserve an impotent rigorism, and will become an accomplice in crimes against humanity. But if, instead, thought takes as its measure the extremity that in both senses eludes the concept, there is at least a slight chance that our future will not repeat the past—a slight chance that our gestures will be moved by our felt sense of moral outrage—and empowered by reminders of redemption.

In a dark and despairing note placed near the beginning of *Minima Moralia*, a note lamenting the absence of a fitting measure and evoking, as he does elsewhere, the involuntary shudder that feels this absence, Adorno wrote: "We shudder [*Es graut uns*] at the brutalization [*die Verrohung*] of life, but lacking any objectively binding morality we are forced at every step into actions and words, into calculations that are by any humane measure [*nach dem Maß des Humanen*] barbaric, and even by the dubious values of good society, tactless [*taktlos*]" (*MM*, §6, 28/27). "There is," he says, "no way out of [our] entanglement." Our entanglement, that is, in the tragic moral dilemmas of the dialectic. Invoking here an involuntary shudder—the body in its situational immediacy touched and moved by the witnessing of brutality—he begins to recognize its significance as a register of the body's originary subjection to morality.[53] So, he adds, "the only responsible course is to deny oneself the ideological misuse of one's own existence, and for the rest to conduct oneself in private as modestly, unobtrusively and unpretentiously [*so bescheiden, unscheinbar und unprätentiös*] as is required, no longer by good upbringing, but by the shame of still having air to breathe, in hell" (*MM*, 28/27–28). But this refuge in the domain of private life is only an illusory shelter. For in the social reality of modernity, there can be no separation of inner and outer, private and public life. And if freedom, responsibility, kindness, and compassion must withdraw into the interiority of the soul or the privacy of the home, the price of their ethical substance is the abandonment of any claim to redeem the utopian promise of a society in which the reconciliation required by a true universality could be realized.

In "Meditations on Metaphysics," which concludes his *Negative Dialectics*, Adorno reflects briefly on some words that Goethe makes Faust say: "I hear the message, yet I lack the faith." These words provoke Adorno to say, "The dramatic poem leaves unsettled whether its gradual progress refutes the skepticism of the thinking adult, or whether its last word is only

another symbol [*nur ein Gleichnis*—only a parable]."[54] Has the poet entirely secularized "transcendence"? And would this secularization totally
reduce it to immanence? Is there any measure befitting the hope registered
by the thought of transcendence? In the *Critique of Practical Reason,* Kant
acknowledges that what he calls, very enigmatically, the "fact of pure reason" (*das Faktum der reinen Vernunft*) can present itself only as a "fact, as
it were," as "like a fact" (*gleichsam ein Faktum*).[55] As perhaps a semblance
of "fact," something that can appear only in the form of a parable. Torn,
as always, between the dialectical extremes of hope and despair, Adorno
can only say, echoing Benjamin's evocation[56] of our "weak Messianic
power":

> Any man who would nail down [*dingfest macht*] transcendence can rightly be
> charged . . . with lack of imagination, and thus a betrayal of transcendence.
> On the other hand, if the possibility, however feeble and distant, of redemp-
> tion in existence [*die schwache Möglichkeit von Erlösung im Seienden*] is cut off
> altogether, the human spirit would become an illusion, and the finite, condi-
> tioned, merely existing subject would eventually be deified as bearer of the
> spirit.[57]

The dialectical twists continue for Adorno:

> All metaphysical speculations are, however, fatally thrust into the apocryphal.
> The ideological untruth in the conception of transcendence is the separation
> of body and soul, a consequence of the division of labor. It leads to an idol-
> ization of the *res cogitans* as the nature-controlling principle, and to the mate-
> rial denials that would founder on the concept of a transcendence beyond the
> context of guilt.

"But what hope clings to," he says, no doubt hesitantly countering that
thought, "is the transfigured body": *der verklärten Leib.*[58] This is the body
that bears the hope, or the promise, of a *material reconciliation,* ending the
diremptions of the past that have opposed manual labor to intellectual labor—and punished the "sensible" in the name of a "supersensible" destination for humanity. But Adorno makes just this one passing reference to
this other body, to this materially significant constellation tempting to
contemplate but, in the end, frustratingly elusive. Could philosophical
reflection take up the challenge in this reference?

"Metaphysics," of course, "will not hear of that." For metaphysics "will
not demean itself to material things, and this is why it passes the line to an

inferior faith in spirits." By leaving his invocation of the "transfigured body" without further elaboration, Adorno leaves it as, in effect, an abstract negation of the metaphysical dualisms that reflect within the philosophical discourse of modernity the material diremptions of an unreconciled society. After his invocation, he attacks both branches of the dualism: first positivism, which turns materialism into an affirmation of what is, and then spiritualism, which relegates our hope for the justice of a material redemption—and for the spiritual awakening it requires—to the interventions of "spirits," giving that hope "a spectral and unreal character [*ein Gespenstisches und Unwirkliches*] that mocks its own concept."[59] Thus, tongue in cheek, Adorno avers that he even prefers Christian dogmatics, with its doctrine of the resurrection of the flesh, to speculative metaphysics, finding it perhaps somewhat more enlightened—"inasmuch as hope means a physical resurrection and feels defrauded of the best part by its [metaphysical] spiritualization."[60] But he has other reasons for repudiating the Christian doctrine, since the resurrection makes heavenly afterlife the objective, and correspondingly devalues life here on earth, offering resignation and consolation instead of a struggle for the material conditions of freedom and justice.

Is the vision motivating this struggle only a parable? Is the "transfigured body" a desperate fantasy? Turning to the Judaic ban on images of the divine, Adorno says: "Now the ban itself has in that form come to evoke suspicions of superstition. The ban has been exacerbated: the mere thought of hope is [now] a transgression against it, an act of working against it. Thus deeply embedded is the history of metaphysical truth—of the truth that vainly denies history, which is progressive demythologization." But, as always with Adorno, we are entangled in the frustrations of the "dialectic of enlightenment," a negative dialectic at work here. Thus he continues this reflection by turning it over: "Yet demythologization devours itself, as the mythical gods liked to devour their children. Leaving behind nothing but what merely is, demythologization recoils into the mythus; for the mythus is nothing else than the closed system of immanence, of that which is. This contradiction is what metaphysics has now coalesced into. To a thinking that tries to remove the contradiction, untruth threatens here and there."[61] Is there any way out of this totalizing immanence, this dialectical dead end? Do our gestures have any chance to break out of the corrupt conventions that accommodate a bourgeois sensibility—and out of the conditions of a society in which true freedom and justice have not yet been realized? Have our gestures really lost their power for tran-scendence—a power that the etymology of the word that names them would seem to have vouchsafed them? Are we incapable of affirming dif-ference and embracing the Other? Have we been reduced to the condition that Edward Said describes as "a self-conscious contemplative passivity . . . , paralyzed gestures of aestheticized powerlessness"?[62] Have our ges-tures really lost touch with their felt sense of the civil and the humane—a sense of the fitting measure that they might have carried, once upon a time, even in the rhythm and the tact that moved them?

"Hope," says Adorno, implicitly answering Kant's question, "is not memory held fast, but the return of what has been forgotten."[63] Perhaps some measure of hope is still to be found—despite the decay of bourgeois tact, despite the disintegration of the traditional conventions—in a cer-tain recollection of those anarchic bodily "impulses": dreams and fantasies arising from the body of the night that have never been tamed by bour-geois institutions. Perhaps a certain process of recollection, operating even within the tactlessness of the most corrupt gestures, could bring to light the mute presence of ciphers of redemption—ciphers that have survived the brutal historical fate to which they have for so long been bound. In *Minima Moralia*, Adorno emphasizes the transformative significance of memory for moral enlightenment: "Thought waits to be awakened one day by the memory of what it has neglected, and to be transformed into teaching" (§50, 90/81). But it is not certain that we may educe even this minimal hope from something Adorno says in *Negative Dialectics*:

> The dawning sense of freedom feeds upon the memory [*Erinnerung*] of the ar-chaic impulse [*Impuls*] not yet steered by any solid I. The more the I curbs that impulse, the more chaotic and thus questionable will it find the pre-temporal freedom. Without an *anamnesis* of the untamed impulse that precedes the ego—an impulse later banished to the zone of unfree bondage to nature [*Naturhörigkeit*]—it would be impossible to derive the idea of freedom, al-though that idea in turn ends up reinforcing the ego. In spontaneity, the philo-sophical concept that does most to exalt freedom as a mode of conduct above empirical existence, there resounds the echo of that by whose control and ul-timate destruction the I of idealistic philosophy means to prove its freedom.[64]

Adorno's expression, here, of a revolutionary or redemptive hope com-ing from the recollection (*anamnesis*) of "archaic impulses" is reminiscent of Benjamin's romantic invocations of such "impulses" in his essay "Sur-realism: The Last Snapshot of the European Intelligentsia."[65] These invo-

cations, never sufficiently elaborated, can only strike us as naïve and un-
convincing. But is there not something profoundly significant in that involuntary shudder Adorno has occasionally invoked? The essay "Progress"
calls our attention to its ethical significance. But, like aphorism 6 in
Minima Moralia, in which, as we saw, Adorno emphasizes that, lacking
any "objectively binding morality," we are often forced into calculations
that are "tactless" and sometimes even "barbaric," this essay also points to
the forces of resistance that threaten to distort or nullify gestures and deeds
moved by the ethical sensibility expressed in the immediacy of the shudder: "In the shudder of horror, the habitus of the system congeals into appearance; the more the system expands, the more it hardens into what it
had been since time immemorial." [66] In *Aesthetic Theory*, the shudder appears as a dialectical trope, constellating the moral significance of the
shudder as historical experience disclosively reflected in the work of art:
"If through the demythologization of the world, consciousness freed itself
from the ancient shudder, that shudder is permanently reproduced in the
historical antagonism of subject and object." [67] For Adorno, there is redemptive hope in the shudder that works of art are especially capable of
inducing: "Art holds true to the shudder, but not by regression to it."
Rather, "art is its legacy." [68]

Is ethical life a "legacy" of the shudder? Does that shudder not shake up
the nihilism asserted in aphorism 39, the note we considered earlier? It
reads: "No measure remains for the measure of all things." Does the shudder not suggest that we are today struggling to find a point of reference for
ethical life, a moral compass to show us the way out of a seemingly hopeless disorientation? But what is this shudder in the presence of brutality if
not, after all, a rudimentary expression of the body's moral sensibility?
Does its involuntariness not tell us that, prior to consciousness, prior to
egoism, the gestural body—social from the very beginning, tragically represented in the history of metaphysics under the category of substance—
is already bound by a moral imperative, a measure, a rhythm, that claims
its disposition? Does the shudder not come from the body's felt sense of
the ancient moral bond? Is it not an undeniable avowal of the humanity
that binds us to one another? The shudder also figures in a passage where
Adorno seems to approach a recognition of the body's archaic, proto-
moral nature, remarking, "Consciousness without shudder is reified consciousness. That shudder in which subjectivity stirs without yet being subjectivity is the act of being touched by the other." [69] The shudder, resisting

philosophical representation, is a moral apprehension without voice, a sudden, involuntary eruption of movement coming from the body's morally sensitive nature. Reducible neither to theoretical interpretation nor to practical reason, the body that shudders nevertheless refuses to remain unmoved by what it has encountered and witnessed.

The blush, like the shudder, is an undeniable sign of such being-touched. Note 116 in *Minima Moralia*, another reflection on "indelicacies" (*Taktlosigkeiten*) that has been "tested on the smallest scale" (*Darauf wird die Probe im Kleinsten gemacht*), reads: "We still get the feel [*spüren*] of morality in our very skin—when we blush." This blush is a sign of the body's involuntary submission to the ethical claim of the other—to what he calls, in this aphorism, "civilization as humanity," in contrast to "civilization as self-preservation." As such, the blush is now, for Adorno, the barely discernible remnant of ethical life in a world in which the feeling that Kant recognized as the sublime authority of the moral law has become more remote, more obscure, than the farthest of stars.

The body's moral disposition, still manifest for Adorno's critical reflection in the spontaneity of the shudder and the blush, is not easily experienced today. In fact, Adorno himself perpetuates the body's abject history and destiny when, despite these reflections on the moral impulse in the shudder and the blush, he posits a body-psyche dualism. Thus, in that same note, he remarks:

> The psychic organism, like the body, is attuned to experience of an order of magnitude bearing some relation to itself. If the object of experience grows out of proportion to the individual, he no longer really experiences it at all, but registers it directly, in concepts divorced from intuitive knowledge, as something external, incommensurable, for which he has the same indifference as the catastrophe has for him.

Adorno's formulation of the moral crisis is unquestionably right. However, I cannot abandon the conviction that, to take the measure of events, we must sooner or later turn to the sense of measure—what Adorno calls "intuitive knowledge"—by which we ourselves, as bodily selves, may be guided. To what alternative sources of moral guidance can we turn? Certainly not to the cacophony of conflicting voices—the norms, standards and values—prevailing in a society that Adorno regards as morally corrupt. To be sure, in a massively corrupt society, not even the body's "ownmost" sense of measure can remain unaffected, undamaged. Alienation from our inner nature, from a felt sense of measure, is one of the ways in which we can become morally damaged. Moreover, the challenge to judgment and action is greatly magnified, as Adorno says, when we are confronted with incommensurable evil; overwhelmed by a catastrophe that demands a moral response but shatters all efforts to take its measure, even the morally sensitive may become critically numbed: separated from bodily felt experience, from the claims of the measure that informs the proto-moral "impulses" with which all human beings are presumably already endowed simply by grace of their bodily nature, even the morally sensitive may find it difficult to bring this measure to bear on the exigent situation.

But the extremely difficult is not the impossible. Is it really impossible, even in the midst of immeasurable catastrophe, for our gestures, despite being greatly alienated from these natural, proto-moral "impulses" or "innervations," and still hostage to the fetishized, brutalizing social practices of a corrupted moral order, to resist corruption and overcome their alienation from measure? In *Negative Dialectics*, Adorno himself seems to suggest that it is possible for a process of recollection, an "anamnesis," to retrieve and activate the proto-moral sensibility already operative in those "impulses," forming it into a "second nature" of moral dispositions. But how can Adorno, so attentive to dialectical aporias, make an argument for ethical life that draws on Platonism?

One must also question Adorno's uncritical appeal to the Freudian theory of drives. Confronted with immeasurable evil, we need more than "impulses" and "innervations" to direct us. His invocations of these spontaneous, reflex-like expressions indicate the extent to which his representation of embodiment is still not liberated from a repressive historicity that makes moral sensibility incomprehensible. At most, only an ephemeral and weak sense of measure, ultimately inadequate for the rational mediations required by ethical life, can be derived from such immediate reactions, valuable though they may be as initial schemata for judgment and action. But could the "anamnesis" that Adorno introduces into his reflections retrieve from the depths of our natural endowment—from a dimension of our embodiment reducible neither to the infantile egoism of instinctual nature nor to the constructed egoism of prevailing social reality—a more trustworthy sense of measure? Adorno's surprising and paradoxical turn to "anamnesis" encourages us to believe that, where we might least have expected it, namely, in the depths of our embodiment, whence the spontaneous expressions of moral emotion originate, a potentially articulate sense of measure may be stirring. However, he leaves no doubt that this sense of measure could be fully realized only from the elusive standpoint of absolute transcendence. Without that reference, it seems, the measure, for Adorno, is inevitably lost. But as we know from a statement in *Negative Dialectics* that we have already read, he would not recognize any claims to "nail down [*dingfest machen*] transcendence." Transcendence is possible only as a dialectical struggle *within immanence*.

In the exceedingly significant note that concludes *Minima Moralia*, Adorno declares, "The only philosophy which can be responsibly practiced in the face of despair is the attempt to contemplate all things as they would present themselves from the standpoint of redemption [*vom Standpunkt der Erlösung*]." "Knowledge," he says, "has no light but that shed on the world by redemption: all else is reconstruction, mere technique." Thus, "perspectives must be fashioned that displace and estrange [*versetzt, verfremdet*] the world, reveal it to be, with its rifts and crevices [*ihre Risse und Schründe offenbart*], as indigent and distorted as it will appear one day in the messianic light." This thought is then rendered in terms of our experience with gestures of tact and contact, although, in the matter of touch, Adorno, like Heidegger, avoids thinking about it in relation to people and, reproducing a certain alienation, contemplates only our involvement with things: "To gain such perspectives without willfulness or violence, entirely from felt contact with its objects—this alone is the task of thought [*Ohne Willkür und Gewalt, ganz aus der Fühlung mit den Gegenständen heraus solche Perspektiven zu gewinnen, darauf allein kommt es dem Denken an*]" (*MM*, §153, 281/247). "But," Adorno insists, returning our thought from the temptations of messianic speculation to the minimal morality of everyday life and the simple gestures that befit it, "beside the demand thus placed on thought, the question of the reality or unreality of redemption itself hardly matters." In an essay on Kafka, Benjamin cites a great rabbi, who once said that the Messiah did not wish to change the world by force, but wanted to make only a "slight adjustment" in it.[70] In keeping with this spirit, perhaps we need to draw on the redemptive powers belonging to our body's memory to begin transforming our gestures in little ways and in relation to the quite ordinary social interactions of everyday life.

Adorno's sharp eye catches many gestures that, seen in the light of redemption, call for transformation. For example: "There is a certain gesture of virility, be it one's own or someone else's, that calls for suspicion. It expresses independence, sureness of the power to command, the tacit complicity of all males. Earlier, this was called with awed respect the whim of the master; today it has been democratized" (MM, §24, 50/45).[71] Another example is the insolence demonstrated by "the nonchalant gestures of teenagers," who, he says, "'don't care a cent for the world' as long as they do not sell it their labor," and who, 'to show that they are dependent on no one and so owe no one respect, put their hands in their trouser pockets," leaving their elbows, stuck outwards, "ready to jostle anyone who gets in their way" (§72, 122/110). Adorno's observations may remind us of other examples: the many gestures of giving that lack real joy, generosity, and warmth of feeling, and the many refusals to engage in genuinely felt gestures. Of people who refuse the Other in these ways, Adorno says: "A chill descends on all they do, the kind word that remains unspoken, the consideration unexercised. This chill finally recoils on those from whom it emanates. Every undistorted relationship, perhaps indeed the conciliation that is part of organic life itself, is a gift. He who through consequential logic becomes incapable of it, makes himself a thing and freezes" (*MM*, §21, 47/43). Now is the time for a handshake between enemies, for a caress instead of a slap, a touch of the hand sharing trust and vulnerability, a friendly embrace. Now is the time to lend a hand without expectation of reciprocity. In "purposiveness without a purpose." Through gestures such as these, gestures seemingly insignificant, seemingly adjusted only slightly, a society worthy of our humanity might perhaps come about.[72]

In a letter to Gershom Scholem, Benjamin touched on the very essence of "tact," describing it as "a feeling for thresholds and distances."[73] On this sublime interpretation, tact becomes an experience of measure sensitive to the enigma that Levinas describes as "transcendence": an experience of the threshold between the "sacred" and the "profane." In *Totality and Infinity*, for example, Levinas gives thought to gestures such as the caress, gestures that in a sense "transcend" the measure of the merely sensible. "It is not," he says, "that it would feel beyond the felt, further than the senses." Rather, such a transcendence

> consists in seizing upon nothing, in soliciting what ceaselessly escapes its form towards a future never future enough, in soliciting what slips away as though it *were not yet.* . . . It is not an intentionality of disclosure but of search: a movement unto the invisible. . . . Anticipation grasps possibles; what the caress seeks is not situated in a perspective and in the light of the graspable.[74]

It is a question, here, of gestures inspired to take care of a material transcendence: gestures that, seen in the light of redemption, seen from this
perspective, belong to a humanity whose time is still to come. Pursuing
what this suggests in terms of Adorno's final note in *Minima Moralia*,
could we imagine the possibility of post-conventional gestures of tact that
retrieve their fitting measure, against all odds, from an inwrought moral
sense of social relations as they would be in a time of redemption? Or
should we concentrate instead on sharpening our critical reflective powers, repudiating whenever we can, and first of all in our own lives, that
mere semblance of a "caring hand" (*bewahrende Hand*) by which what
Adorno calls the "bourgeois revenant" (*MM*, §14, 37/34), living on "like
specters threatening doom," will with one seemingly harmonious motion
lovingly tend his garden and shoo away the stranger who asks for help? Is
this all we can do? Is this enough?

The manifest etymology of the word "gesture," though ultimately withdrawn into the spectral, unquestionably connects the gesture to the process of gestation, to giving birth, to carrying and bringing forth into action. Authentic gestures are accordingly those that bring forth something
new. Such gestures, gestures that still carry within them a memory trace of
the promise of redemption, are what we might call, borrowing a phrase
from Merleau-Ponty, "consecratory gestures." For, as he says, "they draw
affective vectors, discover emotional sources, and create a space of expressiveness as the movements of the augur delimit the *templum*."[75] And as
Levinas observes, there is transformative, redemptive power even in the
simple gesture that says "After you, sir"—and the gesture that confirms the
apologetic "Pardon me!"[76] "Even the little there is" in these humble gestures can make a great difference—a difference that no one can measure.

A fragmentary apothegm in Novalis's "Encyclopedia," obviously familiar to Adorno, reads: "Value of the trifling [*Kleinigkeiten*] in morality
(macrological and micrological morality)."[77] Perhaps redemption has already begun the moment we begin to make kindness and consideration
for others the fitting measure of our deeds and our gestures. "For we are
still in an era of prelude and expectation" (Rilke, Schmargendorf Diary).[78]
But is what would shine through such gestures still, in the end, only mere
semblance? From an ever-fading past, we are still touched by echoes of a
metaphysics of the ethical that we long ago gave up to the realm of dreams:
τὰ φαινόμενα σώζειν, in Adorno's phrase. What could this mean for us
today? What ethics—and what politics—could it still bring forth? In

"The Idea of Natural History," Adorno can see in the culture brought forth by human nature only the melancholy, inevitable fate of the animal nature it can never obliterate: "Whenever 'second nature' appears," he writes, "when the world of convention approaches, its meaning, deciphered, is precisely its transience."[79] The endless vanishing of appearances. Is the "transfigured body," the *verklärter Leib*, in the end only an empty gesture, an enchanting parable? *Nur ein Gleichnis?*

As we ponder this question, we must not forget aphorism 39 in *Minima Moralia*, written before this thought of a transformed embodiment, in which, as if echoing the skepticism and despair in Hölderlin's final poetic thought, Adorno declares: "No measure remains for the measure of all things." Perhaps he is right. But perhaps only partly right, since in the very denial of transcendental measure, there would always remain, at the least, a faint recollection of a desire for that measure.[80] What could be salvaged thereby would represent only a minimal dialectical restitution—a measure that might be sustained, if at all, through our experience of its absence, its negation in contemporary life. And yet, even in this grim experience of our destitution, and in the sustaining of our sense of what has been irredeemably denied to us, is there not still some small measure of hope?

§ 7 What Is Left Intact

Reading the Hand in Benjamin's Writings

The smallest guarantee, the straw that the drowning man clutches . . .
[is] remembrance [*Eingedenken*].

> —Walter Benjamin, "Remarks on 'Theses
> on the Philosophy of History'" [1]

The "magic cobbles piled for barricades," in Baudelaire's draft of an
epilogue, define the limit which his poetry encounters in its immediate
confrontation with social subjects. The poet says nothing of the hands
which moved these cobblestones.

> —Walter Benjamin, "Baudelaire" [2]

These are days when no one should rely unduly on his "competence."
Strength lies in improvisation. All the decisive blows are struck with
the left hand [*mit der linken Hand geführt*].

> —Walter Benjamin, *One-Way Street* [3]

I. Noli Me Tangere

"Tact," according to Walter Benjamin, consists in "a feeling for thresholds and distances." [4] In his introduction to Benjamin's writings, Theodor
Adorno observed that Benjamin, "just like Webern, according to Schön-
berg, imposed on animal warmth a taboo, so that even a friend would
hardly dare to lay a hand on his shoulder." [5] Gershom Scholem, who knew
Benjamin well, wrote of what he called Benjamin's "Chinese courtesy"
(*chinesische Höflichkeit*), a bearing that kept people at a "respectful" distance. [6] Benjamin, he said, using words that will, in the present study, carry
more than their ordinary significance, was "courteous beyond measure"
(*über die Maßen höflich*). [7] Pierre Missac's recollections repeat and elaborate this impression. Benjamin, he says, "could not tolerate a friend's so
much as putting a hand on his shoulder and considered all disgust to originate in touch, in physical contact [*Berührung*]." [8] We might say, then, that
for Benjamin what distinguishes the human from the animal is the social
distance created when the natural impulse to make physical contact is in-
hibited and conventions of tact take its place.

These stories about the man are more than mere curiosities; as we shall see, they bear on matters that carried considerable philosophical significance for Benjamin. For although he may seem at first to be merely articulating a familiar gestural context, distinguishing between the proximity of contact and the distance of tact, his writings reveal dialectical intricacies that profoundly alter the space and time in which he situates not only our gestures but our life. Torsions in this space and time open abruptly into revelatory dimensions of possibility. Because, for Benjamin, the spatiality and temporality of our gestures are not merely material and pragmatic but also ethical, political, and messianic: a space and time of catastrophe, but also of hope; a space and time of aesthetic imagination as well as of perception; a space and time of possibility, which even the slightest gesture, if sufficiently attuned to the messianic, could perhaps evoke and alter beyond recognition.

If Benjamin's aversion to being touched indicates a genuinely philosophical significance, perhaps it lies in his maintaining, between himself and others, a carefully measured opening for an interruption of prevailing social relations—an unsettling of the conventions that, in the final analysis, impose distances of their own: distances not of moral respect and tolerance of difference but of inequality, domination, poverty, and suffering.

This man who could not tolerate being touched—even the intimacies of friendship, the friendly, spontaneous touch, was more of a weight, more of a claim, than he wished to bear—was deeply affected, deeply touched, by the sufferings of others—those, for example, who appeared in his work through the figures of the hunchback, the prostitute, the homeless ragpicker, the estranged flâneur. It was for their sake that he touched pen to paper.

II. The Messianic Dimension: An Unforgettable Measure

In a discussion on morality and anthropology, Benjamin includes an important, if cryptic, fragment concerned with perception (*Wahrnehmung*) and the lived body (*Leib*), in which he briefly invokes the measure of a messianic experience:

> Through our corporeality [*Leiblichkeit*], indeed through our own lived body, we are in the most immediate way imbricated in the world of perception. . . . Nevertheless, [we are] blind and for the most part incapable, here as there a natural body [*Naturleib*], of separating appearance [*Schein*] from being [*Sein*]

according to the measure of the messianic constellation [*nach Maßen der messianischen Gestalt*].[9]

The note continues:

> There is a history of perception, which ultimately is the history of myth. The lived body of perception was not always only the vertical coordinate for the horizontal of the earth. . . . It is in [myth] that those great dispositions of perception slowly form and change which determine the way that our lived body and nature relate to one another: right, left, above, below, in front, behind.

Although Benjamin is not proposing a regression to mythological experience, his insistence on acknowledging this historical connection is motivated by two compelling concerns. First of all, like Horkheimer and Adorno, the two authors of *The Dialectic of Enlightenment*, Benjamin understands the importance of recognizing the intertwining of myth and enlightenment and of acknowledging that, despite the "progress" of enlightenment, mythic constellations of meaning persist within it, inseparable and ineliminable. Second, to some extent like the young Marx, who occasionally turned to such mythic figures as Prometheus, Deucalion, and Odysseus to give to his point the weight of prehistorical consciousness, Benjamin wanted to preserve what he saw as the revolutionary potential in messianic thought and regarded efforts to erase mythology from our historical consciousness as posing a similar threat to the survival of messianic sources for a radical revolutionary movement. These leanings are visible in Benjamin's "Critique of Violence" and "Theses on the Philosophy of History."

It is, I believe, in the spirit of a certain revolutionary messianism—a certain messianic materialism—that Benjamin, in "Surrealism: The Last Snapshot of the European Intelligentsia," calls for a new *physis* or a "new body" for the "corporeal collective" (*leibliche Kollektivum*).[10] But this would require disrupting every prevailing harmony between the individual human body and the sovereign body politic; and the appeal in every corresponding fantasy of aesthetic and political immanence would have to be overcome in a struggle against the "idol" of a "humanity" harmoniously and perfectly formed and against the "phantom of the unpolitical or 'natural' man."[11] For the Platonic vision of a harmony between our bodies and the state—a vision that Aristotle embraced and that even utopian Christianity found a way to adopt—is a vision that could only produce docile, obedient bodies; uniform, conventional gestures; and, correspondingly, an unchanging totalitarian state. For Benjamin, however, it is the body's disruptive mimetic impulses—its capacity for the spontaneous perception of heretofore unrecognized resemblances, its creative and therefore destructive powers of imagination, and its exposure to eruptions of involuntary memory—that ultimately could serve the cause of political revolution. Benjamin's attempts to conceive the gestures of a "new body" derive, at least in part, from the redemptive potential and political promise that he invests—perhaps too extravagantly—in these mimetic impulses.[12] The achievement of a radical justice in the body politic is, after all, not much like child's play. But somehow, we must see our way to transcendence—an irrevocable interruption in the space-time continuum that maintains the injustices and sufferings of a world order ruled by capital. "Salvation," Benjamin declares in a little note, "includes the firm, apparently brutal grasp."[13]

In "The Songs of the Icebergs," the poet W. S. Merwin evokes "hands extended in gestures out of the dreams of men."[14] In the dialectical images of Benjamin's dreams, not all the gestures are gentle and peaceful. Some, as that note shows, may be moved by the cause of justice to acts of revolutionary violence. In an essay on Franz Kafka, Benjamin remarks, "Like El Greco, Kafka tears open the sky behind every gesture [*hinter jeder Gebärde*]; but with El Greco—who was a patron saint of the Expressionists—the gesture remains the decisive thing, the center of the event [*die Mitte des Geschehens*]. . . . What Kafka could see least of all was the *gestus*. Each gesture is an event—one might even say a drama—in itself."[15] Recognizing the limitations of these aesthetic interpretations of the gesture as what we might call, borrowing Heidegger's phrase, a "world-disclosive event," I take this passage to suggest that a revolutionary potential lies immanent within the gesture—but that realizing this potential depends on the gesture's relation to the messianic promise: the measure of justice withdrawn behind every gesture. Since Benjamin is troubled by the injustice that our gestures endure in their bondage to wage labor, he borrows Charles Fourier's voice, in spite of their considerable disagreements, to communicate his own vision of an end to the exploitation of human labor:

> Were this exploitation to come to a halt, work, in turn, could no longer be characterized as the exploitation of nature by man. It would henceforth be conducted on the model of children's play, in which Fourier forms the basis of the "impassioned work" of the Harmonians. To have instituted play as the canon of a labor no longer rooted in exploitation is one of the great merits of

Fourier. Such work, inspirited by play, aims . . . at the amelioration of nature. For it, too, the Fourierist utopia furnishes a model, of a sort to be realized in the games of children. It is the image of an earth on which every place has become an *inn*. The double meaning of the word [*Wirtschaft*] blossoms here: all places are worked by human hands, made useful and beautiful thereby; all, however, stand, like a roadside inn, open to all. An earth that was cultivated according to such an image would cease to be part of "a world where action is never the sister of dream." On that earth, the act would be kin to the dream. ("Baudelaire") [16]

In view of his despair at the magnitude of the forces of oppression, his disappointment with the revolutionary movement, and his admiration for Fourier's dream, we should not be surprised that Benjamin would write about the divine hand of justice. In "The Meaning of Time in the Moral Universe," a note Benjamin left as a fragment, the divine hand in one stroke erases (*vertilgt*) from the world all traces (*Spuren*) of man's brutality and violence.[17] It is an act that expresses not only righteous fury but also the possibility of forgiveness.

III. The Discreet Tact of the Bourgeoisie: Critique

We would not be taking liberties to characterize Benjamin's thought as an exotic, messianic materialism, or even as a utopian materialism, since he does, despite his explicit hostility and protestation, nevertheless continue the tradition of utopian discourse. Like the pious cobbler in the Hasidic tale, who, with every stitch of the awl, brought together the spiritual world of the Torah and the material world of mankind, Benjamin joins together the dream-thought of a world transformed by the justice of the Messiah and the catastrophic world of fallen man. Thus at the same time that he invokes the spiritual power and promise of messianic redemption, he also undertakes an exact, unflinchingly positivistic, almost microscopic analysis of the gestures of the bourgeoisie, revealing, through dialectical images that surprise and disturb, the egoism and cruelty hidden just below the surface of our "civilization."

Benjamin's interest in gestures, which philosophers have so far ignored, has something to teach us about how he understood his work to contribute to the discourse of "dialectical materialism." His scattered comments on gestures communicate a certain baroque melancholy, yet also— paradoxically, ambiguously—a forward-looking nostalgia for an untimely time, a rhythm, tact, and measure given to a past that has never been present and to a future promised by a redemption that is always still to come. For the present, we have only runes and ciphers of fragmentary images, puzzles with pieces missing, the tracework of a subversive optics, a critical perception skilled in dialectical interpretation.

Not even priests can escape Benjamin's critical eye. He remarks with suspicion gestures that, in spite of a spiritual vocation, betray their formation within an economy driven by capitalism. The work "*One-Way Street,* includes a note titled "Costume Wardrobe" ("Maskengarderobe"), in which he recalls:

> At Bellinzona I noticed three priests in the station waiting room. They were sitting on a bench diagonally opposite mine. In rapt attention I observed the gestures of the one seated in the middle, who was distinguished from his brothers by a red skullcap. While he speaks to them, his hands are folded in his lap, and only now and then is one or the other very slightly raised and moved. I think to myself: his right hand must always know what the left is doing.[18]

I take this rather cryptic observation to be suggesting that, if the right hand always knows what the left is doing, these hands must be under the sway of an exchange logic, a commercial logic of strict equivalence. Undoubtedly Benjamin's observation alludes to the biblical scripture that describes the truly generous, truly charitable gesture, beyond all *quid pro quo* motivations, as one in which the hand that gives does so unbeknownst to the other hand. Otherwise, the other hand is ready to take back what the giving hand is giving. Hands moved by greed, moved by envy. Calculating fingers.

Ever the keenest observer of the bourgeoisie, Benjamin recalls for us, in his "Berlin Chronicle," a telling experience from his childhood:

> Only today, it seems to me, am I able to appreciate how much hatefulness and humiliation lay in the obligation to raise my cap to teachers. The necessity of admitting them by this gesture [*Geste*] into the sphere [*Bannkreis*] of my private existence seemed presumptuous. I should have had no objection to a less intimate, and in some way military display of respect. But to greet a teacher as one would a relation or a friend seemed inordinately unfitting.[19]

In this early experience of "school discipline," Benjamin perceives how, in the social formation of our children's gestures, the normalizing exigencies of the modern political economy—its transgression of the traditional boundary between public and private, its consequent invasion of private life—are already at work. "The anarchy of bourgeois society," he elsewhere declares, "is an infernal [*infernalische*] one."[20] The tactful and discreet manners of the bourgeoisie conceal the moral anarchy, the abyssal absence of any authentically moral measure, that these very manners have taken part in producing.

In an essay on the poet and essayist Christoph Martin Wieland (1733–1813), Benjamin approvingly quotes some words the poet wrote at age nineteen: "One who with his wishes goes beyond a kissing of the hand should not say that he loves."[21] Benjamin appreciated the older formalities—formalities that the modern world of the bourgeoisie has destroyed—because they maintained a tactful distance between people, an aura, we might say, that once constituted the attitude of respect, making the tangible intangible, the touchable untouchable. Regardless of Benjamin's intention, the innerworldly effect of his excessive formality, his meticulous adherence to as much of the older, more courtly manners as possible, was to unsettle the manners of the bourgeoisie: he induced a certain discomfiture, an interruption of the conventional expectations, exposing them to a kind of immanent material critique that called attention to their artificiality and contingency. In this dialectic between touchability and untouchability, where those who encountered him were, in effect, compelled to restrain their own gestures, a critical reflexivity could be set in motion, opening up the space for something radically different, as yet unknown: not a return to the older formalities, which were contemptible in their own way, but rather the eventuality of social relations truly mindful, at long last, of the disgrace of the human condition, truly respectful of the moral claims that all human beings as such rightfully make, and truly attentive to opportunities for significant social change.

With similar purpose, Benjamin noted the broken gestures he saw in the early silent films of Charlie Chaplin: the "jerky gait" and "that angular gesticulation which, little by little, would displace the rounded graces of the old world."[22] Benjamin did not want to return to the past; rather, in calling attention to a difference in gestural types, he sought to articulate in historical terms a critique of "modernity" that might ultimately enable us to move beyond it. He seems to have intuitively understood that gestures reveal more than they say, more even than they would want to say—that, despite themselves, and often without recognition, they carry the moral essence, the very conscience, of a society. For Benjamin, the discreet tact of bourgeois gestures can be regarded as "charming" only if that word is understood to accuse the bourgeoisie of re-enchanting the world: giving shape, as did the earlier, courtly era, to the illusions and myths that serve their grip on power by concealing behind beautiful sleight-of-hand the brutality of the conditions they have imposed and applauded. "We have to wake up from the existence of our parents. In this awakening, we have to give an account of the nearness of that existence." [23] What is called for here is an account of nearness that not only acknowledges how slightly we have detached ourselves from that measure of existence but also questions the character of the "nearness" that earlier generations of the ruling class constructed as a measure for their lives and the domination of the others.

IV. "Look, don't touch!"

> The value of commodities is the very opposite of the coarse materiality
> of their substance; not an atom of matter enters into its composition.
> Turn and examine a single commodity by itself, as we will, yet insofar
> as it remains an object of value, it seems impossible to grasp it.
>
> —Karl Marx, *Capital* [24]

In the course of his peregrinations, a perfect flâneur on the streets of Paris, slowly, quietly, almost imperceptibly gathering material for his *Arcades Project*, Benjamin found his glance constantly solicited by the things on display in the shop windows: marvelous mechanical toys, luxurious fabrics, elegant furniture, glamorous dresses and furs, all the booty that colonialism has seized in foreign lands, the threatening disclosure of its provenance rendered as much as possible abstract and unrecognizable. All these things seducing the eye, stimulating desire, creating fantastic needs, tempting the consumer who has money enough to buy them — the phantasmagoria over which a wealthy bourgeoisie celebrates its narrative of progress. But as he takes note of all these "goods," Benjamin is painfully aware that they are forever beyond the reach of most of the people passing them by. With cruel insolence, these goods say to the hardworking people of the manual-labor class: "Look, don't touch!" [25]

In "This Space for Rent," one of his studies for *One-Way Street*, Benjamin observes:

> In face of the huge images across the walls of houses, where toothpaste and
> cosmetics lie handy [*handlich liegen*] for giants, sentimentality is restored to

health and liberated in American style, just as people whom nothing moves or touches [*rührt und anrührt*] any longer are taught to cry again by films. For the man in the street, however, it is money that affects him in this way and brings him into perceived contact [*schlüssigen Kontakt*] with things.[26]

Here he is registering his conviction that, under the spell of capitalism, our capacity for reflective "experience" has atrophied: alienated from the truth of our senses, our perception and sensibility, we have lost much of our capacity to be touched and moved—except by what the marketplace of capitalism puts before us. Is it despite that separation from the hand or, paradoxically, because of it that the ontology of this political economy is, as Heidegger says, determined by what is always ready-to-hand—by the unconditional facticity that everything in the world should present itself, should presence, either as functional and ready-to-hand (*zuhanden*) or as an essence constantly present-at-hand (*vorhanden*)? What kind of "contact" is possible when money is its only motivation and cause? What kind of society sees nothing problematic about celebrating in shop windows all the labor-saving commodities that its manual-labor class manufactures but cannot afford to buy? Under these conditions, the "goods" on display in shop windows reveal without mediation their true demonic face.

Introducing the concept of "aura" in his discussion of the Paris arcades, Benjamin states:

> Looking at someone carries the implicit expectation that our look will be returned by the object of our gaze. Where this expectation is met . . . , there is an experience of the aura to the fullest extent. "Perceptibility," as Novalis puts it, "is a kind of attentiveness." The perceptibility he has in mind is none other than that of the aura. Experience of the aura thus rests on the transposition of a response common in human relationships to the relationship between the inanimate or natural object and man. . . . To perceive the aura of an object we look at means to invest it with the ability to look at us in return.[27]

Now, according to Benjamin, the aura is the "unique manifestation of a distance." And the "essentially distant is the inapproachable: inapproachability is in fact a primary quality of the ceremonial image."[28] Through an aura that says to the workers passing by, "You must look, but don't touch!," the commodities that capitalism displays and celebrates return a mocking gaze—a demonic gaze that cannot but touch the workers with violence and move them to question the system that justifies that unapproachability.

In his notes for "Baudelaire," one of the divisions of his *Arcades Project*, Benjamin wrote:

> The allegorist is in his element with commercial wares. As flâneur, he has empathized with the soul of the commodity; as allegorist, he recognizes in the "price tag" . . . the object of his broodings—the meaning. The world in which this newest meaning lets him settle has grown no friendlier. An inferno rages in the soul of the commodity, for all the seeming tranquility lent it by the price.[29]

We will return to reflect on the broodings of the allegorist. Here, however, we can already get an inkling of the allegorist's deeply felt experience— experience inseparable from an activity, a dialectical practice, that often involves touching things and being touched by them.

Entirely different, as Benjamin observes in "Paris, Capital of the Nineteenth Century," are the desperate, belated efforts of the bourgeoisie to touch and hold onto their material possessions, the substance of their social position: "It is as though the bourgeois made it a point of honor not to lose the trace of his things and accessories. Untiringly, he makes a mold for a myriad of objects; for his slippers and watches, his kitchenware and his umbrellas, he invents sheaths and covers. He has a distinctive preference for velveteen and plush since they keep the imprint of touch."[30] The bourgeoisie longed for permanence in their social position, a status for which their possessions gave enduring tangible evidence; but also, in consequence, they feared losing a subjective connection to the tangible substantiality of their world. Yet the objects—trophies, souvenirs, bibelots— displayed in the nineteenth-century bourgeois interior were only to be seen, not touched. Even much of the elegant furniture was less used than displayed, treasured for its aesthetic and iconographic value, as representative of privileged status. While use-value and exchange-value dominated life outside the bourgeois home, these values were banished from the interior—but with them went the very tangibility the bourgeoisie craved. Such were the contradictions inherent in their historical situation.

The allegorist's passion for the tangible seeks to reveal the stories of things, their secret treasury of historical documentation, archives of dialectical truth, indictments of their social role, intimations of their redemptive afterlife. As we might expect, Benjamin thinks most precisely about such contact with things when he reflects on narratively meaningful

experience (*Erfahrung*) under the rule of capitalism. Indeed, one might argue that experience is at the very heart of his critical-dialectical program.
Many of Benjamin's writings—one must mention at least "On the Program of the Coming Philosophy," "The Storyteller," *One-Way Street*, "On
Some Motifs in Baudelaire," and "Surrealism: The Last Snapshot of the
European Intelligentsia"—take up this question of experience in a major
way, interrogating the atrophy and decay of experience, of course; but also
its potential for redemption.

For Benjamin as for Marx, the fate of the human "sensorium" is a political question—and indeed a matter of urgency. Because sensation, perception, and gesture are not purely natural but are also formations of social practices and institutions, their fate cannot be left to the haphazard
phantasmagoric forces of commodification, impoverishment, and death
that are operative in today's world. The redemption of sensation, perception, and gesture thus becomes an urgent task. For Benjamin, this means
attempting to retrieve anarchic vestiges of their mimetic resources, vestiges
of their nonintentional, auratic "magic," which inherently resist social
control over the realm of the tactile—a realm in which a physiognomic
process of dialectical cognition drawing upon mimetic impulses prior to
socialized consciousness will always and already have begun.

In an essay discussing what was behind Hölderlin's poems "Poet's
Mood" or "Poet's Courage" ("Dichtermuth") and its subsequently revised
version, "Reticence" ("Blödigkeit"), Benjamin criticizes the first version,
arguing that it presents only an abstract form of knowledge and thus fails
as a poem because it does not become *fühlbar*, tangible or "feelable": "We
know this thought," he concedes, but argues that it is disconnected from
sensibility, from the poetic courage (*Dichtermuth*) that is promised by the
title.[31]

It is in the course of these numerous ruminations on "experience," on
our "commerce" (*Verkehr*) with the material world, that Benjamin calls attention to configurations of experience that might be interpreted in terms
of three different types of "contact" between subject and object. Bearing
in mind that summaries of Benjamin are always risky, we might nevertheless usefully differentiate three major moments of experience. (1) *Erlebnis*,
that is, atomic, monadic experience, experience in decay, cut off from any
reflective, critical, and redemptive relation to the historical past, experience whose contact is purely subjective, arrested within the imagination,
incapable of material mediations and of playing a role in dialectical praxis.

(2) *Erfahrung* proper, that is, experience in which contact between subject and object takes place in a narrativized context that relates the historical past to the actualities of the present—but in a way that makes it possible for dialectical praxis to retrieve from remnants of the past some of its still-unrealized potentialities. And (3) *Chock*, a violent and frequently catastrophic event, typical of modern experience, involving excessively stimulating contact that permits no reflective, dialectical mediations—although occasionally the shock of such contact is strong enough to release long-repressed, historically explosive memories and to ignite even in a long-slumbering consciousness a radically new mode of experience. But, as Benjamin eventually realized in exposing another reality, a reality that ideological distortions have concealed beneath the ordinary reality of subject-object commerce, shock can do more than release a repressed historical memory. It can also, even more consequentially, bring us into contact with the traces of the immemorial—traces of the messianic prophecy that are silently waiting to be recognized in the things that, with infinite patience, we touch and handle.

V. Manual Labor

In "Imperial Panorama," the tenth note in his *One-Way Street*, Benjamin registers the following impression:

> Warmth is ebbing from things. The objects of daily use gently but insistently repel us. Day by day, in overcoming the sum of secret resistances—not the overt ones—that they put in our way, we have an immense labor to perform. We must compensate for their coldness with our warmth if they are not to freeze us to death, and handle their spines with infinite dexterity, if we are not to perish by bleeding. From our fellow men we should expect no succor. Bus conductors, officials, workmen [*Handwerker*], salesmen—they all feel themselves to be the representatives of a refractory matter whose menace they take pains to demonstrate through their own surliness. And in the degeneration [*Entartung*] of things, with which, emulating human decay, they punish humanity, the country itself conspires.[32]

This is, however, only the second half of the story. In the first half, what must be brought to light is the character of our gestures, which are only getting what they deserve: the resistance of things, their coldness, is after all just their mimetic revenge. Why are we surprised when, in response to our blind pursuit of absolute ontological presence, the things we turn into objects object to this reification? Hope for us now requires that we learn to touch and handle things differently, imparting our warmth—the warmth of our humanity, a humanity that, however, we have yet to realize here on earth.

In his essay "Baudelaire," Benjamin quotes with approval a remark in Hermann Lotze's *Microcosmos*, bearing on this point:

> Lotze's reflections on the worker who no longer handles a tool but operates a machine aptly illuminate the attitude of the consumer toward the commodity produced under these conditions. "He [the manual worker of earlier times] could still recognize in every contour of the finished product the power and the precision of his own formative touch. The participation of the individual in the work of the machine, by contrast, is limited to . . . manual operations which bring forth nothing directly but merely supply to an inscrutable mechanism the obscure occasion for invisible accomplishments."[33]

"On Some Motifs in Baudelaire" proposes a more intricate historical analysis of the gestures distinctive of our time, a "modernity" that they brought forth, only to be shaped, in turn, by the very conditions of that "modernity":

> The invention of the match around the middle of the nineteenth century brought forth a number of innovations which have one thing in common: one abrupt movement of the hand triggers a process of many steps. This development is taking place in many areas of life. One case in point is the telephone, where the lifting of a receiver has taken the place of the steady movement that used to be required to crank the older models. Of the countless movements of switching, inserting, pressing, and the like, the "snapping" of the photographer has had the greatest consequences. A touch of the finger now sufficed to fix an event for an unlimited period of time. The camera gave the moment a posthumous shock, as it were. Haptic experiences of this kind were joined by optic ones, such as are supplied by the advertising pages of a newspaper or the traffic of a big city. Moving through this traffic involves the individual in a series of shocks and collisions. . . . Baudelaire speaks of a man who plunges into the crowd as into a reservoir of electric energy. . . . Thus technology has subjected the human sensorium to a complex kind of training. There came a day when a new and urgent need for stimuli was met by the film. In a film, perception in the form of shocks was established as a formal principle. That which determines the rhythm of production on a conveyor belt is the basis of the rhythm of reception in the film.[34]

This observation about the rhythm of gestures on the factory assembly line leads into a discussion of Marx:

> Marx had good reason to stress the great fluidity of the connection between segments in manual labor. This connection appears to the factory worker on an assembly line in an independent, objectified form. Independently of the worker's volition, the article being worked on comes within his range of action and moves away from him just as arbitrarily. . . . In working with machines, workers learn to co-ordinate "their own movements with the uniformly constant movements of an automaton." These words [from Marx] shed a peculiar light on the absurd kind of uniformity with which Poe wants to saddle the crowd—uniformities of attire and behavior, but also a uniformity of facial expression. . . . "All machine work," it is said in the above context, "requires early drilling of the worker." This drill must be differentiated from practice. Practice, which was the sole determinant in craftsmanship, still had a function in manufacturing. . . . On the other hand, this same manufacturing produces "in every handicraft it seizes a class of so-called unskilled laborers which the handicraft system strictly excluded. In developing the greatly simplified specialty to the point of virtuosity at the cost of the work capacity as a whole, it starts turning the lack of any development into a specialty. In addition to ranks, we therefore get the simple division of workers into the skilled and the unskilled." The unskilled worker is the one most deeply degraded by the drill of the machines. His work has been sealed off from experience; practice counts for nothing there.

Baudelaire and Poe, two poets who put into unforgettable words the distress of the nineteenth century, recognized in the experience of their time a moment of shock, a moment observable in common gestures. Benjamin epitomizes the moment this way: "The shock experience which the passer-by has in the crowd corresponds to what the worker 'experiences' at his machine."[35] The worker is bound to a process that is designed to eliminate all forms of contingency, all unpredictable possibilities. (One should keep in mind here the connection between the word "contingency" and the experience of touch.) Thus, relating his analysis of the work of the unskilled laborer to Baudelaire's remarks on gambling, Benjamin avers:

> To be sure, [this work] lacks any touch of adventure, of the mirage that lures [for example] the gambler. But it certainly does not lack the futility, the emptiness, the inability to complete something which is inherent in the activity of a wage slave in a factory. Gambling even contains the workman's gesture that is produced by the automatic operation, for there can be no game without the

quick movement of the hand by which the stake is put down or a card is picked up. The jolt in the movement of the machine is like the so-called *coup* in a game of chance. The manipulation of the worker at the machine has no connection with the preceding operation for the very reason that it is its exact repetition.[36]

It is perhaps not surprising, therefore, that Benjamin would be attracted to Fourier's vision of a utopia in which, as Benjamin puts it, "all places are worked by human hands, made useful and beautiful thereby. . . . An earth that was cultivated according to such an image would cease to be part of 'a world where action is never the sister of dream.' On that earth, the act would be kin to the dream."[37] But the imagined transformation of manual labor cannot take place until the work of the hands has been properly recognized. Thus, in spite of his admiration for Baudelaire, Benjamin reproaches the poet for his omission: "The 'magic cobbles piled for barricades,' in Baudelaire's draft of an epilogue, define the limit which his poetry encounters in its immediate confrontation with social subjects. The poet says nothing of the hands which moved these cobblestones."[38] In "The Storyteller," Benjamin is likewise careful to remember the hand that figures in a piece that Paul Valéry wrote about the art of an artist he knew. Valéry had argued that the decisions involved in her work depended on no knowledge and derived from no practice, but drew their inspiration "exclusively from a certain accord of the soul, the eye, and the hand of someone who was born to perceive them [the right gestures] and evoke them in his inner self." (Benjamin gives no source for these words he attributes to Valéry.) While agreeing with Valéry's suggestion of an "accord" but rejecting his denial of a practice, Benjamin is uncomfortable with an intuitionism that overlooks the material conditions of production: "With these words, soul, eye, and hand are brought into connection. Interacting with one another, they determine a practice. We are no longer familiar with this practice. The role of the hand in production has become more modest." Then, returning to his meditation on the historical situation of the storyteller, he adds:

> The place it [the producing hand] filled in storytelling lies waste. (After all, storytelling, in its sensory aspect, is by no means a calling for the voice alone. Rather, in genuine storytelling, the hand plays a part which supports what is expressed in a hundred ways with its gestures trained by work.) That old coordination of the soul, the eye, and the hand which emerges in Valéry's words

is that of the artisan which we encounter wherever the art of storytelling is still at home.[39]

In the world that has passed, the gestures of the artisan's hands mattered: the potter's fingers left their traces in the hardened clay and the weaver's dexterity could be measured by the quality of his knots. Likewise, the storyteller's gestures mattered, a mimetic register not only of the prevailing mode of production but also of that "accord" of soul, eye, and hand that the modern conditions of labor have irrevocably abolished. Along with an economy in which the handicrafts enjoyed a significant role, the marvelous art of the storyteller—and the gestures it kept alive in the collective memory of the culture—was also passing into oblivion. Benjamin, however, could not forget, in spite of his celebration of the mechanical reproduction that was rendering the skillful hand obsolete.

VI. Auras and Traces

Benjamin interprets this historical passage into oblivion in terms of what he calls the "aura": "If we designate as aura the associations which, at home in the *mémoire involontaire*, tend to cluster around the object of a perception, then its analogue in the case of a utilitarian object [*Gegenstand des Gebrauchs*] is the experience which has left traces of the practiced hand."[40] Not even the camera's mechanical reproduction, a photographic memory permanently recording the presence of an absent past, can retard or reverse the historical fate of "practice." The objects produced by machines can have no such auratic presence—although, from the looks of things, commodity fetishism may well have succeeded in re-creating a certain aura of enchantment around the machine-made "goods" that are now offered in hypnotic displays for popular consumption. If this situation constitutes "a crisis in perception"[41] for Benjamin, it is also a crisis for cultural memory, which has lost touch with the tracework of the hands and thereby also with the historical beginnings of the mimetic impulse embodied in "practice."

In "The Work of Art in the Age of Mechanical Reproduction," an essay provoked by Benjamin's recognition of the increasing importance of photography and the "motion picture" in our cultural life, he reflects on the emergence of "a new kind of perception": "During long periods of history, the mode of human sense perception changes with humanity's entire mode of existence. The manner in which human sense perception is organized, the medium in which it is accomplished, is determined not only by nature, but by historical circumstances as well."[42] For Benjamin, it is imperative that we understand "the social transformations expressed by these changes in perception." Thus, he says, "if changes in the medium of contemporary perception can be comprehended as decay of the aura, it is possible to show their social causes."[43] And, moreover, their social consequences.

Benjamin defines the aura as "the unique phenomenon of a distance, however close it may be."[44] It is, as he says in "A Small History of Photography," "a strange weave [*Gespinst*] of space and time: the unique appearance or semblance of a distance, no matter how close the object may be."[45] In another text, part of the *Arcades Project*, Benjamin includes a note entitled "Trace and Aura," which reads: "Trace and aura. The trace is appearance [*Erscheinung*] of a nearness [*Nähe*], however far removed the thing that left it behind may be. The aura is appearance of a distance, however close the thing that calls it forth. In the trace, we gain possession of the *thing* [*werden wir der Sache habhaft*]; in the aura, it takes possession of us [*bemächtigt sie sich unser*]."[46] It may be questioned whether, as Benjamin says, the trace grants us any "possession" of the thing—especially since, in defining the trace, he tells us that the trace is only the "appearance" of a certain nearness. But what he says about the aura seems to fit historical experience. However, while the distinction he draws between trace and aura is useful, one might question its essential stability: doesn't Benjamin's own work show us that modernity has also experienced auratic traces and mourned or celebrated the traces of an aura? We will, for the present, leave this question unresolved.

What, he asks, are the "social bases of the contemporary decay of the aura"?[47] The question presupposes that decay is a fact. Thus, before we consider Benjamin's answer, we should pause to consider whether or not the aura is in fact decaying. Perhaps, as some of Benjamin's writings suggest, there really is no decay in auratic experience as such, but only a radical change with regard to what the aura today surrounds: not, as in the past, the great works of art, the human being, the human body, but rather the seductive commodity, gloriously shining "goods" still unapproachable and untouchable for many people. In any case, answering the question of the "social bases of the contemporary decay of the aura," he says here, calls for research on the increasing significance of the masses in contemporary life, specifically on: "the desire of contemporary masses to bring things 'closer' spatially and humanly, which is just as ardent as their bent toward overcoming the uniqueness of every reality by accepting its reproduction. Every day the urge grows stronger to get hold of an object at very close range by way of its likeness, its reproduction."[48] Heidegger was especially critical of this modern-age compulsion to "get hold" of objects and make them permanently available. Of course, what the masses get hold of by way of photographic reproduction is nothing but a ghostly remnant of the original: "To pry an object from its shell, to destroy its aura, is the mark of a perception whose 'sense of the universal equality of things' has increased to such a degree that it extracts it even from a unique object by means of reproduction." Thus, he says, betraying, once again, a certain ambivalence, "there is manifested in the field of perception what in the theoretical sphere is noticeable in the increasing importance of statistics. The adjustment of reality to the masses and of the masses to reality is a process of unlimited scope, as much for thinking as for perception."[49] We have not yet, I believe, sufficiently taken the measure of these changes.

For Benjamin, perhaps the most poignant experience of the aura is one in which it "emanates from early photographs in the fleeting expression of a human face." In the concluding lines of a short poem reflecting on a photographic portrait of his father as a young man, Rilke gave voice to a haunting experience of loss that Benjamin, in anguished ambivalence, could not in the end avoid sharing:

> You quickly vanishing daguerreotype
> In my slowly perishing hands.[50]

VII. Tact and Contact

In "Gloves," a note for *One-Way Street*, Benjamin briefly touches on the originating connection between tact and contact:

In an aversion [*Ekel*] to animals the predominant feeling is fear of being recognized by them through contact [*Berührung*]. The horror that stirs deep in man is an obscure awareness that in him something lives so akin to the animal that it might be recognized. All disgust [*Ekel*] is originally disgust at touching [*Ekel vor dem Berühren*]. Even when the feeling is mastered, it is only by a drastic gesture [*mit sprunghafter, überschießender Gebärde*] that overleaps its mark: the nauseating [*das Ekelhafte*] is violently engulfed, eaten, while the zone of finest epidermal contact remains taboo. Only in this way is the paradox of the moral demand to be met, exacting simultaneously the overcoming

[*Überwindung*] and the subtlest elaboration [*subtilste Ausbildung*] of man's sense of disgust. He may not deny his bestial relationship [*Verwandtschaft*] with animals, the invocation [*Anruf*] of which revolts him: he must make himself its master [*er muß sich zu ihrem Herrn machen*].[51]

According to Benjamin, then, the birth of tact was a decisive moment in the historical emergence of the human species: that moment when, in a self-conscious effort to obliterate ambiguities and posit an unquestionable biological difference, human beings settled on a substitute for touch, inventing with tactful gestures the proprieties of a reassuring social difference. Tact is the sublimation or sublation of that aversion to the animal, our biological ancestry, simultaneously overcoming it and preserving it. The moral requirement, that the "nature" (*bios*) of the human must be absolutely differentiated from the "nature" (*zoé*) of the animal, accordingly becomes a requirement that every culture somehow translates into recognizable "manners," ritualized forms of "appropriate" social comportment. Instead of touching, we resort to a gesture that demonstrably suspends touch, substituting a movement that bears the sense once borne by touch. The social mediations of tact displace the immediacy of contact, becoming "second nature." The tactful gesture is therefore in two senses a "measured" response: First, in being tactful I prereflectively measure the distance between myself and the other (for knowing the measure that is appropriate to the social relationship becomes "second nature"); and second, in being tactful I restrain my gestures according to a "befitting" measure. Tact may be measured by distance, by spacing; but it may also be measured by temporal rhythm: not only the rhythm of the gesture itself but also the rhythm of a suspended movement, introducing into the encounter a certain delay or deferral. Thus we might say that tact is the measure that gives the appearance of resolving the "double bind" that contact would otherwise incur. And yet, since tact is a sublimation or sublation, it always also remains quietly ambiguous, preserving traces of a kinship with animality that it cannot erase, secretly deconstructing the artificial boundary between the animal and the human, making sure that the nature of our flesh never entirely forgets, or loses contact with, its prehistoric bond. The seemingly immeasurable difference between the human and the animal thus remains—silently, implicitly, tactfully—in question; for breaches, whether pardonable or not, are sometimes tempting, and always possible.

In his essay on Karl Kraus, Benjamin, bringing out the "theological" character of tact, takes the opportunity to consider the ambiguities and in-stabilities inherent in the differentiations posited by tact, by the measure of tact—and the tact of measure:

> If in Johann Peter Hebel we find developed to the utmost the constructive, creative side of tact, in Kraus we see its most destructive and critical face. But for both, tact is moral alertness [*moralische Geistesgegenwart*]—Stössel calls it "conviction refined into dialectics"—and the expression of an unknown convention more important than the acknowledged one. Kraus lived in a world in which the most shameful act was still the *faux pas*; he distinguishes between degrees of the monstrous [*Monströsen*], and does so precisely because his criterion [*Maßstab*] is never that of bourgeois respectability [*Wohlanständigkeit*], which once above the threshold of trivial misdemeanor becomes so quickly short of breath that it can form no conception of villainy on a world-historical scale.
>
> Kraus knew this criterion [*Maßstab*] from the first, and moreover there is no other criterion for true tact. It is a theological criterion. For tact is not [*nicht etwa*]—as narrow minds imagine it—the gift of allotting to each, on consideration of all relationships, what is socially befitting [*gesellschaftlich Gebührende*]. On the contrary, tact is the capacity to treat social relationships, though not departing from them, as natural, even as paradisiac [*paradiesische*] relationships, and so not only to approach the king as if he had been born with the crown on his brow, but the lackey like an Adam in livery.[52]

Here Benjamin develops an understanding of tact and rhythm radically different from the customary interpretation. By situating our social comportment within a theological, indeed messianic context, he submits that comportment to a measure infinitely exceeding the measure to which we conventionally conform our social manners. According to Kraus's critical measure, the studied ease of our tactful gestures unwittingly reveals a deeply suppressed anxiety concerning the socially constructed class hierarchy that our code of manners dissimulates, monstrously, as a product of natural differences among people. Kraus's sharply observant mockery not only exposes "natural" differences as grotesque and fraudulent constructions of bourgeois "tact" but empowers the oppressed class in the process. Tact can no longer assure its survival by taking on the semblance of a natural fate.

For Kraus and Benjamin, the tact of bourgeois respectability is inescapably monstrous: for it measures people's worthiness solely in terms of the conformity of their gestures to a standard of comfortable propriety, while ignoring other, more urgent claims, notably the crimes against humanity that are simultaneously taking place. The monstrosity of the tactful measure stands out in sharpest relief when it is measured against the measure violated by these crimes: the messianic measure articulated by Adorno in the note with which he concludes *Minima Moralia*: the present world must ultimately be judged "from the standpoint of redemption."[53]

Benjamin's retrieval of Krausian tact could undoubtedly be said to announce a new humanism. But if so, it must also be said that it is not a humanism, as in Levinas, of the other person so much as it is a humanism of the in-human—a tact opening toward what lies beyond the "human nature" of social reproduction. Considered in this light, not touching lets a caesura enter into the character of social relations. Not touching would accordingly be a gesture of respect for the promise of a messianic era.

To think the possibility of a radically other future, however, Benjamin realized the need to return to Hegel's notion of the "absolute *Gegenwart,*" the absolute present, of Spirit's total and final self-realization, and to think once again the movement of the dialectic. Otherwise, Spirit would remain hostage to a time continuum that could promise only a counterfeit future, a future that merely repeats the past. So, before we leave one of Benjamin's most astonishing textual passages, I would like to linger over one more matter of consequence, namely, *moralische Geistesgegenwart,* which Edmund Jephcott has quite reasonably translated as "moral alertness."

As we know, the German word *Gegenwart* refers, in its current usage, to the "actuality" or "presentness" of a temporal or historical moment. Thus Benjamin's word *Geistesgegenwart* refers, here, to an awareness, alertness, or watchful attention that is directed upon the presence of that now-present. However, as Benjamin unfolds his reflections on tact in the above passage, that word is so fragmented and dislocated as to undergo a sea change in meaning. The tact he has in mind is an iconoclastic moral alertness, an alertness ceaselessly in touch with its dream of a reconciled world: an alertness, therefore, that is waiting against, or waiting in opposition to, the specious present of bourgeois ideology and idolatry: a watchful waiting, ever alert to the possibility of interruptions in the temporal continuum that constitutes a long history of oppression and suffering, a *Leidensgeschichte.*

The etymology of the word *Gegenwart,* especially as it figures in Benjamin's use of the word *Geistesgegenwart,* calls for further comment. *Gegenwart* breaks up into two parts: *gegen,* meaning "toward," "against," or "in opposition to," and *wart,* which today informs the word for "wait."

Gegenwart entered into modern German by way of the old High German *geginwerti*, meaning "directed toward," "turned toward," derived from the Latin *vertere*. Whence the word *Warte*, referring to a lookout, watchtower, observatory, or belfry. What the vigilance is turned toward, what it is watching out for, is that which is coming toward it, that which is *gegen-über*, in presence before it, or over against it. Significantly, the distinctively temporal sense of *Gegenwart*, that is, in its relation to the past (*Vergangenheit*) and the future (*Zukunft*), seems, however, not to have come into use until the eighteenth century. Although no direct connection has been made between the origin of this usage and the spirit of the Enlightenment, we might note that the distinctly temporal and historical meaning emerged at a time when thinkers and poets of the Enlightenment, men such as Kant and Hölderlin, hoping for progressive social and political changes, began to reflect critically on the cultural experience of the present, the prevailing cultural attitude toward the time in which they were living, ever watchful, ever on the lookout for the signs of a readiness for such changes.

But if the word *Gegenwart* suggests the metaphysical present of Platonism, the presentness of a reified historical moment that stands opposite a serenely contemplative gaze turned toward it in rapt absorption, the "moral alertness" that Kraus attributes to the Enlightenment thinkers and poets, turning, as it did, *toward* the present, was also the beginning of a reflexively critical turn, artfully staged, *against* the metaphysical present of a persistent Platonism. That opposition to a specious promise of difference, to a semblance of fate, Benjamin continues and intensifies, showing that what is at stake is nothing less than a dialectical struggle to release the future from the tyranny of a past that has held it hostage and used repetition to justify long-standing conditions of injustice and oppression.

Thus, although there is no immediate etymological connection between the words *Gegenwart* and *warten*, meaning "to wait," there is an obvious situational connection between the present and being watchful, being on the lookout for something the coming of which is foreshadowed yet still uncertain. So it would not be extravagant to surmise that Benjamin, who gave much thought to the redemptive "deconstruction" of our prevailing experience of time, would have heard echoes of this disruption reverberating throughout his text.[54] If, for Benjamin, the present (*die Gegenwart*) is a moment of "awakening," a moment of reflexive awareness, alert to what is possible, that means that the awakening to the present must turn *against* (*gegen*) the present for the sake of what is always coming, always still to come—the material fulfillment of the messianic promise given to a past that has never been present. "Moral alertness" would then signify not merely a reflexive turn in the direction of the present, nor even merely a gesture turning against (*gegen*) the present, but also a *Warten*, a watchful waiting—the intense but patient waiting of Kafka's "man from the country," the absurd yet not entirely hopeless waiting of the characters in Beckett's *Waiting for Godot*. Benjamin's waiting is an awaiting beyond all measure.

But it is a waiting that takes place in the light of ideas, ideas appearing through *Sternbilder, Konstellationen*, of particulars. Unlike particulars violently subsumed and unified under universalizing concepts, the particulars that "constellations" illuminate are allowed to remain in the "objective interpretation" of their "virtual arrangement." Benjamin is convinced that this ideational procedure lets the material truth-content hidden in certain "elective affinities," certain *Wahlverwandtschaften*, come to light in the form of dialectical images. The "constellation" procedure is, in a crucial sense, the work of a gesture whose manipulations of cultural material invite a *Wiedervergegenwärtigung*, a moment of involuntary recollection in which the elements in the constellation will suddenly appear before the imagination in a rearrangement intimating the messianic fulfillment of a promise that drives the dialectical rhythm of progressive revolutionary forces.[55] (It is important to remember here that, for Kant, the imagination is the root of both practical and theoretical reason. Thus, Benjamin's dialectical images produce reason with a moral force.)

The time of tact—or, say, its rhythm—belongs at once to the dream-thought of a wild "nature" preceding the cultural conventions of our unreconciled society and to the thought of a radically different relationship to the metaphysical delimitation of "nature" and "culture"—a relationship that would overthrow those heavily invested conventions, redeeming all at once both nature and culture. In Benjamin's hands, then, "moral alertness" is given a singular embodiment, cast in the tactfulness of gestures somehow deeply in touch with a memory trace of paradise and a vivid dream of redemption. In moral alertness we await the event—what he calls the *Jetztzeit*—that would interrupt the continuum of history, setting in motion, within but nevertheless against, the *Gegenwart* of that order, a new measure, a new rhythm, of and for the future of historical time.[56]

VIII. Allegorical Gestures: Taking the Measure of the Possible

In an early fragment, "Outline of the Psychophysical Problem," Benjamin describes the human body as a "moral instrument." [57] What does this mean? To answer this question adequately, we need to reflect on Benjamin's dialectical and narrative figures of the collector, the brooder, and the allegorist. We need also to reflect on what he says about the child. The child, he remarks, learns to grasp "by reaching for the moon in the same way he or she reaches for a ball." [58] In other words, what we can learn from observing the child's gestures is that grasping is always projective: even the most concrete gesture is also ideal; even the most immediate is also mediated by anticipations of hopes realized, dreams fulfilled. Merleau-Ponty could perceive the ideality silently moving the mimetic gesture, but he did not see in it what Benjamin could see, namely: the child's anticipations of messianicity, the *promesse de bonheur*.

In a note for "The Collector," one of the Konvoluts making up the *Arcades Project*, Benjamin asserts: "Possession and having are allied with the tactile, and stand in a certain opposition to the optical. Collectors are beings with tactile instincts. Moreover, with the recent turn away from naturalism, the primacy of the optical that was determinant of the previous century has come to an end. . . . The flâneur optical, the collector tactile." [59] The "true collector," according to Benjamin, "detaches the object from its functional relations." But that, he adds, "is hardly an exhaustive description of this remarkable mode of behavior. For isn't this the foundation . . . of that 'disinterested' contemplation by virtue of which the collector attains to an unequaled view of the object?" Although Benjamin seems, in this remark, to be encouraging the primacy of the optical, the collector is also characterized as someone with "tactile instincts" whose reading of historical traces is a way to get in touch with hidden possibilities, some hitherto unrecognizable order. In the collector's seemingly anarchic gestures, Benjamin discerns an obsession with the "interpretation of fate":

> It must be kept in mind that, for the collector, the world is present, and indeed ordered, in each of his objects. Ordered, however, according to a surprising and, for the profane understanding, incomprehensible connection. This connection stands to the customary ordering and schematization of things something as their arrangement in the dictionary stands to a natural

arrangement. We need only recall what importance a particular collector at-
taches not only to his object but also to its entire past, whether this concerns
the origin and objective characteristics of the thing or the details of its osten-
sibly external history. . . . All of these—the "objective" data together with the
other—come together, for the true collector, in every single one of his possessions, to form a whole magic encyclopedia, a world order, whose outline is
the *fate* of his object. . . . It suffices to observe just one collector as he handles
the items in his showcase. No sooner does he hold them in his hand than he
appears inspired by them and seems to look through them into their distance,
like an augur.[60]

In case we might metaphorize and dismiss these invocations of the hands
in Benjamin's descriptions of the collector's practice, another note (Konvolut H 4, 1) declares, "The physiological side of collecting is important."[61]
The art of the collector involves, in every encounter with the collectible
object, the imposition of an order that is also "a sort of productive disorder" (Konvolut H 5, 1), in that the new order allows one to discern the contingency and dispersion that is brought to order. Every construction of the
"natural" assumes it can undo or conceal all potential threats to its imposed
order, thereby making the "natural" appear as an order of "fate." Working
against this semblance and suspending his own rational, order-imposing
impulses, the collector breaks up the established ordering of things, reducing them to mere heaps, pieces of a puzzles still to be assembled into
something meaningful. In this way, the collector hopes to make time for
the remote possibility that, in the sudden eruption of an "involuntary
memory," a radically new constellation of meaning—the image of a radically new social order—could emerge, bearing its directive meaning, first
of all, for the gestures of the hands—in and as a tactile sense.[62]

According to Benjamin, "The dialectical image is defined as the involuntary memory [*unwillkürliche Erinnerung*] of a redeemed humanity."[63]
Influenced, no doubt, by Proust and Baudelaire, Benjamin recognizes that
involuntary memory, which is, for him, at the very heart of the experience
of all three dialectical figures—the collector, the brooder, the allegorist—
comes first of all by way of the body. Involuntary memories come, that is,
as physiognomies that could never have been constructed or predicted by
any cognitive intentionalities. The body of lived experience is for them a
singularly privileged medium for the awakening of memories that can
open the present to the promise in a past that had seemed utterly irre-
trievable. It might be argued that Benjamin has thus adopted in radical-

ized form an observation made by Friedrich Schiller with regard to a program for "aesthetic education." According to Schiller, aesthetic education, the cultivation of sensibility, first of all involves "providing the receptive faculty with the most multifarious contacts with the world as regards feeling, pushing passivity to its fullest extent; and secondly, . . . as regards reason, pushing activity to its fullest extent."[64]

In another note for "The Collector" (Konvolut H 4a, 1), Benjamin attempts to sketch the traits that distinguish the collector from the allegorist:

> Perhaps the most deeply hidden motive of the person who collects can be described this way: he takes up the struggle against dispersion. Right from the start, the great collector is struck by the confusion, by the scatter, in which the things of the world are found. It is the same spectacle that so preoccupied the men of the Baroque; in particular, the world image of the allegorist cannot be explained apart from the passionate, distraught concern with this spectacle. The allegorist is, as it were, the polar opposite of the collector. He has given up the attempt to elucidate things through research into their properties and relations. He dislodges things from their context and, from the outset, relies on his profundity to illuminate their meaning. The collector, by contrast, brings together what he imagines belongs together; by keeping in mind their affinities and their succession in time, he can eventually furnish information about his objects. Nevertheless—and this is more important than all the differences that may exist between them—in every collector hides an allegorist, and in every allegorist, a collector. As far as the collector is concerned, his collection is never complete; for let him discover just a single piece missing, and everything he has collected remains a patchwork, which is what things are for allegory from the very beginning. On the other hand, the allegorist—for whom objects represent only keywords in a secret dictionary, which will make known their meanings to the initiated—precisely the allegorist can never have enough of things. With him, one thing is so little capable of taking the place of another that no possible reflection suffices to foresee what meaning his profundity might lay claim to for each one of them.[65]

"Allegory," for Benjamin, "recognizes many enigmas [*Rätsel*], but it knows no mystery [*Geheimnis*]."[66] "An enigma," as he explains it, "is a fragment [*ein Bruchstück*] that, together with another, matching fragment, indicates a [recognizable] whole. Mystery, on the other hand, was invoked from time immemorial in the image of the veil, which is an old accomplice of distance. Distance appears veiled [*Die Ferne erscheint verschleiert*]."[67] In

other words, whereas the enigma at least hints at the possibility of a reconciled social whole and encourages the allegorist to persist in fitting
the fragments together, the mystery requires veils, barring the way, imposing a forbidding auratic distance. The mystery refuses penetration; the
enigma, although extremely difficult to realize, gives one at least a small
straw of hope to grasp. For Benjamin, realizing the enigma—recognizing,
comprehending, accomplishing its hidden prophecy—is a question of
finding the key to "the procedure whereby meanings [*Bedeutungen*] are
conferred on the set of fragments [*Stückwerk*], on the pieces into which
not so much the whole as the process of its production has disinte-
grated."[68] And he finds in the analysis of manufacturing formulated in
Marx's *Capital* a certain "clue" (*Fingerzeig*) to understanding the allegorist's painstaking and always—inevitably—frustrated efforts. The passage he quotes reads as follows:

> The collective machine . . . becomes more and more perfect, the more the pro-
> cess as a whole becomes a continuous one—that is, the less the raw material
> is interrupted in its passage from its first phase to its last; in other words, the
> more its passage from one phase to another is effected not only by the hand of
> man but by the machinery itself. In manufacture, the isolation of each detail
> of the process is a condition imposed by the nature of division of labor, but in
> the fully developed factory the continuity of those processes is, on the con-
> trary, imperative.[69]

By a procedure reminiscent of Kant's "reflective judgment," the allegorist
and collector struggle to figure out, in the absence of any a priori principles, by what manipulations the pieces of the puzzle can be put together,
so that they can begin to tell a story, begin to complete the emblem that
would reveal the "history of salvation" (*heilsgeschichtlichen Prozesses*).[70]
With only the fragments of a historical truth in his hands, the allegorist,
alienated from the process of production and damaged in a mimesis of the
disintegrating experience of the laborer on the assembly line, fingers
the fragments in hopes of finding some way to make direct contact with
the meaning, the redemptive "Idea," that would not only confer at long
last a tangible integration on the process but also overcome the alienations
and diremptions that have broken the body and diminished the spirit. But
the possibility of immediate contact, of fulfilling the gesture of touch in
an adequate "presentation" (*Darstellung*), always seems to elude the allegorist and collector: he is convinced that the substance of "natural his-

tory," the ruins of which he holds in his hands, can be interpreted only allegorically, only indirectly—and only according to the method of dialectical materialism. Nevertheless, he cannot abandon the desperate hope for a revelation of meaning that would gather all the fragments together and put us in touch with their metaphysical Idea. It is a question of making sensuous—or, say, material—contact with a redemptive meaning. But in the end, all that can be touched is what reminds us of the *absence* of fulfilled experience—and the absence of justice. Benjamin's allegorist will painstakingly endeavor to reproduce within his tactile experience, intimately handling the commodified objects of contemporary life, the felt alienations produced by the "invisible hand" of capitalism.

Benjamin tells us little more than this regarding the concrete, material phenomenology of the allegorist's practice. But this practice is beautifully illuminated by Siegfried Kracauer, whose thought received important "directives" not only from Kafka and Benjamin but also from Kant. In his essay "Those Who Wait,"[71] a critical reflection on the intellectual (*geistige*) situation of his time, Kracauer proposes a typology of attitudes toward the present that, despite significant differences, nevertheless recalls the typology of "forms of prophecy" in Kant's "The Contest of Faculties."[72] Here Kant distinguishes three attitudes toward civilization: (1) the attitude of "moral terrorism," which perceives in civilization only an inevitable decline, only regressions to barbarism; (2) the attitude of eudaimonism, which perceives only the confirmations of a teleology of progress toward moral enlightenment, a realized moral humanity; and (3) the attitude he calls "abderitism," which sees nothing happening of any significance and insists that the moral progress of mankind is at a standstill—a standstill that couldn't be more hostile toward the "standstill" that Benjamin's critical dialectics tries to bring about. Deeply concerned, as is Kant, to think critically about how his contemporaries experience and understand the present in which they are living, Kracauer points to three distinct casts of mind among them—at least among those who, having gone through the disenchantments of modernity and lost their faith, are keenly conscious of their spiritual alienation from "the Absolute" and endure in common a certain "metaphysical suffering" in consequence of this abandonment to a time of nihilism.

The first type that Kracauer considers is the skeptic, "whose intellectual conscience rebels against embarking on any of the paths toward supposed redemption that present themselves at every turn, since these appear to him

as so many wrong tracks and illicit retreats into the sphere of arbitrary limitation." Accordingly, the skeptic courageously "decides out of inner truth-
fulness to turn his back on the absolute: his inability to believe becomes an
unwillingness to believe." In the skeptic's "unequaled heroism," Kracauer
sees an existence "closer to salvation in its self-imposed wretchedness than
is the pampered existence of those who are merely just." Torn between two
forms of suffering, realizing a consolatory significance only in the act of
renunciation, the skeptic struggles to maintain a measure of intellectual
integrity—but "without ever prophetically touching upon meaning" (*ohne
je prophetisch an den Sinn zu rühren*), as Kracauer phrases it.[73]

The second type is what Kracauer calls "short-circuit people" (*kurz-
schluß-Menschen*), whose attitude is that of "metaphysical cowardice."
Unable to endure the withdrawal of the gods, and equally unable to find
within themselves the strength to survive in a totally disenchanted world,
they "flee headlong from the dreariness and the world outside in order to
slip quickly into a sheltering abode." These people, "recognizing the need
for faith and consumed by an impatient yearning, break into a realm of
faith in which . . . they can maintain their ground only artificially and in
self-deception." Thus, even if they once could count on a relation to the
ground of religious experience, "they erect upon it without further ado
(that is, on a very shaky foundation) an entire edifice meant to protect
them against the tribulations they suffered in the empty space" that their
God once occupied without question. And this insecurity drives them
into a fanaticism that becomes ever more extreme the more they feel their
faith threatened by the secularism at work in modernity.

In his essay "Surrealism," Benjamin refers to the passionate reader, the
courageous thinker, the one who patiently waits for the seemingly impossible, and the inveterate flâneur of the boulevards as "types of illuminati"
(*Typen des Erleuchteten*).[74] Thinking perhaps of this essay, Kracauer calls
the third type in his own taxonomy *die Wartenden*, the ones who, like the
man from the country in Kafka's story "Before the Law," stand before a
gate that does not open for them, and nevertheless, with infinite patience,
silently wait for the right moment.[75] "By committing oneself to waiting,"
Kracauer says, "one neither blocks one's path toward faith (like those who
defiantly affirm the void) nor besieges this faith (like those whose yearning is so strong that it makes them lose all restraint)." These waiting ones
are stalled in an "intermediate realm" (*Zwischenbereich*), without any end
in sight:

One waits, and one's waiting is a hesitant openness [*ein zögerndes Geöffnetsein*], albeit of a sort that is difficult to explain. It can easily happen that someone who waits in this manner may find fulfillment in one way or another. Nevertheless, in this context one ought to think primarily of those people who have tarried and still do tarry in front of closed doors, and who thus, when they take it upon themselves to wait, are people who are waiting here and now.

(It is, I think, worth reflecting on the differences between this "hesitant openness" and Heidegger's notion of "anticipatory resoluteness," *vorlaufende Entschlossenheit*.) "Let's assume," Kracauer continues, that "they reject the lust and fervor of messianic enthusiasts just as much as they refuse to be integrated into esoteric circles, that they recognize certain weaknesses in the modern idea of community, and that finally, in their attempt to immerse themselves in the tradition of established religions, they encounter insurmountable difficulties." "In light of all this," he asks, "what is the meaning of their waiting?" The answer he suggests is that, in part, the meaning

> rests upon the fact that the irruption of the absolute [*Einbruch des Absoluten*] can occur only once an individual has committed himself with his entire being to this relationship [with the absolute]. Those who wait will thus be as hard as possible on themselves, so as not to be taken in by religious need. They would much rather lose the salvation of their soul than succumb to the rapture of the moment [*Rausch des Augenblicks*] and fling themselves into adventures of ecstasy and visions.

Rausch des Augenblicks is, I suspect, a phrase intended to suggest a certain mocking criticism of the importance for the inheritance of German culture that Heidegger attributes, in *Being and Time*, to the *Augenblick*, the "moment of vision."

Ever alert to the possibility of an illusory fulfillment, Kracauer's waiting ones expose themselves to a spiritual abyss—an "openness [*Geöffnetsein*] that must not in any way be confused with a relaxation of the forces of the soul directed toward ultimate things; rather, quite the contrary, it consists of tense activity and engaged self-preparation [*angespannte Aktivität und tätiges Sichbereiten*]."[76] In an *Augenblick*, an instant that Benjamin will also call a *Jetztzeit*,[77] the present (*Gegen-wart*) must become a moment of vigilance, a *Geistesgegenwart*, a watchful waiting (*warten*) turning for the sake of what is yet to come against (*gegen*) a present that is hostage to a reified past. We must learn how to wait.

For Benjamin, this exceedingly demanding moment must become, as well, the time of "a certain recognizability" *einer bestimmten Erkennbarkeit*, since what is to come, what is hoped for in the waiting, must, of course, be recognized as such.[78] Thus, while not allowing themselves any magical comfort in false hope, the ones who wait must be exceedingly careful not to exclude the hoped-for gift from another dimension of time. But nothing in the form of knowledge can explain or justify this attitude. Indeed, reflecting back on his sojourn in Moscow, Benjamin warns against appropriating a false empiricism for the cause of revolution, deploying terminology that will remind us, despite the most extreme differences,[79] of Heidegger's *Augenblick*, the extraordinary moment of *vorlaufende Entschlossenheit*, "anticipatory resoluteness": "Only he who has made his dialectical peace with the world in the moment of deciding can comprehend what is concrete. But to him who wishes to make that decision "on the basis of the facts," these "facts" will refuse to offer themselves [*werden diese Fakten ihre Hand nicht bieten*]."[80] Emphasizing this point in one of his notes for the *Arcades Project*, Benjamin comments that, in the lightning flash of the revolutionary *Augenblick*, we would principally experience "things in the moment of their being-no-longer."[81]

Concluding his essay with a statement that one could imagine coming from Heidegger, Kracauer remarks, "Getting oneself ready is only a preparation for that which cannot be obtained by force, a preparation for transformation [*Wandlung*] and for giving oneself over to it." He adds, "Exactly when this transformation will come to pass [*eintritt*] and whether or not it will happen at all is not at issue here, and at any rate it should not worry those who are exerting themselves [*die Sich-Mühenden*]."[82] Nothing could better describe the exquisite patience of the Benjaminian allegorist. But that allegorist seems fated to waver indecisively, inwardly conflicted, torn inconsolably between skepticism and hope, daring only with the greatest hesitation to hope, paradoxically waiting all the more patiently the more he feels compelled by the weight of skeptical arguments to abandon all hope. But even when he has nothing in his hands but some fragments unintelligible to others, the allegorist reads ciphers that stir him to continue hoping—or rather, waiting and almost hoping.

Of Baudelaire, Benjamin writes that the poet, like the historian committed to dialectical materialism, "holds in his hands the fragmented components of authentic historical experience."[83] Unlike the historian committed to historicism, who "lets the sequence of events run through his fingers like the beads of a rosary,"[84] the historian committed to dialectical materialism, who is inevitably therefore an allegorist, struggles to bring into memory a story from the unconscious depths of collective experience that, by virtue of its moral force, would interrupt the continuing violence of history and stop forever the repetition of past injustices.

Using an image that brings to mind the Jewish prayer shawl with its braided tassels of remembrance, Benjamin remarks, "We hold in our hands, usually weakly and loosely, only a few fringes of the tapestry of lived life that has been woven in us by forgetting."[85] Always restraining an impulse toward hope by invoking skeptical concerns, Benjamin again insists: "Only where the course of history glides smoothly as a thread through the historian's hands may he speak of progress. But if it is a frayed rope with a thousand loose ends that hang down like unraveled braids, none of them has its appointed place until all of them have been taken up and braided into a headdress."[86] For Benjamin, this is a task that the allegorical historian must passionately pursue, recognizing all the while, however, that its end cannot possibly be realized without gestures moved in finely tuned correspondence with a messianic intervention.

A practice of the hands also defines the other figure alluded to above, the "brooder." In his portrait of this figure Benjamin says, The brooder [*Der Grübler*], whose glance, in shock and horror [*aufgeschreckt*], falls upon the fragment [*Bruchstück*] in his hand, becomes an allegorist."[87] Carefully handling a jumble of worldly fragments, which is all that remains of the presumption of an originary redemptive meaning, the lost secret of reconciliation and wholeness, the brooder waits in melancholy patience for the shimmering of a redemptive light to assign the fragments a prophetic message. Painfully aware that, as Jacques Derrida says, "one never touches except in touching a limit *at the limit*,"[88] the brooder hopes against all reason—against all sense—to make sensuous contact with that meaning and be touched, at the limit, by the untouchable. But the brooder knows that all he can touch is the absence of that meaning. This is why his efforts are resigned in advance to failure—to a repetition, in mourning, of the allegorical substitution. In this way, the allegorical experience has a certain affinity, I believe, with the Derridean experience of *écriture*.

In another important note, Benjamin draws a distinction between the brooder and the thinker:

> The former not only meditates a thing but also meditates [*nachsinnt*] his meditation [*seinem Sinnen*] of the thing. The case of the brooder is that of the man

who has arrived at the solution of a great problem but then has forgotten it. And now he broods—not so much over the matter itself as over his past reflections on it. The brooder's thinking, therefore, bears the imprint of memory [*Erinnerung*]. Brooder and allegorist are cut from the same cloth.[89]

The brooder's memory, Benjamin says,

> ranges over the indiscriminate mass of dead lore. Human knowledge, within this memory, is something piecemeal—in an especially pregnant sense: it is like the jumble of arbitrarily cut pieces from which a puzzle is assembled. An epoch fundamentally averse to brooding has nonetheless preserved its outward gesture in the puzzle. It is the gesture, in particular, of the allegorist. Through the disorderly fund which his knowledge places at his disposal, the allegorist rummages here and there for a particular piece, holds it next to some other piece, and tests to see if they fit together—that meaning with this image or this image with that meaning. The result can never be known beforehand, for there is no natural mediation between the two.[90]

The hope for justice belongs to the memory of long-suppressed desire—an untimely memory that desires what has never been present: a political dream that, for the allegorical historian looking back in time and brooding over a past of massacred corpses and cities in ruins, the historical past seemed once upon a time to promise, holding it hostage, however, in an almost unapproachable reserve, never granting it more than a ghostly presence. In thinking about the theater of his friend Bertolt Brecht, Benjamin wrote these beautifully resonant words: "The true measure of life is memory. Like lightning, it runs through life, glancing backwards" (*Das wahre Maß des Lebens ist die Erinnerung. Sie durchläuft, rückschauend, das Leben blitzartig*).[91] This point calls for elaboration. The true measure of life is not simply memory, but also how we relate to memory: whether or not historical memory is recognized as the critical measure of life, whether or not we appropriate historical memory as a responsibility defining the task of a critical social theory, whether or not such memory can be released from the spell of endless repetition, whether or not the measure is freed from the grasp of a calculative rationality that denies the truth of the dialectical.

In his *Philosophy of Art*, Friedrich Schelling proposes a definition of rhythm that is pertinent here. Rhythm, he says, is "the transformation of an essentially meaningless succession into a meaningful one. Succession or sequence purely as such possesses the character of chance. The transformation of the accidental nature of a sequence into necessity = rhythm, whereby the whole is no longer subjected to time, but rather possesses time within itself."[92] Further, what Schelling calls "tact" "enters into rhythm . . . wherever something identical is to become different or varied, and is capable of numerous variations itself, whereby an even greater variety enters into the uniformity of the sequence."[93] "Chance," here, refers to the haphazard repetitions of a temporality still immersed in the realm of nature, subject to the whim of fate. "Necessity," by contrast, refers to a different repetition: the rhythm of an "originary" temporality, temporal succession transformed by the tact of a freedom grounded in the moral law and accordingly opened up to endless permutations of genuine originality. The different is the same in its originality. This is the rhythm of freedom—an experience that is heir to Kant's transcendental "causality of freedom."

In his *Gay Science*, Nietzsche remarked that "being the god of rhythm, [Apollo] can bind even the goddesses of destiny."[94] Once upon a time, rhythm bestowed a destinal "potency." Does it still? Could it be operating, for example, through the dialectic of truth in the theater of historiography? In a note for his *Arcades Project*, Benjamin observes: "Every truth clearly refers to its opposite. . . . Truth becomes a living being; it lies only in the rhythm in which sentence and opposition [*Satz und Gegensatz*] are displaced in order to think themselves."[95]

Benjamin's "measure" is thus also the truth in "rhythm," the rhythm of interruptions that create an opening for the possible in the conventional order of time: an appropriate sense of the untimely, of the actual and the potential, in gestures that must retrieve and bequeath fragments of the message of hope that are not yet entirely lost in the trash of our historical existence; and most of all, a keen sense of timing, patiently waiting for signs—Kant, in "The Contest of Faculties," speaks of prophetic prognostications—of the right moment for revolutionary action, the *Jetztzeit*, ὁ καιρός, of messianic judgment. At stake, as the historian Carlo Ginzburg puts it, is the fateful outcome of a long struggle between *res gestae* and *historia rerum gestarum*,[96] a struggle, in Benjamin's words, between gestures moved by "the violent [*gewalttätigen*] rhythm of impatience [*Ungeduld*], in which [what is recognized as] the right finds its justification in the measure [*Zeitmaß*] of the temporal continuum" and gestures moved instead by "the just rhythm of anticipation [*Erwartung*], in which the messianic event [*Geschehen*] comes to pass."[97] (This "just rhythm of anticipation" invites comparison with Heidegger's moment of "resolutely open anticipation.") Do we not, in the endless time of our waiting, endure the absence of what Wallace Stevens calls "a hand of light to turn the page"?[98] Perhaps we are waiting for something that would be enabled to appear only in the moment of its recognition. But perhaps that event is already occurring, just awaiting the time of our recognition before vanishing again into a past lost all too easily to the forces of petrification.

The Cabala says that, from the standpoint of an originary temporality, the Messiah has already passed into the future. Kafka remarks that the Messiah will be known to have come "only on the day after his arrival": "not on the last day, but on the day after."[99] To this Benjamin adds, imparting Kafka's ironic sense of humor, that the Messiah will make in the world only the "slightest adjustment" (*nur um ein Geringes*).[100] The messianic event is a hermeneutic interruption and suspension of the historical order of time; it belongs to a temporality the memory of which, withdrawn into an illegible trace, lies deeply buried in the very flesh of our gestures—in their dialectical sense of appropriate "rhythm" and "measure," and an appropriate exercise of justice. But, as Kafka's remark indicates, messianic temporality is also paradoxical: it involves an uncanny curvature of time.

The idea of a redeemed world, a divided world *made* whole, for which the collector, the brooder, the allegorist patiently wait in melancholy hope as they hold and handle things—the commodity fetishes of capitalism, the ruins and remnants of a vanishing culture—may, however, someday appear, all of a sudden, like a flash of lightning, in a dream image of extraordinary lucidity. But it may also come, I think, in the form of a song; for, in the words of the poet Joseph von Eichendorff,

> There is a song sleeping in all things
> that dream on and on,
> and the world begins to sing
> if you can only find the magic word.[101]

If, for Benjamin, whose political sympathies were different from the poet's, there be such a song sleeping in all things, hope depends not only on words but also on practices of the hands—on the possibility that the collector, the brooder, the allegorist might, in their handling of things, somehow awaken the dream long suppressed within them.

IX. Walter Benjamin, Scrivener, Reader of Runes and the Passages of Time

In *Phenomenology of Spirit,* §§309–17, where individuality and reflexive self-expression become an object for observing Reason,[102] Hegel gives systematic thought to "physiognomy." In a section called "Observation of the Relation of Self-Consciousness to Its Immediate Actuality," he declares that the hand "must represent the in-itself of individuality in respect to its fate." And he explains why this important role falls to the hand:

> Next to the organ of speech, it is the hand most of all by which a man manifests and actualizes himself. It is the living artificer of his fortune. We may say of the hand that it *is* what a man *does,* for in it, as the active organ of his self-fulfillment, he is present as the animating soul; and since he is primarily his own fate, his hand will thus express this in-itself.

The individual, he argues, is a duality, at once "for himself" in a "free activity," a "movement of consciousness," and also "an intrinsic being" with an "original determinate being" of his own, "the fixed being," as he puts it, "of an appearing actuality, an actuality which in the individual is immediately his own." As the inherited embodiment of an individuality, the human body reveals its duality, its being both subject and object. As a subject, the body is an inherited potential for the individual's self-expression. As an object, the body is the medium and product of the subject's actualization, "something through which the individual makes known what he really is, when he sets his original nature to work," and through which the individual learns to recognize himself, gradually appropriating as his own both the expressive activity, expressing what is "inner," and the product of that activity, the "outer" investment.

This prompts Hegel to ask how we are to understand "the 'expression' of the inner in the outer." (We should note the quotation marks around "expression": a singular gesture, occurring only here.) Answering the question, he says:

> This outer, in the first place, acts only as an *organ* in making the inner visible or, in general, a being-for-another; for the inner, insofar as it is in the organ, is the *activity* itself. The speaking mouth, the working hand, and, if you like, the legs too are the organs of performance and actualization which have within them the action *qua* action, or the inner as such. But the externality which

the inner obtains through them is the action as a reality separated from the individual.

However, even though the writing of the writer estranges her from herself, depositing her self-expression in a medium that disseminates her meaning-intentions beyond her control, it also returns her to herself, letting the inner meaning, unknown to her in its pure inwardness, show itself through its outer actualization. But the moment of self-consciousness is always a moment, for Hegel, of self-dispossession, because self-consciousness is possible only through the mediations of the social, the realm of objective spirit. "Speech and work are outer expressions in which the individual no longer keeps and possesses himself within himself, but lets the inner get completely outside of him, leaving it to the mercy of something other than himself." In fact, as Hegel observes,

> in speech and action, the inner turns itself into something else, thus putting itself at the mercy of the element of change, which twists the spoken word and the accomplished act into meaning something else than they are in and for themselves, as actions of this particular individual. Not only do the results of the actions, through this externality of the influences of others, lose their character of being something constant in the face of other individualities, but since, in their relationship to the inner which they contain, they behave as separated, indifferent externality, they can, *qua* inner, *through the individual himself,* be something other than they appear to be.

"The work," as Benjamin says in *One-Way Street,* "is the death mask of its conception."[103] Written works, whether of philosophy or of art, grant their authors' "inner life" an embodiment in the "externality" of a cultural world; but even though works enjoy an afterlife, surviving, like death masks, their authors, they also silently encrypt, with the names of their authors, an inevitable sentence of death. But, for Benjamin, a fate worse than death is now threatening the writer: the diremptions of modern technology are detaching the hand from the words on the page, denying the writer an intimate experience of the rhythms and tact of the hand. Alienated from the gestures of writing, writers must now surrender to the repetition required by the machine. They can no longer feel, as before, the meaning that takes shape in the hand's intervals of hesitation, caesurae measured by the pulse, innervations of anticipation. This technological revolution ultimately portends the writer's fateful alienation from a bodily felt experience of the possible.

Writing of the hand, the hand that writes, Hegel observes that it expresses the essential character of the individual in writing, revealing the inner truth of a singular "fate," giving it not merely appearance and externality but "a more durable existence than does the voice, especially in the particular style of handwriting." [104] But today, handwriting has mostly been abandoned. Benjamin, much like Heidegger, laments this technological development, convinced that it can only be catastrophic: eventually, he says, the typewriter will "alienate the hand of the man of letters from the pen," [105] and "new systems with more variable typefaces . . . will replace the pliancy of the hand with the innervation of commanding fingers." [106]

Why does this substitution matter? Despite his anxieties, Benjamin allows himself to entertain a fugitive moment of hopeful anticipation: "A period that, constructed metrically, afterward has its rhythm upset at a single point yields the finest prose sentence imaginable. In this way a ray of light falls through a chink in the wall of the alchemist's cell, to light up gleaming crystals, spheres, and triangles." [107] But Benjamin's anticipatory turn of mind does not permit itself any counterfeit prophecies:

He who asks fortunetellers the future unwittingly forfeits an inner intimation of coming events that is a thousand times more exact than anything they may say. He is impelled by inertia, rather than curiosity, and nothing is more unlike the submissive apathy with which he hears his fate revealed [*Enthüllung seines Schicksals*] than the alert dexterity [*gefährliche, hurtige Handgriff*] with which the man of courage lays hands on the future. For presence of mind [*Geistesgegenwart*] is an extract of the future, and precise awareness of the present moment [*was in der Sekunde sich vollzieht*] is more decisive than foreknowledge of the most distant events. Omens, presentiments, signals pass day and night through our organism like wave impulses. To interpret them or use them, that is the question. The two are irreconcilable. Cowardice and apathy counsel the former, lucidity [*Nüchternheit*] and freedom the latter. For before such prophecy or warning has been mediated by word or image, it has lost its vitality, the power to strike at our center and force us, we scarcely know how, to act accordingly. If we neglect to do so, and only then, the message is deciphered. We read it. But it is now too late. . . . Like ultraviolet rays memory shows to each man in the book of life a script that invisibly and prophetically glosses the text. But it is not with impunity that these intentions are exchanged, that unlived life is handed over to cards, spirits, stars.[108]

Or handed over, one might add, to processes of mechanical reproduction. The text continues: "We do not go unpunished for cheating the body of its power [*Macht*] to meet [*messen*: measure] the fates [*Geschicken*] on its own ground and triumph. . . . To turn the threatening future into a fulfilled now [*erfüllte Jetzt*], the only desirable telepathic miracle, is a work of bodily presence of mind [*Werk leibhafter Geistesgegenwart*]." In the writer's authentically anticipatory practice, "what would have become a portent of disaster he binds bodily to the moment [*bindet er leibhaft an die Sekunde*], making himself the factotum of his body." [109] As a gesture await- ing messianic revelation, writing must bind itself to the moment in the most intense spiritual alertness—an alertness that is also a watchful wait- ing. Writing, for Benjamin, is thus pressured by what Natalia Ginzburg calls a "creative nostalgia": "a nostalgia for the past that we hope will give rise [*riallacciare*] to a future." [110]

But for writing to make an opening for the "truth-content" of revela- tion—that is, for writing to be truly an infinitely patient gesture of wait- ing, it must be emptied, without expression, without intention. In an of- ten quoted passage from his "Epistemo-Critical Prologue" to *The Origin of German Tragic Drama*, Benjamin declares:

> Truth does not enter into relationships, particularly intentional ones. The ob- ject of knowledge, determined as it is by the intention inherent in the concept, is not the truth. Truth is an intentionless state of being, made up of ideas. The proper approach to it [*Das ihr gemäße Verhalten*] is not therefore one of in- tention and knowledge, but rather a total immersion and absorption [*Einge- hen und Verschwinden*] in it. Truth is the death of intention [*Wahrheit ist der Tod der Intention*].[111]

Revelation is possible only when the willfulness of intentionality has been overcome; for intentionality imposes a certain closure, refusing uncondi- tional exposure. In "On Semblance" ("Über Schein"), Benjamin explains:

> In the expressionless [*das Ausdruckslose*], the sublime force of truth comes to appearance in the same way that truth determines the symbolism of being ac- cording to the laws of the moral world. . . . The expressionless, you see, shat- ters what in all beautiful appearances continues to survive as the heritage of chaos: a false, lying, errant totalization, in short, the absolute totality.[112]

If the historical subject arrests its intentionality and refrains from impos- ing a false expressiveness on things, things might then express the material conditions of modern life. How could the hand learn to communicate and display this drama?

In another essay, a critical review of *Mankind in Handwriting* (*Der Mensch in der Handschrift*), Benjamin remarks:

> Everything ethical is without physiognomy, something expressionless that either invisibly or blindingly leaps out of a concrete situation. It may be prepared for, but never prophesied. . . . Language has a body and the body has a language. Nevertheless—the world is grounded in what, with regard to the body, is not language (the ethical) and with regard to language is not the body (the expressionless).[113]

This review not only critiques graphology, a practice that purports to "deduce" the ethics of the writer from the individual's handwriting, but also attacks causal determinism: a metaphysics of immediacy and constant presence that forecloses the possibility of a victory for justice, reduces the ethical to facticity, and explains away the body's mimetic impulses, its anarchic drives, and its ancient, prelinguistic dreams of freedom as conventions of expression and language. As we know from Kafka's story "In the Penal Colony," programs designed to bring the moral law into immediate tangibility and immediate visibility glisten with political terror. Kafka's writing machine, which inscribes the moral law and the punishment ordained for transgressors into the criminal's flesh, is a machine of death, not enlightenment, because it violates the transcendental withdrawal of the moral law—its partial withdrawal from the tangible and the visible. When Benjamin insists that the world is grounded in an ethics that, with regard to the body, is not language, not expression, not, therefore, intentionality, he is registering his conviction that the ethical requires an overcoming of metaphysical subjectivity, whose will to power precludes an open, responsive receptivity to the solicitations and claims of the radically other.

In "Chinese Curios," one of Benjamin's notes for *One-Way Street*, this question of closure and openness in relation to the radically Other takes an enigmatic turn. Introducing his point, he observes, "The power of a country road is different when one is walking along it from when one is flying over it by airplane. In the same way, the power of a text is different when it is read from when it is copied out." The analogy continues: "Only he who walks the road on foot learns of the power it commands, and of how, from the very scenery that, for the flier, is only an unfurled plain, it calls forth distances, belvederes, clearings [*Lichtungen*], prospects at each of its turns." Arguing for the ethical significance of the expressionless, intentionless art of copying, Benjamin then says:

> Only the copied text thus commands the soul of him who is occupied with it, whereas the mere reader never discovers the new aspects of his inner self that are opened by the text, that road cut through the interior jungle forever closing behind it: because the reader follows the movement of his mind in the free flight of daydreaming, whereas the copier submits it to command. The Chinese practice of copying books was thus an incomparable guarantee of literary culture, and the transcription a key to China's enigmas.[114]

Might this detour through a far-away culture be Benjamin's way of returning to our remembrance the difficult words of Deuteronomy 11:18: "You shall place these commandments of mine in your heart and in your soul, and you shall bind them for a sign on your hand"?

Copywork by the hand is a binding of the hand. A binding to what? And for what? If we think about copywork in the monasteries of mediaeval Europe, we might say this: the most spiritual form of reading and writing was the process of copying. Copying demanded a gesture of intense, self-restrained devotion, reproducing a manuscript of unquestionable authority by a writing that originated in a timeless, allegorical gesture capable of gathering and disseminating the blessings of light. The act itself, the copying, requiring the most intense concentration, steadiness of hand, patience, and humility, brought spiritual fulfillment not so much through the calligraphy as through the compassion of the gesture: copying reached out to other mortals, people in need of care, and handed down to them, beautifully and graciously, the tangible trace of the temporal interruption, that almost imperceptible interval between original and copy, intimating that redemption by which they so desperately needed to be touched.

In concluding his extremely important 1933 essay "On the Mimetic Faculty," Benjamin suggests a connection between "nonsensuous similarity" and the writing of the hand:

> Graphology has taught us to recognize in handwriting images that the unconscious of the writer conceals in it. It may be supposed that the mimetic process that expresses itself in this way in the activity of the writer was, in the very distant times in which script originated, of utmost importance for writing. Script has thus become, like language, an archive of nonsensuous similarities, of nonsensuous correspondences.[115]

A script, a graphology, that in a sudden burst of illumination may even grant us, as he says in the final paragraph, the unforeseeable and unnerving opportunity to read, in a sudden flash of revelation, "what was never written": the messianic promise.

In the "intentionless" copywork of the hand—an intimate process of transcription, pure, unconditional receptivity to what can reveal itself only if it remains unbidden, free of compulsion—a nonsensuous correspondence takes place, in which residues of the divine language of paradise might come to light at any time, appearing in a flash that instantly vanishes, leaving only the faintest of traces—degraded remnants of the sublime Idea—in the ink of mourning that haunts the white page.[116] In considering how "Stone Age" people were able to sketch animals with such skill, Benjamin suggests that "the hand which led the stylus *remembered* the bow with which it killed the animal."[117] A prelapsarian memory persists in the hand, awaiting its time of awakening. Perhaps it will be awakened in the act of a handwriting that copies ancient handwriting gestures. For, as Benjamin says in another context, "man corresponds to every form, to every outline, which he perceives, in the process of creating it. The dancing body, the sketching hand recreates [*bildet nach*] and takes possession of him."[118]

Benjamin dreamed of "writing" a book that would consist of nothing but quotations. The collection of writings bearing the title *Arcades Project* (*Passagenwerk*), recognizing this dream, set down a provocative forcefield of quotations. In his essay on Karl Kraus, Benjamin analyzes Kraus's "mimetic genius," which he characterizes as "imitating while it glosses, pulling faces in the midst of polemics, . . . festively unleashed in the reading of dramas whose authors do not for nothing occupy a peculiarly intermediate position [between writing and reading or enacting what is written]."[119] Benjamin admires Kraus's sense of drama, his mortifying parodies and impersonations, his "flashes of improvisation":

> In them his own voice tries out the abundance of *personae* inhabiting the performer—*persona*: that through which sound passes—and about his fingertips dart the gestures [*Gebärden*] of the figures populating his voice. But in his polemics, too, mimesis plays a decisive role. He imitates his subjects in order to insert the crowbar of his hate into the finest joints of their posture [*den feinsten Fugen seiner Haltung*]. This quibbler [*Silbenstecher*], probing [*sticht*] between syllables, digs out the grubs of humbug. The grubs of venality and garrulity, ignominy and bonhomie, childishness and covetousness, gluttony and dishonesty. Indeed, the exposure to inauthenticity—more dif-

ficult than that of wickedness—is here performed behavioristically [*beha-vioristisch*].[120]

Kraus's critique of society and culture *is* a "physiognomic" art, a critical practice that mockingly mimics the gestures of a bourgeoisie it holds in contempt. The text continues, outlining what could be called Benjamin's theory of citation: "The quotations in *Die Fackel* are more than documentary proof: they are masks stripped off mimetically by the quoter. Admittedly, what emerges in just this connection is how closely the cruelty of the satirist is linked to the ambiguous modesty of the interpreter."[121] Concurring with Brecht on Kraus, Benjamin turns to quotation, letting him say it: "'When the age laid hands upon itself, he was the hands,' Brecht said." But Benjamin notes:

> The fact that the developing man actually takes form not within the natural sphere but in that of mankind, in the struggle for liberation, and that he is recognized by the posture [*Haltung*] that the fight with exploitation and poverty stamp on him, that there is no idealistic but only a materialistic deliverance from myth, and that at the origin of creation stands not purity but purification—all this did not leave its trace [*Spuren*] on Kraus's materialist humanism [*realen Humanismus*] until very late.[122]

Paying tribute to Kraus's courage, the heroic courage of tragedy, Benjamin comments: "Only in despair did he discover in quotation the power not to preserve [*bewahren*] but to purify, to tear from context, to destroy [*zerstören*]; the only power in which hope still resides that something might survive this age [*Zeitraum*]—because it was wrenched away from it."[123] According to Benjamin,

> In the quotation [*Zitat*] that both saves and chastises [*rettenden und strafenden*], language proves the matrix of justice [*Gerechtigkeit*]. It summons the word by its name, wrenches it destructively from its context, but precisely thereby calls it back to its origin. . . . It is in the language of quotation that the two realms—origin and destruction [*Ursprung und Zerstörung*]—come together for the sake of justice. And conversely, only where they interpenetrate—in quotation—is language consummated.[124]

Quoting and copying are a repetition of the same—but with a "slight adjustment," an almost unnoticeable difference. As would happen, perhaps, in the coming of the Messiah.

As Benjamin suggests in "The Task of the Translator," even if all human beings forgot the prophetic event—and, with that, the preoriginary moral-prophetic endowment inscribed in the body—so that its redemptive promise could not now be fulfilled, nevertheless, as long as any rituals that practiced "the remembrance of God" continued, rituals such as the copying by hand of sacred scriptures, there would still be a measure of fulfillment.[125] For, in this "remembrance of God," hands would begin to complete the incomplete, namely, the "promise of happiness," and make incomplete the complete, namely, the injustices, too long forgotten, suffered by all those who received no justice.[126]

Some of these thoughts—though not their radical implications—are anticipated by Emerson's essay "Quotation and Originality," where he remarks on the fact that quotation can bring to light "a new and fervent sense," not noticed before. Moreover, he argues:

Our debt to tradition through reading and conversation is so massive, our protest or private addition to tradition so rare and insignificant,—and this commonly on the ground of other reading and hearing,—that, in a large sense, one would say that *there is no pure originality.* All minds quote. Old and new make the warp and woof of every moment. There is no thread that is not a twist of these two strands. By necessity, by proclivity and delight, we all quote. We quote not only books and proverbs, but arts, sciences, religions, customs, and laws; nay, we quote temples and houses, tables and chairs by imitation. . . . The originals are not original. There is imitation, model and suggestion, to the very archangels, if we knew their history.[127]

Our quotation of Emerson in the context of a reflection on Benjamin is itself an example of how quotation can alter the sense of the text quoted—and also a demonstration that there is no pure originality—no perfectly coinciding return to the origin.

Benjamin's principle, the dialectical principle guiding his work with quotations and binding his gestures, is beautifully conveyed in his "Theses on the Philosophy of History": "In every era, the attempt must be made anew to wrest tradition away from a conformism that is about to overpower it."[128] It is also articulated in Konvolut N 7, 7, a note for his *Arcades Project*, where he states a seeming paradox: "In order for a part of the past to be touched [*betroffen*] by actuality, there must be no continuity between them."[129] By "actuality," Benjamin means not a "factical" present totally enclosed within the continuum of history and consequently determined by its temporal position, but rather a present that the dialectical historian has severed from its bondage to that continuum. This "other" present is accordingly full of explosive potentialities ready to be ignited by sparks from a past that the historian attempts to recall in a freedom that, like Kant's "causality of freedom," has broken out of a historicity bound to the causal order of nature and to the fate it imposes. Because the "past carries with it a temporal index by which it is referred to redemption,"[130] the art of quotation, although undoubtedly only what Benjamin, echoing a phrase from Kant's *Critique of Judgment*, calls a "weak Messianic power,"[131] is a dialectical practice committed to opening an interval in the continuum of time for the possible flashing up of the "image of redemption." Describing the task of the chronicler, Benjamin says:

> A chronicler who recites events without distinguishing between major and minor ones acts in accordance with the following truth: nothing that has ever happened should be regarded as lost for history. To be sure, only a redeemed mankind receives the fullness of its past—which is to say, only for a redeemed mankind has its past become citable in all its moments. Each moment it has lived becomes a *citation à l'ordre du jour* and that day is the Day of Judgment.[132]

In Benjamin's hands, quoting and copying not only model gestures moved by their remembrance [*Eingedenken*] of the idea of redemption, by their "involuntary memory of redeemed humanity"; they also communicate their steadfast faith in "a revolutionary chance" (*revolutionären Chance*) for the fight over the "oppressed past" (*unterdrückte Vergangenheit*).[133]

Quotation and copying are gestures that compel us, of course, to think about origins and originality. In "What Is Epic Theater?," an essay influenced by Brecht's productions for theater, Benjamin observes:

> To quote a text involves the interruption of its context. It is therefore understandable that the epic theater, being based on interruption, is, in a specific sense, a quotable one. There is nothing special about the quotability of its texts. It is different with the gestures which fit into the course of the play. "Making gestures quotable" [*"Gesten zitierbar zu machen"*] is one of the substantial achievements of the epic theater. An actor must be able to space his gestures the way a typesetter produces spaced type. . . . Epic theater is by definition a gestic theater. For the more frequently we interrupt someone in the act of acting, the more gestures result.[134]

Benjamin makes this gestural dialectics of interruption—in effect, a dialectics of destruction—his most powerful strategy for reading and writing history. To set in motion the fourteenth thesis in his "Theses on the Philosophy of History," Benjamin begins with a quotation from Kraus that illuminates his practices of quotation and reproduction: "Origin is the goal." With these four little words, the two men unsettle the fetishistic constructions of time and history in the modern discourse of historiography, shaking their metaphysical grounding.

If authentic history, for Benjamin, "is the subject of a structure whose site is not homogeneous, empty time, but time filled by [the dialectical potentialities of] the now-time [*Jetztzeit*]," if justice cries out for a revolutionary "originality" that has remained unrecognizable within the linear history of bourgeois modernity, then the act of quoting or copying must bring that other temporality to light, denying the origin posited by historicism any refuge in a past that is closed and beyond reach. For Benjamin, the past has no fixed identity: what it "was" is always open to new interpretations that maintain its incompleteness and potential originality. In taking over Kraus's interpretation of "origin," Benjamin not only displaces the "origin" but marks it as an interruption in linear time, so that history can no longer be conceived as an unbroken chain of causally determined events stretching from the origin to the end of time.

Quoting and copying are practices that accordingly attempt to destroy the determinism and fatalism of the origin that has passed in order to rescue its true originality from oblivion. As Giorgio Agamben puts it in an essay entitled "Benjamin and the Demonic": "What is essential for this theory [of the origin] is the intention by which the exposition of the Ideas [i.e., Benjamin's "theory of Ideas"] and the salvation of the phenomena are simultaneous and merge in a single gesture."[135] Like the allegorical gestures of the collector, quoting and copying are practices of freedom, gestures that open up a temporal play-space, not only for the eruption of long-suppressed utopian desires and dream images to question prevailing social reality, but also for the redemptive touch to enter—and forever readjust—our cold, unfeeling world.

Thus, as Benjamin explains in his "Critical Epistemological Preface" to *The Origin of German Tragic Drama*, emphasizing the dialectical experience of originary rhythm:

> Origin [*Ursprung*], although an entirely historical category, has, nevertheless, nothing to do with genesis [*Entstehung*]. The term "origin" is intended to describe not the process by which the existent came into being but rather what emerges [*Entspringendes*] from the process of becoming and disappearance

[*Werden und Vergehen*]. Origin is an eddy in the stream of becoming, and in its rhythm [*Rhythmik*] it swallows the material involved in the process of genesis. What is original is never revealed in the naked and manifest existence of the factual; its rhythm [*Rhythmik*] is recognizable only to a dual insight. It needs to be recognized on the one hand as a process of restoration and reestablishment [*als Restauration, als Wiederherstellung*], but on the other hand, and precisely because of this, as something imperfect and incomplete. There takes place in every original phenomenon [*Ursprungsphänomen*] a determination of the form in which an idea [*Idee*] will constantly confront the historical world, until it is revealed fully, in the totality of its history. Origin is not, therefore, discovered by the examination of actual findings, but it is related to their history and their subsequent development. The principles of philosophical contemplation are recorded in the dialectic that is inherent [*beiwohnt*] in the origin. This dialectic shows singularity [*Einmaligkeit*] and repetition [*Wiederholung*] to be conditioned by one another in all essentials.[136]

In his discussion of this passage, Agamben comments that there are two possible attitudes toward historical consciousness One interprets "all human work (and the past) as an origin destined to an infinite process of transmission that preserves [unchanged] its intangible and mythic singularity"; the other "irresponsibly liquidates and flattens out the singularity of the origin by forever multiplying copies and singularities." But, he argues, neither of these attitudes makes it possible to fulfill or master the origin; rather, they make it possible only to repeat or nullify the origin in a confusion of simulacra: "The Idea of origin contains both singularity and reproducibility, and as long as [either] one of the two remains in force, every intention to overcome both is doomed to fail."[137]

Benjamin's theory of origin is committed to the assumption, born of hope, that the still-concealed truth-content of history is the endless granting of the Ideas of freedom and justice. The origin must accordingly be rendered contingent, for inasmuch as its occurrence is the introduction— or the imparting—of nonactualized potentiality, a certain contingency (Latin present participle: *contingens*) must be inherent in its very logic.[138] Moreover, as the Latin origin of the word reminds us, the contingency that the origin introduces—the contingency that Benjamin's writing hand would struggle to make tangibly intelligible—is what touches on all sides. And if, as Aristotle observes in his *Metaphysics* (1046a, 32), every potentiality is not only a potentiality to be or to do something but also a potentiality not to be or not to do something, then in a paradoxical sense the writer should experience the greatest potential, as writer, in a temporality suddenly opened up when she makes it clear that she prefers not to write. Considered in this light, quoting and copying may be understood as oblique ways of *not* writing: ways for the writer's mimetic gesture, *ausdrucklos*, emptied of expression, to read and decipher the promise of the origin—ways to "read what was never written." [139]

Two textual fragments by Benjamin are pertinent here. One says: "Perception [*Wahrnehmung*] is reading." The second says: "The reader is the true historian." [140] Forsaking what has traditionally been understood as "originality" in order to make way for the transmissibility of an origin still to come, Benjamin shows that he is willing to bind his gestures to the practices of quoting and copying, reproducing by hand what has already been written, so that, in a moment of dialectical confrontation, a moment in which the past and the present meet, what has *not yet* been written— the promise of an origin inaugurating a past that has never been present— may at long last be delivered to a reading. Benjamin's practices accordingly introduce radically original concepts of "origin" and "originality": concepts that radically deconstruct the traditional concepts employed by modern bourgeois historiography to ensure that the originality of the origin remains buried in the past and that the future will remain hostage to the fatalism petrified in the fixed and immutable identity of that past. Thus Benjamin's practices of quoting and copying sacrifice some of their freedom and submit to a rigorous necessity—the responsibilities required for reproduction—for the sake of *a more radical* freedom to come. But moreover, in submitting to a certain necessity, these practices also attempt to put us in touch with the *contingency* of the historical: to rescue for possible future redemption a past that was not, the contingency of a potentiality that, as such, both can be and can not be.

Quoting and copying are gestures of remembrance, attempting to restore possibility to the past, rendering what has happened once again incomplete and completing at long last what has never been. It should not be forgotten that, according to the texts of the cabala, God created the world by an act of writing and revealed His promise of redemption in an enigmatic jumble of letters, leaving to our hands the ethical task of gathering them slowly into the original words that would interpret the meaning of redemption. Relinquishing the *traditional* concept of "originality," a mortified, medusan "originality," Benjamin's mimetic gestures attempt to make contact with *another* originality—the originality of an originary temporality that modern historicism has continued to suppress. The "rhythm" of his gestures is an effort, not entirely hopeless, to make contact with the rhythm of that originary temporality.

Because of a long history of suppression, which has deferred the communication of the utopian and emancipatory meaning in the origin, we can receive genuinely originary meaning only by repeating it: by making nearly vain yet not entirely hopeless efforts to retrieve by repetition the redemptive promise buried in a past that has never been present—and never *will* be present until the temporal order within which it is buried has been destroyed. Copying and quoting works of originary power are Benjamin's ways of waiting: like dread, they have no determinate object, waiting with infinitely destructive patience for a concealed meaning to emerge and hand down the destructive and creative energies constitutive of its originality.

When Benjamin turns to quoting and copying by hand, the truth-content of the origin is imparted not only in words but also in the language of gesture—in the gestural repetition that retraces the *original* gesture of writing, following its traces left in ink, touching on the meaning only at a certain distance.[141] This meaning, never immediately given, never fully present, never complete, never quite reachable, never quite touchable, is therefore irremediably allegorical; and the gestures that attempt to retrieve it are likewise compelled to recognize their allegorical dictation. Something quite similar may be said about how the brooder and the collector handle the fragments of meaning held in the things they gather: here, too, the gestures can only be allegorical, never making contact within the realm of the sensuous with the messianic message that they suppose, in almost vain hope, those things could somehow sensuously, tangibly impart.[142]

Thus, quoting and copying, like the melancholy gestures of the allegorist, undertake an approach to the original meaning of redemption that, in the end, is fated to reveal its impossibility: the only truth they can bring to light is the truth that the origin is inaccessible, beyond the hand's touch. And yet, these gestures are not entirely vain, for they maintain a relationship of proximity to that origin, and enable the hands to be touched and moved, nevertheless, by this sublime truth: That proximity to the origin, a tactful compliance with its distance, is the sense of the "originality" of these gestures: a sense that not only does not contradict their practice of repetition but in fact requires this relation.[143]

At stake, for Benjamin, are gestures of repetition that, while estranged in time from the posited origin, can nevertheless keep in motion the forces at work behind their originality, touched by a powerful sense of the origin. This they can do by virtue of their remembrance, continuing to carry the message of hope for redemptive justice, and by virtue of their keenly felt sense of contingency, a sense of the unexpected that they maintain through their dialectical juxtaposition of textual fragments and images.

As a practice binding his gestures to this difficult realization of originality, Benjamin's writing attempts not only to bring the redemption of meaning into the realm of the tangible, but also somehow to trace the meaning of redemption itself within the contingencies of this realm. The only realm within which it might be possible to touch, or at least approximate, the untouchable truth—to touch, or at least approximate, its absolute untouchability—is the realm of the tangible. Renouncing the tangible for the sake of the purely intelligible avails nothing; one must embrace what in a certain reticence the tangible offers. Benjamin's copywork is a gesture that, in an exemplary way, problematizes not only the distinction between manual and intellectual labor but also the distinction between the sensuous and the cognitive, or, say, the material and the ideal.

But the attempt to touch or approximate the untouchable truth, the originality, of the origin ends, as it must, in failure.[144] Yet, paradoxically, this very failure is the measure that vouchsafes an authentic relation to the origin—the originality that comes only to the one who waits.

Against all reason—even against truth. In a letter to Gershom Scholem (June 12, 1938), Benjamin writes that "wisdom," which is "the haggadic consistency of truth . . . , has been lost." Thus, "Kafka's real genius was that he tried something entirely new: he sacrificed [the positivity of] truth for the sake of clinging to transmissibility, to its haggadic element."[145] In an essay entitled "The Melancholy Angel," Agamben reflects on a number of critical questions surrounding the transmission and reproduction of culture—questions at the center of which is the concept of originality. He notes that, in a "traditional system, culture exists only in the act of its transmission, that is, in the living act of its tradition. There is no discontinuity between past and present, between old and new, because every object transmits at every moment, without residue, the system of beliefs and notions that has found expression in it."[146] Thus, Agamben says, one cannot speak of a culture independently of its transmission. The connection is even tighter in a "mythical-traditional system." Here, "an absolute identity exists between the act of transmission and the thing transmitted, in the sense that there is no other ethical, religious, or aesthetic value outside the act itself of transmission." But in modernity, the situation could not be more different:

> An inadequation, a gap between the act of transmission and the thing to be transmitted, and a valuing of the latter independently of the former appear only when tradition loses its vital force, and constitute the foundation of a characteristic phenomenon of non-traditional societies: the accumulation of culture. For, contrary to what one might think at first sight, the breaking of tradition does not at all mean the [immediate] loss or devaluation of the past: it is, rather, likely that only now the [originary meaning of the] past can reveal itself with a weight and an influence it never had before. Loss of tradition means that the past has lost its transmissibility; and so long as no new way has been found to enter into a relation with it, it can only be the object of accumulation [i.e., an object for the collector] from now on.

"In this situation," Agamben observes, keeping in mind Benjamin's commentary, in his "Theses," on Paul Klee's painting *Angelus Novus,*

> man keeps his cultural heritage in its totality, and in fact the value of this heritage multiplies vertiginously. However, he loses the possibility of drawing from this heritage the criterion of his actions and his welfare, and thus the only concrete place in which he is able, by asking about his origins and his destiny, to found the present as a relationship [of originality and inception] between past and future. For it is the transmissibility of culture that, by endowing culture with an immediately perceptible meaning and value, allows man to move freely toward the future without being hindered by the burden of the past.[147]

Things are very different today:

> But when a culture loses its means of transmission, man is deprived of reference points [i.e., a critical measure] and finds himself wedged between, on the one hand, a past that incessantly accumulates behind him and oppresses him with the multiplicity of its now-indecipherable contents, and on the other hand, a future that he does not yet possess and that does not throw any light on his struggle with the past.

Agamben wants to argue, then, as follows:

> The interruption of tradition, which is for us now a *fait accompli*, opens an era in which no link is possible between old and new, if not the infinite accumulation of the old in a sort of monstrous archive or the alienation effected by the very means that is supposed to help with the transmission of the old. . . . Sus-

pended in the void between old and new, past and future, man is projected into time as into something alien that incessantly eludes him and still drags him forward, but without allowing him to find his ground in it.

According to Agamben, "We are now able to state more precisely what constitutes the alienation value that we have seen to be at the basis both of the quotation and of the activity of the collector, the alienation value whose production has become the specific task of the modern artist: it is nothing other than the destruction of the transmissibility of culture."[148] Benjamin's strategic position on the transmissibility of Western "culture" was accordingly complicated by a "double bind." For in fact he wanted nothing more than the total *destruction* of the oppressive elements and functions of this "culture"—a destruction, however, for the sake of something that that same "culture" has always preserved and handed down, despite its repression, despite its efforts to forget, despite its support of the ruling class, despite its complicity with the enemies of justice for all: a destruction, namely, for the sake of the transmissibility of the meaning of history's redemptive promise, ciphers of a hope for the coming of justice, a relation to a past that has never been present, buried under the idols of culture, withdrawn from our grasp. In *Eros and Civilization*, Herbert Marcuse articulates with admirable lucidity this divided "moral alertness" that I am reading in Benjamin's gestures as an allegorical writer. Marcuse states, "The destructiveness of the present stage [of Western civilization] reveals its full significance only if the present is measured, not in terms of past stages, but in terms of its own potentialities."[149] The dialectically critical words in this passage rightly call our attention to the question of "measure" and the question of "potentialities." The destructiveness inherent in Western culture—what Nietzsche called "passive nihilism," since it is a nihilism passively suffered—must be met by correspondingly destructive gestures—by the gestures of a Nietzschean "active nihilism." For this is, as Marcuse observes, the only way that the "discrepancy between potential liberation and actual repression" will ever become manifest.[150]

It is in precisely this historical context that Benjamin's violent gestures as a writer must be interpreted—most of all, perhaps, his gestures in the practices of quotation and copywork. For these gestures, like those in Benjamin's portrait of Charles Baudelaire, struggle and fail to transmit the originary meaning of redemption in an original way, yet paradoxically achieve originality—a relation to the originary moment. They achieve it by making themselves into a medium that imparts as its truth the cultural destruction of its transmissibility. This in turn begins to destroy the power of the present as absolute fate—as a repetition of the past that excludes any transmission of the posited "originary" moment. Agamben characterizes the Benjaminian project this way: "Since the goal is already present and thus no path exists that could lead there, only the perennially late stubbornness of a messenger whose message is nothing other than the task of transmission can give back to man, who has lost his ability to appropriate his historical space, the concrete space of action and knowledge." [151] If, in the act of transmission, what Benjamin hands down as "truth" is the "deferral" or "withdrawal" of truth, that is because he understands what it means to live with a "vital moral alertness and vigilance" (*leibhafte, moralische Geistesgegenwart*) in the temporality of potential events haunting the present.

Thus, recollecting the dream of a just society entrusted to awakened desire, Benjamin attempts to hand down, as the rhythm and measure of his gestures, the deepest sense of tact—a proximity that renounces presence, renounces touching, in order to be touched by a revelation (*Offenbarung*, not *Enthüllung*) that exceeds every grasp.

X. Handling the Fragment: Problems in Presentation and Judgment

> The activity of dissolution is the power and work of the Understanding, the most astonishing and mightiest of powers, or rather, the absolute power. . . . Death, if that is what we want to call nonactuality, is of all things the most dreadful, and to hold fast to what is dead requires the greatest strength. . . . But the life of Spirit is not the life that shrinks from death and keeps itself untouched by devastation, but rather the life that endures it and maintains itself in it. It wins its truth only when, in utter dismemberment, it finds itself. . . . Spirit is this power only by looking the negative in the face and tarrying with it.
>
> —G. W. F. Hegel, *Phenomenology of Spirit* [152]

> I walk among men as among the fragments and limbs of men. This is what is terrible for my eyes, that I find man in ruins and scattered as over a battlefield or butcherfield. And when my eyes flee from the now to the past, they always find the same: fragments and limbs and dreadful accidents—but no human beings. . . . I [also] walk among men as among fragments of the future—that future which I envision. And this is [the point of] all my creating and striving, that I create

and carry together into One what is fragment and riddle and dreadful accident.

—Friedrich Nietzsche, *Thus Spoke Zarathustra*[153]

In a painful struggle to free himself from the alienations and diremptions of his time, Baudelaire "holds in his hands the scattered fragments of authentic historical experience."[154] In Rilke's *Sonnets to Orpheus*, the poet, made aware by his own terrible isolation and estrangement that the material conditions of life are tearing us apart, speaks intimately to his reader with words of measured hope:

> *We*, with words and finger-pointings [*Fingerzeigen*],
> Gradually make the world our own,
> Perhaps its weakest, most precarious part.

But what this effort requires is that we struggle with a sense of potentiality, a sense of the redeeming whole, which, like a "magic spell" (*Zauberspruch*), seems forever beyond our reach:

> See, now we [two] together must bear
> Piece-work and parts as though [*als sei*] it were the whole.[155]

Everything depends, here, on the fictional *als sei es*, breaking through the false whole of fetishized fragments affirmed by the petrifying repetition of the present.

Now, to understand Benjamin's peculiar obsession with the fragment—all the neglected materializations of European civilization, all the "trash" of history that Benjamin will submit to a dialectically historical critique in the service of a prophetically originated revolution—we must consider it in its historical relation to the Kantian and romantic approaches to the question of the sensible, aesthetically "intuitive" presentation (*Darstellung*) of the rational Idea. Benjamin, however, reorients this question as one concerning the possibility of a sensuous, material, and fragmentary presentation of the messianic Idea of redemption—the Idea underlying, or in any case implicitly inseparable from, Kant's speculative Ideas of freedom, immortality, and God.

Contemplating his research on the German mourning play, Benjamin remarks that, since the messianic Idea presents itself to us in mere fragments and traces, we must "stand with every turn anew before the question of presentation [*Darstellung*]."[156] This also means the question of judgment, *Ur-teil*: a word that, when hyphenated, suggests an originary separation or division, but also the biblical narrative of the Exile imposed by God's Judgment for the originary Fall, and the Day of Last Judgment, when the cry for justice will finally be heard. Thus, "Judgment," or *Urteil* written *without* the hyphen, will refer to the moment of synthesis, reconciliation, the restoration of unity and wholeness, possible only in the deferred time of redemption. Until that time, as Adorno has argued, every reconciliation, every restoration, is belied by the historical reality in which it is undertaken, encrypting traces of catastrophe and a history of guilt.

In its time of recognition, the fragment, for Benjamin, is at once the product of judgment and a presentation or exhibition of this judgment. These fragments appear in five different constellations:

1. In the Judgment of divine Justice, sentencing everything in the world to contingency, finitude, and ruination—from the very beginning.

2. In the judgment of revolutionary justice, taking effect in the theater of history, where the judgment is manifest in the destructiveness of the material dialectic, opposing and subverting oppressive bourgeois institutions from within, according to an immanent pressure for radical change.

3. In the judgment of the allegorist and revolutionary dialectical materialist, which works against history within history to serve, by *Urteilskraft*, by the power of critical thought, the social and political forces slowly gathering to destroy the world of suffering produced by capitalism.

4. In the Judgment that, on the Last Day, is supposed to gather everything into the storm of its destructive but purgative rage before it heralds the beginning of the messianic era.

And finally,

5. In the Judgment of Redemption, in which the divisions and separations familiar to judgment in the time of history are supposed to be transformed, becoming constituents of a synthesis that gathers them into a unity once again, restoring the originary part, the *Ur-teil*, to the wholeness of a redeemed world order.

In "Paris, Capital of the Nineteenth Century," written for his *Arcades Project*, Benjamin remarks: "Each epoch not only dreams the next, but also, in dreaming, strives toward the moment of waking [*Erwachen*]. It bears its end in itself and unfolds it—as Hegel saw—with ruse [*mit List*]. In the convulsions of the commodity economy we begin to recognize the monuments of the bourgeoisie as ruins even before they have crumbled." [157] In these very ruins, these remnants of the bourgeois world—a material world reduced to fragments not only by divine justice but also by the sheer destructive force of allegorical interpretation,[158] gestures unleashing the destructive powers in the Idea of redemption[159]—Benjamin must discern both the critical judgment of human history and the Judgment that belongs to the very Idea of messianicity.

The process that, in the prologue to *The Origin of German Tragic Drama*, Benjamin calls "contemplation" (*Kontemplation*) imposes on itself the "sobriety" of an "intermittent rhythm," halting interruptions, temporal discontinuities, and spatial separations, avoiding a relation—an approach—to its object that would prevent it from communicating itself by and for itself. Confronted with a phantasmagoric world, the observer committed to dialectical materialism has a twofold task: first, to see and "read" the spellbinding artifacts and bibelots of bourgeois society, which *appear* to be original, complete, and whole, as instead already in fragments, fragments of a ruined, never-achieved whole; and second, to collect these fragments and assemble them in a mosaic, or constellation, that resolves their enigmatic reality, revealing the suppressed messianic truth-content—the moral and spiritual universality—that would make them recognizably complete and whole.

Thus the task is ultimately not only to destroy but also to affirm in gestures of remembrance, moved by the need to "save" the redemptive "truth-content" hidden within the material phenomenon. As Benjamin says in "Theses on the Philosophy of History," "a constructive principle underlies materialist historiography."[160] Borrowing a phrase from Goethe, Benjamin refers to this principle as a "tender empiricism."[161] But what can be saved? What can be brought back from oblivion? (With these questions, Benjamin attempts to retrieve the Pauline *apokatastasis*, the hope for restitution.)[162] These questions point toward others: Given that the only "truth" is one that emerges from a field of opposing forces, how are we to put together what has been sundered? How, at the very least, are we to make the fragments present and impart (*mitteilen*) intimations of the restored unity, the reconciled whole? But beyond confronting the incompleteness of the fragments he is handling, Benjamin must also resolve the two-fold problem of presenting the universal by way of a finite, concrete particular and presenting the prophetic by a proleptic invocation of its absence. Could the fragment be handled in such a way that it would make possible a form of historically enacted judgment resembling the "reflective judgment" that consummates, for Kant, the peculiar character of aesthetic experience? An ineluctable problem confronts such a historically enacted judgment: the ciphers of the messianic universal that it seeks and for which it ardently longs can be contacted and presented only through the prophetic contingencies of a particular that will impart its redemptive secrets only in the melancholy and mourning of a reflective procedure that makes tangible its imperative deferment of presence.

But can remembrance handle the fragments, the pieces (*Teile*) in a way that would enable the interpretive task of judgment to transcend the conditions of its own impossibility? Benjamin is convinced that in the fragmentary condition of the particular, there is at least an "immediate" presentation of its historical truth-content, exactly reflecting the true conditions of society under the law of unbridled capitalism.[163]

According to Benjamin, the peculiar metaphysics of the fragment shows that both approaches to the presentation of the rational Idea fall short. The Kantian approach does not fully recognize the materiality of the particular that is supposed to instantiate and exhibit the Idea's universality in a disruption of history and moreover fails to draw on the "power" of reflective judgment—its *Urteilskraft*—to compel the fragment to reveal its *originary*, prophetic historicity. The romantic approach, although seemingly bold in its equation of the system and the fragment, nevertheless succumbs to an excess of "enthusiasm" and does not fully recognize the irredeemable fragmentariness of the fragment.[164]

The failures of these two approaches is precisely what is at stake in Benjamin's easily marginalized distinction, discussed earlier, between the enigma and the mystery. The rational Idea, Benjamin realizes, is inevitably shattered by the materiality of a historical dialectic that entangles it between the two contradictory yet equally exigent imperatives of universality and instantiation. Thus he is satisfied with neither the Kantian nor the romantic approach to the problem of the aesthetic or material presentation of the rational Idea.[165] Instead, Benjamin attempts to work out a theory of presentation, of *Darstellung*, that would enable us to grasp the paradoxical messianicity constitutive of the historically derived fragment. In this theory, Benjamin asks: If we achieve a certain "receptive, intentionless alertness" (*Geistesgegenwart*), a certain "vigilance" (*Aufmerksamkeit*), could the history-destroying meaning of the messianic Idea be rendered sensible to us? If so, in what measure? And could that meaning accordingly be presented in the materiality, contingency, and particularity of the historically derived fragment? If so, in what measure? Or, say, bearing in mind the etymology of the word "contingency": If we handle the fragments constitutive of our cultural life in a suitable way, could the paradoxical temporality of the messianic Idea be presented in an experience of its peculiar rhythmicity, its material contingency, indeed its tangibly critical claim on our commodified tactility? If so, in what measure? As Benjamin says in the third of his reflections in "Theses on the Philosophy of History," he is convinced at least of this: "Only to a redeemed humanity will its past [and thus the messianic promise constitutive of this abandoned past] be fully granted."

Benjamin's obsession with the fragment leads him to question one of the prevailing assumptions about the claims of Reason: its demand for absolutely unconditioned totality. Like Jacobi, Schelling, and Hölderlin, Benjamin holds that Being is not reducible to transcendental reflection, the unconditioned enactment of Reason. Searching for prophetic ciphers of redemption still preserved, against all odds, in the diremptions of the material world, Benjamin attempted to break out of the categorical and conceptual totalizations imposed by Reason. He was accordingly tempted to contemplate reaffirming the dream of German romanticism — the conviction, namely, that, in the wake of this critique of Kantian rationalism, we need to achieve a new type of "intellectual intuition," a new type of immediacy. Thus he hoped to show that, in the redemptive fire of dialectical images ignited by a suitable handling of the fragmentary ciphers of the modern world, we might render intuitively immediate, visible, and tangible the intellectual Idea — the prophetic, messianic potentiality — present, despite its phenomenal particularity, in the immeasurably fragmented material.

Benjamin's approach to the phenomenon thus involves an intricate and paradoxical dialectic. On the one hand, it is destructive, ruthlessly bent on making the object, the phenomenon, appear in its fragmentation. On the other hand, it is resolute in its self-restraint, a "holding back" (*Verhaltenheit*) infinitely respectful of a distance and time that cannot be traversed, recognizing a metaphysical, auratic dimension of the phenomenon that can reveal itself — reveal its prophetically inscribed truth — only insofar as the approach maintains its absolute impotence to coerce the presentation and realization of the Idea. Whatever the cost, the logic of subsumption must be avoided.

Our very recognition of the fragment's fragmentation, its ruination, is what enables us to recover the "truth-content" of the phenomenon and thus the phenomenon itself, and to activate the potential for a radically

new kind of social existence. But inasmuch as the messianic, the temporality of redemption, must not be reduced to the time continuum into
which our lives have been pressed, the dialectical approach to the phenomenon must remain an approximation, forever resisting the temptations of complacency, forever denying itself respite from the struggle
for the most beautiful fulfillment, the prophesied world of truth, universal justice and peace. In *The Origin of German Tragic Drama*, Benjamin
writes that "the value of fragments of thought is all the more decisive the
less they are able to gauge [*messen*] their unmediated relation to the underlying Idea, and the brilliance of the presentation depends as much on
this measure [*Maße*] as the brilliance of the mosaic does on the quality of
the glass paste."[166] Paradoxically, everything depends on permitting the
fragments to resist the violence that would be inherent in their subordination to, or subsumption under, the universal Idea—and thereby depends on encouraging the free articulation of the unified whole that the
Idea represents. In other words, the fragmentation is not imposed from
the top down, deductively, as in Kant's determinant judgment, but is accomplished from the bottom up, as in Kant's reflective judgment. In this
way, the contemplative process makes the fragments work dialectically
against any linear master narrative and ideology and *for* the prophetically
charged dream of messianic fulfillment. But the possibility of such a presentation requires a double movement, a rhythm and a counterrhythm: a
destructive movement and a movement that approaches in such a way that
the phenomenon can withdraw, so that the closer the gesture comes to it,
the farther away it recedes, its messianic Idea rescued from destructiveness
by the caesura, the interruption, the intention-suspending epokhē.

   This epokhē brings ordinary, profane time to a standstill, in which—
as Heidegger says of the "resolute, anticipatory openness" (*vorlaufende
Entschlossenheit*) of the authentic "moment of vision" (*Augenblick*)—
"nothing can happen." Nothing can happen, because the chain of causalities has been broken, opening the way for the eventual intervention—
who knows when?—of another temporality, and another moral order.

XI. With Hope Intact

In "The Concept of Enlightenment," a sentence almost certainly written
by Adorno laments the atrophy of experience in the our time: "The regression of the masses today is their inability to hear the unheard-of with

their own ears, to touch the unapprehended with their own hands [*Unergriffenes mit eigenen Händen tasten zu können*]—the new form of delusion which deposes every conquered mythic form." [167] And yet, Frederick Sachs surely has hold of a truth when he observes, "The first sense to ignite, touch is often the last to burn out; long after our eyes betray us, our hands remain faithful to the world." [168] But what is this fidelity? To what "world" must we be faithful? In his essay "Nature," Emerson, despite all the obvious differences separating him from Benjamin's politics, addresses this question, invoking in the transcendentalist spirit that he derived from German romanticism a notion of childhood that bears a priceless gift—a gift that Benjamin, too, never forgets: "Infancy is the perpetual Messiah, which comes into the arms of fallen men, and pleads with them to return to paradise." [169] Benjamin attached great philosophical and allegorical significance to the experience of childhood: in the freedom of the child's imagination, the child's mimetic impulses, playfulness, and fantasies of magical transformation. In the child, for whom nothing is what it is and everything can be turned into something else, the spirit that awakens to revolution has not yet been suppressed. Thus, the possibility of radical social change would always be, for Benjamin, in part a question of our fidelity to the free originality of our earliest years, a question, therefore, of reconnecting our life as adults to our experience of life at the beginning.

I would like to connect this reflection to an apocalyptic fragment of pre-Socratic thought attributed to Alcmaeon of Croton. It reads: "Men perish because they cannot join the beginning to the end." [170] The struggle to join them—in the "now-time" (*Jetztzeit*) of world history as well as in the biographical time of our individual lives—could be said to define the allegorical fate of Benjamin's dialectical gestures. But in Benjamin's hands, writing becomes a dialectical practice with no end in sight. It is a practice that derives its measure from the time of remembrance—a practice of vigilance, of the utmost "attentiveness," *Aufmerksamkeit*,[171] holding the now of the present in a state of exceptional openness to the contingency and potentiality of another temporality.

In one of his short studies, an essay inspired by Kafka and bearing the title "In the Sun," Benjamin recalls:

The Hasidim have a saying about the world to come. Everything there will be arranged [*eingerichtet*] just as it is with us. The room we have now will be just the same in the world to come; where our child lies sleeping it will sleep in the

world to come. Everything will be the same as here—only a little bit different [*nur ein klein wenig anders*]. Thus it is with phantasy [*Phantasie*]. It merely
draws a veil over the distance. Everything remains just as it is, but the veil flut-
ters and everything changes imperceptibly beneath it.[172]

Everything remains the same, but everything also changes. In *One-Way
Street*, with revolutionary action always in mind, Benjamin declares:
"All the decisive strokes are accomplished with the left hand."[173] In
Minima Moralia, as if he were replying to Benjamin, Adorno argued:
"There is nothing innocuous left."[174] Even the most tactful of gestures,
seemingly without guile or malice, must be subjected to reflectively medi-
ated suspicions.

    I am reminded to quote here a remarkable statement confronting us at
the beginning of Nietzsche's *Ecce Homo*: "The lightning bolt of truth
struck precisely what was highest so far: let whoever comprehends what
has here been destroyed see whether anything is left in his hands."[175] This
statement might direct our attention to the rhythmic peculiarities of Benjamin's writings, "where," to cite a line from Celan, "the pulse has dared
the counter-beat [*Gegentakt*]."[176] Something of this "counter-beat" figures in one of Benjamin's early textual "fragments," "The Meaning of
Time in the Moral Universe," written in 1921.[177] One should read it bearing in mind, as I am sure Benjamin did, the allegorical significance of
Michelangelo's representation, in the Sistine Chapel, of God's benevolent
hand reaching down to touch—and empower—the extended hand of
Adam. "The Last Judgment," Benjamin says,

> is regarded as the date when all postponements are ended and all retribution
> is allowed free rein. This idea, however, which mocks all delay as vain pro-
> crastination, fails to understand the immeasurable significance of the Last
> Judgment, of that constantly postponed day which flees so determinedly into
> the future after the commission of every misdeed. This significance is revealed
> not in the world of law, where retribution rules, but only in the moral uni-
> verse, where forgiveness comes out to meet it. In order to struggle against ret-
> ribution, forgiveness finds its powerful ally in time. For time, in which Ate
> pursues the evildoer, is not the lonely calm of fear but the tempestuous storm
> of forgiveness which precedes the onrush of the Last Judgment and against
> which she [Ate] cannot advance.

The text continues, invoking now the righteous hand of God, bringing
the absolute gift of forgiveness in the purity of its divine violence:

This storm is not only the voice in which the evildoer's cry of terror is drowned; it is also the hand that obliterates the traces of his misdeeds, even if it must lay waste to the world in that process. . . . God's fury roars through history in the storm of forgiveness, in order to sweep away everything that would be consumed forever in the lightning bolts of divine wrath.

"In this," Benjamin says in the final sentence of the fragment, "time not only extinguishes the traces of all misdeeds, but also—by virtue of its duration, beyond all remembering or forgetting—helps, in ways that are wholly mysterious, to complete the process of forgiveness [*Vergebung*], though never of reconciliation [*Versöhnung*]." Forgiveness is not reconciliation: there must be no moral complacency, no acquiescence in evil. The hand of God, the hand that gives the blessing of life, has become the hand that shows us the blessing of forgiveness—a deeply mysterious gesture on which, beyond all calculation, beyond all measure, the time of redemption depends. If, as Benjamin's "Theologico-Political Fragment" observes, "the rhythm of messianic time is happiness," this is a rhythm that our own hands must somehow learn, extending themselves in gestures of forgiveness, benevolence, charity.[178]

In keeping with his way of thinking about the metaphysics of the fragment, Benjamin acknowledges the inherent limitations in allegorical and metaphorical presentations: "What we have expressed here metaphorically," he notes, "must be capable of being formulated clearly and distinctly in conceptual form: the meaning of time in the economy of the moral universe."

But the fragmentary state of the text suggests that the way to that conceptual form is still to be learned; and it undoubtedly will depend in considerable measure on the favor of certain material conditions. Consequently, with the rhythms of restrained hope in his fingers and the strength of messianic justice in his arm, Benjamin the masterful *Scheidekünstler*,[179] artist of alchemical separations and affinities, leaves us for the time being with a jumble of fragments in our hands and four importunate questions, which, if we recall Nietzsche's admonition, we may ignore only at our peril: What, in the end, is left intact? What is left of tact? What is Left—what does "Left" mean—in relation to tact? And what is or could be, in our time, an intact Left?

These are questions for the left hand to take on, since "All the decisive blows are struck by the left hand."[180]

§ 8 Usage and Dispensation

Heidegger's Meditation on the Hand

πάντων χρημάτων μέτρον ἐστὶν ἄνθρωπος, τῶν μὲν ὄντων ὡς
ἔστιν, τῶν δὲ μὴ ὄντων ὡς οὐκ ἔστιν.

[Of all things in customary use, man is the measure: of those that
are present, that they are, but of those that are not present, that they
are not.]

—Protagoras, Fragment 1

A strange measure . . . , certainly not a palpable stick or rod but,
in truth, simpler to handle than they, provided our hands do not
abruptly grasp but are guided by gestures befitting the measure
here to be taken.

—Martin Heidegger, ". . . Poetically Man Dwells . . ." [1]

Each human being has its own measure [*ein eignes Maß*], likewise a
distinctive attunement [*Stimmung*] of all his bodily felt meanings
[*sinnlichen Gefühle*] with one another. [However, the human is also
called to live according to another measure:] That he become the
organ of sense of his god among all the living beings of Creation,
according to the measure of their relation to him.

—Johann Gottfried von Herder, *Ideas* [2]

Between the stars, how far; and yet, by how much still farther,
what we learn from the here and now.
. . .

Fate [*Schicksal*], it measures us [*es mißt uns*] perhaps with the span of being
[*mit des Seinenden Spanne*],
that it seems strange to us.
. . .

Everything is far—, and nowhere does the circle close.

—Rainer Maria Rilke, *Sonnets to Orpheus* [3]

Even before the technical ascendancy over things which the knowledge
of the industrial era has made possible and before the technological
development of modernity, knowledge, by itself, is the project of an
incarnate practice of seizure, appropriation, and satisfaction. The
most abstract lessons of the science of the future will rest upon this
familiarity with the world that we inhabit in the midst of things

which are held out to the grasp of the hand. *Presence, of itself,* becomes the now.

—Emmanuel Levinas, "Transcendence and Intelligibility"[4]

We too serve, are sent to be of use [*geschickt*]
When we come, with our art, and of the heavenly powers
Bring one with us. But fitting,
Skillful hands [*schickliche Hände*] we ourselves contribute.

—Friedrich Hölderlin, "Reticence"[5]

This thought of the hand belongs to the essence of the gift, of a giving that would give, if this is possible, without taking hold of anything.

—Jacques Derrida, "Geschlecht II"[6]

One would be tempted to say that a subject as such never gives or receives a gift. It is constituted, on the contrary, in view of dominating, through calculation and exchange, the mastery of this *hubris* or of this impossibility that is announced in the promise of the gift. There where there is subject and object, the gift would be excluded. A subject will never give an object to another subject. But the subject and the object are arrested effects of the gift: arrests of the gift. At the zero or infinite speed of the circle.

—Jacques Derrida, "Given Time: The Time of the King"[7]

The foundation of consciousness is justice and not the reverse. Objectivity reposing on justice. To the extravagant generosity of the for-the-other is superimposed a rational order, ancillary or angelic, of justice through knowledge, and philosophy here is a *measure* brought to the infinity of the being-for-the-other of peace and proximity, and is like the wisdom of love.

—Emmanuel Levinas, "Peace and Proximity"[8]

I. Originary Ethics

What is it to be human? To be, that is, a human being, a being that is human? When Heidegger considers these questions, he attempts to twist free from the spell of metaphysics, within which "the human" is an "essential nature" presumed to be, in its being, its way of being, already determined—presumed, moreover, according to a metaphysics that has "forgotten" to think the human in relation to the question of being. In his "Letter on Humanism," Heidegger writes: "If then, in accordance with the basic meaning of the word *ethos*, the name 'ethics' says that it considers the true habitation of human beings, then the thinking that thinks the import of being as the primary element of human beings, as something that exists, is already an originary ethics."[9] With modernity increasingly trapped in an extreme subjectivism and relativism that he is convinced threatens to destroy civilization, Heidegger attempts to restore a sense of measure to freedom. Heidegger's "originary ethics" must derive its measure—its directive, its normativity, and its point of reference—from the questioning of being: from our thoughtful exposure to the ontological dimensionality into which that questioning throws us. This is why Heidegger insists that *Dasein*, the *being* of the human, is not something human. But this means that originary ethics is an ethics in which the human is always exposed, always open to questioning, open to the most radical otherness—the groundlessness of an ethical life measured by what is beyond all human measure. Hence a life always *unheimlich*, unsettled, uncanny, radically homeless. Our "essence" as human beings is to be without any essence. This is of course a deprivation, but it is also a gift that no other being has received: the gift, namely, of freedom. But freedom is possible only if it can transgress the limits constitutive of measure. So "originary ethics" would be a way of dwelling, a way of living with the humble dignity of a freedom that attempted to measure itself and give itself limits in the light of the measurelessness, the groundlessness, without which there could be no freedom, no human being.

In this chapter, we will consider the possibility of an "originary ethics," an ethics, namely, that originates in the freedom of our preontological attunement, as human beings, to the conditions of being. Because of the nihilism threatening our time, such an ethics is needed now more than ever—and yet, precisely because of the prevailing "forgetfulness" of being, such a possibility has never before been so difficult even to imagine. But, for Heidegger, success depends on our commitment to the task of "remembrance," since remembrance requires that we come into a thoughtful relation to the question of being—and to the existential situation of humanity that we have been given most destinally to ponder. As he says in *Identity and Difference*, bearing in mind the *Es gibt* of being as *Ereignis*, as epochal "eventuality," and the questions that Parmenides provoked by his claim of a "measure-giving" relation between thinking and being: "We get into the proximity of what has been sent only through the abruptness of the moment of remembrance and commemoration [*die Jähe des Augenblickes eines Andenkens*]."[10]

Now, *Andenken*, for Heidegger, is indeed "a remembrance"; "but," he asserts, it is a remembrance "of something to come," of *das Künftige*: "Such a 'thinking about' what is to come can only be a thinking about what has been [*Erwesenes*], through which we think the difference between what is past [*Vergangenes*] and that which is still in process [*das fernher noch Wesende*]."[11] *Ereignis* is the name Heidegger gives to the history-shattering "event" that bears the claim of the ontology still-to-come, interrupting the causality that chains what has been to its pastness. If, as Hölderlin says in his "Remarks on *Antigone*," "time is always measured in suffering," and if the soul is most "in tune" with the passing away of time, then perhaps Heidegger's seemingly paradoxical way of remembrance is the only way to receive in our suffering a future of redemptive possibilities.[12]

II. Writing the Future

In his *Notes to Literature*, Adorno sketches a portrait of the Benjamin he came to know, recalling the peculiarities of his friend that came to light in the course of their many years of correspondence.[13] Attempting to explain how Benjamin could, as it were, turn himself, with "his touchy subjective form of response," into "an organ of objectivity," Adorno conjectures, "Whatever Benjamin may have lacked in immediacy, whatever it must early on have become second nature for him to hide, has been lost in a world that is governed by the abstract law of human relations." Adorno continues, exploring what the gestures of writing meant for Benjamin: "Within himself, and in his relationships with others, he gave unreserved primacy to spirit, and this, rather than immediacy, became his form of immediacy." According to Adorno, Benjamin's "private demeanor approached ritual." Thus, for example: "In his letters, ritual extends even into the typography and the choice of paper, which played an uncommonly significant role with him."

Adorno recalls that Benjamin "had a passion for writing letters":

> The letter became a literary form for Benjamin. The form transmits the primary impulses but interposes a third thing between them and the addressee, the artistic shaping of what is written, as if under a law of objectification— despite and also by virtue of the occasion of time and place, as though only the occasion gave legitimacy to the impulse. . . . The letter was so congenial to

him because from the outset it encourages a mediated, objectified immediacy. Writing letters creates a fiction of life within the medium of the frozen word. In a letter one can disavow one's isolation and nevertheless remain separate and at a distance.

Although, as Adorno points out, "the letter form is now anachronistic and was already becoming so in Benjamin's lifetime," nevertheless Benjamin found some of his deepest consolation and power in the hand-written letter: "It is significant that whenever possible he wrote letters by hand, at a time when the typewriter had long been dominant; in the same way, the physical act of writing brought him pleasure—he liked to make excerpts and fair copies—as mechanical aids repelled him." "But," Adorno concludes, "in the age of the disintegration of experience human beings are no longer subjectively disposed to the writing of letters." For Benjamin, however, "the letter represented the wedding of something in the process of disappearing and the utopia of its restoration. . . . For him, letters were natural-philosophical images of something that survives transience and decay." Letters were crucibles for an alchemy in which a concrete particular could manifest its objective universality. Consequently, it was imperative that the letter be written by a gesture befitting this allegorical moment.[14]

Though for different reasons, Heidegger, too, passionately insisted on writing by hand, shunning the use of the typewriter. In a discussion of the word πρᾶγμα, a discussion important for the unfolding logic of his lecture course on Parmenides (winter semester 1942–43), Heidegger remarked:

It is not accidental that modern man writes "with" the typewriter and "dictates" [*diktiert*] (the same word as "poetize" [*Dichten*]) "into" a machine. This "history" of the kinds of writing is one of the main reasons for the increasing destruction of the word. The latter no longer comes and goes by means of the writing hand, the properly acting hand, but by means of the mechanical forces it releases. The typewriter tears writing from the essential realm of the hand, i.e., the realm of the [incarnate] word. The word itself turns into something "typed." Where typewriting, on the contrary, is only a transcription and serves to preserve the writing, or turns into print something already written, there it has a proper, though limited, significance. In the time of the first dominance of the typewriter, a letter written on this machine still stood for a breach of good manners. Today a hand-written letter is an antiquated and undesired thing; it disturbs speed reading. Mechanical writing deprives the hand of its rank in the realm of the written word and degrades the word to a means of communication. In addition, mechanical writing provides this "advantage," that it conceals the handwriting, and therefore the character. The typewriter makes everyone look the same.[15]

We shall have to give thought to Heidegger's claims here, regarding "the properly acting hand" and "the essential realm of the hand." Although Benjamin did not share Heidegger's ontological concerns, he, too, lamented the degradation of the word to an instrument for the communication of "factual information" and thought that in this seemingly insignificant historical change something "destinal," something bearing on the possibility of that more radical inception promised as a time of redemption, was ultimately at stake.

In the "Recapitulation" of the lecture course, Heidegger turns historical fact into an "originating essence," contending, "Writing, in its originating essence [*Wesensherkunft*], is hand-writing [*Hand-schrift*]." Further, in the melodic gesture of writing with the hand, the letters and words are connected with one another and gathered into a felt unity that the typewriter cannot bring about. Thus:

> We call the disclosive taking up and perceiving of the written word "reading" or "lection" [*Lesen*], i.e., col-lection, gathering—"gleaning" [*Ähren lesen*]), in Greek λέγειν, λόγος; and this latter, among the primordial thinkers, is the name for Being itself. Being, word, gathering, writing denote an original essential nexus, to which the indicating-writing hand belongs. In handwriting, the relation of Being to man, namely the word, is inscribed in beings themselves. The origin and the way of dealing with writing is almost itself a decision about the relation of Being and of the word to man and consequently a decision about the comportment of man toward beings and about the way both, man and thing, stand in unconcealedness or are withdrawn from it.

"Therefore," he says,

> when writing was withdrawn from the origin of its essence, i.e., from the hand, and was transferred to the machine, a transformation occurred in the relation of man to Being. It is of little importance for this transformation how many people actually use the typewriter and whether there are some who shun it. It is no accident that the invention of the printing press coincides with the inception of the modern period. The word-signs become type, and the writing stroke [the gesture of embodied meaning] disappears. . . . The typewriter veils the essence of writing and of the script [*Die Schreib-maschine verhüllt das Wesen des Schreibens und der Schrift*]. It withdraws from man the essential rank

of the hand, without man's experiencing this withdrawal appropriately and recognizing that it has transformed the relation of his essence to Being.

These assertions provoke questions that cannot be avoided. What is the "essence" of writing? What is the "essential rank" of the hand? What ontological event does the triumph of the typewriter conceal? What would be an "appropriate" experience of this historical transition and the "withdrawal of Being" that it implies? By what measure is the "proper" use of the hand to be determined? Indeed, is there a proper use? And is there a measure?

Feeling compelled to defend his claims, since their truth is far from obvious, Heidegger says:

> I have not been presenting a disquisition on the typewriter itself, regarding which it could justifiably be asked what in the world that has to do with Parmenides. My theme was the modern relation, transformed by the typewriter, of the hand to writing, i.e., to the word, i.e., to the unconcealedness of Being. . . . In the typewriter the machine appears, i.e., technology appears, in an almost quotidian and hence unnoticed and hence signless relation to writing, i.e., to the word, i.e., to the distinguishing essence of man [of man, that is, in contrast to the essence of the animal].

He seems to think that, when we write by hand, we are in closer, if not immediate, contact with the event of meaning, for what is written in this way preserves the bodily felt dimensions of meaning—affective, conative, reflexive—carried by the gesture. The typewriter is a mediation that obliterates virtually all traces of this contact. But in laying down letters in a standardized type, the machine not only, in a certain sense, alienates the writer from meaning; it also imposes uniformity, making thought conform in very subtle ways to conceptual formations of meaning deprived of all subjective and reflective character. "The typewriter makes everyone look the same." What is at stake—the future of humanity—can be detected in our relations with others: Heidegger reminds us that there was a time when a typed letter, by suggesting a certain indifference, could seem tactless, "a breach of good manners." What is at stake is also manifest, according to Heidegger, in our relation to being: an absolutely fundamental relation that the typewriter has irreparably altered. Its neutralization and alienation diminish our sense of responsibility in relation to the prevailing ontology. It denies us the *tangibility* of our responsibility to, and for, the presencing of being, to and for our representations of this presencing. If the hand, in its "essential co-belonging" (*Wesenszusammengehörigkeit*) to language, manifests what is hidden (*die Hand Verborgenes entbirgt*), the typewriter, *zeichenlos*, withdrawn in a decisive way from the signifying process, draws us toward a fatefully deep ontological forgetfulness. Thus Heidegger says: "Λήθη and the typewriter—this is indeed not a digression for anyone not submerged in the oblivion of Being." For the question of Λήθη "interrogates this relation of man to Being, and therefore our elucidation of the essence of πρᾶγμα, the action of the hand, had to refer to the typewriter, assuming that a thoughtful meditation is a thinking that thinks of our history (the essence of truth), in which the future comes toward us." Although we tend to fall into ontological forgetfulness even when writing by hand, using the typewriter makes this oblivion a greater temptation, for we lose touch with the historical connection between the hand and our ontology—our experience of the way beings presence. And as we surrender to the alienations and reifications of technology, we slowly begin to forget that the destiny of being is still very much in our hands.

But, as Derrida astutely remarks, Heidegger's preference for handwriting may indicate that even he encountered difficulty in twisting free of the usage determined long ago by the metaphysics of constant, totalized presence—although, as Derrida also points out, writing cannot avoid the contingencies of meaning that contest the grip of this ontology.[16] Equivocations, disseminations, errancies, absences, corruptions, failures: vicissitudes of meaning that can easily seem, if only at first, to be averted by the living "presence" of the voice engaged in conversation. But Heidegger's preference for handwriting over typewriting is not a vestige of his entanglement in the metaphysics of presence but rather a result of his recognition of the importance of a contact that necessarily enjoins a sense of responsibility for the ontology one is bringing forth.

Heidegger's brief reflections on the "history" of writing derive from his prolonged questioning of the nature of language. But since writing involves the hand, his reflections on writing inevitably turn his thought in the direction of the hand. In writing, the gestures of the hand bring the words of language into visibility, into a certain presence. As he says in his 1942–43 lecture course on Parmenides, "The word as inscribed [*eingezeichnete*], and such that it shows itself thus to the gaze is the written word, that is, writing [*d.h. die Schrift*]." "But," he adds, "the word as writing is handwriting. [*Das Wort als die Schrift aber ist die Handschrift*]."

For Heidegger, this history portends the "destruction of the word"

(*Zerstörung des Wortes*), because, even though the hand is still involved in the typewriter, typographic mechanization destroys the gesture's intimate sense of bringing words into being. The typewriter "wrests" (*entreisst*) the process of writing from the "essential" domain of the hand and "degrades" (*degradiert*) the word, reducing it to a *Verkehrsmittel*, a mere instrument of commerce and information. Thus, making an argument reminiscent of Plato's argument in the *Republic* about the image of the bed, Heidegger asserts that the "word" produced by the machine is really nothing but a copy (*Abschrift*), a second-order reality.

Using his hand, Heidegger writes a history of ontology, a history that fears the technology that began with the hand, and attempts to set in motion, within the realm of thought, the "destruction" of this ontology.[17] Lending his hand, then, to an eschatology without end, he writes toward a possible future.

He writes! Writes volumes, in fact. But how extensive is his "destruction"? To what extent is he still himself spellbound by the metaphysics of constant and totalized presence? To be sure, Heidegger indicates a preference for the living presence of speech over the sedimentations of meaning in the written language. But is Derrida right that this is further proof of Heidegger's inability to think beyond what he calls "the metaphysics of presence"?[18] It is not, I think, so clear that a preference for the "presence" of speech necessarily implies a commitment to the "presence" desired by transcendental idealism—or, for that matter, by positivism and empiricism.

For Heidegger, Socrates is the "purest thinker" because, writing nothing, entrusting his thought only to dialogue, he understood that "anyone who begins to write out of thoughtfulness must inevitably be like those people who run to seek refuge from any draft too strong for them." And concluding this train of thought, he adds, provocatively: "An as yet hidden history still keeps the secret why all great Western thinkers after Socrates, with all their greatness, had to be such fugitives."[19] Could it be that this "as yet hidden history" is a history of being in which, unrecognized as such, the spellbinding "presence" of the voice still echoes? Could it be that, although the voice has withdrawn before the reach of writing, before the powerful technologies of the hand, its peculiar presence, even if only an illusory refuge, nevertheless continues to hold sway, echoing and beckoning from the reserve of its concealment in an *Ort der Stille*, a "place of silence"?

Perhaps. But Heidegger never ceased to write! He devoted much of his life to writing, giving his hand to the task of thinking, so that thinking, in turn, could give itself to the hand, thereby bestowing that guardianship of being in which the hand most properly "rests." And what the philosopher's hand writes inclines, as we know, toward a future decidedly untimely, out of line: a future retrieving from a past that has never been present the originary possibility of another ontological epoch. A future that could have been apprehended only through the temporality of writing. For he understood, long before Derrida, that in writing, this future can no longer be securely maintained under the spell and rule of an absolute present.

III. The Hold of the Hand in the History of Ontology

Surprising though it may seem, the hand is the object of a sustained meditation extending through years of Heidegger's writings: at least from *Being and Time* (1929), where, though not yet thematized as such, its "pragmatic" involvement in the history of ontology figures implicitly; through the Parmenides lecture course (1942–43), where its ontological significance is explicitly recognized and examined at length; to his commentary on "usage" in "The Anaximander Fragment" (1946) and the lectures that constitute *What Is Called Thinking?* (1952). But Heidegger's discussion of ontology, in *Being and Time*, makes this attention to the hand completely understandable, for it emphasizes how much our experience of what is, and of being as such, has been formed and informed by the functions, activities, and experiences of our hands. *Dasein* would not have the ontology it has if it could not gesture, using the hands.

In the Parmenides lecture course, taking up for questioning the Greek words πρᾶγμα, πρᾶξις, and πράττειν (as a first approximation, we may say "thing," "practice," or "activity," and "to handle"), Heidegger notes that these words, significantly, were from the outset related to activities of the hand, although the Greeks left the gestures of the hand as such in the dark, because, despite their concern for practical life and the work of the hands, and despite the practical derivation of their ontology, their reflections on this ontology gave pride of place to the theoretical relation to beings—the contemplative relation par excellence of the philosopher. Emphasizing that πρᾶγμα "originally means, and still in Pindar," both an activity and that activity's object or end, Heidegger writes:

> More precisely, πρᾶγμα means the original unity of both in their relation— the still unseparated and essential unity of the setting up in the arrival at some-

thing and of what is reached in the arrival and is then present as unconcealed. Πρᾶγμα is here not yet distinguished and set apart and separated as thing and fact from πρᾶξις as presumed "activity." Πρᾶγμα is not yet narrowed down to the concept of "thing," the matter "at hand" to be dealt with, to be acted upon. Nevertheless, we have translated πρᾶγμα precisely by "action" [*Handlung*]. Although "action" is not the literal translation of πρᾶγμα, yet, correctly understood, "action" does touch the originally essential essence [*das ursprünglich wesentliche Wesen*] of πρᾶγμα. Things "act" [*handeln*], insofar as the things present [*Vorhandenen*] and at hand [*Zuhandenen*] dwell within the reach [*im Bereich*] of the "hand." The hand reaches out for them and reaches them: πράττειν, the reaching arrival at something (πρᾶγμα), is essentially related to the hand.[20]

But Heidegger's turn to the Greeks of antiquity set the stage for a critique of the subject-object structure that prevails in the modern epoch, for it indicates, as Heidegger says explicitly elsewhere,[21] that this structure is a historical contingency and could perhaps be overcome in the future. The point of this return is to bring to the fore the ontological significance — one might even say the "destinal," that is, *geschicklich*, significance — of the hand. This also set the stage for his "destruction" of modern ontology.

Now, according to the analysis Heidegger proposes in *Being and Time*,[22] things, πράγματα, have been presenting themselves "in the domain of the hand" (*im Bereich der Hand*) as being either present-at-hand (*vorhanden*) or ready-to-hand (*zuhanden*): presenting themselves in these two ways since a time beyond recall, but most overwhelmingly in the modern epoch of technological domination. The term "ready-to-hand" names that modality of presencing, or being, in which things such as tools are within reach of our hands, or are in some other way available for the activities of the hand, ready for our use. The term "present-at-hand" names that modality of presencing, or being, we experience when, for example, something — say, a tool or a machine — has broken down and we are at a loss to go on; or when manipulability (*Handlichkeit*) as such is in question; or when we pause simply to behold the presencing of something; or when we abstract a sensuous quality — say, the indigo lines on a vase or the rustling of leaves — from its object and referential totality. Thus things are experienced as *vorhanden*, present-at-hand, when they are treated or regarded as subsisting in a certain "theoretical" independence, isolated or detached from our more "practical" concerns.

Being present-at-hand (*Vorhandensein*) is always a latent potentiality in our experience with equipment, things of use; but that potentiality with-draws into latency when our interests and concerns require that these things be ready-to-hand. Pure presence-at-hand—the thing as such, what-ever it may be—comes thematically to the fore only through a shift of at-tention, when what is at first proximally ready-to-hand is no longer our concern. According to Heidegger:

> The Greeks had an appropriate term for "things": πράγματα—that is to say, that which one has to do with [*zu tun*] in one's concernful dealings [*im besorgenden Umgang*] (πρᾶξις). But ontologically, the specifically "pragmatic" character of the πράγματα is just what the Greeks left in obscurity [*im Dunkeln*]; they thought of these "proximally" as "mere things" [*bloße Dinge*]. We call those entities which we encounter in concern [*im Besorgen*] "equip-ment" [*Zeug*]. In our everyday dealings and undertakings [*im Umgang*], we come across equipment for writing, sewing, working, transportation, mea-surement [*Schreibzeug, Nähzeug, Werk-, Fahr-, Meßzeug*]. The kind of being that equipment [*Zeug*] possesses must be shown. The clue for doing this lies in our first defining what makes an item of equipment—namely, its equip-mentality [*Zeughaftigkeit*].[23]

But, as Derrida points out,[24] the ancient Greek philosophers also left the gestures of the hand "in the dark" because, even though their practical life, especially the work of the hand, in many ways decisively conditioned their paradigmatic way of thinking about the world, still the formal ontology that they brought to theoretical formulation gave pride of place to the the-oretical relation—the relation, in effect, of the philosopher—to being.

In introducing the distinction between two modalities of presencing, the present-to-hand and the ready-to-hand—Heidegger is able to set in motion the most radical attempt ever undertaken to question the prevail-ing ontology and prepare thinking for the possibility of another epoch of being, differently presencing out of its concealment. Moreover, he is able to dispute the ancient and still compelling opposition of πρᾶξις (action, activity) and θεωρία (theory, contemplation, purely theoretical apprehen-sion), an opposition he rejects. Strongly influenced by Aristotle, Heideg-ger argues that thinking is also an activity, and that what we call "theo-retical activity," registering what presences in its *Vorhandenheit*, always emerges from what we call "practical activity": an activity of the hands.

Moreover, the distinction between the two modalities of presencing en-ables him to argue against the reification and commodification of the hu-man being that is taking place in our time. Thus, while acknowledging

that *Dasein*—our given potentiality as human beings and the true measure of our humanity—"can with some right and within certain limits
be *regarded* as merely present-at-hand,"[25] for example, in the ontological
commitments of the natural and human sciences, he nevertheless insists
that *Dasein* is "in its essence" neither *vorhanden* nor *zuhanden*. Accordingly, in thinking about the essence of our humanity, about what it means
to be human, Heidegger says, we must think our way beyond the domination of these two ontological modalities.

To common sense, it is not surprising that our experience of how entities presence—how they are present—derives from manual activities in
the practical life of archaic cultures. But over the course of the history of
philosophical thought, recognition of this practical derivation has virtually disappeared. Indeed, transcendental idealism thought the practical as
deriving from the theoretical, and thus inevitably neglected or denied the
role of the hand in shaping our ontological commitments.

Heidegger's argument for the practical derivation of our *zuhanden* and
vorhanden ontology is therefore not an unnecessary exercise. Moreover, he
needs this argument for two further reasons. First, he wants to show that
this ontology and the will to power are essentially connected. Second,
he wants to argue that giving the gift of thought to the gestures of our
hands—or, say, "rooting" (*berühen*) the gestures of our hands in thinking—might prepare our world for the possibility of another epoch in the
history of being: a time when the being of beings would presence (*ereignet*)
otherwise than in those two pragmatically constituted ways of unconcealment. For if our world is increasingly compelled to suffer the consequences of our will to power, if our technologies of power increasingly
threaten us with nihilism in all its guises, then it makes sense for thinking
to return to the gestures of the hand. By giving them the gift of thought,
would we not be enabling our hands to "rest" (*berühen*) in thinking? And
could this not be the most appropriate (*geeignete, schickliche*) way for the
gestures (*Gebärden*) of our hands to bring forth (*gebärden*) conditions favoring another ontological epoch—another way, at present beyond our
grasp, for beings to be?

IV. Animals and Mortals: A Metaphysical Difference

"We are trying," Heidegger says, "to learn thinking. Perhaps [*Veilleicht*]
thinking . . . is something like building a cabinet. At any rate, it is a craft,

a handicraft" (*WHD*, 50–51/16–17).[26] Then, remarking that "craft" literally means "the strength and skill in our hands," he reflects on the thought that the hand is a peculiar thing, something truly singular (*mit der Hand hat es eine eigene Bewandtnis*): "In the common view [*gewöhnliche Vorstellung*], the hand is part of our bodily organism. But the hand's essence [*Wesen*] can never be determined, or explained, by its being an organ which can grasp [*ein leibliches Greiforgan*]." In opposition to the common representation, we must think of the hand as essentially, and most properly, *withdrawn* from the realm of animal nature. In other words, although we must worry about essentialism, we must recognize that the *essence* of the hand is withdrawn from this realm. Destined to this withdrawal, released into the interplay of presence and absence. He argues:

> Apes, too, have organs that can grasp [*Greiforgane*], but they do not have hands [*hat keine Hand*]. The hand is infinitely different from all grasping organs—paws, claws, or fangs—different by an abyss of essence [*durch einen Abgrund des Wesens*]. Only a being [*Wesen*] who can speak, that is, think, can have hands [*kann die Hand haben*] and be handy in achieving works of handicraft [*in der Handlung Werke der Hand vollbringen*].

So goes the argument in Heidegger's 1951 and 1952 lectures, published under the title *What Is Called Thinking?* But even drawing on Heidegger's existential phenomenology in *Being and Time*, we could already have said that the "essence" of the difference lies in *Dasein*'s hermeneutical capacity to be disclosive—aletheically disclosive. Unlike a stone, which is "worldless," and an animal, which is world-poor (*weltarm*), *Dasein* inhabits a world disclosively, exists disclosively, building a world for the human (*der Mensch ist weltbildend*).[27] Using our hands, we build a world that extends beyond their reach (*begreifen*), beyond the tangible, into the realm of the *Begriff,* the realm of intelligible sense, the realm of conceptual comprehension—and of truth. Thus Heidegger will assert that the hand comes into its ownmost essence (*west*) only in the movement toward truth, only, therefore, in its participation in the eventing of language: a double movement, hermeneutical in character, involving what hides and causes to leave its reserve (*Verbergung/Entbergung*).

In "What Are Poets For?" (final version, 1950), this being-disclosive, which for Heidegger is the ownmost (*eigenste*) distinction of the human being, receives further clarification, resuming an argument against Rilke that Heidegger had already formulated in the 1942–1943 lecture course on

Parmenides.[28] In the 1950 essay, sharply differentiating his understanding of the animal from Rilke's, Heidegger argues that even if, as Rilke believes, animals live more immediately, more openly than we do, live in the Open without reducing it to the manipulability of determinate objectivity, nevertheless whatever is unconcealed in this openness will not reveal itself to the animal in the "essentiality" of a hermeneutical experience—namely, *as* that which is unconcealed. Thus, animals are not "admitted" into the enigma of unconcealment. Thus, too, animals are deprived of hands because they do not live within the world of language. As Heidegger says in "The Origin of the Work of Art" (1950), "language alone brings what is, as something that is, into the Open for the first time. Where there is no language, as in the being of the stone, plant and animal, there is also no openness of what is . . . and what is not."[29] But there is language in our gestures. And let us not forget that the hand which brought writing into the world participated, through its writing, in bringing our world itself into being.

Heidegger neither says nor implies that a biological, evolutionary abyss separates human beings from animal beings: their biological, evolutionary kinship is indisputable. Yet he nevertheless insists that an abyss of "essence" separates the human hand from the animals' counterparts—paws, claws, talons. Even between the chimpanzee's "hands" and our hands there is, for him, an essential difference, since we are the only beings able to "use" our hands apophantically and hermeneutically to signify and disclose—and indeed, able not only to be conscious of the intentionality engaged in such use, but also to give an account of our gestures in language. For Heidegger, the essential difference comes down to the fact that, even if it has been compellingly demonstrated that the biological, evolutionary difference between animal beings and ourselves depends on the conjunction of numerous contingencies, it somehow remains inconceivable—as a necessary "a priori" truth—that the animals, such as they are, could ever acquire a "proper" language and hands we would ever recognize, or be willing to recognize, as capable of hermeneutic unconcealment. But why wouldn't it be sufficient to remark the differences and resemblances without making any abstract, "a priori" claims about what is of the essence and what not? It seems that, for Heidegger, it is not just a question of making explicit the prevailing "grammar" of our concepts. But what else could it be?

In his lecture course on Parmenides, devoted to the historiography and phenomenology of "truth," Heidegger gives a more elaborate statement of this argument from language, beginning with the Aristotelian proposition that the human is the living being who "has" speech, that being "whose being is determined by φύσις [the power to bring into unconcealment], emergence and self-opening":

> Man himself acts [*handelt*] through the hand [*Hand*]; for the hand is, to-gether with the word, the essential distinction of man. Only a being which, like man, "has" the word (μῦθος, λόγος), can and must "have" "the hand." ... *The hand exists as hand only where there is disclosure and concealment.* No animal has a hand, and a hand never originates from a paw or a claw or talon. Even the hand of one in desperation (it least of all) is never a talon, with which a person clutches wildly. The hand sprang forth [as such] only out of the word and together with the word. [Strictly speaking, therefore], the human does not "have" hands; rather, the hand holds the essence of the human [*die Hand hat das Wesen des Menschen inne*], because the word as the essential realm of the hand is the ground of the essence of the human. The word as what is inscribed and what appears to the regard is the written word, i.e., script. And the word as script is handwriting.[30]

The hand may be used for writing. This is, for Heidegger, a "proper" or "appropriate" use of the hand. Would it also be the *most* proper or appropriate? Heidegger calls to mind other uses of the hand, leaving such characterizations in question. Hands that are moved in greeting and thanking, saluting and waving, hands raised to take an oath or give a signal, hands that weave or chisel, hands that come together in prayer can also be "abused"—used to commit monstrous acts of murder.[31]

This abuse compels one to reflect on a question: Is the human hand separated from the prehensile organs of the animal "through the abyss of its being" (*durch einen Abgrund des Wesens*)? In "Geschlecht II," Derrida questions Heidegger's reinscription of the old metaphysical doctrine that an abyssal difference separates the human from the animal:

> Dogmatic in its form, this traditional statement presupposes an empiric or positive knowledge whose titles, proofs, and signs are never shown. Like most of those who ... speak of animality, Heidegger takes no account of a certain "zoological knowledge" ... concerning this so general and confused word "animality." He does not criticize it and does not even examine the sorts of presuppositions, metaphysical or otherwise, it can harbor. This nonknowing [is] raised to a tranquil knowing, then exhibited as essential propositions.[32]

Thus, for Derrida, Heidegger's comprehension of the hand is still framed within the very discourse of humanism out of which he insists one must break free. I am not persuaded that Heidegger's claims about the hand commit him to the entirety of traditional humanism, although they certainly commit him, as he freely acknowledges, to some version of humanism, if by that we simply mean a doctrine that insists on a crucial and irreducible ontological difference between animal beings and human beings—a difference in their relation to the presencing of being—without denying their indisputable evolutionary kinship. In light of this kinship, what would it mean to insist, as Heidegger does, on an essential difference between the human hand and the animal counterpart?

Although he does not propose an answer to this question, Heidegger wants to think of the hand in terms of what might be called its "vocation." Derrida uses this word "to recall that, in its destination (*Bestimmung*), the hand holds on to speaking." "This vocation," Derrida says, "is double, but gathered together or crossed in the same hand." [33] For the hand that receives can also give: can in fact give and receive in one and the same gesture. It can also yield: meaning at once giving up or handing over and also receiving or giving in to.

According to Heidegger, we must recognize that "the craft of the hand is richer than we commonly imagine [*meinen*]." Thus, for example:

> The hand not only grasps and catches [*greift und fängt nicht nur*], or pushes and pulls. The hand reaches and extends, receives and welcomes [*reicht und empfängt*]—and not just things: the hand extends itself, and receives its own welcome in the hand of the other. The hand holds [*hält*]. The hand bears [*trägt*]. The hand designs and signs, presumably because [as Hölderlin said] man is a sign.

In his commentary on this text, Derrida remarks, "This passage from the transitive gift, if such can be said, to the gift of what gives itself, which gives itself as being-able-to-give, which gives the gift, this passage from the hand that gives something to the hand that gives itself, is evidently decisive." [34] This becomes even more apparent, perhaps, as Heidegger's text continues: "Two hands fold into one [*falten sich*], a gesture [*Gebärde*] meant to carry man into the great oneness [*in die große Einfalt*]. The hand is all this, and this is the true handicraft [*das eigentliche Hand-Werk*]. Everything is rooted here that is commonly known as handicraft, and commonly we go no further" (*WHD*, 51/16). In his commentary on the first of these sentences, Derrida says that he is "not sure of comprehending" what is at stake for Heidegger in the play on *sich falten* and *Einfalt*: "whether it be a matter of prayer or of more common gestures." [35] But in any case, Derrida continues, "what matters most of all is that the hands can touch each other as such, in autoaffection, even at the touch of the other's hand in the gift of the hand": as when, for example, two people shake hands in greeting or confirming an agreement. (We will return to the question of autoaffection, two hands touching each other as such, in the chapters on Merleau-Ponty and Levinas.)

The hand is manifestly capable of many things, gestures and skills infinitely exceeding the capabilities of the animal: Commonly we go no further in thinking about the hand. But, for Heidegger, the absolutely decisive difference between human hands and the animal's prehensile organs shows itself (*zeichnet sich*) in the hands' gestures of touching and being touched—and in their ways of giving and receiving. The animal organ can of course take hold of something, can grasp something and let go of it; but it cannot possibly let the thing it touches be what it is "as such," that is, in its hermeneutical "essence." It can neither experience nor manifest any relation to the very "essence" of the being as such.[36] Thus, the animal's ways of giving and taking are fundamentally deprived of the disclosively signifying relation.

Although expressing the next step in his argument with questionable assurance, Heidegger asserts, "The hand's gestures [*Gebärden*] pass everywhere through language, in their most perfect purity precisely when man speaks by being silent." This passage through language is necessary, he says, for thinking. But if our gestures always pass through language, then "every motion [*Bewegung*] of the hand in every one of its works carries itself [*sich trägt*] through the element of thinking, everywhere a bearing of the hand that bears itself [*gebärdet sich*] in that element. All the work of the hand is rooted [*beruht*] in thinking. Therefore, thinking is man's simplest, and for that reason hardest, *Hand-Werk*, if it would be properly [*eigens*] accomplished." How are we to understand the proposition that the gestures of the hand are "rooted" in thinking? We must be careful not to interpret it in a way that reinscribes what Heidegger wants to say within the dualism of a metaphysical system that attributes "thinking" to an immaterial mental substance and would regard the gestures of the hand as the motions of a material substance separate from the mental. We must also be careful, therefore, to refrain from privileging a pure activity of thought; otherwise, we will not be able to recognize Heidegger's decisive departure from the ontological commitments at work in the historical forms of idealism.

If Heidegger is attempting here to say something radically different, then his words cannot be taken to mean that the gestures of the hand are steered by an act of thinking, just as a ship is steered by its pilot. This is how Plato and Descartes understand the matter, picturing the body to be moved by the soul's intentional acts. Nor can Heidegger's words mean what is commonly meant when one says of someone that she "thinks with her hands." For this grants the gesture a merely supplementary role, as when gesticulation is exceptionally expressive, accenting the pure thought that is moving into speech. If this were all that Heidegger meant, it would not be very significant; indeed, it would not need to be said. Thus, what Heidegger is saying calls for further thought. But how to say what needs to be said is, as he acutely realizes, extremely difficult.

Perhaps the hands' "rootedness" in thinking could be clarified by reference to experiences such as tying one's shoes and playing a musical instrument. Once one has learned how to tie one's shoes, thinking about doing it, when "thinking" has become an abstract, purely "intellectual" act, only makes the task more difficult. We tie our shoes most easily when we abandon what is commonly called "thinking" and let our hands do what they already "know" how to do perfectly well—as it were, καθ' αὑτό, on their own, from out of themselves. A great musician experiences playing the piano or the oboe in much the same way: the music, the musical knowledge, is immediately present "in" the hands, operative "in" and "from" the hands. Perhaps the historical significance of Heidegger's claim can be represented only when we abandon the pictures of "mind" and "body" that have dominated thought since Plato, and recognize that it could be through the hands themselves that thinking becomes "rooted," tangibly involved, in the interplay of the tangible and the intangible, that peculiar field of concealment and unconcealment as which being presences in opening the realm within which our hands are enabled to move.

But can we also twist free of the metaphysical determination of the difference between the animal deprived of hands and the animal, the human animal, favored with hands? Could we acknowledge a difference without insisting that it has a metaphysical origin and destination?

V. Critique: The Use of the Hand and the Will to Power

> I take this evanescence and lubricity of all objects, which lets them slip
> through our fingers then when we clutch hardest, to be the most
> unhandsome part of our condition.
>
> —Ralph Waldo Emerson, "Experience"[37]

Because of the decisive historical connection that Heidegger establishes
between the "pragmatics" of the hand and our ontology, the hand's complicity in the negation of being must be critically examined. Reflecting, in
Contributions to Philosophy, on what he regards as the nihilism that is increasingly overtaking our contemporary world, Heidegger posits the alternatives he thinks we are facing: Whether we will leave the will to power
(*Machtraum*) of metaphysics, which is completed in "machination"
(*Machenschaft*) and "total mobilization of resources" (*Ermächtigung*), or
whether we will remain in this "endless etcetera of what is most desolately
transitory [*endlosen Undsoweiter des ödesten Flüchtigsten*]."[38]

   In *Being and Time*, Heidegger argues against philosophies that take
truth to be determined solely by the correspondence between an assertion
and a state of affairs. For Heidegger, the possibility of such an attribution
essentially depends on a prior moment of disclosure, opening up a certain
field of significance and making the state of affairs in question accessible.
And if, as he suggests, the stare is the analogue, in vision, of the assertion
as understood by the discourse of truth he is disputing, we might likewise
consider violent grasping and clutching to be the analogue of such assertion in the use of the hand.

   In "The Turning," Heidegger calls our attention to "the injurious neglect of the thing" that is common in our time.[39] In "The Age of the
World Picture," where he connects this neglect to the character of contemporary technology, he registers an even stronger indictment, describing the gestures constitutive of this technology as an "assault," a violence
designed to order and dominate the object: "In truth, it is the coming to
presence of man that is now being ordered forth to lend a hand to the
coming to presence of technology [*dem Wesen der Technik an die Hand zu
gehen*]."[40] In modern technology the hand has increasingly served processes of objectification, processes that Heidegger calls *das Ge-stell* ("enframing"). In the world of the *Ge-stell*, all "things" are reduced to mere
"objects," their reduced being ordered within a realm of constant availability, total control, and efficient manipulation. Such a reduction by ob-

jectification constitutes a "certain loss of being" (*es geht das Seiende in gewissen Weise des Seins verlüstig*").[41]

In "The Origin of the Work of Art," Heidegger therefore asks us to consider whether "such an assault [*Überfall*] could perhaps be avoided—and how?" "Only," he suggests, "by granting the thing, as it were, a free field [*ein freies Feld*] to display its thingly character directly. Everything that might interpose itself between the thing and us in apprehending and talking about it must first be set aside. Only then do we yield ourselves [*überlassen wir uns*] to the unreified presence [*unverstellten Anwesen*] of the thing."[42] But can we accomplish this? What can our gestures accomplish, even if moved by the best of intentions, without the favor of a dispensation of presencing over which they must first learn to renounce all control? What can they accomplish, when even this act of renunciation can set in motion a willfulness of incalculable violence?

I would like to carry forward this critique by considering a darkly brooding poem by Rilke, "The Hand," written in 1921:

> Look at the little titmouse,
> astray in this room:
> twenty heartbeats long
> it lay within my hand.
> Human hand. One resolved to protect,
> unpossessing protect.
> But
> now on the window-sill
> free
> in its fear it remains
> estranged
> from itself and what surrounds it,
> the cosmos, unrecognizing.
> Ah, so confusing a hand is
> even when out to save.
> In the most helpful of hands
> there is death enough still
> and there has been money.[43]

The poet, who elsewhere wrote of "the merchant's hand,"[44] is here reminding us that the hand is a force for harm as well as for good. The *bewahrende Hand*,[45] the hand moved by care, the hand that offers protection without expecting anything in return, cannot banish from the world the brutal hand that brings injury and death. The poet's reference to money suggests that, in a profit-driven economy, hands all too often inflict pain and death. They are the instruments of economic injustice, which for Levinas as for Rilke, is symbolized with exceptional clarity by the metal gold.[46] But Heidegger, as was his wont, did not seize the opportunity here to develop his reflections into a material and dialectical critique, a move that could have shed much light on this problematic. (One could perhaps argue that Leibniz's "preestablished harmony" and Hegel's "cunning of Reason" are precursors of Adam Smith's "invisible hand," an ideological phantasm peculiar to the administrative rationality of modern economies.)

In his historical survey of the projection of the "thing" in philosophical constructions, Heidegger contends that "in the [Kantian] thing-concept . . . there is not so much an assault upon the thing as rather an inordinate attempt to bring it into the greatest possible proximity [*Unmittelbarkeit*] to us." In the Aristotelian interpretation, by contrast, the thing is put "at arm's length" from us (*völlig Leibe hält und zu weit weggestellt*).[47] That is, the thing is granted a certain auratic "respect," freeing it in its "thing-being" (*Dingsein*) from our domination (*Herrschaft*), letting it remain, so to speak, in itself: *auf sich beruhen lassen*.[48] This theoretical construction, Heidegger argues, reflects a way of using things that "is nothing passive, but a doing in the highest degree."[49] It reflects a *Gebrauch*, a using, that is neither a *verbrauchen*, a using up, nor a *mißbrauchen*, a misusing. The thing remains a thing; it is not reduced to the ontology of the object—to being an object for a subject.

The hand is normally capable of grasping and clutching. But, breaking away from the "pragmatic" paradigm that has been axiomatic within the entire history of philosophical thought, Heidegger insists that the essential and most proper being of the hand is to be determined not by its function as a bodily organ of grasping (*als ein leibliches Greiforgan*), nor even, in truth, by its function as an organ for the enactment of volition, but rather by its belonging to the *Es gibt*, the gift of being, as an asymmetrical giving that takes nothing in return.

The paradigm operative in Heidegger's claims about the hand is the "essential nature" of thinking itself, since thinking, as he understands it—in the light, namely, of the Greek concepts of *legein* and *noein*—is a kind of "handicraft," indeed "the finest [*ausgezeichnete*] of handicrafts" (*WHD*, 53/23). But thinking "is not a grasping [*Greifen*], neither the grasp [*Zugriff*] of what lies before us, nor an attack [*Angriff*] upon it. . . . In the high youth of its unfolding essence, thinking knows nothing of the grasping concept (*Begriff*)" (128/211). For the same reason, thinking is not essentially a matter of representation.

In lectures addressing the question "What is called thinking?" Heidegger thus finds himself reflecting on the "proper" use of the hands. Taking as his point of departure what it means to learn to think, he remarks, "To learn means to make everything we do answer to whatever essentials address themselves to us at a given time" (*WHD*, 49–50/14–15). The cabinetmaker's craft is then proposed "as an example" of an activity—in fact, a use of the hands—that fits this conception of learning. For the apprentice learning the trade,

> learning is not mere practice, to gain facility in the use of tools. Nor does he merely gather knowledge about the customary forms of the things he is to build. If he is to become a true cabinetmaker, he makes himself answer and respond above all to the different kinds of wood and to the shapes slumbering within the wood—to wood as it enters into man's dwelling with all the hidden riches of its nature.

Indeed, he says, "this relatedness to wood is what maintains the whole craft. Without that relatedness, the craft will never be anything but empty busywork, any occupation with it will be determined exclusively by business concerns." Still not free of a metaphysics that posits an ontological abyss between thinking and gesturing, he declares, "Thinking guides and sustains every gesture of the [apprentice's] hand" (*Das Denken leitet und trägt jede Gebärde der Hand*) (*WHD*, 53/23). By virtue of a mindful relatedness (*besinnendes Bezug*) to the wood—in a sensitive, tactful dialogue with it—the cabinetmaker, unlike the industrial worker, resists turning the activity into a "mere manipulation [*bloße Hantieren*] of tools" (53/23).

This leads Heidegger to ask about the machine. For in today's industrial world, the worker's hands are not free: they are the servants of our money-making machines. However, in spite of this critical observation, he explicitly takes issue with Hegel and Marx, turning away from the concerns of critical social theory: "Important as the economic, social, political, moral, and even religious questions may be which are being discussed in connection with technological labor or handicraft, none of them reach to the core of the matter" (*WHD*, 55/24). For what still needs to be thought, he maintains, is its ontology, the very essence of technology as such, which has "long been withdrawing": "the way in which anything that is under the dominion of technology has any being at all." In particular, what calls for thought is the unchallenged relation of technology to the will to power. But what is "most thought-provoking," he says, not averse to thinking of the tangibility of being, "is even closer to us than the most palpable closeness of our everyday handiwork [*das nächste Handgreifliche der gowöhnlichen Handgriffe*]—and yet it withdraws" (55/25).

Withdraws from our power to take its measure. Withdraws into a measure that we cannot possibly measure. And yet, as Hölderlin says in "The Titans," even useful things, things ready-to-hand, lay down, as conditions for their proper usefulness, reminders and hints of this intangible measure:

> For under the firm measure,
> The crude, too, is useful,
> That the pure may know itself.
>
> (*Denn unter dem Maaße,*
> *Das Rohen brauchet es auch,*
> *Damit das Reine sich kenne.*)

Heidegger quotes these lines in the eighth lecture, part two, of *What Is Called Thinking?* He then comments: "The crude is not an addition to the pure. Nor does the pure have need [*benötigt*] of the crude. But the crude must be there in order that the pure may become manifest to itself as the pure and thus as that which is other, and thus may have its own being." A being not reducible to our customary uses, or to the measures that fall within the reach and comprehension of our will to power.

In order to get a better handle on the pragmatic character of use in our time, Heidegger reverts to the pre-Socratics, guided into the enigmas of their thinking—as he so often was—by the poetic spirit of Hölderlin. Specifically, the question of the connection between measure and use draws Heidegger's thinking back to a saying by Parmenides: χρὴ τὸ λέγειν τε νοεῖν τ' ἐὸν ἔμμεναι. In a commonly accepted translation, it reads: "One should both say and think that being is" (quoted in *WHD*, 114/178). Attempting to measure up to the sublimity of this thought, Heidegger observes:

"To use" means, first, to let a thing be what it is and how it is [*etwas in dem belassen, was es ist und wie es ist*]. To let it be this way requires that the used thing be cared for in its essential nature [*in seinem Wesen gepflegt werde*]—we do so by responding [*entsprechen*] to the demands [*Ansprüchen*] which the used thing makes manifest [*von sich her Kund gibt*] in the given instance. (*WHD*, 168/191)

He adds:

Once we understand "using" in this sense, which is more natural to us [than relating use to the presencing of being], and in which using designates a human activity, we have already differentiated it from other modes of acting with which it is easily and readily confused and mixed up: from utilizing [*Benützen*], and from needing [*Benötigen*]. In common usage, however, χρή may mean those things as well.

In the third lecture of part two, Heidegger suggests: "The highest and really most lasting gift [*während Gabe*] given to us is always our essential nature, with which we are gifted [*begabt*] in such a way that we are what we are only through it. That is why we owe thanks for this endowment [*Mitgift*]" (*WHD*, 94/142). This elicits the question "How can we give thanks for this endowment?" "The supreme thanks," he says, could be given only in our thinking. Thinking must become a way of thanking. But, rooting his thought in the archaic historicity of the German language, in its ability to be *maßgebende*, a source of measure (91/139), he learns that the etymology of *Denken*, "thinking," draws it back to the claim of memory, of memory as the mindful giving of thanks.

This puts Heidegger in mind of a line in Hölderlin's poem "Mnemosyne": "we are a sign bereft of meaning." Heidegger proposes an interpretation of this claim: "Memory [*Gedächtnis*] is the gathering [*Versammlung*] and convergence of thought upon what everywhere demands to be thought about first of all: Memory is the gathering of recollection, thinking back [*des Andenkens*]. It safely keeps and keeps concealed within it [*birgt bei sich und verbirgt in sich*] that to which at each given time thought must be given before all else" (*WHD*, 7/11). What is it that calls so urgently for thought? What is it that thinking is called upon to recollect? "Thinking is thinking," he says, "only when it *recalls* in thought the ἐόν, . . . , and that is the duality of beings and being" (149/244). Immediately following this, Heidegger asks a question that will return us to the gestures of our hands and the distinctively modern ways that they commit themselves to use: "Can thinking take this gift into its hands [*in seinem Empfang*], that is, take it to heart, in order to entrust it in λέγειν, in the telling statement, to the original speech of language?" This understanding of thinking constitutes the discursive space within which Heidegger situates the fulcrum of his critique of modernity as the age of nihilism, when the will to power—and not the ἐόν, the presencing of being—has appropriated our gestures, giving them the law and measure that will motivate and direct them.

It is also within this space that Heidegger approaches a translation of Parmenides' word χρή, noting that it comes from χράω ("I handle"), χρῆσθαι ("to handle, have use for, and use"), and ἡ χείρ ("the hand"). Starting from this constellation of words, he attempts to get at the essential nature of using—and thus, also, at the essential nature of the human hand. In the etymological connection between χρή, meaning "need" or "necessity," and χείρ, the Greek word for "hand," one should realize that the hand both expresses and responds to need; although confined to the realm of necessity, the hand nevertheless manifests our freedom. "Using," he says, "does not mean the mere utilizing [*das bloße Benützen*], using up, exploiting [*Ab- und Aus-nützen*]. Utilization is only the degenerate and debauched form of use. When we handle [*handhaben*] a thing, for example, our hand must fit itself or measure up to [*anmessen*] the thing" (*WHD*, 114/187). "Use implies fitting [measured] response" (*Im Brauchen liegt das sich anmessende Entsprechen*). It calls for a responsiveness in the gesture, in the hand, that co-responds to the condition of the thing being used. Thus, "Proper use [*Das eigentliche Brauchen*] does not debase what is being used—on the contrary, use is determined and defined by leaving the thing used in its essential nature." "But," he adds, "leaving it that way does not mean carelessness, much less neglect. On the contrary: only proper use brings the thing to its essential nature and keeps it there. So understood, use itself is the summons [*Anspruch*] which demands that a thing be admitted [*eingelassen*] to its own essence and nature [*Wesen*], and that the use keep to it." In other words, "To use something is to let it enter into its essential nature, to keep it safe in its essence." (This should be understood in relation to the radical definition of hermeneutical phenomenology that Heidegger formulates in the introduction to *Being and Time*, viz., an approach to disclosiveness that lets the phenomenon show itself from out of itself. Such an understanding would, of course, confirm a deep continuity between his earlier and later thought.)

It follows from this interpretation of the Greek words—and of the cultural world in which the gestures of the hand moved—that "utilizing" and "needing," two common ways of translating the Greek, cannot carry us into that world. For the gestures that those words describe will always "fall short" of "proper use":

> Proper use is rarely manifest, and in general is not the business of mortals. Mortals are at best illumined by the radiance of use. The essential nature of use can never be adequately clarified by merely contrasting it with utilization and need. We speak of usage [*Brauch*] and custom [*Sitte*], of what we are used to. But even such usage is never of its own making. (*WHD*, 195/187)

Defending his hermeneutical translation, which he acknowledges to be an attempt at hearing Parmenides' words in keeping with their "highest" normative sense, Heidegger argues that, in translating χρή as "it is useful" (*es braucht*),

> we co-respond [*entsprechen*] to a meaning of χρή that echoes in the root word. Χράομαι means turning something to use by handling it [*ist das handhabende Verwenden*]—which has always been a turning to the thing in hand according to its nature, thus letting that nature become manifest by the handling [*das sich an das Gehandhabte immer so gewendet hat, daß es dessen Wesen entspricht und es so durch die Handhabung erscheinen läßt*]. (*WHD*, 118/195)

The user accordingly must let the used thing "enter into the property [*das Eigene*] of its own nature" and "preserve" (*verwahrt*) it there: "This admitting [*Einlassen*] and preserving [*Wahren*] is what distinguishes the using of which we are speaking here, but in no way exhausts its nature" (*WHD*, 119/196).

Directly opposing the will to power that determines how our gestures today make use of things, Heidegger brings out the teaching to be derived from Parmenides' saying: Using, thought in this way, is no longer, is never merely, the effect of man's doing. On the contrary, "all mortal doing belongs within the realm in which the χρή makes its appeal." Nothing could more radically, more uncompromisingly oppose the instrumental rationality that Heidegger takes to be determinative today of our gestures than the evocations of hands and use in this hermeneutical rendering of Parmenides. Although Heidegger had good reasons for his reluctance to acknowledge any normative implications in his account, it is difficult to avoid reading a far-reaching critique of modernity in the comparison he is unquestionably proposing between the use of the hands implied in Parmenides' thought and the uses of the hands that figure in Heidegger's descriptions of modernity. Could we accuse him, as some have accused Foucault, of "cryptonormativism"? However we answer, we must at least recognize that if, as Heidegger has insisted, the normativity of the ontological has been neglected, forgotten, and lost in its concealment, then the accusation must be directed not at Heidegger but at the nihilism of the modern world.

If, for Parmenides, there is a "proper" use of the hands, a "proper" measure by which our gestures should be moved, that measure would consist, according to Heidegger, in the mindfulness of our gestures—in their capacity to "let be." By contrast, the distinctive trait of our gestures in the modern world, according to Heidegger, is their will to power, a technologized "rationality" obliterating all awareness of the ontological dimension in which they move. Thus Heidegger remarks on the process of rationalization that reduces Parmenides' sense of the fitting measure to the terms of a "ratio": "But the original nature of λέγειν and νοεῖν disappears as *ratio*. As *ratio* assumes dominion, all relations are turned around, are upset" (*WHD*, 127/210). *Ratio* is, of course, a Latin term for "measure." Ontological reductionism was already taking hold in the Roman and medieval translations; the philosophical discourse of modernity only took over and reinforced the sway of an instrumental rationality—rationality as "ratiocination"—deepening and concealing its forgetfulness. Giving his argument further historical reference, Heidegger adds that the "explanation" (*Erklärung*) of Parmenides' words that we have inherited from the tradition "no longer enlightens [*klärt nicht mehr auf*]—it obfuscates." The Enlightenment, the *Aufklärung*, committing our gestures to the ratios and ratiocinations of an egoism that reduces the presencing of being to the structure of subject and object, the structure imposed by a modernity obsessed with power, "obscures [*verfinstert*] the essential origin [*Wesensherkunft*] of thinking." And therewith, accordingly, the ontological nature of our gestures and hands—the ontological claim on their use.

Heidegger's critical reference here to the Enlightenment suggests that one could usefully compare his critique with that of Adorno, who eventually turned the dialectic of history against the Enlightenment (having called upon that era's resources with far less reserve before the Holocaust). This comparison becomes especially appropriate in view of Rilke's deep influence on Heidegger: Rilke repeatedly called attention to the economic dimension of the technological transformation of the world, and accordingly provides the terms we need in order to connect Heidegger's critique of technology to Adorno's.

In a letter to Benjamin, Adorno describes the figure of the collector "as the one who liberates things from the curse of utility."[50] For Adorno, as for Heidegger,

> technology is making gestures [*Gesten*] precise and brutal, and with them, men. It expels from movements [*Gebärden*] all hesitation, deliberation, civility [*Zögern, Bedacht, Gestaltung*]. It subjects them to the implacable [*unversöhnlichen*], as it were ahistorical demands of objects. . . . The movements machines demand of their users already have the violent, hard-hitting, unresting jerkiness [*Mißhandlungen*] of Fascist maltreatment. Not least to blame for the withering [*Absterben*] of experience is the fact that things, under the law of pure functionality, assume a form that limits contact [*Umgang*] with them to mere operation [*auf bloße Handhabung beschränkt*].[51]

While it seems true that technology is dehumanizing us and making our gestures ill-mannered, tactless, even brutal, I think it is also true that we hastened to invent such technology—and adopted it eagerly, without anxiety, without hesitation—because our gestures had already lost some of their personal warmth, their care, and their humanity. With our technology we have created an "expressionless" world, which, as Adorno astutely remarks, "bears no traces [*keine Spur*] of the human hand": a world "without the mild, soothing, un-angular quality of things that have felt the touch of hands or their immediate implements" (*Dingen, an denen Hände oder deren unmittelbare Werkzeuge das ihre getan haben*). A world that is, moreover, "uncomforted and comfortless."[52] Whatever things in our world do bear the traces of our gestures, and thus modes of behavior, inscribed in them, they are, as Adorno puts it, accusatory "monuments" to our indifference, our carelessness, our diminished capacity for feeling— and to our reduction of the beauty in genuine freedom to the ugliness of an exercise in the will to power.[53] For, according to Adorno,

> whatever was once good and decent [*anständig*] in bourgeois values, independence, perseverance, forethought [*Vorausdenken*], circumspection [*Umsicht*], has been corrupted utterly. For while bourgeois forms of existence are truculently conserved, their economic pre-condition has fallen away. . . . The caring hand [*bewahrende Hand*] that even now tends the little garden as if it had not long since become a "lot," but fearfully wards off the unknown intruder, is already that which denies the political refugee asylum.[54]

Thus, the world instituted by the bourgeoisie becomes increasingly inhuman, *unmenschlich*, increasingly "spectral."[55] Resistance from subjective experience, which might otherwise testify to this condition, is discredited and weakened, since "anything that is not reified, that cannot be counted and measured, ceases to exist."[56]

In "Articles may not be exchanged," a note in *Minima Moralia* that anticipates Derrida's critique of our customary practice in the giving and receiving of gifts, Adorno laments the reduction of the exorbitant spirit of generosity in gift-giving to a calculated exchange of equivalents and discerns in this reduction the total triumph of the logic of identity. He remarks:

> We are forgetting how to give presents. . . . Instead we have charity, administered beneficence, the planned plastering-over of society's visible sores. In its organized operations there is no longer room for human impulses; indeed the gift is necessarily accompanied by humiliation through its distribution, its just allocation, in short through the treatment of the recipient as an object. . . . Real giving had its joy in imagining the joy of the receiver. It means choosing, expending time, going out of one's way, thinking of the other as a subject.[57]

Arguing for a time of nonsymmetry favoring the other, a notion with which Levinas would certainly concur, Adorno maintains that, even if we achieved a society of abundance and ended poverty, rendering charitable giving no longer necessary for the maintenance of social stability and political legitimacy, "the people who no longer gave would still be in need of giving." Adorno explains:

> In them wither the irreplaceable faculties which cannot flourish in the isolated cell of pure inwardness, but only in live contact with the warmth of things [*nur in Fühlung mit der Wärme der Dinge*]. . . . Every undistorted relationship, perhaps indeed the conciliation that is part of organic life itself, is a gift. He who through consequential logic becomes incapable of it, makes himself a thing and freezes.[58]

The final note in *Minima Moralia* returns to this question of contact, but here conceives it "from the standpoint of redemption."[59] "The only philosophy which can be responsibly practiced in the face of despair," he declares, "is the attempt to contemplate all things as they would present themselves from the standpoint of redemption." Thus, "Perspectives must be fashioned that displace and estrange the world, reveal it to be, with its rifts and crevices, as indigent and distorted as it will appear one day in the messianic light." Then, shifting from a rhetoric of vision to a rhetoric of sensibility, a rhetoric that brings out the redemptive responsibility to be borne by touch and tact, he asserts: "To gain such perspectives without velleity or violence, entirely from the felt contact with its objects—this alone is the task of thought" (*Ohne Willkür und Gewalt, ganz aus der Fühlung mit den Gegenständen heraus solche Perspektiven zu gewinnen, darauf allein kommt es dem Denken an*). Implicitly, Adorno here assigns to our capacity for felt contact a role in the bringing-forth of the truth hidden in the very nature of things—a historical and ultimately messianic "promise"[60] that the objects we handle contain and maintain, in spite of reifications that powerfully operate to suppress it. Knowledge of this redemptive truth, he says, must be "wrested [*abgetrozt*] from what is": but wrested from things by gestures no longer moved by a will to power, gestures that have renounced their "natural" violence.

Adorno's *Negative Dialectics*, a later work, again touches on the emancipatory potential in felt contact, reaffirming his earlier thought. He contends that "the commanding freedom of the subject intends in the object even that of which the object was deprived by objectification [*Zurüstung*]."[61] "What will not have its law prescribed for it by given facts transcends them even in the closest contact with the objects [*noch in der engsten Fühlung mit der Gegenständen*], and in repudiating a sacrosanct transcendence."[62] There is a certain rhythm and measure to be learned from felt contact with things. A redemptive truth that neither detached contemplation nor violent appropriation can retrieve.

Our excursus through Adorno brings to light intriguing parallels with Heidegger. Both thinkers formulate a critique of technology and its reifying "technologization" of the hand and its gestures. Both connect the current historical form of technology to nihilism, which they see as destructive to our very sense of the human—and as portending an unimaginable danger to our relationship with the natural world on which our existence depends. Both speak of a withering of experience, the spiritual emptiness of the subject, and a loss of meaningfulness, all of which degrade our sense of the moral and the corresponding sense of tact—our sense of what is situationally appropriate, a "knowledge" that is inscribed in the very flesh of our gestures.

The two philosophers do, however, differ significantly. If Heidegger connects nihilism to the ontological conditions imposed by the will to power, Adorno connects it to the historical form that egoism assumes with the ascent of the bourgeoisie and to the material conditions imposed by contemporary capitalism. Although Heidegger touches on the injustices of an exchange economy, the dangers of industrialization and mass consumption, and the commodification of subjectivity, his ontological diagnosis fails to get at the factors that Adorno considers to be fundamental. For Heidegger, the threat with which nihilism confronts us is ultimately ontological, consisting in the historical withdrawal and self-concealment of being—a process that is accelerating in the epoch of technology's planetary domination, imposing on subjectivity, at the moment of its greatest power, an objectification that denies the human will to power a spiritually meaningful lifeworld. For Adorno, the threat with which nihilism confronts us is ultimately psycho-sociological, consisting in the injustice and dehumanization incurred under modern capitalism and the economic class-structure that is at once its product and its engine of reproduction.

Despite these important differences, both philosophers experienced a certain ambivalence about tradition—for example, about our sense of tact in social relations and about the touch of our gestures in relation to natural objects and human artifacts. In both Heidegger and Adorno, one can hear a tone of lament, a painfully conscious nostalgia, for what we moderns have lost: in the technological skill of our gestures, a spirit of craftsmanship that once imbued them with care and respect for the materials and the processes of production. For both philosophers, craftsmanship is not only a way of bringing forth an artifact that protects the *being* of the object and grounds "subjectivity" in a meaningful material existence, but also a way of bringing forth those qualities of character and disposition (ἔθος) essential for the realization of our humanity. In *Minima Moralia*, Adorno remarks that "dwelling, in the proper sense, is now impossible."[63] Heidegger would have readily concurred with this melancholy judgment. Indeed, in his essay "Building Dwelling Thinking," he argues for essentially that same indictment. Neither Heidegger nor Adorno could forget the historically distinctive beauty and virtue—the sense of fitting measure—to be found in an economy still ruled by the spirit of craftsmanship embodied in thoughtful and carefully measured gestures, rhythms of tact and touch, as a way of living the ontology of the modern subject-object structure.

But their nostalgia never succumbed to the temptations of a regressive romanticism; it was always tempered by the realization that we cannot return to some original Paradise. What we must do, rather, is to see more clearly, through interpretation of a past that holds an unfulfilled dream we cannot forget, a present that we experience without understanding, and a future that we might think our way toward, in which we and our world would be different, be otherwise. Their effort to remember the spirit of craftsmanship, the tact and touch in which that spirit moved, was always intended to serve the ends of critique—a critique that would free us from a conviction of fate; free us, as Heidegger puts it so simply in "The Origin of the Work of Art," from our fateful "captivity in that which is." [64] Thus freed, we would be open to new historical possibilities. Possibilities that concern the ways we use our hands: possibilities belonging to a past that is still to come, possibilities—if we are ready—already close at hand. For "thinking is genuine activity, genuine taking a hand, if to take a hand means to lend a hand to . . . the coming to presence of Being" (*Denn das Denken ist das eigentliche Handeln, wenn Handeln heißt, dem Wesen des Seins an die Hand gehen*). [65] If we are to disrupt metaphysics, we must understand this to be a matter of thoughtful gestures, uses of the hand that, by virtue of their mindfulness (*Besinnung*), do actually lend a hand to a historically eventful presencing of being, breaking the grip of the present *Ge-stell*, which, like a magic spell, makes the temporality of our world seem petrified, fated to endless repetition.

But Heidegger insists that he

> chose the cabinetmaker's craft as our example, assuming that it would not occur to anybody that this choice indicated any expectation that the state of our planet could, in the foreseeable future, or indeed ever, be changed back into a rustic idyll. The cabinetmaker's craft was proposed as an example for our thinking [*Nachdenken*] because the common usage of the word 'craft' is restricted to human activities of that sort. (*WHD*, 54/23)

Adorno would no doubt have said something very similar about his own evocations of a past in which skilled manual labor—the work of the cabinetmaker, the wheelwright, the blacksmith, the mechanic—was a matter of pride, showing the carefulness of the hand's intimate dialogue with its tools and materials.

In *Negative Dialectics*, Adorno speaks of remorse and the need for philosophical thought to suggest possibilities for "restitution," ending a history of violence. Not even exempting Kant's critical theory of knowledge from his indictment, he writes (retracing Benjamin's description of the allegorical process): "While doing violence to the object of its syntheses, our thinking heeds a potential that waits in the object, unconsciously obeying the idea of making amends [*wiedergutzumachen*] to the fragments for what it has done to them; in philosophy, this unconscious tendency becomes conscious."[66] Heidegger would have little disagreement with this representation of the task that awaits philosophical thinking. His essay "The Origin of the Work of Art," in which he examines different historical conceptual constructions of the being of the thing—including the construction alluded to by Adorno in this passage—explicitly connects these philosophical theories to the problem of violence. At the same time, moreover, it directs our thinking toward the unconcealment of an epoch in which that ontological violence would be no more. Other essays by Heidegger—for example, "The Thing," "The Question Concerning Technology," and "The Age of the World Picture"—take us into the very heart of a thinking that, as Adorno puts it so eloquently, "heeds a potential that waits in the object."

VI. Fitting Measure

For Plato, the measure revealed itself to the mind in its most beautiful, most ideal dimensionality, a metaphysical measure manifesting rhythmic and harmonic qualities, and in relation to which the individual must learn to become attuned in his ethical life. Aristotle said: ζῷον λόγον ἐχον. That is: we are the living beings who have been granted the word—and the measure it brings. The Roman philosophers translated λόγος as *ratio*, thereby bringing out the connections they wanted to recognize. The measure to which the Romans gave thought was the measure appropriate for the citizen's participation in the civic life of the state, a measure constitutive of speech, the public and political use of reason. For the Romans, the λόγος is to be brought forth in an appropriately measured speech of reason. But it was only in the enigmatic pre-Socratics—in Parmenides and Heracleitus—that Heidegger would find some hints to direct him toward the measure in its ontological dimensionality.

If, however, as Merleau-Ponty observes,[67] our gestures bear and communicate meaning—so that there is always a certain "gestural meaning" immanent in speech—then to be endowed with λόγος must also mean that, as living beings, as animals, we always carry, informing our gestures, a vital sense of proper proportion, the right measure, befitting the intuitive wisdom of φρόνησις. What Plato and Aristotle say about theater bears out this implication regarding gesture.

But what is the measure, the ratio, by which our gestures should be moved? To what measure, what ratio, should they be attuned? In his *Theaetetus,* Plato submits Protagoras's claim—that the human is the measure—to anxious critical reflection. Protagoras said, "Of all things in customary use, man is the measure: of those things that are present, that they are, but of those that are not present, that they are not" (Πάντων χρημάτων μέτρον ἐστὶν ἄνθρωπος, τῶν μὲν ὄντων ὡς ἔστιν, τῶν δὲ μὴ ὄντων ὡς οὐκ ἔστιν). In "The Age of the World Picture," Heidegger offers a new interpretation of Protagoras's claim and argues against the standard interpretation, which, ignoring questions of historicity, reads into it an anthropocentric relativism that is distinctly modern. Thus he observes:

> This belongingness to what presences in the open fixes the boundaries between that which presences and that which absents itself. From out of these bounds *man receives and keeps safe* the measure of that which presences and that which absents itself. Through man's being limited to that which, at any particular time, is unconcealed, there is given to him the measure that always confines a self to this or that. Man does not . . . set forth the measure to which everything that is, in its being, must accommodate itself. Man . . . is μέτρον in that he accepts restriction [*Mäßigung*] to the horizon of what is and the insusceptibility to any decision [*Unentscheidbarkeit*] of the latter's presencing or absencing and to a like degree acknowledges the insusceptibility to decision of the visible aspect of that which endures as present.[68]

For, as Protagoras also says, "manifold is that which *prevents* the apprehending of whatever is as what it is, i.e., both the non-disclosedness of what is and the brevity of man's historical course" (βίος). This is obviously not an early formulation of our modern relativism; nor is it an expression of skepticism. Rather, as Heidegger contends, "the fundamental metaphysical position of Protagoras is only a narrowing down, but that means nonetheless a preserving, of the fundamental position of Heracleitus and Parmenides."[69] The "narrowing down" consists in the fact that, unlike his predecessors, Protagoras explicitly thinks the question of measure in terms of its significance for human life—thus, from that standpoint, that perspective. But by making the relation to that standpoint explicit, he opened up for philosophical thought the consequent possibility of a relativism never before imagined. Bringing out the irreducible difference that separates Protagoras's understanding of measure from that of modern philosophers, such as Descartes, Heidegger says: "It is one thing to preserve the horizon of unconcealment that is limited at any given time through the apprehending of what presences (man as *metron*). It is quite another to proceed into the unlimited sphere of possible objectification, through the reckoning up of the representable that is accessible to every man and binding for all."[70] In other words, for Protagoras, our ability to measure finite things is a gift that points toward a measure that we cannot measure; whereas for us moderns the world is taken to "found and confirm" us as "the authoritative measure for all standards of measure with which whatever can be accounted as true . . . is measured off and measured out."[71] The standard modern interpretation is justified to this extent: it is correct to read Protagoras as explicitly thinking about measure *from the standpoint of the human experience.* But what he says about that standpoint from that standpoint, far from confirming ἄνθρωπος as the authoritative measure, instead acknowledges our limited measure of power, our limited power to measure, bounded as we are and always will be by the cosmic law that lays down the interplay of concealment and unconcealment within which we can take the measure of the things we are involved with in our daily lives. Moreover, we have not been given the power of measure without having submitted to the overwhelming authority of a measure that metes out the temporal limits of our mortality. Recognition of our mortality is thus the inescapable condition to which we have submitted in receiving the power to measure. (This is the tragic wisdom that fate compels Hölderlin's Empedocles to learn.) In receiving measure, we ourselves are being measured. Do we measure up?

And it is surely not to be forgotten here that τὸ μέτρον has other ancient names, besides λόγος: most important to recall are νόμος, originally referring to the law that lays down boundaries, dividing the earth into propertied land; and Μοῖρα, referring to the deity who appears when mortals must make their most difficult, most extreme ethical decisions and who metes out to mortals their blessings and their curses in just proportions, marking the time and the place for the enigma of a singular destiny to reveal what is at stake.

But νόμος also implies the use of geometry, the necessity for measurements of the earth. Whenever we mortals measure the earth, however, we ourselves are being measured. Measured by the earth—measured in a reversal that overturns our anthropocentric relativism, our arrogance, revealing the delusion in all our claims of domination. When we measure and divide, build and dwell, the earth is always taking our measure. For the conditions laid down by the earth itself determine how we can measure and mark off divisions of land to create a world for ourselves. And there is eternal strife between earth and world: a strife that chronically reminds us not only of our finitude, the measure of our lives, and the vulnerability of the world we have built with the labor of our hands, but also of the generosity of the earth, whose wealth we are today gathering and enjoying beyond all reasonable measure. But when our brief life ends, the earth reclaims us, in accordance with its own inhuman laws, its own eternal geometry.

Our being is such that the preeminent question confronting us is, What is the meaning of our being? Our being is such that we also must confront the question, What is the appropriate measure of our being? What is the nature of the normativity, the νόμος, by which we should live and by which the ethical character of our lives should be measured and judged? As Heidegger says in the 1965 Zollikon seminars: "The relationship of the human being to what gives us measure is a fundamental relationship to what is. It belongs to the understanding of being itself."[72] That relationship accordingly calls on us to think of our own being in terms of the measure that constitutes and discloses it.

But everything seems to hinge on whether and, if so, how we are able, as Heidegger says in "The Turning," "to correspond at all to being and its claim" (*vermag, dem Sein und dessen Anspruch zu entsprechen*).[73] Whether and how we might measure up—for it is a question of corresponding to what gives us the measure. "In this regard [*Demgemäß*]," Heidegger asserts,

> modern man must first and above all find his way back into the full breadth of the space proper to his essence [*in die Weite seines Wesensraumes*]. That essential space of man's essential being receives the dimension [*empfängt seine ihn fügende Dimension*] that unites it to something beyond itself solely from out of the conjoining relation [*Ver-hältnis*] that is the way in which the safekeeping [*die Wahrnis*] of being itself is given to belong to the essence of man as the one who is needed and used by being [*als dem von ihm gebrauchten vereignet ist*]. Unless man first establishes himself beforehand in the space proper to his essence and there takes up his dwelling [*in seinem Wesensraum sich anbaut*], he will not be capable of anything essential within the destining now holding sway [*des jetzt waltenden Geschickes*].[74]

In this quotation, two passages are especially noteworthy. First is the term *die Weite*, "the breadth." As we shall see when we conclude this section with an examination of the Heracleitus lectures, this term, together with *das Offene*, "the open," is Heidegger's hermeneutical translation of μέτρον (fragment 30). Second is the passage about man's being "needed and used by being." This notion connects to the ontological significance that Heidegger draws out of Parmenides' word χρή, as we have already seen.

In "Poetically Man Dwells," one of Heidegger's most sustained meditations on measure, the philosopher turns to Hölderlin's later poetic works for provocations regarding the question of measure. Heidegger notes that, according to the poet, mortals span the dimension between earth and sky by measuring themselves against the heavenly ones. For Hölderlin, poetry is a form of measuring, a *Maß-nahme*. But the philosopher asks: What is it to measure? His answer: Measuring is "the taking of measure" (*das Nehmen des Maßes*).[75] In the experience of poetry, mortals enjoy the power to measure not because they have taken or seized that power but because they are above all compliant and receptive, listening well to the λόγος and willing to "receive the measure for the breadth of their being" (*das Maß für die Weite seines Wesens empfängt*).[76] Again we should note the way in which *die Weite* figures in Heidegger's interpretation of measure.

But if, for the poet, an unknown god, *dieser Unbekannte*, is the measure—or the giver of the measure, *das Maß-gebende*—the philosopher is compelled to ask: "how can that which by its very nature remains unknown ever become a measure"?[77] The poet, however, has an answer: According to Heidegger, the measure, god, appears through the sky "in a disclosing that lets us see what conceals itself, but lets us see it by not seeking to wrest what is concealed out of its concealedness, guarding the concealed in its self-concealment." This is a strange (*seltsames*) and perplexing (*verwirrend*) measure. Moreover, Heidegger continues, it is "certainly not a palpable stick or rod [*ein handgreifliches Stecken und Stab*], but in truth simpler to handle [*handhaben*] than they, provided our hands do not abruptly grasp [*greifen*] but are guided by gestures [*durch Gebärden geleitet sind*] befitting the measure [*die dem Maß entsprechen*] here to be taken." "This is done," he says, "by a taking [*in einem Nehmen*] which at no time clutches [*sich reißt*] at the standard [*Maß*]."[78] Here again, Heidegger insists that the measure-taking (*Maß-Nahme*) is not a clutching (*Zugriff*) at something that can be quantified or in any other way handled as if it were objectifiable. Thus, it is a question of a "poetic taking of measure" (*dichtendes Maß-Nahme*), "a letting-come [*Kommen-lassen*] of what has been meted out [*des Zu-Gemessenen*]."[79] But, according to the poet, in light of the extraordinary nature of the measure, such an attitude—we might think of it as an attitude of "reception"—requires a deep change of heart, so that, as Heidegger puts it, one would "turn to give heed to the measure" (*daß dieses sich an das Maß kehrt*) and be responsive to the appeal, the claim (*Anspruch*), of the measure.[80]

The ontological measure, ground of ontic measures, demands an *andenkende Hingabe*, a "thoughtful devotion"; but, according to Heidegger, this must be understood as an unconditional openness to the possibility of another dispensation (*Geschick*) of being. For this openness is the only possible normative "directive" that can come from *die Weite*. Moreover, the required "devotion" must be understood as a gesture of freedom that is at the same time an "active" appropriation *of* the measure and a "submissive" appropriation *by* it. For it is this metaphysically incomprehensible doubleness, this deconstruction of the metaphysical representation of agency, that constitutes the ontological character of reception.

Although an ontological measure may be present in our world, its "presence," which Hölderlin in his later years doubted, is like the afterimage of a flash of lightning: an ephemeral presence, leaving only a fading, intangible trace of its passage. It cannot be made hostage to the calculative, instrumental rationality that rules our world. And while that elusiveness is precisely the measure's authority, its poetic power, the elusiveness also means that the bearing of the measure, its concrete situational "relevance" or "application," can never be unproblematic—can never be decidable according to prior rules or procedures, nor, therefore, beyond the possibility of conflicting interpretations and judgments.

Nowhere is this problematic made clearer, perhaps, than in Heidegger's reflections on Parmenides and Heracleitus. So we cannot leave the question of fitting measure without submitting our thought to the measure that, in fragment 30, Heracleitus attempts to make visible in the sublime depth of its invisibility. Heidegger discusses this fragment in his 1943–44 lecture series published in the Heracleitus volume as "The Inception of Western Thinking" ("Der Anfang des abendländischen Denkens").[81] Fragment 30 says: πῦρ ἀείζωον, ἁπτόμενον μέτρα καὶ ἀποσβεννύμενον μέτρα. These enigmatic words, which refer to the uncreated nature of the cosmos, have often been translated as saying: "It was ever and is and shall be ever-living Fire, kindled in measure and quenched in measure."[82] In this short utterance, one word, occurring twice, stands out: μέτρον, commonly translated as "measure." As Heidegger notes, πῦρ, the word for fire, is written here together with the word for measure. "But what," he asks, "does 'measure' [*Maß*] mean here?" Can we get close to the sense of what Heracleitus understood by this word? And how are we to comprehend that what he is saying is said "according to measure"? For Heidegger, it is utterly impossible to measure this "measure" according to calculative procedures. It is not a *ratio*, a "standard," a *Zollstab*. The "essence" of μέτρον is, says Heidegger, "the wide [*die Weite*], the open [*das Offene*]": a measure the dimensionality of which *cannot* be measured, not only because it exceeds our capacity to measure and understand the measurable, but also because, like a spark shooting up from a blazing fire, it resists objectification, resists apprehension in the form of an object, resists all attempts to submit it to modern rationalization processes—processes that would reduce it to an instrumental function in the calculation of means and ends.

The measure that Heracleitus names is an-archic, withdrawing authority from all merely instrumental measures—but also from all measures that we, within our limited realm of life, might think to posit as absolute. Thus, it is a measure that compels us to confront our situations in an openness that lets *them* disclose the appropriate character—the appropriate measure—for our comportment. As befits the essence of the ontological measure, it grounds the possibility of ontic measures only by granting a certain "wisdom," the wisdom, namely, of our finitude, while withdrawing before our freedom, leaving us free to determine our actions—either with or without its guidance. But of course this also means that all claims to absolute normative authority on the part of our ontic measures are subject to delimitation and deconstruction within the freedom granted by the incommensurability of the ontological measure.

In Heidegger's lecture course on Parmenides, we find implicit support for this reading of μέτρον in Heracleitus. There, Heidegger writes that "without the open, which is how being itself comes to presence, being could be neither unconcealed nor concealed." But he hastens to add, immediately reminding us of the measure of our limits, "Man and he alone sees into the open—though without beholding it. Only the essential sight of authentic thinking beholds being itself." [83]

The measure that Heracleitus names is an "adornment" (*Zier*) of the cosmos, a measure beyond measure, sublime in its beauty. Sublime—if we may advert to a phrase in Wilhelm von Humboldt's essay "On the Imagination"—like "an abyss that grows all the deeper, the more one strains to fathom it." [84] It is the originary cosmos (*anfängliche Zier*) itself that is measure-giving (*Maß-gebende*); and the measure that it gives is the wide, the open, the full breadth of being in its interplay of concealment and unconcealment: a natural world, within which and by the grace of which what is (*ein Seiendes*) can forever come to presence, appearing as such. Thus it is a measure that summons us to maintain an openness, a wide-open attitude—toward the ontological possibility of the absolutely other—a measure directing us to submit our gestures to a discipline of letting-be, so that, no longer captive to what is, we would no longer impose a consolatory ontology, but would instead let the ontological possibilities of what is absolutely other come, in their own time, into presence.

How could our gestures be moved by this understanding of measure? How could our gestural ways of relating to the world—the way we handle and use things, the way we touch other living beings and are moved by the sympathy they evoke—maintain this sense of sublime measure, with which they are always already favored whether we recognize it or not? And could the most fitting measure also appear on the horizon of our lives as the vanishing reference-point for the question of how our gestures bear a sense of our mortality—bear a sense of this dispensation? The image that Heraclitus proposes for thought in fragment 30—the image of a fire that blazes up and in time dies out, an image representing the sublime "harmony" of φύσις—might be read allegorically as reminding us that all beings come into being, remain a while, and perish according to their nature. In terms of this reading, Heidegger would perhaps be saying that it is our finitude, our mortality in its cosmological significance, that has been given to our gestures as their most fitting measure: an intangible measure to be borne in the vigilance of a guardian awareness, in an *Aufmerksamkeit* and *Wächterschaft* carefully maintained by all our gestures.[85] A sublime measure reminding us to be measured in all of our gestures.

In *Contributions to Philosophy*, Heidegger adverts again and again to the thought that, as human beings, we must live "with *Da-sein* as [our] measure": *daseinsmäßig* is his word.[86] *Da-sein* is thus, for us, ineluctably measure-giving. But what is the measure that the *Da-sein* "within us" gives to us—or rather, passes on to us? According to the text, it is a summons to live our lives in a guardian awareness of *die Weite, das Offene*.

We of today live so far from this measure—absolute as it is in its normative claim for alterity—that it is difficult to imagine how we could live any farther. And yet, however far we may stray, seeming to lose touch with it in its "externality," Heidegger feels deeply that we nevertheless still bear within us, in a closeness that is also farthest from us, disavowed and alienated, a "preontological understanding of being." I would describe this "understanding" as the ontological attunement *standing under* us as the embodied normative claim in our *daseinsmäßig* relation to being—an experience that becomes, in consequence of its originary withdrawal, its originary repression, a bodily sustained memory lost to awareness but summoning us to remember and retrieve its claim, its gift of the most fitting measure. This is a measure that would draw us into the depth and breadth of its ontological dimensionality, compelling our acknowledgment of the openness to alterity that constitutes its normative claim.

This "preontological understanding of being" would best be read, I believe, as an innate predisposition through which our bodily nature, manifesting as the incarnation of *Da-sein*, receives and takes up the measure that befits our ownmost humanity. Our humanity, however, as Heidegger's "Letter on Humanism" makes clear, must no longer be conceptualized within the discursive configurations of humanism. Nor, *a fortiori*, would it be wise to think of it in naturalistic or mechanistic terms—as "the blind impress all our behavings bear," to borrow Richard Rorty's words.[87] Instead, we must ultimately conceive of our humanity as measured by its openness to the untimely eventuality of another way of being.

In his "Schmargendorf Diary," with words reminiscent of Adorno's reference to our need for "live contact with the warmth of things,"[88] Rainer Maria Rilke recorded thoughts that bring us into the very heart of the sensibility called upon to prepare us for this different experience of presencing:

> Why say what *is*? Why afflict the things with their meaning? I can imagine only a longing that with continual wandering traverses the world. All things are so ready to host for a short time our many and often confused thoughts and desires.—I want to rest for one night in each thing when by day I have gone with my doings through the other things.—I want to sleep one time beside each thing, grow drowsy from its warmth, on its breathing dream up and down, sense in all my limbs its dear relaxed naked being-near and become strong through the scent of its sleep and then in the morning, early, before it wakes, ahead of all farewells, pass on, pass on.[89]

VI. Hermeneutical Gestures

In his 1943–44 lecture course on Parmenides, Heidegger tells how the deity Aletheia, welcoming the mortal traveler, "clasps his hand." Heidegger uses this lovely scene to call attention to the aletheic, or disclosive, character of the hand, which, "like the word, safeguards the claim [*Bezug*] of being on man, and only thereby the relation [*Verhältnis*] of man to beings."[90] It is in the hand's ability—its *Geschicklichkeit*—to be a destinally attuned (*schickliches*) medium for disclosiveness that the essence of human freedom is to be discerned. Thus, in "The Question Concerning Technology," Heidegger writes:

> The essence of freedom is *originally* not connected with the will [*Willen*] or even with the causality of human willing. . . . It is to the happening of revealing [*Geschehnis des Entbergens*], i.e., of truth [understood as "aletheia"], that freedom stands in the closest and most intimate kinship. . . . All revealing comes out of the open [*aus dem Freien*], goes into the open [*ins Freie*], and brings into the open. . . . Freedom is that which conceals in a way that opens to light.[91]

According to this conception of freedom, most of our gestures—if not all—are not yet moving in freedom, bound as they are to the ontologically "forgetful" structure of subject and object.

In "The Anaximander Fragment," Heidegger asserts that the human is "that present being [*derjenige Anwesende*] which . . . lets what is present as such become present in unconcealment [*in der Unverborgenheit wesen läßt*]."[92] In keeping with the principal argument of *Being and Time*, chapters 5 and 6, what this implies with regard to our gestures is that, while they can serve to indicate or signify a truth, their more essential nature consists in their capacity for disclosiveness. This is a question not only of their ποίησις, but also of their ἀλήθεια, their capacity to bring something forth into unconcealment. This capacity is "hermeneutically phenomenological" in the precise and most demanding sense that Heidegger formulates in the introduction to *Being and Time*: here, radically overturning Husserl's transcendental idealism, the capacity becomes instead a question of φαίνεσθαι, letting something show itself from out of itself.

Just as "apophantic" questions about the correctness of our assertions depend on, and derive from, the prior unconcealment of a field of discursive meaningfulness that orients the inquiry, so the gestures that signify depend on, and derive from, the disclosiveness of gestures of a more originary, hermeneutical nature that open and lay out a prior motility-field of potential gestural trajectories within which the meaningfulness, the very intelligibility, of our signifying acts can be understood. Pointing with a finger can be either a hermeneutic or an apophantic λέγειν, either bringing forth—

gathering and laying out—an ontological field of intelligibility for possible gestures of signification, or bringing forth into the light of ontic presence something of interest posited within that field of recognition.

Discussing the ostensive gesture, Jacques Lacan formulates the argument for these two dimensions in a way that nicely parallels Heidegger's argument for the crucial difference between, on the one hand, *aletheia*, the ontological event of unconcealment, opening-up, gathering, and laying-down a field of semantic intelligibility, and, on the other hand, the ontic truth-claim, the very possibility of which depends on that prior moment. According to Lacan, "There is only one gesture, known since Saint Augustine, which corresponds to nomination: that of the index-finger which shows, but in itself this gesture is not even sufficient to designate what is named in the object indicated."[93] That is because the gesture of pointing requires the opening, or clearing, of a context of referential intelligibility. Without that, the gesture's communication is fated to fail. For "no signification can be sustained other than by reference to another signification," and consequently it requires a "whole field" of signification.[94]

But do we know what our gestures are capable of in their hermeneutic role? Perhaps they open our world to ciphers that would intimate the presencing of ontological possibilities as yet unrecognizable in their absolute being-otherwise. It is conceivable that a time could come when our demonstrative finger-pointing, instead of imposing determinate reference, as happens during our present epoch of *das Ge-stell*, could become capable of an extraordinary hospitality, welcoming a gathering of earth and sky, mortals and gods, and making for it, there where we are pointing, a fitting place, a clearing, prepared by the hermeneutical memory of the gesture.[95] But of course *that* gesture could take place only in the time, if it ever should come, of another *Ereignis*, another ontological dispensation.

In the meantime, it would be wise to remember some lines from Rilke's *Sonnets to Orpheus*:

> *We*, with words and finger-pointings [*Fingerzeigen*],
> gradually make the world our own,
> perhaps its weakest, most precarious part.[96]

In the lectures assembled under the title *What Is Called Thinking?*, Heidegger turns his thinking toward this λέγειν, and toward its relation to νοεῖν:

Λέγειν and νοεῖν, both by virtue of their conjunction [*Gefüge*], achieve what later, and only for a short time, is specifically called ἀληθεύειν: to disclose and protect in disclosure what is unconcealed. The veiled nature of λέγειν and νοεῖν lies in this, that they correspond [*entsprechen*] to the unconcealed and its unconcealedness. Here we receive an intimation of how χρή, which governs the conjunction of λέγειν and νοεῖν, is expressed through ἀλήθεια. (*WHD*, 126/209–10)

For us to be appropriately *mindful* of being and appropriately *say* that being is, it is necessary that this "mindfulness" not be reduced to a subjective act of the rational intellect and that the "truth-content" said by the saying not be reduced to a question of mere correctness. What is involved is an anamnestic experience of unconcealment—an unconcealment through which being would nevertheless be allowed to withdraw into the depths of its self-concealment.

Fragment 50, attributed to Heracleitus, together with Heidegger's commentary on it, will enable us to pursue somewhat further our argument concerning the ontological significance of hermeneutical gestures.[97] Fragment 50 reads as follows:

Οὐκ ἐμοῦ ἀλλὰ τοῦ Λόγου ἀκούσαντας
ὁμολογεῖν σοφόν ἐστιν ῞Εν Πάντα.

This is a difficult saying to translate. But for the time being we may perhaps read it as saying: "When you have listened not to me but to the *Logos*, you receive the wisdom that comes from being appropriately attuned, for everything is One." Now, what I want to give thought to here is this ὁμολογεῖν, this "attunement" or "correspondence," this *Entsprechung*. Can it be thought as telling us something of fateful importance for the λέγειν (i.e., the articulative-disclosive capacity) of our gestures? For the *character* of our gestures? And about their appropriation by the measure that is laid down as most fitting, most appropriate for them? Since our gestures cannot be understood apart from the *logos* that moves them, it would be wise—if Heracleitus is right—to ponder these questions, for they are asking about the attunement of our gestures to and by the *logos*—asking about our ability to co-respond.

About this ὁμολογεῖν, Heidegger comments: "῾Ομολογεῖν occurs when the hearing of mortals has become proper hearing. When such a thing happens, something destinal [*geschicklich*] comes to pass."[98] But, since our gestures are also manifestations of λέγειν, we can and indeed must give thought to *their* essential "propriety": the nature of *their* ὁμολογεῖν. Later in the same essay, Heidegger writes, "Mortals, whose essence remains appropriated [*vereignet*] in [by] ὁμολογεῖν, are destinal [*geschicklich*] when they measure [*ermessen*] the Λόγος as the ἕν πάντα and submit themselves to its measurement [*seiner Zumessung gemäß werden*]."[99] And, he adds, "'Ομολογεῖν dispatches itself without presumption into the measuring of the Λόγος." This, he thinks, is why, in fragment B43, Heracleitus says: Ὕβριν χρὴ σβεννύναι μᾶλλον ἢ πυρκαιήν. ("Measureless pride [*Vermessenheit*] needs to be extinguished sooner than a raging fire"). As Heidegger puts this counsel in other words: "Before you play with fire, whether it be to kindle or extinguish it, put out first the flames of presumption [*Vermessenheit*], which overestimates itself [*sich vermißt*] and takes poor measure [*in der Maßnahme versieht*], because it forgets the essence of Λέγειν."

Now, if our gestures are forms of λέγειν, and if this word in Heracleitus is taken to mean, as Heidegger proposes, "the laying that gathers," then we need to think what the character of our gestures would be if, as layings-that-gather, they were to be measured by the way in which, recollecting the Λέγειν of the Λόγος, they were appropriated in (by) the ὁμολογεῖν. What we are asking about is, as Heidegger would put it, "a certain kind of comportment [*Verhalten*]," namely:

> That which maintains itself [*sich hält*] in the abode [*Aufenthalt*] of mortals. This abiding holds to what the primordial Laying-that-gathers [*die lesende Lege*] lets lie before us, which in each case *already* lies before us. . . . Because it is appropriate [*ein Schickliches*], such comportment becomes skillful [*geschickt*]. . . . In this way, we hit upon the genuine meaning of σοφόν, which we translate as "destined" [*"geschicklich"*].[100]

With the ὁμολογεῖν as their destinal measure, measure of what is most befitting, our gestures would need to *become* the λέγειν, the laying-that-gathers, which, by grace of their preontological relation to being, they always already are—and are accordingly destined to be. This means, first of all, that our gestures must, by virtue of a certain recollection or "anamnesis," get in touch with our preontological experience of being, a corporeal memory and felt sense of being that they carry within them—as if their originary appropriation by the λέγειν of the Λόγος had somehow been inscribed in their very flesh.

Accomplishing this "anamnesis," however, is extremely difficult in our present time. Our epoch, as the epoch of *das Gestell,* draws us away from our preontological experience of (or, say, our participation in, our μέθεξις in) being, draws us away from its law, its measure, its Νόμος, into the temptations of forgetfulness and, finally, into the nihilism of the will to power.[101] To defend against an unbearable distress, an inconsolable loss we hardly understand, we attempt to repress or deny our experience of the "loss of being," and we disavow our corporeal memory, our power of recollection kept in reserve by the very nature of the flesh—adopting a metaphysics that denies even the conceptual intelligibility of such a corporeal memory. There is also, however, another motivation driving this metaphysical negation of corporeal memory—and its neglect, thereby, of our preontological experience of being—namely, the ego's realization that its will to power can neither completely suppress nor completely master this experience and the ontological claim to which it exposes us.

For Heidegger, this claim, registered by our preontological experience of being, constitutes our historical task. Yet he conveys only the most obscure sense that our only hope in this age of nihilism is to solicit the corporeal memory borne by our gestures, retrieving from the depths of originary forgetfulness some trace of our preontological experience of being, bringing it into the understanding of our guardian awareness, and letting that understanding bestir us deeply, through our gestures. (We could perhaps recall that preontological experience by drawing on Aristotle's notion of the *arkhē tēs kinēseōs.*) The recognition of this preontological experience *as* a corporeal memory was something for which Heidegger, as he was the first the acknowledge, was not well prepared, and which therefore could appear within his thought only in the form of an unsettling *Vorhabe* or *Vorbegriff,* a merely formal indication. Thus, as we pursue the logic of Heidegger's thinking beyond the point where he has left us, we must try to elicit the philosophical significance of gestures that are gathered by recollection, by "Mnemosyne,"[102] into the ontological dimension (*die Weite, das Offene*) of their deepest nature. Such gestures move, or are moved, as follows:

1. They hermeneutically unconceal the operation of an *originary* Laying-that-gathers, *a more primordial nomological field,* laying down and gathering the ontologically normative conditions of possibility for the motility of our gestures.

2. They hermeneutically disclose themselves to be *themselves* (becoming) a laying-that-gathers, that is, an ontic laying-that-gathers.

3. They enact a *mimesis* whereby they hermeneutically disclose themselves to be *moved* by their obedient and skillful (*geschickt*) attunement to this more originary, more primordial Laying-that-gathers.

4. By virtue of this *mimesis*, they hermeneutically disclose themselves to be *dependent* on their attunement to the conditions of that originary Laying-that-gathers.

What does it mean, in terms of our gestures, to say, with Heidegger, that human being "is grounded in the opening of the being of entities"?[103] Perhaps it means that our gestures are grounded in—take place in—the *Ereignis*, the epochal opening that grants a *Zeit-Raum*, a field of possible movements and orientations. For, according to Heidegger's *Contributions to Philosophy*, the *Da-* of *Dasein* means "the clearing [*Lichtung*] of being itself, whose openness first of all opens up the space for every possible here and yonder and for arranging beings in historical work and deed."[104] *Dasein* is thus a disclosive being-there that can act through our gestures. And through these disclosive, hermeneutical gestures, it can become manifest *that and how* being *is*, that is to say, presences as, the clearing of a space-time in which beings can emerge in their concrete historical forms.

Gestures that move or are moved in accordance with the above four conditions would measure up to the ὁμολογεῖν. Its normativity would appropriate them for appropriately tactful enactments of ontological disclosiveness, and let being be made visible and palpable in its sensible presencing, its ἀληθεύειν, as the originary, primordial, most elemental Laying-that-gathers. Thus, in *What Is Called Thinking?*, Heidegger concludes his sequence of lectures by recalling the gift of the ἐον (that there are beings) and asking, "Can thinking take this gift into its hands, that is, take it to heart, in order to entrust it in λέγειν, in the telling statement, to the original speech of language?" Can thinking take this gift into its hands? Perhaps it could, but only if thinking can twist free of the historical grip of a metaphysics that denies us the very possibility of a corporeal memory and is unable to conceive a gesture of thinking that is not merely "with the hands," as if the hands were just an interpretative accompaniment of thought, or merely "by the hands" as if they were just a contingent instrument of thought. The hands are, as Merleau-Ponty says, with words coming after Heidegger, "an ontological organ."[105]

VII. *Gelassenheit*: Tactfully Yielding

If our gestures were to correspond appropriately to their ontological appropriation, they would need to relate to the being of the beings we touch and handle with a tactfulness that leaves their being intact, while also letting their transience, their perishability, and their intangible relation to nothingness become manifest. Such tactfulness is a question of "yielding," a word that is especially fitting because of its semantic duality. "Yielding" can refer both to an "active" gesture of giving, or handing over and, with equal sense, to a "passive" gesture of giving in, allowing-to-come, and thus receiving. In later years, however, Heidegger tried to think this ontological tactfulness in terms of *Gelassenheit*, "releasement" or "letting-go," a comportment characterized by *Verhaltenheit*, reserve and restraint, appropriately measured gestures.[106] Such tactfulness does not involve a renunciation of the will, for that could only be an intensification of willfulness, the will to power in the form of self-mastery. Nor is it mere passivity. Rather, it involves a certain "caesura," a certain "suspension" or "neutralization" of the will, made possible by our openness, the level of our guardian awareness, our *Wächterschaft der Wahrheit*. We might call it, for want of a better term, "non-willing."

Now, as ontic gestures, letting-go and letting-be would not always be the right comportment. For example, letting go as a way of rescuing someone who is drowning or as a way of relating to a thief one could easily seize would certainly not be meritorious action. It is therefore absolutely essential to differentiate an ontological from an ontic interpretation of releasement. Heidegger's concept of *Gelassenheit* is often accused of overcorrecting his earlier concept of *Entschlossenheit*, advocating inaction instead of resolute decisiveness, and thus even, in effect, tolerating what is evil. But this accusation mistakes an *ontological* attitude for an ontic one. Moreover, it fails to realize that *Gelassenheit* is actually a rewriting of *Entschlossenheit*, for this latter term never meant, as its critics charged, an arbitrary resolve of the will; rather, it means a resolute commitment to openness.

As referring to an *ontic* mode of comportment, an *ontic* gesture, releasement *may or may not* be fitting, *may or may not* be appropriate. But the situation is radically different when releasement, non-willing is understood as referring to the ontological dimension of comportment. For then releasement concerns our capacity for disclosiveness, our openness-to-being, as the very condition (in Kantian terms, the transcendental condition) for the possibility of *ontically appropriate* gestures. Releasement thus understood is an attitude or attunement that, precisely by virtue of its reserve, its restraint, its neutralization of the will to power, becomes *disclosive* of the situation in a way that makes gestures of *situationally appropriate* willing possible—and actually more feasible. In this way, *ontological Gelassenheit* discloses our situation as a referential field within which reflective mediations can orient us in advance of action; in this way, it discloses possibilities for appropriately measured deeds, actions, gestures— *praxis* guided by *phronesis*—in the *ontic* realm of life.

But how is this neutralization or suspension to come about? How are we, in effect, to will—but otherwise than we now do? How is non-willing to be achieved without another exercise of the will? This is a difficult question, a seeming paradox for which Heidegger, in spite of much thought, never finds a satisfactory answer.[107] But perhaps an example from the realm of touch could give us some direction here. Suppose one is presented with a fabric of exceptional softness and delicacy. If one applies a forceful touch of great pressure instead of handling it lightly and gently— as in a caress—the fabric's soft texture cannot come forth; our hands will not bring out its "true" quality. As Heidegger points out, "there must always be preservation of self-concealing."[108] But if one caresses the fabric too lightly, one will likewise have no experience of the texture. The pressure of one's touch must have the right measure: neither too much nor too little.

A similar point is expressed by Mallarmé's beautiful phrase, "the absent of all bouquets," indicating in terms of scents the originary absence, the self-concealment, at the very heart of presence.[109] In the summer, one is treated to many subtly fragrant scents. But as soon as one attempts to capture them, approaching the object and sniffing intensely to hold on to the fragrance, one is inevitably disappointed: the fragrance withdraws itself and vanishes, refusing to yield its delicate and ephemeral pleasures. Fragrances are intricate and subtle. They cannot be mastered, seized, fixated, or made into stable presences. They give themselves only to those who are truly open to receiving them and letting them go, letting them withdraw from presence. Thus, ironically, the more intense the will, the more willful the effort to objectify, the greater the closure. The object will object! In the dialectic of subject and object set in motion by the will to power, the fragrance either vanishes into thin air or intensifies to such a degree that it becomes disagreeable, compelled in response to become repellent.

We moderns cannot easily acknowledge the unapproachable inner life of nature—a nature upon which our modern world has imposed a will to power that can only cause it to wither and die, as Kant's *Critique of Judgment* warned. To the extent that human nature, and consequently the nature of our embodiment, will have been sentenced to endure this same fate, the originary gift of a preontological experience, its traces preserved as a memory buried in the flesh, will remain threatened with endless obliteration.

Even though, as I said, Heidegger never attained a satisfying philosophical elucidation of *Gelassenheit*, it would be useful at this point to follow his suggestion of taking a "step back" (*Schritt zurück*).[110] But the step back we will be taking here is not one that he himself takes—nor is it one that he even explicitly recognizes. For in our step back, we will be returning—by way of recollection—to a felt sense of the primordial attunement (*Grundstimmung*) that is constitutive of our body's preontological and proto-moral experience of being. That is to say, it is similar to but not the same as a "step back" toward something akin to a transcendental condition for the possibility of action, a condition of neutrality and thus of a disclosive openness to being that prepares one for appropriately measured gestures. Why "step back" in this particular direction? Since the experience of being toward which we will be moving belongs to the most primordial dimension of our bodily nature, it enters social history with a dispensation, a predisposition, that is not and cannot be totally corrupted by the nihilism of our time.[111] This elemental attunement, a yielding of the will functioning at the very heart of the will, is not and cannot be under the sway of the *Gestell*, the universal imposition of an order that makes everything that presences ready-to-hand. This originary experience of being has been suppressed, concealed, forgotten; and as such, it can manifest, as Nietzsche understood so well, only in a multitude of distortions and disguises, symptoms of disavowed suffering, defensiveness, and aggression. Thus the return to this preontological experience, this attunement, needs to take place through an arduous process of recollection, or "anamnesis." I am suggesting that this recollection must be understood as the return to a *corporeal memory* of the ontological—a return taking us into the uncanny normativity of the open, there "where," as Rilke puts it, "the law touches us [*uns anrührt*]."[112]

Thus, to the extent that our gestures let themselves be guided by this recollection of their preontological attunement, getting "from being itself the assignment of those directives that must become law and rule for human beings," as Heidegger says in his "Letter on Humanism," to this extent it would seem that our gestures could perhaps begin to learn the strange "ethos" of non-willing.[113] In the next passage from the "Letter on Humanism," Heidegger points out that "in Greek, to assign is νέμειν. Νόμος is not only law but more originally the assignment contained in the dispensation of being." "Only this assignment," he says,

> is capable of enjoining human beings into being. Only such enjoining is capable of supporting and obligating. Otherwise, all law remains merely something fabricated by human reason. More essential than instituting rules is that human beings find their way [back] to their abode [*Aufenthalt*] in the truth of being. This abode first yields the experience of something we can hold on to [*halten*]. The truth of being offers a hold for all conduct [*Verhalten*].

In regard to this "hold," he observes: "'Hold' in our language means protective heed." Making contact with the preontological dimension of our existence, and thus with the "originary ethics" into which it casts us, we might begin to receive some hints concerning the most appropriate measure for gestures of an ethical life no longer ruled by the will to power, an ethical life that would realize its freedom as "subject to the claim that presencing makes."[114]

In a letter included in his "Schmargendorf Diary," Rilke reflects on the character of hands and evokes their passage from the will to power to releasement. His eloquent words, akin both in spirit and in substance to Emerson's words in "Experience," are worth reading here:

> For in our gazing lies our truest acquiring. Would to God our hands were as our eyes are: so ready in grasping, so bright in holding, so carefree in letting all things go; then we could become truly rich. But we do not become rich by having something dwell in our hands and wither there: everything is meant to stream through their grip as through the festive gate of entrance and homecoming. Our hands are not meant to be coffins; rather beds, in which the things engage in twilight slumber and accomplish many a dream, out of whose darkness their fondest secrecies speak. But the things are meant to wander on beyond our hands, sturdy and strong, and we are meant to retain nothing of them but the courageous morning song that floats and shimmers behind their fading steps. For possession is poverty and worry; having possessed is the only unconcerned possessing.[115]

VIII. Tangible/Intangible

> Come, and do not touch me, but let me find the sacred tomb by
> myself, where it is fated for this man to be hidden in this earth.
>   —Sophocles, *Oedipus at Colonus*, ll. 1544–46

Having survived the ravages of time, two ancient words attributed to
Heracleitus, words that resist efforts to transfer them from the language
of their world into a language that can speak in our own world, come
to mind as provocations for the reflections pursued in this section: ἀγχιβασίην, fragment 122, meaning "approximation," "nearing," or "unending approach," and ἅπτεται, fragment 26, meaning "touch on" or "touch
without touching," but also "kindle."[116]

Attempting, in *Being and Time*, to break away from the metaphysical
obsessions of Cartesianism—especially its subject-object structure, its
inner-outer structure, and its consequent picture of the human body,
Heidegger maintains:

> When Dasein directs itself toward something and grasps it, it does not some-
> how first [need to] break out of an inner sphere in which it has been proxi-
> mally encapsulated; but its primary kind of being is such that it is always
> [already] "outside" alongside the entities which it encounters. . . . And fur-
> thermore, the perceiving [*Vernehmen*] of what is known is not a process of re-
> turning with one's booty to the "cabinet" of consciousness after one has gone
> out and grasped it.[117]

This phenomenological argument is resumed in "Building Dwelling
Thinking," where Heidegger observes:

> Spaces open up by the fact that they are let into the dwelling of man. To say
> that mortals *are* is to say that *in dwelling* they persist through spaces by virtue
> of their stay among things and locations. And only because mortals pervade,
> persist through, spaces by their very nature are they able to go through spaces.
> But in going through spaces, we do not give up our standing in them. Rather,
> we always go through spaces in such a way that we already experience them by
> staying constantly with near and remote locations and things.[118]

Thus, he says, "when I go toward the door of the lecture hall, I am already
there, and I could not go to it at all if I were not such that I am there. I
am never here only, as this encapsulated body [*abgekapselte Leib*]; rather,
I am there, that is, I already pervade the room, and only thus can I go

through it." The same, *mutatis mutandis*, may also be said of our sensory experience and perception. When I look at something located at the far end of this room, I am already "in touch" with it—already, in a sense, "touching" it. In consequence, as Merleau-Ponty observes,

> One can see the hardness and brittleness of the glass, and when, with a tin-kling sound, it breaks, this sound is conveyed by the visible glass. One can see the springiness of steel, the ductility of red-hot steel, the hardness of a plane blade, the softness of shavings. . . . [Similarly,] the form of a fold in linen or cotton shows us the resilience or dryness of the fiber, the coldness or warmth of the material.[119]

For, as he says there, the senses "intercommunicate by opening on to the structure of the thing."

Heidegger does not have much to say about touch, but he does not en-tirely neglect it. Elaborating what he intends by insisting on our "being-in-the-world," he says in *Being and Time*: "Only because the "senses" be-long ontologically to an entity whose kind of being [*Seinsart*] is a bodily [*befindlichen*] being-in-the-world can they be 'touched' [*gerührt*] by any-thing or 'have a sense for' [*Sinn haben für*] something in such a way that what touches them [*das Rührende*] shows itself as an affect [*in der Affek-tion zeigt*].[120] This passage merits our attention because it brings out the inherent connection between the corporeal and affective dimensions of touching—but without remarking the semantic ambiguity or duplicity that sustains this connection. This connection is, nevertheless, at the bot-tom of the distinction Heidegger makes between the nature of the human and the nature of the thingly, with regard to touching: "in principle," he says, "the chair can never touch the wall, even if the space between them should be equal to zero."[121] Expanding his phenomenological account of this distinction, he writes:

> There is no such thing as the "side-by-side-ness" of an entity called "Dasein" with another entity called "world." Of course when two things are present-at-hand together alongside one another, we are accustomed to express this occa-sionally by something like "the table stands 'by' [*bei*] the door" or "The chair 'is touching' [*berührt*] the wall." Taken strictly, however, "touching" is never what we are talking about in such cases, not because accurate re-examination will always eventually establish that there is a space between the chair and the wall, but because in principle the chair can never touch the wall. . . . If the chair could touch the wall, this would presuppose that the wall is the sort of thing "for" which a chair would be *encounterable*. An entity present-at-hand

within the world can be touched [*berühren*] by another entity only if by its very nature the latter entity has being-in as its own kind of being—only if, with its being-there [*Da-sein*], something like the world is already revealed to it, so that from out of that world another entity can manifest itself in touching [*Berührung*], and thus become accessible in its being-present-at-hand. When two entities are present-at-hand within the world, and furthermore are *worldless* themselves, they can never "touch" each other.[122]

It is worth noting here that there is no discussion of the animal; but we may assume that the animal can touch and be touched, despite its "world-poor" or "world-bereft" condition, neither belonging, as humans do, to a proper world nor being located, as are trees, stones, and clouds, in a world that is not theirs at all, and despite its not having hands, which (according to Heidegger) only human beings have. And the animal can touch in a way that is much closer to the human way than to the way in which the inanimate things of our world may be said to touch and be touched by one another—perhaps by mimetic projection, the vestiges of mythic animism.

Heidegger returns to the question of touching in § 67 of *Being and Time*, where he once again takes up the difference between the human and the animal—but, as always, only with a surprising brevity. He asserts, "Only an entity which, in existing, is as already having been [*je schon gewesen ist*], and which exists in a constant mode of what has been [*in einem ständigen Modus der Gewesenheit existiert*] can become affected [*affiziert*]."[123] Only the human measures up to that requirement. The animal is without the temporality, the temporal integrity, of self-awareness—without what Kant would call "the unity of transcendental apperception." Heidegger continues: "Ontologically, such affection [*Affektion*] presupposes making present [*das Gegenwärtigen*], and indeed in such a manner that, in this making present, Dasein can be brought back to itself as something that has been [*als Gewesenes*]." To which he adds, in closing all-too-brief reflections on the difference between the human and the animal: "It remains a problem in itself to define ontologically the way in which the senses can be stimulated and touched [*Reiz und Rührung*] in a being that merely has life [*in einem Nur-Lebenden*], and how and where the being of animals, for instance, is constituted by some kind of time." Among human beings, however, touching and being touched demonstrate in the most immediate way that, in the first instance, we do not and cannot possibly experience others as mere things, as being either merely ready-to-hand or merely present-at-hand. Thus, in *Being and Time*, laying out his phenomenology of *Dasein's* being-with-others, Heidegger writes: "In concernful solicitude, the other [person] is proximally disclosed. . . . But just as opening oneself up [*Sichoffenbaren*] or closing oneself off is grounded in one's having being-with-one-another . . . , so even the explicit disclosure of the other in solicitude grows out of one's primarily being *with* him in each case." [124] In the realm of the human, touching and being touched are forms of solicitude, ways of experiencing, through the sensibility of the flesh, our being with others. Through touching, we solicit and bring forth from the other a responsiveness we can feel. In being touched, we feel ourselves being solicited, aroused, brought forth into responsiveness. Touching and being touched are therefore modes of unconcealment—gestures that must be understood, at least in the realm of the human, in terms of a certain hermeneutics.

In "What Are Poets For?," Heidegger comments on some lines from a poem by Rilke in which the poet invokes the fateful touch of what we might take to be the law of being, measuring out, for each one of us, the beginning and end of our lifetime. The lines read as follows:

> in the end,
> it is our unshieldedness on which we depend,
> and that, when we saw it threaten, we turned it
> so into the Open that, in widest orbit somewhere,
> where the Law touches us [*wo das Gesetz uns anrührt*], we may
> affirm it. [125]

To this Heidegger responds, saying:

> When we are touched [*angerührt*] from out of the widest orbit [*Umkreis*], the touch [*das Anrühren*] goes to our very nature [*Wesen*]. To touch [here] means to touch off, to set in motion [*in Bewegung bringen*]. Our nature is set in motion. The will is shaken by the touch [*Im Rühren wird das Wollen erschüttert*], so that only now is the nature of willing made to appear and set in motion. Not until then do we will willingly [*Dann wird das Wollen erst ein Williges*]. [126]

The touch of *this* law is a touch that penetrates our egological defenses so deeply, so disarmingly, that it could perhaps even bring about a radical alteration in the disposition of the will, overcoming its inveterate will to power. "But what is it that touches us directly [*uns unmittelbar anrührt*] out of the widest orbit?" Heidegger answers: "Death. Death is what touches mortals in their nature, and so gets them on their way to the other side of life. . . . Our unshieldedness, so converted [by our realizing death as something infinitely precious], finally shelters us within the Open, outside all protection." [127] Death is the law, the measure of life, whose touch, taking its time, could perhaps bring about in the very nature of the will a "conversion" or "turning" that would open it, in an approximation to the way of *Gelassenheit*, for the dispensations of being.

Late in his life, nearing the time of his death, Husserl, still obsessed by the nature of the human body, put into words one of the philosophical lessons that he found hidden within the reflexivity of perception and the experience of touching, a lesson that he had resisted for years: "The same lived-body [*Leib*], which serves me as a means for all my perception [*Wahrnehmung*], obstructs me in the perception of it itself and is a remarkably imperfectly constituted thing [*ein merkwürdig unvollkommen konstitutiertes Ding*]." [128] In the reflexivity that is its very essence, the human body compels us to encounter a finitude it bears within itself—a measure the will to power cannot take in hand and master, a law that, by recognizing in our subjectivity the ciphers of materiality, registers the inevitable approach of our death.

Shaken—and thus solicited—by the touch of death, shaken so profoundly as to be released from the grip of the will to power, our gestures could perhaps become capable to some extent of a more hermeneutically tactful mode of unconcealment.

Heidegger also records some ruminations on touch in the lectures assembled under the title *What Is Called Thinking?* He observes:

What must be thought about, turns away [*sich abwenden*] from man. It withdraws [*sich entziehen*] from him. But how can we have the least knowledge of something that withdraws from the beginning, how can we even give it a name? Whatever withdraws, refuses arrival. But—withdrawing is not nothing. Withdrawal is an event [*Entzug ist Ereignis*]. In fact, what withdraws [*das Sichentziehen*] may even concern [*angehen*] and claim man [*in den Anspruch nehmen*] more essentially than anything present that strikes and touches [*trifft und betrifft*] him. Being struck [*Betroffenheit*] by actuality is what we like to regard as constitutive of the actuality of the actual. However, in being struck by what is actual, man may be debarred precisely from what most concerns and touches him [*was ihn angeht*]—touches him in the surely mysterious way of escaping [*entgeht*] him by its withdrawal. The event of withdrawal [*Das Ereignis des Entzugs*] could be what is most present [*Gegenwärtigste*] in all our present [*Gegenwärtigen*], and so infinitely exceed the actuality of everything actual. (*WHD*, 5/8−9)

Thus, bearing in mind Hölderlin's claim that "Man is a sign," Heidegger reflects on the fact that the human is the one being capable of pointing. The human, he says, is not just contingently and occasionally a being capable of pointing, but is rather that being who first becomes what it is by virtue of realizing its essential nature in and as pointing, in and as that being whose being is destined to be drawn toward what withdraws: "To say 'drawing toward' is to say 'pointing toward what withdraws'" (*"Auf dem Zuge zu . . . " sagt schon: "zeigend auf das Sichentziehende"*). Such hermeneutically attuned pointing could not be a gesture moved by the will to power, for the will to power would not tolerate withdrawal, beyond its grasp, into the depths of concealment.

Heidegger returns to the theme of touch—but touch, now, in the sense of contact—in one of the later lectures, in which he connects it to thinking as recollecting and thanking:

> The *thanc*, the heart's core, is the gathering of all that concerns us [*was uns angeht*], all that we care for [*was uns anlangt*], all that touches us [*woran uns liegt*] insofar as we are—as human beings. What touches us [*uns anliegt*] in the sense that it defines and determines our nature, what we care for, we might call contiguous or contact [*das Anliegende oder auch das Anliegen*]. For the moment, the word may strike us as odd. But it grows out of the subject matter it expresses, and has long been spoken. (*WHD*, 157–58/144–45)

Explaining what he means, Heidegger continues:

> Whenever we speak of subject and object, there is in our thoughts . . . an oppositeness [*ein Gegenüber-liegen*]. There is always contact [*das Anliegen*] in the widest sense. It is possible that the thing which touches us and is in touch with us [*was uns anliegt und woran uns liegt*] if we achieve our humanity [*Menschsein*], need not be represented by us constantly and specifically. But even so it is concentrated, gathered toward us in advance [*im voraus auf uns zu versammelt*]. In a certain manner, though not exclusively, we ourselves are that gathering [*Versammlung*].

Heidegger wants to say that we ourselves *could become* that very gathering that we essentially already are if, deeply touched in our hearts by what we have been given to think, we undertake a process of recollection—a process that bears within it the possibility of radically altering the character of our worldly relations, our worldly "gatherings." The gatherings that take place, for example, by virtue of the way we approach, touch, make contact, and remain with. The lecture continues: "The gathering of what is next to us [*Versammlung des Anliegens*] here never means an after-the-fact collection of what already exists, lying before us [*ein nachträgliches Einsammeln von Vorliegendem*], but the tidings that overtake all our doings, the tidings [*Botschaft*] of what we are committed to beforehand [*schon angeboten sind*] simply by our being human beings." He explains what this means as follows:

> Only because we are by nature [*im Wesen*] gathered in contiguity [*in das Anliegen versammelt*] can we remain concentrated [*bei dem gesammelt bleiben*] on what is at once present and past and to come. The word "memory" [*"Gedächtnis"*] originally means this incessant concentration on the contiguity of what lies near [*gesammelte Nicht-Ablassen vom Anliegenden*]. In its original telling sense, memory means as much as devotion [*An-dacht*]. This word possesses the special tone of the pious and piety, and designates the devotion of prayer, only because it denotes the all-comprehensive relation of concentration [*Sammlung*] upon the holy and the gracious. The *thanc* unfolds in memory, which persists as devotion [*als die An-dacht währt*]. Memory in this originary sense later loses its name to a restricted denomination, which now signifies no more than the capacity to retain things that are in the past.

"But," Heidegger now argues,

> if we understand memory in the light of the old word *thanc,* the connection between memory and thanks will dawn on us at once. For in giving thanks, the heart in thought recalls where it remains gathered and concentrated [*im Dank gedenkt das Gemüt dessen, worein es versammelt bleibt*], insofar as that is where it belongs. This thinking that recalls in memory [*andenkende Gedenken*] is the original thanks.

These remarkable passages enable us to bring together the primary traits we have considered in the course of this ontological interpretation of touching—in particular, its measure, its tact, its *Gelassenheit.* I want to suggest that, if our touching were in touch with its ontological measure, the measure by which it is most deeply affected and moved, and in that sense most deeply appropriated, it might begin to learn from its attunement in that contact how to become skillful, *geschickt,* in the tactfulness of *Gelassenheit.* But, educing the implications of Heidegger's philological reflections here, I must again stress that our contact with the ontological measure would need to be a work of recollection, and that, in its appropriation of our gestures, such recollection, rendering them ontologically thoughtful, would draw them into the depths of an experience in which they would eventually encounter the untouchable—an experience, manifest only through touch, of the very limits of the touchable, the very limits of what could be approached, even by the most tactful of engagements. Finally, I want to suggest that, as thoughtful recollection, the tactfulness of *Gelassenheit* would require gestures moved by the spirit (*Gemüt*) of thanksgiving, gestures that would express their thankfulness for their being by keeping within a tradition of memory the opening up of a tactile world perpetually taking shape from out of the depths of what absolutely withdraws from touch. For what must in the end be remembered is the primordial Λέγειν, the claim that lays hold of our gestures, a claim, or Νόμος, which comes from the abyssal realm of what, in opening a space for our gestures and granting them natural powers, withdraws from our reach and touch.

In his "Worpswede Diary," Rilke wrote down in verse what might at first be read only as words of weary mourning:

> even the slightest
> gesture is hard for me.
> My life is: the stillness of final form.
> I am gesture's beginning and end.
> I am so old
> That I can't grow older.[129]

Every gesture bears within it a story, a memory of beginning and end. On another occasion, the poet writes: "desires are the memories from our future."[130]

In time, there is loss. And yet in our hands, we already carry the gift of their *Gesetzmäßigkeit*. Could our fingers, our hands, our gestures remember? Could they remember—as it were—for us? Could they remember the measure laid down for us to live by? Could they, remembering for us, gather us into the nomological layout, the λέγειν, that has always already—but also, not yet—appropriated our ethical life for the fitting unconcealment of its measure?

IX. Gathering into the Future: A Destiny Beyond Fate

Rilke's "Worpswede Diary" also touches on the moment when the gesture, in taking leave of its time, offers itself to another time:

There comes a time when every past sheds its heaviness. . . . And the darker and more colorful our various pasts were, the richer the images will be by which our quotidian life redeems itself. And that holds true as much for the course of history as for an individual life. . . . All heirs bear deceased fates like jewelry. Dead eyes full of lament have been transfigured into precious stones, the gesture of a great leave-taking repeats itself, scarcely noticed, in an inconspicuous fluttering of their garments.[131]

Fate can be left behind—perhaps even redeemed in the destiny of a new beginning.

If in the German word for gathering, or harvesting, a process of reading is also registered, the hands involved in reading possibilities into the future would also be engaged in the gathering of those possibilities. Gathering them into the breach of a destiny (*Geschick*) that must be differentiated from the continuum of fate (*Schicksal*). It is a question of lending a hand (*an die Hand geben*)[132] to the gathering of ontological possibilities that could take place in the expanse opened up by that difference. Lending a hand, for example, by a writing that gathers the history of metaphysics into an interpretive project of reading and therein discloses possibilities for a different ontological dispensation within our experience of the present field of presencing.

Inspired by Hölderlin's poetic thought, Heidegger allows himself to imagine the possibility of a new inception, a different dispensation, taking place as a gathering of earth and sky, gods and mortals. Perhaps, he seems to suggest, if our gestures could truly be moved by the hermeneutics of remembrance, this "Fourfold" might gather once again to inaugurate, in the realm where the tangible and the intangible meet, a great new destiny. A new destiny not only for us, the mortals, but also for the benevolent gods, embodiments of our ideals and dreams—and for the earth and the sky, in danger today of seemingly irreparable devastation. If there is sincere remembrance, the heartfelt devotion of thought, perhaps even what takes place in a gathering at our fingertips could bring forth intimations, *Winke*, of the possible destiny offered to each of the Four in the time of their harmony.

But we have lost our memory—perhaps even lost our desire and capacity. And the semblance of memory with which we now live is a formula that utterly obliterates it. In *Being and Time*, Heidegger contends that, because of our lapse into the forgetfulness of a reified historicality that abandons the past, thinking it finished and done, the way in which fate has been primordially stretched along has been hidden. With the inconstancy of the self that is anyone-and-everyone [*das Man*], Dasein makes present [*gegenwärtigt*] its "today." In awaiting [*Gewärtig*] the next new thing, it has forgotten the old one. The "one that is anyone-and-everyone" [*das Man*] evades choice. Blind for possibilities, it cannot repeat what has been, but only retains and receives the "actual" that is left over, the world-historical that has been, the leavings [*die Überbleibsel*], and the information about them that is present-at-hand.[133]

The text continues:

> Lost in the making present of the "today," it [*Dasein* lost in its forgetfulness of the ecstatic, ontological dimension of temporality] understands the "past" only in terms of the present [*aus der Gegenwart*]. On the other hand, the temporality of authentic historicality, as the moment of vision of anticipatory repetition, *deprives* the "today" of its character *as present*, and weans one from the conventionalities of the anyone-and-everyone. When, however, one's existence is inauthentically historical, it is loaded down with the legacy of a "past" that has become unrecognizable [*unkenntlich*] and it seeks the modern [the "new"]. But when historicality is authentic, it understands history as the "recurrence" of the possible, and knows that a possibility will recur only if existence is open for the destiny it can bring in a moment of vision, in resolute repetition.

For Heidegger, authentic historicity requires a resolute commitment to the openness of anticipation (*vorlaufende Entschlossenheit*), an attitude in which the claims of a past that has never been present could be for the first time "recognized." Nonetheless, one can glean from the text no specific indication that these "leavings" (*Uberbleibsel*) could perhaps be redeemed if they were to be handled with an authentic sense of historicity—handled by hands moved in a time of remembrance, carefully preparing an opening to greet a future when presence-at-hand and readiness-to-hand might no longer rule in the presencing of being. But the text does hint at the possibility of a transformation that would redeem the originary inheritance of the past, which, in today's marketplace, consists of nothing but remnants left to be forgotten.

Like Heidegger, Benjamin also contemplates the recognizability of the remnants of the past. In his historiographical writings, he attempts to explain how we can recognize in these leavings, these world-historical ruins, prophetic messages, legible traces of the messianic, foretelling the time of justice. From his early writings to his last, Benjamin makes the material and dialectical presentation of the redemptive future and the time of its specific recognizability (*das Jetzt einer bestimmten Erkennbarkeit*) a principal matter for his thought. For thought and the hand of thought.

But between Heidegger and Benjamin, irreconcilable differences ultimately prevail. Whereas the remnants that Benjamin attempts to retrieve bear the promise of a cosmopolitanism even more radical than the one Kant imagines in his speculative philosophy of history, the remnants that Heidegger wants to retrieve in *Being and Time* belong to a specific cultural tradition—the heritage of his Germany. Later, after the so-called "turn" in Heidegger's thinking, the task is to retrieve from the remnants that ontological forgetfulness has not yet destroyed the true history of being. After this "turn," it is no longer only the heritage of Germany that is at stake, but indeed the fate or the destiny of the entire human world.

In a brief text entitled "Hölderlin's Earth and Heaven," written after *Being and Time*, Heidegger continues to emphasize the inevitability of finitude and fragmentation, noting that even though, with the thought of the gathering of the Fourfold, we have been granted intimations of the "infinite relation," we are still denied its presencing as a unified whole.[134] Consequently, he says, we are still not able to hear the "voices of destiny" coming from its gathering. One might justly say the same, I think, with regard to the use of our hands. What we have been granted to touch and handle are nothing but the fragmentary remains, the *Überbleibsel*, of this infinite relation—fragments that are nothing but intimations of the unified whole. We are still denied any tangible sense of the destinal possibilities that nevertheless are summoning us to remembrance, awaiting their time in concealment, preserved within the secret intimacies of the things we touch, handle, and use.

But Heidegger never abandons the claims of remembrance—the origin of remembrance and the coming of another inception. In a meditation on the spirit of "remembrance" invoked in Hölderlin's poem "Andenken," Heidegger points out that "remembrance is a kind of greeting":

> From the used-up and empty greeting of thoughtless exchanges to the rarity of the true greeting, and indeed up to the uniqueness of this poetic greeting, we come across many levels. In a greeting, the one who greets does indeed name himself, but only to say that he wants nothing for himself; rather, he addresses everything to the one who is greeted, all that is fitting [*was diesem gebührt*]. A true greeting acknowledges what is greeted in its own proper being, and yet it takes its own place, belonging in a different and therefore dis-

tant will. The greeting unfolds the distance between what is greeted and the one who sends the greeting, so that in such [respectful] distance there may be established a [tactful] nearness that does not need to breed familiarity.[135]

"A true greeting," he says, "accords to the one greeted the harmony of its essence" (*Der echte Grüß schenkt dem Gegrüßten den Anklang seines Wesens*). In still other words: "Greeting is a re-thinking [*An-denken*] whose mysterious rigor again shelters what is greeted and the greeting one in the distance of their own essential being. The greeting wants nothing for itself, and precisely for this reason receives thereby everything that helps the greeted one to enter into his own [way of] being." These reflections invite one to imagine a world yet to come, in which the presencing of earth and sky, mortals and gods would be greeted in its unconcealment by gestures born of remembrance.

Gestures moved by remembrance, moved by the solicitations of Mnemosyne, would belong to an ontological order of time in which, as Heidegger puts it in the second division of *Being and Time*, "nothing can occur." They would belong there since that order is a temporality no longer organized according to an instrumental rationality (the pragmatic order of means and ends) and a metaphysics of total, constant presence. It is a temporality no longer structured by a pragmatic causality of discrete now-points, directed in their endless succession toward ends that neither recognize the contingency and transience of all these worldly ends nor permit the return of the great potentialities granted in a past that has never been present, a past that is not completely past.

Unlike gestures whose disclosiveness would be moved by remembrance, the conventional gestures of bourgeois tact—everyday manners—not only are superficial but also participate in the growth of nihilism, because they substitute themselves for an ontologically attuned form of tact, which they conceal and deny. Whereas the tact of the modern bourgeois subject serves the self-preserving interests of the will to power and its calculative, instrumental rationality, an ontologically mindful tact, letting beings be, would serve the possibilities of a different presencing. Whereas bourgeois tact serves to maintain the familiar, ontological tact would recognize the claims of the uncanny, the unrecognizable, the absolutely other. For of all beings, the human is the most unknowable, the most unpredictable—the most uncanny. Only the human is described, in Greek tragedy, as δεινός: strange, awesome, and frightening. It is precisely that dimension of the human—human nature—from which our conventions of tact are alienating us, reducing us in our singularity to a socially proper identity.

We are free to give ourselves—to assert—our own proper measure. But the *use* of our freedom is in question. It seems that the question, for Heidegger, must be whether or not the measure that guides us as we take the measure of our circumstances keeps us open to the dimension of the ontological. Nothing could be more important than an ontological principle that keeps us open to the different, because when freedom denies all sense of an ontological measure, it inevitably becomes self-destructive and violent. Thus, paradoxically, in our freedom we must learn a resolute commitment to submission: the ownmost use of our freedom to take over and make our own the measure that, even for the conscience born of our heart, withdraws its origin from the categories of empirical understanding. In touch, nevertheless, with this measure—with its imperative claim on our responsibility—we must learn the use of our freedom to affirm that measure, letting it—making it—ground the conduct of our lives. The measure that we must thus realize and actualize is, however, a post-metaphysical measure, for its moral normativity summons us in its categorical presence, but only as an originary condition of possibility, a "meta-ethical principle," providing *no specific directives* for our comportment in everyday social life. So Heidegger urges that we listen with care to the originary attunement constitutive of our preontological experience of that measure, and that we turn away from the measure whose false universality always tempts us to follow it into the smug comfort of moral indifference, the measure that is nothing but an idol and fetish of *das Man*, a projection of a brutal social reality constructed by the will to power.

Freedom lies in the difference of a "repetition" that creatively renews the originary measure, "using" it to determine situationally appropriate measures for living, measures we must make for ourselves, but in obedience to the logic of difference and alterity that forever functions in the tangible interplay of concealment and unconcealment. It is the immeasurable that remains concealed within the measure which gives it its "justice": recollecting ontological reminders from its echoes and traces, we learn what it means for us mortals to build, to dwell, to live with others according to the principle of nonidentity, the principle that renounces totality.

Referring his project in "The Anaximander Fragment" to an "eschatology of Being,"[136] Heidegger attempts to think the possibility of another way for beings of all kinds to presence. A way for which, in fact, even the word "eschatology," positing an ordering of time and history that he rejects, can only be a misleading, albeit indispensable, formal indication. It is this question, he says, that now lays claim to (*er-eignet*) the essence of *Dasein*. Much depends (*anliegt*), he says, using a word that Benjamin holds dear, "on the way we are mindful [*eingedenk*] of what is destined [*des Geschicklichen*]." [137] Hope for the coming of another destiny (*Ankunft eines anderen Geschickes*) cannot and must not be abandoned. [138] "Another destiny, yet veiled, is [perhaps] waiting" (*ein anderes, noch verhülltes Geschick wartet*). [139] But the destiny in question is a destiny that "does not allow itself either to be logically and historiographically predicted, or to be metaphysically construed as [the end of] a sequence" belonging to the causal continuum of history. [140] (The seer's "foresight," the "moment of vision," is not at all predictive; rather, it is a visionary, prophetic capacity to draw from the past the absolutely unforeseeable.) Much depends, therefore, on our not enduring history as if it were "an ordained fate": history is "no blind destiny" (*kein blindes Geschick*), [141] "never a destiny [*Geschick*] that compels," but rather a "gathering [*jenes versammelnde Schicken*] that brings humans to the way of unconcealment [*auf den Weg des Entbergens*]." [142] It is essential to keep in mind the distinction between "fate" (*Schicksal*) and "destiny" (*Geschick*). Whereas fate denies us freedom, destiny is an ontological dispensation that grants it. Freedom must, however, renounce its reduction to the causal power of the will and open the realm of history to a temporal dimension within which destiny can be effective and the experience of being that destiny grants can be made actual. Authentic freedom originates, therefore, not in relation to the course of ontic events but only in relation to the deeper, self-concealing origin of destiny. (In *Being and Time*, Heidegger uses *Schicksal* to refer to the individual *Dasein*'s appropriation of its ownmost potentiality-for-being and reserves *Geschick* for the (German) people's authentic historical appropriation of their cultural inheritance. In other, mostly later works, however, this way of differentiating the two terms is less clear. Although we must certainly recognize a difference between the individual's relation to its "potentiality-for-being" and the relation that a community can have to its historical possibilities, I suggest that the more fundamental distinction, equally applicable, *mutatis mutandis*, to the life of an individual and to the historicality of a community, is the distinction between fate and destiny. In both the life of the individual and the historical life of the community, it is our realization of freedom as responsibility for an authentic relation to ontological possibilities that Heidegger wants us to question.) Although so far we have known "only *one* mode of presencing" (*nur immer eine Art des Anwesens*), we have no reason to suppose that things must necessarily appear (*unbedingt erscheinen*) in that way forever.[143]

Freedom, for Heidegger, is the human condition that, through its attention to destiny, makes what destiny grants possible, defeating the tragic work of fate. Thus, instead of consisting, like fate, in the denial of freedom, destiny is an ornament of freedom: destiny challenges freedom to rise to the occasion and contribute to destiny's very fulfillment.

Joining critique to lamentation, Heidegger asserts that in today's world, people "believe that their trafficking [*Verkehr*] in what is present [*Anwesenden*] by itself creates for them a sufficient familiarity [*eine gemäße Vertrautheit*] with it."[144] But if, as he suggests in his meditation on Heracleitus fragment B16, the "revealing-concealing gathering" of being—thus the presencing of beings—"is entrusted [*zuspricht*] to mortals in such a way that their essence unfolds only in . . . their corresponding [*Entsprechen*] to the Λόγος,"[145] then the prospect of another epoch of ontological dispensation—the prospect of our release from historical fate—would seem to require that we contemplate how we entrust our hands to what it is given to them to receive, so that with them we may bring to tangible articulation in a radically different affective attunement the presencing of what we touch and handle.

In his *Phenomenology of Perception*, Merleau-Ponty tries to recall us from the depths of an ontological forgetfulness to which we inevitably succumb and evoke in us a sense of the gesture as ontologically "initiatory," and even "consecratory," bringing the things we encounter into unconcealment.[146] The gestures he calls "initiatory" and "consecratory" are gestures that "draw affective vectors, discover emotional sources, and create a space of expressiveness as the movements of the augur delimit the *templum*." They are gestures that get in touch with our originary attunement, gestures that come from the ontological "clearing" that is their most appropriate "templum." In this manner, as Rilke says, "the bearers of the farthest future pass by all struggles with a quiet smile, like monks who have the cloister's treasure in their safekeeping. They have only to protect."[147] Bearing in guardian awareness the dream of that farthest future, when the time of our hope might offer us the conditions of another ontology, our gestures have only, as the poet says, to keep safe and protect. This is their only truth.

But how are we to understand "saving" and "protecting"? What meaning do those words carry for the "handiwork" of memory, of recollection? If the rescuing powers of recollection, of *Erinnerung* as a process of *Wiederholung*, are necessary for the "destruction" or "overcoming" of the world-historical rule of a metaphysics of presentness, then we need to recognize in the work of memory two different ways of rescuing and protecting—ways that must also be understood in terms of their gathering into "destructiveness." This is already configured in *Being and Time*, where Heidegger stakes out the difference between "authentic" and "inauthentic" types of historicality. Unfolding what is tightly folded into that work's division two, chapter five, we might say that the "inauthentic" type of historical memory destroys the past it "gathers" by a process of dispersion, *Zerstreuung*, first reducing it to a succession of monadic now-points and then leaving it behind as irrevocably finished, as *das Vergangene*, embalmed in an identity beyond amendment, without origin and destiny. In effect, this type of remembering is the dismemberment of the past—its betrayal, death, and burial. "Authentic" memory, however, is also destructive, also a process of dispersion or dissemination; but its way of destroying actually saves and protects. For, although it tears times past out of their assigned textuality, their unity and identity, turning them into historical fragments without totally determinate identity, it also, by virtue of this very operation, brings them back from death to life, opening them up as "what has been" (*das Gewesene*) to endlessly renewed interpretation. The repetitions of "authentic" memory re-collect unrealized potentialities concealed within those times past, making possible critical interruptions in the course of the present. Such processes of re-collection expose us in our historical being to new questions: in re-collection, we let ourselves be haunted by the "afterlife" of our past, by a historicality that persists in calling us to overcome the spell of presentness that binds us to the law of fate. In the authentic form of memory, the origin self-destructs endlessly—it is in fact the very origin of a destruction that inaugurates what is renewing. And "tradition," authentically understood and practiced, will correspondingly be a preservation that preserves by destroying.

If one bears this in mind, one might adopt the "spirited" attitude that Nietzsche attributed to the ancient Greeks when he said, writing of their relation to the laws decreed by the gods, "One worships them, certainly, but one also keeps in one's hands a final trump to be used against them."[148] There is a certain type of skepticism that keeps safe and protects, respecting the authority of the ontological measure by *maintaining* its self-concealment, its absolute withdrawal from the will's realm of decidability. All the will's efforts to master the past serve only to strengthen the power of fate surviving in these reifications.

There must already be—in our hands, in our gestures—a way of measuring up to the claims of destiny without succumbing to the temptations of the will to power. And realizing what destiny grants to human freedom when freedom becomes a way of recollecting the historical conditions of being. In question is our capacity for remembrance, remembrance enacted in the way that our hands "greet" whatever may give itself to be taken in hand, touched, felt, handled, used. What would our hands be if they were deprived of the possibility of remembrance—if they lost that possibility?

If there is a possibility of a destiny beyond fate, it may well lie in our hands. In their capacity to gather things into the disclosive dimension of another dispensation. Only in this way would our gestures become ontologically fitting and appropriate in their measure. Gestures of the hand in the time of remembrance—the time that belongs to an uncertain future.

X. Monstrous Errancy

Reflecting, in his 1936 Frankfurt lectures entitled "The Origin of the Work of Art," on the "strife between measure and unmeasure" (*Streit von Maß und Unmaß*), Heidegger laments what he takes to be a decisive historical truth: that "everything ordinary and hitherto existing becomes an unbeing [*Unseienden*]. This unbeing has lost [*eingebüßt*] the capacity [*Vermögen*] to give and keep being as measure."[149] What is involved in keeping being as our measure? And how would keeping being as our measure bear on the questions of morality we are responsible for answering? In his lectures on Nietzsche, this measure is again invoked, and our historical relation to it is again asserted to be decisive: "We today are witnesses to a mysterious law of history which states that one day a people no longer measures up to the metaphysics that arose from its own history; that day arrives precisely [*in dem Augenblick*] when such metaphysics has been transformed into the absolute [*das Unbedingte*]."[150] That is to say: transformed into "a new kind of human being," a being who, living in the modern machine economy, measures up to the technological and political possibilities for "absolute dominion over the earth."

I share this concern. For the earth—and for the kind of human being that the global economy of capitalism is demanding. But I am compelled to conclude this chapter with a sobering reflection. For the philosopher who urged us to let our judgment be guided by the ontological measure was not "saved" by that counsel from some exceedingly disturbing failures of judgment—failures that reveal him to be without a normal sense of proportion, a normal sense of the appropriate measure. My purpose here is not to take the measure of the man but rather to question the ability of ontological understanding to motivate a morally appropriate sense of proportion and measure. Two examples unequivocally reveal a shocking absence of this sense of proportion and measure in Heidegger.

The first example appears in "Enframing" ("Das Ge-stell"), the original version of his lecture "The Question Concerning Technology," where he wrote, "Agriculture [*Ackerbau*] is now a mechanized food industry, in essence the same as the manufacturing of corpses in the gas chambers and extermination camps, the same as the blockade and starvation of nations, the same as the production of hydrogen bombs."[151] As if it were morally appropriate even to consider balancing these events on the scale of justice! But in the later, published version, this equation of the mechanization of agriculture and the Nazi technology of genocide was omitted, leaving only the reference to agriculture. The second example is only slightly less reprehensible. In a letter dated January 20, 1948, responding to Herbert Marcuse's pleas for some signs of remorse for his participation in the evil of the Nazi regime, Heidegger wrote:

> To the severe and justified reproaches formulated "over a regime that has exterminated millions of Jews, that has made terror the norm and transformed everything connected to the concepts of spirit, freedom, and truth into its opposite," I can only add that, instead of the "Jews," one could equally well put the "East Germans," and that everything which has happened since 1945 is known to all the world, while the bloody terror of the Nazis was kept secret from the German people.[152]

This prompts him to equate the devastation and deaths caused by Nazi bombs with the Allied bombing of Dresden. Such failures to put matters in proper balance would perhaps be more comprehensible, though not more forgivable, were they not the failures of a philosopher for whom the question of proper measure was of paramount importance. These failures are moral failures of immeasurable proportions, warning us not to believe that orientation to the normativity of the ontological in the realm of thought can somehow guarantee ontic gestures of solicitude. In "The Turning," Heidegger declares, "We locate history in the realm of happening [*des Geschehens*], instead of thinking history in accord with its essential origin [*Wesensherkunft*] from out of destiny." Keeping one's gaze fixed on the sublime destiny of being can blind one all too easily to the specific fate of history's victims.[153]

How could a thinking committed to the proposition that the dignity of the human being lies in a mindful relation to the incommensurable so readily assert these moral equations? Is critical reason not being reduced to ratios? Is thinking itself not being reduced to mere calculation? How could a thinking that declares its submission to the ontological as the sole appropriate measure for mortal dwelling have been so tragically bereft of any ontic sense of proportion concerning matters of such moral gravity? Heidegger's moral coldness sends a chilling storm over the whole of his thought. We cannot simply ignore the obligation to question what he says about measure. Such errancy in thought compels us to take its measure. But in the court of world history, the immeasurable suffering of the victims of nationalism and racism will not have received that measure of recognition which Heidegger wanted to deny to it until judgment can finally declare the time of a fully realized humanity.

§ 9 Two Hands Touching

Chiasmatic Gestures in Merleau-Ponty

I. When Hands Think and Poetize

> I really do think with my pen, because my head often knows nothing
> about what my hand is writing.
>
> —Ludwig Wittgenstein, *Culture and Value* [1]

> Yes or no: do we have a body—that is, not a permanent object of
> thought, but a flesh that suffers when it is wounded, hands that touch?
> We know: hands do not suffice for touch—but to decide for this
> reason alone that our hands do not touch, and to relegate them to
> the world of objects or of instruments, would be, in acquiescing
> to the bifurcation of subject and object, to forgo in advance the
> understanding of the sensible and to deprive ourselves of its lights.
>
> —Maurice Merleau-Ponty, "The Intertwining
> —The Chiasm" [2]

In his *Meditations on First Philosophy*, Descartes makes what today can
only be regarded as an astonishing assertion: "If a foot or an arm or some
other part is separated from my body, I am aware that nothing has been
taken away from the mind." [3] For Merleau-Ponty, however, the body acquires, remembers, carries a great wealth of knowledge. Tying one's shoes,
playing the piano, and typing are examples of embodied skills, forms of
"knowledge [immediately] in the hands." [4] Once such knowledge becomes
a habitual, interventions by the intellect can only interrupt and obstruct
it. In "Cézanne's Doubt," Merleau-Ponty argues that the brushstrokes on
the painter's canvases demonstrate that "a hand is not simply part of the
body, but the expression and continuation of a thought which must be

captured and conveyed."⁵ Until the emergence of phenomenology, philosophy failed to understand or even recognize this experience of the hand. The body is of course an object, a thing among things. As Adorno says, "in the attributes that seem to be attached to [the object] by the subject alone, the subject's own objectivity comes to the fore."⁶ For Merleau-Ponty, this means that we are capable of seeing only because we belong to the visible, capable of hearing only by belonging to the audible, and capable of touching only if we are part of the tangible. There is a certain "kinship" between my hand, for example, and the things it touches: a kinship "according to which my gestures are not only, like the pseudopods of the amoeba, vague and ephemeral deformations of the corporeal space, but the initiation to and the opening upon a tactile world" (*VI*, 175/133).

The nature of the body is thus double, for the body is also a subject. Hence, Merleau-Ponty will say that this "opening" can happen "only if my hand, while it is felt from within, is also accessible from without, itself [something] tangible" (*ibid.*). Accordingly, while my body is a thing among things, it is so "in a sense stronger and deeper than they," because it is also "of them," not just "among" them, detaching itself from things in the movement whereby, as body-subject, it experiences their presence—sees, hears, touches. Taking its place among the things it touches, my hand "is in a sense one of them" (ibid.). But even as a tangible being among them, indeed precisely because it is "of them," it creates an expressive space within which they become present. Things in the world can of course touch one another; but there is an abyss of difference between their way of touching one another and our way of touching them (*VI*, 175, 181/133, 137).

Gotthold Ephraim Lessing's theatrical work *Emilia Galotti* raises questions about the Cartesian mortification of the body by putting the established doctrine in the mouth of one of the characters, a painter who, without the slightest hesitation, puts it into words: "Alas! That we cannot paint directly with our eyes! On the long journey from the eye through the arm to the pencil, how much is lost!"⁷ One may read in Merleau-Ponty's phenomenology—and especially in his writings on painting, one of the gestural arts—a rejoinder to this Cartesian view, for he shows, on the contrary, how much is to be gained by that sensuous journey.

Attempting to defend his assertion, and indeed his reputation and ambitions, Lessing's painter says: "But, as I have already said, though I know what is lost, and how and why it is lost, I am as proud and prouder of this loss than of what I have preserved. For by the former, I perceive more than by the latter, that I am a good painter, though my hand is not always so." And he concludes with a question for another character, the Prince: "Or do you hold, Prince, that Raphael would not have been the greatest genius in painting [*das größte malerische Genie*] even if he had unfortunately been born without hands?" Nietzsche could not resist getting into the act, writing his rebuttal of Lessing's painter with a sneer:

> *The problem of those who are waiting.*—It requires strokes of luck and much that is incalculable if a higher man in whom the solution of a problem lies dormant is to get around to action in time—to "eruption," one might say. In the average case it does not happen, and in the nooks all over the earth sit men who are waiting, scarcely knowing in what way they are waiting, much less that they are waiting in vain. Occasionally the call that awakens—that accident which gives the "permission" to act—comes too late, when the best youth and strength for action has already been used up by sitting still; and many have found to their horror when they "leaped up" that their limbs had gone to sleep and their spirit had become too heavy. "It is too late," they said to themselves, having lost their faith in themselves and are henceforth forever useless.

"Could it be," Nietzsche asks, bringing the aphorism to its stinging conclusion, "that in the realm of the spirit 'Raphael without hands,' taking this phrase in its widest sense, is perhaps not the exception but the rule?"[8]

Nietzsche's efforts to rescue the human body from its long history of misrepresentations and mortifications in idealism and intellectualism have been continued by a number of scholars,[9] but with exceptional dedication and methodological rigor in the work of Merleau-Ponty. Thus, in *Eye and Mind*, for example, he argues, against Descartes, that "a closer study of painting would lead [him] to another philosophy."[10] And in "Cézanne's Doubt," he reflects on the philosophical significance of the gestures whose movements remain to be seen in the intense brushstrokes that are their material traces: "Other minds are given to us only as incarnate, as belonging to faces and gestures. Countering with the distinctions of soul and body, thought and vision is of no use here, for Cézanne returns to just that primordial experience from which these notions are derived and in which they are inseparable."[11] This great painter, who "motioned his friends, when still far away, not to approach him," and who often could not bear friendly physical contact, seems to have found something in the gestures of painting—in the strong brushstrokes, thick and heavy with an insistent

materiality—that would compensate for what Merleau-Ponty characterizes as "this loss of flexible human contact."

In these two essays on painting, Merleau-Ponty calls our attention to
the poetry of the gesture, sometimes hesitant, sometimes assured, sometimes forceful, sometimes delicate, moving in rhythms of the most intimate collaboration with the painter's vision to create, within the world,
the magical substance of semblance. The two essays supplement the arguments that Merleau-Ponty had formulated earlier, in the *Phenomenology of
Perception*, and also enrich the still-schematic reflections—left unfinished
by his untimely death and posthumously gathered into *The Visible and the
Invisible*—that boldly attempt to break the spell of a metaphysics that has
held philosophical thought in thrall since Plato and Aristotle. In these
works, Merleau-Ponty deploys the testimony of phenomenology to question not only the prevailing representations of subjectivity and objectivity,
including accounts committed to the temporal primacy of the subject-
object structure, but also the prevailing representations of our embodiment as we experience it in the chiasmatic intrigue of nature and culture.
With equal force, he challenges, in his last writings, the assumptions of
both idealism and realism, both intellectualism and empiricism, in an effort to release the body from its reification as a material substance and to
turn inside-out the "mind" that philosophers had kept hidden within the
thinglike body. In the course of this effort, he reveals the emergence of the
body from a more elemental dimension of experience that he calls "flesh,"
weaving the flesh of the body into the flesh of the world, and drawing perception into a dimension where subject and object, although differentiated, are intertwined in a perpetual dance of reversibility.

Thus, in the company of Merleau-Ponty's writings, we are privileged to
see hands gifted with intelligence, hands that bring wondrous things into
our world. More precisely, we are returned to the intricacies of our native
experience, free of some very old philosophical illusions, free to behold the
magic of poetizing, the creative event of meaning happening right there
before our eyes—right there, in the gestures of the hands. Thus, Merleau-
Ponty, despite manifest differences from Adorno, could easily agree with
Adorno's assertion that the task of the philosophical essay should be not
"to seek the eternal in the transient and distill it out" but rather "to render the transient eternal."[12] It is in this light, I believe, that we should interpret Merleau-Ponty's "rehabilitation of the sensible."

II. Enlightenment and Disenchantment: Merleau-Ponty's Critical Inheritance

Implicitly responding to the "disenchantment" set in motion by the Enlightenment, through which the ensouled body was denied its already fading aura, Merleau-Ponty attempted to bring the body back to life. To the body-object, body-instrument, body-machine, body-puppet, he opposed the body-subject, the living, lived body-of-experience that I am. As early as *The Structure of Comportment*, he was already working to free the human body from its reification within the metaphysics of substances that has held sway since Aristotle. If Merleau-Ponty's concepts of the body-subject and the lived body may be said to begin this difficult process, his later concept of the flesh, introduced with its chiasmatic intertwinings in *The Visible and the Invisible*, takes this project of deconstruction much further.

As George Santayana observed, the concept of the flesh is an allegorical figure, originating in and belonging to a discourse of the spirit: it is a spiritual matter, a matter of the most intense concern in the life of the spirit. As such, it is proto-ethical, proto-moral, the bearer of a utopian, eschatological potentiality—a normative demand waiting to be realized. Thus, the concept of flesh does not repudiate the Enlightenment but rather, on the contrary, gives practical Reason new resources, new inspiration, and new capacities upon which to draw.

But the Enlightenment's "disenchantments" incurred a serious disconnection between the cognitive and the affective-motivational dimensions of our ethical life. The concept of the flesh enables us to see and reaffirm their connection, because, prior to acts of cognition, the flesh is *already* affected, touched, and moved, already responsive to the other, already implicitly acknowledging the ethical claim—we might call it an organismic a priori—inherent in that relation. For Merleau-Ponty, the flesh is by its very nature, thus from the very beginning, ethically disposed, ethically exposed, and ethically dispossessed. "The Child's Relations with Others," a late essay summarizing a series of lectures given at the Collège de France, makes this indisputably clear. But this rudimentary ethical predisposition can easily be damaged and aborted. Its ideal development into a mature, reflectively autonomous, self-critical ethical character is in no sense necessary, inevitable, or preordained.

Merleau-Ponty was an astute reader of Schelling, as even his early work reveals. But Schelling's philosophical concerns can also be discerned in Merleau-Ponty's later thinking. Thus, for example, the concept of the flesh nicely dissolves the so-called "paradoxes of reflection" that have troubled German idealism and romanticism ever since Descartes and Kant. For if the paradoxes are a consequence of one-dimensional thinking, thinking remaining at the level of thematic cognition, the concept of flesh introduces a prereflective, fluid, nontotalizable unity-in-difference. The reflecting "I" identifies with the "I" that is the object of this act of reflecting; but the identity does not and moreover cannot take place for the first time at the level of reflection. Rather, the identity—what Kant thought of in terms of the "transcendental unity of apperception"— occurs first of all in the organismic unity of the prereflective, pre-personal lived body, the auto-nomous body-subject moving about and gesturing, actively engaged in the exploration of the natural and social world.

III. Measure: Normativity In Motion

Aristotle was the first philosopher to analyze and categorize in a thoroughly systematic way the various possible modes of movement proper to entities of different ontological types, beginning with the difference between the capacity for self-caused movement distinctive of living beings and the absence of that capacity in plants and nonliving beings. Human beings are endowed with an ability (*dunamis*) to move themselves—for example, to move their arms in an intentional gesture. This capacity or potentiality for self-caused movement, and the actualization, or setting-in-motion (*energeia*), of this potentiality, are what the philosopher considers to be most proper to the human being—although, whether living or dead, the human body also lends itself to being moved by causes external to the body.

Aristotle returned again and again to the question of movement, discussing it in numerous chapters of the *Physics*, *De Anima*, and *Metaphysics*. His interest in motion was principally motivated by questions concerning the nature and functioning of the soul, for, although the soul itself, being immaterial, cannot be said to move, its capacity to cause movement in the body it temporarily inhabits is "what is closest [most proper] to the nature of the soul" (*De Anima* 404a20–24). Thus, our gestures receive their measure, their rhythm, their timing, their direction and sense from the soul. And if reason rules in the soul, the measures it imparts to our gestures would cause them to move in the way most natural to the life of reason:

with deliberate moderation, in harmony with the nature of things, moved only to realize a desire informed by knowledge of the Good. Pursuing his metaphysical reflections on the nature of living beings, Aristotle attained a deep physiognomic understanding of the ethical motivation—the desire for the Good—operative in human motility. These reflections led him to the *arkhē kinēseōs tou kinouménon kath' autó*, the principle, ground, or origin of the self-initiated movement that human beings—animals endowed with reason—are capable of.

One can find something like this "origin" in Merleau-Ponty's phenomenology. According to Merleau-Ponty, unless some pathology is present, our gestures obey the "melody" and "rhythm" of an "intentional arc." Hence they are always in some way measured, endowed with a capacity to *give themselves* the measure befitting their situation. For example, in "normal" subjects, gestures are self-measured in their timing, momentum, rhythm, force, directionality, reach, and expressiveness. What Merleau-Ponty, following Husserl, called our "functioning intentionality" always expresses itself in a bodily schematized normativity conditioning our existential "opening upon the world." [13] The chapter in *Phenomenology of Perception* entitled "The Spatiality of One's Own Body and Motility" is the principal source for our reflections here on the ways in which our gestures are the bearers of measure in the spatialized, practical world they have participated in making.

In fact, the possibility of autonomy—the capacity to give oneself the moral law—could accordingly be said to have been already registered by the body as a deeply inscribed commandment—the normativity constitutive of the "corporeal schema," calling the motility system to action. Autonomy itself would therefore begin with the very first gestures—gestures not only self-motivated, self-moved, self-caused, and self-determined, but also, though at an elementary level, self-regulated, their movement measured by an immanent norm: their attunement to the "coordinates" of the immediate situation into which they are gathered, as into a certain *legein*, a certain "setting." [14]

Describing the intertwining of the gestural movement and its setting, Merleau-Ponty observes: "For the normal person, every movement has a background, and . . . the movement and its background are 'moments of a unique totality.' The background to the movement is not a representation associated or linked externally with the movement itself, but is immanent in the movement [itself], inspiring and sustaining it at every moment" (*PP*, 128/110). In other words, the setting or background, in its

"immanence," functions as a law, norm, or measure for the "motor intentionality" of the gesture: a law, norm, or measure to which the gesture
yields, which it takes into itself, and which it carries with it throughout its
duration. Thus, for example, "my gesture of impatience emerges from the
situation without any intervening thought" (*PP*, 129/111).

Our gestures receive their measure, their end—end in both senses—
from their felt sense of the concrete situation. But this does not mean that
they are bound to the present, bound to actuality, bound to the positivity
of their situation. Rather, our gestures require for their very possibility a
relation to the possible or the nonexistent, projecting or "throwing out,"
as it were, their own background: "The normal function which makes abstract movement possible is one of projection, whereby the subject of
movement keeps in front of him an area of free space in which what does
not naturally exist may take on a semblance of existence" (*PP*, 129/111).
Thus, "when I move about my house, I know without thinking about it
that walking towards the bathroom means passing near the bedroom, that
looking at the window means having the fireplace on my left, and in this
small world each gesture, each perception, is immediately located in relation to a great number of possible co-ordinates" (*PP*, 150–51/129). In these
coordinates, in relation to which our gestures are attuned and adjusted,
there is always law, normativity, measure. But this measure cannot be located in the objective space of the natural sciences, because the measure
exists neither solely "outside" nor solely "inside" the gesture: the space of
the gesture as gesture is an expressive or physiognomic space, a phenomenological space: "My flat is, for me, not a set of closely associated images.
It remains a familiar domain round about me only as long as I still have
'in my hands' or 'in my legs' the main distances and directions involved,
and as long as from my body intentional threads run out towards it."
Moreover, as Merleau-Ponty puts it in another passage:

> I am not *in* space and time [like some inanimate object], nor do I conceive
> space and time [as if I were a transcendental subject]; I belong to them, my
> body combines with them and includes them. The scope of this inclusion
> is the *measure* of that of my existence; but in any case, it can never be all-
> embracing. The space and time which I inhabit are always in their different
> ways indeterminate horizons. . . . The synthesis of both time and space is a task
> that always has to be performed afresh. (*PP*, 164/140)

Thus it is that, bearing a felt sense of the time and space of the situation
within it, "each instant of the movement embraces its whole span, and

particularly the first which, being the active initiative, institutes the link between a here and a yonder, a now and a future" (*PP*, 164/140). In a note he left behind, Wittgenstein attests to the truth in this description, drawing on his own body of experience to evoke a felt sense of this dynamic embrace, the gesture's unifying flow and rhythm: "Piano playing," he writes: "a dance of human fingers." [15] Moving with a physiognomic sense of this span, this measure, the gestures of a "normal" subject, in noticeable contrast to the gestures of (say) brain-damaged subjects, will always have a certain "melodic character," however awkward, abrupt, or incoherent they may be (*PP*, 122/105). Merleau-Ponty also describes this immanently organized gestural span, the melodic measure of our situational attunement, as an "intentional arc." With this descriptive concept, Merleau-Ponty may indeed be said to "flesh out" Kant's critical epistemology, locating in the body-subject the earliest moment in the unifying function of transcendental apperception, a function that the body continues to perform despite the eventual role of reflexive consciousness:

> The life of consciousness—cognitive life, the life of desire or perceptual life—is subtended by an "intentional arc" which projects round about us our past, our future, our human setting, our physical, ideological and moral situation, or rather, which results in our being situated in all these respects. It is this intentional arc [and not the transcendental apperception of a transcendental ego no longer entangled in bodily existence] which brings about the unity of the senses, of intelligence, of sensibility and motility. And it is this which "goes limp" in illness. (*PP*, 158/136)

Situating the gesture "in the realm of the potential," this "intentional arc" accordingly spans, or measures out, not only the spatialization of the gesture but its temporality. "The normal person *reckons with* the possible, which thus, without shifting from its position as a possibility, acquires a sort of actuality" (*PP*, 126–27/109). Thus, he observes, "At every moment, previous attitudes and movements provide an ever-ready standard [or norm] of measurement. It is not a question of a visual or motor 'memory' of the starting position of the hand; cerebral lesions may leave visual memory intact while destroying awareness of movement" (*PP*, 163/140). Acknowledging the psychological research that shows how different gestures of "grasping" or "touching" are from gestures of "pointing," Merleau-Ponty nevertheless deems it necessary to add a phenomenological comment: "From the outset the grasping movement is magically at its [temporalized and spatialized] completion; it can begin only by anticipating its end, since to disallow taking hold is sufficient to inhibit the action" (*PP*, 120/103–4). Once again, we are reminded that, in order to make sense of gesture, one must recognize the measure that it bears from its beginning to its end.

Measure is involved not only as the gesture's setting, not only in the gesture's spatialization and temporalization, but also in the immanence of the gesture's "toward-which" of referentiality: "In the action of the hand which is raised towards an object is contained a reference to the object, not as an object represented, but as that highly specific thing toward which we project ourselves, near which we are, in anticipation, and which we haunt" (*PP*, 160–61/138). Measure is likewise involved in the gesture's referential "in-order-to" or "for-the-sake-of." Thus, Merleau-Ponty argues:

> The subject, when put in front of his scissors, needle and familiar tasks, does not need to look for his hands or his fingers, because they are not objects to be discovered in objective space: bones, muscles and nerves [are] but potentialities already mobilized by the perception of scissors or needle, the central end of those "intentional threads" which link him to the objects given. It is never our objective body that we move, but our phenomenal body, and there is no mystery in that, since our body, as the potentiality of this or that part of the world, surges towards objects to be grasped and perceives them. . . . The bench, scissors, pieces of leather offer themselves to the subject as poles of action, [and] through their combined values they *delimit* a certain situation, an open situation moreover, which calls for a certain mode of resolution, a certain kind of work. The body is no more than an element in the system of the subject and the world, and the task to be performed elicits the necessary movements from him by a sort of remote attraction, as the phenomenal forces at work in my visual field elicit from me, without any calculation on my part, the motor reactions which establish the most effective balance between them . . . (*PP*, 123–24/106)

Significantly, the sentence goes on to propose another way in which a certain "remote attraction" solicits the appropriate gestures: "or," he says, "as the conventions of our social group, or our set of listeners, immediately elicit from us the words, attitudes and tone which are fitting [*qui leur conviennent*]." This brings out the fact that our gestures are often moved by measures whose origins, emerging through a dialogue with the social world, can be assigned exclusively neither to the realm of social conventions nor to the nature of the gesture.

In another passage, this "remote attraction," which is constitutive, for the gesture, of a certain measure, is described as a "calling": "A movement is learned when the body has understood it, that is, when it has incorporated it into its "world," and to move one's body is to aim at things through it; it is to allow oneself to respond to their call, which is made upon it independently of any representation" (*PP*, 161/139). In the solicitation that calls the gesture forth, guides it to its destination, and continues until the gesture ends, the normativity of measure is in effect regulating at a pre-reflective level such things as the rhythm and momentum of the gesture, the pressure and delicacy of the touch, the tightness and duration of the grip, the direction and duration of the referential monstration, and the tactfulness of the timing.

Learning these habit-forming measures is an essential part of socialization. Mastering table manners, which require finely attuned movements of arm and hand, is a striking example of this process. Merleau-Ponty gives the examples of typing and the playing of a musical instrument, habitual skills that also involve precisely self-regulated movements of arms and hands. As for typing, he remarks:

> To know how to type is not, then, to know the place of each letter among the keys, nor even to have acquired a conditioned reflex for each one, which is set in motion by the letter as it comes before our eye. If habit is neither a form of knowledge nor an involuntary action, what then is it? It is a *knowledge in the hands* [*un savoir qui est dans les mains*], which is forthcoming only when bodily effort is made, and cannot be formulated in detachment from that effort. The subject knows where the letters on the typewriter are as we know where one of our limbs is, through a knowledge bred of familiarity which does not give us a position in objective space. The movement of her fingers is not presented to the typist as a path through space which can be described, but merely as a certain adjustment of motility, physiognomically distinguishable from others. . . . When I sit at my typewriter, a motor space opens up beneath my hands, in which I am about to "play" what I have read. The reading of the word is a modulation of visible space, the performance of the movement is a modulation of manual space, and the whole question is how a certain physiognomy of "visual" patterns can evoke a certain type of motor response. (*PP*, 168/144; italics added) [16]

To understand skills such as typing and playing the piano is, therefore, to "experience the *harmony* between what we aim at and what is given, between the intention and the performance"—and to get a feeling for the way in which "the body is our anchorage in a world" (*PP*, 169/144; italics added). To experience this "harmony" is to experience the normative functioning of a measure—a measure no longer mediated by conscious attention: "When the typist performs the necessary movements on the typewriter, these movements are governed by an intention, but the intention does not posit the keys as objective locations. It is literally true that the subject who learns to type incorporates the keyboard space into his bodily space" (*PP*, 169/145). Now, according to Merleau-Ponty,

> The example of instrumentalists shows even better how habit has its abode neither in thought nor in the objective body, but in the body as mediator of a world. It is known that an experienced organist is capable of playing an organ with which he is not at all familiar. . . . He needs only an hour's practice to be ready to perform his program. Such a short preparation rules out the supposition that new conditioned reflexes have been substituted for the existing sets, except where both form a system and the change is all-embracing, which takes us away from the mechanistic theory, since in that case the reactions are mediated by a comprehensive grasp of the instrument.

"Are we to maintain," he then asks, "that the organist analyses the organ, that he conjures up and retains a representation of the stops, pedals and manuals and their relation to each other in space?" Having argued against physicalism, he argues now against cognitivism:

> But during the short rehearsal preceding the concert, he does not act like a person about to draw up a [cognitive] representation. He sits on the seat, works with the pedals, pulls out the stops, *gets the measure of the instrument with his body* [*il prend mesure de l'instrument avec son corps*], incorporates within himself the relevant directions and dimensions, and settles into the organ as one settles into a house. He does not learn objective spatial positions for each stop and pedal, nor does he commit them to "memory." During the rehearsal, as during the performance, the stops, pedals and manuals are given to him as . . . possibilities of achieving certain emotional or musical values. (*PP*, 169–70/145; italics added)

When the organist sits down at the keyboard and begins to play, fingers moving and touching as if instinctively, the instrument "comes to life," as we say. This is not merely a fanciful figure of speech, for the keyboard was nothing but a silent, dead object before this magical moment when the musician's dancing fingers intertwine with it, virtually obliterating the metaphysical distinction between hand and instrument. As the fingers simultaneously bring forth and respond to the "physiognomy" of keyboard and sounds, they are "obedient" to a measure that originates neither solely in the instrument nor solely in the fingers—a measure that can originate only in their chiasmatic intertwining.

IV. Sensus Communis: The Ideal Dimension
   of Gestural Experience

In an extremely significant aphorism in *Minima Moralia*, virtually ignored by critical-social theorists, Adorno remarks, "We still get the feel of morality in our very skin—when we blush." [17] A passage from *Arcadia*, by Sir Philip Sydney, offers this surpassingly charming description of the blush as a touching that can happen even at a distance: "And once his eye cast upon her and finding hers upon him, he blushed: and she blushed, because he blushed: and yet streight grew paler, because she knew not why he had blushed." [18] What the young lovers see at a distance in the interaction of their eyes touches them so forcefully that they involuntarily blush. This "touch effected by the eyes," traversing a "quasi-spatial tactile field" of sense and sensibility is not a mere metaphor, since the affect visibly alters the color of the cheeks (*PP*, 258/223). The blush is indeed causal action at a distance. For the traditional theories of empiricism and intellectualism, this experience can only remain an enigma. Not so for Merleau-Ponty's phenomenology. In his *Phenomenology of Perception*, he declares, "We must rehabilitate the experience of others which has been distorted by intellectual analyses" (216/185); for "insofar as I have sensory functions, a visual, auditory and tactile field, I am already in communication with others" (406/353). [19] He argues:

> We must rediscover after the natural world, the social world, not as an object or sum of objects, but as a permanent field or dimension of existence. . . . Our relationship to the social is, like our relationship to the world, deeper than any express perception or any judgment. It is as false to place ourselves in society as an object among other objects, as it is to place society within ourselves as an object of thought, and in both cases, the mistake lies in treating the social as an object. We must return to the social with which we are in contact by the mere fact of existing, and which we carry about inseparably with us before any objectification. . . . The social is already there when we come to know or judge it. . . . Prior to the process of becoming aware, the social exists obscurely and as a summons. (*PP*, 415–16/362)

It is evident from this passage that, as early as the *Phenomenology*, Merleau-Ponty was working his way toward the phenomenological disclosure of the social bonds through which we are appropriated—originally in an anonymous, pre-personal existence, prior to the stable formation of the egological subject, prior to the emergence of "intentional consciousness," prior even to the slightest velleity—for a life within the community, in the hold of which we are always already beholden to the other.[20] Calling attention to our experience in gesturing, Merleau-Ponty brings out its immanent acknowledgment of the other: "The communication or comprehension of gestures comes about through the reciprocity of my intentions and the gestures of others, of my gestures and intentions discernible in the conduct of other people. It is as if the other person's intention inhabited my body and mine his" (*PP*, 215/185).

In a later text, published in *The Prose of the World*, he continues reflecting on the deep communicativity of gestures: "It is characteristic of cultural gestures to awaken in all others at least an echo, if not a consonance."[21] In Merleau-Ponty's phenomenology, especially in his very late writings, we can therefore discern an attempt to elicit from our gestural experience, from the traces recovered as a felt sense, the corporeal origin of the ideal of sociality—an origin that Jürgen Habermas, neglecting the phenomenology, posits in the physical "mechanisms" of language. According to Habermas, the ideal of sociality can be traced back to our *biological* nature, and accordingly is an end objectively authorized by nature itself. In a recent work, he claims, "The utopian perspective of reconciliation and freedom is ingrained in the conditions for the communicative sociation of individuals; it is built into the linguistic mechanism of the reproduction of the species."[22] In contrast, Merleau-Ponty directs our attention to a utopian experience we actually live—an experience of embodiment through which he thinks we could get in touch with our dream of "an ideal community of embodied subjects, of an intercorporeality."[23] In another late writing, "The Intertwining—The Chiasm," he asks himself, in a challenge to the ontologies of empiricism and idealism: "Is my body a thing, is it an idea?" His answer could not be more emphatic: "It is neither," he says; rather, it is "the *measurant* of the things." To consummate this thought, he makes an extremely bold yet frustratingly obscure assertion: "We will therefore have to recognize an ideality that is not alien to the flesh, that gives it its axes, its depth, its dimensions" (*VI*, 199/152). This represents a task that it is surely imperative for phenomenology to undertake—a task that I think promises—if we follow out the logic of his indications—to exhibit the schematism of a certain moral ideality, a certain social order, that is already functioning—if only at the most rudimentary level, and without any teleological power, any biological predestination—as a predisposition inscribed in the very nature of the body of experience. In the *Critique of Pure Reason* (A808/B836), Kant adverts, though all too briefly, to the metaphysical thought that there is a *"corpus mysticum* of rational beings."

I believe that Adorno's aphorism about the blush and his comments elsewhere about the shudder[24] must be affirming a related metaphysical thought: that the flesh, even when badly damaged by the brutalities of history, preserves within itself a normative orientation toward a certain enlightened utopian ideality. But it is left to us to think the realization of this ideality, this "sublimation of the flesh" (as Merleau-Ponty phrases it), within our experience (*VI*, 203/155). In "The Intertwining—The Chiasm," Merleau-Ponty writes, "We touch here the most difficult point, that is, the bond between the flesh and the idea, between the visible and the interior armature which it manifests and which it conceals" (*VI*, 195/149). But he is ready to say at least this: that what is to be thought is an ideality that is not the contrary of the sensible, but rather "its lining and its depth" (ibid.). An ideality that constitutes a certain pro-mise, a pro-mise made to the flesh, registering in its paradoxical substance the dream of an ethical transformation of the social world, a transformation redeeming the sensuous and the sensible—and mutely calling for realization.

Contemplating the Platonism in Christianity, Santayana once said with regard to the flesh: "The difference between the life of the spirit and that of the flesh is itself a spiritual difference."[25] In other words, the life of the spirit constitutes and marks a difference within the life of the flesh: it cannot be denied its disquieting dwelling—precisely as inscription of difference, as register of a negative dialectics—within the identity of the flesh.

We know that, at some point in the years following his writing of *Phenomenology of Perception*, Merleau-Ponty returned to the task of thinking this utopian perspective in the context of his phenomenology. Although he glimpsed a connection between the "ideal community" posited by a certain moral-political project and the primordially social nature of our embodiment, he never completed an "archaeology" of this connection, showing the emergence and schematic projection of the ideal from a schematism of the *sensus communis* already inscribed, as a "gift of nature," into the nature of our flesh. In speaking of "the eternal body" and the "glorious body," did Merleau-Ponty name the dream of this impossible task (*VI*, 318/265)?[26]

Influenced by Heidegger, but saying something that Heidegger could never have said, Merleau-Ponty situates our bodies in "a field of being," a

field of multiple dimensions (*VI*, 293/240). Thus, "my body is made of the
same flesh as the world" (*VI*, 302/248), and in this dimension, the I and
the other exist in the world "like organs of one single intercorporeality,"[27]
flesh that has emerged into separate and autonomous structures of existence from "one sole tissue" (*VI*, 315/262). In "The Child's Relations with
Others," Merleau-Ponty refutes speculative theories of skepticism and
solipsism by calling attention to the "tissue" of intercorporeality that en-
twines the lives of infants. This is an intersubjective dimension of our experience as embodied beings that not only *temporally precedes* the emergence of the subject-object structure, but also continues to function in
sublated form, *structurally underlying* that structure.[28] This structural dimension of our embodiment, I would suggest, might be what would
allow us to retrieve and experience "once again"—albeit with adequate
consciousness only for the first time, and to a limited extent—the reci-
procities of existential acknowledgment that, from observations of children, we may surmise took place during our infancy and childhood, in a
past that never was present to consciousness. Is it even possible for us
to retrieve from the depths into which it has withdrawn any traces of an
experience of that originary "pre-communication" within which, as we
surmise, an "initial sympathy" first awakened in us, arousing, in its turn,
the body's obscurely felt sense of belonging to an "initial community," a
"sensus communis"? These phenomenological conceptualizations powerfully challenge ideologies and economies that commodify social relations.
Unfortunately, Merleau-Ponty does not elaborate the ethical and social-
political implications that his intriguing phenomenological appropria-
tions of the empirical research on infant behavior suggest. I am inclined to
think, however, that these implications were always in his mind.

In "The Intertwining—The Chiasm," this corporeal register of the social is attributed to the body's "ontological framework" (*VI*, 203/155), a
"universal flesh" (181/137) within which the gestures of the other receive
their "motor echo" (190/144) in mine, and our gestures are so intricately
intertwined that, if we were to abstract them from the field of their interaction, we would find it impossible to determine their meaning—or even
to individuate them, since we would have lost the metaphysical difference
that once secured their identity.[29] For the Merleau-Ponty that my reading
here is representing, it is to the phenomenologically reflective retrieval of
this experience of our chiasmatic intertwining—a retrieval, however fragmentary, however faint and ephemeral, of the remaining traces of a nor-

mative experience into which we were already initiated in the time of our infancy—that the utopian dreams of a moral community must turn for material encouragement. It is there, he seems to imply, there in traces of the *logos* and *nomos* already inscribed in the flesh, already buried within its nature, that the Kantian "*corpus mysticum* of rational beings," the promise of a moral community—the "carnal existence of the idea," as he refers to it in that text—will continue to summon and haunt us (*VI*, 203/155).

But this implication always remains, in his writings, a silent, unwritten thought, no matter how near he comes to the gesture. Thus I want to argue explicitly that, by virtue of this retrieval, an anonymous, pre-personal responsiveness to the other could be taken up into consciousness to become a personal responsibility to the other, a commitment of one's own name. In this way, an intersubjectivity functioning beneath the level of consciousness could be turned into a conscious commitment to the endless task of realizing the elusive utopian potential inherent in this intersubjectivity. In other words, by virtue of this endeavor, the schematism of a corporeal intersubjectivity, precariously preserved in sublated but damaged form by the self-interested sociability of the modern bourgeois subject, might be given a chance to fulfill the promise of enlightened sociability that it has secretly maintained. After all, the reversibility to which Merleau-Ponty calls our attention—a reversibility taking place prereflectively in the intertwinings of the flesh—is the experiential origin of the reciprocity essential to the realization of social justice. If, then, an initial schematization of this possible justice is already inscribed in the flesh, Merleau-Ponty's phenomenology may be used to suggest a "practice of the self" that could contribute to this realization.

This hope depends on recognizing in the intertwining, the chiasmic nature of the flesh, a dimension of the body that is to some extent *beyond the reach* of socialization, beyond the control of social normalization—to some extent, therefore, a "wild nature," human nature in the form of a dream, a desire that eludes to some extent the normative violence of social forces. But hope also depends on recognizing in the very nature of the flesh a certain preliminary normativity, the schematism of an ethical relation to the other.

In "The Philosopher and His Shadow," Merleau-Ponty argues that phenomenology must undertake "an ontological rehabilitation of the sensible."[30] Here he was in his own distinctive way consciously inheriting the philosophical project that Schelling described, drawing inspiration from the language of theology to express the sublime vision of romanticism, as "releasing even the realm of nature from the curse which weighs upon it."[31] For Merleau-Ponty, the way to approach this "redemption" of fallen nature is to begin an ontological retrieval of the sensible. That project, as he recognized, would demand an argument, validated by phenomenology, that boldly revisions the nature of human embodiment and defeats the hostile representations of the experiencing body that appear in Platonism, Cartesianism, and even transcendental idealism. This argument was set in motion in the last writings of Edmund Husserl, in spite of its unresolved ambiguities, intricate inconsistencies and disquieting paradoxes.

The first gesture in this direction must be to rescue the human body from the ontology of substances into which it has been cast. In his early work, *Phenomenology of Perception*, Merleau-Ponty began this rescue. But he eventually realized that the rescue required a more extreme move. He made this move in his lectures on research in child psychology and, even more vividly, in writings published posthumously under the title *Le visible et l'invisible*, in which "the body"—the body of experience—is represented in its elemental ecstatic dehiscence as flesh. Thus Merleau-Ponty argues that, if the identity of the subject is essentially and irreducibly intersubjective, then the embodiment of this subject must be recognized, correspondingly, in terms of an intercorporeality. Thus, moreover, he shows that ultimately there can be no redeeming of the nature of the body without a retrieval of its originary sociality: an intertwining that, without compelling or predetermining, nevertheless already disposes the infant to acknowledge the other in an experience of sympathy. This experience forms the basis for subsequent stages in one's psychosocial, ethical, and even political maturation.[32]

In "The Philosopher and His Shadow," Merleau-Ponty writes that "the constitution of others does not come after that of the body; others and my body are born together from an originary ecstasy."[33] For better or worse, our individual destinies, from the time of our birth to the time of our death and beyond, in the afterlife we are given in the memories of those who survive us, are inextricably entangled in the destinies of others—not only in the existence of individuals, communities, and nation-states, but also in the existence of the minerals, plants, and animals belonging to the world of nature.

Schelling—who strongly influenced Merleau-Ponty's thought, especially Merleau-Ponty's bold, early work *The Structure of Comportment*—

argued in *Clara; or, On Nature's Connection to the Spirit World* for a philosophical understanding of nature and our place in it that would encourage an ethics rooted in the body's felt sense of that "originary ecstasy," that originary destinal entanglement. Schelling observed there that "the lower level [of our corporeal life] contains prophecies of the higher, but this level nevertheless still remains the lower one."[34] (I am reminded of Emerson's remark in his unquestionably Schellingian essay "Nature": "Infancy is the perpetual Messiah, which comes into the arms of fallen men and pleads with them to return to paradise.")[35]

Undoubtedly Merleau-Ponty would have been able to hear his own thought sympathetically resonating in a statement that Adorno once made, arguing for a society that has overcome its contradictions and learned the reconciliation that surely can happen only through what Merleau-Ponty calls "intercorporeality." Adorno said: "In its proper place, even epistemologically, the relationship of subject and object would lie in the realization of peace among humans as well as between humans and their Other. Peace is the state of distinctness without domination, with the distinct *participating* in each other."[36] Could an experience of the intertwining some day bring together people now divided, gathering them into the sense and sensibilities of a moral community? Could retrieving that intercorporeality bring people together for the realization of its normative universality, its equality, reciprocity, and sense of justice?

But, strange to say, from Merleau-Ponty's writings we can in fact get no unequivocal answers to these questions. Perhaps he did not believe that we could retrieve from our intercorporeality the gift one might suppose it could proffer. As I will argue, bearing in mind the two senses of "realization," what I think ultimately made Merleau-Ponty's realization of the retrieval impossible for him was his dire misunderstanding of the experience of touching. I suspect that his error stemmed at least in part from a misapplication of analogy: having learned, from earlier work, about the intertwining of the senses, and most of all about the intertwining of the tactile with the visual, he was led to contemplate the experience of touch in terms of the same dialectic of mirroring that had seemed quite fitting in regard to the reversibilities taking place in the field of vision, where intricately intertwined glances visibly mirror one another, and where he consequently saw a certain "narcissism" in operation. This claim regarding the narcissism of vision may be disputed—as I have done elsewhere.[37] But in any case, importing the dialectic of mirroring that is operative in the exchange of glances into a hermeneutic phenomenology of touching is a mistake of major proportions.

One cannot ignore the problem that he bequeaths. As Levinas justly remarks, "the overall phenomenon [that Merleau-Ponty articulates] is structured as if the touch were [merely] a reflection on touching."[38] But Merleau-Ponty's error must be understood in its proper historical context. Specifically, it must be seen, on the one hand, against the blinding light of a Cartesianism still dominant in the philosopher's academic circles, and on the other hand, against the no less blinding light of a naturalism that, in appropriating the paradigm of the natural sciences, reduced social life to the externality of biophysical substances separated from one another by a space of absolute indifference.

Although Levinas, with evident approval, discerns in the intercorporeality of Merleau-Ponty's late phenomenology of the flesh a sublime maneuver away from the essentializing and reifying presuppositions of nineteenth-century humanism, he erroneously attributes to him an ontology borrowed from Heidegger. Thus Levinas writes: "The human is only a moment or an articulation of an event of intelligibility, the heart of which is no longer enveloped or situated within the human being. Note must be taken of this anti-humanist or non-humanist tendency to connect the human to an ontology of anonymous being."[39] But the "anonymous being" in question here is not what Heidegger would recognize as "being"; for Merleau-Ponty, it is, rather, the flesh, that pre-personal dimension of carnal existence in which my life and the lives of others are chiasmatically intertwined—a dimension of potentialities in which the emergence of the ethical relation is already anticipated.

If Merleau-Ponty pushed chiasmatic intercorporeality to an extreme that threatens to obliterate the other's alterity, he did so because only such a gesture would have seemed capable of sweeping away the vestiges of solipsism—the metaphysics of an individualism that supports a body politic, a form of sociality, that the philosopher believed inimical to the recognition of rights and responsibilities and to the overcoming of injustice.

V. Touching Hands

In his late writings, Merleau-Ponty gives himself a unique philosophical task. "The essential," as he formulates it, "is to describe the vertical or wild being as that pre-spiritual milieu without which nothing is thinkable, not

even the spirit, and by which *we pass into one another*, and ourselves into
ourselves" (*VI*, 257/204; italics added). In keeping with this tempting but
questionable claim, he argues that "reversibility . . . is the ultimate truth"
(204/155).[40] "Reversibility" is certainly one of the principal concepts in
Merleau-Ponty's late work. Its importance, for me, is that it recalls the root
meaning of reciprocity, the practical condition essential for the material
realization of justice. Through intertwining reversibility, the body is already *schematizing* the possibility of reciprocity. Thus, in his late writings,
especially those on research into the psycho-social maturation of infants
and young children, Merleau-Ponty calls attention to a corporeal schema
encoded in the flesh, an order that anticipates and calls for the achievement of reciprocity in social and political life.

According to Merleau-Ponty, where there is an intertwining of the I and
the other, there is always a potential reversibility of positions and roles—
even, to an extent, of identities. Nevertheless, identities can never completely coincide, never totally substitute for each other, since, as he says in
"Interrogation and Intuition," the intertwining is an encounter between
conscious beings, and not between two objects: "Every [conscious] being
presents itself at a distance—which does not prevent us from knowing it;
on the contrary, it is the very guarantee for knowing it" (*VI*, 169/127; also
see 163–66/122–24). Arguing against Husserl's intuitionism, Merleau-
Ponty emphatically insists that, even in the supposed "immanence" of intuition, there can be no immediate contact, no real coincidence, between
the subject's consciousness and the object intended by that consciousness.[41] "We are," he says, "interrogating our experience precisely in order
to know how it opens us to what is not ourselves. This does not ever exclude the possibility that we find in our experience a movement toward
what could not in any event be present to us in the original and whose irremediable absence would thus count among our originating experiences"
(*VI*, 211/159). Thus, even in the reflexivity of our experience with vision,
there is always a certain *punctum caecum* (*cecité*): even when I see myself
reflected in the eyes of the other, something always escapes the reflexive
moment (*VI*, 300, 301/247, 248). Thus it is necessary to admit that "in the
very measure that I see, I do not know what I see" (300/247). Analogously,
the flesh that the I and the other share and in whose intertwinings they
participate cannot itself and as such be touched. Escaping objectification,
the flesh to which they belong is, as such, neither visible nor tangible (301–
2/248).

But in *Phenomenology of Perception,* his earlier work, Merleau-Ponty shows that he is still under the spell of Husserlian immanentism—even in the very struggle to escape from the suspicion of solipsism that haunts the transcendental project and to formulate what is at stake in terms more faithful to our experience of the other: "The perceiving subject must, without relinquishing his place and point of view, and in the opacity of sensation, reach out towards things to which, in advance, he has no key, and for which he nevertheless carries *within himself* the project, and open himself to an absolute Other, *which he is making ready in the depths of his being* (*PP,* 376/325–26). I have italicized the troublesome—indeed duplicitous—elements in this description. Precisely here, where the philosopher attempts to "reach out" and "open himself to an absolute Other," we find instead a subversion of alterity and a reinscription of the metaphysics of immanence. The subject of this account dominates and reduces the other to the condition of the same. Assimilation, incorporation, and the violence of nonrecognition.

It is certainly true that Merleau-Ponty resists intuitionism, vehemently denying the possibility of immediate cognitive contact, total comprehension, total conceptual possession, and that he introduces chiasmatic intertwining in order to leave behind the metaphysics of presence involved in intuitionism. Nonetheless, his approach to the experience of the other ultimately fails to recognize the alterity that this experience registers.

Even in his very last writings, the treacherous duplicity persists, unrecognized and unresolved. Thus in *The Visible and the Invisible,* when he touches on the phenomenology of touching, he writes: "Every reflection is after the model of the reflection of the hand touching by the hand touched, open generality, a prolongation of the body's reserve [*volant*], hence reflection is not an identification with oneself . . . but non-difference with self = silent or blind identification" (*VI,* 257/204). The problem here is that Merleau-Ponty has inherited Husserl's visualism and the paradigm of reflection it promotes, all the while attempting to articulate within its overpowering logic a phenomenology of alterity and *différance.* His commitment to that ocularcentric paradigm means that, without his knowing it, he is being led astray by vestiges of a metaphysics of immanence—a metaphysics, in fact, of the will to power. He erases with one hand what the other hand has written. Only a phenomenology that is no longer a "photology," a "heliotropism," only a phenomenology free from the narcissism of reflection, can solicit for our ethical life the significance of the intercorporeality involved in the experience of touching.

First and foremost, we must abandon the conviction, which the paradigm of reflection encourages, that the experience of touching, and the experience of being touched and moved, can be understood only through a certain intermediate auto-affection.[42] As if, in these experiences, I could never really touch the other, but only ever touch myself—and as if I could encounter another only through the mediation of that auto-affection. In the realm of vision, the analogue would be the thesis that, strictly speaking, I am never justified in claiming really to *see* another person, and must concede that what I can see is nothing but an image—an image that obstructs and foreshortens my view, and never warrants more than a probabilistic inference regarding the "transcendent" reality of other persons.

Hostage to the paradigm of reflection, Merleau-Ponty's phenomenological account of touching turns the vulnerability of one's exposure to the other into a reflexivity that double-crosses alterity, handing it over to a Cartesian narcissism of mirroring that the post-metaphysical concepts of intertwining, intercorporeality, flesh, and reversibility were supposed to abolish forever. Insufficiently critical of this paradigm, he can articulate the experience of touching only in a way that, ironically, subverts and defeats the intention behind the entire demonstration, namely, the intention to break out of Cartesian metaphysics, working with new concepts—ecstasis, flesh, intercorporeality, intertwining, chiasm, reversibility—to deconstruct the prevailing representations: the metaphysical structure of subject and object, the reification of the body in both empiricism and intellectualism, the failure to recognize the dynamics of intersubjectivity constitutive of our corporeal nature, and finally, the failure to recognize alterity in the very heart of identity. Merleau-Ponty's account thus enables us to understand that, and why, both subjectivism (idealism, intellectualism) and objectivism (empiricism, physicalism, positivism) destroy the presence of the other as singularity, as alterity: the one by internalization or incorporation, the other by reification, the most extreme exclusion, the most extreme denial of recognition that can be conceived. Nevertheless, his own phenomenology of intersubjective life is not without problems. For example, in "The Child's Relations with Others," he describes the intercorporeality of infancy in terms of the child's "alienation" from itself through its relation with the other, and describes the child's experience of the other as that of a certain "encroachment" and "transgression" by the other. These terms— "alienation," "encroachment," and "transgression"—contradict the experience of intercorporeality. And in "The Intertwining—The Chiasm," his account of reversibility contradicts the experience of alterity, making the other appear to be nothing but a sublated moment in the self's reflexive return to itself.[43]

Reflecting, in *The Muses*, on the nature of aesthetic experience, Jean-Luc Nancy takes up the question of touch. I am not convinced, however, that his account settles all the questions that Merleau-Ponty leaves us with. In response to Freud and Derrida, Nancy writes:

> Now, for all of tradition, touch . . . is nothing other than "the sense of the body in its entirety," as Lucretius puts it. Touch [*Le toucher*] is nothing other than the touch or stroke [*la touche*] of sense altogether and of all the senses. It is their sensuality as such, felt and feeling. But touch itself—inasmuch as it is a sense and consequently inasmuch as it feels itself feeling, or more than that, inasmuch as it *feels itself feeling itself*, since it only touches by touching also itself, touched by what it touches *and* because it touches—touch presents the proper moment of sensuous exteriority; it presents it *as such and as sensuous*. What makes for touch is this "interruption," which constitutes the touch of the *self-touching*, touch *as self-touching*. Touch *is* the interval and the heterogeneity of touch. Touch is proximate distance. It makes one sense what makes one sense (what it *is* to sense): the proximity of the distant, the approximation of the intimate.[44]

In Merleau-Ponty, this self-touching, this reflexivity in the nature of touch, risks losing touch with the other. From the role that he assigns to autoaffection, one might conclude that it is a mediation which interrupts and prevents felt contact with the other, and that, strictly speaking, I can never really touch another but can only ever touch myself. But Merleau-Ponty does not draw this conclusion; on the contrary, he asserts, in phrasing reminiscent of Schelling, that identity is always "difference of difference" (*VI*, 318/264). I can indeed touch the other, but my touching of the other is always an experience in which the alterity of the other is irrefutably tangible. Yet it is difficult to overcome the suspicion that a problematic ambiguity in Merleau-Ponty's phenomenological account remains.

Thus we must examine in greater detail the intricately intertwining dialectic in Merleau-Ponty's phenomenological description of the gesture involved in touching. The trouble begins with his interpretation of the flesh. For he holds that "the flesh is a mirror phenomenon." Now, to be sure, he has warned against solipsistic reductionism, stating, immediately prior to this, that "the flesh, the *Leib*, is not a sum of self-touchings (of 'tactile sensations'), but also not a sum of tactile sensations plus 'kinaes-theses'; it is an 'I can'" (*VI*, 309/255). Moreover, it is clear from other passages that he introduces the concept of flesh precisely in order to deny solipsism—and even skepticism—any anchorage:

> What we are calling flesh, this interiorly worked-over mass, has no name in any philosophy. [But it enables us to recognize it in its anteriority as] the formative medium of the object and the subject. . . . We must not think the flesh starting from substances, from body and spirit—for then it would be the union of contradictories—but we must think it, as we said, as an element, as the concrete emblem of a general manner of being. (*VI*, 193/147)

The text continues, calling attention to the reversibility that characterizes the intertwinings of the flesh, but also arguing against any coincidence of subject and object:

> We spoke earlier of a reversibility of the seeing and the visible, of the touching and the touched. But it is time to emphasize that it is a reversibility always imminent and never realized in fact. My left hand is always on the verge of touching my right hand touching the things, but I never reach coincidence: the coincidence eclipses at the moment of realization.

However, an unexamined ocularcentrism continues to work its mischief, so that the image of reflective mirroring haunts the concept of flesh, secretly unraveling what the philosopher thinks he has woven together. Thus, for example, he says:

> Once again, the flesh we are speaking of is not matter. It is the coiling over of the visible upon the seeing body, of the tangible upon the touching body, which is attested in particular when the body sees itself, touches itself seeing and touching the things, such that, simultaneously, *as* tangible it descends among them, *as* touching it dominates them all and draws this relationship and even this double relationship from itself, by dehiscence or fission of its own mass. This concentration . . . , this bursting forth of the mass of the body toward the things, which makes a vibration of my skin become the sleek and the rough, makes me *follow with my eyes* the movements and the contours of the things themselves, this magical relation, this pact between them and me according to which I lend them my body in order that they inscribe upon it and give me their resemblance, this fold . . . , *these two mirror arrangements* of the seeing and the visible, the touching and the touched, form a close-bound system that I count on. . . . The flesh (of the world or my own) is not contin-

gency, chaos, but *a texture that returns to itself* and conforms to itself. (*VI*, 191–92/146; italics added)

It is in this "return" that the duplicity lies. For, although it *could* break the grip of the subject-object paradigm, and thereby also of solipsism, it risks incorporating—that is to say, denying—the otherness that is essential to the experience.

Addressing Husserl's account of the experience in *Ideas* II, according to which, when my right hand touches my left hand, the left not only is touched by but also touches the right, Merleau-Ponty expresses his agreement with the proposition first adumbrated by Kant's discussion of the right-hand and left-hand gloves,[45] that there can be no coincidence (*Deckung*) of the touching and the touched: "In the very moment when my touched hand becomes the touching hand, it is no longer being touched: reciprocity bursts open [*éclate*] the moment it is about to come into being."[46] But essential though it is to reflect on this experience, one must wonder how the philosophical narrative would have been written if, instead of taking as exemplary point of departure for phenomenological interrogation the touching of two hands belonging to one and the same person, Merleau-Ponty had examined—as Levinas does—experiences of touching between two subjectivities, two individuals.

Merleau-Ponty's earliest sustained discussion of touching is in his *Phenomenology of Perception*. Arguing against the representation of the tactile body in "classical psychology," he says there:

> If I can, with my left hand, feel my right hand as it touches an object, the right hand as an object is not the right hand as it touches: the first is a system of bones, muscles and flesh brought down at a point in space, the second shoots through space like a rocket to reveal the external object in its place. In so far as it sees or touches the world, my body can therefore be neither seen nor touched. What prevents its ever being an object, ever being "completely constituted," is that it is that by which there are objects. It is neither tangible nor visible in so far as it is that which sees and touches. (*PP*, 108/92)

The argument continues:

> My body, it was said, is recognized by its power to give me "double sensations": when I touch my right hand with my left, my right hand, as an object, has the strange property of being able to feel too. We have just seen that the two hands are never simultaneously in the relationship of touched and touch-

ing to each other. When I press my two hands together, it is not a matter of two sensations felt together as one perceives two objects placed side by side, but of an ambiguous set-up in which both hands can alternate the roles of "touching" and "being touched." What was meant by talking about "double sensations" is that, in passing from one role to the other, I can identify the hand touched as the same one which will in a moment be touching. In other words, in this bundle of bones and muscles which my right hand presents to my left, I can anticipate for an instant the integument or incarnation of that other right hand, alive and mobile, which I thrust toward things in order to explore them. The body catches itself from the outside engaged in a cognitive process; it tries to touch itself while being touched, and initiates "a kind of reflection" which is sufficient to distinguish it from objects, of which I can indeed say that they "touch" my body, but only when it is inert, and therefore without ever catching it unawares in its exploratory function.

In *The Visible and the Invisible*, the phenomenology of touching assumes an even more prominent role. In the texts assembled in this book, Merleau-Ponty seizes every opportunity to deny any coincidence of the "subjective" hand touching and the "objective" hand being touched: "Either my right hand really passes over to the rank of touched, but then its hold on the world is interrupted; or it retains its hold on the world, but then I do not really touch *it*—my right hand touching, I palpate with my left hand only its outer covering" (*VI*, 194/148). "But," he writes,

> this incessant escaping, this impotency to superpose exactly upon one another the touching of things by my right hand and the touching of this same right hand by my left hand, or to superpose, in the exploratory movements of the hand, the tactile experience of a point and that of the "same" point a moment later . . . —this is not a failure. For if these experiences never exactly overlap, if they slip away at the very moment they are about to rejoin, if there is always a "shift," a "spread" [*écart*] between them, this is precisely because my two hands are part of the same body, because it moves itself in the world.

Moreover, "this hiatus between my right hand touched and my right hand touching . . . is not an ontological void, a non-being: it is spanned by the total being of my body, and by that of the world." Thus, although reversals are taking place, so that "to touch is to touch oneself" (*VI*, 308/255), it is nevertheless "not an actual identity of the touching and the touched" (326/272). This point is elaborated in an intriguing "working note" in which Merleau-Ponty invokes the "negativity that inhabits the touch," and states that, because of this negativity, the body is not an empirical fact but has an ontological significance, for there is an *untouchable dimension* of the touch—the reverse or beyond of sensible being (*VI*, 308/255).

Since "the touch is formed in the midst of the world and as it were in the things," Merleau-Ponty pays much attention to the synaesthetic intertwinings of vision and touch: "the visible spectacle," he says, "belongs to the touch neither more nor less than do the "tactile qualities." We must habituate ourselves to think that every visible is cut out in the tangible, every tactile being in some manner promised to visibility, and that there is encroachment, infringement, not only between the touched and the touching, but also between the tangible and the visible" (*VI*, 176/134). Although what he says is obviously true, Merleau-Ponty's obsession with this "intimacy" of touch and vision introduces some treacherous consequences into the phenomenology of touch. And this "promise" to visibility will be disputed by Levinas, since it amounts to handing over all modalities of touch to the possessive totalizing violence of vision. But touch, for its part, delimited though it is by what exceeds it, raises the specter of a certain narcissism—a narcissism not easily rendered immune to the philosophical pathology in solipsism.

Merleau-Ponty evokes the untouchable again in another important passage, in which he takes pains, as he does elsewhere, to distance himself from Husserlian idealism:

> To touch and to touch oneself. . . . They do not coincide in the body: the touching is never exactly the touched. This does not mean that they coincide "in the mind" or at the level of "consciousness." Something else than the body is needed for the junction to be made: *it takes place in the untouchable.* That of the other which I will never touch. But what I will never touch, he does not touch either; no privilege of oneself over the other here. (*VI*, 307/254; italics added)

This "untouchable" inhabits and envelops the touched; in relation to the realm of the tactile, it constitutes the ontological difference. It is the condition of possibility, necessarily intangible, that gives us the things that can be touched. The tangible presents itself in a sensory field organized by the interplay of the tangible and the intangible—a field first opened up by an event whose origin belongs to the intangible, into which it has forever withdrawn. Thus Merleau-Ponty must argue: "The untouchable is not a touchable in fact inaccessible. . . . The negative here is not a positive that is elsewhere (a transcendent)————. It is a true negative, i.e., an *Unver-*

borgenheit of the *Verborgenheit, Urpräsentation* of the *Nichturpräsentierbar*" (*VI*, 308/254). Touching is consequently not only a relation to the being touched but always also an experience of the untouchable. Touching the untouchable is not, of course, like touching a tactile being; rather, it is an experience of the limits of the touchable, a tangible experience of our finitude—and the death of intentionality.

But Merleau-Ponty's potentially momentous recognition of this experience of finitude is diminished by the narcissism that overcomes it in his narrative, as a consequence of his assimilating touch to vision. To touch is always, he says, to touch oneself: "Accordingly, [it] is not to apprehend oneself as an ob-ject; it is to be open to oneself, destined to oneself (narcissism)." What he says immediately following this statement in no way avoids the problem: "Nor, therefore, is it to reach *oneself*; it is on the contrary to escape *oneself*, to be ignorant of *oneself*; the self in question is by divergence [*d'écart*]" (*VI*, 303/249).

Using a vision-generated paradigm for the reflexivity experienced in touching can mean only that the ambiguity surrounding alterity remains, despite his insistence that no coincidence is possible:

> The quasi-"reflective" redoubling, the reflexivity of the body, the fact that it touches itself touching, sees itself seeing, does not consist in surprising a connecting activity behind the connected, in reinstalling oneself in this constitutive activity; the self-perception . . . does not convert what it apprehends into an object and does not coincide with a constitutive source of perception: in fact, I do not entirely succeed in touching myself touching, in seeing myself seeing; the experience I have of myself perceiving does not go beyond a sort of *imminence*, it terminates in the invisible. (*VI*, 303/249)⁴⁷

And yet, he will argue, for example in "The Philosopher and His Shadow," that "my right hand was present at the advent of my left hand's active sense of touch. It is in no different fashion that the other's body becomes animate before me when I shake another man's hand or just look at him."⁴⁸ So "he and I are like organs of one single intercorporeality."⁴⁹ But can we agree to the words "no different"? How can this avoid assimilating the other to the same? And is there not an unexamined ocularcentrism in his use of the word "or," a use that in effect equates the gesture of shaking someone's hand with the act of "just looking"? There certainly seem to be some problematic claims here.

In the essay "On Intersubjectivity: Notes on Merleau-Ponty,"⁵⁰ Levinas disputes the phenomenology of touching proposed in "The Philosopher and His Shadow," arguing that Merleau-Ponty turns the relation to the other into a representation of knowledge. But in so arguing, has Levinas not, to some extent, confused Merleau-Ponty's characterization of that relation with Husserl's? After all, the whole of Merleau-Ponty's work in phenomenology, beginning with his early *Phenomenology of Perception*, is intended to undermine philosophies that make the originary relation between ego and alter a question of knowledge, ignoring the precedence of a more primordial interaction. In "The Philosopher and His Shadow," Merleau-Ponty says, "If the other is to exist for me, he must do so to begin with in an order beneath the order of thought."[51] His point of course speaks against the arrogance of idealism, but just as much against the pretensions of empiricism, which remains stubbornly oblivious to the fact that the "reality" it represents as independent of thought is nothing but a reification of its unavowed projections. When Merleau-Ponty adverts to the moment of *connaissance*, he is pointing not to a moment of knowledge (*savoir*) but to the simultaneous "birth" (*naissance*) of ego and alter from an "original ecstasy,"[52] a moment without any absolute identity, a moment that, from the very beginning, is already fissured, differentiated, chiasmatic. Thus, to defend against the kind of objection that Levinas makes, simply ignoring the texts of his interlocutor, Merleau-Ponty repeatedly states that there can be no possibility of a "coincidence" or "confusion" of identities. Moreover, after the passage quoted above from "The Philosopher and His Shadow," Merleau-Ponty hastens to add the following remark, no doubt thinking that he is disputing Husserl's Cartesian phenomenology:

> It is imperative to recognize that we have here neither comparison, nor analogy, nor projection or "introjection." The reason why I have evidence of the other man's being-there when I shake his hand is that *his hand is substituted for my left hand,* and my body *annexes* the body of another person in that "sort of reflection" it is paradoxically the seat of. My two hands "coexist" or are "compresent" because they are one single body's hands. The other person appears through an extension of that compresence; he and I are like organs of one single intercorporeality. (Italics added)

But is the other person (merely) an "extension" of my embodied existence—or instead a disruption of my identity? Is it true that, when I shake someone's hand, that hand is experienced, is felt, as a substitution for my own? In "The Child's Relations with Others," Merleau-Ponty describes the presence of the other as an "encroachment" and "transgression"—terms that do not fit easily into the picture of intercorporeal extension and

annexation. But could one read the concept of intertwining as both a phenomenologically generated concept and a critically effective concept, intended to make the relation between myself and the other a dialectical
interaction?

In "Subject and Object," a major essay, Adorno argues that the truth of
my relation with the other can be rendered only in terms of such a dialectical interaction. He writes:

> The separation of subject and object [in the discourse of philosophy] is both
> real and illusory. True, because in the cognitive realm it serves to express the
> real separation, the dichotomy of the human condition, a coercive develop-
> ment. False, because the resulting separation must not be hypostatized, not
> magically transformed into an invariant. . . . Though they cannot be thought
> away, as separated, the *pseudos* of the separation is manifested in their being
> mutually mediated—the object by the subject, and even more, in different
> ways, the subject by the object.[53]

In this light, it would be desirable to interpret Merleau-Ponty's concepts
of "intertwining" and "flesh" as preserving both the separation and the
connection—and to do so in terms of what might be called a dialectical
interaction. The flesh, he says, is to be understood as "the formative
medium of the object and the subject" (*VI*, 193/147). However, getting entangled in a reflexivity that threatens to erase his efforts to free phenomenology from the narcissism of transcendental metaphysics, he also says,
"The flesh is a mirror phenomenon" (*VI*, 309/255).

Continuing his argument against the vestiges of Cartesianism remaining in phenomenology, Merleau-Ponty asks: "If my left hand can touch
my right hand while it palpates the tangibles, can touch its touching, can
turn its palpation back upon it, why, when touching the hand of another,
would I not touch in it *the same power* to espouse the things that I have
touched in my own?" (*VI*, 185/141; italics added). Now, as an immanent
critique, this may be an appealing argument; but its victory—if there is
one—is not without a tragic price. For, although the argument may be an
attempt (borrowing Adorno's words) "to use the strength of the subject to
break through the fallacy of constitutive subjectivity,"[54] it makes its case
only by presupposing that the starting point for reflection on my relation
to the other must be my subjectivity, necessarily posited—regardless
of Merleau-Ponty's good intentions—in its absolute, metaphysical self-
containment: my subjectivity in its moment of enclosure within reflexivity. To be sure, he says that "to feel one's body is also to feel its aspect for

the other." And as he acknowledges, "One would here have to study in what sense the other's sensoriality is implicated in my own" (*VI*, 299/245). But he is already conceding too much by formulating his phenomenological description of my tactile interactions with the other by way of a description of my experience of touching myself.

Why, he asks, would the "universality" of the flesh, elemental medium of all possible human interactions, not render my body "open" to other bodies? "The handshake too," he says, "is reversible":

> I can feel myself touched as well and at the same time as touching, and surely there does not exist some huge animal whose organs our bodies would be, as, for each of our bodies, our hands, our eyes are the organs? Why would not the synergy exist among different organisms, if it is possible within each? Their landscapes interweave, their actions and their passions fit together exactly. (*VI*, 187/142)

How would Merleau-Ponty's late phenomenology be altered, if, instead of beginning from the experience of my left hand touching the right, he had begun with the handshake? What implications would follow?

After acknowledging that there is still much to be learned about how "the other's sensoriality is implicated in my own," he writes: "But the correlation is not always thus of the seer with the seen, or of speaking with hearing: my hands, my face also are of the visible. The case of reciprocity (seeing seen), (touching touched in the handshake) is the major and perfect case, where there is *quasi-reflection* (*Einfühlung*)" (*VI*, 299/245). But is empathy (*Einfühlung*) rightly understood in terms of the model of reflection? And does the concept of "empathy" not in a sense perpetuate the very metaphysics we are trying to escape, by assuming that my access to the "interiority" of other persons is obstructed by the virtually impenetrable "exteriority" formed by the massive substance of their bodies?

What if the two hands touching were yours and mine? What if the phenomenological theater opened with a handshake? Could the felt experience of reversibility that joins these hands have communicated something crucial about the meaning of equality and justice? Could a simple handshake activate the *promesse de bonheur* touched upon ever so lightly in "The Child's Relations with Others," where the presence of an "initial sympathy" and an "initial community" is invoked? Could our intertwined hands begin to awaken the universal body to its dream of ethical life?[55]

She stretches out her hand to the poor;
She reaches out her hands to the needy.

        —Proverbs 31

I remember the manifold cord—the thousand or the million stranded cord which my being and every man's being is, . . . so that, if everyone should claim his part in me, I should be instantaneously diffused through creation and individually decease. . . . I am an alms of all and live but by the charity of others.

        —The Early Lectures of Ralph Waldo Emerson

No dejéis morir a los viejos profetas
pues alzaron su voz contra la usura que ciega nuestros ojos con óxidos oscuros,
la voz que viene del desierto, el animal desnudo que sale de las aguas
para fundar un reino de inocencia,
la ira que despliega un mundo en alas, el pajaro abrasado de los apocalipsis,
las antiguas palabras, las ciudades perdidas,
el despertar del sol como dádiva cierta en la mano del hombre.

[Do not let the old prophets die,
for they raise their voices against the usury that blinds our eyes with dark oxides,
voice that comes from the desert, naked animal that emerges from the waters
to found a reign of innocence,
rage that unfolds the world in wings, the bird charred in the apocalypse,
ancient words, lost cities,
the awaited wakening of the sun as sure gift in the hand of the human.]

—José Ángel Valente, *Obra poética 2: Material memoria 1977–1992*

§ 10 Arrhythmia in the Messianic Epokhē

Opening the Gate with Levinasian Gestures

How can we be fair, kindly, and humane towards others, let our
maxims be as praiseworthy as they may be, if we lack the capacity
to make strange natures genuinely and truly a part of ourselves,
appropriate strange situations, make strange feelings our own?

— Friedrich Schiller, *Letters on the Aesthetic Education
of Man*[1]

The reconciled condition would not be the philosophical imperialism
of annexing the alien. Instead, its happiness would lie in the fact
that the alien, in the proximity it is granted, remains what is distant
and different, beyond the heterogeneous and beyond that which is
one's own.

— Theodor W. Adorno, *Negative Dialectics*[2]

All that is visible rests on [*haftet an*] the invisible—the audible on
the inaudible—the felt on the unfelt [*das Fühlbare am Unfühlbaren*].
Perhaps thinking rests on unthinking.

— Novalis, "Logological Fragments"[3]

Obey the law that reveals, and not the law revealed.

— Henry David Thoreau, *A Writer's Journal*[4]

I. A Different Modernity: The Ethics and Politics of Alterity

In this final chapter, we continue our reflections on the ethics of gesture
by engaging the work of Emmanuel Levinas. In its entirety, Levinas's
philosophical work radically contests the principal investments—ethical,
political, and spiritual—of Western modernity. To provide context for
our thematic questions, I will begin with a brief exposition of the most important elements in this Levinasian "critique" of modernity.

1. Invoking a new humanism, a humanism "for the other one," Levinas
criticizes modernity's prevailing conception of humanism, questioning its
most enduring assumptions: for instance, that the very "essence" of the
human consists in a monadic subjectivity motivated by egoistic pursuit of
individual interests and ends, and that a concern for the plight of the other
is accordingly not constitutive of our humanity, our very dignity and iden-

tity as human. Against a humanism that affirms the absolute sovereignty of Mankind over a world closed to transcendence, Levinas proposes a humanism that encourages a certain "vigilance," attentive to the intimations and traces of transcendence that reveal the disruptive presence of the other in a world otherwise reduced to total immanence.

2. Levinas also contests the ethics we have inherited from the Enlightenment. In this project he questions the normative role of rationality in our ethical life, emphasizing how the ethical subject is subordinated and violated when its singular concerns are recognized only in terms of the formal universalism required by an impersonal reason. Similarly, he interrogates Kantian deontologism, whose ideal of moral symmetry subjects the unique individual will and the ethical relation to a procedure for the imaginative reversibility of equivalent subjective positions. Finally, Levinas questions the demands of an instrumentalized rationality that reduces our subjectivity to its utility or to a calculable objectivity.[5]

3. The dominant ontological and epistemic paradigm at work in ethics and politics, according to Levinas, is the drive to dominate and control, to reduce the world to a totality, a predictable presence, and to privilege the theoretical over the practical, the cognitive over the affective, the objective over the subjective, knowledge of being over concern for ethical life, and the disclosure of truth over the achievement of social justice.

In many ways, the critique of modernity that Levinas undertakes continues the critique that Heidegger set in motion. I am thinking, for example, of Heidegger's critique of technologization, the prevailing paradigm of objectivism, philosophical commitments to totality, and an individualism that encourages a freedom indifferent to responsibility. Levinas sharply rejects Heidegger's obsession with the question of being; nevertheless, he happily takes over Heidegger's argument concerning the derivation of our ontology from the gestures of our hands. With it, he not only joins Heidegger in questioning the character of our relation to things, but also moves beyond Heidegger to question the character of our relations with others. Thus, in his essay "Transcendence and Intelligibility," Levinas observes that the prevailing philosophical understanding of the being of beings has come to reflect "a society seemingly delivered over to technological domination," "the promise of *satisfaction* made to a greedy and hegemonic ego." Accordingly, this philosophical understanding has degenerated into an ideological discourse not only supporting the morally corrupt fantasy of "a plenitude of adequation in the *satis*," but even dismissing as "unintelligible" whatever "surpasses its measure," whatever does not lend itself to "the grasp and to manipulation."[6] In this discourse, Levinas thus discerns telltale traces of the hand:

> Even before the technical ascendancy over things which the knowledge of the industrial era has made possible and before the technological development of modernity, knowledge, by itself, is the project of an incarnate practice of sei-zure, appropriation, and satisfaction. The most abstract lessons of the science of the future will rest upon this familiarity with the world that we inhabit in the midst of things held out to the grasp of the hand. Presence, of itself, be-comes the now.[7]

"Total presence" defines an ontology that originates in the desires aroused by what our hands make possible—desires to seize, possess, master, and control. Desires that cannot handle even the thought of transcendence, infinity, what is beyond presence, beyond all manipulable measure. Re-flecting on the literal meaning of *maintenant*, the French word for "now," Levinas stresses that the hand's typical use consists in maintaining the pri-macy of the now-present moment, *le main-tenant*, literally, "the hand's holding." The hand has become the organ of the ego's impatient demand for immediate satisfaction, fulfilled intentionality. Thus, whereas Heideg-ger connects the hand to ontologies of totalized presence, heeding what the German language gives one to hear in *Vorhandensein* and *Zuhanden-sein*, Levinas, attentive to the language of his adoptive France, connects the hand to the "maintenance" of a temporality dominated by the imme-diacy of the "now." But although Levinas indicts the ontology that origi-nates with the hand, he also offers thoughts that make it possible to con-ceive the redemption of the hand in its prophetic employment.

4. Levinas also challenges the liberalism of enlightened politics, espe-cially its enthusiasm for the prevailing culture of freedom and individual-ism: "What is an individual, a solitary individual," he asks, "if not a tree that grows without regard for everything it suppresses and breaks, grab-bing all the nourishment, air and sun, a being that is fully justified in its nature and its being? What is an individual if not a usurper?"[8] He believes that by giving priority to freedom, to freedom of the individual and pri-vate satisfactions, this politics inevitably subordinates our responsibility for the others in our community and cannot avoid supporting irreconcil-able inequalities, grave injustices, attitudes of intolerance, intractable so-cial antagonisms, and even violence.

In many ways, therefore, Levinas wants to salvage remnants of a premodern experience of ethical and political life without abandoning the
values, virtues, and ideals of the Enlightenment project. In fact, in some
decisive ways, Levinas's work is a thought that arrives to disturb the present, bringing with it, from its years of absorption in the hermeneutics of
old talmudic teachings, both an ethics and a politics: an ethics that elevates
the other in recognition of a sacred singularity; and a messianic politics
moved by its hope for justice, peace, and an end to unnecessary suffering.

For Levinas, Kant's deontological ethics of rationally derived duty does
not realize the truly sublime dignity of the ethical relation. For in the highest phase of development of that relation, what should call forth from me
a gesture of pure benevolence toward a stranger in need is not a categorical imperative, the inner voice of the moral law, appearing as if alien to my
nature and appealing to my conscience only at the end of a procedure of
rational reflection,[9] but rather an immediately receptive, spontaneously
responsive "perception," appropriately realizing what the situation in its
uniqueness requires of me. I encounter someone in distress—and I do
whatever I can to be of help. I am passively acting, then, in immediately
receptive responsivity to the appeal, the summons, that comes within the
perception itself and is constitutive of its very sense as such. As Franz
Rosenzweig puts it in *The Star of Redemption*, we are now realizing all too
painfully what it means to live in a world ruled by egoism, a world in
which "no one could feel the human element as the human element in
others, [in which] each one [could feel it] immediately only in his own
self."[10] For Levinas, who was profoundly influenced by Rosenzweig, the
source of the ethical is not to be found, as it is for Kant, in the rationally
determined universality of a will that has ignored all instruction by sense
and sensibility, rendering itself indifferent toward the singular; nor does
the ethical derive, as it does for the utilitarians, from a rational calculation
of the maximum measure of happiness. Instead, the ethical is inherent in
the very experience of the encounter, which is constitutive of the relationship between self and other.

According to Levinas, the seemingly progressive, enlightened conditions of bourgeois modernity, conditions promoting emancipation, autonomy, and rights, have also—paradoxically—thrown our ethical and
political life into a deepening crisis. Kant was certainly acutely aware of
this crisis, long before Nietzsche's diagnosis of nihilism, proclaiming the
devaluation of all values; but Kant thought his procedure of rational re-

flection, telling us how to discern what is right from the universal stand-point of the rational will, could somehow overcome this crisis. But since, in effect, Kant's proceduralism *presupposes* a certain individualism, a certain monadic egoism, his effort to subordinate action to the principles of an "impersonal reason,"[11] instead of overcoming the crisis, creates a compromising accommodation that only exacerbates it by leaving this egoism—the very root of the crisis—almost completely intact. What is more, his proceduralism ends up denying to the judgment of reason the motivating force it needs, locked away in sense and sensibility. The excesses of bourgeois Enlightenment rationalism only deepen this alienation from our senses and our sensibility and attenuate our felt proximity to the other, so that, despite an intention to encourage a greater feeling of responsibility toward the other, such rationalism empties the ethical relation of bodily felt value, meaningful value, and leaves the universal principle without motivational mooring in experience. Hence Levinas argues that the persistence of such rationalism can only continue the destruction of ethical experience.

In a statement with which Levinas could certainly agree, Walter Benjamin argued: "Tactile reception is accomplished not so much by attentiveness [*Aufmerksamkeit*] as by habit. . . . The tasks which face the human apparatus at the turning points of history cannot be solved by optical means—that is, by contemplation alone. They are acquired gradually by habit, under the tutelage of tactile reception."[12] Not satisfied with the forms of enlightenment brought by intuition, contemplation, and "sovereign" reason, Benjamin here reconnects us to a deeply motivating sense of our ethical and political responsibilities, and thereby puts the historical task of moral awakening squarely in our hands.

Instead of proposing a rational reconstruction of moral experience, Levinas hopes to return us to the compelling authority of our lived experience—to the immediately felt, bodily felt imperatives and the preoriginarily guilty conscience that constitute our ethical relations with others. Drawing on the rhetorical resources of language, its resources for invocation and exhortation, he attempts to awaken our moral sense and sensibility, convinced that the authority invested by philosophers in an abstract, formal reason has displaced and weakened our capacity to feel proprioceptively the immediate claim of our ethical responsibilities to the other. If I am "bound" to the other "by a plot which knowing can neither exhaust nor unravel,"[13] then my responsibilities for the other—responsibilities whose absolutely imperative character Levinas describes in the most extreme terms, namely as "traumatic" and "persecutory"—cannot be rendered motivationally meaningful in formal representations of principle, which appeal to the methodically detached indifference of a contemplative or deliberative rationality. Instead my responsibilities must, he thinks, be bodily felt in all their situational immediacy and uniqueness. No unconditional rational necessity can substitute for the passive, traumatic, ethically motivating experience of another's distress and need.

Thus, as Adorno also understood,[14] the originary, natural impulse to respond to the other that is the very heart of the ethical relation, already severely repressed by the disenchantments of Enlightenment and the ruthless individualism of the modern bourgeois spirit of freedom, is threatened with even deeper oblivion by well-intentioned efforts to encourage this impulse through the mediations of abstract ratiocination. Hence Levinas's ethical project is an anamnestic one, born of trauma and mourning: an evocation of a moral sensibility that we have forgotten—forgotten and lost touch with. At stake, for him, is the ethical character of a sensibility that has been subjected, subordinated, to the most radical heteronomy: a heteronomy absolutely different from the Kantian, but so extreme that even the critical conception of autonomy, which is obliged to renounce what Kant calls "heteronomy," is still not, in fact, free of its egoism. In Levinas's ideal of the ethical relation, "heteronomy" displaces Kantian autonomy as the height of that relation, because the welfare of the other is "higher" and more "urgent" than the symmetry—the equality and reciprocity—required for Kantian autonomy. Therefore, from the standpoint of Levinasian heteronomy, Kant's conception of moral autonomy is still entangled in the egoism that defines Kantian heteronomy.

In his preface to *Totality and Infinity*, Levinas commits himself to conceiving an ethical "lucidity" capable of penetrating the shadow "that 'falls' over the actions of men[,] . . . divests the eternal institutions and obligations of their eternity[,] and rescinds *ad interim* the unconditional imperatives," ultimately rendering morality itself "derisory" (ix/21). The words *"ad interim"* deserve particular attention since, with the finest discretion, they invoke the prophecy of redemption that Levinas considers in the concluding pages of his book. But "in the meantime," that is, for now (*maintenant*), social relations and institutions are haunted by cold indifference, gratuitous cruelty, and ruthless violence. Our world is torn apart by the primitive justice of retaliation and by wars of ever-increasing destructiveness: indeed, "does not lucidity, the mind's openness upon the true, consist in catching sight of the permanent possibility of war?" (*TI*, ix/21). For Levinas, we will see no end of such horrors until moral lucidity develops into a revolutionary messianic consciousness that finally breaks the spell of fatality, the "truth of being" operative in the logic of identity, the ideology of totality, and the rule of a cold objectivity (*TI*, ix/21).

The almost obliterated traces of our radical, preoriginary heteronomy, the one-for-the-other, which Levinas wants memory to retrieve from ethical experience are traces of an exorbitant claim on our generosity, our compassion, our willingness to sacrifice for the benefit of the other—a categorical claim on our response-ability and humanity that we cannot in good conscience decline. This unquestionably requires an ethics at odds with the contemporary spirit: an ethical life motivated by unconditional responsibility to and for the other. But in the heart of its difference there also lies an uncompromising passion for justice—and, to keep it vigilant, a concern for the welfare of others that is immeasurable, a concern that therefore defies representation by gestures of greeting, recognition, and respect, the normative practices idealized by the Enlightenment and its heirs. Thus, even when his politics recognizes the "dignity" of citizenship, Levinas will propose understanding it as a dimension of our "spiritual nature." [15]

In this light, the concept of "freedom" that Levinas affirms demands that we renounce an egoism motivated by "solitary salvation" and commit ourselves to "the difficult task of living an equitable life [*une vie équitable*]" in community with others. [16] This formulation of course recognizes the moral imperative of just measure, of fairness, in the politics of freedom. But, claiming for freedom an origin that modernity has repudiated, he boldly asserts that "to the objectivism of war we oppose a subjectivity born from the eschatological vision" (*TI*, xiv/25). [17] Yet even when we take such eschatology seriously, between the thought of "an equitable life" and the thought with which John Rawls concludes *The Theory of Justice* there can be, I believe, only the slightest difference—as Kafka said of the Messiah's intervention. With words that recall Kant and Hegel, but also draw near to the perspective of redemption, which Levinas invokes in *Totality and Infinity* and Adorno defines in *Minima Moralia*, Rawls writes:

> The perspective of eternity is not a perspective from a certain place beyond the world, nor the point of view of a transcendent being; rather it is a certain form of thought and feeling that rational persons can adopt within the world. And

having done so, they can, whatever their generation, bring together into one scheme all individual perspectives and arrive together at regulative principles that can be affirmed by everyone as he lives by them, each from his own standpoint. Purity of heart, if one could attain it, would be to see clearly and to act with grace and self-command from this point of view.[18]

If Rawls is invoking the religious spirit here, it is what Max Horkheimer calls "religion in the good sense," reactivating its charity, benevolence, and commitment to justice: "What is religion in the good sense? The not-yet-strangled impulse that insists that reality should be otherwise, that the spell will be broken and turn toward the right direction." Horkheimer concludes by saying, "Where life points this way in every gesture, there is religion."[19]

II. The Measure of Our Responsibility

> Rabbi Rafael said: "Measured behavior is a dreadful evil. It is a dreadful evil when a man measures his behavior to his fellow humans. It is as if he were always manipulating weights and measures."
>
> —Martin Buber, *Tales of the Hasidim*[20]

> We must be human. We need eternity, for it alone provides our gestures room; and yet we know ourselves in cramped finality. We must, then, create an infinity within these barriers, since we no longer believe in boundlessness.
>
> —Rainer Maria Rilke, "The Florence Diary"[21]

Reflecting on his impressions of America, profoundly troubled by the distinctly new form of individualism that he observed, Alexis de Tocqueville wrote:

> Each person behaves as though he is a stranger to the destiny of all the others. . . . As for his transactions with his fellow citizens, he may mix among them, but he sees them not; he touches them, but does not feel them; he exists only in himself and for himself alone. And if on these terms there remains in his mind a sense of family, there no longer remains a sense of society.[22]

In the opening sentence of *Émile*, Jean-Jacques Rousseau laments the fact that "everything is good as it leaves the hands of the Author of nature, everything degenerates in the hands of men."[23] Is this true? Have we not struggled to build with our hands a good and just society? And have we not, in some measure, succeeded? We may disagree with Rousseau, but we cannot ignore the truth touched on by de Tocqueville.

On the last page of *Otherwise Than Being*, bringing his thought to a sober and humbling conclusion, Levinas writes: "For the little humanity that adorns the earth, a relaxation [*relâchement*] of essence . . . is needed: *in the just war waged against war, to tremble or even to shudder* [frissoner] *at every instant because of this very justice.* This weakness is needed. This relaxation of virility without cowardice is needed for the little cruelty our hands repudiate."[24] What is our responsibility to the other and for the other? Is it something that can be measured? Levinas advances four principal arguments in regard to this question. Since, in each case, Levinas oscillates between phenomenological description and ethical exhortation, I will use the phrase "cannot and must not" to sustain, in all its tension, the critical force of the ethical that is carried by his rhetorical ambiguity. The four arguments are as follows.

1. Against the aggrandizement of the human in humanism and the optimism of the Enlightenment, Levinas argues that, despite our seemingly limitless power to measure and compare, the human cannot and must not be taken as the measure of all things (see, e.g., *TI*, 30/59). Both of these discursive systems assume a totality that he categorically rejects: a faith in the comprehensiveness of knowledge and in our ability—indeed, our sovereign right—to master the ends and means of nature.

2. Against the prevailing egoism of our time, he argues that the ego cannot be, and must not assert itself to be, the measure for the other, the one "who, precisely in his uniqueness [*dans son unicité*], is refractory [*réfractive*] to every measure."[25] On the contrary, it is the other who must always be my measure, my judge.

3. Moreover, the "presence" of the other is "infinite," and constitutes for me an "infinite" obligation. As "infinite," this "presence" is also an "absence," and consequently it exceeds all measure—not only my own but all conceivable measures (*TI*, 21/51). For Levinas, ethical life can be a question only of "measuring oneself against the perfection of the infinite," the sublime "perfection" that Kant invoked with the idea of "humanity in our person."[26]

4. To this Levinas adds the argument that the "presence" of divinity in the other further undermines my right to claim that the measure of "human being" is something I could know and dominate. Rejecting Heidegger's onto-theology, Levinas denies that "being" can give us any useful

measure for ethical life: "There can be meaning in being," he says, "only through him who is not measured according to being. . . . For the pre-originary responsibility for the other is not measured by being."[27] Thus he will argue that we must somehow find in the experience of mankind, "lost in history and in [institutional] order," the "traces" of this assignment of responsibility.[28] Our measure for ethical life is in these "traces." But that means that the measure is beyond the reach of calculation.

Matthew 6:3 says, "When thou doest alms, let not thy left hand know what thy right hand doeth." This counsel invites a number of important interpretations. Perhaps the most obvious invokes the difference between good and evil, right and left, and urges us to avoid the temptations of evil. Another interpretation emphasizes the priority of good deeds over mere knowledge of the good. Levinas would be sympathetic to both of these readings. But he would undoubtedly also wish to venture a third inter-pretation, bringing out the verse's admonition concerning the appropria-tion of alms-giving within an exchange-economy of equivalences. On this reading, one must avoid the temptation to subordinate kindness, generos-ity, sacrifice, to a rationality of calculations. The giving of alms is an act that must be beyond symmetry, reciprocity, beyond the very possibility of calculation, an infinitely fitting measure. Confronted by another human presence, by a "face" that bespeaks a destitution exceeding my compre-hension and my capacity for benevolence, one must hope that "avidity" can turn into a "generosity incapable of approaching the other with empty hands" (*TI*, 21/50). But Levinas will not even permit what two full hands can give or share to determine the measure of generosity.

For Levinas, the ethical takes hold of our consciousness in the form of an idea: the idea of the infinitely Good. But before that, it has taken hold of us in the form of a certain desire: a desire that is "the commencement of moral consciousness." Compelling me to measure myself "against the perfection of infinity," this desire that Levinas describes as the "desire for the absolutely other" calls into question my freedom—and my assump-tion of sovereign authority (*TI*, 56/84). It is a "metaphysical" form of de-sire "which understands the remoteness, alterity, and exteriority of the other" and appropriates our gestures in a way that profoundly shapes them, binding them to a measure of which they could not possibly be the origin: "Metaphysics desires the other beyond satisfactions, where no ges-ture by the body to diminish the aspiration is possible, where it is not pos-sible to sketch out any known caress nor invent any new caress" (*TI*, 4/34).

The metaphysical, which Levinas identifies with the Good, a measure infinitely transcending all empirical determinations, thus "arouses" us and takes hold of us in the form of a "desire that measures the infinity of the infinite"; however, the measure that this desire engages "is a measure [only] through the very impossibility of measure." And this "inordinateness" (*démesure*) is measured by a desire that, when in the presence of the other, cannot avoid confronting the demand for its subordination to the absolute authority of the ethical (*TI*, 33/62).

Levinas understands that the desire for freedom "is not realized outside social and political institutions" (*TI*, 218/241). Thus, in "Freedom and Command," he observes, "Freedom consists in instituting outside of one-self an order of reason, in entrusting the rational to a written text, in resorting to institutions. Freedom, in its fear of tyranny, leads to institutions, to a commitment of freedom to a state in the very name of freedom."[29] But even though, as he concedes, "it is not possible to do without [the State] in the extremely politicized world of our time,"[30] he contemplates these institutions from the transcendent and therefore critical perspective of metaphysics—a point of reference that he identifies with a messianic ethics and politics, and that requires a "superposition" of messianic eschatology over the political order of the state. It is this "prophetic" orientation that gives the infinitely demanding measure by which our ethical and political life is to be guided. And it is for the sake of a justice and a freedom still to come, a justice and a freedom at the heart of this orientation, that he argues passionately against the reduction of political life to the law of the state. Accordingly, in "Space Is Not One-Dimensional," he argues that, beyond the "three dimensions" of the modern constitutional state—liberty, equality, and fraternity—our only real hope for the fulfillment of political life lies in a "work of justice" both haunted and inspired by its remembrance of a "fourth dimension": the messianic time of prophetic revelation.[31] For the time being, however, we can enter this dimension only by virtue of this endless work of justice.

This work ultimately requires, for Levinas, the "recollection" of the prophetic messianic promise—the recollection of the idea of a universal justice that, however far from realization, will always put the law of the state into question, submitting it to the "an-archy" of a justice that cannot be compromised by inclusion in any calculus. Somehow, the "work of the state," even that of a state constitutionally framed to bear responsibility for "liberty, equality, and fraternity," must be radically transformed, so that the state begins to realize a prophetic "work of justice." In the meantime, we must struggle toward the moral ends of a truly universal history, all the while deeply inspired by the idea of redemption—as if touched by the messianic light of a "holy history." Acting with this messianic inspiration, we must not let the politics of the state be completely absorbed into the immanence of "profane" history; but we must also not let that politics continue undisturbed, unquestioned by the ideal of making "profane" history the achievement of universal reason. Politics must work *within* history in order to be a critical part of the struggle to make history fulfill the moral requirement of universality, and first of all, therefore, to persist in reminding us of the suffering that is not yet alleviated. But politics must not ignore the suffering for which this Enlightenment ideal of universality is itself partly responsible. Without rejecting this glorious ideal, politics must nevertheless struggle with the fact that the very logic of universality can prevent us from recognizing its inadequate respect for difference. We must remember the differences that universality was meant to protect.

In a late essay, "Utopia and Socialism," Levinas invokes the historical task of memory, which requires us to draw out from the immemorial depths of embodied memory the sense of "a destiny confusedly felt" (*un destin confusément pressenti*),[32] a sense of something haunting the precincts of memory, patiently summoning us into a prophetic inheritance, a *pressentiment*, of the future. With this in mind, Levinas entertains the following thought:

> Perhaps this recollection, the ever-renewed quest for a society in which the *being-together* of men should be realized, a resistance to the forgetting of this utopian *should-be* at the very heart of State structures setting themselves up as ends-in-themselves, and the resurgence of conscience against the State's deterioration of social relations—are themselves objective events. Events that mark, in the society-State dialectic, the moment of morality limiting politics—an indispensable and unforgettable moment.[33]

For Levinas, the ethical imperative, according to which my responsibility to and for the other must determine my use of freedom, has a correlate: what might be termed a political imperative, according to which the public realm of freedom must be determined by the requirements of justice for all. This is a justice that must not be quantified by reference to any measure not submitted to critical questioning from the metaphysical perspective of the prophetic tradition (see *TI*, 54–57/82–84).

Although the political "work of justice" manifestly requires the existence of a state, this requirement means that justice is always in danger of being arrested or compromised, not only by the corruption that is endemic—even when the rule of law prevails—to the very form of the state, but also by the force of the law. For the law can recognize no source of authority, no principles of justice, transcending the jurisdiction of the state "unless," as Levinas says, politics can create conditions hospitable to "possibilities for political invention" that could radically alter the ontology of the modern state.[34] If politics were to accomplish this, the law would be provoked to recognize the state-transcending authority of the messianic: historical possibilities for the "superposition" or "supervenience" of the messianic—the only "measure" that does not abandon the hungry, the homeless, the stranger.

In *Difficult Freedom*, concluding with a stinging rebuke of those who, like one of Kierkegaard's characters, would find a way to make the messianic measure easy to live with, Levinas writes: "If we cannot feel the absurd element in history, a part of our messianic sensibility is lost. One cannot lay claim to the prophetic vision of truth, and go on to participate in the values of the world which has surrounded us since the Emancipation. There is nothing more hypocritical than the messianic prophetism of the comfortably bourgeois."[35] Thus, the orientation that Levinas invites us to consider is this: "Each historical event transcends itself, taking on a metaphysical meaning that guides its literal significance. . . . In this sense, human history is a spiritual work."[36] Not a measure immanent in history, but only the messianic, the prophesied life that will "adorn" the earth at the end of history as we know it, can be the measure of ethical life. Arguing against the totalization of history that, by an abuse of interpretation, he reads into Hegel and Heidegger, Levinas writes:

> Between a philosophy of transcendence that situates elsewhere the true life to which man, escaping from here, would gain access in the privileged moments of liturgical, mystical elevation, or in dying—and a philosophy of immanence in which we would truly come into possession of being, when every "other," encompassed by the same, would vanish at the end of history—we propose to describe, within the unfolding of territorial existence, of economic existence . . . , a relationship with the other that does not result in a divine or human totality, that is not a totalization of history but the idea of infinity. Such a relationship is metaphysics itself. (*TI*, 23/52)

History as we know it is a continuum, a chain of causes and effects, an oppressive immanence that the singular existence of the other (*l'autrui*) and irrepressible cries for justice disturb, compelling recognition of a measure that cannot be contained within the inherent totalization of the historical. The argument continues:

> History would not be the privileged plane where Being disengaged from the particularism of points of view (with which reflection would still be affected) is manifested. If it claims to integrate myself and the other [*l'autre*] within an impersonal spirit, this alleged integration is cruelty and injustice, that is, it ignores the Other [*l'Autrui*]. History as a relationship between men ignores a position of the I before the other [*l'autre*] in which the other remains transcendent with respect to me. Though of myself I am not exterior to history, I do find in the Other [*l'Autrui*] a point that is absolute with regard to history—not by amalgamating with the Other [*l'Autrui*], but in speaking with him.

The argument concludes with a statement to which we will return near the end of this chapter: "History is worked over by the ruptures of history, in which a judgment is borne upon it. When man truly approaches the Other [*l'Autrui*], he is uprooted from history." This conception of history challenges even the "speculative" conception formulated by Kant: despite the noumenal origin of freedom that figures aporetically in Kant's theory of causality, and despite the demand that reason makes—namely, that we find in the meaning of historical events the moral ends of reason—Kant nevertheless does not ground his philosophy of history in the moral claims of the other. Nor does he break open the historical continuum to admit the messianic spirit in these claims, even though he invokes the hidden work of "Providence" guiding history toward its realization of the Enlightenment project.

In a conversation with Richard Kearney that bears on the moral desire for transcendence, for an interruption in the order of history as we know it, Levinas had this to say:

> It is not by superlatives that we can think of God, but by trying to identify the particular interhuman events that open towards transcendence and reveal the traces where God has passed. The God of ethical philosophy is not God the almighty being of creation, but the persecuted God of the prophets. That is why I have tried to think of God in terms of desire, a desire that cannot be fulfilled or satisfied—in the etymological sense of *satis*, measure. I can never have enough in my relation to God, for he always exceeds my measure, remains forever incommensurate with my desire. In this sense, our desire for God is without end or term: it is interminable and infinite because God reveals himself as absence rather than as presence. . . . What is a defect in the

finite order becomes an excellence in the infinite order. In the infinite order, the absence of God is better than his presence, and the anguish of man's concern and searching for God is better than consummation or comfort.[37]

But if to acknowledge traces of the presence of God in history is to recognize in the singularity of the other (*l'autrui*) imperative moral claims that disturb the order of history, refusing its finite measures and compromises, then no historical mediation by the rationality of means and ends—not even a mediation that would posit an image of the "kingdom of ends"—could avoid moral offense, violence, and injustice.

A passage from Levinas's essay "The Rights of Man and the Rights of the Other" bears on this point:

> To limit oneself, in the matter of justice, to the norm of pure measure, or moderation, between mutually exclusive terms, would be to revert to assimilating the relations between members of the human race to the relation between individuals of logical extension, signifying between one another nothing but negation, additions or indifference. In humanity, from one individual to another, there is established a proximity that does not take its meaning from the spatial metaphor of the extension of a concept.[38]

It is in the other's cries for justice, and in the uncompromising commitment to work for justice on the part of the one who is in proximity to the other—the one who must therefore assume absolute, unconditional responsibility for "the just man who suffers"—that the gate for the coming of the Messiah will be opened. But, as Levinas reminds us, "The Messiah comes only to him who waits."[39] Thus, for Levinas, as for Kant, Kracauer, Benjamin, and Heidegger, we "late moderns" must learn how to wait, must learn the virtues of patience. In "The Virtues of Patience," Levinas interprets this attitude in relation to the "revolutionary spirit" motivating the work of Enlightenment within the order of history that, meanwhile, is still in effect: "The modern world has forgotten the virtues of patience. . . . We must recall these virtues of patience, not so as to preach a sense of resignation in the face of revolutionary spirit, but so that we can feel the essential link which connects the spirit of patience to true revolution. This revolution comes from great pity."[40] It is no ordinary revolution. To give this point dramatic emphasis, Levinas concludes his thought thus: "The hand that grasps the weapon must suffer in the very violence of that gesture. To anesthetize this pain brings the revolutionary to the frontiers of fascism." And yet, I am compelled to ask: what am I to do? I am compelled to ask this even though, as Levinas insists in "Peace and Proximity," my "responsibility for the other human being is, in its immediacy, anterior to every question." There are many questions to be addressed here. But the "first question in the interhuman" is, he says, "the question of justice":

> Henceforth it is necessary to know, to become consciousness. Comparison is superimposed onto my relation with the unique and the incomparable, and, in view of equity and equality, a weighing, a thinking, a calculation, the comparison of incomparables, and, consequently, the neutrality—presence or representation—of being, the thematization and the visibility of the face in some way de-faced as the simple individuation of the individual; the burden of ownership and exchange; the necessity of thinking together under a synthetic theme the multiplicity and the unity of the world; and, through this, the promotion in thought of intentionality; of the intelligibility of the relation, and of the final signifyingness of being; and through this, finally, the extreme importance in human multiplicity of the political structure of society, subject to laws and thereby to institutions where the for-the-other of subjectivity—or the ego—enters with the dignity of a citizen into the perfect reciprocity of political laws which are essentially egalitarian, or held to become so.[41]

With the question of justice, the concept of measure, excluded from the ethical relation, enters into the realm of history, bearing the revolutionary judgment of the objective spirit. But inasmuch as this history is still a realm of conflict and violence, Levinas deems it important that we remind ourselves that the desire for peace and justice is always at their origin, always their only possible justification, and always their most uncompromising critical measure. As he says in "Peace and Proximity," it is necessary to remind ourselves

> that this justice, which can legitimate them ethically—that is, preserve for the human its proper sense of dis-inter-estedness under the weight of being—is not a natural and anonymous legality governing the human masses, from which is derived a technique of social equilibrium, placing in harmony the antagonistic and blind forces through transitory cruelties and violence, a State delivered over to its own necessities that it is impossible to justify.[42]

Insisting accordingly on the ethical, hence on the divine beyond all measure, as the sole ultimate measure for determining the "justice" entangled in the law-positing measures making our history, he argues: "Nothing would be able to withdraw itself from the control of the responsibility of the 'one for the other,' which delineates the limit of the State and does not cease to appeal to the vigilance of persons who would not be satisfied with the simple subsumption of cases under a general rule." Concluding the essay, he writes, "The foundation of consciousness is justice and not the reverse. Objectivity reposing on justice. On the extravagant generosity of the for-the-other [i.e., the ethical relation] is superimposed a reasonable order, ancillary or angelic, of justice through knowledge." And what can philosophical thought contribute to this order? "Philosophy here is a *measure* brought to the infinity of the being-for-the-other of peace and proximity, and is like the wisdom of love." With these words, the essay ends. But the reference to the "angelic" order will not let us forget that only the metaphysical standpoint, which Levinas is not embarrassed to call an experience of "the divine," can judge, can take the measure of our commitment to justice. In "Place and Utopia," he writes that "the ethical order," deriving its measure from the realm of messianic prophecy, "does not [merely] prepare us for the Divinity; it is the very accession to the Divinity. All the rest is dream."[43]

How could this orientation by reference to an infinite measure instruct our hope? How could it bring human beings together—people of different sexualities, different ethnicities, different races, different tribes and families, different nations and states? How could it guide us toward the revolutionary spirit promised in our ethical proximity? What if, as Levinas says, there is an "anarchic responsibility which summons me from nowhere into a present time"? What if the response to this responsibility is "the measure . . . of an immemorial freedom that is older than being, or decisions, or deeds"?[44]

III. Impossible Contact: The Limits of Mourning

Following the death of his young son, Emerson mourned with an intense need to maintain some vital contact with the beloved boy. All that he found, however, was a sense of loss and emptiness so overwhelming that nothing in ordinary life could remain untouched by it. While sinking deeper and deeper into a terrible numbness, Emerson wrote "Experience," in which he permitted himself to lament: "The only thing grief has taught me, is to know how shallow it is. That, like all the rest, plays about the surface, and never introduces me into the reality, for contact with which, we would even pay the costly price of sons and lovers."[45] "Was it Boscovich,"

he asks, "who found out that bodies never come in contact?" "Well," he
says, "souls never touch their objects." Thus:

> Grief too will make us idealists. . . . If tomorrow I should be informed of the
> bankruptcy of one of my principal debtors, the loss of my property would be
> a great inconvenience to me, perhaps, for many years; but it would leave me
> as it found me,—neither better nor worse. So it is with this calamity: it does
> not touch me: something which I fancied was a part of me, which could not
> be torn away without tearing me, nor enlarged without enriching me, falls off
> from me, and leaves no scar. . . . I grieve that grief can teach me nothing, nor
> carry me one step into real nature.

Our relations to each other, he concludes, are, in the end, "oblique and
casual," merely contingent, accidental, and without immediacy. Nonetheless, he continues his exertions, for he cannot abandon all hope that meaningful contact will eventually come: "Two human beings are like globes,
which can touch only in a point, and, whilst they remain in contact, all
other points of each of the spheres are inert; their turn must also come,
and the longer a particular union lasts, the more energy of appetency the
parts not in union acquire."

   "Substitution," the fourth chapter of Levinas's *Otherwise Than Being*,
opens with a quotation from Paul Celan in which the poet attempts to redeem the social and ethical content in the "I am I" (*Ich bin ich*), first principle of Johann Gottlieb Fichte's *Theory of Knowledge*, joining it with the
"I am you" (*Ich bin Du*), Novalis's critical reformulation of Fichte's principle, to say "I am you when I am I" (*Ich bin du, wenn ich ich bin*).[46] Could
a deeper experience of contact, of contact as communicative intercorporeality, connecting the flesh of the living to the flesh of the elemental, an
elemental from which we mortals come and to which, in death, we are always returned, have granted any real consolation to this grieving father?

   In Celan's "Alchemical," a poem bearing a title in which there are, perhaps, buried echoes reminding us of Chelmno, one of the most hellish of
Nazi extermination camps, six lines of verse that call into question our capacity to remember, to mourn the dead, and to offer consolation to the
living. The poet invokes the hands of the victims, hands that still bear witness, hands speaking in accusation, but also in prayer:

> Silence, cooked like gold, in
> charred, charred
> hands.

Fingers, insubstantial as smoke.
Like crests,
crests of air.[47]

These incinerated hands need to come to life again in our remembrance. Could a deeper experience of intercorporeality enable the traces of ethical proximity still binding our hands to keep more securely in remembrance the hands of the victims incinerated in the ovens of the Nazi death camps? Is there any way for our own hands to remain connected with theirs? We need to think of hands connected, perhaps, as if themselves charred in mourning—but also, of hands connected, across the expanse of time, beyond the resignation in mourning, by virtue of their commitment to working and sacrificing for the coming of a time in which such holocausts could never happen.

In *If This Is a Man*, Primo Levi tells about his deportation to the camps in Auschwitz:

> The doors had been closed at once, but the train did not move until evening. . . . Next to me, crushed against me for the whole journey, there had been a woman. We had known each other for many years, and the misfortune had struck us together, but we knew little of one another. Now, in the hour of decision, we said to each other things that are never said among the living. We said farewell [*Ci salutammo*] and it was short; everybody said farewell to life through his neighbor [*ciascuno salutò nell'altro la vita*]. We had no more fear.[48]

Crushed against one another: a time, perhaps, even in such brutal, dehumanizing conditions, for what Levinas calls "proximity." For, according to this witness, everybody said farewell to life "through his neighbor." A striking phrase! Must we not, then, recognize in this phrase the ethical significance to which it testifies—namely, that in this proximity of neighbors, this terrible intertwining of fates, there was also the revelation of an uncanny intercorporeality, a redemptive experience of the neighbor in which the facticity of "substitution," the truth of the one-for-the-other, the sense of human affinity, was compellingly revealed?

IV. The Corpus Mysticum

> The hint half guessed, the gift half understood, is
> Incarnation.
>
> —T. S. Eliot, "The Dry Salvages"

Hence it is so important to recognize (1) that the body, in and of itself, already contains a spiritual principle, and (2) that it is not the body which infects the spirit, but the spirit the body; the good man kindles the body with the goodness of his spirit, the bad with the evil of his spirit. The body is a soil that accepts every seed, a soil in which both good and evil can be sown.

—F. W. J. von Schelling, "Stuttgart Lectures" [49]

The lower level [of our corporeal nature] contains prophecies of the higher, but this level nevertheless remains the lower one.

—F. W. J. von Schelling, *Clara; or, On Nature's Connection with the Spirit World* [50]

The purely corporeal can be uncanny [*Das rein körperliche kann unheimlich sein*]. Compare the way angels and devils are portrayed. So-called "miracles" must be connected with this. A miracle must be, as it were, a sacred gesture [*eine heilige Gebärde*].

—Ludwig Wittgenstein, *Culture and Value* [51]

The difference between the life of the spirit and that of the flesh is itself a spiritual difference.

— George Santayana, *Platonism and the Spiritual Life* [52]

The texts and teachings [of the Torah] that concern conduct and the formulation of practical laws . . . give to the Judaic Revelation, written and oral, its distinctive physiognomy [*sa physiognomie propre*] and have sustained the unity of the very body [*l'unité du corps même*] of the Jewish people across the Diaspora and History.

—Emmanuel Levinas, *Beyond the Verse* [53]

Rabbi Leib, son of Sarah, the hidden zaddik who wandered over the earth, following the course of the rivers in order to redeem the souls of the living and the dead, said this: "I did not go to the maggid in order to hear Torah from him, but to see how he unlaces his felt shoes and laces them up again."

—Martin Buber, *Tales of the Hasidim* [54]

The maggid of Zlotchov was asked by one of his disciples: "The Talmud says that the child in the womb of his mother looks from one end of the earth to the other, and knows all the teachings, but the instant it comes into contact with the air of earth, an angel strikes it on the mouth, and it forgets everything. I do not understand why this should be: first one knows everything, and then one forgets it." "A trace is left behind in man," the rabbi answered, "by dint of which he can re-acquire knowledge of the world and the teachings."

—Martin Buber, *Tales of the Hasidim* [55]

> Attached to the ring, which is offered as a symbol of Reason, there is
> a piece of skin from the hand that offers it; and if Reason is scientific
> connection, and has to do with concepts, we can very well do without
> that piece of skin.
>
> —G. W. F. Hegel, *Faith and Knowledge* [56]

In the *Critique of Pure Reason* (A808, B836), Kant evokes the "corpus mys-ticum of rational beings," [57] knowingly appropriating the Catholic liturgi-cal doctrine for a displacement that the faithful in the Roman Church could contemplate, no doubt, only with some horror. But the thought it-self is cryptic, and introduced only in passing, only to be spirited away— or say, rather, buried, encrypted, forgotten—within the architecture of a rational reconstruction. But can ethics, which for Levinas is "first philos-ophy," really "do without" the gift of embodiment—that medium that bears the life of Reason and an urgent sense of responsibility for the wel-fare of the other? The argument to be unfolded here will make the very strong claim that the ethics Levinas proposes is not possible without the phenomenology of a "mystical body": a body the conception of which, in-spired by Talmudic and cabalistic sources, could not be more different both from the Catholic and from the Kantian.

However, as I have argued in detail elsewhere,[58] although Levinas rec-ognizes an "embodied spirituality" (*une spiritualité incarnée*),[59] he leaves this "mystical" body—or, as I would prefer to say, this "hermeneutically prophetical" body—insufficiently fleshed out. The principal shortcom-ing is that he does not realize that his ethics requires the differentiation of body and flesh, and, correspondingly, a careful exposition of the intrica-cies—the intrigues—of the flesh. (See "The Moral Journey" and "The Palimpsest of the Flesh," the two tables, with their corresponding expla-nations, printed at the end of this chapter.) What is called for, I suggest, is a hermeneutical phenomenology that recognizes in the flesh a prophetic palimpsest. The oldest of its layers, constitutive of the preoriginary self, is the medium of a "preoriginary election" by the Good that subjects this self to its ethical assignment of responsibility, while the most fully spiritual-ized layer is the medium that would bear the sense and sensibility of the zaddik, the one who realizes this vocation in the piety of an ethical life at the heart of which is an unconditional responsibility to and for the other.

The second shortcoming of Levinas's conception of the "mystical" body is that, despite his concern for moral education, he does not recognize the need to correlate this hermeneutical reading of the synchronically operative layers in the palimpsest of the flesh with a diachronic phenomenology of the stages in moral development. This phenomenological task is made necessary by (to name only a few of the matters begging for elaboration) his figure of the "trace," claimed to bear a prophetic message from an order of time beyond memory; his conception of the "preoriginary," the logic of which seems to imply, or call for, a process of moral development; his discussions of ego and self, in which their temporal relations are left undecidable; his inadequately explained doubling of the terms "self" and "heteronomy"; and his invocation of a "preoriginary election," which leaves unsettled how this passive, involuntary "assignment," which I would like to interpret as a moral sense registered in the sensibility of the flesh, is related to the gestures that enact a conscious will. In particular, he leaves unexplained how our "preoriginary election" by the Good—an "event" that is supposed to happen *prior to consciousness and volition*—is even possible. Would it not have to be an event that appropriates and binds my flesh? Moreover, he leaves unexplained how that "election" can influence our conscious choices and decisions. What difference does this unconscious and involuntary "election" make—what difference could it make—in how I live my life? How could it figure in the way of life that I knowingly "elect"? What role does it play? What role *could* it play? Must it not be a question of somehow willingly "retrieving" and "reactivating" the body's felt sense of that "preoriginary election"—even if it be only in some ephemeral traces of traces—and "electing" to make its claim on us the source of inspiration and guidance for the way we live? And would this attempt at retrieval and reactivation not involve a process of recollection?

"Attachment to the Good," Levinas says, "precedes the choosing of the Good. . . . The Good is good precisely because it chooses you and grips you before you have had time to raise your eyes to it."[60] But what bearing does this preoriginary "election" have on the choices I actually make? How does it, or how could it, influence me? How does it—how could it—figure in my freedom? These are pressing questions, because Levinas makes it clear that the preoriginary "election" is not a causal or metaphysical determinism, preordaining the use of my freedom; yet he never explains how it might otherwise enter into the ethical formation of my conscious life.

What is needed, I suggest, is a hermeneutical phenomenology of incarnate recollection, enabling us to understand the possibility of voluntarily retrieving and reactivating, if only from the faintest of traces, a certain bodily felt sense of this preoriginary "election," which we nevertheless carry with us by grace of the extraordinary medium that is our flesh. But we also desperately need a much more intricate phenomenological account of social interactions than Levinas provides, because what motivates such a retrieval and reactivation is always, after all, the "face," or "proximity," of the other. The other's proximity is what arouses and provokes this process of recollection, recalling me to myself, reminding me to make contact with my body's never entirely obliterated felt sense of its preoriginary "election" by the Good. In his much later work, *Otherwise Than Being*, Levinas refers to this "election" as the "traumatism" of a "substitution": my responsibility to and for the other. Even identifying incarnate recollection as a "practice of the self," a practice opening the self to the claims of the other, still does not sufficiently flesh out that process of recollection phenomenologically.

But, as is well known, Levinas seems to have repudiated every kind of anamnestic "recuperation," arguing not only against the positivities of empiricism but also against philosophies of consciousness—whether Cartesian, Hegelian, or Husserlian—for they all assume the possibility of a total recuperation of the subject's past experience in the form of knowledge or self-knowledge. For Levinas, "recuperation" presupposes that there is, or can be, a "unity of consciousness and essence," "a recuperation in which nothing is lost," a correlation in memory that would overcome the ethical anachronisms, imposing continuity between past and present and effectively reducing the claims of the past to the ambitions of the present: The past that bears on our ethical life "cannot be recuperated by reminiscence not because of its remoteness, but because of its incommensurability with the present" (*AE*, 13–14, 36, 112/11, 28, 29, 88). In fact, it is a past that never was present and therefore even escaped retention. Giving the question a twist that threatens to fictionalize the entire phenomenology, Levinas says that, in the experience of the other person's "proximity," what gives itself to be "heard" is a moral command that has come "as though" from an immemorial past" (*AE*, 112/88).[61] This might seem to preclude the peculiar role that we are assigning to "recollection" in this chapter; but, as should become apparent, it could do so only by sacrificing everything that makes Levinas's phenomenology of ethical life distinctive and compelling. I agree with his critique of recuperation and accordingly offer in this chapter a conception of recollection that avoids making the claims that Levinas rightly repudiates.

According to Sanhedrin 99a of the Talmud, in the time of messianic *tikkun*, or "mending," the just will be able at long last to taste "the wine preserved in the grapes since the six days of creation." This certainly seems to support a notion of recollection. But we must first agree with Levinas that recollection cannot—and must not—be characterized in terms of "representation" and "intentionality" as he construes them. So if "recollection" requires reducing the immemorial past to the synchrony of the present; if it involves re-presenting that past in the pure immanence of consciousness; if it is taken to claim a noetic-noematic correlation; if it claims total recuperation and makes this past a possession of knowledge or self-knowledge, then—to be sure—we must concur that no such process could possibly serve the exigencies of our ethical life as Levinas understands it. Indeed, it could only betray the preoriginary moral assignment, retrieving a counterfeit normativity.

But if there were no possibility of recollection—if the retrieval of a preoriginary moral assignation made no sense here at all—by what right, what criterion of justification, could Levinas make any phenomenological claims about the preoriginary, about our "election" to ethical responsibility, our submission, in a time before egological consciousness, to the law of "substitution"? If the preoriginary cannot be retrieved in any sense, then either the obligation would become effective in total independence of my volition, my consciousness—in which case my actions would be both blind and without freedom, subject to a rigorous corporeal determinism—or else that obligation would play no role in my ethical life and have no effect on my conduct. Without some confirmation by a process of "recollection" that reactivates the preoriginary "assignment" of responsibility, his entire phenomenology of the trace would become nothing more than an architecture of empty, speculative postulates, completely detached from ethical experience.

Furthermore, as it will be presented here, the process of recollection is itself an ethical act, not a procedure for the acquisition of empirical knowledge about the world. It is a solemn commitment, already an assumption of the greatest responsibility. I must respond to the "call of conscience" by attempting to get in touch with its origin—even though that origin is infinitely transcendent, immemorial, beyond retrieval. What matters is therefore precisely not the "fulfillment" of the intentionality, but instead the simple fact of intense effort: the exertion by itself and as such is a demonstration of ethical virtue. Consequently, even though I must concede the impossibility of a completed retrieval, or indeed, in a certain crucial sense, the impossibility of access, I am nevertheless responsible for undertaking the process of recollection with wholehearted commitment.

Be that as it may, Levinas clearly wants to argue that it is the other's "presence," or "proximity," always somehow disquieting, that compels me—as an adult—to question myself, demanding that I find within myself a felt sense of obligation to the other that I have always already been carrying: a sense that, unbeknownst to me, my embodiment has, from its very beginning, been given to carry, but that *only* the proximity of the other can motivate a consciousness already "guilty," already in default in its response to the other, to adopt. Of course, in the case of the infant or child, what is absolutely decisive for the initiation and outcome of this process is that the character of the proximity be loving and caring. Abuse, cruelty, violence in the early years of life can permanently damage the moral sense that the body carries—or make it virtually impossible for the older child later to contact and retrieve it.

As indicated above, another major problem with which Levinas leaves us concerns the temporality of the relation between ego and self. Some passages in *Otherwise Than Being* describe the self as "older" than the ego (e.g., 150/117). But other passages in that same work suggest that he (also) wants to think of the self as installed in a time *after* the ego, perhaps as a stage of moral development that would come *after* egoism, sublating or transforming the ego—perhaps through a process of recollection that would attempt to retrieve, from the inscription of the moral law borne in the flesh, the ethical orientation registered in the depths of this flesh. The need for a process of recollection seems to be suggested by the assertion that "egoism is neither first nor last" (*AE*, 162, 165/126, 128). What could this possibly mean? The most compelling answer, I believe, is that it calls for a phenomenology that would make use of recollection to lay out the *stages* of moral maturation. More specifically, I suggest that Levinas's ethics requires that there be, in the first stage, a preoriginary self; in the second stage, ego-formation; and, in a merely possible third stage, never fully realized, a self-formation of greater moral "height," which would struggle to overcome egoism and consecrate its life to the other, and to the others of the other. In this ongoing struggle against itself, the ego would find guidance and encouragement by recollecting, retrieving, and activating, to whatever extent possible, something of the bodily felt sense of the assignment of obligation, of responsibility, that took hold of the flesh—the flesh of the "preoriginary self"—in a time before consciousness, before memory, before volition, before ego. Lifting up into egological consciousness this sense of responsibility that informs the preoriginary self, the self "before egoism," recollection might begin to displace the self-centered ego, installing, where it was, a self of greater moral height. This, it seems to me, sketches a narrative that proposes a compelling reading of his assertion that "egoism is neither first nor last."

In *Otherwise Than Being*, Levinas asserts, "The body is neither an obstacle opposed to the soul, nor a tomb that imprisons it, but that by which the self is susceptibility itself" (*AE*, 139/195 n. 12). This point is reiterated in many other texts, for example, in "Without Identity," where he declares, "The subject is already [living] for the other on the level of sensibility." [62] So he might have added that the body is also not to be despised as a cauldron of unruly drives and ego-centered desires—for his acknowledgment of the body as the medium of a preoriginary "susceptibility" implies that it is not *by nature* totally inimical to the ethical order. But his attitude toward the body is not without ambiguities, since there are many textual passages that either state or imply that the ethical is inherently "contrary to nature": as when it is supposed to be an experience of "trauma," and even a "persecution." [63] But how can the nature of the body be inherently inimical to the ethical, when it is, as it must be, the medium that bears my "involuntary election by the Good" (*AE*, 19/15)? [64]

I say "as it must be" because, if my "election" by the Good is prior to memory, prior to volition, prior, in fact, to consciousness, then it can only be an "election" that takes place in the body: an "election" that is "inscribed" for safekeeping—and for the possibility of remembrance—in the very secrecy and intimacy of our flesh. But this preoriginary "election" preordains nothing, determines nothing. I am completely free to ignore it. Indeed, since it takes place in a time prior to consciousness, and nothing compels its becoming conscious, nothing compels an attempt to retrieve it for memory—nothing other than the claims the ego may feel when facing the plight of the other—it could remain deeply repressed, despite occasional eruptions into the form of consciousness we call "guilty conscience." How else could this "pre-originary election" enter into the life one *elects* to live?

In his preface to *Beyond the Verse*, a collection of Talmudic commentaries, Levinas, never released from the work of mourning imposed by the Shoah, asks a question that continues to haunt and obsess him: "Can anyone amongst mankind wash his hands of all this flesh gone up in smoke?" [65] As Howard Caygill points out, Levinas intends this question not only to draw us into the struggle to accomplish the universal history posited by the Enlightenment project, but also to summon us to the heights of a "sacred history that touches the flesh of all humanity." [66] But "flesh" here must be taken more seriously than Caygill assumes. What we regard as our "flesh" is, as it has always been, the site of a struggle unto death between the spirit of the moral law and the unbound dispositions of nature—its "aorgic" impulses, drives, appetites, and desires. However, it is by grace of the flesh as medium of prophetic transmission that the appeal of the messianic—sacred history—enters into the struggle of consciousness, of reason, to realize, for the sake of each and every human singularity, the principles of justice constitutive of universal history.

I think that a "reconstruction" of the distinctions Kant attempts to draw in Book One of his late work, *Religion Within the Bounds of Reason Alone*, might make it possible to illuminate, if not resolve, some of the questions about our embodiment that Levinas's phenomenology leaves insufficiently addressed. Kant there introduces three critical terms to clarify how human nature is related to good and evil. In effect, these terms set up a palimpsest of the flesh: (1) *Anlage* refers to our preoriginary natural predisposition: although we are born neither good nor evil, we are given a nature enduringly *capable* at any time of enacting either one of these potentialities. Nevertheless, with this nature, we are also given the moral law, a moral "compass" designed to guide us on our journey through life. For Kant as for Levinas, the origin of this "equipment," bestowed in a time "older" than any originary time, exceeds our finite comprehension. Using Levinas's terminology, this predisposition may accordingly be described as "preoriginary," because the origin or ground of this predisposition precedes whatever origin or ground we could possibly know. It is not available to a knowledge of origins and grounds. (2) *Hang* refers to our natural "propensity" to succumb to the temptations of our desire-driven nature and the corruptions of social existence, with the consequence that we exercise our freedom of will in ways that disregard the moral law. Of course, this propensity can in principle always be resisted. Indeed all three forms of this propensity—weakness of will, moral ignorance and confusion, and the wicked subordination of the moral law to other considerations— can always, in principle, be resisted. In spite of this propensity, however, nothing in our nature denies the will its freedom to heed the moral law.

(3) *Gesinnung* refers to our "cast of mind," the accumulated precipitate of the will's actions, the actual disposition of our character—whether or not, over time, the will in the acts of its freedom has struggled against its natural propensity, demonstrating a consistent pattern of concern, a habitual respect, for the good and the right. If interpreted as referring to the nature of the body, these terms make it possible to formulate a coherent and compelling picture of the body within the altered phenomenology that Levinas leaves us. Moreover, perhaps this picture could give new life to the interpretation of the Kantian categorical imperative, investing the flesh with the spirit of the moral law.[67]

In "Humanism and An-archy," Levinas effects an astonishing reversal, overturning the picture of the body that has dominated Greek and Christian philosophy. He writes:

> It is not because the ego is an incarnate soul that temptation troubles the antecedent obedience to the Good and promises sovereign choice to man; it is because the obedience free of servitude to the Good is an obedience to the other that remains other that the subject is carnal, on the limit of eros, and becomes a being.[68]

I experience myself not as merely corporeal but as flesh, to the extent that I experience myself as an ethical creature—because the flesh of the body is a vessel, a medium, that carries the "tracework" of my ethical assignment, the prophecy of my ethical vocation, and because that assignment compels me to struggle with the corporeal nature of my desires. It is my prophetic, or my "supersensible," destination that grants me a body of flesh, a body that is not mere substance, mere matter—nor even mere animality.

"But," Levinas says there, "nothing in this passivity of possession by the Good . . . becomes a natural tendency. The relationship with the other is not convertible into a nature."[69] These words suggest that the ethical does not belong to, does not emerge from, the nature of the body. But I think they should rather be understood as insisting that, despite our preoriginary "election" by the Good, our ethical comportment, our actual choosing the Good, is not preordained by the moral "assignment" constitutive of our preoriginary nature—by what Kant calls our *Anlage*, our preoriginary "predisposition." It is always possible for us to turn away from this "election." In this sense, the Good is certainly not a "natural tendency."

Calling attention to the "feeling of identity between self and body," Levinas rejects the discourses of idealism and rationalism, arguing in an early paper, "To separate the spirit from the concrete forms in which it is already involved is to betray the originality of the very feeling from which it is appropriate to begin."[70] This "affirmation" of the body unquestionably supports the argument in this chapter. But it must not be construed as supporting a doctrine of biologism. Nothing could be more hostile to the project within which Levinas attempts to think what might be called the "redemption" of the body ("of" the body in both the objective and subjective grammatical senses) than a doctrine of human corporeity that assigns fate according to consanguinity and offers ideological shelter to a violent struggle for domination based on biological inheritance. Thus, in *Otherwise Than Being*, Levinas states, "The schema that corporeality outlines submits the biological itself to a higher structure" (*AE*, 139/109). This very significant claim seems to allude to a process of moral self-development, the full potentiality of which seems to be, for Levinas, already prophetically "inscribed" as a supersensible "assignment" in the very nature of corporeality. Something like this thought had already emerged in Schelling—for example, in his never-completed work, *Clara; or, On Nature's Connection to the Spirit World*, where one of the interlocutors in the conversation remarks, "The lower level [of our corporeal nature] contains prophecies of the higher, but this level nevertheless still remains the lower one."[71] (This reference to Schelling is not, as it may seem, far-fetched, because his philosophy of nature and cosmology greatly influenced Rosenzweig, who in turn inspired Levinas.) But unfortunately, Levinas does not undertake a phenomenology of moral self-development—nor, *a fortiori*, does he sufficiently acknowledge the role of the experienced body in relation to such a narrative. This, however, is a task that his ethical philosophy certainly requires.

If this interpretation is correct, the argument I am proposing in this chapter—which derives in part from the Old Testament and claims that, in a time before memory, a time before time, the moral law, pure trace of the assignment, the difference, that makes us human, was "inscribed" in the flesh of all mortals[72]—cannot be construed as a version of naturalism. But however much the moral life is, and must be, a perpetual struggle against certain desires and habits of the body, one cannot deny without lapsing into nonsense that a moral life is nevertheless "natural," in the precise though still minimal sense that moral comportment is, and must be, educed from the endowed nature of our embodiment—from the spiritual resources of our flesh. Moral life is intricately related to the body of needs, desires, and intentions; the body of sense and sensibility; the body of gesture; the body of judgment and speech. To be sure, moral life is not "natural," if by that one means that morality can come forth from corporeity spontaneously, without the countless civilizing mediations of socialization. All this is so obviously true that it would scarcely bear mentioning, were it not for the fact that "naturalism" has consistently been interpreted to imply the causal determinism of an organic machine or the reduction of the normativity of human life to the facticity of biological processes.

The "naturalism" for which I am arguing here, however, and which I think Levinas's ethics requires, is committed only to the following claims: (1) The ethical relation emerges from the nature of the body. (2) It is in the nature of the body to carry and preserve the ethical, if only in suppression or sublation. (3) Neither 1 nor 2 means that the ethical is not, despite this incarnation, "contrary to nature"; it is contrary to nature, just as Levinas insists, but in the specific sense that the ethical calls upon us to struggle against certain natural inclinations, notably the temptations of egoism and the corruptions inherent in social existence. Lastly, (4) the outcome of this struggle is never a foregone conclusion, because, even if I am always "elected" by the Good in a preoriginary appropriation and subjection of my corporeal nature, I am always nevertheless free to ignore or defy this ethical assignment.

Otherwise Than Being contains a statement bearing on these points that merits much more attention than it has received. It too supports the argument unfolding in this chapter. Levinas says, "The incarnation of the [moral] self [must be understood as] a passivity prior to all passivity at the bottom of matter becoming flesh [*la matière se faisant chair*]" (*AE*, 150/196 n. 21).[73] We should note here, first of all, that Levinas uses the reflexive *se faisant*, a grammatical construction perhaps even suggesting something that only a language with a "middle voice" could adequately express. The English translation unfortunately conceals this grammar—and consequently its philosophical implications. What Levinas is surely saying here is that the matter constitutive of our bodies bears *within itself* the potential—the prophetic assignment—to become flesh, medium for the realization of the ethical life, responsible for the other, and committed to *res gestae*, the historical "work of justice." It is in this sense that Levinas must be understood when he asserts that "to be flesh [*l'être-là-en-chair*] is to enter into time and history" (*TI*, 89/116–17; and see 90–91/117–19). Time engages the flesh as diachronic—and is prophetically inflected.

I suggested above that Kant's terminology for addressing the nature of the self in relation to evil and Santayana's definitions of flesh and spirit could prove extremely useful in elucidating matters that Levinas leaves in the dark. The cryptic passage just cited from *Totality and Infinity* is a central instance. Thus, I would like to deploy those resources here to differentiate body from flesh. Specifically, I would suggest that the flesh is the spiritual *potential* of the body, granted to the body through the preoriginary gift of bodily predisposition. The flesh is the body in the mode of its spiritual sublimation, the body in regard to its prophetic, supersensible "destination"—a "destination" that Levinas, recalling the Old Testament, will describe more than once as an "inscription," an "assignment" given to us, that is, to the flesh of the body, in an immemorial time, the time of "a past that has never been present." The flesh is the body in its assumption of responsibility as medium for the realization of a prophetic spirit; it is the preoriginary dimension of the body out of which this spirit emerges into the light of consciousness; it is the body in its preoriginary passivity, its submission to the spirit of the moral law. The flesh is also, therefore, the "traumatic" body in its moment of subjection and spiritual struggle; it is that preoriginary disposition, that peculiar commitment of the body that, for the sake of the Good, urges us to oppose certain inclinations arising from the very nature of the body that bears it. (Santayana's differentiation of flesh and spirit gives us a way, perhaps, to clarify Levinas's extraordinarily obscure notion of the trace. What that differentiation suggests is that we might take the "trace" to be nothing but the preoriginary *difference*, the "primordial *Ur-teil*," between the flesh and its prophetic realization in and as spirit—the difference also, therefore, between inclination and its realization in and as indeclinable obligation—that re-marks the opening and subjection of the human being to the imperative claims of the ethical relation. As such, it would signify a preoriginary assignment of moral responsibility for the other, opening and thus making the decisive difference between the human and the merely biological. What, on my reading, Levinas leaves unthought here is the *bearing* of this trace on ethical life: as I cannot emphasize too strongly, we need a narrative—a phenomenologically intricate hermeneutics—to explain how a bodily felt sense of this trace could be retrieved, despite its preoriginary "inscription," so that it would make a difference in the character of our ethical experience, our ethical relations with others.) However, the opposition to the body's "lower" desires, to its propensity for temptation by egological satisfactions, which of course takes place through the flesh, attests at the same time to the body's glorification, the consecration of this corporeal nature: in other words, the opposition reveals the possibility of a higher reconciliation between the nature of the body and the spirit of the moral law, in which the body, the site of moral struggle, would be dedicated to serving others and working for the triumph of the Good.

From the early writings to the late, Levinas insists on the importance of sensibility for our ethical life. As he wants us to understand and experience it, sensibility is the medium of my exposure to the other, my vulnerability, my susceptibility to being touched and moved by the plight of the other. For it is also the medium of my subjection to the other: a subordination so profound, so overwhelming, so inescapable, that Levinas resorts to the word "hostage"—a word that also indicates my absolute passivity—to describe the condition of my experience, and at the same time to arouse slumbering sympathies. Sensibility will also be described as the medium of a "substitution": substitution in the sense of an indeclinable responsibility to and for the other, even to the extreme of sacrificing myself to avert the sacrifice or the suffering of the other. Such substitution must not be mistaken, however, for a sympathetic absorption of the differences that separate the one from the other. On the contrary, my willingness to sacrifice myself comes from my ethical assumption of the sufferings of the other, an assumption that is not permitted to acknowledge and respect in any other way the alterity, the withdrawal of the other from the violence of ontology.

Now, it would seem that, according to Levinas, we cannot understand the "incarnate subjectivity" of ethical life unless we distinguish the ego from the self. The self, he says, is "older than the ego, prior to principles." Thus, the ego has a "prehistory": "in the 'prehistory' of the ego posited for itself [there] speaks a responsibility," an indeclinable "election" by the Good that is "prior to freedom" (*AE*, 149–50/116–17; and see 108–9/86). In other words, prior to our formation as egological, we are already in a certain "contact" with the other: not in what would commonly be called "physical contact," nor even in what would commonly be called the "presence" of the other, but rather in what Levinas calls "proximity" to the other: prior to any actual encounter with the other, I am already sensibly predisposed, predisposed by the very nature of my sensibility, to be concerned, to feel some responsibility to and for the good of the other (*AE*,

178/139). This does not mean that I am not free to disregard this bodily felt summons to responsibility. I am always free to decline this preoriginary "election," despite the fact that it demands and grants no exception. Indeed I am free to neglect this "election" to such a degree that I can no longer hear its summons, as when, in Arendt's example, Adolf Eichmann could no longer hear the voice of conscience—or rather, could hear it only through a corrupted echo that reduced the moral maxim to the "law of the land," and, finally, to the absolute will of the Führer.[74]

The final chapter of *Otherwise Than Being* commences with a passage from Goethe's *Faust*, in which Faust declares that "the shudder [*Der Schaudern*] is the best part of humanity" (*AE*, 221/175; and see 101/83–84). In the paragraph that closes the book, Levinas returns to this shudder, a manifestation of moral sensibility: "For the little humanity that adorns the earth, a relaxation of essence . . . is needed: *in the just war waged against war to tremble or shudder* [trembler—encore frissonner] *at every instant because of this very justice*" (*AE*, 233/185). Furthermore, he adds, this is a "weakness" deeply needed. Like Adorno, Levinas invokes the shudder, an experience beyond volition and beyond rationality, to get at something crucial about our moral nature. In proximity, Levinas says, subjectivity is overtaken by the other, bound and beholden to the other in an experience "in which difference shudders as non-indifference." In more concrete phenomenological terms, this experience is a "recurrence in awakening" that one can describe as "a shudder of incarnation through which giving takes on sense, as the primordial *dative* of the *for-another*, in which a subject becomes a heart, a sensibility, and hands which give" (*AE*, 105, 110/83–84, 87).[75] The shudder is an experience in which the body, confronted by an evil, spontaneously expresses its moral outrage, its horror. From what "dimension" of our bodily nature does this shudder come? Surely not from its egological dimension, but from a much "deeper" dimension, where intercorporeality makes us susceptible to being moved by the horror of something evil. In his earlier work, *Totality and Infinity*, Levinas had written: "Without philosophically 'demonstrating' eschatological 'truths,' we can proceed from the experience of totality back to a situation where totality breaks up" (*TI*, xiii/24–25). Such an experience could certainly be registered in the shudder—and not only in "the gleam of exteriority or of transcendence in the face of the other."

Shame is another experience that could be said to attest to a preoriginary "election" by the Good. In *Being and Nothingness*, Sartre writes: "I have just made an awkward or vulgar gesture. This gesture clings to me; I neither judge it nor blame it. I simply live it. I realize it in the mode of the for-itself. But now suddenly I raise my head. Somebody was there and has seen me. Suddenly I realize the character of my gesture, and I am ashamed."[76] Although the shame occurs *after* his awareness that someone witnessed the gesture, it nevertheless indicates an ethical predisposition that *preceded* the moment of awareness—a predisposition that always presents itself in the paradoxical, immemorial temporality of the preoriginary.[77] As Levinas says, in the presence of the other, the ego (*le Moi*) is always subject to judgment—even in regard to "the rightness, or straightforwardness, of its movement" (*la droiture même de son mouvement*).[78]

The ego is compelled by sensibility to undergo a certain passivity, rendering it more susceptible to the moral claims of the other. These claims take hold of us not through the body's "passivity of inertia, persistence in a state of rest or of movement," but through a passivity immeasurably more passive than the passivity that is contrasted to activity. This passivity occurs because the moral assignment of responsibility for the other is, as it were, "inscribed" in the flesh, a condition suggesting—according to the hermeneutic phenomenology that Levinas proposes—a covenant with God belonging to a time that only messianic prophecy can recognize: a time before the time of memory, before the emergence of volition, before the beginning of consciousness (*AE*, 94/75). Sensibility "refers [us] to an irrecuperable, pre-ontological past"—in fact, it comes from "a past that has never been present" (*AE*, 99/78). A past the traces of which are recognizable only through the body's receptivity to their revelation, a past in which the messianic promise of redemption is spelled out in the moral assignment prophetically "inscribed" in the universal flesh of our individual bodies.

The most important reference to this "inscription" that I can find appears in *Otherwise Than Being*, in a passage that we cannot, and must not, reduce to metaphorical arabesques. Once again using a reflexive grammar that perhaps approximates the middle voice, Levinas says: "It is because . . . there is inscribed or written [*s'inscrit ou s'écrit*] the trace of infinity, the trace of a departure—the trace of what is inordinate, does not enter into the present, and inverts the *arkhē* into an an-archy—that there may be . . . responsibility and a [morally disposed] self" (*AE*, 149/117; translation revised). The nature of the flesh is such that, because of its peculiar impressionability, its capacity to bear the moral law in feeling, the body is "elected" to be the medium—the prophetically designated site—for the first revelation of the law. If we take "the word" to represent the moral law, then Schelling's observation, in *Of Human Freedom*, could also shed some light on the Talmudic hermeneutics in Levinas's phenomenology. Schelling writes: "The word which is fulfilled in man exists in nature as a dark, prophetic (still incompletely spoken) word."[79] Perhaps it would also be useful at this point to recall what Benjamin says in his *Origin of German Tragic Drama*:

> The sanctity of what is written is inextricably bound up with the idea of its strict codification. . . . So it is that . . . the script of sacred complexes . . . takes the form of hieroglyphics. The desire to guarantee the sacred character of any script—there will always be a conflict between sacred standing and profane comprehensibility—leads to complexes, to hieroglyphics.[80]

But a much likelier source of encouragement for Levinas's recuperation of the hermeneutics of inscription—if indeed any were needed, other than the Holy Scriptures—would have been Moses Mendelssohn's *Jerusalem*, which says: "The prescriptions [*Vorschriften*] for action and rules of life [are] in large part to be regarded as a mode of script [*Schriftart*] and have, as *ceremonial laws*, significance and meaning [*Bedeutung und Sinn*]."[81] Thus Mendelssohn urges "a kind of midwifery" (*Geburtshülfe*): faithful observance of the liturgical ceremonies and diligent study of the Talmud, the written and oral teachings, translating the visible and invisible texts into a way of life—"a living mode of script."[82] Levinas would seem to agree with this. For example, in his preface to *Beyond the Verse*, he declares that the "writing" with which he is concerned "is always prescription and ethics, . . . holy writing [*écriture sainte*] before being a sacred text [*texte sacré*]."[83] In any case, for the interpretation of Levinas proposed in this chapter, particularly with regard to my narrative of moral development, I want to claim Mendelssohn's *Jerusalem* as a valuable source of encouragement.

Returning to Levinas's phenomenological hermeneutics of the trace, inscription of the moral law, we cannot avoid the fact that there arises just such a question of comprehensibility as Benjamin indicates—but it is a comprehensibility inextricably connected to the disposition of the will, the strength or weakness of the "desire for the Good" that would resist temptations to evade the prophetic inscription.[84] Thus, the "incomprehensibility" or "illegibility" attributed to the inscription is symptomatic of the ego's *evasion* of the categorical summons to responsibility already consecrating and commanding the nature of its flesh. But if all that remains of the inscription are traces of traces, the seeming facticity of the philosophical claim must be called into question, its hermeneutics suspended in a disconcerting moment of undecidability. Is it revelation or mere construction? Is it straightforwardly empirical—or does it belong, instead, to the allegorical register of prophecy? Does the inscription belong to an immemorial past or only to a present that assumes its belatedness, its *Nachträglichkeit*?

Whatever the answers to these questions, I think it incontestable that Levinas's ethics needs the body, needs to distinguish flesh from body, and needs the flesh of the body to bear the prophetic assignment in its covenant with God, to live in mindfulness of the moral law, understood as the law that, hosted by the flesh, makes me "hostage" to the other. Not that this makes the facticity of this embodiment, its anachronistic temporality, its metaphysical origin, its legibility, entirely comprehensible in the phenomenological register! It has not—not even when phenomenology has turned hermeneutical in a concession to the hiddenness of the trace. But could we not argue that in the shudder, in the blush, in the disquieting obsession with guilt, and in the need to confess, there are symptomatic indications, decipherments of the otherwise illegible moral "inscription"?

How are we to ascertain the truth of Levinas's claims regarding the preoriginary, when, according to their logic, they must be withdrawn from the possibility of thematization within the realm of the phenomenon? His claims regarding an "a priori" more ancient than the one posited by the tradition; his claims regarding an inscription of the moral law, supposed to take hold of me in a preoriginary time prior to consciousness, prior to volition, and prior to the time of memory; and his claims regarding a responsibility, an obligation, and a guilt incurred in a past that has never been present, and attested only by traces of traces impossible to represent in the phenomenal order—all these propositions certainly seem to defy demonstration by the phenomenological method. But the alternative to phenomenological experience would return the preoriginary "a priori" to its traditional figure of thought: transcendental conditions for the theoretical possibility of ethical experience. Not at all, we have reason to think, what Levinas wants to maintain. Hence it seems necessary for us to give thought to whatever our bodily felt experience reveals, using a hermeneutically sensitive phenomenology—a phenomenology hospitable to the unapparent that reveals itself within such experience—to indicate that in

telling moments, a deeply felt sense of the corporeal remnants of preoriginary experience can suddenly overcome us, disturbing our composure,
revealing, as beyond our grasp and beyond our powers of denial, our involuntary *subjection* to the "law"—the welfare—of the other. We might
say, with Hölderlin: "And that which happened before, but hardly was
felt, / Only now is manifest." [85] Once again, we must confront the question of belatedness—and an anachronistic temporality.

But the interpretation I am presenting here might be thought to contradict what Levinas explicitly argues regarding the "recuperation" by
memory of the preoriginary moral command. In "Diachrony and Representation," for instance, he invokes the paradoxical thought of "an immemorial past, signified without ever having been present, signified on the
basis of responsibility 'for the other,'" and then unequivocally denies the
memory that the invocation of such a past would seem to require:
"Harkening to a commandment that is therefore not the recall of some
prior generous dispositions toward the other man, which, forgotten or secret, belong to the constitution of the *ego*, and are awakened as an *a priori*
by the face of the other . . . " [86] But such paradoxical claims must be
worked through in terms of a critique of the prevailing conceptions that
Levinas is contesting. Obviously, there must be, for Levinas, some way by
which an experience of this "immemorial past" could figure in our current
lives. And there must be some means of retrieving it, retrieving it at least
to some extent—otherwise the philosopher's words would be nothing but
empty rhetorical gestures, signifying nothing. The means in question, I
suggest, is memory in a different mode: not a memory, therefore, driven
by empirical or transcendental egoism. The moral law, carried by preoriginary predispositions that precede the formation of the ego, is absolutely
beyond any "recuperation" that would make its preoriginary authority an
objective possession of empirical or transcendental consciousness. The retrieval of the moral commandment—always, perhaps, in the form of
traumatic conscience—requires, as I have argued, a distinctive corporeal
anamnesis, a process of recollection that can never bring back more of its
preoriginary history than—as Levinas puts it—the trace of a trace. Nor
can such a retrieval ever capture the preoriginary past of the moral law in
the transcendental form of a constitutive *Sinngebung*. The "memory" for
which I have argued is thus not in the service of any transcendental constitution; nor is it the kind of "recall" represented in the passage last
quoted, a memory reliving the ego's worldly deeds and claiming for them

an origin in "a priori" dispositions. In brief, what Levinas is rejecting here are all representations that would betray the diachronic character of ethical experience, reducing it either to the conditions of objective presentness, as happens in empiricism, or to the conditions of subjective presentness, as occurs in transcendental idealism.[87]

Now, with regard to the role of embodiment in the phenomenology that Levinas proposes, one of the most decisive texts appears near the beginning of *Otherwise Than Being*, where the philosopher writes: "There is a paradox in responsibility, in that I am obliged without this obligation having begun in me, as though an order slipped into my consciousness like a thief. . . . But this is impossible in a consciousness, and clearly indicates that we are no longer in the element of consciousness" (*AE*, 16/13). What "element" could we be in, then, if not that of the body—the "mystical" medium of corporeity that is invoked by the word "flesh"? Because of the radical priority or originality of the obligation, taking hold of me in a time even before volition, Levinas will describe this "incarnation" as "an extreme passivity" (*AE*, 139/195 n. 12). In "Language and Proximity," he says:

> But there is a consciousness which is a passive work of time, with a passivity more passive still than any passivity that is simply antithetical to activity, a passivity without reserve, . . . when there is [yet] no subject to assume the creative act. . . . Consciousness as the passive work of time which no one activates cannot be described by the categories proper to a consciousness that aims at an object.[88]

Indeed! This passivity is the consciousness encrypted in the flesh: a flesh in subjection to the other, host to the moral law; a flesh entrusted with the prophetic spirit of this law, the blessing of a moral "compass."

But as soon as intentional consciousness presides, the originary hold of the "proximity" that could once secretly make me experience my responsibility to and for the other as absolutely urgent, unconditional, and indeclinable, tends to weaken, for the logic of ego-consciousness inevitably "represses" the sensibility of a "subjectivity older than knowing or power" (*AE*, 104–5/63). Nevertheless, the obligatory character of the ethical responsibility that subjects and binds the flesh continues to haunt and obsess the ego, never releasing it altogether from its commandment and persistently urging it to become the mature moral self already traced out for it as an existential potentiality in the corporeal schematism of a "preoriginary self."

No matter how thick one's skin, as the surface of an "embodied spirituality" (*une spiritualité incarnée*),[89] it remains exposed: it can never completely defend itself against the importunings of a conscience that originates in the depths of the flesh it covers; for it cannot remain completely untouched by the hesitant gestures that, compelled by the other's dire needs, appeal to its reserve of compassion, charity, and love. Rejecting Merleau-Ponty's account, which sees in the exposure of the face-to-face relation a moment of encroachment, transgression, and alienation, and which accordingly misrepresents the way—or the spirit—in which the other figures in the self's formation of identity, Levinas observes: "I exist through the other and for the other, but without this being alienation. . . . This inspiration is the psyche. The psyche can signify this alterity in the same without alienation in the form of incarnation, as being-in-one's-skin, having-the-other-under-one's-skin" (*AE*, 146/114 –15). As Levinas explains, "The tenderness of the skin is the very gap between approach and approached, a disparity, a non-intentionality, a non-teleology. Whence the 'disorder' of the caress, the diachrony, . . . without a present" (*AE*, 114/90). Racisms obsessed by the color of skin thus reveal their inherent inhumanity, their inherent violence, since they must deny "the very flesh of the spirit" (*la chair même de l'esprit*), as Levinas puts it.[90]

But in what sense was Hegel right and in what sense tragically wrong when he said, in the passage from *Faith and Knowledge* quoted at the beginning of this section, that reason can "do without" skin? Is Hegel asserting the triumph of human reason over the animal flesh of its origins? Does reason require the sacrifice of our skin? Would he not then be rejecting the flesh as the medium of our *Anlage*, the medium bearing the originary assignment of obligation—obligation to the extremity of substitution, sacrificing myself for the other—that is supposed to be "inscribed" within its already differentiated predisposition? Could Hegel be implying a dialectic of Enlightenment, implying that the time could come when we would discern, hidden in the universal reason of history—in that idealized ontology in the name of which we struggled to end the violence against skin—a logic that also brings violence, obliterating the differences that entreat recognition? Or is he proclaiming reason's exile of the *corpus mysticum*, the body of prophecy whose flesh carries and hands down its deeply felt sense of the moral law?

Writing on the cabala, Gershom Scholem comments, "The exile of the body in outward history has its parallel in the exile of the soul in its mi-

grations from embodiment to embodiment."[91] Racism is one of those ex-
iles of body and soul that have marked the course of history. Nationalisms
of consanguinity also mark that history with their violence and brutality.
But in spite of its suffering, its "passion," the ancient flesh of the body continues to bear its moral assignment, its immemorial gift of prophetic revelation, received and passed on through the cunning work of natural history—above all, through the infinitely patient gestures of consecrated
lives.[92] Can we turn "avidity" into a "generosity incapable of approaching
the other with empty hands" (*TI*, 21/50)?

V. Proximity: Approaching the Unapproachable

> [Micrological moral myopia] subjects the intimate sphere to critical
> scrutiny because intimacies estrange, violate the imponderably delicate
> aura of the other which is his condition as a subject. Only by the
> recognition of distance in our neighbor is strangeness alleviated,
> accepted into consciousness. The presumption of undiminished
> nearness present from the first, however, the flat denial of strangeness,
> does the other supreme wrong, virtually negates him as a particular
> human being and therefore the humanity in him, "counts him
> in," incorporates him into the inventory of property. Whenever
> immediateness posits and entrenches itself, the bad mediateness
> of society is insidiously asserted. The cause of immediacy is now
> espoused only by the most circumspect reflection. This is tested
> on the smallest scale.
>
> —Theodor W. Adorno, *Minima Moralia*[93]

What ethical factors are involved in my approaching the other person?
Approaching the other as other, approaching the other in a way that recognizes the other's humanity, and thus also his otherness, is what now
comes in question: a proximity that is also a certain distance—indeed, a
proximity, a nearness or closeness, that maintains this distance precisely
out of respect for the other in her absolute alterity as another human. The
question of proximity arises because the other is, as Levinas says, "exposed
to all my powers. . . . But he can also . . . oppose himself to me *beyond all
measure*, with the total uncoveredness and nakedness of his defenseless
eyes, the straightforwardness, the absolute frankness of his gaze."[94] The
other can oppose me, in fact, merely with the proximity of her "presence,"
for this "presence" is "the very presence of infinity."[95] Thus, in *Totality
and Infinity*, proximity is said to be a disruptive relation, an "ineluctable
moment" of "revelation," compelling me to acknowledge the "absolute

presence" of the other as constitutive of absolute ethical obligations (*TI*, 50/78). One's gestures in relation to others must accordingly take place in the ethical spacing of respectful, tender, discreet proximity—a nearness or closeness that is also, in a uniquely ethical sense, an infinite distance. This proximity, according to Levinas, is a presence that "contests its own presence." So much so that one might even say that it is "an absence on the verge of nothingness."[96] Proximity is totally "different from some 'short distance' measured in geometrical space separating the one from the others."[97] It is not "a certain measure of the interval narrowing between two points or two sectors of space, toward a limit of contiguity or even co-incidence" (*AE*, 102/81). Rather, its "absolute and proper meaning pre-supposes 'humanity.'" But if "proximity" cannot be measured, cannot be understood in objective, physical terms, Levinas also warns against the op-posite, namely, the temptation to represent this ethical relation in the sub-jective terms of a Husserlian type of phenomenology:

> Humanity, to which proximity properly so-called refers, must then not be first understood as consciousness, that is, as the identity of an ego endowed with knowledge or . . . with powers. Proximity does not resolve into the conscious-ness a being would have of another being that it would judge to be near in-asmuch as the other would be under one's eyes or within one's reach, and in-asmuch as it would be possible for one to take hold of that being, hold on to it or converse with it, in the reciprocity of handshakes, caresses, struggle, col-laboration, commerce, conversation. (*AE*, 104/83)

Levinas withdraws proximity not only from the phenomenology of con-sciousness but even from the realm of cognition: "Proximity, which should be the signification of the sensible, does not belong to the move-ment of cognition" (*AE*, 79/63; and see 119–20/94). Only in the language of another phenomenology could proximity be approached and thema-tized with minimal distortion. But this much, at least, is clear: in the con-text of an ethical relation, proximity calls for restraint in one's gestures: a restraint that releases the social space from the entelechies of instrumental intentionalities: "[Proximity] is not a simply asymptotic approach to its 'term.' Its term is not an end. The more I answer, the more I am respon-sible; the more I approach the other . . . , the further away I am" (*AE*, 119/93).[98] The spacing that proximity establishes between the I and the other is no longer organized around ends which turn the other into a means. Thus, according to Levinas, proximity forms a "null site," a place or space that cannot be measured, cannot be represented by any geometrical topology: "Never close enough, proximity does not congeal into a structure, save when represented in the demand for justice as reversible, and reverts into a simple relation. . . . It attains its *superlative* as my incessant restlessness, becomes unique, then one forgets reciprocity, as in a love that does not expect to be shared" (*AE*, 103/82). The other's "presence" as proximity, throwing me outside both objectivity and subjectivity, demands of me endless self-examination concerning my motives and intentions—and the utmost tact and discretion in my gestures: "This being thrown outside of objectivity cannot consist [merely] in a becoming conscious of this situation, which would annul the non-indifference or fraternity of proximity" (*AE*, 104/82). So if proximity cannot be understood in terms of objectivity, it also cannot be understood in terms of transcendental subjectivity—as a "state of soul" or of consciousness. "Not all spirituality is that of theoretical, voluntary or affective representation in an intentional subject. . . . Proximity is not a state, a repose, but a restlessness, a null site, outside the place of rest" (*AE*, 104/82). It is an *anarchic* relationship with a singularity that is, as such, released from mediation by any principle, any ideality—a relationship, ultimately, released even from intentionality, which, for Levinas, is always an imposition (*AE*, 127/100).[99] In "Language and Proximity," describing proximity as a mode of contact, he says: "This relationship of proximity, this contact unconvertible into a noetico-noematic structure . . . is the original language, a language without words or propositions, pure communication. . . . Proximity, beyond intentionality, is the relationship with the neighbor in the moral sense of the term."[100] Proximity is, one might say, an "auratic" experience, a "purely" ethical gesture, absolutely free of the calculus of means and ends. For the neighbor's proximity, according to Levinas, is a "presence" that "summons me with an urgency so extreme that we must not seek its measure in the way this presence is presented to me."[101]

For Levinas, then, the concept of "proximity" must be invoked to describe the paradoxical character of the ethical relation involved in gestures of contact and touch. What he has to say about such gestures is undoubtedly inspired by his reflections on how the Torah says the ethical relation should be handled. For the human is, in a sense, an embodiment of the Torah. Hands, he says, are

> always busy, taking hold of everything. Indeed, nothing is more mobile, more impertinent, more restless than the hand. Moreover, we are told that the hand that has touched the Torah cannot touch the *terumah* and becomes impure.

The text of *Shabbat* 14a therefore asks the question: "Are the hands impure because they have been declared impure as hands, or were they first declared impure after they touched the scroll of the Torah?"[102]

"The answer," Levinas says, "is obvious": "The hands were declared impure only after they had touched the scroll of the Torah. If all hands had been declared impure in general from the beginning, it would have been unnecessary to declare specifically that hands that had touched the scroll of the Scriptures were impure." Consequently:

> It is after the hands touched the uncovered scroll of the Torah that they are declared impure. But why? Is it certain that the nakedness of the scroll means only the absence of a covering around the parchment? I am not sure that that absence of covering does not already and especially symbolize a different nakedness. And is the hand just a hand and not also a certain impudence of spirit that seizes a text savagely, without preparation or teacher, approaching the verse as a thing or an allusion to history in the instrumental nakedness of its vocables . . . ? Without precautions, without mediation, without all that has been acquired through a long tradition strewn with contingencies, but which is the opening up of horizons through which alone the ancient wisdom of the Scriptures reveals the secrets of a renewed inspiration. Touched by the impatient, busy hand that is supposedly objective and scientific, the Scriptures, cut off from the breath that lives within them, become unctuous, false, or mediocre words.

Levinas thus insists, "It was not absurd to warn readers of the dangers brought about by the very sanctity of the Torah, and to declare it impure in advance. Hands off!" For the "impurity returns to and strikes back at the hand from which it came." Our gestures expose us to certain dangers, then, "despite the good reputation attaching to directness in gaining access to the things of the world—things the 'com-prehension' of which still means a 'grasping-together.'" So, "it may sometimes be necessary in today's world to 'get one's hands dirty,' and the specific merits of 'objective research' applied to the Holy Scriptures must not be belittled. But the Torah eludes the hand that would hold it unveiled."

In another text, "God and Philosophy," Levinas asserts that the "strange fire" of spirit burning within the Holy Scriptures, miraculously burning without consuming its divine substance, effects "an ignition of the skin that touches and [yet] does not touch that which burns beyond the graspable."[103] Thus, with regard to our gestures—gestures, for example, of touching, grasping and holding, Levinas introduces the term "proximity" in order to situate them in a hodological space as paradoxical as the topology to be traversed by Zeno's arrow: no matter how near our gestures get to the flesh of the other, there is a sense in which they can never reach and touch, never make contact. The flesh of the other withdraws from our approach—withdraws into the untouchable dimension, the infinitude, of its ethical existence. Even when I grasp the other's hand, there is a sense in which that hand remains ungrasped and, indeed, ungraspable. In the spatiality of the ethical relation, our gestures take place in a condition of betweenness: between the approachable and the unapproachable, between the touchable and the untouchable, between what can be grasped and what is forever beyond the possibility of our grasp. Thus, in "Language and Proximity," Levinas says that, in proximity, "the skin [of the other] is neither a container nor the protection of an organism, nor purely and simply the surface of a being," but "presence abandoned by a departure" [104]

So gestures characterized by proximity would not take place in the order of conventional time: they would experience temporality otherwise. Nor is such proximity an experiential distance between the I and the other that some metric system could possibly measure. If we want to speak of measure, then we must say that it concerns the spacing of a relationship that can be measured only in terms of the ethical responsibility that I willingly take on in regard to—and for—the other. Thus, just as my responsibility for the other is, according to Levinas, infinite, so my proximity to the other is beyond the possibility of measure, since my responsibility brings me close to the other, yet it is precisely in that ethical relation that the other is infinitely withdrawn from my approach and my power. Withdrawn—and by virtue of a strenuous discretion and tact, enabled to remain intact. For, as the idea of infinity recognizes, "contact with the intangible" is always an ethical possibility; but it is "a contact that does not compromise the integrity of what is touched" (*TI*, 21/50). And because this ethical gesture resists with its tact the temptations of a corrupt social order, it is also true, as the philosopher tells us, that "when man truly approaches the Other, he is uprooted from history" (*TI*, 23/52).

VI. Touching the Other

> [In] ethics, in the sense given to it by Levinas, the principal, central
> prohibition is that of contact. . . . But one must not expect . . . to
> snatch speech away from light, to speak while a Hand hides Glory.
>
> —Jacques Derrida, "Violence and Metaphysics" [105]

In the moment of contact, there is no touch![106] For, while mere contact is always a superficial relation, often indifferent, a gesture typically of the instant, touching is always a gesture of deeper commitment, greater extension, and longer duration. Moreover, unlike mere contact, touching another person is a gesture that always bears within it ethical implications—and an inherently ethical potentiality. But even mere contact is a proximity that can never reduce the skin of the other to a mere surface, something that could be totally possessed—or, hence, typified and classified, as racism always attempts to do. Even the briefest contact encounters a flesh that withdraws into the intangible.

In an entry in his *Journals*, Emerson records a beautiful fragment of a conversation he had with his young son: "Waldo asks if the strings of the harp open when he touches them."[107] Perhaps only a child not yet corrupted by the normalization of the ordinary could experience in this simple gesture the extraordinary nature of the ordinary—would experience his touching as a marvelous hermeneutic event of opening. Perhaps it is to just such an experience that Benjamin was alluding when, in the 1920 fragment "World and Time," he wrote of a "perception turned toward revelation" (*offenbarenden Wahrnehmung*).[108]

But such revelatory opening is possible only if the sensibility that issues in touching is not "subordinated to the disclosure [*découverte*] of being"[109] but instead enters into a relation with the other that means the ego's exposedness, vulnerability, and even risk to life (*AE*, 94/75). This represents, for Levinas, a major point of divergence from Merleau-Ponty's phenomenological account, according to which touching another—for example, in the handshake—may be understood as a variation on my experience of touching myself, "as if both [of us] belonged to the same body."[110] Levinas concurs with Merleau-Ponty's argument that, if there is to be a phenomenological ethics, it must re-cognize "the flesh of a thought"—the fact of "thought having a flesh."[111] He also agrees with Merleau-Ponty that there is "a modality of meaning older than that of the dualistic metaphysics in Cartesianism or in the subject-object correlation [of transcendental idealism]." For, in sensation, in sensibility, "something comes to pass" below, or before, the activation of consciousness.[112] But he objects to Merleau-Ponty's assumption that this older modality is a relation of cognition, rather than our preoriginary ethical relation.[113] Accordingly, Levinas argues that "the immediacy of contact is not spatial contiguity, visible to a third party and signifying through the 'syntheses of the understanding.' Proximity is *by itself* signification."[114] The argument continues:

> The ethical does not designate an inoffensive attenuation of passionate partic-
> ularisms, which would introduce the human subject into a universal order and
> unite all rational beings, like ideas, in a kingdom of ends. It indicates a rever-
> sal of the subjectivity which is open upon beings and always in some measure
> represents them to itself, . . . into a subjectivity that enters into contact with
> . . . an absolute singularity, as such unrepresentable [in terms of any set of
> categories].

What can be said, however, is this: "The precise point at which this mutation of the intentional into the ethical occurs, and occurs continually, at
which the approach breaks through consciousness, is the human skin and
face. Contact [thus confronts the appeal, the moral presence, of the other
to become] tenderness and responsibility."[115] Thus, if the sensibility involved in touching is an openness, it is so in a way that could not be more
at odds with the ontological reification that Levinas (I think erroneously)
understands to be constitutive of the "openness-to-being" in Heidegger's
late thinking: "Here the event does not lie in the openness upon the palpable quiddity of the touched being, even though, here, too, contact can
turn into [mere] palpation [i.e., a touching that objectifies, categorizes,
seeking knowledge or information]." However, Levinas adds, touch, before turning into impersonal palpation, "is pure approach and a proximity that is not reducible to the [intentional] *experience* [at once monado-
logically subjective and impersonally objectifying] of proximity."[116] For,
as the philosopher argues:

> In contact, things are near, but are so in a quite different sense from the sense
> in which they are rough, heavy, black, agreeable, or even existing or nonexist-
> ing. The way in which they are "in flesh and bone" . . . does not characterize
> their manifestation, but their proximity. . . . The sensed is defined by this re-
> lationship of proximity. It is a tenderness: it exists in the face and nudity of the
> skin [*le peau*].[117]

Tenderness is an openness, but not the openness invoked by Heidegger's
hermeneutics. It is touching as receptive, touching as an "unlimited undergoing," an active passivity more passive than any passivity we might
normally contrast with activity, because it is "the passivity of being-for-
another" (*AE,* 80, 91, 94–95, 149/63, 72, 75, 117). This passivity, taking
away from me all my "self-possession," is my "subjection" to the other,
compelling the most uncompromised openness to the moral claims of the
other—even if against my inclinations. In the passivity of touching, "the
other in me" is sensible—sensible as a claim against my ethical conscience.

The synesthesia that entangles the touch in the "madness" of vision constitutes a serious challenge: there is more than just an affinity between touch and vision; there is also a certain kinship that, for Levinas, tempts the touch to move with the aggression and violence that vision encourages: contact, he says, is, like vision, a "forgetting" of the infinite. Nevertheless, despite this temptation, "The connection between vision and touch . . . remains essential. Vision moves into grasp. Vision opens upon a perspective, upon a horizon, and . . . invites the hand to movement and contact. . . . The forms of objects call for the hand and the grasp. By the hand, the object is in the end comprehended, touched, taken" (*TI*, 165–66/191). Our hands are all too often moved in coordination with the imperialism of the gaze:

> Inasmuch as the movement of the hand that touches traverses the "nothing" of space, touch resembles vision. Nevertheless, vision has over touch the privilege of maintaining the object in this void and receiving it always from this nothingness . . . whereas in touch nothingness is manifested to the free movement of palpation. Thus, for both vision and touch, a being comes as though from nothingness, [as if by a miraculous *creatio ex nihilo*], and in this precisely consists their traditional philosophical prestige. (*TI*, 163–64/189)

But touch is even less capable of concealing its intentionality than is vision, although Levinas is willing to qualify this "indictment": "To be sure, the intentionality of consciousness does not designate voluntary intention only. Yet it retains the initiating and inchoative pattern of voluntary intention" (*AE*, 129/101). But when contact between two persons is prolonged, and the touching becomes mere "palpation," then the "intactness" of the other is being violated for the sake of knowledge (*AE*, 96/76; and see 104/82–83). Palpation is the objectification of the other's body, a reduction of the other to a tangible possession—in effect, an obscene form of knowledge. In "Diachrony and Representation," Levinas asserts: "Seeing and knowing, or taking in hand, are tied together in the structure of intentionality. It remains the intrigue of a thought that recognizes itself in consciousness: the "now" [main-tenance] of the present [imposed and maintained by *la main*, the hand,] emphasizes immanence as the very excellence of this thought." The intentionality in touching—the "ethos" of the hand—is consequently a diachrony that desires the synchrony of the present, reducing the other to total availability, the immediacy of the same.[118]

But, according to Levinas, contact and touch always carry within themselves the capacity to become, instead, interactions of "tenderness and responsibility." As he explains, "The precise point at which this mutation of the intentional into the ethical occurs, . . . the point at which the approach breaks through [*perce*] consciousness, is the human skin."[119] This point of transformation is so wondrous, so uncanny, that Levinas does not hesitate, there, to call it "kerygmatic." Thus, recognizing the need to characterize the ethical alternative to the violence of touch, he says, using (as he often does) the present indicative to invoke ethical obligation: "To be in contact is neither to invest the other and annul his alterity, nor to suppress myself in the other. In contact itself, the touching and the touched separate, as though the touched moved off, was always already other, did not have anything in common with me" (*AE*, 109/86). But as a phenomenological description, this provides a very minimal characterization of the ethical experience.

In a letter to a friend, Henry James said, with customary delicacy: "You are more than tactful; you are tenderly, magically tactile."[120] Does this not imagine with marvelous exactitude something important about the bodily felt sense of tact—about its way of touching and about the "proximity" that is proper to it?

VII. The Caress: An Infinite Discretion

> The word *modestia* (moderation) is derived from *modus* (measure), and the word *temperantia* (restraint) from *temperies* (proper mixture, limit). Wherever *modus* and *temperantia* are, there is nothing either too much or too little. . . . The measure of the soul is [in] wisdom. . . . Thus, whoever is happy possesses his measure, that is, wisdom [*Modus ergo animi [in] sapientia est. Habet ergo modum suum, id est sapientiam, quisquis beatus est*]. The truth, however, receives its being through a supreme measure [*summum modum*], from which it emanates and into which it is converted when perfected. No other measure is imposed upon the supreme measure. For if the supreme measure exists through the supreme measure, it is measure through itself [*per seipsum modus est*]. Of course, the supreme measure must also be the true measure [*verus modus*]. But just as the truth is engendered [*gignitur*] through measure, so measure is recognized [*cognoscitur*] in truth. Thus, truth has never been without measure, nor measure without truth. . . . Whoever attains the supreme measure through the truth is happy. This means, to have God within the soul.
>
> —St. Augustine, *De Beata Vita*[121]

Rabbi Barukh said: "If the righteous man is to serve God in the right way, he must be a man who, no matter what fires he may feel within

him, does not allow the flame to burst from the vessel, but performs
every tangible action in the manner proper to it."
—Martin Buber, *Tales of the Hasidim*[122]

In an essay honoring Alphonse de Waelhens, Levinas asks: "Should it be
said that there is a waiting-for-God in this pre-sentiment [*pressentiment*]
of the absolutely other?" To suggest an answer, he calls attention to "the
touch itself, the possibility of a helping hand [*une main secourable*]. Or the
possibility of the caress."[123] It would, I think, be a grave mistake to suppose that, in the phenomenology of Levinas, the caress is necessarily or
primarily an erotic gesture. It may, of course, be so; but in the reflections
below, the caress is to be understood, rather, as a gesture of tenderness, affection, and caring, a gesture also of infinite discretion, tact, and respect.
"Caress" will accordingly serve here as our name for the distinctively virtuous character of the gesture in the ethical relation. The caress is, moreover, a way of holding and withholding one's hand that is receptive to the
paradoxical temporality that would be involved in the messianic realization of the ethical relation.

In *Time and the Other*, an early work, Levinas was already making the
ethical distinctions that he would continue to affirm even in his late writings: approach, proximity, contact, touch, and caress. Regarding the caress, he argued there:

> The caress is a mode of the subject's being, where the subject who is in con-
> tact with another goes beyond this contact. Contact as sensation is part of the
> world of light. But what is caressed is not touched, properly speaking. It is not
> the softness or warmth of the hand given in contact that the caress seeks. The
> seeking of the caress constitutes its essence by the fact that the caress does not
> know what it seeks. This "not knowing," this fundamental disorder, is the es-
> sential. It is . . . without project or plan, not with what can become ours or us,
> but with something other, always other, always inaccessible, and always still to
> come [*à venir*]. *The caress is the anticipation of this pure future* [avenir] *without
> content.*[124]

Anachronistic, welcoming the other's ungraspability, belonging to no one,
the caress, always in this sense "improper," does not "properly speaking"
ever touch what it caresses. This makes it a worthy instantiation of what
Benjamin calls an "auratic" experience, describing it as "the unique phenomenon of a distance, however close it may be."[125]

In *Totality and Infinity*, Levinas states that "transcendence is not an

optics, but the first ethical gesture" (*TI*, 149/174). Nonetheless, he wants
to say that even the tenderest of touches, touches moved by love and its
corresponding responsibilities,[126] will always fall short of the "infinite discretion"[127] that the other's humanity demands. For the ethical requires
gestures not motivated by "disclosure" (*dévoilement*) but receptive to the
eventuality of "revelation" (*révélation*): a revelation necessary for the ultimate ethical experience of the humanity of the other as other (*TI*, 37/65;
and see 50/78). When Levinas speaks of the "caress," he names the ethical
character of the gesture when it is most deeply touched and moved by its
sense of the alterity of the other. Hence, as Levinas points out, the caress
shelters, hosts in its depths the paradox of "substitution": "Substitution is
not an act; it is a passivity inconvertible into an act" (*AE*, 149/117; and see
23–24, 160–61/19 and 125). *It is the other as "sensible within me," sensible in
the form of an ethical imperative.*

In the care of the caress and sensitive to the need for a certain "modesty" (*AE*, 233–35/256–57), the I makes a "gift" of its own skin, moved by
a generosity, an affection, a tenderness so deep that the ego's thematization
cannot approach it (*AE*, 127–28, 176/101, 138).[128] In this interaction, the
subject, moved by a caring without reserve, without conditions, finds itself "denuding itself of its skin, sensibility on the surface of the skin, at the
edge of the nerves, offering itself [to the other] even in suffering" (*AE*,
18/15; and see 65–66/51). Transforming the skin as mere surface into a
flesh of unfathomable spirituality, a flesh irreducible to presence, the caress is, as Jean-Luc Nancy puts it, "the gesture of the limit," or "the gesture at the limit."[129] Levinas says: "In the caress, what is there is sought as
though it were not there, as though the skin were the trace of its own withdrawal. . . . The caress is not the coinciding proper to contact but a denuding never denuded enough [*La caresse est le ne pas coïncider du contact,
une dénudation jamais assez nue*]" (*AE*, 114/90). For my caress, the other
person's "skin is neither a container nor the protection of an organism, nor
purely and simply the surface of a being, but nudity, presence abandoned
by a departure, exposed [to my touch]."[130] The caress touches on infinity:
an infinity that is, as Levinas says, pressing his claim to the point where it
conflicts with our normal experience, "an absence on the verge of nothingness," an absence that "always flees," leaving nothing but a mere trace
of its passage through the void.[131] Elaborating the phenomenology of the
caress in a way that makes this characterization both more compelling and
more perplexing, Levinas states:

The caress, like contact, is sensibility. But the caress transcends the sensible. It is not that it would feel beyond the felt, further than the senses. . . . The caress consists in seizing upon nothing, in soliciting what ceaselessly escapes its form towards a future never future enough, in soliciting what slips away as though it were not yet. . . . It is a movement unto the invisible. In a certain sense, it expresses love, but suffers from an inability to tell it. . . . It is not that the caress would seek to dominate a hostile freedom, to make of it its object or extort from it a consent. (*TI*, 235/257–58)

Reiterating the paradoxical, anachronistic temporality of the caress, he continues:

Beyond the consent or the resistance of a freedom, the caress seeks what is not yet, a "less than nothing," closed and dormant beyond the future, consequently dormant quite otherwise than the possible, which would be open to anticipation. . . . Anticipation grasps possibles; but what the caress seeks [to let reveal itself] is not situated in a perspective and in the light of the graspable.

Consequently, "the carnal [that the caress engages] is to be identified neither with the body-thing of the physiologist, nor with the lived body [*corps propre*] of the 'I can,' nor with the body-expression." If, under the ethically tender touch of the caress, the body of the other becomes withdrawn to some extent from the realm of the tangible, it also is allowed to withdraw—from its presence in the plenitude of the present: "The not-yet-being is not to be ranked in the same future in which everything I can realize already crowds . . . , offering itself to my anticipations and soliciting my powers. The not-yet-being is precisely not a possible that would only be more remote than other possibles" (*TI*, 236–37/259). In other words, by virtue of its "inaction," its self-abandonment in an ethical relation without design or intention, the caress whose ethical character Levinas is attempting to evoke makes time for a temporality that is absolutely other than the calendar time and clock time of our worldly instrumental entanglements.

In his recent critical study on touch, written in response to Jean-Luc Nancy, Derrida recognizes in this character, ultimately anachronistic, paradoxical, metaphysical, something not merely ethical but also potentially messianic, potentially revelatory: "I admit to being tempted," he writes, "by the inadmissible temptation to go as far as to say not only that the caress touches or borders on [*confine*] the messianic, but that it is the only experience capable, possible, meaningful for the surfacing [*affleurement*] of the messianic." He concludes this thought by stating "The messianic can only be caressed."[132] "But just barely" (*Mais à peine*), Derrida adds, insisting on his reservations.[133] Regarding Levinas's phenomenology of the caress, Derrida permits himself to say only this: "One might be tempted . . . to call it virtually [*quasiment*] messianic."[134] Why such caution? One reason for his reserve pertains to the diachronic, anachronistic character of the caress, its tact always restraining the gesture at the very moment of touch, submitting to the other's ethical withdrawal from the realm of the tangible. Whence its "virtuality." But the much deeper reason is that, for Derrida, messianicity must be without messianism and without a Messiah, that is, without expectation, without any teleology or eschatology, in which an end would be immanent. Derrida insists that "messianicity" refers to an alteration in the world that must take place and yet also never take place—for it must never come to an end. It must remain as a disruptive, interruptive excess, forever immeasurable in relation to its conditions of possibility; otherwise it would be hopelessly entangled in the causalities of the historical continuum.

In the caress, as Levinas suggests in his later writings, the hand becomes "the hand of the to-God" (*la main de l'à-Dieu*)." Derrida's comment about Levinas's "virtual" messianicity may even be excessively cautious. In any event, Levinas is right to conclude that what is caressed is "not touched, properly speaking." For by virtue of its "tact" (*tact*), the caress "touches upon [*touche à*] the origin of the [moral] law." In "Diachrony and Representation," Levinas explains the sense of his phrase "to-God": "The to-God is neither the thematization of theologies, nor a finality which goes toward an end-point instead of to the infinite, nor an eschatology preoccupied with ultimate ends or promises, rather than with obligations to other people."[135] Moreover, since the caress is a form of spiritual life released from instrumental relationships, a form expressing absolutely unconditional tenderness, generosity, and love, perhaps it could be argued, borrowing a term from Benjamin's "Critique of Violence," that the gesture consecrated in the *à-Dieu* is preparing for the "pure means" of the messianic intervention.

In the context of the ethical relation, what would make such a gesture the "pure means" of an *à-Dieu* is not only that it is absolutely unconditional but also that its end, no longer part of an instrumental relation, has been returned to the other in a substitution that makes your well-being my end—my only end. But when your end, your well-being, is substituted for my own, the end of my gesture is, in a certain sense, indefinitely postponed, since I can never do enough for the welfare of the other. There is no end to what I can and should do for the other.

But ethical relations are also social relations. Just as, in the ethical relation, I must substitute the other's ends for my own, so, in the political realm, I must assume as my own the needs of the moral community in the future of which I have always already, in fact, taken part. But the "ends" of this coming community must be kept open, responsive to continued interrogation, their finality always deferred. We still need to learn "purposiveness without a purpose": the gestures of "pure means," released from all finalities and instrumentalities, all egological calculations. We still need to learn what it would mean for our gestures to be moved by the *à-Dieu*.[136]

VIII. Arrhythmia

> To the spiritual *restitutio in integrum* . . . corresponds a worldly restitution that leads to the eternity of downfall; and the *rhythm* of this eternally transient worldly existence, transient in its totality, . . . the *rhythm* of Messianic nature, is happiness. For nature is Messianic by reason of its eternal and total passing away. To strive after such passing . . . is the task of world politics, whose method must be called nihilism.
>
> —Walter Benjamin, "Theologico-Political Fragment"[137]

> The "mourning-play" [*Trauerspiel*] is in no way characterized by immobility, nor indeed by slowness of action . . . , but by the irregular rhythm of the constant pause, the sudden change of direction, and consolidation into a new rigidity [*die intermittierende Rhythmik eines beständigen Einhaltens, stoßweisen Umschlagens und neuen Erstarrens*].
>
> —Walter Benjamin, *Origin of the German Tragic Drama*[138]

Benjamin's reflections on rhythm and arrhythmia were inspired, as we saw in Chapter 3 above, by Hölderlin's "Remarks on *Oedipus*," a fragment the poet left behind. In it he says: "What in poetic meter is called caesura, the pure word, the counterrhythmic interruption [*die gegenrhythmische Unterbrechung*], becomes necessary in order to encounter the rupturing alteration of representations at its summa in such a manner that forthwith no longer the change of representation, but representation itself appears."[139] But Benjamin, putting into practice his theory of quotation, seizes upon this concept of counterrhythmicity and, taking it out of its original context, he recontextualizes it, assigning it a new and extremely disruptive political meaning. The device designed by the poet to interrupt the weight of the meter and reestablish a certain balance, a certain symmetry becomes, in Benjamin's hands, a dialectical weapon in the service of justice: an opening for the rhythm of messianic politics. As Benjamin says in Konvolut N, notes written for his *Arcades Project*: "What for others are deviations, for me are data by which to set my course. I base my reckoning on the *differentiae of time* that disturb the 'main lines' of the investigation for others." [140]

Levinas also invokes an interrupted rhythm, using the concept initially to formulate a critique of the ontological and transcendental phenomenologies of temporality, and ultimately to characterize what he interprets as the eschatological, or messianic, dimension of the ethical relation.

In "The Ruin of Representation," Levinas argues against Husserl's phenomenological representation of social relations, insisting that what the "objectivating acts" supposedly "constituting" intersubjectivity actually demonstrate is the irreducibility of these relations to a process of transcendental constitution "claiming to nurture [*bercer*] them in its rhythm." [141] Rhythm, for Levinas, is associated with a "dangerous ontology": synchronicity, predictability, symmetry, determinate ratios, the comparison of comparables, a calculus of equivalences, and repetitions of the same. But the time of the ethical relation can be neither represented as nor measured by rhythm: "The neighbor," he says in "Language and Proximity," "is not to the measure and rhythm of consciousness." [142] In *Otherwise Than Being*, he writes:

> The other as other, as neighbor, is in his presence never equal to his proximity. . . . Between the one I am and the other for whom I am responsible there gapes open a difference, without a basis in community. The unity of the human race is in fact posterior to fraternity [i.e., the preoriginary responsibility for the welfare of the other]. Proximity is a difference, a non-coinciding, an *arrhythmia* in time, a diachrony refractory to thematization, refractory to the reminiscence that synchronizes the phases of a past. (*AE*, 211/166)

This arrhythmia manifests the an-archy, the dis-order of the ethical relation relative to the temporality otherwise in effect. For if the temporality otherwise in effect is ordered according to instrumental considerations, means and ends, causal chains, and the teleologies of egological intentionality—representations that inevitably objectify others—by contrast, the temporality in effect in the ethical relation is an interruption of all these ontological orders. Also at stake, for Levinas, is the very pulse of our impulses: the ethical relation depends on whether what moves our gestures can be subjected to a rhythm, a pulse, belonging by substitution to the other. Moreover, as a passage from *In the Time of Nations* confirms, rhythm and arrhythmia are, for Levinas, important not only in our ethical life but also in our political life. Driven by the laws of capitalism, the modern world has become, he remarks, "a forgetting, a failure to recognize the other [*méconnaissance de l'autre*]! A piling up, amassing, unending totalization of the objects and money that mark the rhythm and essential structure of the perseverance of being in its being. Its concrete modes: stockpiling and banks. But also men at war. A dangerous ontology." [143] Our time, as Levinas says, quoting Shakespeare, is very much "out of joint." Its rhythms are the rhythms of egological intentionality, ego-centered impulses, industry and commerce. But, with their potential for counterrhythmic tension, gestures that are ethically motivated can interrupt these rhythmic orders, orders constitutive of the world of the same. Breaking the spell of these rhythms, ethically motivated gestures move in the keeping of a different dimension of time and a different dimension of space. Thus, if our violent social order, an order inseparable from the pulse of selfish impulses and the "dangerous" rhythms of economic life, is ever to be brought to its just end, it will be through the arrhythmia, the anarchy, of gestures that, by virtue of their generosity, courage, and respect for difference, prepare for the messianic interruption, holding in untimely suspension the historical power of the same.

IX. Anachronism: The Paradoxical Temporality of Ethical Life

> He expounded the passage in the Talmud which states that the first hasidim waited for a time before they began to pray, in order to concentrate their hearts on God: "During the time they were waiting, they prayed to God to help them concentrate their hearts on him" [i.e., they prayed to be made capable of prayer].
>
> —Martin Buber, *Tales of the Hasidim*

> The Messiah will come only when he is no longer necessary; he will come only on the day after his arrival; he will come, not on the last day, but on the day after.
>
> —Franz Kafka, *Parables and Paradoxes* [144]

> The past carries with it a temporal index by which it is referred to redemption. . . . For every second of time [is] the little gate [*die kleine Pforte*] through which the Messiah might enter.
>
> —Walter Benjamin, "Theses on the Philosophy of History"[145]
>
> The other, like the Messiah, must arrive whenever he or she wants.
>
> —Jacques Derrida, Round Table remarks[146]

Nothing exhibits anachronism, the paradoxical temporality of Levinas's messianic, prophecy-oriented phenomenology with more fidelity than his use, for the time being, for the time of the "meanwhile," of the present indicative—the usually inconspicuous little word "is," for example. His intricate rhetoric is uncompromisingly ambiguous, always oscillating between supposedly phenomenological descriptions of our lived ethical experience and hortatory descriptions of what ought to be. This rhetorical ambiguity is always disquieting, for it displaces our experience, situating it in the suspended time of the "meanwhile"—between the sensible and the supersensible, the real and the ideal, the actual and the potential, the immanent and the transcendent, the historical and the prophetic. His is an aporetic use of language, torn between the time of the present, which is ruled by an oppressive and violent ontology, and the anachronism of another temporality: a use of language stretched between the urgency of a past that has never been present, impossible for memory to retrieve and make present, except, perhaps, in the ephemeral and hieroglyphic form of mere traces of traces, and a future of messianic fulfillment, the possibility of which has already been revealed, if only in the endlessly contestable hermeneutics of prophecy.

When our gestures are moved by ethical concerns, they no longer belong to the present; nor do they belong to a past that would move them according to the dictates of fate; nor do they belong straightforwardly to the future, still an order ruled by presentness. After withdrawing ethical gestures from all intentionalities, Levinas also withdraws them from all universal teleologies, all theologically represented eschatologies, all orders of time that would in the end submit the sense of the moral law to an ontology that cannot admit the immeasurable.

In *Time and the Other*, Levinas asserts that the relationship with the other "is the absence of the other; not absence pure and simple, not the absence of pure nothingness, but absence in [or, say, from] a horizon of the future, an absence that is time."[147] The other comes to meet me in (or from) a time that cannot be made present. For this reason, touching and being touched by the other can put us in touch with an ethical dimension of our relationship—an anachronistic dimension in which a past that has not been and never will be present is nevertheless at work. Levinas indicates this paradoxical anachronism when he writes, in *Totality and Infinity*: "Corporeity is the mode of existence of a being whose presence is postponed at the very moment of presence. Such a distension in the tension of the instant can only come from an infinite dimension, which separates me from the other, both present and still to come" (*TI*, 200/225). Later, in *Otherwise Than Being*, he withdraws the "presence" of the other from objective orders of time: "Proximity does not enter into the common time of clocks. . . . It is a disturbance." He argues, "The common hour marked by the clock is the hour in which the neighbor reveals himself and delivers himself in his image—but it is precisely in his image that he is no longer near" (*AE*, 112–13/89). Encountering the other in the objectivity of common time, the affectively significant dimension of the ethical relation is neglected and damaged. But, in any event, ethical consciousness is "always late" for the encounter (*rendez-vous*) with the neighbor, since, by way of the flesh in its spiritual consecration, the law of the ethical relation will have always already taken hold.[148] Moreover, it will have been always already betrayed, subordinated to the rhythms of egoism. Thus Levinas says: "The neighbor's presence summons me with an urgency so extreme that we must not seek its measure in the way this presence is presented to me, that is, manifests itself and becomes representation." "Here," he adds, "urgency is not a simple lack of time, but an anachronism: in representation, presence is already past."[149] The proximity of the other—even the merest contact with the other—will always be "a disturbance of the rememberable time." For such contact happens in "a diachrony without a common present," whereby "difference" is "the past that cannot be caught up with" and a future that resists betrayal in the form of an image (*AE*, 113/89).

Describing the commanding temporality of the ethical, Levinas resorts to the phrase "posteriority of the anterior" (*TI*, 25/54), for the ethical relation is (to use phrases explained in the following section) "in effect," or "in force," prior to all volition, prior to consciousness, prior to egological memory—although it is realized and becomes significant and recognizable only in a later moment of life. There is a "pre-history" at work in the ego's life, for a moral sensibility "older than any present" has already taken hold of this life, taken it over in "a past more ancient than any present," and already put it radically into question — even before the actual appearance of another person (*AE*, 94–95, 126–27, 150/75, 100–101, 117). Since this prehistory, this preoriginary moral responsibility, which is said *now* to be "what was," "what is past," according to an a priori status "more ancient" than can be expressed in terms of the a priori of modern philosophy, belongs not to a straightforward, irreversible linear series of now-points but to the uniquely structured temporality of ethical experience, it becomes, in its anamnestic retrieval, "what will have been" for a phenomenological interpretation that articulates one's current sense, bodily felt, of the temporality through which the moral law manifests its compelling command.

In the present, according to Levinas, I am affected, touched, moved, by the urgency of a moral assignment coming from a past that I cannot make present, cannot possibly fully recuperate or re-present: "A linear, regressive movement, a retrospective back along the temporal series toward a very remote past, would never be able to reach the absolutely diachronous pre-original which cannot be recuperated by memory or history" (*AE*, 12/10). For Husserl, on the contrary, the "time-structure of sensibility," and consequently its existential orientation, can always be fully recovered and possessed in an appropriately transcendental act of consciousness (*AE*, 43/34). Within his phenomenology, it makes no sense to conjure up "a past more ancient than every representative origin," since only what consciousness can re-present to itself through its constitutive acts will be recognized as valid (*AE*, 10–11/9). "This anarchy, this refusal," says Levinas, "has its own way to concern me: the lapse [*le laps*]." But, he adds,

> the lapse of time irrecuperable in the temporalization of time is not only negative, like the immemorial. Temporalization as lapse, the loss of time, is neither an initiative of the ego, nor a movement toward some telos of action. The loss of time is not the work of a subject. Already the synthesis of retentions and protentions in which Husserl's phenomenological analysis . . . recuperates the lapse, bypasses the ego. Time passes [*se passe*]. (*AE*, 66–67 in the French; p. /51)

What matters to Levinas is a "time that does not return": a "diachrony" that is in force, in effect, even though its meaning, a meaning one might call "allegorical," remains inaccessible in the form of representation. "This diachrony," he states, "is not due to the length of the interval, which representation would not be able to take in. It is a disjunction of identity where the same does not yet rejoin the same" (*AE*, 67/52). Thus, he says, the "Good" that commands this diachrony "cannot enter into the present of consciousness, even if it were to be remembered" (ibid.).

Benjamin argues in his "Theses on the Philosophy of History" that "the past carries with it a temporal index by which it is referred to redemption."[150] Although the truly ethical gesture always responds immediately to the present needs of the other, reflection recognizes in the character of the ethical gesture a motivationally compelling, bodily felt sense of humanity springing from an ancient and unfathomable depth within the self, an origin belonging to a past so originary that it must have preceded every origin that memory might retrieve. The ethical gesture takes place in a present that it disturbs, for the gesture belongs to, is moved by, and expresses the "passion" of a past still to come. In other words, the ethical gesture is always intricately diachronic, moved by a moral command that is at once present and absent: a command operative as a bodily felt obligation to the present need of the other, but operative, too, both as an obligation coming from an immemorial past, a past beyond the *adequatio* of re-presentation in which it was always already "in force" (i.e., prior to the present solicitation of the other), and as an obligation whose fulfillment will always belong to an indefinitely postponed future, an obligation never to be met, therefore, in any future present.

There is diachrony in gestures that are truly ethical, because the spirit of the moral law has been revealed through the body, in a memory-inscription carried from a time before consciousness, before the arousing of the ego, carried by way of gestures that, through their "weak messianic power," bring forth the moral law, a law already in force but lacking the innerworldly "referentiality" that would realize and fulfill its allegorically promised meaning. There is a prophetic diachrony in gestures of forgiveness, gestures of sympathy, kindness, and generosity. Neither the origin nor the fulfillment or completion of such gestures can be reduced to the temporality of the present. There is prophetic diachrony also in gestures that serve justice and peace. For such gestures participate in the peculiar rhythm and tact of a paradoxical temporality, by completing what was incomplete, namely, the flourishing of ethical life, and by making incomplete what was complete, namely, the injustices that the victims are still obliging us to rectify.

In the meantime, only in the "passivity of patience," which is more passive than the passivity recognized by modern philosophical thought, can the temporality of the social relation shelter the other from the sovereignty of the same. Perhaps this patience could begin to transform the "now," the *main-tenant*, of a social order always on the verge of violence into a different "now": a "now-time" for the sake of the other, in which caring for the other would be what moved our gestures to take in hand, *main-tenant*, the other's plight.

X. The Epokhē of the Meanwhile: Prophetic Contraction, Prophetic Opening

> A hand that extends itself, that refuses itself, that we cannot take hold of in any way.
>
> —Maurice Blanchot, *The Step Not Beyond*[151]

> The rays of Messianic light [keeping the promise of prophecy] break the evil spell of *having* [i.e., the greed, indifferent to others, that the modern world serves] by which being insists on being. They offer a glimpse at a future suspension [*interruption*] of the heaping up, the amassing, the accumulation by which, for being . . . , it is ever and again a question of its own being.
>
> —Emmanuel Levinas, *In the Time of Nations*[152]

In his *Ideas Toward a Pure Phenomenology and Phenomenological Philosophy*, a work strongly influenced by Descartes, Edmund Husserl introduced a methodological procedure that he labeled with a term borrowed from the Stoics: "epokhē." This procedure, Husserl declared, would put into effect, as a temporary speculative hypothesis, "an annihilation of the world of things"—an "annihilation" in which the human spirit, achieving the status of transcendental consciousness, would remain absolutely "undisturbed" (*unberührt*).[153] In other words, by means of the epokhē, we can temporarily suspend our habit of taking the existence of the world for granted, in order to bring to "self-evidence" the world-constituting acts of the transcendental ego.

In a 1931 essay published in *Discovering Existence with Husserl and Heidegger*, Levinas expressed his admiration for Husserl's critique of objectivism, but at the same time formulated far-reaching objections to Husserl's method, including the procedural epokhē. To be sure, Levinas is not entirely unsympathetic to this methodology. For, as he says, "the phenomenological method wants to destroy the world falsified and impoverished by the naturalistic tendencies of our time—which certainly would have their rights, but also their limits. It wants to rebuild; it wants to re-cover the lost world of our concrete life." [154] Levinas, too, wants to recover the world of concrete life—above all the ethical dimension of our social life. But he will not permit the move into transcendental idealism that Husserl's epokhē sets in motion, because, in sovereign acts of transcen-dental constitution, and in spite of certain "passive syntheses" analogically pairing the one and the other, it ultimately reduces the "being" of the other, the "presence" of the other, to a mere *Sinngebung*, a meaning that the transcendental ego has constituted in the solitude of its freedom. Again and again, Levinas objects to the role that Husserl assigns to inten-tionality, insisting that, while it is acceptable in the context of knowledge, it cannot be tolerated in the context of our ethical relations, since it re-quires a reductive correlation between the subject and the other, its con-stituted "object"—or, in other words, strange as this may seem, an ethical relation structured by symmetry and equivalence. Consequently, inten-tionality always sets in motion a relation of domination, a relation already implicated in violence. [155]

Intentionality, which Levinas takes to impose a correlation, a symme-try, between noesis and noema, subject and object, the "myself" and "the other person," is always, for Levinas, in the service of possession and dom-ination, inasmuch as it involves the act of re-presenting—an act, that is, whereby the encounter with the other is temporarily delayed, in order to give oneself an interval of time—time that would make it possible to pre-sent the other to oneself entirely on one's own terms. *Main-tenance*, a pos-sessive "taking in hand," always threatens the other in every act of inten-tionality. [156] In effect, this critique leads to the conclusion that, in the context of Husserl's phenomenology, no gesture could truly be moved by a generosity or love beyond all measure. Nor could any gesture be moved by the other's needs in a radical substitution of those needs for one's own.

Levinas sympathizes with Husserl's critique of the time-order posited by objectivism and his recuperation of an experience of temporality that is lived otherwise. But he objects to Husserl's phenomenology of time-consciousness: structured as it is by an intricate weave of protentions and retentions, that consciousness cannot recognize the seemingly impossible possible event, the occurrence that could not possibly have been antici-pated. And since, according to Husserl, no experience is possible outside the continuum of this weave, we are able to encounter other people only through the terms of an already familiar typology: thus we experience others only insofar as they become comparable to what we already know.[157] What the Husserlian phenomenology of time-consciousness precludes, for Levinas, is a past still to come in a future no longer determined by a linear temporality, a past bearing redemptive potentials that can be realized only at the end of the prevailing order of time and that must accordingly always be represented, within this order, as a prophetic fulfillment indefinitely deferred.

In his preface to *Phenomenology of Perception*, Merleau-Ponty states that "the most important lesson which the [phenomenological] reduction teaches is the impossibility of a complete reduction."[158] This lesson comes as an unwelcome reminder of our limitations—a warning that commitment to a transcendental rationalism is always in danger of arrogance and dogmatism. But it also recognizes what the epokhē has revealed, namely, the claims of an absolute moral singularity, whose alterity can never be reduced to an identity within my categories. An absolute moral singularity, whose irreducible alterity suspends the totalizing authority of the transcendental ego, arrests its ontology, and puts the sensibility of the empirical ego into question. So instead of taking the epokhē in a Husserlian sense, namely, as a methodically produced *closure* to what falls outside the boundaries it posits, we could construe it in a Levinasian sense, as a "deformative" event, interrupting egological order, breaking open its imposed limits, and exposing it, in a condition of the most extreme vulnerability, to the moral claims of the other. Could one think of such a Levinasian epokhē as an event of laceration?

Perhaps we could go so far as to say that Levinas introduces his own version of the epokhē through his conception of the ethical, a version appropriate to ethics as "first philosophy." After all, in "The Trace of the Other," Levinas points out that "the epiphany of the Other carries [*comporte*] a proper significance [*signifiance*] independent of the signification [*signification*] received from the world." Moreover, this worldly signification "finds itself deranged and unsettled [*bousculée*] by this other presence," which resists integration into the objective totality of the world.[159] Levinas's epokhē ar-rests—stops, puts to rest—the transcendental *Sinngebung*, this meaning-conferring, meaning-constituting act.

This epokhē contained in Levinas's conception of the ethical would be a doubled event: taking hold preoriginarily in our passivity, it could subsequently be actively taken up by our freedom. On one hand, it must be an "elective" procedure—but one which, in contrast with the Husserlian epokhē, freely submits to the moral law and lets it take effect, restraining the ego's motivations and subordinating the ego's intentionalities to the categorical imperative. On the other hand, it would be the work of the moral law itself, which, prior to our consciousness, volition, and memory, is to be understood as having always already been "in effect," "in force," even if no innerworldly fulfillment of its referentiality, no realization of its significance or potential to signify, is—for the time being—possible. Thus, the inscription of the moral law could perhaps be described as "allegorical." In any event, what I would like this to suggest is an interpretation of the epokhē according to which the ego, embodied in gestures and manifesting its character through them, would "elect" to submit itself to the imperative of the moral law, allowing its intentionality to be suspended or contracted by the moral law. In this way the moral law, which already requires us to substitute the other's ends for our own, could take more immediate effect through the "weak messianic power" buried in the flesh of our gestures. This would be the beginning of the law's meaning or referentiality.

In Husserl's epokhē, we suspend our involvement in the world and withdraw from "distracting" entanglements and commitments in order to master and possess the world in the form of a pure, constituted, intentional meaning. In Levinas's epokhē, however, we suspend our egoistic intentionality in order to open ourselves to the other, making ourselves as radically vulnerable to the other as open wounds. Instead of strengthening the sovereignty of the subject, this ethical epokhē dismantles the subject's defenses and contracts the ego; it thus makes possible the infinitely discreet, infinitely tactful self-restraint of our gestures—for the sake of unconditional service to the other. (For Benjamin, *Vorbehalt*, a certain reserve or restraint, is the most essential requirement for the task of remembrance at the heart of ethical life, since it enjoins an attitude of openness.)

Levinas himself suggests this radical reinterpretation of the epokhē in *Otherwise Than Being*, where he proposes "an inversion of intentionality," "the contrary of intentionality," a "counter-intentionality," and calls upon a "counterconsciousness, reversing consciousness" to recognize its "responsibility for the Other, going contrary to intentionality" (*AE*, 61, 67, 180/47, 53, 141).[160] Ethics demands that this countermovement operate in our gestures.

In "No Identity," Levinas directly challenges the Husserlian epokhē, denying it the power to com-prehend as a totality the very existence of the world: "The phenomenological reduction that seeks the pure ego, beyond being, could not be secured by the effect of a writing, when the ink of the world stains the fingers that put this world between parentheses." "But," he continues, "the philosopher must return to language to convey, even if in betraying them, the pure and the unutterable."[161] There is an irreducible dimension, beyond the grasp of the epokhē: a dimension, however, that the very limitations of the epokhē reveal. In regard to the ethical relation, my experience, not of the world as such, but of another person, a being vulnerable and suffering, this irreducibility assumes the greatest possible significance. To emphasize this significance, Levinas (with a touch of humor) embodies Husserl's epokhē in a gesture—a gesture, in fact, of writing, a gesture that, as the concluding sentence insists, is not without its own philosophical implications.

Levinas's colorful remark is remarkable in a number of ways, provoking rich trajectories of thought. To begin with, the very body that Husserl wants to capture within the epokhē, reducing it to the status of a transcendentally constituted meaning, temporarily assumes, in this passage from Levinas, the sovereign, constitutive role that Husserl assigns to the transcendental ego, putting the reduction into effect. But Levinas's image of ink staining the fingers is no less consequential than Husserl's transcendental ego, suggesting, I believe, that the world whose existence is to be "reduced" is a world stained by suffering and violence—a world, moreover, whose carnage will always also stain us and always hold us responsible, giving us no possibility of evasion. It will be, moreover, through the very flesh of the body that this obligation takes hold and lays claim to our ethical life, its exigency and urgency a traumatism, a permanent stain on our flesh. In the ethical epokhē, the body once again loses its sovereignty—but for reasons that are not those of Cartesian, Kantian, or Husserlian idealism.

The ink-stained fingers also suggest that with the writing of phenomenology—a writing taking upon itself the task of remembering, against all the destructive forces, the indeclinable claims of our ethical obligation— there always comes, for the philosopher mindful of what cannot be denied, evaded, forgotten, an interruption of thought marked, stained, by trauma, always marked by inevitable complicity in the causes of suffering even if also by a sympathetic suffering, imposing a time of lamentation—a pause or epokhē taken over by guilt, remorse, atonement, and mourning.

There are no innocent hands, no clean hands, For our hands become indelibly stained with the blood of others, whether we inflict or merely know of their suffering. My hands are also stained because they themselves are wounded: the traumas suffered by others are, through substitution, my own. But why can't the stains of guilt fade with time? Is there no *end* to our "history of guilt," our *Schuldgeschichte*?

According to *Totality and Infinity*, ethics involves "an order different from historical time in which totality is constituted," an order different from what Benjamin describes, in his "Theses," as "empty, homogenous time." For Levinas, the ethical is "an order in which everything is pending [*pendant*], where what is no longer possible historically [i.e., according to historiography and prevailing philosophical thought] remains always possible" (*TI*, 26/55–56). This ethically originated order of suspended time, of time rendered "pending," is also, as the French word *pendant* suggests, a "meanwhile," a time passed through in the meantime: a time for patient waiting, its epokhē casting us into a time of judgment that stretches on indefinitely from the present epoch of corruption to the futural epoch of prophetic redemption.

At work in our ethical gestures, always pending, there is, therefore, a certain hermeneutics of memory. The passage just cited continues:

> Memory recaptures and reverses and suspends what is already accomplished in birth—in nature. . . . By memory, I ground myself after the event, retroactively: I assume today what in the absolute past of the origin had no subject to receive it and had therefore the weight of fatality. By memory, I assume and put back in question. Memory realizes impossibility: memory, after the event, assumes the passivity of the past and masters it.

Levinas seems to be telling us here that another, non-Husserlian understanding and experience of the epokhē is necessary. Not at all a Pyrrhonian "ataraxia," a suspension of judgment and action for the sake of freedom from disturbance, our epokhē must be precisely the contrary, a suspension or contraction of the ego's aggressive defenses that restrains us in order to expose us to the ethical "presence" of the other.[162]

The hope for the future that Levinas invokes is thus, I would say, a hope depending on a Benjaminian "weak messianic power" to "break the evil spell of having"—to arrest the greed that, in the modern world, the hand so readily serves.[163] Hope consequently depends on "a future suspension of the heaping up, the amassing, the accumulation."[164] In the between-time of the meanwhile, hope depends on an *ethically* motivated epokhē, already in force but not yet fully realized, to make room within the present order of time for the time of fulfillment, a time not of "disclosure" (*dévoilement*) but rather of "revelation," when a messianic potential would be recognized as already operative in the spiritual motivation of our gestures. So it might be said that, in the interruption that is the anamnestic epokhē, the almost intangible suspension of the gesture in "non-indifference," there nevertheless would be an acknowledgment that the time of redemption has been indefinitely delayed. But in the meantime, in obedience to a preoriginary ethical sensibility that is binding our gestures to a moment of passivity and heteronomy prior to memory, prior to volition, our gestures would already have submitted to a certain interruption of their intentionality, a suspension, contraction, and delay of their egoism, waiting to be touched and moved by the anachronistic proximity of the messianic.

In a letter dated September 20, 1934, Gershom Scholem, writing to Walter Benjamin, took up the vexing question of law and revelation in Kafka's novel *The Trial*, and suggested that Kafka is attempting to evoke "a stage in which revelation [*Offenbarung*] does not signify or refer [*bedeutet*], yet still affirms itself by the fact that it is in force."[165] The messianic is unrealizable in our prevailing order of time; but in the meantime, by no means is it simply absent. It exists, for Scholem, as an allegorical *Geltung ohne Bedeutung*: a prophetic promise already "in force," already "operative," but not yet referentially signifying—because the time for the completion of the messianic process has not yet come and the meaning of the promise is therefore not yet realized. This is precisely what, in Levinas's first philosophy, I am claiming the epokhē involves. And, as we have seen, the life of "interiority," according to Levinas, requires the infinite "postponement" of representation, its preoriginary ethical epokhē resisting integration into any totality, any universalism (*TI*, 26/55).

But one must recognize, therefore, at least *two distinct moments* in the gestural experience bearing this radicalized epokhē: first, a passivity more passive than any passivity that philosophical thought is capable of adequately representing; second, a velleity that, in obedience to the moral law bodily sensed within, freely contracts, subtracting itself from the conceits and ends, intensities and impulses of the intentional gesture. The first takes place as a preoriginary inscription of the moral law, a "disruption of our being-in-the-world that [prior to volition] opens us to the other." The second, by contrast, would take place as an ethically motivated self-restraint, an "elective" suspension of the egoism directing intentionality, whereby I would be opened to the other, somehow enabled, beyond my habitual moral resources, beyond my vulnerabilities and defenses, to receive the neighbor in the time of her need.[166] This election of epokhē entails a certain *closure* to what Husserl termed the "natural attitude"—an attitude which for Levinas means the primacy of the ego over the other—and also an *opening* to the other, which this closure makes possible. For the restraint of egoism, the ar-resting of its pulses, impulses, and desires, means an opening to the other that consists in exposure, vulnerability, the peculiar "trauma" of a moral subjectivity touched and moved by its responsibilities to and for the other.

One might even say that, whereas Husserl's epistemically motivated epokhē brings intentionality as such to light, the epokhē that Levinas's critique implicitly invokes is an ethical moment that, calling to mind Benjamin's prologue to *The Origin of the German Mourning Play*, effectuates the very death of ego-generated intentionality. Destroys it, for example, in the gesture of touching. For in the interval of measured tension and contraction prepared by the epokhē of self-restraint, a moment of remembrance can take place; and it is in just such a moment that the preoriginary "law" of obligation, having already taken hold of our gestures in a past that has never been present, could finally reveal something of its promised utopian or messianic meaning in and for the redemption of ethical life.

In "Humanism and An-archy," Levinas adverts to the "emergence" of morality in "a pre-originary susceptibility" that precedes the investment in egoism: an ethical experience more ancient than any origin we have ever represented, "a susceptibility provoked in the subject without the provocation ever becoming present or becoming a logos presenting itself to assumption or to refusal and situating itself in the bi-polar field of values." This leads him to conclude that the subject is "a responsibility before being an intentionality."[167] Should this responsibility subsequently become "electively" operative in our gestures, then—I want to argue—a bodily felt, anamnestic sense of the involuntary, preoriginary event of epokhē could reinforce the "elective" assumption of responsibility, enabling the sense of tact inherent in this preoriginary relationship with the other to guide our gestures' rhythm and measure. Such gestures would consequently proceed in "elective" obedience to that "preoriginary" responsibility, inscribing the suspension, an ethical caesura, in the very heart of touch. This, I submit, is the ethical character that is manifest, for example, in gestures of kindness, gestures moved by solicitude, outpourings of generosity, compassion, and love: gestures in which the ends of the other, though never sufficiently realized, are received in unconditional substitution for the ends of the ego.

Arguing that "justice interrupts history," Levinas implies that the politics of justice also sets an epokhē in motion, opening in history a breach in which "a justice of redemption" might be substituted for "the infernal or vicious circle of vengeance and pardon" and for "the common measure of money" distorting social relations. Warning that the "Angel of Reason" can bring with it a violent and destructive freedom,[168] Levinas seems to be obliquely commenting on the discussion of Klee's *Angelus Novus* in Benjamin's "Theses" and the "divine violence" of "pure means" in Benjamin's "Critique of Violence." Despite the danger against which he warns us, Levinas suggests that the epokhē at work in the ethical relation must also be applied to our "normal" way of experiencing history, suspending the validity of our ontological assumptions and preparing this experience for the possibility of a time when the gift of Creation could be realized and fulfilled in a community of welcoming and receiving beyond all use of measure. For this epokhē, this inhibition of force, coming from a time outside history, compels "a relation with alterity, with mystery": "That is to say, with the future, with what . . . is never there, with what cannot be there when everything is there—[a relation] not with a being that is not there, but with the very dimension of alterity."[169] But the epokhē cannot fully take effect until, through terrible suffering, we have finally learned to submit to the law of its inhibition or prohibition. As Benjamin puts it in his "Critique of Violence":

> To motivate human beings to the peaceful resolution of their interests beyond all legal orders, there is, in the end, regardless of all virtues, one effective motivation that often enough puts into the hands of even the most recalcitrant will pure instead of violent means: it is the fear of mutual disadvantages that threaten to arise from violent confrontations, whatever the outcome might be.[170]

If one is reluctant to accept the ethically compromised motivation proposed by this narrative, one should recall the prominence of war in the reflections Levinas commits to the pages of *Totality and Infinity*. As Kant argued, morality requires that we never treat others as means to our ends but always as ends in themselves. To be sure, we cannot live without instrumental involvements in the world; nor can the means we adopt be detached from the ends they implicate and serve. But if, for the time being, these ends were to be transferred, by substitution, to the other, and "our own" ends accordingly indefinitely deferred—if, that is, our own ends were to be kept in a state of suspension—then the character of the means could eventually, perhaps, be morally "purified." "Purified," that is, in four distinct but inseparable ways: (1) my ends are not my own but instead are yours, by substitution; (2) there are no preconditions or terms to impose their measure; (3) my own ends are therefore indefinitely postponed; and (4) the end I have by substitution is also indefinitely postponed, but in a different sense, because I can never do enough for the other. A "purification" for the meantime: the time in-between, *l'entretemps*, the time of separations that prepares for the realization of the messianic epoch (*AE*, 138/109).

But are we capable of this contraction and suspension? Are we willing to let our gestures be moved by the "weak messianic power" with which we have always and already been blessed—if this is what that suspension, that contraction, that epokhē should require of us in order that an opening for the messianic might appear? How might we give thought to the possibility of gestures in which any end posited by egoism has been suspended indefinitely? How might we give thought to the possibility of gestures in which the "means" have been "purified"? As a preliminary answer to these questions, we need to give thought to the *felt character* of such gestures— and more specifically, their absolute unconditionality and their substitution of ends. We must approach this task for the sake of the alterity at the heart of the ethical relation. For the sake of a justice that would lift our existence out of its corruption in the present order of historical time.

XI. Universal History

Not even ashes can entirely conceal the traces of evil from the judgment of history; nor can they refute the hope that is preserved, despite so many traumas, in remembrance. There is a redemptive history that we must attempt to write, a history, however, that we are still learning to write. To do so, we must breach the defenses of a memory that time and again takes refuge in a historicism of the present that petrifies the past, betraying it in the very process of making it present, and thereby denying its persistent and still unrealized promise to a past yet to come.

Although Levinas readily acknowledges that the ideal of "universal history"—as it figures, for example, in the Enlightenment writings of Kant—has promoted human rights and social justice, in *Otherwise Than*

Being he attempts to think "a temporality different from that which scans consciousness." Such a temporality, he writes, "takes apart the recuperable time of history and memory in which representation continues. For [while], in every experience, the making of a fact precedes the present of experience, [in contrast] the memory, history, or extra-temporality of the a priori recuperates the divergence and creates a correlation between the past and this present." He explains this thought, declaring that, in ethical proximity, there is felt "a command that has come as though from an immemorial past which was never present" (*AE*, 112/88). The reflection on time and history continues: "One can call that, apocalyptically, the breakup of time. But it is a matter of an effaced but untamable diachrony of non-historical, non-said time, which cannot be synchronized in any present by memory and historiography, and where the present is but the trace of an immemorial past" (*AE*, 113/89). History has always been written by the victors, denying the vanquished their own story. Moreover, history has mainly told of "great individuals" and "great moments, events, and movements," neglecting the quotidian lives of ordinary people. Even the most enlightened canvases of such history represent a past in which the speculative idea of universality unwittingly conceals the singularities whose abject ethical life it is intended to redeem. In *Totality and Infinity*, with words reminiscent of Benjamin's "Theses," Levinas argues:

> Totalization is accomplished only in history—in the history of the historiographers, that is, among the survivors. It rests on the affirmation and the conviction that the chronological order of the history of the historians outlines the plot of being itself, analogous to nature. The time of universal history remains as the ontological ground in which particular existences are lost, are computed, and in which at least their essences are recapitulated. . . . In the time of the historiographer, interiority is the non-being in which everything is possible, for in it nothing is impossible—the "everything is possible" of madness. (*TI*, 26/55)

Defending ethical "interiority," ethical "singularity," against the assumption implicit in "the time of universal history" that it has a right to be "the measure of reality," he asserts: "Interiority is the very possibility of a birth and a death that do not derive their meaning from [universal] history. Interiority institutes an order different from the historical time in which totality is constituted." He then, in a statement of great tropic significance, contends that, unlike the ontologized time of universal history, the historical time of ethical interiority is "an order where everything is *pending*, where what is no longer possible historically remains always possible." But here, the reference to an inconceivable possibility, an order where everything is, so to speak, always "pending," could not be more at odds with the "madness" of a historical order in which the totalitarian will to power, brutally enforcing the law of identity, makes come true the terrifying proposition that "everything is possible." For it is a reference to the *breaking open* of historical time, invoking a gate of hope through which the messianic redemption might eventually enter.

"Commencement and end," Levinas says, if "taken as points of universal time, reduce the I to the third person, such as it is spoken by the survivor." Here he comes near to Primo Levi's reflections on the claims of the Shoah survivor to bear witness.[171] Levinas explains his remark as follows:

> Interiority is essentially bound to the first person of the I. The separation is radical only if each being has its own time, that is, its *interiority*; only if each time is not absorbed into the universal time. By virtue of the dimension of interiority, each being declines the concept and withstands totalization—a refusal necessary for the idea of Infinity. [Interiority] does not exhibit itself in history; the discontinuity of the inner life [i.e., most deeply, its ethical life] interrupts [the continuum of] historical time. (*TI*, 28–29/57–58)

Continuing this reflection on history, Levinas declares that "mortal existence unfolds in a dimension that potentially intersects the time of history." He explains:

> Between a philosophy of transcendence that situates elsewhere the true life to which man, escaping from here, would gain access in the privileged moments of liturgical, mystical elevation, or in dying—and a philosophy of immanence in which we would truly come into possession of being when every "other" (cause for war), encompassed by the same, would vanish at the end of history—we propose to describe, within the unfolding of terrestrial existence, of economic existence . . . , a relationship with the other that does *not* result in a divine or human totality, that is not a totalization of history but the idea of infinity. Such a relationship is metaphysics itself. (*TI*, 23/52)

Levinas's repudiation of all totalities, all closures, all ontologies of presence, all logics of identity—a repudiation with which Adorno would certainly agree—prepares for the evocation, in terms very modest and subtly hermeneutic, of the "rupture of history," which, as for Benjamin, signifies and portends the messianic intervention or supervenience, a parallel temporality. Obliquely contesting Heidegger's eschatology of history, which surrenders history to the intangible forces and dispensations of an impersonal, indifferent destiny, together with all the other eschatologies that posit an end in the finitude of history, Levinas cautiously sets down his own stakes: "History would not be the privileged plane where Being disengaged from the particularism of points of view (with which reflection would still be affected) is manifested. If it claims to integrate myself and the other within an impersonal spirit, this alleged integration is cruelty and injustice; that is, it ignores the Other." Levinas proceeds to affirm the priority of the ethical relation over the relations of power that history not only documents but invariably reinforces, owing to ontological commitments that deny the very possibility or meaning of transcendence. He accordingly states: "History as a relationship among humankind ignores a position of the I before the other in which the other remains transcendent with respect to me. Though of myself I am not exterior to history, I do find in the Other a point that is absolute with regard to history—not by amalgamating with the other, but in speaking with him." "History," he says, now suggesting the prophetic sense of its end, "is worked over by the ruptures of history, in which a judgment is borne upon it." The reflection concludes with an image of the ethical relation in the era of its redemption. This era belongs to the end of history—an end that may, however, last a very long time. But meanwhile, in the ethical relation, what is decisive is its character: "When one truly approaches the Other, the one is uprooted from history." And history, *for that moment*, comes to an end. No measure immanent in history—or somehow entangled in its rage—but only the messianic, proclaimed through revelation and prophecy, can serve as the measure of ethical life, determining its rhythm: the peculiar arrhythmia, for example, of its gestures, the ends of their desire held back in suspension, indefinitely deferred. Such gestures reach beyond the frame of universal history, touched and moved by moral commitments that connect the present to an immemorial past and a future that in the prevailing historiography remains unrecognizable. Such gestures are otherwise determined.

XII. Messianicity: When the Time Comes

> God's truth conceals itself from those who reach for it with one
> hand only, regardless of whether the reaching hand is that of . . . the
> philosopher, which preserves itself free of preconceptions, soaring
> above its objects, or that of . . . the theologian, proud of its experience

and secluding itself from the world. God's truth wants to be entreated
with both hands.

—Franz Rosenzweig, *Star of Redemption*[172]

In his preface to *Totality and Infinity* (x–xii/22–23), Levinas invokes eschatology—but it is a messianic eschatology, a divinely purified means, that refuses to represent the correlative end. "Morality," he states,

> will oppose politics in history and will have gone beyond the functions of prudence or the canons of the beautiful to proclaim itself unconditional and universal [only] when the eschatology of messianic peace will have come to superpose itself upon the ontology of war. Philosophers distrust it. . . . For them, eschatology—a subjective and arbitrary divination of the future, the result of a revelation without evidences, tributary to faith—belongs naturally to Opinion.

But Levinas's defense of eschatology is decisively qualified:

> However, the extraordinary phenomenon of prophetic eschatology certainly does not intend to win its civic rights within the domain of thought being assimilated to a philosophical evidence. In religions and even in theologies, eschatology, like an oracle, does indeed seem to "complete" philosophical evidences . . . , as though eschatology added information about the future by revealing the finality of being. But . . . its real import lies elsewhere. It does not introduce a teleological system into the totality; it does not consist in teaching the orientation of history. Eschatology institutes a relation with being *beyond the totality* or beyond history, and not with being beyond the past and the present.

He emphasizes the ethical contestation of every measure, even that of "Being": "It is a relationship with a *surplus always exterior to the totality*, as though the objective totality did not fill out the true measure of being; as though another concept, the concept of infinity, were needed to express this transcendence with regard to the totality, non-encompassable within the totality and as primordial as totality." This "beyond," however, "is not to be described in a purely negative way." It is not merely privation—of rational evidence, legitimate knowledge, final totality—for it is "reflected *within* the totality and history, *within* experience": "The eschatology, as the "beyond" of history, draws beings out of the jurisdiction of history and the future; it arouses them in and calls them forth to their full responsibility. Submitting history as a whole to judgment, exterior to the wars that mark its end, it restores to each instant its full signification in that very in-

stant." Thus, "it is not the Last Judgment that is decisive, but the judgment of all the instants in time, when the living are judged." Each instant
matters infinitely, because each one is, as the last thesis of Benjamin's "Theses" puts it, "shot through with chips of Messianic time."[173] Levinas's preface continues: "The eschatological notion of judgment . . . implies that
beings have an identity 'before' eternity, before the accomplishment of history, before the fullness of time, while there is still time. . . . The eschatological vision breaks with the totality of wars and empires, in which one
does not speak." Levinas concludes these reflections by appropriating Heidegger's "moment of vision" (*Augenblick*) for an experience that could not
be more divergent: "The first 'vision' of eschatology (hereby distinguished
from the revealed opinions of positive religions) reveals the very possibility
of eschatology, that is, the breach of the totality, the possibility of a signification without a context." Would not Scholem's eloquent phrase *Geltung ohne Bedeutung* ("being in force without referentially realized significance," "validity without reflectively fulfilled meaning") provide an insightful name for this Levinasian eschatology, this possibility of a "reality"
already in force but without (as yet) any thematized experience of its
meaning? Could we experience such a possibility? Levinas suggests that we
watch for this possibility with extreme vigilance, for every situation in
which we find ourselves is potentially "a situation where totality breaks
up" (*TI*, xiii/24). Never is this more keenly to be felt than in one's ethical
relation with another. Whenever one person truly enters into an ethical relation with another, the relation constitutes "a rupture of continuity" in
history. But the ethical relation also generates a certain "continuity across
this rupture" (*TI*, 260/284): a continuity of the hope that defies history to
approach with imagination the redemption of a destitute humanity.

But behind this stirring of hope, Levinas, like Benjamin, finds what
might be called "divine violence": "What, in action, breaks forth as essential violence is the surplus of being over the thought that claims to contain
it: the marvel of the idea of infinity" (*TI*, xv/27).[174] In "World and Time,"
a fragment written in 1920, Benjamin comments, "Authentic divine
power can manifest itself *other than destructively*, [but it can do so] only in
the world to come (the world of fulfillment)." Whenever divine power enters into the secular world, however, "it breathes destruction."[175] His argument continues, "In its present state, the social is a manifestation of
spectral and demonic powers, often, admittedly, in their greatest tension
to God, their efforts to transcend themselves." "The divine," Benjamin

says, expressing a view in which Levinas could have recognized some surprising affinities, "manifests itself in [those powers] only in revolutionary force. Only in the community, nowhere in 'social organizations,' does the divine manifest itself either with force or without. (In this world, divine power is higher than divine powerlessness; in the world to come, divine powerlessness is higher than divine power.)" Benjamin claims further that such manifestations of divine power "are to be sought not in the sphere of the social, but in perception oriented toward revelation and, first and last, in language, sacred language above all." This sacred language must somehow, however, make it possible for divine power to take possession of the profane human body, giving it the message of redemption through the inscription of moral law: "The Mosaic laws," he says, "belong to the legislation governing the realm of the body in the broadest sense . . . and occupy a very special place: they determine the location and method of *direct* divine intervention. And just where this location has its frontier, where it retreats, we find the zone of politics, of the profane, of a bodily realm that is without law in a religious sense." In this "revelation of the divine," the world must undergo "a great process of decomposition," transformations affecting even the nature of our embodiment, "while time—the life of him who represents it—is subjected to a great process of fulfillment." This fulfillment cannot succeed, however, without the "redemption of history"—a process requiring that we, the ones who "represent" it, prepare our present world for "the world to come," holding it open for the utopian, messianic moment.

Levinas remains close to the spirit of Benjaminian thought, for when he returns to the question of messianic time, near the end of *Totality and Infinity*, he avers: "The completion of time is not death, but messianic time, where the perpetual is converted into the eternal. Messianic triumph is the pure triumph; it is secured against the revenge of evil, whose return the infinite time does not prohibit" (*TI*, 261/285). He then asks us to consider: "Is this eternity a new structure of time, or an extreme vigilance of the messianic consciousness?" Perhaps we should prefer the second option, since the first risks a return to the illusory eternity of totalizing ontologies. In any case, "infinite time" must be understood as "putting back into question the very truth it promises" (*TI*, 261/284). But in spite of this necessary skepticism—if that is what it is—Levinas will insist that "the dream of a happy eternity . . . is not a simple aberration." For *the messianic requires that we live simultaneously in two absolutely distinct but—as it were*—*parallel dimensions of time*: "both an infinite time and a time it will be able to seal, a completed time." (When the parallel intersects!)

Although Levinas opposes Benjamin's political anarchism, even if it hopes to prepare for the messianic era, he, like Benjamin, is convinced that the conditions for the appearance of the messianic—in particular, our achievement of social justice and the peace it brings—require a radical transformation in the social and political institutions of the nation-state, including fundamental alterations in regard to its laws of inclusion and exclusion. Such changes are essential to the achievement of tolerance and hospitality, an openness beyond patriotism and nationalism, in the social and political institutions of the nation-state—institutions determining the conditions of its very existence.[176]

Thus, while Levinas believes, with good reason, that "messianic deliverance cannot ensue from individual effort [alone]," [177] such effort does create an opportunity for the messianic to enter history; and no individual effort serves this purpose more effectively than the charity and hospitality in individual gestures of forgiveness.[178] In *Totality and Infinity*, Levinas points out how messianicity structures the paradoxical diachrony of such gestures:

> The paradox of pardon lies in its retroaction; from the point of view of common time it represents an inversion of the natural order of things, the reversibility of time. . . . Pardon refers to the instant elapsed; it permits the subject who had committed himself in a past instant to be as though that instant had not passed on, to be as though he had not committed himself. Active in a stronger sense than forgetting, which does not concern the reality of the event forgotten, pardon acts upon the past, somehow repeats the event, purifying it. But in addition, forgetting nullifies the relations with the past, whereas pardon conserves the past pardoned in the purified present. (*TI*, 259/283)[179]

The paradox of pardon is "time constituting itself." The instants do not connect up with one another in a straightforward linear succession of now-points; nor do they "connect up with one another indifferently, but extend from the other unto me" (*TI*, 259–60/283). Consequently, "the future does not come to me from a swarming of indistinguishable possibles which would flow from my present and which I would grasp; it comes to me across an absolute interval whose other shore the Other [that is] absolutely other . . . is alone capable of marking and connecting with the past." And if, as Levinas says, "each instant of historical time in which action commences is, in the last analysis, a birth, and hence breaks the continuous time of history" (*TI*, 29/58), forgiveness is a gesture that can accomplish just that, anachronistically enabling us—not only victim and perpetrator but also many others—to be moved by the time of redemption. In the ethical relation, the gesture will always be one that is moved by the "weak messianic power" in forgiveness. Moved even to forgive the unforgivable.

But forgiving does not mean condoning, excusing, or justifying the wrongful act; nor does it imply fully understanding or even fully sympathizing with the perpetrator. There can be no absolution of responsibility and no annulment of the evil character of the deed. And *a fortiori*, no quid pro quo: no bargain, no calculated exchange between repentance and forgiveness. No doubt this is why Benjamin, in an early fragment entitled "The Meaning of Time in the Moral Universe," refuses to support "reconciliation," although he encourages forgiveness, which he describes as a "purifying destruction" that overcomes the archaic, mythic justice of retribution, "fundamentally indifferent to the passage of time." Thus he states:

> The Last Judgment is regarded as the date when all postponements are ended and all retribution is allowed free rein. This idea, however, . . . fails to understand the immeasurable significance of the Last Judgment, of that constantly postponed day which flees so determinately into the future after the commission of every misdeed. This significance is revealed not in the world of [profane] law, where retribution rules, but only in the moral universe, where forgiveness comes out to meet it.[180]

"In order to struggle against retribution," Benjamin says, "forgiveness finds its powerful ally in time. For time . . . is not the lonely calm of fear but the tempestuous storm of forgiveness which precedes the onrush of the Last Judgment." "This storm," he adds, "is not only the voice in which the evildoer's cry of terror is drowned; it is also the hand that obliterates the traces of his misdeeds, even if it must lay waste to the world in the process. . . . God's fury roars through history in the storm of forgiveness." In this storm, the divine hand of forgiveness becomes the human hand, extended in good will, lending a hand to God's work. Taking place through the patience of time, forgiveness is not only, as Levinas puts it, "a movement stronger than death" but also a movement, a gesture, infinitely stronger than revenge, beyond all calculation, all measure—and consequently, as he also says, "a movement toward the other that does not come back to its point of origin."[181]

Benjamin's fragment closes with a final thought concerning "the meaning of time in the economy of the moral universe": "In this, time not only
extinguishes the traces of all misdeeds but also—by virtue of its duration,
beyond all remembering and forgetting—helps, in ways that are wholly
mysterious, to complete the process of forgiveness [*Vergebung*], though
never of reconciliation [*Versöhnung*]." If time can heal, if it can make forgiveness possible, that is much to be desired. But encouraging "reconciliation" would be tantamount, for Benjamin, to ceding ultimate victory to
the agents of injustice. There must be no bargaining with the demonic—
and no compromising of the redemptive hope, the messianic pro-mise.
Levinas, on the other hand, does invoke the "strange happiness of reconciliation" (*TI*, 259/283)—but it is certain that he does not mean to con-
done evil deeds. What I think he hopes for when he welcomes "reconciliation" is the distinctive moral proximity that can take place only through
the miracle of forgiveness—a miracle that may sometimes move through
gestures of the most unimposing physiognomy.

    Difficult Freedom contains a lecture in which Levinas refers to "a ritual-
ization regulating all the gestures [*gestes*] of the complete Jew's day-to-day
life, which the pious experience as something joyful."[182] Messianicity can
manifest itself in even the seemingly most inconsequential of everyday
gestures.

    A striking instance of this point, extraordinary in its way, appears in
Simon Wiesenthal's *The Sunflower*, in which he narrates the event that
prompted him to undertake the research culminating in this book.[183] In
1942, under German occupation, Wiesenthal was imprisoned in a concentration camp. At the end of a day of hard labor in the military hospi-
tal there, he was taken by a nurse to visit a young German soldier, seriously wounded and about to die. This man, torn apart by remorse for the
atrocities he had committed during his time in the SS, told Wiesenthal his
story and then asked for forgiveness. But Wiesenthal immediately rose
and left the room without a word. But he became disturbed by his action
to the point of obsession, consumed by the thought that perhaps he
should have granted the man a word of forgiveness. So he undertook to
ask a number of people of different nationalities about this question of forgiveness, and eventually prepared a collection of their answers for publication. Despite many differences of opinion among the interviewees,
there was considerable agreement on at least one crucial point: forgiveness, passing beyond the temptations of revenge, is always morally desir-

able, but it must not be extended in the name of others—and it must never erase our memories.

Reading the Italian translation of this translation, Norman Gobetti noticed something in Wiesenthal's story that all the contributors seem to have overlooked:

> The physical presence in the room of the hospital of those two persons torn apart by their suffering, left to themselves and confronting one another face to face. In the middle of Karl's horrible confession, Wiesenthal was distracted: "For an instant," he wrote, "I forgot where I found myself, and I heard a buzzing sound. A fly, obviously attracted by the odor of the wounds, landed on the head of the dying man. He didn't see it, and couldn't even see my hand, which chased it away. But perhaps he felt it. 'Thanks,' he murmured. And only then did I realize that I, helpless *Untermensch*, had given relief to the Overman, likewise helpless, as a natural thing to do, without having first given it any thought." [184]

This gesture, exemplifying the "banality" of the good, happened "naturally," as we are wont to say, without deliberation, without decision—happening as if, "in the everyday, nothing has happened." But it is a gesture that breaks out of the prevailing order of history—a history of crimes against humanity—to reach the other in his or her ethical transcendence.

Arguing for the idea of infinity, Levinas points out that its metaphysical transcendence breaks the spell of totalization that historicism casts over history. "History," he writes, no doubt intent on expressing his disagreements with Hegel and Heidegger,

> would not be the privileged plane where Being disengaged from the particularism of points of view is manifested. If it claims to integrate myself and the other within an impersonal spirit, this alleged integration is cruelty and injustice, that is, it ignores the Other. History as a relationship between men ignores a position of the I before the other in which the other remains transcendent with respect to me. Though of myself I am not exterior to history, I do find in the Other a point that is absolute with regard to history.

He concludes this thought with a reminder: "History is worked over by the ruptures of history, in which a judgment is borne upon it. When man truly approaches the Other, he is uprooted from history" (*TI*, 23/52). Yet in spite of its burning desire to see love, justice, and peace transform this world, Judaic messianism has always resisted totally separating life in the messianic era from life in the present time. Many Talmudic texts confirm this interpretation of messianicity, for example, the story about a man who is planting a tree when he is told that the Messiah has arrived. After debating whether he should immediately interrupt his work and go at once to see the Messiah, he concludes that his first obligation is to finish the planting. The Messiah can be postponed![185] It is, I think, in something of the same spirit that the Israeli poet Yehuda Amichai wrote:

> Once I was sitting on the steps near the gate at David's Citadel and I put down my two heavy baskets beside me. A group of tourists stood there around their guide, and I became their point of reference: "You see that man over there with the baskets? A little to the right of his head there is an arch from the Roman period. . . . " Hearing this, I said to myself: Redemption will come only when they are told: "Do you see that arch over there from the Roman period? It doesn't matter; but near it, a little to the left and then down a bit, there's a man who has just bought fruit and vegetables for his family."[186]

With this story, the poet shows us a profound paradox: from one point of view, the coming of the Messiah will involve an infinitely consequential alteration in the way we live together; and yet, from another point of view, the coming of the Messiah will involve, as Kafka said, "only the slightest adjustment." Perhaps Levinas must be read in such a way that both these perspectives are kept equally in mind. The ethical life accordingly requires of us an infinitely rigorous moral vigilance: a messianic vigilance even in regard to the smallest of gestures.

The Tables

> I liked . . . feeling her touch my arm in the same spot where Hector had touched me only a moment before. Two different gestures, two different memories—one on top of the other. My skin had become a palimpsest of fleeting sensations and each layer bore the imprint of who I was.
>
> —Paul Auster, *The Book of Illusions* [187]

In an essay entitled "Persecution: The Self at the Heart of Metaphysics," I propose an interpretation of Levinas's claims regarding the experiences of accusation and persecution that brings out the ethical complexity and the intricacy of these experiences. I also propose there a phenomenological account of the stages of moral self-development, arguing that Levinas's exposition of these experiences requires such a narrative.

TABLE 10.1
The Moral Journey

The four faces of subjectivity

The Saintly Self (by an effort to recuperate traces carried by the Preoriginary Self) (Transpersonal)	Transpersonally responsive, open, vulnerable and exposed in its compassion Heteronymous: the-one-for-the-other Anonymous: selfless, joyous self-sacrificing Asymmetrical relations with others, in favor of the other Nonreversible, nonreciprocal responsibility, in favor of the other Assumes supererogatory responsibilities: saintly volition Experience of "accusation" and "persecution": sympathetically shares the sufferings of others and feels pain at being unable ever to do enough
The Enlightened Ego (Impersonal)	Capable of an impersonal, universalizable moral standpoint (Kant's "mature" moral development) Autonomous (in the Kantian universalizable sense) Not necessarily anonymous: anonymity is, at this stage, an option that may or may not be taken Symmetrical relations with others: mutual recognition, reversibility, reciprocity, equality Builds institutions of justice to achieve a pragmatic accommodation with an enlightened egoism Assumes obligatory responsibilities, in a critical, reflective, dialogical spirit Experience of "accusation" and "persecution": sympathetically understands the sufferings of others and works for social justice, equality, and peace
The Narcissistic Ego (Narrowly personal)	Unable or unwilling to adopt the impersonal, third-person standpoint of justice Heteronymous: actions conform more or less prereflectively or unreflectively to ego-satisfying desires; no reversibility of positions; only a pragmatic mutual recognition; quid pro quo exchanges; no principled reciprocity (immature moral development in the Kantian sense) Not anonymous: insists on being named when giving Asymmetrical relations with others, in ego's favor Oriented toward self-preservation (*conatus essendi*) Assumes obligatory responsibilities, in a self-centered, self-interested spirit Narcissistic experience of "accusation" and "persecution": regards responsibility for others as an unwanted burden
The Preoriginary Self (Prepersonal)	Substitutes the self for the other preconsciously, prepersonally, prior to volition Heteronymous: acts in favor of the other, in irreversible, nonreciprocal substitution for the other Anonymous: preconsciously, prepersonally selfless Asymmetrical relations with others, in favor of the other Involuntary subjection to the other: "accusation" and "persecution" (being called to service by the voice of conscience) prior to consciousness, memory, volition Traumatized Assumes responsibilities unconsciously: the self is taken hold of by an indeclinable responsibility for the other Experience of persecution: taken hold of in the flesh by responsibility for the suffering of others

TABLE 10.2
The Palimpsest of the Flesh

To the four faces of subjectivity, there correspond four layers or dimensions of our embodiment:
the flesh as text and texture of the moral journey

The Saintly Self (Transpersonal) Possible only by elective retrieval of the experience undergone by the preoriginary self	The flesh in its apotheosis, e.g., in tenderness and compassionate work, in service to the community, especially to the needy: "She stretches out her hand to the poor; She reaches out her arms to the needy" (Proverbs 31:20).
The Enlightened Ego (Impersonal)	The flesh in its universality as the medium of mutual recognition, mutual respect, and peace.
The Narcissistic Ego (Narrowly personal)	The flesh in its social role as egological skin, site of sensuous pleasure, defining boundaries between ego and other, establishing and protecting the interiority and immanence of subjectivity, expressive and assertive, even to the point of aggressivity and violence. (Hence the problem of racism.)
The Preoriginary Self (Prepersonal)	The flesh prophetically inspired: the passive receiver and entrusted bearer of the prophetic message, bearer of the moral law, which accuses, persecutes, and takes possession of the flesh, binding it to an indeclinable responsibility for the other, endowing it with a sensibility that makes it responsive to and capable of suffering for the other.

The two tables are representations: the first, of the moral self; the second, of that self's palimpsest of flesh. Each table represents its subject matter both diachronically, as a temporal process of spiritual development, and synchronically, as sedimented structural hypostases. For the diachrony, the tables should be read from the bottom (the earliest stage) to the top (the final stage), with the understanding that each stage is surpassed by the one above it but remains effective in the mode of traces. For the synchrony, the tables should be read as exhibiting the spiritual layers or dimensions of the self and the structural layers or dimensions of the flesh: read, one might say, as if each were a palimpsest of texts, with the text underneath, almost illegible, faintly showing through the one above it, which it has, in a certain sense, anticipated and configured.

In a fragment entitled "Physiology," Novalis remarked: "The largest part of our body, our humanity itself, is still sleeping a deep sleep."[188] In the context of Levinas's phenomenology, I suggest interpreting this "sleeping" stage—when the endowment and disposition that Kant would call "the humanity within us" remains to be developed by consciousness in the light of reason—as the preoriginary and proto-moral self.

The first stage, or layer, is our preoriginary predisposition, which endows us with a moral assignment—but also with a capacity, a freedom, to disregard that assignment and its prophetic promise.

The egoism of the self's second stage will in normal circumstances inevitably emerge, its character taking shape according to the particular interaction between our biological inheritance and the character of our experience in the order of social life.

The third stage is, however, an entirely "elective" development: a virtuous moral life in which the ego-character of the self expands, committed to the values and ideals of an enlightened humanism and working to realize them not only in personal ethical relations but also in the theater of politics. This stage represents the ego's achievement of moral maturity (*Mündigkeit*) in the Kantian sense.

The fourth stage, that of the pious and holy one, the saint or zaddik, is likewise purely elective, but not many of us ever rise to that moral height. The character of this stage requires the enlightened ego to undertake a hermeneutical process of recollection, attempting as much as possible to retrieve, for continued activation in living, traces of the preoriginary moral assignment that are still carried in its sense and sensibility, its bodily felt sense of that elusive beginning in a time before consciousness and memory. In other words, the ego must finally be willing to sacrifice itself—even its proper name—by accepting a certain anonymity or self-effacement for the sake of the other, and the other of the other. It must *elect* the very substitution of the-one-for-the-other that, in a time before the time of the ego, elected it without passing through volition. What could provoke the ego to abandon its egological character? Levinas answers this question by invoking the face of the other. In other words, the ego must find its motivation in actual encounters with others. The election of this stage depends on whether the ego can be sufficiently touched and moved by such encounters, perhaps even to the point of shuddering and blushing in shame, so that it finally begins to heed the urgings of the preoriginary sensibility in command of its flesh. Emerson invokes this preoriginary sensibility, this intertwining "corporeality," when he says: "I remember the manifold cord—the thousand or million stranded cord which my being and every man's being is, . . . so that, if everyone should claim his part in me, I should be instantaneously diffused through creation and individually decease." From this he draws a lesson for morality that could have been written by Levinas: "I am an alms of all and live but by the charity of others." [189]

The tables allow ready comparison of the four stages, or layers, with respect to several important moral characteristics. Heteronomy, for example, occurs in all but the third of the stages, though it takes a different form in each case. The Kantian heteronomy of the ego in the second stage, for example, could not be more at odds with that of the zaddik in the fourth, whose heteronomy is a life consecrated to serving others. Another moral trait, an elective anonymity, is lacking in the second stage and is often lacking in the third stage, for the ego is disposed to insist that its name be publicly recognized. Anonymity does occur, however, in the first and fourth stages: in the first, there is an anonymity assigned prior to consciousness, prior to volition; by contrast, in the fourth, there is an anonymity that the self "elects." The character of this "elective" anonymity draws inspiration from whatever traces of the preoriginary experience it has retrieved from the sublime sense and sensibility of the flesh. Moral asymmetry is also present in the first and fourth stages, in that the self is committed to living for the sake of the other. The second stage exhibits moral asymmetry of the opposite form, with the self living for its own sake, regardless of the other. Moral symmetry is achieved in the enlightenment of the third stage: here the symmetry of reversibility and reciprocity prevails, always requiring comparison and equal measure between self and other. As for the experience of accusation and persecution, the tables show that the obligations they involve are passively received in the first, "accusative" stage, resisted and denied in the second, recognized within the limits of reason in the third, and voluntarily and joyfully accepted in the fourth, where they impose upon the self an endless task, an endless vigilance. For as Paul Celan reminds us:

> the poles
> are in us,
> not to be crossed
> waking,
> we sleep across, up to the Gate
> of Mercy." [190]

Reference Matter

Notes

All English quotations from non-English works are my translations unless published translations are cited in the notes below. In most cases in which I have used a published translation, I cite the source for the original language first, then follow it with a citation of the English edition.

Preface

1. Novalis [Friedrich von Hardenberg], "Logologische Fragmente," in *Schriften*, vol. 2: *Das philosophische Werk*, pt. 1, ed. Richard Samuel (Stuttgart: Kohlhammer, 1965), p. 524; translated as "Logological Fragments," in *Philosophical Writings*, ed. and trans. Margaret M. Stoljar (Albany: SUNY Press, 1997), p. 49. The German text also appears in Novalis, *Werke und Briefe*, ed. Alfred Kelletat (Munich: Winkler, 1968), p. 417.

2. Friedrich Hölderlin, "Anmerkungen zur *Antigone*," in *Sämtliche Werke*, ed. Friedrich Beißner and Adolf Beck (Stuttgart: Kohlhammer, 1943–85), vol. 5, p. 272; also in *Sämtliche Werke*, ed. Paul Stapf (Berlin: Tempel-Verlag, 1960), p. 1067.

3. See Walter Benjamin, *Einbahnstraße*, in *Gesammelte Schriften*, ed. Rolf Tiedemann and Hermann Schweppenhäuser, vol. 4 (Frankfurt am Main: Suhrkamp, 1991), pt. 1, p. 89; translated as *One-Way Street*, in *Reflections: Essays, Aphorisms, Autobiographical Writings*, ed. Peter Demetz, trans. Edmund Jephcott (New York: Schocken, 1986), p. 65. The rumination entitled "Chinese Curios" begins with the thought: "These are days when no one should rely on his 'competence.' Strength lies in improvisation. All the decisive blows are struck left-handed."

4. Walter Benjamin, *Gesammelte Briefe*, ed. Rolf Tiedemann and Hermann Schweppenhäuser (Frankfurt am Main: Suhrkamp, 1955), vol. 3, p. 14; for the

English translation, see *The Correspondence of Walter Benjamin: 1910–1940*, ed. Gershom Scholem and Theodor W. Adorno, trans. Manfred R. Jacobson and Evelyn M. Jacobson (Chicago: University of Chicago Press, 1994), p. 261.

5. Maurice Blanchot, *Friendship*, trans. Elizabeth Rottenberg (Stanford, Calif.: Stanford University Press, 1997), p. 270.

6. Ludwig Wittgenstein, *Philosophical Investigations*, ed. and trans. G. E. M. Anscombe (New York: Macmillan, 1953), §129, p. 50.

7. Martin Heidegger, *Wegmarken* (Frankfurt am Main: Klostermann, 1967), p. 187; translated as *Pathmarks*, trans. William McNeill (Cambridge, Eng.: Cambridge University Press, 1998), p. 271.

8. Giorgio Agamben, *Infancy and History: Essays on the Destruction of Experience*, trans. Liz Heron (London: Verso, 1993), p. 140. "Notes on Gesture" did not appear in the original 1978 Italian edition of the book, published by Einaudi.

9. Ralph Waldo Emerson, "Education," in *The Portable Emerson*, ed. Mark Van Doren (New York: Viking, 1975), pp. 254–55.

10. W. S. Merwin, *The Miner's Pale Children* (New York: Atheneum, 1976), p. 124.

11. Friedrich Nietzsche, "On the Uses and Disadvantages of History for Life," in *Untimely Meditations*, trans. R. J. Hollingdale (New York: Cambridge University Press, 1983), p. 95.

Introduction

1. Johann Wolfgang von Goethe, "Einschränkung," in *Sämtliche Werke*, ed. Karl Eibl, vol. 1: *Gedichte 1756–1799* (Frankfurt am Main: Klassiker, 1987), p. 305. The German, which in its entirety also invokes "destiny," reads:

> O wäre doch das rechte Maß getroffen!
> Was bleibt mir nun
> als eingehüllt,
> von holder Lebenskraft erfüllt,
> in stiller Gegenwart die Zukunft zu erhoffen!"

2. Horace, *Satires*, in *Satires, Epistles, Ars Poetica*, trans. H. Rushton Fairclough, Loeb Classical Library (Cambridge, Mass.: Harvard University Press, 1991), ll. 106–7, p. 13: "Est modus in rebus, sunt certi denique fines, / quos ultra citraque nequit consistere rectum."

3. Theodor W. Adorno, *Minima Moralia: Reflexionen aus dem beschädigten Leben*, in *Gesammelte Schriften*, vol. 4 (Frankfurt am Main: Suhrkamp, 1980), §39, p. 69; translated as *Minima Moralia: Reflections from Damaged Life*, trans. E. F. N. Jephcott (London: Verso, New Left Books, 1984), p. 63.

4. Hannah Arendt, *The Origins of Totalitarianism* (New York: Harcourt Brace Jovanovich, 1975), p. 459.

5. Hannah Arendt, "Understanding and Politics," *Partisan Review*, 20, no. 4 (July–Aug. 1953): 391.

6. Friedrich Hölderlin, "Über Religion," in *Sämtliche Werke*, ed. Paul Stapf (Berlin: Tempel-Verlag, 1960), pp. 1004–5; translated as "On Religion," in *Friedrich Hölderlin: Essays and Letters on Theory*, ed. and trans. Thomas Pfau (Albany: SUNY Press, 1988), pp. 91–92. I have modified Pfau's translation.

7. Jürgen Habermas, *Der philosophische Diskurs der Moderne: Zwölf Vorlesungen* (Frankfurt am Main: Suhrkamp, 1993), p. 16; translated as *The Philosophical Discourse of Modernity: Twelve Lectures*, trans. Frederick Lawrence (Cambridge, Mass.: MIT Press, 1987), p. 7. See G. W. F. Hegel's observation, in *Hegel's Logic*, part 1 of the *Encyclopedia of Philosophical Sciences* (1830), trans. William Wallace (London: Oxford University Press, 1975), pp. 28–29: "Thought deprived existing institutions of their force. Constitutions fell victim to thought: religion was assailed by thought; firm religious beliefs that had always been looked upon as revelations were undermined, and in many minds the old faith was upset. . . . Thought, in short, made itself a power in the real world, and exercised enormous influence. The matter ended by drawing attention to the influence of thought, and its claims were submitted to a more rigorous scrutiny."

8. Maurice Merleau-Ponty, *Phénoménologie de la perception*, 2nd ed. (Paris: Gallimard, 1945), pp. 498, 501–2; translated as *Phenomenology of Perception*, trans. Colin Smith (London: Routledge & Kegan Paul, 1962), pp. 436, 439.

9. Jacques Derrida, *Voyou* (Paris: Galilée, 2003), pp. 48–49.

10. Maurice Blanchot, *L'entretien infini* (Paris: Gallimard, 1969), pp. 86, 91–92; translated as *The Infinite Conversation*, trans. Susan Hanson (Minneapolis: University of Minnesota Press, 1993), pp. 60, 64.

11. G. W. F. Hegel, *Phänomenologie des Geistes* (Hamburg: Felix Meiner, 1952), par. 32.

12. Ibid., par. 8.

13. Theodor W. Adorno, *Aesthetic Theory*, trans. Robert Hullot-Kentor (Minneapolis: University of Minnesota Press, 1997), p. 133.

14. Blanchot, *L'entretien infini*, p. 46; *Infinite Conversation*, p. 33.

15. Theodor W. Adorno, *Negative Dialektik*, in *Gesammelte Schriften*, vol. 6 (Frankfurt am Main: Suhrkamp, 1973), pp. 30–31; translated as *Negative Dialectics*, trans. E. B. Ashton (New York: Continuum, 1973), p. 19.

16. See Martin Heidegger, *Satz vom Grund*, 5th ed. (Pfullingen: Neske, 1978), pp. 147, 177.

17. Friedrich Hölderlin, "Aphorismen," in *Sämtliche Werke*, ed. Stapf (1960), pp. 991–92; translated as "Reflection," in *Hölderlin: Essays and Letters*, pp. 45–46.

18. Ibid. And see Friedrich Hölderlin, "Über das Gesetz der Freiheit," in *Sämtliche Werke*, ed. Stapf (1960), pp. 987–88; translated as "On the Law of Free-

dom," in *Hölderlin: Essays and Letters*, p. 33: "There is an aspect of the empirical faculty of desire, the analogue of what is called nature, which is most prominent where necessity and freedom, the restricted and the unrestricted, the sensuous and the sacred seem to unite . . . a morality of the instinct [*eine Moralität des Instinkts*], and the fantasy in tune with what is heavenly." To this remark the poet then adds, "However, this natural state as such is dependent on natural causes." Therefore, he says, "it is [a] sheer fortune to be thus attuned [*Es ist ein bloßes Glück, so gestimmt zu sein*]." Later, Nietzsche will echo this misguided idea, urging it as a "new" morality. They should have called instead for a morality of spontaneity, because a morality obedient to instinct could only regress to animality.

19. Maurice Blanchot, "Lentes funérailles," in *L'amitié* (Paris: Gallimard, 1971), pp. 107–8; translated as "Slow Obsequies," in *Friendship*, trans. Elizabeth Rottenberg (Stanford, Calif.: Stanford University Press, 1997), p. 92.

20. F. W. J. von Schelling, "Allgemeine Übersicht der neuesten philosophischen Literatur" (later titled "Abhandlungen zur Erläuterung des Idealismus der Wissenschaftslehre"), in *Sämtliche Werke*, ed. K. F. A. Schelling (Stuttgart: Cotta, 1856–61), vol. 1, p. 389; translated as "Treatise Explicatory of the Idealism in the Science of Knowledge," in *Idealism and the Endgame of Theory*, ed. and trans. Thomas Pfau (Albany: SUNY Press, 1994), p. 94.

21. Novalis, "Die Enzyklopädie," in *Werke und Briefe*, ed. Alfred Kelletat (Munich: Winkler-Verlag, 1968), p. 490; translated as "The Encyclopedia," in *"Pollen" and Fragments*, trans. Arthur Versluis (Grand Rapids, Mich.: Phanes, 1989), p. 100.

22. Ibid., pp. 509–10 in the German; pp. 114–15 in the English. Also see Davide Stimilli, *The Face of Immortality: Physiognomy and Criticism* (Albany: SUNY Press, 2005).

23. Ludwig Wittgenstein, *Philosophical Investigations*, ed. and trans. G. E. M. Anscombe (New York: Macmillan, 1953), pt. 1, §568, p. 151.

24. Theodor W. Adorno, "Cultural Criticism and Society," in *Prisms*, ed. and trans. Samuel Weber and Shierry Weber (Cambridge, Mass.: MIT Press, 1984), p. 30.

25. Herbert Marcuse, *Eros and Civilization: A Philosophical Inquiry into Freud* (New York: Vintage, 1962), p. 34.

26. Richard Sennett, *Flesh and Stone: The Body and the City in Western Civilization* (New York: Norton, 1994), pp. 370, 373–74.

27. As Hans Jonas says, the living body is a "reminder of the still unsolved questions of ontology" and must not be consigned any longer to the margins of philosophical thought. In this sense, the body is a symptom of the "latent crisis" disturbing our inheritance of ontology and must be taken as "the criterion of any future one [i.e., ontology] which could emerge as a science." Hans Jonas, *The*

Phenomenon of Life: Toward a Philosophical Biology (Chicago: University of Chicago Press, 1982), p. 35.

28. Ibid., p. 1: "the organic, even in its lowest forms, prefigures mind, and mind, even in its highest reaches, remains part of the organic." Regarding the "transcendental unity" accomplished at the corporeal level, see, e.g., Merleau-Ponty, *Phénoménologie de la perception*, pp. 173–75 and 278; *Phenomenology of Perception*, pp. 148–50 and 241–42. The transcendental unity of apperception is an intellectual representation of "a rigorous ideality" that initially belongs, for Merleau-Ponty, to an experience of the flesh, "a cohesion without concept, that is of the same type as the cohesion of the parts of my body, or that of my body and the world." Maurice Merleau-Ponty, *Le visible et l'invisible* (Paris: Gallimard, 1964), p. 199; translated as *The Visible and the Invisible*, trans. Alphonso Lingis (Evanston, Ill.: Northwestern University Press, 1968), p. 152.

29. I more or less agree with Claude Levi-Strauss, who wrote, in *Les structures élémentaires de la parenté* (The Hague: Mouton, 1947), p. 108: "Each child brings with him, at birth, and in an embryonic form, the sum total of possibilities of which each culture, and each period of history, will choose only certain ones to retain and develop. Each child brings at birth, and in the form of certain mental structures, the entirety of means that humanity will draw upon to define his relations to the world and his relations to the Other [*Autrui*]." In his Sorbonne lectures, Merleau-Ponty drew on Hegel's notion of *Aufhebung* to argue, "The true development, the true maturation, consists in a double phenomenon of the surpassing [*dépassement*] and the *maintaining* [*maintien*] of the past. Surpassing really is also preserving; in becoming other, one should not refuse to acknowledge what one has been." Maurice Merleau-Ponty, *Merleau-Ponty à la Sorbonne: Résumé de cours, 1949–1952* (Lagrasse: Cynara/Verdier, 1988), p. 501.

30. See, e.g., Merleau-Ponty, *Phénoménologie de la perception*, pp. 193 and 254; *Phenomenology of Perception*, pp. 219 and 165–68.

31. Wittgenstein, *Philosophical Investigations*, pt. 2, §iv, p. 178.

32. Walter Benjamin, "Schicksal und Charakter," in *Schriften*, ed. Theodor W. Adorno and Gretel Adorno (Frankfurt am Main: Suhrkamp, 1955), vol. 1, p. 39; translated as "Fate and Character," in *Walter Benjamin: Selected Writings*, ed. Marcus Bullock, Michael W. Jennings, et al., trans. Rodney Livingstone (Cambridge, Mass.: Belknap Press of Harvard University Press, 1996–2003), vol. 1, *1913–1926*, p. 206. Also see Walter Benjamin, *Gesammelte Schriften*, ed. Rolf Tiedemann and Hermann Schweppenhäuser (Frankfurt am Main: Suhrkamp, 1972–89), vol. 6, p. 91, for a perplexing textual fragment, written, I suspect, in the 1920s, bearing the title "Zum Problem der Physiognomik und Vorhersagung" ("On the Problem of Physiognomics and Prophecy"), concerned with the "time of fate" in the "order of guilt," the "order of indebtedness."

33. See Benjamin, *Gesammelte Schriften*, vol. 2, pt. 1, pp. 208, 209, 213; vol. 4, p. 432; and vol. 6, pp. 170–72.

34. Maurice Merleau-Ponty, "Indirect Language and the Voices of Silence," in *Signs*, trans. Richard C. McCleary (Evanston, Ill.: Northwestern University Press, 1964), p. 68.

35. Merleau-Ponty, *Phénoménologie de la perception*, pp. 153–54; *Phenomenology of Perception*, p. 132.

36. See Maurice Merleau-Ponty, "Le langage indirect," in *La prose du monde* (Paris: Gallimard, 1969), pp. 85–86; translated as "The Indirect Language," in *The Prose of the World*, trans. John O'Neill (Evanston, Ill.: Northwestern University Press, 1973), pp. 60–61. The notion of a "melodic arc" is introduced by Merleau-Ponty in *Phénoménologie de la perception*, pp. 122, 135, 154, 158, and 184; *Phenomenology of Perception*, pp. 105, 116, 132, 135–36, and 157.

37. Maurice Merleau-Ponty, "Les relations avec autrui chez l'enfant," in *Cours de Sorbonne* (Paris: Centre du Documentation Universitaire, 1975), p. 69; translated as "The Child's Relations with Others," trans. William Cobb, in *The Primacy of Perception* (Evanston, Ill.: Northwestern University press, 1964), p. 146.

38. See Friedrich Nietzsche, *Daybreak: Thoughts on the Prejudices of Morality*, trans. R. J. Hollingdale (Cambridge, Eng.: Cambridge University Press, 1982), §551.

39. Sennett, *Flesh and Stone*, p. 161. Also see two works by Jean-Claude Schmitt: *La raison des gestes dans l'Occidente médiévale* (Paris: Gallimard, 1990) and "The Ethics of Gesture," trans. Ian Patterson, in Michel Feher, Ramona Nadaff, and Nadia Tazl, eds., *Fragments for a History of the Human Body*, Part 2 (New York: Urzone, 1989); Andrea de Jorio, *Gesture in Naples and Gesture in Classical Antiquity*, trans. Adam Kendon (Bloomington: Indiana University Press, 2001).

40. Walter Benjamin, *Ursprung des deutschen Trauerspiels*, in *Gesammelte Schriften*, vol. 1, pt. 1, p. 353; translated as *The Origin of German Tragic Drama*, trans. John Osborne (London: Verso, New Left Books, 1998), p. 177.

41. Theodor W. Adorno and Max Horkheimer, *The Dialectic of Enlightenment*, trans. John Cumming (New York: Continuum, 1986), p. 33.

42. Friedrich Hölderlin, "Über das Gesetz der Freiheit," in *Sämtliche Werke*, ed. Stapf (1960), pp. 987–88; translated as "On the Law of Freedom," in *Hölderlin: Essays and Letters*, pp. 33–34.

43. See Carlo Ginzburg, *Occhiacci di legno: Nove riflessioni sulla distanza* (Milan: Feltrinelli, 1998), p. 173. Also see Frantz Fanon, *Black Skin, White Masks*, trans. Charles Markmann (New York: Grove, 1967), p. 8. Fanon helps one see that and how the body can get in touch with its destitution and can resist, or "talk back" to, oppressive social forces.

44. Italo Calvino, "La pompa di benzina," in *Prima che tu dica "pronto"* (Milan: Arnoldo Mondadori, 1996), p. 157.

45. Friedrich Nietzsche, "Truth and Lies in a Non-Moral Sense," in *Philosophy and Truth: Selections from Nietzsche's Notebooks of the Early 1870's*, ed. and trans. Daniel Breazeale (Atlantic Highlands, N.J.: Humanities Press International, 1979), p. 84.

46. Adorno, *Aesthetic Theory*, p. 128. And see Rudolf Bernet, "The Other in Myself," trans. Simon Critchley, in Simon Critchley and Peter Dews, eds., *Deconstructive Subjectivities* (Albany: SUNY Press, 1996).

47. Baruch Spinoza, *Ethics*, in *The Collected Works of Spinoza*, ed. and trans. Edwin Curley (Princeton, N.J.: Princeton University Press, 1986), vol. 1, pt. 3, prop. 2, scholium.

48. Louis Althusser, "The Only Materialist Tradition," pt. 1: "Spinoza," in W. Montag and T. Stolze, eds., *The New Spinoza* (Minneapolis: University of Minnesota Press, 1998), pp. 12–13.

49. Novalis, "Blutenstaub," in *Schriften*, vol. 2, *Das philosophische Werk*, pt. 1, ed. Richard Samuel (Stuttgart: Kohlhammer, 1960, 1965), pp. 428–29; also in *Werke und Briefe*, p. 417; translated as "Pollen," in *"Pollen" and Fragments*, p. 29.

50. Schelling, "Allgemeine Übersicht der neuesten philosophischen Literatur," p. 418; "Treatise Explicatory of the Idealism," p. 114.

51. Paul Celan, "Chymisch," in *Poems of Paul Celan*, ed. and trans. Michael Hamburger (New York: Persea, 1988), pp. 178–79. This is a bilingual edition.

52. Paul Celan, "Atemkristall," in *Werke: Historisch-kritische Ausgabe*, ed. Beda Allemann, Rolf Bücher, et al. (Frankfurt am Main: Suhrkamp, 1990), vol. 7, pt. 1, p. 120.

53. Friedrich Schlegel, *Seine prosaischen Jugendschriften* (Vienna, 1906), vol. 2, p. 358.

Epitaph for the Handshake

1. G. W. F. Hegel, *Aesthetics: Lectures on Fine Art*, trans. T. M. Knox (Oxford: Clarendon, 1975), vol. 2, p. 732.

2. Maurice Merleau-Ponty, *Phenomenology of Perception*, trans. Colin Smith (London: Routledge & Kegan Paul, 1962), p. 354.

3. Giorgio Agamben, "Notes on Gesture," in *Infancy and History: Essays on the Destruction of Experience*, trans. Liz Heron (London: Verso, 1993), pp. 135, 139.

4. Theodor W. Adorno, "On Proust," in *Notes to Literature*, trans. Shierry Weber Nicholsen, vol. 2 (New York: Columbia University Press, 1992), p. 317.

5. Emmanuel Levinas, "In Memoriam Alphonse de Waelhens: De la sensibilité," in *Hors Sujet* (Montpellier: Fata Morgana, 1987), p. 167; translated as "In

Memory of Alphonse de Waelhens," in *Outside the Subject*, trans. Michael B. Smith (Stanford, Calif.: Stanford University Press, 1994), p. 112. Translation modified. Also see his "De l'intersubjectivité: Notes sur Merleau-Ponty," in *Hors Sujet*, p. 151; translated as "On Intersubjectivity: Notes on Merleau-Ponty," in *Outside the Subject*, p. 101.

　　6. Jacques Derrida, *Spectres de Marx* (Paris: Galilée, 1993), p. 15; translated as *Specters of Marx*, trans. Peggy Kamuf (New York: Routledge, 1994), p. xix.

　　7. Maurice Merleau-Ponty, "The Concept of Nature," pt. 1, in *Themes from the Lectures at the Collège de France, 1952–1960*, trans. John O'Neill (Evanston, Ill.: Northwestern University Press, 1970), p. 82.

　　8. Martin Heidegger, *Sein und Zeit*, 5th ed. (Halle: Niemeyer, 1941), p. 394; translated from the 7th ed. as *Being and Time*, trans. John Macquarrie and Edward Robinson (New York: Harper & Row, 1962), p. 446.

Chapter 1

　　1. Rainer Maria Rilke, *Lou Andreas Salomé Briefwechsel*, ed. Ernst Pfeiffer (Frankfurt am Main: Insel-Verlag, 1975), pp. 246–47. See the translators' "Commentary," in Rainer Maria Rilke, *Duino Elegies*, trans. J. B. Leishman and Stephen Spender (New York: Norton, 1939), p. 95. The poem, "Orpheus, Eurydike, Hermes," published in both German and English, can be found in Rainer Maria Rilke, *New Poems*, ed. and trans. J. B. Leishman (London: Hogarth, 1964), pp. 142–47. In his introduction to the edition, Leishman points out Eurydice's "intactness and intangibility"—qualities to which the bas-relief is marvelously faithful. In addition to evoking the gesture in that poem and in the Duino Elegies, Rilke evokes it in two other poems: "Mehr nicht solst du wissen als die Stele" (1922) and "An der sonngewohnten Straße" (1924). See his *Späte Gedichte* (Leipzig: Insel-Verlag, 1934), pp. 101 and 152; and his *Late Poems*, ed. and trans. J. B. Leishman (London: Hogarth, 1938), pp. 85 and 174. In the second of these is a line that reads: "nur ein leichtes Anruhn meiner Hände." The Museo Capitolino in Rome houses another bas-relief worth noting: a sarcophagus showing the life of Achilles. (See the front cover.) Here, too, we find the representation of a hand on the shoulder, a gesture of the most exquisite beauty, grace, and tact. And, if we may presume, as would be reasonable, that the gesture depicts the bond between Achilles and Patroclus, it appears to be moved by a sense of foreboding, an intimation of imminent parting, as if tenderly haunted by death.

　　2. Rilke, *Duino Elegies*, pp. 32–33. The German reads:

> Erstaunte euch nicht auf attischen Stelen die Vorsicht
> menschlicher Geste? war nicht Liebe und Abschied
> so leicht auf die Schultern gelegt, als wär es aus anderm
> Stoffe gemacht als bei uns? Gedenkt euch der Hände,

wie sie drucklos beruhen, obwohl in den Torsen die Kraft steht.
Diese Beherrschten wußten damit: so weit sind wirs,
dieses ist unser, uns so zu berühren; stärker
stemmen die Götter uns an.

3. Rainer Maria Rilke, "The Schmargendorf Diary," in *Diaries of a Young Poet*, trans. Edward Snow and Michael Winkler (New York: Norton, 1997), p. 87. The entry is dated March 10, 1899.

4. *Letters of Rainer Maria Rilke, 1910–1926*, trans. Jane B. Greene and M. D. Herter Norton (New York: Norton, 1972), p. 139.

Chapter 2

1. For an English translation by Paul Shorey, see Plato's *Republic*, vol. 2, Loeb Classical Library (Cambridge, Mass.: Harvard University Press, 1963), p. 411: "but he will always be found attuning the harmonies of his body for the sake of the concord in his soul." For my discussion of the *Republic*, I have used the two-volume Loeb Classical Library set and also Benjamin Jowett's translation in *The Dialogues of Plato*, 2 vols. (New York: Random House, 1937), occasionally altering these translations after reading the original Greek and consulting *Liddell and Scott's Greek-English Lexicon*.

2. For the Greek and a French translation, see Platon, *Les lois*, ed. and trans. Éduard des Places, in *Platon, oeuvres complètes*, ed. and trans. A. Diès (Paris: Collections des Universités de France, l'Association Guillaume Budé, Société d'Édition "Les Belles Lettres," 1951), vol. ii, pt. 2, p. 66; for an English translation, see Plato, *The Laws*, trans. Trevor J. Saunders (New York: Penguin, 1970), p. 175. The Greek, answering the question "what conduct [πρᾶξις] is pleasing to God and recommends itself to him?," says, "to the like, if he keep the measure, like will be a friend, while beings without measure are in harmony neither with themselves nor with beings which do have measure." The Athenian goes on to say, "Now, in our view, divinity must be the pre-eminent measure of all things, much more so than any man, which is what some say." And the Athenian speaks eloquently against those who let their souls become inflamed beyond measure by hubristic pride (φλέγεται τὴν ψυχὴν μεθ' ὕβρεως) (4.716a7, trans. Saunders; translation slightly modified).

3. Aristotle argued that, in regard to pleasure and pain, the "right measure" depends not only on sheer quantity (whether too much or too little), but also on such other singular factors as motive, situation, the character and quality of an action, the ends to be achieved, and the means employed.

4. For the Greek, see Plato, *The Statesman*, ed. Harold N. Fowler and W. R. M. Lamb, trans. W. R. M. Lamb, Loeb Classical Library (New York: G. P. Putnam's Sons; London: William Heinemann, 1925), vol. 3, pp. 96–109. For the

basic translation by Jowett, which, however, I have occasionally modified, see *The Dialogues of Plato*, vol. 2, pp. 310–14. Here I want to thank John Sallis for reminding me of Plato's discussion of measure in *The Statesman* and for the enjoyable conversation on measure that took place on this occasion.

5. Hannah Arendt, "Understanding and Politics," *Partisan Review*, 20, no. 4 (July–Aug. 1953): 391.

6. Plato, *Statesman*, pp. 152–53 in the Loeb; p. 327 in Jowett.

7. Immanuel Kant, *Critique of Judgment*, trans. Werner S. Pluhar (Indianapolis: Hackett, 1987), §43, pp. 170–71. Translation modified.

8. Maurice Blanchot, *L'entretien infini* (Paris: Gallimard, 1969), p. 67; translated as *The Infinite Conversation*, trans. Susan Hanson (Minneapolis: University of Minnesota, 1993), p. 4.

9. My citations refer to these Greek and English editions of Aristotle: *Nicomachean Ethics*, trans. H. Rackham, Loeb Classical Library (Cambridge, Mass.: Harvard University Press, 1962); and *Politics*, trans. H. Rackham, Loeb Classical Library (Cambridge, Mass.: Harvard University Press, 1950).

10. For the Greek, I have used Platon, *Les Lois*; for the English, I have used Saunders's translation in Plato, *The Laws*. After consulting the original Greek and the French translation, I have occasionally modified the Saunders translation.

11. See Aristotle, *Politics* 7.1324a28 and 1325b16: the best life (ἄριστος βίος) is the life of contemplation (βίος θεωρητικός). But the next best is the life of practical wisdom and good citizenship (ὁ πολιτικὸς καὶ πρακτικὸς βίος).

12. Martha Nussbaum, *Love's Knowledge: Essays on Philosophy and Literature* (New York: Oxford University Press, 1990), pp. 160, 182.

13. See Aristotle, *Nicomachean Ethics* 10.6.1177a11; and *Politics* 7.11.1332a40, where he speaks of ἔθος, ἦθος, and ἕξις. A fascinating book just came to my attention: Allen L. Boegehold, *When a Gesture Was Expected: A Selection of Examples from Archaic and Classical Greek Literature* (Princeton, N.J.: Princeton University Press, 1999). In this work, the author catalogues the sites in texts by Plato, among others, in which the written words assume their accompaniment—or even, in many cases, their substitution—by a culturally familiar gesture.

14. Walter Benjamin, "Baudelaire," in *The Arcades Project*, trans. Howard Eiland and Kevin McLaughlin (Cambridge, Mass.: Belknap Press of Harvard University Press, 1999), p. 339.

Chapter 3

1. *Sophocles: Plays. "Antigone,"* ed. and trans. Richard C. Jebb (London: Bristol Classical Press, 2004), lines 1347–53, pp. 236–39. See Heidegger's expansive and problematic interpretation of *Antigone*, in Martin Heidegger, *Hölderlins Hymne "Der Ister"* (Frankfurt am Main: Klostermann, 1984). In his *Introduction*

to Metaphysics as well as in other lectures and texts, Heidegger also takes up the "monstrosity" or "uncanniness" of the human in his commentary on freedom in the tragedy *Antigone*. Also see Maurice Merleau-Ponty, *Notes des Cours au Collège de France, 1958–1959 et 1960–1961* (Paris: Gallimard, 1996), p. 148, where he comments, regarding Heidegger's "Letter on Humanism," that the living being (*l'être vivant*) is our closest relative (*parent*) and at the same time is "séparé de nous par un abîme," a "parenté qui nous est plus étrange que la distance de l'homme à dieu, si immense soit-elle."

2. Martin Heidegger, *Beiträge zur Philosophie (Vom Ereignis)*, in *Gesamtausgabe*, vol. 65 (Frankfurt am Main: Klostermann, 1989), §5; translated as *Contributions to Philosophy (from Enowning)*, trans. Parvis Emad and Kenneth Maly (Bloomington: Indiana University Press, 1999). For Heidegger, the poet Hölderlin exemplifies this attitude. In the *Beiträge*, he remarks: "the historical vocation [*Bestimmung*] of philosophy culminates [*gipfele*] in the recognition [*Erkenntnis*] of the necessity of making Hölderlin's word be heard." §258, p. 422 in the German; p. 297 in the English.

3. Martin Heidegger, "Wozu Dichter?," in *Holzwege* (Frankfurt am Main: Klostermann, 1950), p. 248; translated as "What Are Poets For?," in *Poetry, Language, Thought*, trans. Albert Hofstadter (New York: Harper & Row, 1971), p. 92.

4. Walter Benjamin, "Theologisch-Politisches Fragment," in *Gesammelte Schriften*, ed. Rolf Tiedemann and Hermann Schweppenhäuser (Frankfurt am Main: Suhrkamp, 1972–89), vol. 2, pt. 2, p. 438; translated as "Theologico-Political Fragment," in *Reflections: Essays, Aphorisms, Autobiographical Writings*, ed. Peter Demetz, trans. Edmund Jephcott (New York: Schocken, 1986), p. 313. Italics added.

5. Friedrich Hölderlin, "In lieblicher Bläue . . . ," in *Sämtliche Werke*, ed. Paul Stapf (Berlin: Tempel-Verlag, 1960), pp. 415–17; my translation. For another English translation, see "In lovely blueness . . . ," in Friedrich Hölderlin, *Poems and Fragments*, trans. Michael Hamburger, bilingual edition (Cambridge, Eng.: Cambridge University Press, 1980), p. 601. It is not certain that these are the poet's own words. When I refer to works from the "late" or "last" period of his poetic life, I mean works written soon after 1800. Hölderlin died in 1843, but he apparently had ceased concentrated writing long before that time.

6. Walter Benjamin, "Geschichtsphilosophische Thesen," in *Schriften*, ed. Theodor W. Adorno and Gretel Adorno (Frankfurt am Main: Suhrkamp, 1955), vol. 1, p. 498; translated as "Theses on the Philosophy of History," in *Illuminations*, ed. Hannah Arendt, trans. Harry Zohn (1968; reprint, New York: Schocken, 1969), p. 257. For a provocative and illuminating discussion of the issues involved in Benjamin's appropriation of the concept of a state of exception, see Giorgio Agamben, "The Messiah and the Sovereign: The Problem of Law in Walter Benjamin," in Agamben, *Potentialities: Collected Essays in Philosophy*, ed.

and trans. Daniel Heller-Roazen (Stanford, Calif.: Stanford University Press, 1999), pp. 160–74. My reading of Hölderlin is indebted to Agamben's essay: though he does not attempt there, as I have here, to interpret Hölderlin's poetic thought in terms of Benjamin's theory of history, reading his essay set in motion a sequence of thoughts that enabled me to carry forward my reflections on freedom and measure in the poet's work. For a meditation on freedom that draws inspiration from Schellingian romanticism, see Slavoj Žižek, *The Abyss of Freedom* (Ann Arbor: University of Michigan Press, 1997)

7. Friedrich Hölderlin, "Brot und Wein," first version, in *Sämtliche Werke*, ed. Stapf (1960), p. 279; my translation. The German reads: "wozu Dichter in dürftiger Zeit?" For another English translation, see "Bread and Wine," in Hölderlin, *Poems and Fragments*, p. 250. See Martin Heidegger's discussion of this question in "Wozu Dichter?," pp. 248–343; "What Are Poets For?," pp. 91–142. For some other important texts where Heidegger discusses the question of measure, see the following: (1) "Die Zeit des Weltbildes," in *Holzwege*, pp. 69–104; translated as "The Age of the World Picture," in *"The Question Concerning Technology" and Other Essays*, trans. William Lovitt (New York: Harper & Row, 1977), pp. 115–54. This text challenges the confident affirmation of anthropocentric relativism in the most widespread interpretation of Protagoras's saying "The human is the measure of all things." (2) "Logos (Heraklit, Fragment 50)," in *Vorträge und Aufsätze* (Pfullingen: Neske, 1954), p. 225; translated as "Logos (Heraclitus, Fragment B50)," in *Early Greek Thinking*, trans. David Farrell Krell and Frank A. Capuzzi (New York: Harper & Row, 1975), especially p. 75. Here, interpreting "logos" as "maßgebend," the philosopher says, "Mortals . . . are fateful when they measure the Logos . . . and submit themselves to its measurement." (3) "Moira (Parmenides VIII, 34–41)," in *Vorträge und Aufsätze*, pp. 231–56; translated under the same title in *Early Greek Thinking*, pp. 79–101. And (4) "Aletheia (Heraklit, Fragment 16)," in *Vorträge und Aufsätze*, pp. 257–82, especially p. 275; translated as "Aletheia (Heraclitus, Fragment B16)," in *Early Greek Thinking*, pp. 102–23, especially p. 117. Here the philosopher reads the Heracleitean "fire" as a figure for the *Lichtung*, the *Ereignis* "which gives measure and takes it away." In formulating my interpretation of Hölderlin with regard to the question of measure, I have also benefited from Christoph Jamme and Otto Pöggler, eds., *Jenseits des Idealismus: Hölderlin's letzte Hamburger Jahre 1804–1806* (Bonn: Bouvier, 1988); and Jochen Schmidt, *Hölderlins geschichtsphilosophischen Hymnen* (Darmstadt: Wissenschaftliche Buchgesellschaft, 1990).

8. *Friedrich Hölderlin: Essays and Letters on Theory*, ed. and trans. Thomas Pfau (Albany: SUNY Press, 1988), p. 140.

9. Friedrich Hölderlin, "Wie wenn am Feiertage . . . ," in *Sämtliche Werke*, ed. Stapf (1960), p. 295; translated as "As when on holiday . . . ," trans. Michael Ham-

burger, in *"Hyperion" and Selected Poems*, ed. Eric Santner, bilingual edition (New York: Continuum, 1990), pp. 194–95.

10. Friedrich Hölderlin, "Sonst nemlich, Vater Zeus...," in *Sämtliche Werke*, ed. Stapf (1960), p. 368; translated as "There was a time...," in *Hymns and Fragments*, trans. Richard Sieburth (Princeton, N.J.: Princeton University Press, 1984), pp. 162–63.

11. Implicit in the parts, the fragments, there are hints of divine judgment (*Ur-theil*) and its "originary division," or "originary allotment." *Ur-theil* as "originary division": Hölderlin appears to have borrowed this controversial but nevertheless illuminating etymology from Fichte.

12. Regarding the question of the *Untheilnehmende*, "those who do not take part," see Friedrich Hölderlin, "Die Titanen," in *Sämtliche Werke*, ed. Stapf (1960), p. 362.

13. I want to thank Daniel Brandes for raising this question.

14. See §§44–49 of Heidegger's *Beiträge zur Philosophie*, a work of thought written as if in conversation with the poet, where the philosopher struggles to give proper recognition to this question of undecidability (*Unentschiedenheit*).

15. Friedrich Hölderlin, "Der Tod des Empedokles," second version, in *Sämtliche Werke*, ed. Stapf (1960), act 1, scene 3, p. 719.

16. Friedrich Hölderlin, "Hyperions Jugend," in *Sämtliche Werke*, ed. Stapf (1960), p. 586.

17. Friedrich Hölderlin, "Der Rhein," in *Sämtliche Werke*, ed. Stapf (1960), p. 319.

18. Martin Heidegger, "Die Metaphysik als Geschichte des Seins," in his *Nietzsche* (Pfullingen: Neske, 1961), vol. 2, p. 423; translated as "Metaphysics as History of Being," in *The End of Philosophy*, trans. Joan Stambaugh (New York: Harper & Row, 1973), p. 21.

19. Ibid., p. 421 in the German; p. 20 in the English.

20. Friedrich Hölderlin, *Sämtliche Werke*, ed. Friedrich Beißner, Grosser Stuttgarter Ausgabe, 15 vols. (Stuttgart: Cotta, 1943–85), vol. 3, p. 163. Also see Dieter Henrich, *Der Grund im Bewußtsein: Untersuchungen zu Hölderlins Denken 1794–1795* (Stuttgart: Klett-Cotta, 1992); and Manfred Frank, *"Unendliche Annäherung": Die Anfänge der philosophischen Frühromantik* (Frankfurt am Main: Suhrkamp, 1997). Regarding Empedocles, see the first version of Hölderlin's unfinished tragedy, "Der Tod des Empedokles" ("The Death of Empedocles"), and his short 1798 poem "Empedokles," where he addresses the hero and reflects on his own sentiments, saying: "Yet you are holy to me as the power / Of earth that took you from us, the boldly killed! / And gladly, did not love restrain us, / Deep as the hero plunged, down I'd follow." Hölderlin, "Empedocles," trans. Michael Hamburger, in *"Hyperion" and Selected Poems*,

pp. 138–39. Also see the second version of "Der Tod des Empedokles," act 1, scene 3, in *Sämtliche Werke*, ed. Stapf (1960), pp. 719–20, where Empedocles boasts of his abilities, achievements, and knowledge, and asserts "effecting" (*Wirken*) as the measure of the human. He also expresses his faith, there, that "Man" can accomplish much (*viel vermag er*) to transform the world that lies ready to hand (*unter den Händen*). But, as Panthea laments in the first version of "Empedocles": "O eternal mystery, what we are / And seek, that we cannot find; what / We find, that we are not" (Hölderlin, "Der Tod des Empedokles," in *Sämtliche Werke und Briefe*, ed. Günther Mieth [Berlin: Aufbau, 1995], vol. 3, p. 18). This realization calls to mind Hölderlin's fragment "Judgment and Being" ("Urteil und Sein"), where he argues that the ground we can comprehend is not the ground. I also want to acknowledge an essay by Véronique Fóti, "Empedocles and Tragic Thought: Heidegger, Hölderlin, Nietzsche," in David C. Jacobs, ed., *The Presocratics After Heidegger* (Albany: SUNY Press, 1999), pp. 297–94.

21. Friedrich Hölderlin, "Hyperions Schicksaalslied," translated as "Hyperion's Song of Fate," both in *Poems and Fragments*, p. 79.

22. Ralph Waldo Emerson, *Emerson in His Journals*, ed. Joel Porte (Cambridge, Mass.: Harvard University Press, 1982), p. 452.

23. Ralph Waldo Emerson, "Nature," in *Emerson: Essays and Lectures*, ed. Joel Porte (New York: Library of America, 1983), p. 47.

24. Ibid., pp. 7 and 42.

25. Friedrich Hölderlin, "We set out from the abyss . . . " ("Vom Abgrund nehmlich . . . "), in *Hymns and Fragments*, pp. 198–99. The German reads: "nach der Gestalt, die / Abdruck ist der Natur zu reden / Des Menschen nehmlich, . . . "

26. Hölderlin, "Brot und Wein," first version, in *Sämtliche Werke*, ed. Stapf (1960), p. 279; "Bread and Wine," in *Poems and Fragments*, p. 250. Also see Michel de Montaigne, "Du repentir," in his *Essais* (Paris: Bibliothèque de la Pléiade, 1961), bk. 3, chap. 2, p. 900. Montaigne makes use of a similar image, but Hölderlin's interpretation of the image, a *mise en abîme*, could not be more different. Montaigne says: "Chaque homme porte la forme entière de l'humaine condition" ("Each man bears the entire form or imprint of the human condition").

27. Hölderlin, "Die Titanen," in *Sämtliche Werke*, ed. Stapf (1960), p. 362; my translation. For another English translation, see Hölderlin, *Poems and Fragments*, p. 531.

28. Friedrich Hölderlin, "Mnemosyne," a late poem, in *Sämtliche Werke*, ed. Stapf (1960), p. 350; translated as "Mnemosyne," in *Hymns and Fragments*, pp. 116–19. The German reads: "Ein Zeichen sind wir, deutungslos / Schmerzlos sind wir und haben fast / Die Sprache in der Fremde verloren."

29. Friedrich Hölderlin, "Der Einzige," early version, in *Sämtliche Werke*, ed. Stapf (1960), p. 325; my translation. For another English translation, see "The

Only One," in Hölderlin, *Poems and Fragments*, p. 451. My translation differs significantly and fatefully from Hamburger's.

30. Maurice Blanchot, *The Step Not Beyond*, trans. Lycette Nelson (Albany: SUNY Press, 1992), p. 17.

31. Walter Benjamin and Gershom Scholem, *Briefwechsel 1933–1940*, ed. Gershom Scholem (Frankfurt am Main: Suhrkamp, 1980), p. 175; translated in *The Correspondence of Walter Benjamin and Gershom Scholem, 1932–1940*, ed. Gershom Scholem, trans. Gary Smith and Andre Lefevere (New York: Schocken, 1989), p. 142.

32. Agamben, *Potentialities*, p. 169.

33. Friedrich Hölderlin, "Über das Gesetz der Freiheit," in *Sämtliche Werke*, ed. Stapf (1960), p. 988; translated as "On the Law of Freedom," in *Hölderlin: Essays and Letters*, pp. 33–34.

34. Friedrich Hölderlin, "Über den Begriff der Strafe," in *Sämtliche Werke*, ed. Stapf (1960), pp. 989–90; translated as "On the Concept of Punishment," in *Hölderlin: Essays and Letters*, pp. 35–36. In his *Genealogy of Morals* and *Beyond Good and Evil*, Friedrich Nietzsche will strongly attack this argument for punishment, while supporting the spirit of transgression.

35. See Hölderlin, "Über das Gesetz der Freiheit," in *Sämtliche Werke*, ed. Stapf (1960), pp. 987–88; "On the Law of Freedom," in *Hölderlin: Essays and Letters*, p. 33.

36. Friedrich Hölderlin, "Heimkunft," in *Sämtliche Werke*, ed. Stapf (1960), p. 281; my translation. For another English translation, see "Homecoming," in Hölderlin, *Poems and Fragments*, pp. 255–57.

37. Friedrich Hölderlin, "Friedensfeier," final version, in *Sämtliche Werke*, ed. Stapf (1960), pp. 308–9; my translation. For another English translation, see "Celebration of Peace," in Hölderlin, *Poems and Fragments*, p. 437.

38. Hölderlin, "Friedensfeier," first version, in *Sämtliche Werke*, ed. Stapf (1960), p. 302; translated as "Celebration of Peace," in *Poems and Fragments*, p. 433.

39. See Heidegger, *Beiträge zur Philosophie*, for example, §256, p. 414.

40. One might also, I think, use Siegfried Kracauer's term *Geistesgegenwart* ("extreme vigilance and attentiveness") to describe this attitude. See his essay "Die Wartenden," in *Das Ornament der Masse: Essays* (Frankfurt am Main: Suhrkamp, 1963), pp. 106–19; translated as "Those Who Wait," in *The Mass Ornament: Weimar Essays*, trans. Thomas Y. Levin (Cambridge, Mass.: Harvard University Press, 1995), pp. 128–40.

41. Hölderlin, "Brot und Wein," first version, in *Sämtliche Werke*, ed. Stapf (1960), p. 280.

42. Ibid., p. 278.

43. I submit that it is misleading to translate the poet's word *das Wilde* as "savage," as Michael Hamburger does, although this is certainly the normal, literal meaning in English. If we take into account Hölderlin's translations of the tragedies of Sophocles, in which the daimonic (τὸ δαίμων) figures preeminently, it is not at all an arbitrary violence to translate his word as I have done. Moreover, we should not forget the semantic connection in the Greek language, of which the poet was certainly aware, between the experience of happiness (eudaimonia) and the "presence" of the daimonic. The figure of a "holy wildness" or "holy wilderness" (*heilige Wildniß*) in which spirit (*Geist*) dwells appears both in "The Titans" and in "Tinian" (*Sämtliche Werke*, ed. Stapf [1960], pp. 362 and 374, respectively). Martin Heidegger refers to this figure in his *Erläuterungen zu Hölderlins Dichtung*, 4th ed., in *Gesamtausgabe*, vol. 4 (Frankfurt am Main: Klostermann, 1981), pp. 60–61.

44. Hölderlin, "Friedensfeier," final version, in *Sämtliche Werke*, ed. Stapf (1960), p. 309; "Celebration of Peace," in *Poems and Fragments*, pp. 436–37. See also the first version of "Brot und Wein," where the "Halbgott," heralding the possibility of a coming god, is described as "almost regarding as sacred / Trash [*Unheiliges*] which he with [a well-meaning] blessing hand [*mit segnender Hand*] foolishly, kindly has touched [*thörig und gütig berührt*]" (Hölderlin, "Brot und Wein," in *Sämtliche Werke*, ed. Stapf [1960], p. 278; "Bread and Wine," in *Poems and Fragments*, p. 247). The Heavenly Ones look down on many hands deficient in appropriate skill.

45. Hölderlin, "Friedensfeier," final version, in *Sämtliche Werke*, ed. Stapf (1960), p. 309.

46. Hölderlin, "Friedensfeier," first version, in *Sämtliche Werke*, ed. Stapf (1960), p. 302; second version, ibid., p. 305; "Celebration of Peace," in *Poems and Fragments*, pp. 425, 429, 437. *Wahn* must be translated, I think, as "daimonic madness," not as "delusion." This is not an inconsequential point.

47. Hölderlin, "Brot und Wein," second version, in *Sämtliche Werke und Briefe*, ed. M. Knaupp, vol. 2 (Munich: Carl Hanser Edition, 1992), p. 379.

48. Ibid., p. 378.

49. Jacques Derrida, *Speech and Phenomenon*, trans. David B. Allison (Evanston, Ill.: Northwestern University Press, 1973), p. 102.

50. See Giorgio Agamben, *The End of the Poem: Studies in Poetics*, trans. Daniel Heller-Roazen (Stanford, Calif.: Stanford University Press, 1999). Agamben suggests that the very essence of the poem consists in the necessity of a certain unresolvable strife between sound and sense.

51. Hölderlin, "Brot und Wein," first version, in *Sämtliche Werke*, ed. Stapf (1960), p. 278.

52. Hölderlin, "Brot und Wein," second version, and "Bread and Wine,"

trans. Michael Hamburger, both in *"Hyperion" and Selected Poems*, pp. 180–81. Translation modified. The German reads: "Fest bleibt Eins; es sei um Mittag oder es gehe / Bis in die Mitternacht, immer bestehet ein Maas, / Allein gemein, doch jeglichem auch ist eignes beschieden, / Dahin gehet und kommt jeder, wohin er es kann." Also see *Sämtliche Werke*, ed. Stapf (1960), p. 277.

53. Emmanuel Levinas, *Totality and Infinity: An Essay on Exteriority*, trans. Alphonso Lingis (Pittsburgh: Duquesne University Press, 1969), pp. 229, 231.

54. Hölderlin, "Der Rhein," in *Sämtliche Werke*, ed. Stapf (1960), p. 317; translated as "The Rhine," in *Hymns and Fragments*, p. 75. Also see Heidegger, *Hölderlin's Hymn "The Ister"*; and his *Erläuterungen zu Hölderlins Dichtung*, pp. 97–102.

55. Hölderlin, "Der Rhein," in *Sämtliche Werke*, ed. Stapf (1960), p. 319; "The Rhine," in *Hymns and Fragments*, p. 79.

56. See Heidegger, *Beiträge zur Philosophie*, §§248–55. The ones who "go under" are the ones who, in their time and for their time, question and prepare for the future, exhorting their people to avoid the danger of *das Unbedingten zu vergötzen* (§251, p. 398): "idolizing as its unconditioned [and as its absolute ground and measure] what are only [contingent and transient] conditions for its existence." Also see the lectures in Martin Heidegger, *Hölderlins Hymne "Andenken,"* in *Gesamtausgabe*, vol. 52 (Frankfurt am Main: Klostermann, 1982).

57. Regarding the figure of "Chaos," see Heidegger, *Erläuterungen zu Hölderlins Dichtung*, p. 61.

58. Friedrich Hölderlin, "Der Wanderer," second version, in *Sämtliche Werke*, ed. Stapf (1960), p. 269; my translation. For another English translation, see Hölderlin, *Poems and Fragments*, p. 621. The German reads as follows: "auch hier sind Götter und walten, / Groß ist ihr maß, doch es mißt gern es mit der Spanne der Mensch."

59. Heidegger, *Beiträge zur Philosophie*, §250, p. 398; *Contributions to Philosophy*, p. 279.

60. Hölderlin, "Der Einzige," first version, in *Sämtliche Werke*, ed. Stapf (1960), p. 325; translated as "The Only One," first version, in *Poems and Fragments*, pp. 450–51. Translation somewhat modified. The poet's *wenn kommet* is grammatically ambiguous: it could refer either to the god or to "what I wish for." Also ambiguous is *das Beste*, which could mean either that the god knows best what I wish for or that the god knows that what I wish for is the best.

61. Friedrich Hölderlin, "Der Ister," in *Sämtliche Werke*, ed. Stapf (1960), p. 347; translated as "The Ister," in *Poems and Fragments*, pp. 492–93.

62. See Immanuel Kant, *On History*, trans. Lewis White Beck (New York: Library of Liberal Arts Press, 1963), p. 173: For Kant, the French Revolution was a sign of hope (*signum, demonstrativum, prognostikon*) showing that the desire

for social enlightenment, freedom, and justice was still very much alive. The German text may be found in Kant's *Gesammelte Schriften*, ed. Königliche Preußische Academie der Wissenschaft (Berlin: De Gruyter, 1902–38).

63. Hölderlin, "Der Rhein," in *Sämtliche Werke*, ed. Stapf (1960), p. 319; my translation. For Hamburger's translation, see "The Rhine," in Hölderlin, *Poems and Fragments*, pp. 420–21.

64. Hölderlin, "Der Einzige," concluding lines of a second version, in *Sämtliche Werke und Briefe*, ed. Knaupp, vol. 2, p. 458; translated as "The Only One," second version, in *Poems and Fragments*, p. 457.

65. Friedrich Hölderlin, "Blödigkeit," in *Sämtliche Werke*, ed. Stapf (1960), p. 260; translated as "Timidity," in *Poems and Fragments*, p. 205.

66. Hölderlin, "Wie Wenn am Feiertage . . . ," in *Sämtliche Werke*, ed. Stapf (1960), p. 295; "As when on holiday . . . ," in *Poems and Fragments*, pp. 375–77. Also see Heidegger, *Gesamtausgabe*, vol. 4 and vol. 39 (Frankfurt am Main: Klostermann, 1983 and 1989).

67. Friedrich Hölderlin, "Griechenland," in *Sämtliche Werke*, ed. Stapf (1960), p. 383.

68. Hölderlin, "Der Einzige," second version, in *Sämtliche Werke und Briefe*, ed. Knaupp, vol. 2, p. 458; "The Only One," second version, in *Poems and Fragments*, p. 457. These lines do not appear in the "final" or "complete" version.

69. For the Greeks of antiquity, the deity who pursues the cause of judgment, punishing the disregard of due measure (τὸ μετρόν), is Νέμεσις, whose rule, as Herder noted in a 1786 essay, calls for compliance with an internal, spiritual norm, and not a merely external one. See Johann Gottfried von Herder, "Nemesis: Ein lehrendes Sinnbild," in *Zerstreute Blätter*, 2nd ed., in *Sämtliche Werke*, ed. Bernhard Suphan, vol. 15 (Berlin: Weidmannsche Buchhandlung, 1888), p. 417. Also see F. W. J. von Schelling, "Philosophie der Mythologie," in *Sämtliche Werke*, ed. K. F. A. Schelling (Stuttgart: Cotta, 1856–61), vol. 2, pt. 2, p. 145: "Nemesis," he says there, noting its etymological connection to νόμος (law, the ordinances recognizing the immemorial divisions, *Ur-teile*, of land), is a power of judgment that comes *before* the law, and even *before* what mortals think of as "justice." Νέμεσις is also related, of course, to Μοῖρα, the goddess of fate, of fateful crossroads, fateful decisions, the goddess who metes out, allots, assigns portions (*Teile*). She it is through whom primordial judgment (*Ur-teil*) is ultimately dispensed (*ge-teilt*).

70. Regarding "those who refuse to take part," see Hölderlin's "Die Titanen," in *Sämtliche Werke*, ed. Stapf (1960), p. 362.

71. Blanchot, *Step Not Beyond*, p. 101.

72. Agamben, *Potentialities*, p. 182.

73. Friedrich Hölderlin, "Patmos," in *Sämtliche Werke*, ed. Stapf (1960), p. 328; translated as "Patmos," in *Hymns and Fragments*, pp. 88–89. The Ger-

man reads: "Nah ist / Und schwer zu fassen der Gott. / Wo aber Gefahr ist, wächst / Das Rettende auch." For one of Heidegger's most important discussions of this time of danger, see his *Beiträge zur Philosophie*, §46.

74. Blanchot, *Step Not Beyond*, p. 106.

75. Novalis's words appear in Friedrich Schlegel, *Philosophical Fragments*, trans. Peter Firchow (Minneapolis: University of Minnesota Press, 1991), p. 58. These words are echoed in the concluding note of Theodor W. Adorno's *Minima Moralia: Reflections from Damaged Life*, trans. E. F. N. Jephcott (London: Verso, New Left Books, 1984), p. 247: "The only philosophy which can be responsibly practiced in face of despair [*Angesicht der Verzweifelung*] is the attempt to contemplate all things as they would present themselves from the standpoint of redemption [*vom Standpunkt der Erlösung*]." For the German, see *Minima Moralia: Reflexionen aus dem beschädigten Leben*, in *Gesammelte Schriften*, vol. 4 (Frankfurt am Main: Suhrkamp, 1980), p. 281.

76. Hölderlin, "Die Titanen," in *Sämtliche Werke*, ed. Stapf (1960), pp. 362–64. I have drawn on two different translations in recording this poem: Hamburger's in Hölderlin, *Poems and Fragments*, pp. 532–35); and Sieburth's in Hölderlin, *Hymns and Fragments*, pp. 144–49.

77. Hölderlin, "Die Titanen," in *Sämtliche Werke*, ed. Stapf (1960), p. 363.

78. The quotation is from Heidegger's meditation on the poet's word χρή, "use," in *Was Heißt Denken?* (Tübingen: Niemeyer, 1954), p. 118; translated as *What Is Called Thinking?*, trans. J. Glenn Gray (New York: Harper & Row, 1968), pt. 2, lecture 8, p. 194. According to Heidegger, we need to hear the poet's word, "use," in relation to the χρή of Parmenides' saying (6): χρὴ τὸ λέγειν τε νοεῖν τ' ἐὸν ἔμμεναι.

79. Hölderlin, "Vom Abgrund nemlich . . . ," in *Sämtliche Werke*, ed. Stapf (1960), pp. 379–80; translated as "For from the abyss . . . ," in *Poems and Fragments*, pp. 552–53. The German reads as follows: "Vom Abgrund nemlich haben / Wir angefangen und gegangen / Dem Leuen gleich . . . " On the abyss in this poetic fragment, see Rainer Nägele, *Theater, Theory, Speculation: Walter Benjamin and the Scenes of Modernity* (Baltimore: Johns Hopkins University Press, 1991), chap. 6, pp. 108–34.

80. Heidegger, *Beiträge zur Philosophie*, §271, p. 487; *Contributions to Philosophy*, p. 343.

81. Hölderlin, "Mnemosyne," in *Sämtliche Werke*, ed. Stapf (1960), pp. 348–49; "Mnemosyne," in *Hymns and Fragments*, pp. 116–17. The German reads: "Nicht vermögen / Die Himmlischen alles. Nehmlich es reichen / Die Sterblichen eh'in den Abgrund." Also see Heidegger, *Erläuterungen zu Hölderlins Dichtung*, pp. 67ff.

82. See the discussion of this transformation *vom Grund aus* in Heidegger, *Beiträge zur Philosophie*, §170. Also see §133 and §177, where the philosopher

interprets our vocation (*Bestimmung*) as a question of our capacity for opening ourselves to the "truth of being" in all our activities on earth—in "thinking, poetizing, building, leading, sacrificing, suffering, celebrating."

83. On the question of "grounding" as our historical calling, see Heidegger, *Beiträge zur Philosophie*, §168–§274.

84. Heidegger, *Beiträge zur Philosophie*, §57, p. 120; *Contributions to Philosophy*, p. 84. See also §8, p. 28 in the German; p. 20 in the English.

85. Ibid., §227, p. 356 in the German; p. 249 in the English. I have modified the translation, rewriting the final clause beginning with "while." Hereafter, *Beiträge zur Philosophie* will be cited in the text as *B*, followed by the section number and the page numbers, first in the German, then in the English. I will sometimes modify the translation.

86. Hölderlin, "Der Ister," in *Sämtliche Werke*, ed. Stapf (1960), p. 346; "The Ister," in *Poems and Fragments*, p. 493. Also see Jacques Derrida, *De l'esprit* (Paris: Éditions Galilée, 1987).

87. Heidegger, *Beiträge zur Philosophie*, "Vorblick," §2, p. 7.

88. Novalis, *Heinrich von Ofterdingen*, in *Gesammelte Werke*, ed. Hildberg Kohlschmidt and Werner Kohlschmidt (Gütersloh: Sigbert Mohn, 1967), p. 254.

89. Heidegger certainly thought so. See his *Erläuterungen zu Hölderlins Dichtung*, p. 61. As he points out there, for the poet, "Chaos" is a figure representing "the Holy."

90. See Theodor W. Adorno, "Parataxis: Zur späten Lyrik Hölderlins," in *Noten zur Literatur* (Frankfurt am Main: Suhrkamp, 1981), vol. 3, pp. 452ff.; translated as "Parataxis: On Hölderlin's Late Poetry," in *Notes to Literature*, trans. Shierry Weber Nicholsen, vol. 2 (New York: Columbia University Press, 1992), p. 139. Also see Heidegger, "Wozu Dichter?," pp. 248–95; "What Are Poets For?," pp. 91–142, for the philosopher's discussion of Hölderlin's concern for measure in its relation to his poetry. And see Aris Fioretos, ed., *The Solid Letter: Readings of Friedrich Hölderlin* (Stanford, Calif.: Stanford University Press, 1999), especially the contributions by Jean-Luc Nancy, "The Calculation of the Poet," pp. 44–73; and Peter Fenves, "Measure for Measure: Hölderlin and the Place of Philosophy," pp. 25–43. Fenves pursues the question of Hölderlin's caesura in another thought-provoking essay, "The Scale of Enthusiasm: Kant, Schelling and Hölderlin," published in his *Arresting Language: From Leibniz to Walter Benjamin* (Stanford, Calif.: Stanford University Press, 2001), pp. 98–128.

91. See Friedrich Hölderlin, "Anmerkungen zum Ödipus," in *Sämtliche Werke*, ed. Stapf (1960), p. 1056. Calling attention to the two words *aber Dank* is one of the many merits of Adorno's essay "Parataxis: On Hölderlin's Late Poetry."

92. Hölderlin, "Anmerkungen zum Ödipus," in *Sämtliche Werke*, ed. Stapf (1960), p. 1060. "Rhythm" and "arrhythmia" are ontological notions, figures for modalities of presencing that indicate a sense of temporality radically other

than ordinary time. They are "preliminary names" for "the truth of a being that is yet to be experienced." See Martin Heidegger, introduction to "Was ist Metaphysik?," in *Wegmarken*, rev. ed. (Frankfurt am Main: Klostermann, 1976), p. 206; translated as "What Is Metaphysics?," in *Pathmarks*, trans. William Mc-Neill (Cambridge, Eng.: Cambridge University Press, 1998), p. 287. Also see Heidegger's discussion of these notions in his commentary on Aristotle's *Physics* B.1, in "Vom Wesen und Begriff der Physis," in *Wegmarken*, pp. 337–38, 342–44, 352; translated as "On the Essence and Concept of Physis," in *Pathmarks*, pp. 204–5.

93. Friedrich Hölderlin, "Anmerkungen zur *Antigone*," in *Sämtliche Werke*, ed. Stapf (1960), p. 1064.

94. Hölderlin thought deeply about the caesura (*die Zäsur*), which he describes as a *gegenrhythmische Unterbrechung*, in his "Anmerkungen zum Ödipus," in *Sämtliche Werke*, ed. Stapf (1960), p. 1056. His discussion there illuminates the connection between his rhetorical and philosophical intentions. With regard to Hölderlin's caesurae and the question of a "change of measure," see Adorno's essay "Parataxis: Zur späten Lyrik Hölderlins," in *Noten zur Literatur* (Frankfurt am Main: Suhrkamp, 1981), vol. 3, pp. 447–91; and Nägele, *Theater, Theory, Speculation*, chap. 7, pp. 135–66. Also see Philippe Lacoue-Labarthe, "La césure du speculatif," either in *Friedrich Hölderlin: "L'Antigone" de Sophocle*, ed. and trans. Philippe Lacoue-Labarthe (Paris: Christian Bourgeois, 1978), pp. 183–223, or in *L'imitation des modernes* (Paris: Galilée, 1986). For the English translation of this work, see "The Caesura of the Speculative," trans. Robert Eisenhauer, in *Typography: Mimesis, Philosophy, Politics* (Cambridge, Mass.: Harvard University Press, 1989), pp. 208–35. Hölderlin's writings on the caesura concern its function in Greek tragedy, wherein it serves to create a certain "balance," a certain "stillpoint," a pause or a moment of narrative and dramatic suspension, between alternating "tones": a rhythm balancing the unfolding of the tragedy between a movement toward unification and a movement toward separation. Could one relate Hölderlin's use of this "stillpoint" of the caesura to Benjamin's *Jetztzeit*? Perhaps. But in any case, I want to argue that the poet's own deployment of the caesura in his poetic works does not function solely or even primarily as a balancing device; rather, it serves primarily to manifest the disruption and breakdown of revelatory meaning—the abyss of impossibility into which our language has fallen.

95. In this regard, see these works by Walter Benjamin: "Theses on the Philosophy of History," pp. 253–64; "Theologico-Political Fragment," in *Reflections*, pp. 312–13; and "Critique of Violence," in *Reflections*, pp. 277–300.

96. Benjamin, *Gesammelte Schriften*, vol. 1, pt. 3, p. 1233.

97. Hölderlin, "Friedensfeier," third version, in *Sämtliche Werke*, ed. Stapf (1960), p. 307; translated as "Celebration of Peace," in *Poems and Fragments*, pp. 428–29. I have modified Hamburger's translation.

98. Hölderlin, "Friedensfeier," final version, in *Sämtliche Werke*, ed. Stapf (1960), p. 309; "Celebration of Peace," in *Poems and Fragments*, pp. 438–39.

99. See Walter Benjamin, "Über das mimetische Vermögen," in *Gesammelte Schriften*, vol. 2, pt. 1, p. 213; translated as "On the Mimetic Faculty," in *Reflections*, p. 336. Benjamin "rescued" this phrase, which he abstracted from Hugo Hofmannsthal.

100. On this theme of a memory that by its very forgetfulness preserves and protects, see Maurice Blanchot, *L'entretien infini* (Paris: Gallimard, 1969), pt. 3, chap. 5.

101. Friedrich Hölderlin, "Sophokles," in *Sämtliche Werke*, ed. Stapf (1960), p. 211; translated as "Sophocles," in *Poems and Fragments*, pp. 70–71. The German reads: "Viele versuchten umsonst das Freudigste freudig zu sagen / Hier spricht endlich es mir, hier in der Trauer sich aus."

102. Adorno, *Minima Moralia*, §128, p. 200 in the English.

103. See Heidegger, *Beiträge zur Philosophie*, §253–§255.

104. See ibid., §281.

105. Friedrich Hölderlin, "Grund zum Empedokles," in *Sämtliche Werke: Kritische Textausgabe*, ed. D. E. Sattler (Frankfurt am Main: Luchterhand, 1986), vol. 13, p. 365.

106. *Letters of Rainer Maria Rilke, 1910–1926*, trans. Jane B. Greene and M. D. Herter Norton (New York: Norton, 1969), pp. 139–40.

107. Hölderlin, "In lieblicher Bläue . . . ," in *Sämtliche Werke*, ed. Stapf (1960), p. 416; "In lovely blueness . . . ," in *Poems and Fragments*, p. 601; and see Sieburth's translation in Hölderlin, *Hymns and Fragments*, p. 249. The German reads: "Voll Verdienst, doch dichterisch, wohnet der Mensch auf dieser Erde." Also see Martin Heidegger, " . . . Dichterisch wohnet der Mensch . . . ," in *Vorträge und Aufsätze*, pp. 187–204; translated as " . . . Poetically Man Dwells . . . ," in *Poetry, Language, Thought*, pp. 213–29. And see Heidegger, *Erläuterungen zu Hölderlins Dichtung*, pp. 38–45 and 73–80, for his meditation on "Andenken," especially on the line "Was bleibet aber, stiften die Dichter" ("But what remains, that the poets found"). According to Heidegger, "'*Dichterisch*' is Dasein in its ground—which says at the same time: it is, as founded [*gestiftetes*] (*gegründetes*), not [only a question of] *Verdienst* but [also the question of] a gift [*Geschenk*]" (p. 39). In §190 of the *Beiträge* (*Beiträge zur Philosophie*, p. 310; *Contributions to Philosophy*, p. 218), Heidegger presents a diagram showing the dimensions of the *Ereignis*. On the horizontal plane of the diagram, "mankind" (*Mensch*) appears on the left, "gods" (t/here: "Da") on the right; on the vertical axis, a plane of strife, "earth" is below and "world" is above it. Is this a diagram of the Fourfold (*das Geviert*)? According to Heidegger, in the *Ereignis* of the Fourfold, there takes place a gathering of earth and sky, gods and mortals. For us human beings to dwell "poetically" (*dichterisch*) would be for us to live our lives in such a way that we would make wherever we happen to be (namely, our *Da-*

sein, our "being t/here") a site (*Stätte*) within the world welcoming such a gathering. Heidegger's emphasis on the strife between earth and world, not only in the *Beiträge* but also in his essay "The Origin of the Work of Art," could be read, I think, as an oblique disagreement with Plato's politics, which makes the ideal republic a community of pure immanence dependent on the myth of autochthony.

108. Hölderlin, "Der Ister," in *Sämtliche Werke*, ed. Stapf (1960), p. 347; "The Ister," in *Poems and Fragments*, pp. 492–93.

109. See Hölderlin, "Anmerkungen zum Ödipus," in *Sämtliche Werke*, ed. Stapf (1960), pp. 1060ff.; translated as "Remarks on *Oedipus*," in *Hölderlin: Essays and Letters*, p. 102. And see Maurice Blanchot, *L'écriture du désastre* (Paris: Gallimard, 1980), pp. 172–74; translated as The *Writing of Disaster*, trans. Ann Smock (Lincoln: University of Nebraska Press, 1986), pp. 112–13.

110. F. W. J. von Schelling, "Allgemeine Übersicht der neuesten philosophischen Literatur" (later titled "Abhandlungen zur Erläuterung des Idealismus der Wissenschaftslehre"), in *Sämtliche Werke*, vol. 1, p. 389; translated as "Treatise Explicatory of the Idealism in the Science of Knowledge," in *Idealism and the Endgame of Theory*, ed. and trans. Thomas Pfau (Albany: SUNY Press, 1994), p. 94.

111. Hölderlin, "Der Rhein," in *Sämtliche Werke*, ed. Stapf (1960), p. 319; "The Rhine," in *Poems and Fragments*, p. 421. The apparent tension between the lines from "The Ister" just cited and this line from "The Rhine" reminds me of Kafka's "man from the country," who posits the requirements of an unfathomable Law to which he may not measure up. He waits outside the entrance to the Law, only to be told, as he nears his death, that the door was kept open just for him. What seemed to be a measure beyond him turns out to be a measure befitting him precisely.

112. Hölderlin, "In lieblicher Bläue . . . ," in *Sämtliche Werke*, ed. Stapf (1960), p. 416. The German reads: "Größeres zu wünschen, kann nicht des Menschen Natur sich vermessen." Also see Andrew Bowie, *From Romanticism to Criticism: The Philosophy of German Literary Theory* (New York: Routledge, 1997); Manfred Frank, *Das Problem "Zeit" in der deutschen Romantik* (Munich: Schöningh, 1994); Thomas Weiskel, *The Romantic Sublime* (Baltimore: Johns Hopkins University Press, 1976); Géza von Molnar, *Romantic Vision, Ethical Context: Novalis and Artistic Autonomy* (Minneapolis: University of Minnesota Press, 1987); and Dieter Henrich, *Der Gang des Andenkens: Beobachtungen und Gedanken zu Hölderlins Gedicht* (Stuttgart: Klett-Cotta, 1986).

Chapter 4

1. F. W. J. von Schelling, *Philosophische Untersuchungen über das Wesen der menschlichen Freiheit und die damit zusammenhängenden Gegenstände*, in *Werke*,

unaltered reproduction of the celebratory printing in Munich in 1927, ed. Manfred Schröter (Munich: Beck'sche Verlagsbuchhandlung, 1958), p. 281; translated as *Of Human Freedom*, trans. James Gutmann (Chicago: Open Court,
1936), §389, p. 68. Also see Jean-Luc Nancy, *The Experience of Freedom*, trans.
Bridget McDonald (Stanford, Calif.: Stanford University Press, 1993), pp. 129–
30, for a provocative discussion of Martin Heidegger's commentary on Schelling,
Schelling's Treatise on the Essence of Human Freedom, trans. Joan Stambaugh
(Athens: Ohio University Press, 1985), pp. 142–43: "If man is the being in whom
the 'ground' (the divine essence as the ground-without-ground of absolute indifference) is separated from the existence of God (as his proper possibility of existence revealed in humanity), and if it is man who, acceding in his autonomy to
understanding and language, lays claim to existence itself as the ground, which
means to the 'tendency to return to oneself' or to 'ego-centrism,' then *evil occurs
when 'the ground elevates itself to existence and puts itself in the place of existence'
and when man wants to be 'as separated selfhood the ground of the totality.'"* (Italics added.)

2. Schelling, *Philosophische Untersuchungen*, §370, p. 262; *Of Human Freedom*, §370, p. 46.

3. Ibid., §372, p. 264 in the German; p. 48 in the English. I have corrected and
in other ways modified the translation.

4. Nancy, *Experience of Freedom*, p. 134. Also see Martin Heidegger, "Brief
über den 'Humanismus,'" published as a supplement in *Platons Lehre von der
Wahrheit* (Bern: A. Francke, 1954), p. 112; translated as "Letter on Humanism,"
in *Basic Writings*, trans. David Farrell Krell, rev. ed. (San Francisco: Harper,
1993), p. 260: "With healing, evil appears all the more in the clearing of being
[*Mit dem Heilen zumal erscheint in der Lichtung des Seins das Böse*]. The essence
of evil does not consist in the mere baseness of human action, but rather in the
malice of rage [*im bösartigen des Grimmes*]. Both of these, however, the healing
and the raging [*das Heilige und das Grimmige*], can essentially occur only in being, insofar as being itself is what is contested." A more recent edition of the
German text appears in Martin Heidegger, *Wegmarken* (Frankfurt am Main:
Klostermann, 1967), pp. 145–94.

5. Theodor W. Adorno, *Minima Moralia: Reflexionen aus dem beschädigten
Leben*, in *Gesammelte Schriften*, vol. 4 (Frankfurt am Main: Suhrkamp, 1980),
§67, pp. 114–16; translated as *Minima Moralia: Reflections from Damaged Life*,
trans. E. F. N. Jephcott (London: Verso, New Left Books, 1984), pp. 103–4. I
have modified the translation of *entzieht sich* and *vorweggenommene*. Also see
Emil Fackenheim, *To Mend the World: Foundations of Post-Holocaust Jewish
Thought* (Bloomington: Indiana University Press, 1994); Hans Jonas, *Mortality
and Morality: A Search for the Good After Auschwitz* (Evanston, Ill.: Northwestern University Press, 1996); Hannah Arendt, *The Origins of Totalitarianism* (New

York: Harcourt Brace Jovanovich, 1975); and Hannah Arendt, *Eichmann in Jerusalem: A Report on the Banality of Evil* (New York: Penguin Books, 1994).

6. See Primo Levi, *"Se questo è un uomo" e "La tregua"* (Torino: Einaudi, 1989); translated as *Survival in Auschwitz*, trans. Stuart Woolf (New York: Simon & Schuster, 1996); and his *I sommersi e i salvati* (Torino: Einaudi, 1991), translated as *The Drowned and the Saved*, trans. Raymond Rosenthal (New York: Vintage International, 1989).

7. Levi, *I sommersi e i salvati*, pp. 83–84; *The Drowned and the Saved*, p. 106.

8. Ibid.

9. Ibid.

10. Ibid., p. 152 in the Italian; p. 186 in the English.

11. Ibid., p. 153 in the Italian; p. 187 in the English.

12. Ibid.

13. Ibid., p. 114 in the Italian; p. 141 in the English.

14. Martin Heidegger, *Sein und Zeit*, 5th ed. (Halle: Niemeyer, 1941), p. 284; translated from the 7th ed. as *Being and Time*, trans. John Macquarrie and Edward Robinson (New York: Harper & Row, 1962), p. 330.

15. Martin Heidegger, *Nietzsche*, vol. 1, *Der Wille zur Macht als Kunst* (Pfullingen: Neske, 1961), pp. 55–56; translated as *Nietzsche*, vol. 1, *The Will to Power as Art*, trans. David Farrell Krell (New York: Harper & Row, 1979), pp. 47–48.

16. Lawrence J. Hatab, *Ethics and Finitude: Heideggerian Contributions to Moral Philosophy* (Lanham, Md.: Rowman & Littlefield, 2000), p. 76.

17. Immanuel Kant, *Critique of Practical Reason*, trans. Lewis White Beck (New York: Library of Liberal Arts, 1956), p. 166.

18. Martin Heidegger, *Was Heißt Denken?* (Tübingen: Niemeyer, 1954), p. 43; translated as *What Is Called Thinking?*, trans. J. Glenn Gray (New York: Harper & Row, 1968), pt. 1, lecture 10, pp. 103–4.

19. Adorno, *Minima Moralia*, §66, p. 103 in the English.

20. Friedrich Hölderlin, "Wurzel alles Übels," in *Poems and Fragments*, trans. Michael Hamburger, bilingual edition (Cambridge, Eng.: Cambridge University Press, 1980), p. 70; my translation. I was not happy with the interpellations in Hamburger's translation.

21. Emmanuel Levinas, *Totality and Infinity: An Essay on Exteriority*, trans. Alphonso Lingis (Pittsburgh: Duquesne University Press, 1969), p. 229. Also see p. 231: "The will thus moves between its betrayal and its fidelity, which, simultaneous, describe the very originality of its power."

22. Emmanuel Levinas, "Transcendence and Evil," in *Of God Who Comes to Mind*, trans. Bettina Bergo (Stanford, Calif.: Stanford University Press, 1998), pp. 127–28.

23. Theodor W. Adorno, *Metaphysics: Concepts and Problems*, ed. Rolf Tiede-

mann, trans. Edmund Jephcott (Stanford, Calif.: Stanford University Press, 2000), pp. 127, 129.

24. Vasco Pratolini, *Allegoria e derisione* (Milan: Arnoldo Mondadori Editore, 1983), p. 353: "O ritroviamo una misura dell'uomo comparata sugli sceletri di Buchenwald e di Horoshima, o ci scopriremo di nuovo a intonare palinodie." Pratolini was quick to denounce his early, youthful involvement with fascism and became a passionate and articulate critic of fascist politics.

25. I am especially indebted to David Wood, whose thoughtful questions on an earlier draft of this chapter encouraged me to write this third section. I also want to thank Daniel Brandes, Peter Fenves, Robert Gooding-Williams, Lawrence Hatab, Nikolas Kompridis, Roger Levin, and Edith Wyschogrod for valuable comments, questions, and suggestions.

Chapter 5

1. Friedrich Nietzsche, *Thus Spoke Zarathustra*, trans. Walter Kaufmann (New York: Penguin, 1978), pt. 2, p. 138. Nietzsche seems to be echoing Hölderlin's "Hyperion," where Hyperion says, "You see artisans, . . . but no human beings" ("Hyperion," in *Sämtliche Werke*, ed. Paul Stapf [Berlin: Tempel-Verlag, 1960], p. 552). And echoing also, perhaps, a fragment by Friedrich Schlegel; see note 18 below. In his *Traité de la vie élégante*, Honoré de Balzac articulates with remarkable lucidity the transition into a world of industrialization and managed labor, which his generation was the first to experience: "Once he starts working with his hands, man abdicates his destiny; he becomes a means. . . . Workers are nothing but pulleys and stay welded to their wheelbarrows, shovels, pickaxes. . . . A worker, a bricklayer, a soldier are the featureless fragments of one mass. . . . Work is to them like an enigma whose solution they seek till they die." See Honoré de Balzac *La comédie humaine*, ed. Pierre-Georges Castex (Paris: Gallimard, 1976–81), vol. 12, pp. 212–13. Balzac also perceived the phantasmagoric and ideologically determined character of the transition: the fact that, for the consciousness of the workers it binds, capitalism requires that the process appear absolutely enigmatic.

2. David Harvey, *The Limits to Capital* (Oxford: Oxford University Press, 1982), p. 157. And see Tom McCall, "Momentary Violence," in David S. Ferris, ed., *Walter Benjamin: Theoretical Questions* (Stanford, Calif.: Stanford University Press, 1996), p. 206: "Law, the means by which the state marks its language on bodies, is structured like a curse. . . . Who is subject to the speech acts of contracts and laws is accursed. The curse offers a paradigm for the pure positional power of law, its nomothetic force, its power to mark the body politic. The violence of law, like that of myth, has to do with just this constitution and marking of bodies. Yet law remains an ideality that decays whenever it is applied."

3. Theodor W. Adorno, *Aesthetic Theory*, trans. Robert Hullot-Kentor (Minneapolis: University of Minnesota Press, 1997), p. 206.

4. Walter Benjamin, "Kaiserpanorama," in *Einbahnstraße*, in *Schriften*, ed. Theodor W. Adorno and Gretel Adorno (Frankfurt am Main: Suhrkamp, 1955), vol. 1, p. 527; translated as "Imperial Panorama," in *One-Way Street*, in Walter Benjamin, *Reflections: Essays, Aphorisms, Autobiographical Writings*, ed. Peter Demetz, trans. Edmund Jephcott (New York: Schocken, 1986), p. 72.

5. Novalis, "Neue Fragmente," in *Werke und Briefe*, ed. Alfred Kelletat (Munich: Winkler-Verlag, 1968), p. 415. The German reads: "Handlungsweise der schönen, rhythmischen Seele . . . Gang im Lande der Schönheit—überall leise Spur des Fingers der Humanität—freie Regel—Sieg über die rohe Natur in jedem Worte . . . Humanisierung—Aufklärung—Rhythmus."

6. Denis Diderot, *Oeuvres esthétiques* (Paris: Classiques Garnier, 1959), p. 260. The French reads: "Chez un peuple esclave, tout se dégrade. Il faut s'avilir par le ton et le geste, pour ôter à la vérité son poids et son offense."

7. Ibid. The French reads: "plus un peuple est civilisé, poli, moins ses moeurs sont poétiques."

8. George Sturt, *The Wheelwright's Shop* (Cambridge, Eng.: Cambridge University Press, 1963), p. 23. Hereafter, the abbreviation *WS* will be used in citations of this work in my text.

9. Ronald Blythe, *Akenfield: Portrait of an English Village* (New York: Dell, 1969), p. 166.

10. Ibid., p. 131.

11. Ibid., p. 136.

12. See David Ross's interview with Ilya Kabakov, quoted in Gregg M. Horowitz, *Sustaining Loss: Art and Mournful Life* (Stanford, Calif.: Stanford University Press, 2001), p. 147.

13. André Breton, *Nadja*, in *Oeuvres complètes* (Paris: Gallimard, Bibliothèque de la Pléiade, 1988), vol. 1, pp. 683, 697ff. Also see Gérard de Nerval, "La main enchantée," in *Nouvelles et fantaisies*, in his *Oeuvres complètes* (Paris: Librairie Ancienne Honoré Champion, 1928), vol. 3, pp. 181–236. In this tale, Eustache Bouteroue, a young clothier, is executed for certain crimes and misdemeanors, but his bloody severed hand continues for a while to make mischief, terrorize, haunt, and entertain. Reminiscent in some ways of certain tales by Kleist, this tale is prefaced, and thereby its moral significance is contextualized, in terms of the history of La Place Dauphine in Paris, raising questions about "intellectual emancipation," social progress, inequalities in property, and the justice of the courts of law.

14. Maurice Merleau-Ponty, *Phenomenology of Perception*, trans. Colin Smith (London: Routledge & Kegan Paul, 1962), p. 98. Hereafter, this work will be cited in the text by the abbreviation *PP*.

15. Karl Marx, *Capital: A Critique of Political Economy*, trans. Samuel Moore and Edward Aveling, vol. 1: *The Process of Capitalist Production* (New York: International, 1967), p. 72.

16. See, for example, Karl Marx, *Capital*, in *Karl Marx: Selected Writings*, ed. David MacLellan, trans. Ewald Osers (New York: Oxford University Press, 1977), p. 429, where Marx observes that, in a capital-driven economy, it is "impossible to grasp" the value of commodities.

17. Karl Marx, *Economic and Philosophical Manuscripts of 1844*, trans. Martin Milligan (New York: International, 1964), pp. 138–39. Hereafter, this work will be cited in the text by the abbreviation *EPM*.

18. Friedrich Schlegel, *Philosophical Fragments*, trans. Peter Firchow (Minneapolis: University of Minnesota Press, 1991), p. 66. Also see Hölderlin, "Hyperion," in *Sämtliche Werke*, ed. Stapf (1960), p. 552. Echoing a passage in Rousseau's "Discours sur les sciences et les arts," but giving the disintegration due to division of labor a more materialist, more violent interpretation, more also in the spirit of the baroque "Trauerspiel," the poet has Hyperion say, near the end of book 2, "You see artisans [*Handwerker*], but no human beings, thinkers but no human beings, priests but no human beings, masters and servants, but no human beings—is this not like a battlefield on which hacked-off hands and arms and every other member are scattered about, while the life-blood flowing from them vanishes into the sand?" (my translation).

19. Following Kant on this point, Marx makes this same distinction.

20. Rainer Maria Rilke, "The Hand," in *Poems 1912–1926*, trans. Michael Hamburger, a bilingual edition (Redding Ridge, Conn.: Black Swan Books, 1981), pp. 72–73.

21. Rainer Maria Rilke, *Gesammelte Werke*, vol. 3 (Leipzig: Insel-Verlag, 1927), p. 438; quoted in Hofstadter's translation in Martin Heidegger, "What Are Poets For?," in *Poetry, Language, Thought*, trans. Albert Hofstadter (New York: Harper & Row, 1971), p. 136. In *Totality and Infinity*, Levinas enters into a lengthy discussion of labor and political economy, giving considerable attention to the uses and abuses of our hands. See Emmanuel Levinas, *Totalité et infini: Essai sur L'extériorité* (The Hague: Nijhoff, 1961); translated as *Totality and Infinity: An Essay on Exteriority*, trans. Alphonso Lingis (Pittsburgh: Duquesne University Press, 1969), esp. pp. 131–42 in the French and pp. 158–68 in the English.

Chapter 6

1. Johann Wolfgang von Goethe, *Elective Affinities*, trans. David Constantine (New York: Oxford University Press, 1994), p. 151. The passage is a remark written by the character Ottilie in her diary.

2. Immanuel Kant, *Lectures on Ethics*, trans. Louis Infield (Indianapolis: Hackett, 1963), p. 198.

3. Friedrich Schlegel, *Philosophical Fragments*, trans. Peter Firchow (Minneapolis: University of Minnesota Press, 1991), §83, p. 10.
4. Friedrich Schleiermacher, "Athenaeum Fragments," in Schlegel, *Philosophical Fragments*, §351, p. 71.
5. Pierre Bourdieu, *Outline of a Theory of Practice* (Cambridge, Eng.: Cambridge University Press, 1977), p. 82.
6. Pierre Bourdieu, *The Logic of Practice* (Cambridge: Polity, 1990), p. 67.
7. Søren Kierkegaard, *The Concept of Dread*, trans. Walter Lowrie (Princeton, N.J.: Princeton University Press, 1980), p. 118.
8. Sigmund Freud, *Totem and Taboo*, trans. James Strachey (New York: Norton, 1989), pp. 52–53, 91. Also see p. 35: as in the case of taboos, the main prohibition in certain obsessional neuroses is against any touching. Freud calls this the "touching phobia," or the *délire de toucher*. It is not always only immediate physical contact that is feared and avoided, but any situation in which one might possibly come into contact with the forbidden objects.
9. Maurice Merleau-Ponty, *Phénoménologie de la perception*, 2nd ed. (Paris: Gallimard, 1945), pp. 220–21; translated as *Phenomenology of Perception*, trans. Colin Smith (London: Routledge & Kegan Paul, 1962), p. 189.
10. Georg Lukács, *Die Theorie des Romans: Ein Geschichtsphilosophischer Versuch über die Formen der großen Epik* (Neuwied: Luchterhand, 1974), p. 55; translated as *The Theory of the Novel*, trans. Anna Bostock (Cambridge, Mass.: MIT Press, 1971), p. 64.
11. See G. F. W. Hegel, *The Phenomenology of Spirit*, trans. A. V. Miller (New York: Oxford University Press, 1977), p. 493. The figure is introduced at the very end of the work, in the section on the historicity of Spirit in the attainment of "Absolute Knowing." Lukács and Levinas each give Hegel's figure a significantly different twist.
12. Emmanuel Levinas, "Textes messianiques," in *Difficile liberté: Essais sur le judaïsme* (Paris: Éditions Albin Michel, 1976), p. 91; translated as "Messianic Texts," in *Difficult Freedom: Essays on Judaism*, trans. Sean Hand (Baltimore: Johns Hopkins University Press, 1997), p. 60.
13. See Theodor W. Adorno, *Negative Dialektik* (Frankfurt am Main: Suhrkamp, 1966), pp. 347–53; translated as *Negative Dialectics*, trans. E. B. Ashton (New York: Continuum, 1973), pp. 354–60. Unless otherwise noted, the German edition cited below in this chapter is this one. Occasionally, I will cite the edition published as vol. 6 of *Gesammelte Schriften* (Frankfurt am Main: Suhrkamp, 1973); these citations will be explicitly indicated. Also see his early essay, translated by Robert Hullot-Kentor: Theodor W. Adorno, "The Idea of Natural History," *Telos*, 60 (Summer 1984): 111–21.
14. Adorno, "Idea of Natural History," p. 121.
15. Lukács, *Die Theorie des Romans*, pp. 73 and 77–78; *Theory of the Novel*, pp. 84 and 89.

16. Ibid., p. 63 in the German; p. 74 in the English.

17. Theodor W. Adorno, *Minima Moralia: Reflexionen aus dem beschädigten Leben,* in *Gesammelte Schriften,* vol. 4 (Frankfurt am Main: Suhrkamp, 1980), §5, p. 26; translated as *Minima Moralia: Reflections from Damaged Life,* trans. E. F. N. Jephcott (London: Verso, New Left Books, 1984), p. 25. Hereafter, *Minima Moralia* will be cited in the text as *MM,* followed by the section number and the page numbers, first in the German, then in the English.

18. Theodor W. Adorno, *Aesthetic Theory,* trans. Robert Hullot-Kentor (Minneapolis: University of Minnesota Press, 1997).

19. Immanuel Kant, *Schriften zur Anthropologie, Geschichtsphilosophie, Politik und Pädagogik,* vol. 2, in *Werkausgabe,* vol. 12 (Frankfurt am Main: Suhrkamp, 1977), pp. 444–45; translated as *Anthropology from a Pragmatic Point of View,* trans. Mary J. Gregor (New York: Nijhoff, 1974), p. 32. Kant also says there, pragmatically: "But we are better off having token money [*Scheidemünze*] in circulation than no money at all; and it can eventually be converted into pure gold, albeit at a considerable loss."

20. Kant, *Lectures on Ethics,* p. 222.

21. See Immanuel Kant, "Idea for a Universal History with a Cosmopolitan Intent," in *"Perpetual Peace" and Other Essays on Politics, History, and Morals,* trans. Ted Humphrey (Indianapolis: Hackett, 1983), pp. 30–32.

22. See Kant, *Schriften zur Anthropologie; Anthropology from a Pragmatic Point of View.*

23. Kant, *Schriften zur Anthropologie,* pp. 444–45; *Anthropology from a Pragmatic Point of View,* p. 32.

24. Ibid.

25. Walter Benjamin, *Gesammelte Schriften,* ed. Rolf Tiedemann and Hermann Schweppenhäuser (Frankfurt am Main: Suhrkamp, 1972–89), vol. 4, pt. 1, pp. 402–3.

26. Kant, *Schriften zur Anthropologie,* pp. 444–45; *Anthropology from a Pragmatic Point of View,* p. 32. See Stephen L. Carter, *Civility: Manners, Morals and Etiquette of Democracy* (New York: Basic Books, 1998); and Peter France, *Politeness and Its Discontents* (Cambridge, Eng.: Cambridge University Press, 1992). Also see Dena Goodman, "Difference: An Enlightenment Concept," in Keith M. Baker and Peter H. Reill, eds., *What's Left of Enlightenment?* (Stanford, Calif.: Stanford University Press, 2001), pp. 129–47. Goodman claims that, beginning in the seventeenth century, aristocratic salons taught the practice of "civility," a code of nobility based not on birth but on manners, comportment, and conversation. But, according to her, it is necessary to distinguish between "civility" and "politeness," because one sees aristocratic "civility" yielding in the eighteenth century to "the broader and more egalitarian notion and practice of politeness." She supports her historical analysis, quoting from the chevalier de Jancourt:

"'Civility' does not say as much as politeness, and makes up but a portion of it." Moreover, civility, which maintained rank and status, was increasingly thought to be superficial, even hypocritical. Thus, for example, "true" politeness would not resort, as "civility" might, to obsequious words of flattery. According to Goodman, "before the [French] Revolution, civility was criticized for the artificiality it tended to produce, for its attention to form and appearance. (The substitution of politeness for 'mere' civility was an attempt to rescue civility from this critique). . . . Before the Revolution, only Rousseau really worried about freedom being sacrificed on the altar of civility; his contemporaries were more concerned about the destructive and deceptive potential of language for human society. . . . Indeed, . . . the value of civility in the view of Rousseau's contemporaries was its role in the 'tightening' of men's interdependence" (p. 139).

27. Kant, *Schriften zur Anthropologie*, pp. 444–45; *Anthropology from a Pragmatic Point of View*, pp. 32–33.

28. Ibid.

29. Ibid., pp. 688–89 in the German; p. 192 in the English.

30. Immanuel Kant, *The Critique of Judgment*, trans. Werner Pluhar (Indianapolis: Hackett, 1987), §60, p. 231.

31. *The Wisdom of Laotse*, ed. and trans. Lin Yutang (New York: Random House, 1948), p. 49.

32. Adorno, *Negative Dialektik*, pp. 394–95; *Negative Dialectics*, pp. 404–5. On the importance of a "space of appearance" for understanding the realm of politics, see Hannah Arendt, *The Human Condition* (Chicago: University of Chicago Press, 1958), pp. 57, 197–99; and her *On Revolution* (New York: Penguin, 1962), p. 98. But, whereas she here seems to inscribe this space in a logic of identity (appearance-reality), Adorno will always insist on a logic of nonidentity, without which critique for him is not possible. These logics clash on the question of hypocrisy. In *On Revolution*, p. 101, Arendt asks: "Was not hypocrisy, since it paid its compliment to virtue, almost the vice to undo the vices? . . . Why should the vice that covered up the vices become the vice of vices? Is hypocrisy then such a monster?" In her work "French Existentialism," in *Essays in Understanding: 1930–1954* (New York: Harcourt, Brace, Jovanovich, 1994), she turns the freedom in appearance into the freedom of nonidentity, observing, "By play-acting at what one is, one guards one's freedom as a human being from the pretenses of one's [socially imposed] functions; moreover, only by playing at what one really is, is man able to affirm that he is never identical with himself as a thing is identical with itself." In this 1946 essay, therefore, she showed an Adornian appreciation of the moment of nonidentity, the negative dialectics, at the heart of both freedom and critique.

33. Adorno, *Negative Dialectics*, p. 169.

34. Theodor W. Adorno, "Veblen's Attack on Culture," in *Prisms*, ed. and

trans. Samuel Weber and Shierry Weber (Cambridge, Mass.: MIT Press, 1984), p. 84.

35. Martin Heidegger, *Sein und Zeit*, 5th ed. (Halle: Niemeyer, 1941), §44, p. 222; translated from the 7th ed. as *Being and Time*, trans. John Macquarrie and Edward Robinson (New York: Harper & Row, 1962), pp. 264–65.

36. Adorno, *Negative Dialektik*, pp. 394–95; *Negative Dialectics*, pp. 404–5.

37. Ibid., p. 388 in the German; p. 398 in the English.

38. Theodor W. Adorno, "Odysseus oder Mythos und Aufklärung," in Theodor W. Adorno and Max Horkheimer, *Dialektik der Aufklärung: Philosophische Fragmente* (Frankfurt am Main: Fischer, 1969), p. 53; translated as "Odysseus or Myth and Enlightenment," in Theodor W. Adorno and Max Horkheimer, *The Dialectic of Enlightenment*, trans. John Cumming (New York: Continuum, 1986), p. 57. There is now a much better translation in print: *Dialectic of Enlightenment: Philosophical Fragments*, ed. Gunzelin Schmid Noerr, trans. Edmund Jephcott (Stanford, Calif.: Stanford University Press, 2002).

39. See Peter Dews, *Logics of Disintegration: Post-Structuralist Thought and the Claims of Critical Theory* (London: Verso, New Left Books, 1987).

40. Henry James, *Letters 1883–1895*, ed. Leon Edel, vol. 3 (Cambridge, Mass.: Belknap Press of Harvard University Press, 1980), p. 483. The occasion was the death of Walter Pater. The letter, dated August 10, 1894, was addressed to Edmund Gosse.

41. Adorno and Horkheimer, *Dialektik der Aufklärung*, p. 4; *Dialectic of Enlightenment*, trans. Cumming, p. xv.

42. Henry James, *Letters 1895–1916*, ed. Leon Edel, vol. 4 (Cambridge, Mass.: Belknap Press of Harvard University Press, 1984), p. 12. The letter is dated April 28, 1895.

43. See Theodor W. Adorno's reflections on these gestures in "Über Tradition," in *Gesammelte Schriften*, vol. 10 (Frankfurt am Main: Suhrkamp, 1977), pt. 1, pp. 310–20. And see his note on "Les Adieux," in *Minima Moralia*, p. 289 (in the German edition only), where he argues against any restoration of the traditional gestures of farewell, while also lamenting the loss of a certain experience of distance and absence. "What would hope be without distance? [*Was wäre Hoffnung ohne Ferne?*]," he asks. For "Humanity," he says, was once a "consciousness of the presence of the not-present [*Gegenwart des Nichtgegenwärtigen*]."

44. Immanuel Kant, "Die Tugendlehre," in *Gesammelte Schriften*, ed. Königliche Preußische Akademie der Wissenschaften, vol. 6 (Berlin: De Gruyter, 1902), p. 379; translated as "The Doctrine of Virtue," in *The Metaphysics of Morals* (Philadelphia: University of Pennsylvania Press, 1964), p. 37. In Kant's exact phrase, it is a question of "the humanity in my own person."

45. Theodor W. Adorno, *Metaphysics: Concept and Problems*, ed. Rolf Tiedemann, trans. by Edmund Jephcott (Stanford, Calif.: Stanford University Press,

2000), p. 116. A comment by Adorno following one of his lectures is instructive. Asked what his absolutely foundational justification for morality is, he repudiated foundationalism and spoke about the limited motivational role of reason in our moral life and emphasized the role of immediate bodily reactions as a major, if not always ultimate, moral source: "[As soon as] one asks about absolutely ultimate values, one is already in the devil's kitchen, and I think that in answer to this a certain minimum amount of enlightenment suffices. . . . I mean, to get involved in theoretical discussions about whether people should be tortured or not, let's rather stop that. I think that in a higher sense breaking off [questions of] rationality at such a point better serves reason than a kind of pseudo-rationality that erects systems where it is first and foremost a question of immediate reaction" (Theodor W. Adorno, "The Meaning of Working Through the Past," in *Critical Models: Interventions and Catchwords*, trans. Henry V. Pickford [New York: Columbia University Press, 1998], p. 304). This remark comes from a philosopher renowned for his insistence on dialectical mediations. It would be useful to contrast Adorno's position in this regard with the postmetaphysical, antitheoretical, antisystematic approaches to ethics eloquently argued for by Bernard Williams and Richard Rorty.

46. Adorno, *Metaphysics*, p. 116.

47. Adorno, *Negative Dialektik*, in *Gesammelte Schriften*, vol. 6, p. 358; *Negative Dialectics*, p. 365.

48. Adorno and Horkheimer, *Dialektik der Aufklärung*, p. 36; *Dialectic of Enlightenment*, trans. Cumming, also p. 36.

49. Martin Heidegger, "Aletheia (Heraklit, Fragment 16)," in *Vorträge und Aufsätze* (Pfullingen: Neske, 1954), pp. 262–66; translated as "Aletheia (Heraclitus, Fragment B16)," in *Early Greek Thinking*, trans. David Farrell Krell and Frank A. Capuzzi (New York: Harper & Row, 1975), pp. 106–9.

50. Adorno, *Negative Dialektik*, p. 395; *Negative Dialectics*, p. 405.

51. Adorno, *Negative Dialektik*, in *Gesammelte Schriften*, vol. 6, p. 344; *Negative Dialectics*, p. 351.

52. Adorno, *Negative Dialektik*, p. 358; *Negative Dialectics*, p. 365.

53. Adorno makes several references to the shudder in his *Aesthetic Theory*: "Artworks are images as *apparition*, as appearance, and not as copy. If through the demythologization of the world consciousness freed itself from the ancient shudder, that shudder is permanently reproduced in the historical antagonism of subject and object. The object became as incommensurable to experience, as foreign and frightening, as manna once was" (pp. 84–85). "Art is redemptive in the act by which the spirit in it throws itself away. Art holds true to the shudder, but not by regression to it. Rather, art is its legacy. The spirit of artworks produces the shudder by externalizing its objects. Thus art participates in the actual movement of history in accord with the law of enlightenment. . . . The uncheckable

movement of spirit toward what has eluded it becomes in art the voice that speaks for what was lost in the most distantly archaic" (p. 118). "Ultimately, aesthetic comportment is to be defined as the capacity to shudder, as if goose bumps were the first aesthetic image. What later came to be called subjectivity, freeing itself from the blind anxiety of the shudder, is at the same time the shudder's own development; life in the subject is nothing but what shudders, the reaction to the total spell that transcends the spell. Consciousness without shudder is reified consciousness. That shudder in which subjectivity stirs without yet being subjectivity is the act of being touched by the other. Aesthetic comportment assimilates itself to that other rather than subordinating it" (p. 331).

54. Adorno, *Negative Dialektik*, p. 390; *Negative Dialectics*, pp. 399–400.

55. Immanuel Kant, *Kritik der praktischen Vernunft*, in *Gesammelte Schriften*, ed. Königliche Preußische Akademie der Wissenschaften (Berlin: George Reimer, 1900–), vol. 5, p. 47; translated as *Critique of Practical Reason*, trans. Lewis White Beck (New York: Library of Liberal Arts, 1956), p. 31.

56. Walter Benjamin, "Geschichtsphilosophische Thesen," in *Schriften*, ed. Theodor W. Adorno and Gretel Adorno (Frankfurt am Main: Suhrkamp, 1955), vol. 1, p. 495; translated as "Theses on the Philosophy of History," in *Illuminations*, ed. Hannah Arendt, trans. Harry Zohn (1968; reprint, New York: Schocken, 1969), p. 254.

57. Adorno, *Negative Dialektik*, p. 390; *Negative Dialectics*, p. 400.

58. Ibid., p. 393 in the German; p. 400 in the English.

59. Ibid., p. 391 in the German; pp. 400–401 in the English.

60. Ibid.

61. Ibid., p. 392 in the German; p. 402 in the English.

62. Edward Said, *Reflections on Exile* (Cambridge, Mass.: Harvard University Press, 2000), p. 19.

63. Theodor W. Adorno, "On the Final Scene of Faust," in *Notes to Literature*, trans. Shierry Weber Nicholsen, vol. 1 (New York: Columbia University Press, 1991), p. 120. This remark on memory is the final sentence, closing with the opening of hope. Kant's question "What may I hope?" is the last of three questions formulated at A805/B833, near the end of his *Critique of Pure Reason*. Using these questions to indicate the different tasks constitutive of his three critical works, Kant says there, "all hoping is directed to happiness."

64. Adorno, *Negative Dialektik*, in *Gesammelte Schriften*, vol. 6, pp. 221–22; and by a strange coincidence, the passage is to be found on the same pages in the English.

65. Walter Benjamin, "Surrealism: The Last Snapshot of the European Intelligentsia," in his *Reflections: Essays, Aphorisms, Autobiographical Writings*, ed. Peter Demetz, trans. Edmund Jephcott (New York: Schocken, 1986), pp. 177–92.

66. Theodor W. Adorno, "Fortschritt," in *Stichworte. Kritische Modelle 2* (Frankfurt am Main: Suhrkamp, 1970), p. 49; translated as "Progress," trans. Eric Krakauer, in *Benjamin: Philosophy, Aesthetics, History*, ed. Gary Smith (Chicago: University of Chicago Press, 1989), p. 100.

67. Adorno, *Aesthetic Theory*, pp. 83–84.

68. Ibid., p. 118.

69. Ibid., p. 331.

70. Walter Benjamin, "Franz Kafka: Zur zehnten Wiederkehr seines Todestages," in *Gesammelte Schriften*, vol. 2, pt. 2, p. 432; translated as "Franz Kafka: On the Tenth Anniversary of His Death," in *Illuminations*, p. 134.

71. For another example of Adorno's theoretical interest in gesture and his acute powers of observation and insight, see his description of the bearing (*Haltung*) and gestures (*Gesten*) of the smoker in the unpublished typescript (pp. 11–13) of his work on Richard Wagner: "The gesture of smoking is rather the opposite of that involved in listening to a concert: for it is directed against the aura of the work of art, and it blows smoke in the face of sound. The gesture of smoking indicates a certain turning away from the thing in question, or at least from its power to enchant: the person who smokes is experiencing himself. At the same time, smoking can also serve to concentrate attention." Quoted in *Theodor W. Adorno and Walter Benjamin: The Complete Correspondence 1928–1940*, ed. Henri Lonitz, trans. Nicholas Walker (Cambridge, Mass.: Belknap Press of Harvard University Press, 1999), p. 238.

72. See Adorno's intensive meditation on gestures in "Über Tradition," pp. 310–20. Here he gives thought to the gestures involved in the handing down and the receiving of tradition: gestures that, even as they take part in this "handwerkliche Überlieferung," can only, inevitably, betray it. For a fine discussion of Adorno's theoretical interest in gestures—gestures such as the hand kiss, the handshake, the farewell—see Eva Geulen, "Theodor Adorno on Tradition," in Max Pensky, ed., *The Actuality of Adorno: Critical Essays on Adorno and the Postmodern* (New York: SUNY Press, 1997), pp. 183–92.

73. See *The Correspondence of Walter Benjamin and Gershom Scholem, 1932–1940*, ed. Gershom Scholem, trans. Gary Smith and Andre Lefevere (New York: Schocken, 1989), p. 221. Benjamin's letter bears the date June 12, 1938.

74. Emmanuel Levinas, *Totalité et infini: Essai sur l'extériorité* (The Hague: Nijhoff, 1961), p. 235; translated as *Totality and Infinity: An Essay on Exteriority*, trans. Alphonso Lingis (Pittsburgh: Duquesne University Press, 1969), pp. 257–58.

75. Merleau-Ponty, *Phénoménologie de la perception*, p. 170; *Phenomenology of Perception*, p. 146.

76. Emmanuel Levinas, *Autrement qu'être, ou Au-delà de l'essence* (The

Hague: Nijhoff, 1974), p. 150; translated as *Otherwise Than Being, or Beyond Essence*, trans. Alphonso Lingis (Pittsburgh: Duquesne University Press, 1998), p. 117.

77. Novalis, "Die Enzyklopädie," in *Werke und Briefe*, ed. Alfred Kelletat (Munich: Winkler-Verlag, 1962), §503, p. 509; translated as "The Encyclopedia," in *"Pollen" and Fragments*, trans. Arthur Versluis (Grand Rapids, Mich.: Phanes, 1989), pp. 114–15. According to Hegel, in Jewish law and the daily life it once commanded, "the non-being of man and the littleness of an existence maintained by favor was to be recalled . . . in every human activity." G. W. F. Hegel, *Hegels Theologische Jugendschriften*, ed. Herman Nohl (Tübingen: J. C. A. Mohr, 1907), p. 251; translated as *Early Theological Writings*, trans. T. M. Knox (Philadelphia: University of Pennsylvania Press, 1971), p. 192.

78. Rainer Maria Rilke, *Diaries of a Young Poet*, trans. Edward Snow and Michael Winkler (New York: Norton, 1997), p. 166.

79. Adorno, "Idea of Natural History," p. 120. Translation modified.

80. See Theodor W. Adorno, "Motive nach metaphysischen Denkens," in *Nachmetaphysisches Denken* (Frankfurt am Main: Suhrkamp, 1988), p. 60. Only contact with the extraordinary can remind us of our loss and bring about a progressive transformation of the everyday.

Chapter 7

1. Walter Benjamin, "Anmerkungen zu Seite 691–704, 'Über den Begriff der Geschichte,'" in *Gesammelte Schriften*, ed. Rolf Tiedemann and Hermann Schweppenhäuser (Frankfurt am Main: Suhrkamp, 1972–89), vol. 1, pt. 3, pp. 1243–44.

2. Walter Benjamin, "Baudelaire," Konvolut J 74, 4, in *Gesammelte Schriften*, vol. 5, pt. 1, p. 454; translated as "Baudelaire," in *The Arcades Project*, trans. Howard Eiland and Kevin McLaughlin (Cambridge, Mass.: Harvard University Press, Belknap Press, 1999), p. 359. The Baudelaire draft in question can be found in Charles Baudelaire, *Oeuvres complètes* (Paris: Pléiade, 1976), vol. 1, p. 192.

3. Walter Benjamin, "Chinawaren," in *Einbahnstraße*, in *Gesammelte Schriften*, vol. 4, pt. 1, p. 89; translated as "Chinese Curios," in *One-Way Street*, in Walter Benjamin, *Reflections: Essays, Aphorisms, Autobiographical Writings*, ed. Peter Demetz, trans. Edmund Jephcott (New York: Schocken, 1986), p. 65.

4. Walter Benjamin's letter to Gershom Scholem, June 12, 1938, in *The Correspondence of Walter Benjamin and Gershom Scholem, 1932–1940*, ed. Gershom Scholem, trans. Gary Smith and Andre Lefevere (New York: Schocken, 1989), p. 221.

5. Theodor W. Adorno, "Einleitung," in Walter Benjamin, *Schriften*, ed.

Theodor W. Adorno and Gretel Adorno (Frankfurt am Main: Suhrkamp, 1955), vol. 1, p. xxiv.

6. Gershom Scholem, *Über Walter Benjamin* (Frankfurt am Main: Suhrkamp, 1975), pp. 31–34; and Gershom Scholem, *Die Geschichte einer Freundschaft* (Frankfurt am Main: Suhrkamp, 1975), p. 47.

7. Gershom Scholem, "Interview mit Lisa Fittko," in Ingrid Scheurmann and Konrad Scheurmann, eds., *Für Walter Benjamin* (Frankfurt am Main: Suhrkamp, 1992), p. 145.

8. Pierre Missac, *Walter Benjamin's Passages*, trans. Shierry Webber Nicholsen (Cambridge, Mass.: MIT Press, 1995), p. 18. Also see Walter Benjamin, "Zum Bilde Prousts," in *Gesammelte Schriften*, vol. 2, pt. 1, p. 321; translated as "The Image of Proust," in *Illuminations*, ed. Hannah Arendt, trans. Harry Zohn (1968; reprint, New York: Schocken, 1969), p. 212: "There has never been anyone else with Proust's ability to show us things; Proust's pointing finger [*weisender Finger*] is unequaled. But there is another gesture [*Geste*]—one of amicable togetherness, in conversation: physical contact [*Berührung*]. To no one is this gesture more alien than to Proust." And see Sigmund Freud's discussion of touch, contact, and contagion in his *Inhibitions, Symptoms and Anxiety*, trans. Alix Strachey (New York: Psychoanalytic Quarterly Press and Norton, 1959), chap. 6.

9. Walter Benjamin, "Wahrnehmung und Leib," a fragment in "Zur Moral und Anthropologie," in *Gesammelte Schriften*, vol. 6, p. 67. Regarding the "measure of the messianic constellation," see Irving Wohlfarth, "The Measure of the Possible, the Weight of the Real, and the Heat of the Moment: Benjamin's Actuality Today," *New Formations*, 20 (Summer 1993): 16–17. According to Wohlfarth, Benjamin always recognized that even gestures appropriated by the most threatening features of capitalist technology can be seen to have a *revolutionary function*, in the sense of "a purely preventive measure, intended to avert the worst."

10. See Walter Benjamin, "Der Sürrealismus: Die letzte Momentaufnahme der europäischen Intelligenz," in *Gesammelte Schriften*, vol. 2, pt. 1, pp. 307–10; translated as "Surrealism: The Last Snapshot of the European Intelligentsia," in *Reflections*, p. 192. Also see Benjamin's *Einbahnstraße*, in *Gesammelte Schriften*, vol. 4, pt. 1, p. 148; and his "Anmerkungen," in *Gesammelte Schriften*, vol. 2, pt. 3, p. 1041, on the question of a "new body": "The collectivity [*das Kollektivum*] too," he says in this latter text-fragment, "has a body." And it is this "embodied collectivity [*leibliche Kollectivum*]," and not some merely "abstract material," which must be the basis of a true dialectical materialism.

11. Walter Benjamin, "Karl Kraus," in *Gesammelte Schriften*, vol. 2, pt. 1, p. 364; translated as "Karl Kraus," in *Reflections*, p. 270.

12. See Walter Benjamin, "Über das mimetische Vermögen," in *Gesammelte*

Schriften, vol. 2 pt. 1, pp. 210–13; and in *Schriften,* vol. 1, pp. 507–10; translated as "On the Mimetic Faculty," in *Reflections,* pp. 332–36.

13. Walter Benjamin, "Erkenntnistheoretisches, Theorie des Fortschritts," Konvolut N 9a, 3, in *Gesammelte Schriften,* vol. 5, pt. 1, p. 592; translated as "Re: Theory of Knowledge, Theory of Progress," trans. Leigh Hafrey and Richard Sieburth, in *Benjamin: Philosophy, Aesthetics, History,* ed. Gary Smith (Chicago: University of Chicago Press, 1989), p. 64. The German reads: "Zur Rettung gehört der feste, scheinbar brutale Zugriff."

14. W. S. Merwin, *The Miner's Pale Children* (New York: Atheneum, 1976), p. 124.

15. Walter Benjamin, "Franz Kafka: Zur zehnten Wiederkehr seines Todestages," in *Schriften,* vol. 2, pp. 207–8; translated as "Franz Kafka: On the Tenth Anniversary of His Death," in *Illuminations,* p. 121.

16. Benjamin, "Baudelaire," Konvolut J 75, 2, in *Gesammelte Schriften,* vol. 5, pt. 1, pp. 455–56; and in *Arcades Project,* p. 361.

17. Walter Benjamin, "Die Bedeutung der Zeit in der moralischen Welt," in *Gesammelte Schriften,* vol. 6, frag. 71, pp. 97–98; translated as "The Meaning of Time in the Moral Universe," trans. Rodney Livingstone, in *Walter Benjamin: Selected Writings,* ed. Marcus Bullock, Michael W. Jennings, et al. (Cambridge, Mass.: Belknap Press of Harvard University Press, 1996–2003), vol. 1, *1913–1926,* pp. 286–87.

18. Benjamin, *Einbahnstraße,* in *Schriften,* vol. 1, p. 576; *One-Way Street,* p. 90. One might profitably consider this remark about right and left hands in light of Maurice Merleau-Ponty's discussion, in *The Visible and the Invisible,* of the experience we have when one of our hands is touching the other hand.

19. Walter Benjamin, "Berliner Chronik," in *Gesammelte Schriften,* vol. 6, p. 508; translated as "A Berlin Chronicle," in *Reflections,* p. 49.

20. Walter Benjamin, "Kommentare zu Gedichten von Brecht," in *Schriften,* vol. 2, p. 357.

21. Walter Benjamin, "Christoph Martin Wieland," in *Gesammelte Schriften,* vol. 2, pt. 1, p. 399.

22. Benjamin, "Baudelaire," Konvolut J 11a, 4, in *Gesammelte Schriften,* vol. 5, pt. 1, p. 322; and in *Arcades Project,* p. 248. See Eugène Marsan, *Les Cannes de M. Paul Bourget et le bon choix de Philinte* (Paris, 1923), pp. 239–40. Judging by the notes he wrote for the *Arcades Project* study of Baudelaire, Benjamin seems to have taken more than a passing interest in eyewitness descriptions of Baudelaire's gestures, thinking of them as a dialectical measure for interpreting the historical "decline" of gesture.

23. Walter Benjamin, "Paris, die Hauptstadt des XIX. Jahrhunderts. Anmerkungen zu Seite 45–59," in *Gesammelte Schriften,* vol. 5, pt. 2, p. 1216; translated as "Materials for the Exposé of 1935," in *Arcades Project,* §8, p. 908.

24. Karl Marx, *Capital*, in *Karl Marx: Selected Writings*, ed. David MacLellan, trans. Ewald Osers (New York: Oxford University Press, 1977), p. 429.

25. See Benjamin, *Gesammelte Schriften*, vol. 5, pt. 2, p. 1267.

26. Walter Benjamin, "Diese Flächen Sind zu Vermieten," in *Gesammelte Schriften*, vol. 4, pt. 1, pp. 131–32. Also see Benjamin, *Einbahnstraße*, in *Schriften*, vol. 1, p. 565; *One-Way Street*, p. 86.

27. Walter Benjamin, "Über einige Motive bei Baudelaire," in *Gesammelte Schriften*, vol. 1, pt. 2, p. 646; translated as "On Some Motifs in Baudelaire," in *Illuminations*, p. 188. On the aura, also see Benjamin, "Baudelaire," Konvolut J 47, 6, in *Gesammelte Schriften*, vol. 5, pt. 1, p. 396 : "Hierzu meine Definition der Aura als der Ferne des im Angeblickten erwachenden Blicks."

28. Benjamin, "Über einige Motive bei Baudelaire," in *Gesammelte Schriften*, vol. 1, pt. 2, p. 646; "On Some Motifs in Baudelaire," p. 188.

29. Benjamin, "Baudelaire," Konvolut J 80, 2, and J 80a, 1, in *Gesammelte Schriften*, vol. 5, pt. 1, p. 466; and in *Arcades Project*, p. 369.

30. Walter Benjamin, "Paris, die Hauptstadt des XIX. Jahrhunderts," in *Gesammelte Schriften*, vol. 5, pt. 1, p. 68.

31. Walter Benjamin, "Zwei Gedichte von Friedrich Hölderlin," in *Schriften*, vol. 2, pp. 375–400; translated as "Two Poems by Friedrich Hölderlin," trans. Stanley Corngold, in *Benjamin: Selected Writings*, vol. 1, pp. 18–36.

32. Walter Benjamin, "Kaiserpanorama," in *Einbahnstraße*, in *Gesammelte Schriften*, vol. 4, pt. 1, p. 99; translated as "Imperial Panorama," in *One-Way Street*, pp. 74–75.

33. Benjamin, "Baudelaire," Konvolut J 83a, 2, in *Gesammelte Schriften*, vol. 5, pt. 1, p. 472; and in *Arcades Project*, p. 373.

34. Benjamin, "Über einige Motive bei Baudelaire," in *Gesammelte Schriften*, vol. 1, pt. 2, p. 630; "On Some Motifs in Baudelaire," pp. 175–77.

35. Ibid.

36. Ibid.

37. Benjamin, "Baudelaire," Konvolut J 75, 2, in *Gesammelte Schriften*, vol. 5, pt. 1, p. 456; and in *Arcades Project*, p. 361.

38. Ibid., Konvolut J 74, 4, p. 454 in the German; p. 359 in the English.

39. Walter Benjamin, "Der Erzähler," in *Gesammelte Schriften*, vol. 2, pt. 2, pp. 463–64; translated as "The Storyteller," in *Illuminations*, p. 108.

40. Benjamin, "Über einige Motive bei Baudelaire," in *Schriften*, vol. 1, pp. 459–63; "On Some Motifs in Baudelaire," pp. 186–90. The German reads: "so entspricht die Aura am Gegenstand einer Anschauung eben der Erfahrung, die sich an einem Gegenstand des Gebrauchs als Übung absetzt." The English translation here is not exact or literal, though it is, I think, entirely faithful to the meaning.

41. Ibid.

42. Walter Benjamin, "Das Kunstwerk im Zeitalter seiner technischen Reproduzierbarkeit," in *Schriften*, vol. 1, pp. 372–73; translated as "The Work of Art in the Age of Mechanical Reproduction," in *Illuminations*, pp. 222–23.

43. Ibid.

44. Ibid.

45. Walter Benjamin, "Kleine Geschichte der Photographie," in *Gesammelte Schriften*, vol. 2, pt. 1, p. 378; translated as "A Small History of Photography," in *"One-Way Street" and Other Writings* (London: Verso, 1985), pp. 240–57.

46. Walter Benjamin, "Spur und Aura," a note in "Der Flaneur," Konvolut M 16a, 4, in *Das Passagenwerk*, in *Gesammelte Schriften*, vol. 5, pt. 1, p. 560; translated as "Trace and Aura," in "The Flâneur," in *Arcades Project*, p. 447.

47. Benjamin, "Das Kunstwerk im Zeitalter seiner technischen Reproduzierbarkeit," p. 373; "The Work of Art in the Age of Mechanical Reproduction," p. 223.

48. Ibid.

49. Ibid.

50. Rainer Maria Rilke, "Jugend-Bildnis meines Vaters," in "Neue Gedichte," in *Gesammelte Gedichte* (Frankfurt am Main: Insel-Verlag, 1962), p. 278: "Du schnell vergehendes Daguerrotyp / in meinen langsamer vergehenden Händen."

51. Benjamin, "Handschuhe," in *Einbahnstraße*, in *Schriften*, vol. 1, p. 521; "Gloves," in *One-Way Street*, p. 66.

52. Benjamin, "Karl Kraus," in *Gesammelte Schriften*, vol. 2, pt. 1, p. 339; and in *Reflections*, p. 244.

53. Theodor W. Adorno, *Minima Moralia: Reflexionen aus dem beschädigten Leben*, in *Gesammelte Schriften*, vol. 4 (Frankfurt am Main: Suhrkamp, 1980), p. 281; translated as *Minima Moralia: Reflections from Damaged Life*, trans. E. F. N. Jephcott (London: Verso, New Left Books, 1984), p. 247.

54. I want to take this opportunity to express my gratitude to Jürgen and Ute Habermas for their research and reflections concerning the etymology of the word *Gegenwart*. Their enthusiasm for the philological research my questioning put before them set in motion thoughts I might otherwise not have pursued.

55. See Walter Benjamin, *Ursprung des deutschen Trauerspiels*, in *Gesammelte Schriften*, vol. 1, pp. 209, 214, 215; translated as *The Origin of German Tragic Drama*, trans. John Osborne (London: Verso, New Left Books, 1998), pp. 29, 34, 35.

56. See two books by Reinhart Koselleck: *Futures Past: On the Semantics of Historical Time* (Cambridge, Mass.: MIT Press, 1985) and *Critique and Crisis: Enlightenment and the Pathogenesis of Modern Society* (Cambridge, Mass.: MIT Press, 1988). These are works of extraordinary critical insight, conceptual imagination, and analytical depth, profoundly rich and provocative.

57. Walter Benjamin, "Outline of the Psychophysical Problem," in *Benjamin: Selected Writings*, vol. 1, pp. 393–96.

58. Benjamin, *Gesammelte Schriften*, vol. 7, p. 360.

59. Walter Benjamin, "Der Sammler," Konvolut H 2, 5, in *Gesammelte Schriften*, vol. 5, pt. 1, p. 274; translated as "The Collector," in *Arcades Project*, pp. 206–7. Also see Konvolut H 4, 1; H 4a, 1; and H 5, 1.

60. Ibid., Konvolut H 2, 7; H 2a, 1; pp. 274–75 in the German; p. 207 in the English.

61. Ibid., p. 278 in the German; p. 210 in the English.

62. Ibid., p. 278–80 in the German; p. 211 in the English. See Irving Wohlfarth's important essay "Measure of the Possible, the Weight of the Real, and the Heat of the Moment," pp. 1–20.

63. Benjamin, *Gesammelte Schriften*, vol. 1, pt. 3, p. 1233. And see Benjamin, "Über einige Motive bei Baudelaire," in *Gesammelte Schriften*, vol. 1, pt. 2, pp. 607–53; "On Some Motifs in Baudelaire," pp. 155–200.

64. Friedrich Schiller, *On the Aesthetic Education of Man: In a Series of Letters*, trans. Reginald Snell (New York: Ungar, 1965), p. 126.

65. Benjamin, "Der Sammler," pp. 279–80; "The Collector," p. 211.

66. Benjamin, "Baudelaire," Konvolut J 77a, 8, in *Gesammelte Schriften*, vol. 5, pt. 1, pp. 461–62; and in *Arcades Project*, p. 365.

67. Ibid.

68. Marx, *Capital*, quoted ibid., Konvolut J 78, 4, p. 462 in the German; pp. 365–66 in the English.

69. Ibid.

70. Ibid.

71. Siegfried Kracauer, "Die Wartenden," in *Das Ornament der Masse: Essays* (Frankfurt am Main: Suhrkamp, 1963), pp. 106–19; translated as "Those Who Wait," in *The Mass Ornament: Weimar Essays*, trans. Thomas Y. Levin (Cambridge, Mass.: Harvard University Press, 1995), pp. 128–40.

72. Immanuel Kant, "The Contest of Faculties," in *Kant's Political Writings*, ed. Hans Reiss, trans. H. B. Nisbet (Cambridge, Mass.: Cambridge University Press, 1977), pp. 176–90.

73. Kracauer, "Die Wartenden," p. 114; "Those Who Wait," p. 136.

74. Benjamin, "Der Sürrealismus," p. 308; "Surrealism," p. 190.

75. Kracauer, "Die Wartenden," p. 107; "Those Who Wait," p. 130: without mentioning Kafka by name, Kracauer uses Kafka's image.

76. Ibid., pp. 116–17 in the German; pp. 138–39 in the English.

77. See Benjamin, "Erkenntnistheoretisches, Theorie des Fortschritts," Konvolut N, in *Gesammelte Schriften*, vol. 5, pt. 1, pp. 570–611; "Re: Theory of Knowledge, Theory of Progress," in *Benjamin: Philosophy, Aesthetics, History*,

p. 43–83. Also see Walter Benjamin, "Geschichtsphilosophische Theses," in *Schriften*, vol. 1, pp. 494–506; translated as "Theses on the Philosophy of History," in *Illuminations*, pp. 253–64.

78. Benjamin, "Erkenntnistheoretisches, Theorie des Fortschritts," Konvolut N, in *Gesammelte Schriften*, vol. 5, pt. 1, pp. 570–611; "Re: Theory of Knowledge, Theory of Progress," in *Benjamin: Philosophy, Aesthetics, History*, p. 43–83. Concerning the extraordinary time of *Erkennbarkeit*, see also Heidegger's appropriation of this issue in Martin Heidegger, *Sein und Zeit*, 5th ed. (Halle: Niemeyer, 1941), div. 2, chap. 5, pp. 391–92; translated from the 7th ed. as *Being and Time*, trans. John Macquarrie and Edward Robinson (New York: Harper & Row, 1962), p. 444. He speaks, there, of a past become unrecognizable, "unkenntlich."

79. Whereas for Heidegger in *Being and Time* it was a question of retrieving the greatness in the cultural tradition of a bygone Germany, for Benjamin it was a question of retrieving, for the achievement of social justice, certain revolutionary energies—a "weak messianic power"—preserved in anamnestic images that repeat the prophetic promise and illuminate the critical historical task, if only in a flash of recognizability that reveals what needs to be destroyed.

80. Walter Benjamin, "Moscau," in *Gesammelte Schriften*, vol. 4, pt. 1, p. 317; translated as "Moscow," in *Reflections*, pp. 97ff.

81. Benjamin, *Das Passagenwerk*, in *Gesammelte Schriften*, vol. 5, p. 1001.

82. Kracauer, "Die Wartenden," pp. 118–19; "Those Who Wait," p. 140.

83. Benjamin, "Über einige Motive bei Baudelaire," in *Gesammelte Schriften*, vol. 1, pt. 2, p. 643; "On Some Motifs in Baudelaire," p. 185.

84. Benjamin, "Geschichtsphilosophische Thesen," p. 506; "Theses on the Philosophy of History," p. 263.

85. Benjamin, *Schriften*, vol. 2, p. 133.

86. Benjamin, *Gesammelte Schriften*, vol. 1, pt. 3, pp. 1233–34.

87. Benjamin, "Baudelaire," Konvolut J 53, 3, in *Gesammelte Schriften*, vol. 5, pt. 1, p. 408; and in *Arcades Project*, p. 324.

88. Jacques Derrida, *Le toucher: Jean-Luc Nancy* (Paris: Galilée, 2000), p. 333.

89. Benjamin, "Baudelaire," Konvolut J 79a, 1, in *Gesammelte Schriften*, vol. 5, pt. 1, p. 465; and in *Arcades Project*, p. 367.

90. Ibid., Konvolut J 80, 2, and J 80a, 1, p. 466 in the German; pp. 368–69 in the English.

91. Walter Benjamin, "Gespräche mit Brecht," in *Versuche über Brecht* (Frankfurt am Main: Suhrkamp, 1966), p. 124; also see *Gesammelte Schriften*, vol. 6, p. 529.

92. F. W. J von Schelling, *The Philosophy of Art*, ed. and trans. Douglas W. Stott (Minneapolis: University of Minnesota Press, 1989), §79, p. 111.

93. Ibid.

94. Friedrich Nietzsche, *Gay Science*, trans. Walter Kaufmann (New York: Vintage, 1974), aphorism 84.

95. Benjamin, "The Flâneur," Konvolut M 1a, 1, *Arcades Project*, p. 418.

96. Carlo Ginzburg, *Occhiacci di legno: Nove riflessioni sulla distanza* (Milan: Feltrinelli, 1998), p. 173, where the historian comments on Yosef Yerushalmi, *Zakhor: Jewish History and Jewish Memory*.

97. Benjamin, *Gesammelte Schriften*, vol. 6, frag. 69, p. 95; and frag. 76, p. 104.

98. Wallace Stevens, "Things of August," in *The Palm at the End of the Mind* (New York: Knopf, 1971), p. 357.

99. For Kafka's remark, see *Franz Kafka: Parables and Paradoxes*, ed. Nahum Glatzer, trans. Clement Greenberg, bilingual edition (New York: Schocken, 1975), pp. 80–81. Thus: "The Messiah will come only when no longer necessary." I take this to refer to the *Nachträglichkeit* involved in our recognition of the Messiah's presence: He arrives on day D; but we do not realize he has come until the next day, D + n. His work of transforming us *takes time*. Thus, he will have come only when no longer needed; because, if we are able to recognize him, able to recognize his presence among us, that means we have already been deeply affected, deeply transformed. But if we have been altered, we no longer need him. What does his coming "at the right time" mean then?

100. Benjamin, "Franz Kafka: Zur zehnten Wiederkehr seines Todestages," in *Gesammelte Schriften*, vol. 2, pt. 2, p. 432; "Franz Kafka: On the Tenth Anniversary of His Death," in *Benjamin: Selected Writings*, vol. 2, *1927–1934*, p. 811. Benjamin writes that, regarding the coming of the Messiah, a great rabbi is reported to have said, "daß er [*der Messias*] nicht mit Gewalt die Welt verändern wolle, sondern nur um ein Geringes sie zurechtstellen werde."

101. Joseph Freiherr von Eichendorff, "Wünschelrute," in the "Sängerleben" series of poems, in *Neue Gesamtausgabe der Werke und Schriften*, ed. Gerhard Baumann and Siegfried Grosse (Stuttgart: Cotta'sche Buchhandlung, 1957), vol. 1, p. 112. Also see vol. 4, p. 243, "Die Neuere Romantik," where the poet urges us to hold in memory the time of romanticism, "eine Feenzeit, da das wunderbare Lied, das in allen Dingen gebunden schläft, zu singen anhob, da die Waldeinsamkeit das uralte Märchen der Natur wiedererzählte, von verfallenen Burgen und Kirchen die Glocken wie von selber anschlugen, und die Wipfel sich rauschend neigten."

102. G. W. F. Hegel, *The Phenomenology of Spirit*, trans. A. V. Miller (New York: Oxford, 1977), pp. 185–90.

103. Benjamin, *Einbahnstraße*, in *Schriften*, vol. 1, p. 538; *One-Way Street*, p. 81.

104. Hegel, *Phenomenology of Spirit*, p. 189.

105. Benjamin, *Einbahnstraße*, in *Schriften*, vol. 1, p. 536; *One-Way Street*, pp. 79–80. And see Theodor W. Adorno, "Benjamin the Letter Writer," in *Notes to Literature*, trans. Shierry Weber Nicholsen, vol. 2 (New York: Columbia University Press, 1992), pp. 233–39. Adorno comments, "The letter was so congenial to him [Benjamin] because from the outset it encourages a mediated, objectified immediacy. Writing letters creates a fiction of life within the medium of the frozen word. In a letter one can disavow one's isolation and nevertheless remain separate and at a distance." Noting that the letter form was already becoming anachronistic in Benjamin's lifetime, Adorno says: "It is significant that whenever possible he wrote his letters by hand, at a time when the typewriter had long been dominant; in the same way, the physical act of writing brought him pleasure— he liked to make excerpts and fair copies—just as mechanical aides repelled him." Heidegger seems to have had a very similar preference for writing by hand—and a similar objection to using the typewriter. Suggesting that Benjamin's attitude toward letter writing was that of the allegorist, Adorno remarks, "for him, the letter represented the wedding of something in the process of disappearing and the utopia of its restoration." There is no evidence, however, that Heidegger shared this allegorical relation to writing.

106. Benjamin, *Einbahnstraße*, in *Schriften*, vol. 1, p. 536; *One-Way Street*, pp. 79–80.

107. Ibid.

108. Ibid., p. 574 in the German; pp. 88–90 in the English.

109. Ibid., pp. 575 in the German; p. 90 in the English.

110. Natalia Ginzburg, *È difficile parlare di sé: Conversazione a più voci condotta da Marino Sinibaldi, a cura di Cesare Garboli e Lisa Ginzburg* (Torino: Einaudi, 1999), pp. 234–35.

111. Benjamin, *Ursprung des deutschen Trauerspiels*, in *Schriften*, vol. 1, pp. 150–51; *Origin of German Tragic Drama*, pp. 35–36.

112. Walter Benjamin, "Über Schein," in *Gesammelte Schriften*, vol. 1, pt. 3, p. 832.

113. Benjamin, *Gesammelte Schriften*, vol. 3, pp. 137–38. Also see *Benjamin: Selected Writings*, vol. 2, p. 285, for a note in which Benjamin discusses the writing hand of a child.

114. Benjamin, *Einbahnstraße*, in *Schriften*, vol. 1, p. 520; *One-Way Street*, p. 66. On the significance of the phrase "I prefer not to" in "Bartleby the Scrivener," a story about copywork as an act of "pure writing," also see Maurice Blanchot, *L'écriture du désastre* (Paris: Gallimard, 1980), p. 219; translated as *The Writing of Disaster*, trans. Ann Smock (Lincoln: University of Nebraska Press, 1986), p. 145.

115. Benjamin, "On the Mimetic Faculty," pp. 335–36.

116. See Johann Gottfried von Herder, "Die Bildung einer Sprache," in *Frühe*

Schriften 1764–1772, ed. Ulrich Gaier, in *Werke*, vol. 1 (Frankfurt am Main: Deutscher Klassiker, 1985), pp. 613–14. Herder noticed that communication had undergone a certain loss of gesture because, in the course of history, language had become more abstract and idealized, less dependent on bodily expressiveness.

117. Benjamin, *Gesammelte Schriften*, vol. 6, p. 127.

118. Ibid., vol. 4, p. 613.

119. Benjamin, "Karl Kraus," in *Gesammelte Schriften*, vol. 2, pt. 1, p. 347; and in *Reflections*, p. 252.

120. Ibid.

121. Ibid.

122. Ibid., p. 365 in the German; p. 271 in the English.

123. Ibid.

124. Ibid., p. 363 in the German; p. 269 in the English. Translation modified.

125. Walter Benjamin, "Die Aufgabe des Übersetzers," in *Gesammelte Schriften*, vol. 4, pt. 1, p. 10; translated as "The Task of the Translator," in *Illuminations*, p. 70.

126. Benjamin, *Das Passagenwerk*, in *Gesammelte Schriften*, vol. 5, pt. 1, p. 589. Hebrew grammar distinguishes between completed and uncompleted time, which traverses or crosses the three dimensions (past, present, future). Consequently, a verb conjugated in the past could in fact indicate a future action if preceded by the letter *vav* in a usage called "conversion" or "inversion," syntactically showing the past as in the future and the future as in the past. In this way the grammar of time can unfold a sense of the messianic.

127. Ralph Waldo Emerson, "Quotation and Originality," in *The Complete Works of Ralph Waldo Emerson*, ed. Edward Waldo Emerson (Boston: Houghton Mifflin, 1903–4), vol. 8, pp. 178–80, 194. The essay may also be found in *The Portable Emerson* ed. Mark Van Doren (New York: Viking, 1975), pp. 285–86 and 296. Also see *Emerson in His Journals*, ed. Joel Porte (Cambridge, Mass.: Harvard University Press, 1982), pp. 546–47, for a journal entry on quotation and originality.

128. Walter Benjamin, "Über den Begriff der Geschichte," in *Gesammelte Schriften*, vol. 1, pt. 2, p. 695; translated as "Theses on the Philosophy of History," in *Illuminations*, p. 255. And see *Gesammelte Schriften*, vol. 1, p. 571: "Quotations in my work are like robbers by the roadside who make an armed attack and relieve an idler of his convictions."

129. Benjamin, Konvolut N7, 7, in *Das Passagenwerk*, in *Gesammelte Schriften*, vol. 5, pt. 1, p. 187.

130. Benjamin, "Über den Begriff der Geschichte," pp. 693–94; "Theses on the Philosophy of History," p. 254.

131. Ibid. Benjamin's phrase is "schwachen messianische Kraft." Kant's phrase is "schwachen Strahl der Hoffnung" ("faint ray of hope"); see Immanuel Kant,

The Critique of Judgment, trans. Werner Pluhar (Indianapolis: Hackett, 1987), §80, p. 304.

132. Benjamin, "Über den Begriff der Geschichte," pp. 693–94; "Theses on the Philosophy of History," p. 254.

133. Ibid., pp. 694 and 703 in German; pp. 254 and 263 in the English.

134. Walter Benjamin, "Was ist das epische Theater?," in *Gesammelte Schriften*, vol. 2, pt. 2, p. 536; translated as "What Is Epic Theater?," in *Illuminations*, p. 151.

135. Giorgio Agamben, *Potentialities: Collected Essays in Philosophy*, ed. and trans. Daniel Heller-Roazen (Stanford, Calif.: Stanford University Press, 1999), p. 156. And see David Michael Levin, "The Living Body of Tradition," pp. 184–89 in *The Body's Recollection of Being* (London: Routledge & Kegan Paul, 1985). The latter is the first volume of my trilogy on the emerging body of understanding, wherein I discuss the significance of Benjamin's practice of writing as a spiritual discipline binding the gestures of the hand in relation to the question of the transmissibility of religious traditions. I argue there that the mediaeval practice of copying by hand sacred texts written by hand retraces and reproduces the gesture that originally produced the text as well as the cognitive meaning and inscribes in the very flesh of the copyist the rhythm, timing, and melody of the original gesture—inscribes, indeed, the emotional quality and moral character motivating that original gesture. Thus, both the cognitive meaning and the normative meaning are literally handed down and performatively embodied, transmitted both as cognitive meaning and as a bodily-felt normative sense.

136. Benjamin, *Ursprung des deutschen Trauerspiels*, in *Schriften*, vol. 1, pp. 161–62, or *Gesammelte Schriften*, vol. 1, pt. 1, p. 226; *Origin of German Tragic Drama*, p. 45. Translation modified.

137. Agamben, *Potentialities*, p. 155.

138. See Giorgio Agamben, "Bartleby, or On Contingency," pp. 243–71, another remarkable essay in his *Potentialities*.

139. Walter Benjamin, "Das dialektische Bild," in *Gesammelte Schriften*, vol. 1, pt. 3, p. 1238. Benjamin is quoting Hugo von Hofmansthal: "Was nie geschrieben wurde, lesen." Also see Benjamin's frags. 16 and 17, in *Gesammelte Schriften*, vol. 6, p. 32: "Wahrnehmung ist Lesen."

140. See Benjamin, *Gesammelte Schriften*, vol. 6, p. 32, frags. 16 and 17; and *Gesammelte Schriften*, vol. 1, pt. 3, p. 1238

141. See Derrida, *Le toucher*, p. 138, for an indication of his critique of "haptic intuitionism"—touching (on) meaning—in the history of philosophy.

142. See Benjamin's quotation from volume 1 of Proust's "Du côté de chez Swann," in Benjamin, "Baudelaire," Konvolut J 90, 1, in *Gesammelte Schriften*, vol. 5, pt. 1, p. 484; and in *Arcades Project*, p. 383: "Proust on the allegories by Giotto in Santa Maria dell'Arena: 'In later years, I understood that the arresting

strangeness . . . of these frescoes lay in the great part played in each of them by its symbols, while the fact that these were depicted not as symbols (for the thought symbolized was nowhere expressed) but as real things, *actually felt or materially handled*, added something more precise and more literal to their meaning, something more concrete and striking to the lesson they imparted.'" My italics are intended to emphasize that Benjamin's references to the allegorical handling of fragments should not be read as nothing but figures of speech, although it is nevertheless true that the references are themselves, in a certain crucial sense, allegorical.

143. For a useful discussion of "origin" and "originality," one to which I am obviously greatly indebted, see Giorgio Agamben, *L'uomo senza contenuto* (Milan: Quodlibet, 1994); translated as *The Man Without Content*, trans. Georgia Albert (Stanford, Calif.: Stanford University Press, 1999), chaps. 7 and 10.

144. See Walter Benjamin, "Paul Scheerbart: Lesabendio," in *Gesammelte Schriften*, vol. 2, pt. 2, pp. 619 –20: "Von dem Größeren—der Erfüllung der Utopie—kann man nicht sprechen—nur zeugen." ("About the realization of utopia one cannot, in a certain sense, speak; one can only work to bring it about.")

145. *Correspondence of Benjamin and Scholem, 1932–1940*, p. 225.

146. Agamben, *Man Without Content*, p. 107.

147. Ibid., p. 108.

148. Ibid., p. 107.

149. Herbert Marcuse, *Eros and Civilization: A Philosophical Inquiry into Freud* (New York: Vintage, 1962), p. 92.

150. Ibid., p. 91.

151. Agamben, *Man Without Content*, p. 114.

152. Hegel, *Phenomenology of Spirit*, pp. 18–19. Also see Hegel's §427 of the Zusätze, *Philosophy of Mind*, part 3 of *The Encyclopedia of Philosophical Sciences* (1830), trans. William Wallace (London: Oxford University Press, 1971), pp. 168 –69. Concerned here with the satisfaction of desire in its moment of immediacy, he observes that, in the process whereby the self-conscious subject takes possession of the object, "the object must perish" in a unity only possible by the "negation of the immediacy." Moreover: "In the destruction of the object by self-consciousness, the former perishes by the power of its own inner Notion, which, just because it is inner, seems to come from outside. The object is thus made explicitly subjective. But by this annulment of the object, the subject . . . removes its own defect, its diremption." This approximates a description of Benjamin's practice in the handling of the objects he collects for critique and revelation.

153. Friedrich Nietzsche, *Thus Spoke Zarathustra*, trans. Walter Kaufmann (New York: Penguin, 1978), pp. 138–39. Nietzsche goes on to say: "To redeem those who lived in the past and to recreate all 'it was' into a 'thus I willed it'—

that alone should I call redemption." Benjamin could agree with this remark up to the "thus I willed it." At that point, his interpretation of "redemption" would be radically different. Concerning the diremptions that damage the body, also see Friedrich Schlegel, *Philosophical Fragments*, trans. Peter Firchow (Minneapolis: University of Minnesota Press, 1991), p. 66. Fragment 330 says: "Many people have spirit or feeling or imagination. But because singly these qualities can only manifest themselves as fleeting, airy shapes, nature has taken care to bond them chemically to some common earthly matter. To discover this bond is the unremitting task of those who have the greatest capacity for sympathy, but it requires a great deal of practice in intellectual chemistry as well. The man who could discover an infallible reagent for every beautiful quality in human nature would reveal to us a new world. As in the vision of the prophet, the endless field of broken and dismembered humanity would suddenly spring into life."

154. Benjamin, "Über einige Motive bei Baudelaire," p. 643; "On Some Motifs in Baudelaire," p. 185.

155. Rainer Maria Rilke, *Die Sonnette an Orpheus*, pt. 1, sonnet 16, in *Gesammelte Gedichte*, p. 497; translated as *Sonnets to Orpheus*, trans. M. D. Herter Norton (New York: Norton, 1962), pp. 46–47.

156. Benjamin, *Gesammelte Schriften*, vol. 1, p. 207. And see Walter Benjamin, *Was Heißt Darstellung?*, ed. Christian Hart-Nibbrig (Frankfurt am Main: Suhrkamp, 1994).

157. Benjamin, "Paris, die Hauptstadt des XIX. Jahrhunderts," in *Gesammelte Schriften*, vol. 5, pt. 1, §6, p. 59; translated as "Paris, Capital of the Nineteenth Century," in *Reflections*, §6, p. 162.

158. See Benjamin, *Gesammelte Schriften*, vol. 1, p. 661.

159. See Walter Benjamin, "Der destruktive Charakter," in *Gesammelte Schriften*, vol. 4, pp. 396–98; translated as "The Destructive Character," in *Benjamin: Selected Writings*, vol. 2, pp. 541–42.

160. Benjamin, "Über den Begriff der Geschichte," pp. 701–2; "Theses on the Philosophy of History," p. 262.

161. Walter Benjamin, "Der Begriff der Kunstkritik in der deutschen Romantik," in *Gesammelte Schriften*, vol. 1, pt. 1, p. 60; translated as "The Concept of Criticism in German Romanticism," trans. David Lachterman, Howard Eiland, and Ian Balfour, in *Benjamin: Selected Writings*, vol. 1, p. 183.

162. See Benjamin, *Gesammelte Schriften*, vol. 5, p. 573.

163. See Walter Benjamin, "Über Sprache Uberhaupt und Über die Sprache des Menschens," in *Gesammelte Schriften*, vol. 2, pt. 1, p. 153; translated as "On Language as Such and On the Language of Man," in *Benjamin: Selected Writings*, vol. 1, p. 71.

164. See Samuel Weber, "Criticism Underway: Walter Benjamin's Romantic Concept of Criticism," in Kenneth R. Johnston, ed., *Romantic Revolutions*

(Bloomington: Indiana University Press, 1990). And see Benjamin, *Ursprung des deutschen Trauerspiels*, in *Schriften*, vol. 1, p. 143; p. 29 in John Osborne's 1998 translation, *Origin of German Tragic Drama*: "The value of fragments of thought is all the more decisive the less they are able to gauge [*messen*] their unmediated relation to the underlying Idea, and the brilliance of the presentation depends as much on this measure [*Maße*] as the brilliance of the mosaic does on the quality of the glass paste." Everything depends on the strength of the fragments to resist subordination to, or subsumption under, the Idea—and thereby to increase the articulation of the whole that the Idea represents. In other words, the fragmentation is imposed not from the top down, deductively, as in Kant's determinant judgment, but from the bottom up, as in Kant's reflective judgment. In this way, the contemplative process makes the fragments work dialectically *against* any linear master narrative and ideology.

165. See Benjamin, "Der Begriff der Kunstkritik in der deutschen Romantik," pp. 7–122; "Concept of Criticism in German Romanticism," pp. 116–200. And see the admirably lucid and insightful discussion of these issues by Rodolphe Gasché, in his foreword to Friedrich Schlegel, *Philosophical Fragments*, trans. Peter Firchow (Minneapolis: University of Minnesota Press, 1991), pp. vii–xxxii.

166. Benjamin, *Ursprung des deutschen Trauerspiels*, in *Schriften*, vol. 1, p. 143; *Origin of German Tragic Drama*, p. 29.

167. Theodor W. Adorno and Max Horkheimer, *Dialektik der Aufklärung: Philosophische Fragmente* (Frankfurt am Main: Fischer, 1969), p. 36; translated as *Dialectic of Enlightenment*, trans. John Cumming (New York: Continuum, 1986), p. 36.

168. Frederick Sachs, "The Intimate Sense of Touch," *The Sciences*, 28, no. 1 (Jan./Feb. 1988): 28–34.

169. Ralph Waldo Emerson, "Nature," in *Emerson: Essays and Lectures*, ed. Joel Porte (New York: Library of America, 1983), p. 46.

170. Quoted in *Ancilla to the Pre-Socratic Philosophers*, ed. and trans. Kathleen Freeman (Cambridge, Mass.: Harvard University Press, 1978), p. 40.

171. Benjamin, "Franz Kafka: Zur zehnten Wiederkehr seines Todestages," in *Gesammelte Schriften*, vol. 2, pt. 2, p. 432; "Franz Kafka: On the Tenth Anniversary of his Death," in *Illuminations*, p. 134. Benjamin wrote here, "Even if Kafka did not pray—and this we do not know—he still possessed in the highest degree what Malebranche called 'the natural prayer of the soul': attentiveness [*Aufmerksamkeit*]. And in this attentiveness he included all living creatures, as saints included them in their prayers."

172. Walter Benjamin, "In der Sonne," in *Gesammelte Schriften*, vol. 4, pt. 1, pp. 419–20; translated as "In the Sun," in *Benjamin: Selected Writings*, vol. 2, p. 664.

173. Benjamin, *Gesammelte Schriften*, vol. 4, pt. 1, p. 89.

174. Adorno, *Minima Moralia*, aphorism 5, p. 26 in the German; p. 25 in the English.

175. Friedrich Nietzsche, "Why I Am a Destiny," in *"On the Genealogy of Morals" and "Ecce Homo,"* trans. Walter Kaufmann (New York: Vintage, 1984), section 1.

176. Paul Celan, "Allerseelen," in *Werke: Historisch-kritische Ausgabe*, ed. Beda Allemann, Rolf Bücher, et al. (Frankfurt am Main: Suhrkamp, 1983–), vol. 1, p. 183. In *Origin of German Tragic Drama*, Benjamin writes: "The *Trauerspiel* is in no way characterized by immobility [*Unbeweglichkeit*], nor indeed by slowness of action, but by the irregular rhythm of the constant pauses, the sudden change of direction, and consolidation into new rigidity [*intermittierende Rhythmik eines beständigen Einhaltens, stoßweisen Umschlagens und neuen Erstarrens*]" (*Ursprung des deutschen Trauerspiels*, in *Schriften*, vol. 1, p. 322; *Origin of German Tragic Drama*, p. 197). Benjamin's dialectical rhythms struggle against this rigidity.

177. Benjamin, "Die Bedeutung der Zeit in der moralischen Welt," pp. 97–98; "Meaning of Time in the Moral Universe," pp. 286–87. In the course of a recent return to Hölderlin, I was surprised to discover that Benjamin's fragment bears remarkable similarities to some verses in Hölderlin: "the noble spirit flies, like the eagle / Ahead of the thunderstorm, prophesying / The coming of the gods." See the poet's *Sämtliche Werke*, ed. Friedrich Beißner and Adolf Beck (Stuttgart: Kohlhammer, 1943–85), vol. 4, p. 135.

178. Walter Benjamin, "Theologisch-Politisches Fragment," in *Schriften*, vol. 1, p. 512; translated as "Theologico-Political Fragment," in *Reflections*, p. 313.

179. See Immanuel Kant's use of the term *Scheidekünstler*, in *Critique of Pure Reason*, trans. Norman Kemp Smith (London: Macmillan, 1956), A652–53, B680–81, pp. 538–39.

180. Concerning Benjamin's "favoring" of the left hand, see his *Einbahnstraße*, in *Gesammelte Schriften*, vol. 4, pt. 1, p. 89; *One-Way Street*, p. 65: "These are days when no one should rely unduly on his 'competence.' Strength lies in improvisation. All the decisive blows are struck left-handed."

Chapter 8

1. Martin Heidegger, " . . . Dichterisch wohnet der Mensch . . . ," in *Vorträge und Aufsätze* (Pfullingen: Neske, 1954), p. 198; translated as " . . . Poetically Man Dwells . . . ," in *Poetry, Language, Thought*, trans. Albert Hofstadter (New York: Harper & Row, 1971), p. 223.

2. Johann Gottfried von Herder, *Ideen zur Philosophie der Geschichte der Menschheit*, book 8, sec. 1, in *Sämtliche Werke*, ed. Bernhard Suphan (Berlin: Weidmann, 1877–1913), vol. 13, p. 291. And see his reference to measure in Johann Gottfried von Herder, *Vom Erkennen und Empfinden der menschlichen*

Seele: Bemerkungen und Träume 1778, in *Sämtliche Werke,* vol. 8, p. 200; for a newer edition, see *Werke, Schriften zu Philosophie, Literatur, Kunst und Altertum 1774–1787,* ed. Jürgen Brummack and Martin Bollacher (Frankfurt am Main: Deutscher Klassiker, 1994), vol. 4, p. 361.

3. Rainer Maria Rilke, *Sonnets to Orpheus,* trans. M. D. Herter Norton, bilingual edition (New York: Norton, 1962), pt. 2, sonnet 20, pp. 108–9. Also see Rilke's "Die Sonnette an Orpheus," in *Gesammelte Gedichte* (Frankfurt am Main: Insel-Verlag, 1962), pp. 520–21. The German reads:

> Zwischen den Sternen, wie weit; und doch, um wievieles noch weiter,
> was man am Hiesigen lernt. . . .
> Schicksal, es mißt uns vielleicht mit des Seienden Spanne,
> daß es uns fremd erscheint. . . .
> Alles ist weit—, und nirgends schließt sich der Kreis.

4. Emmanuel Levinas, "Transcendence and Intelligibility," trans. Simon Critchley and Tamra Wright, in *Basic Philosophical Writings,* ed. Robert Bernasconi, Simon Critchley, and Adrian Peperzak (Bloomington: Indiana University Press, 1996), p. 152.

5. Friedrich Hölderlin, "Blödigkeit," in *Sämtliche Werke,* ed. Paul Stapf (Berlin: Tempel-Verlag, 1960), pp. 259–60. The word *Blödigkeit* in this context resists easy translation. It means a certain reserve or self-restraint coming from a deep, awe-stricken reverence for the sublimity of the Holy. It is a "metaphysical" shyness, a "metaphysical" reticence, brought into "*grundstimmender*" *Gesang* by the poet. See Walter Benjamin, "Zwei Gedichte von Friedrich Hölderlin," in *Schriften,* ed. Theodor W. Adorno and Gretel Adorno (Frankfurt am Main: Suhrkamp, 1955), vol. 2, pp. 388, 399.

6. Jacques Derrida, "Geschlecht II: Heidegger's Hand," trans. John P. Leavey, Jr., in *Deconstruction and Philosophy: The Texts of Jacques Derrida,* ed. John Sallis (Chicago: University of Chicago Press, 1987), p. 173.

7. Jacques Derrida, "Given Time: The Time of the King," trans. Peggy Kamuf, *Critical Inquiry,* 18, no. 2 (Winter 1992): 180.

8. Emmanuel Levinas, "Peace and Proximity," in *Basic Philosophical Writings,* p. 169.

9. Martin Heidegger, "Brief über den 'Humanismus,'" in his *Wegmarken,* 2nd ed. (Frankfurt am Main: Klostermann, 1978), p. 353. And see John Llewellyn, "Ontological Responsibility and the Poetics of Nature," *Research in Phenomenology,* 19 (1989): 3–26.

10. Martin Heidegger, "Die Onto-Theo-Logische Verfassung der Metaphysik," in *Identität und Differenz* (Pfullingen: Neske, 1957), p. 65; translated as "The Onto-Theo-Logical Conception of Metaphysics," in *Identity and Difference,* trans. Joan Stambaugh (New York: Harper & Row, 1969), p. 135. With regard to the question of measure, of *Maß* and *das Maß-gebende,* see Heidegger's

chapter "Der Satz der Identität," in *Identität und Differenz*, pp. 13–34. Also, on the question of "Andenken," ontological recollection, preserving what is never past but remains always to come, see Martin Heidegger, *Wegmarken*; translated as *Pathmarks*, trans. William McNeill (Cambridge, Eng.: Cambridge University Press, 1998).

11. Martin Heidegger, *Erläuterungen zu Hölderlins Dichtung*, 2nd ed. (Frankfurt am Main: Klostermann: 1951), pp. 79–80.

12. Friedrich Hölderlin, "Anmerkungen zur *Antigone*," in *Sämtliche Werke*, ed. Stapf (1960), pp. 1061–67. And see Paul Celan, *Gesammelte Werke*, ed. Beda Allemann, Stefan Reichert, and Rolf Bücher (Frankfurt am Main: Suhrkamp, 1983), vol. 1, p. 251. For Heidegger, *Ereignis* is the way that being appropriates us in regard to our historicity, above all our historical relation to being, claiming our capacity to open ourselves to other ways for the being of beings to presence. This requires the resolute openness of *Gelassenheit*. Celan connects the possibility of such an Ereignis to a heartfelt greeting: "Something that can vanish without greeting / Like a heart in transformation / comes" (*Etwas, das gehn kann, grußlos / Wie Herzgewordenes, / kommt*).

13. Theodor W. Adorno, *Notes to Literature*, trans. Shierry Weber Nicholsen, vol. 2 (New York: Columbia University Press, 1992), pp. 234–37.

14. See Henry James, *Letters 1895–1916*, ed. Leon Edel, vol. 4 (Cambridge, Mass.: Belknap Press of Harvard University Press, 1984), pp. 41–95. Beginning in 1897, James, compelled by writer's cramp to resort to a Remington and the services of a typist, apologizes profusely in numerous letters for this abandonment of the hand's personal gesture, communicating his great embarrassment and complaining about the alterations in his style of self-expression imposed by the use of a machine. In a letter to Charles Eliot Norton (December 26, 1898), James connects the use of the typewriter to alterations in manners.

15. Martin Heidegger, *Parmenides*, ed. Manfred Frings, in *Gesamtausgabe*, vol. 54 (Frankfurt am Main: Klostermann, 1982), pp. 118–29; translated as *Parmenides*, trans. André Schuwer and Richard Rojcewicz (Bloomington: Indiana University Press, 1992), pp. 80–87.

16. Derrida, "Geschlecht II," pp. 178–79.

17. See Martin Heidegger, *Sein und Zeit*, 5th ed. (Halle: Niemeyer, 1941), "Einleitung," §6; translated from the 7th ed. as *Being and Time*, trans. John Macquarrie and Edward Robinson (New York: Harper & Row, 1962), Introduction, §6. The page references to the German text that appear in the margin of the English translation correspond to the pages in this German edition.

18. Derrida, "Geschlecht II," p. 180.

19. Martin Heidegger, *Was Heißt Denken?* (Tübingen: Niemeyer, 1954), p. 52; translated as *What Is Called Thinking?*, trans. J. Glenn Gray (New York: Harper

& Row, 1968), p. 15. Hereafter, this work will be cited in the text as *WHD*, followed by the page numbers, first in the German, then in the English.

20. Heidegger, *Parmenides*, pp. 117–18 in the German; p. 80 in the English. Also see §6 of the "Einleitung" to *Sein und Zeit*; Introduction to *Being and Time*, where Heidegger remarks that the ancient Greek philosophers interpreted being without any explicit realization that their conception was committed to thinking of being as parousia, as constantly present, always in the present.

21. See Martin Heidegger, "Die Kehre," in *Die Technik und die Kehre* (Pfullingen: Neske, 1962), pp. 25, 38–39, and 45; translated as "The Turning," in *"The Question Concerning Technology" and Other Essays*, trans. William Lovitt (New York: Harper & Row, 1977), pp. 37 and 47. Also see Martin Heidegger, "Wissenschaft und Besinnung," in *Vorträge und Aufsätze*, p. 64; translated as "Science and Reflection," in *"Question Concerning Technology" and Other Essays*, p. 176.

22. See Heidegger, *Sein und Zeit*, §§15, 16, and 32; *Being and Time*, §§15, 16, and 32.

23. Ibid., p. 68 in the German; pp. 96–97 in the English.

24. Derrida, "Geschlecht II," p. 177.

25. Heidegger, *Sein und Zeit*, p. 55; *Being and Time*, p. 82.

26. For critical commentary on this, see Derrida, "Geschlecht II," pp. 172–78.

27. See Martin Heidegger, *Die Grundbegriffe der Metaphysik: Welt—Endlichkeit—Einsamkeit*, in *Gesamtausgabe*, vols. 29–30 (Frankfurt am Main: Klostermann, 1983), pt. 2, chap. 4, §50, pp. 307ff.; translated as *The Fundamental Concepts of Metaphysics: World, Finitude, Solitude*, trans. William McNeill and Nicholas Walker (Bloomington: Indiana University Press, 1995), §50, pp. 209ff.

28. Martin Heidegger, "Wozu Dichter?," in *Holzwege* (Frankfurt am Main: Klostermann, 1950), pp. 262–63, 266; translated as "What Are Poets For?," in *Poetry, Language, Thought*, pp. 107–10. The argument against Rilke appears in Heidegger's *Parmenides*, pp. 225–40 in the German; pp. 151–61 in the English.

29. Martin Heidegger, "Der Ursprung des Kunstwerkes," in *Holzwege*, p. 60; translated as "The Origin of the Work of Art," in *Poetry, Language, Thought*, p. 73.

30. Heidegger, *Parmenides*, pp. 100, 118–19 in the German; pp. 63, 80 in the English. Italics added.

31. Ibid., pp. 118–19 in the German; p. 80 in the English.

32. Derrida, "Geschlecht II," pp. 173–74.

33. Ibid., p. 174.

34. Ibid., p. 175.

35. Derrida, "Geschlecht II," p. 175.

36. Derrida brings out this point very nicely in "Geschlecht II," p. 175, calling attention to Heidegger's *Gesamtausgabe*, vols. 29–30, p. 290.

37. Ralph Waldo Emerson, "Experience," in *Emerson: Essays and Lectures*, ed. Joel Porte (New York: Library of America, 1983), p. 473.

38. Martin Heidegger, *Beiträge zur Philosophie (Vom Ereignis)*, in *Gesamtausgabe*, vol. 65 (Frankfurt am Main: Klostermann, 1989), pp. 287, 408; translated as *Contributions to Philosophy (from Enowning)*, trans. Parvis Emad and Kenneth Maly (Bloomington: Indiana University Press, 1999), pp. 202–3, 286–88. Also see *Beiträge zur Philosophie*, p. 16: *Machenschaft* is "the arranging of things with a view to the makability of everything, namely, in such a way as to prearrange the irresistibility of the unconditional calculation of each thing."

39. Heidegger, "Die Kehre," pp. 45; "The Turning," pp. 45, 48.

40. Ibid., p. 37 in both the German and the English.

41. Martin Heidegger, "Die Zeit des Weltbildes," in *Holzwege*, p. 93; translated as "The Age of the World Picture," in *"Question Concerning Technology" and Other Essays*, p. 142.

42. Heidegger, "Der Ursprung des Kunstwerkes," pp. 14–15, 19 and 20; "Origin of the Work of Art," pp. 30, 31. Also see pp. 20 and 25 in the English.

43. Rainer Maria Rilke, "The Hand," in *Poems 1912–1926*, trans. Michael Hamburger, a bilingual edition (Redding Ridge, Conn.: Black Swan Books, 1981), pp. 72–73. In another poem, "Handinneres" ("Palm of the Hand"), from October 1924 (*Poems 1912–1926*, pp. 94–95), Rilke suggests, in a biblical image, that there may be hands that, having wandered the desert in exile, arrive with a message of arrival, a messianic message, a message of what is yet to arrive, yet *à-venir*. Hands that are *l'envoi*, an expression of *das Geschick*.

44. For Heidegger's discussion of this unfinished poem by Rilke, see Heidegger, "Wozu Dichter?," p. 290; "What Are Poets For?," p. 136. The poem that Heidegger is discussing here was never finished.

45. Theodor W. Adorno, *Minima Moralia: Reflexionen aus dem beschädigten Leben*, in *Gesammelte Schriften*, vol. 4 (Frankfurt am Main: Suhrkamp, 1980), §14, pp. 36–37; translated as *Minima Moralia: Reflections from Damaged Life*, trans. E. F. N. Jephcott (London: Verso, New Left Books, 1984), p. 34.

46. See Emmanuel Levinas, "The Ego and Totality," in *Collected Philosophical Papers*, ed. and trans. Alphonso Lingis (Pittsburgh: Duquesne University Press, 1998), p. 39.

47. Heidegger, "Der Ursprung des Kunstwerkes," p. 15; "Origin of the Work of Art," p. 26.

48. Ibid., p. 20 in the German; p. 31 in the English.

49. Ibid., p. 83 in the English edition's "Addendum."

50. *Theodor W. Adorno and Walter Benjamin: The Complete Correspondence 1928–1940*, ed. H. Lonitz, trans. Nicholas Walker (Cambridge, Mass.: Belknap Press of Harvard University Press, 1999), letter dated August 1935, p. 107.

51. Adorno, *Minima Moralia*, §19, pp. 43–44 in the German; p. 40 in the English.

52. Ibid., §28, p. 54 in the German; p. 48 in the English.

53. Ibid., §72, p. 122 in the German; p. 110 in the English.

54. Ibid., §14, pp. 36–37 in the German; p. 34 in the English. Note Adorno's use of two words reminiscent of Heidegger's terminology in *Being and Time*.

55. Adorno, *Minima Moralia*, §14, pp. 36–37 in the German; p. 34 in the English.

56. Ibid., §25, p. 52 in the German; p. 47 in the English.

57. Ibid., §21, p. 46 in the German; pp. 42–43 in the English.

58. Ibid. Adorno is probably responding here to Benjamin's remark in *One-Way Street*: "Warmth is ebbing from things. . . . We must compensate for their coldness with our warmth if they are not to freeze us to death." Walter Benjamin "Kaiserpanorama," in *Einbahnstraße*, in *Schriften*, vol. 1, pp. 529–30; translated as "Imperial Panorama," in *One-Way Street*, in Walter Benjamin, *Reflections: Essays, Aphorisms, Autobiographical Writings*, ed. Peter Demetz, trans. Edmund Jephcott (New York: Schocken, 1986), pp. 74–75.

59. Adorno, *Minima Moralia*, §153, p. 281 in the German; p. 247 in the English.

60. Theodor W. Adorno and Max Horkheimer, *Dialektik der Aufklärung: Philosophische Fragmente* (Frankfurt am Main: Fischer, 1969), p. 4; translated as *Dialectic of Enlightenment*, trans. John Cumming (New York: Continuum, 1986), p. xv.

61. Theodor W. Adorno, *Negative Dialektik*, in *Gesammelte Schriften*, vol. 6 (Frankfurt am Main: Suhrkamp, 1973), p. 31; translated as *Negative Dialectics*, trans. E. B. Ashton (New York: Continuum, 1973), p. 19.

62. Ibid., p 29 in the German; p. 17 in the English.

63. Adorno, *Minima Moralia*, aphorism 18, p. 42 in the German; p. 38 in the English. The German reads: "Eigentlich kann man überhaupt nicht mehr wohnen."

64. Heidegger, "Der Ursprung des Kunstwerkes," p. 55; "Origin of the Work of Art," p. 67.

65. Heidegger, "Die Kehre," p. 40; "The Turning," p. 40. On the difference between thinking and the instrumental rationality that rules in our time, see Heidegger, "Zur Seinsfrage," in *Wegmarken*, rev. ed. (Frankfurt am Main: Klostermann, 1976), p. 216; translated as "On the Question of Being," in *Pathmarks*, trans. William McNeill (Cambridge, Eng.: Cambridge University Press, 1998), p. 293: "Reason and its representational activity are only *one* kind of thinking and are by no means self-determined. They are determined, rather, by that which has called thinking to think in the manner of *ratio*. That the domination of *ratio* is

erecting itself as the rationalization of all order, as standardization, and as leveling out in the course of the unfolding of European nihilism, should give us just as much to think about as the accompanying attempts to flee into the irrational."

66. Adorno, *Negative Dialektik*, p. 31; *Negative Dialectics*, p. 19.

67. Maurice Merleau-Ponty, *Phénoménologie de la perception*, 2nd ed. (Paris: Gallimard, 1945), p. 209; translated as *Phenomenology of Perception*, trans. Colin Smith (London: Routledge & Kegan Paul, 1962), p. 179.

68. Heidegger, "Die Zeit des Weltbildes," pp. 96–97; "Age of the World Picture," pp. 145–46. Italics added.

69. Ibid., p. 97 in the German; p. 146 in the English.

70. Ibid., p. 98 in the German; p. 147 in the English.

71. Ibid., p. 101 in the German; p. 151 in the English.

72. Martin Heidegger, *Zollikoner Seminare: Protokolle—Gespräche—Briefe*, ed. Medard Boss (Frankfurt am Main: Klostermann, 1987), p. 130; translated as *Zollikon Seminars: Protocols, Conversations, Letters*, trans. Franz Mayr and Richard Askay (Evanston, Ill.: Northwestern University Press, 2001), p. 100.

73. Heidegger, "Die Kehre," p. 40; "The Turning," p. 41.

74. Ibid., p. 39 in the German; pp. 39–40 in the English.

75. See Heidegger, " . . . Dichterisch wohnet der Mensch . . . ," pp. 187–204; " . . . Poetically Man Dwells . . . ," pp. 213–29.

76. Ibid., p. 196 in the German; pp. 221–22 in the English.

77. Ibid., p. 197 in the German; p. 222 in the English.

78. Ibid., p. 198 in the German, p. 223 in the English.

79. Ibid., pp.199, 202 in the German; pp. 224, 227 in the English.

80. Ibid., p. 204 in the German; p. 229 in the English.

81. Martin Heidegger, "Der Anfang des abendländischen Denkens," in *Heraklit*, in *Gesamtausgabe*, vol. 55 (Frankfurt am Main: Klostermann, 1979), pp. 168–71.

82. Translation from Diels in *Ancilla to the Pre-Socratic Philosophers*, ed. and trans. Kathleen Freeman (Cambridge, Mass.: Harvard University Press, 1978), p. 26.

83. Heidegger, *Parmenides*, pt. 2, §8, p. 237 in the German; p. 159 in the English.

84. Wilhelm von Humboldt, "On the Imagination," trans. Ralph R. Read III, in A. Leslie Willson, ed., *German Romantic Criticism*, vol. 21 (New York: German Library, Continuum, 1982), p. 139.

85. Heidegger, *Beiträge zur Philosophie*, pp. 346, 350; translated as *Contributions to Philosophy (from Enowning)*, trans. Parvis Emad and Kenneth Maly (Bloomington: Indiana University Press, 1999), p. 291.

86. See, for example, ibid., §271.

87. Richard Rorty, *Contingency, Irony and Solidarity* (Cambridge, Eng.: Cambridge University Press, 1989), p. 34.

88. Adorno, *Minima Moralia*, aphorism 21, p. 47 in the German; p. 43 in the English. Also see the reference to "felt contact," in aphorism 153, p. 281 in the German; p. 247 in the English.

89. Rainer Maria Rilke, *Diaries of a Young Poet*, trans. Edward Snow and Michael Winkler (New York: Norton, 1997), p. 88.

90. Heidegger, *Parmenides*, p. 125 in the German.

91. Martin Heidegger, "Die Frage nach der Technik," in *Die Technik und die Kehre*, pp. 24–25; translated as "The Question Concerning Technology," in *"Question Concerning Technology" and Other Essays*, p. 25.

92. Martin Heidegger, "Das Spruch des Anaximander," in *Holzwege*, p. 323; translated as "The Anaximander Fragment," in *Early Greek Thinking*, trans. David Farrell Krell and Frank A. Capuzzi (New York: Harper & Row, 1975), p. 38.

93. Jacques Lacan, *Maurice Merleau-Ponty* (private edition) (Paris, n.d.), p. 13. Cited and translated by Peter Dews in his essay "The Truth of the Subject: Language, Validity and Transcendence in Lacan and Habermas," in Simon Critchley and Peter Dews, eds., *Deconstructive Subjectivities* (Albany: SUNY Press, 1996), p. 168.

94. Jacques Lacan, "L'instance de la lettre dans l'inconscient," in his *Écrits* (Paris: Editions du Seuil, 1966), p. 498.

95. Regarding the disclosive capacity of the hand, see Martin Heidegger, "Das Ding," in *Vorträge und Aufsätze*, pp. 164–80; translated as "The Thing," in *Poetry, Language, Thought*, pp. 167–81. Also see Heidegger, *Parmenides*, §5, pp. 118–30 in the German; §5, pp. 80–87 in the English.

96. Rilke, *Sonnets to Orpheus*, pt. 1, sonnet 16, first strophe, pp. 46–47.

97. Martin Heidegger, "Logos (Heraklit, Fragment 50)," in *Vortrüage und Aufsätze*, pp. 207–29; translated as "Logos (Heraclitus, Fragment B50)," in *Early Greek Thinking*, pp. 59–78.

98. Ibid., p. 218 in the German; p. 68 in the English.

99. Ibid., p. 226 in the German; p. 75 in the English.

100. Ibid., p. 217 in the German; p. 68 in the English.

101. On "methexis," see Heidegger, *Was Heißt Denken?*, p. 135; *What Is Called Thinking?*, p. 222.

102. On "Mnemosyne," see ibid., pp. 6–8 in the German; pp. 10–12 in the English.

103. Martin Heidegger, *Einführung in der Metaphysik*, 3rd ed. (Tübingen: Niemeyer, 1953, 1966), p. 134.

104. Heidegger, *Beiträge zur Philosophie*, p. 298; *Contributions to Philosophy*, p. 210.

454 *Notes to Pages 251–256*

105. Maurice Merleau-Ponty, "Interrogation et intuition," in *Le visible et l'invisible* (Paris: Gallimard, 1964), p. 162; translated as "Interrogation and Intuition," in *The Visible and the Invisible*, trans. Alphonso Lingis (Evanston, Ill.: Northwestern University Press, 1968), p. 121.

106. Martin Heidegger, *Wegmarken*, in *Gesamtausgabe*, vol. 9 (Frankfurt am Main: Klostermann, 1996), pp. 310, 363.

107. But see Martin Heidegger, "Feldweg-Gespräche (1944–1945)," in *Gesamtausgabe*, vol. 77 (Frankfurt am Main: Klostermann, 1995); translated as "Conversation on a Country Path about Thinking," in *Discourse on Thinking* (New York: Harper & Row, 1966).

108. Heidegger, *Beiträge zur Philosophie*, p. 391; *Contributions to Philosophy*, p. 273.

109. Stéphane Mallarmé, *Oeuvres complètes*, ed. Henri Mondor and G. Jean-Aubry (Paris: Éditions Pléiade, 1945), p. 361. And see Mary Oliver, "In Blackwater Woods," in *New and Selected Poems* (Boston: Beacon, 1992):

> To live in this world
> you must be able
> to do three things:
> to love what is mortal; to hold it
> against your bones knowing
> your own life depends on it,
> and, when the time comes to let it go,
> to let it go.

This is an incomparable evocation of the *ontic* attitude of *Gelassenheit*.

110. Heidegger, "Das Ding," p. 180; "The Thing," in *Poetry, Language, Thought*, p. 181.

111. See, e.g., Martin Heidegger, *Bremer und Freiburger Vorträge*, in *Gesamtausgabe*, vol. 79 (Frankfurt am Main: Klostermann, 1994).

112. See Heidegger's discussion of a poem by Rilke, "Wozu Dichter?," p. 255; "What Are Poets For?," p. 99.

113. Heidegger, "Brief über den 'Humanismus,'" in *Wegmarken*, vol. 9 of *Gesamtausgabe*, pp. 360–61; translated as "Letter on Humanism," in *Pathmarks*, p. 274.

114. Heidegger, *Zollikoner Seminare*, p. 273; *Zollikon Seminars*, p. 217.

115. Rilke, *Diaries of a Young Poet*, p. 87. The letter in question is marked "10 March, 1899, Arco." For the Emerson text referred to here, see the epigraph to Section V above in this chapter.

116. *Die Fragmente der Vorsokratiker*, ed. Walter Kranz, trans. Hermann Diels, a bi-lingual Greek-German edition (Berlin: Weidmann, 1974), vol. 1, pp. 156, 178. See Heidegger's discussion of "touching" in Martin Heidegger, 1966–67 Hera-

clitus seminar with Eugen Fink, in *Heraclitus Seminar 1966–1967*, trans. Charles Seibert (University: University of Alabama Press, 1979); and Heidegger, *Heraklit.*

117. Heidegger, *Sein und Zeit*, chap. 2, §13, p. 62; *Being and Time*, p. 89.

118. Martin Heidegger, "Bauen Wohnen Denken," in *Vorträge und Aufsätze*, p. 158; translated as "Building Dwelling Thinking," in *Poetry, Language, Thought*, p. 157.

119. Merleau-Ponty, *Phénoménologie de la perception*, p. 265; *Phenomenology of Perception*, p. 229.

120. Heidegger, *Sein und Zeit*, chap. 5, §29, pp. 137; *Being and Time*, pp. 176–77.

121. Ibid., p. 55 in the German; p. 81 in the English.

122. Ibid.

123. Ibid., p. 346 in the German; p. 396 in the English.

124. Ibid., p. 124 in the German; p. 161 in the English.

125. Rilke, quoted in Heidegger, "Wozu Dichter?," p. 255; "What Are Poets For?," p. 99.

126. Ibid., p. 280 in the German; p. 125 in the English.

127. Ibid., p. 280 in the German; p. 126 in the English.

128. Edmund Husserl, *Ideen zu einer reinen Phänomenologie und phänomeno-logischen Philosophie*, vol. 2: *Phänomenologische Untersuchungen zur Konstitution*, ed. Marly Biemel, in *Husserliana*, in *Gesammelte Werke*, ed. Rudolf Boehm and Samuel Ijsseling, vol. 4 (The Hague: Nijhoff, 1952), p. 159; translated as *Ideas Pertaining to a Pure Phenomenology and to a Phenomenological Philosophy*, bk. 2: *Studies in the Phenomenology of Constitution*, trans. Richard Rojcewicz and Andre Schuwer, in *Collected Works*, vol. 3 (Dordrecht: Kluwer Academic, 1989), p. 167.

129. Rilke, *Diaries of a Young Poet*, pp. 223–24.

130. Ibid., p. 87. This thought appears in the letter of March 10, 1899, in the "Schmargendorf Diary."

131. Ibid., pp. 221–22.

132. Heidegger, "Die Kehre," p. 40; "The Turning," p. 40.

133. Heidegger, *Sein und Zeit*, pp. 391–92; *Being and Time*, pp. 443–44. The echoes, resonances, and reverberations to be found between Heidegger and Benjamin are quite remarkable, and indeed surprising, though one should never minimize the most extreme divergence one can imagine in their political loyalties and programs. But, for example, Benjamin's Konvolut N, notes he prepared for his Arcades Project, is likewise concerned with the decay of memory, the reification of the past, the transmission (*Überlieferung*) of the past, and the "recognizability" or "legibility" of the past, an uncanny past whose potentialities are to be gathered up in what Benjamin terms a *Jetztzeit* and Heidegger would think

of as the moment of "anticipatory resoluteness." Thus, also like Heidegger, Benjamin is vehement in insisting on (1) the difference between the punctate "now" of the empty historical continuum and the disruptive "now" of renewal (Heidegger's *Augenblick*, Benjamin's *Jetztzeit*), in which the past returns, interrupting the continuum, and (2) the distinction between understanding the past as *das Vergangene* and understanding it as *das Gewesene.*

In regard to Heidegger, one must note, of course, a difference between the task of memory assigned in *Being and Time* and the task assigned in his later works. Whereas in *Being and Time* authentic historical memory is to destroy the experience of the present and recover the German nation-state's cultural heritage (memory thus serving a culture of nationalism) in order to create an "authentic" future for the present, in his subsequent work authentic historical memory is to destroy the forgetfulness of the present in order to repeat the originality of the historical origin, contributing to the possible inauguration of a new epoch of being, a new ontological dispensation. Unfortunately, we cannot here explore these matters any further.

134. Martin Heidegger, "Hölderlins Erde und Himmel," in *Erläuterungen zu Hölderlins Dichtung*, 6th ed. (Frankfurt am Main: Klostermann, 1996), p. 178; translated as "Hölderlin's Earth and Heaven," in *Elucidations of Hölderlin's Poetry* (Amherst, Mass.: Humanity Books, 2000), p. 202.

135. Martin Heidegger, "Andenken," in *Erläuterungen zu Hölderlins Dichtung*, 2nd ed., pp. 91–92; translated as "Remembrance," in *Elucidations of Hölderlin's Poetry*, pp. 119–20. For more on questions of memory, see Martin Heidegger, *Besinnung*, in *Gesamtausgabe*, vol. 66 (Frankfurt am Main: Klostermann, 1997); and Martin Heidegger, *Die Geschichte des Seyns*, in *Gesamtausgabe*, vol. 53 (Frankfurt am Main: Klostermann, 1988). Also see Alexander Düttman, *The Memory of Thought* (New York: Continuum, 2000).

136. Heidegger, "Das Spruch des Anaximander," p. 302; "Anaximander Fragment," p. 18.

137. Ibid., pp. 311–12 in the German; p. 27 in the English.

138. Heidegger, "Die Kehre," pp. 38–39; "The Turning," p. 39.

139. Ibid., p. 39 in both the German and the English.

140. Ibid., p. 45 in the German; p. 47 in the English.

141. Ibid.; and Heidegger, "Die Frage nach der Technik," p. 24; "The Question Concerning Technology," p. 24.

142. Heidegger, "Die Frage nach der Technik," pp. 24–25; "The Question Concerning Technology," pp. 24–25: "For humans are truly free only insofar as they belong to the realm of destiny" (*Denn der Mensch erst frei wird, insofern er den Bereich des Geschickes gehört*).

143. Heidegger, "Wissenschaft und Besinnung," p. 64; "Science and Reflection," p. 176.

144. Martin Heidegger, "Aletheia (Heraklit, Fragment 16," in *Vorträge und Aufsätze*, p. 281; translated as "Aletheia (Heraclitus, Fragment B16," in *Early Greek Thinking*, p. 122.

145. Ibid., p. 280 in the German; p. 122 in the English.

146. Merleau-Ponty, *Phénoménologie de la perception*, pp. 170, 226; *Phenomenology of Perception*, pp. 145–46, 194.

147. Rainer Maria Rilke, "The Florence Diary," in *Diaries of a Young Poet*, p. 24.

148. Friedrich Nietzsche, *Daybreak: Thoughts on the Prejudices of Morality*, trans. R. J. Hollingdale (Cambridge, Eng.: Cambridge University Press, 1982), aphorism 130.

149. Heidegger, "Der Ursprung des Kunstwerkes," pp. 58–59; "The Origin of the Work of Art," in *Basic Writings*, trans. David Farrell Krell, rev. ed. (San Francisco: Harper, 1993), pp. 195, 197.

150. Martin Heidegger, *Nietzsche* (Pfullingen: Neske, 1961), vol. 2, pp. 165–66; translated as *Nietzsche*, vol. 4: *Nihilism*, trans. David Farrell Krell (New York: Harper & Row, 1982), pp. 116–17.

151. Martin Heidegger, "Das Ge-stell," in *Bremer und Freiburger Vorträge*, p. 27; and see Wolfgang Schirmacher, *Technik und Gelassenheit* (Freiburg: Alber, 1983), p. 25. Heidegger's lecture on "das Ge-stell" took place in 1949. Also see "Das Ge-stell," p. 56, for the no less chilling discussion of the exterminations: "Sterben sie? Sie werden Beständstücke eines Bestandes der Fabrikation von Leichen. Sterben sie? Sie werden in Vernichtungslagern unauffällig liquidiert. Und auch ohne Solches—Millionen verelenden jetzt in China durch den Hunger in ein Verenden."

152. Quoted in Victor Farias, *Heidegger and Nazism*, ed. Joseph Margolis and Tom Rockmore (Philadelphia: Temple University Press, 1989), p. 285. Also see Rüdiger Safranski, *Martin Heidegger: Between Good and Evil* (Cambridge, Mass.: Harvard University Press, 2001).

153. Heidegger, "Die Kehre," p. 38; "The Turning," p. 38.

Chapter 9

1. Ludwig Wittgenstein, *Culture and Value*, ed. G. H. von Wright and Heikki Nyman, trans. Peter Winch (Chicago: University of Chicago Press, 1984), p. 17.

2. Maurice Merleau-Ponty, "L'entrelacs—Le chiasme," in *Le visible et l'invisible* (Paris: Gallimard, 1964), p. 180; translated as "The Intertwining—The Chiasm," in *The Visible and the Invisible*, trans. Alphonso Lingis (Evanston, Ill.: Northwestern University Press, 1968), p. 137. Hereafter, this volume will be cited in the text as *VI*, followed by the page numbers, first in the French, then in the English.

3. René Descartes, *Meditations on First Philosophy*, in *The Philosophical Works of Descartes*, ed. and trans. Elizabeth Haldane and G. R. T. Ross (New York: Dover, 1955), vol. 1, meditation 6, p. 196.

4. Maurice Merleau-Ponty, *Phénoménologie de la perception*, 2nd ed. (Paris: Gallimard, 1945), p. 168; translated as *Phenomenology of Perception*, trans. Colin Smith (London: Routledge & Kegan Paul, 1962), p. 144. Hereafter, this work will be cited in the text as *PP*, followed by the page numbers, first in the French, then in the English.

5. Maurice Merleau-Ponty, "Le doute de Cézanne," *Sens et non-sens* (Paris: Éditions Nagel, 1948), p. 31; translated as "Cézanne's Doubt," in *Sense and Non-Sense*, trans. Hubert L. Dreyfus and Patricia A. Dreyfus (Evanston, Ill.: Northwestern University Press, 1964), p. 18.

6. Theodor W. Adorno, "Subject and Object," in Andrew Arato and Eike Gebhardt, eds. and trans., *The Essential Frankfurt School Reader* (New York: Continuum, 1987), p. 503.

7. Gotthold Ephraim Lessing, *Emilia Galotti*, in *Gesammelte Werke*, ed. Wolfgang Stammler, vol. 1 (Munich: Hauser, 1959), act 1, scene 4, pp. 133–34; translated as *Emilia Galotti*, in *The Dramatic Works of G. E. Lessing*, trans. Ernest Bell (London: George Bell & Sons, 1878), p. 141. See Maurice Merleau-Ponty, *L'oeil et l'esprit* (Paris: Gallimard, 1964), p. 60, where he says that the moment of painting takes place when vision becomes gesture—an observation that could not disagree more with Lessing's intellectualism.

8. Friedrich Nietzsche, *Beyond Good and Evil*, trans. Walter Kaufman (New York: Vintage, 1966), aphorism 274, p. 222. I wonder whether Siegfried Kracauer's essay "Die Wartenden" was inspired by this aphorism.

9. For works on gesture, see the following: André Leroi-Gourhan, *Le geste et la parole*, vol. 2: *La mémoire et les rhythmes* (Paris: Albin Michel, 1964); Moshe Barash, *Gestures of Despair in Mediaeval and Early Renaissance Art* (New York: New York University Press, 1976); Jean-Claude Schmitt, "The Ethics of Gesture," trans. Ian Patterson, in Michel Feher, Ramona Nadaff, and Nadia Tazl, eds., *Fragments for a History of the Human Body*, Part 2 (New York: Urzone, 1989); Richard Brilliant, *Gesture and Rank in Roman Art* (New Haven: Connecticut Academy of Arts and Sciences, 1963); Jan Bremmer and Herman Roodenburg, eds., *A Cultural History of Gesture* (Ithaca, N.Y.: Cornell University Press, 1991), and, the most recent, Michael C. Corballis, *From Hand to Mouth: The Origins of Language* (Princeton, N.J.: Princeton University Press, 2002).

10. Merleau-Ponty, *L'oeil et l'esprit*, p. 42; translated as *Eye and Mind*, trans. Carleton Dallery, in *The Primacy of Perception* (Evanston, Ill.: Northwestern University Press, 1964), p. 171. Also see Maurice Merleau-Ponty, "L'ontologie cartésienne et l'ontologie d'aujourd'hui," in *Notes de cours 1959–1961* (Paris: Gallimard, 1996), pp. 159–268. In *L'oeil et l'esprit*, Merleau-Ponty points out that

"the cartesian model of vision is touch" (p. 37). This generates two temptations, or risks two dangers: on the one hand, it suggests a vision without mediations, a vision that can achieve the peculiarly compelling evidence reserved for the tangible; on the other hand, it suggests an experience with touch that is too optical, too mirrorlike. It is therefore surprising that, in *Le visible et l'invisible*, Merleau-Ponty falls prey to the second temptation, modeling the experience of touching on the oneiric reflexivity of vision.

11. Merleau-Ponty, "Le doute de Cézanne," p. 27; "Cézanne's Doubt," p. 16.

12. Theodor W. Adorno, "Der Essay als Form," in *Gesammelte Schriften*, vol. 2 (Frankfurt am Main: Suhrkamp, 1974), p. 18; translated as "The Essay as Form," in *Notes to Literature*, trans. Shierry Weber Nicholsen, vol. 1 (New York: Columbia University Press, 1991), p. 11.

13. Merleau-Ponty, *Phénoménologie de la perception*, p. 136; *Phenomenology of Perception*, p. 117.

14. Regarding the laying-down of a layout or "setting," see ibid., pp. 126 and 160 in the French; pp. 108 and 137 in the English. Also see p. 117 in the French; p. 100 in the English. Here, discussing the movement of the hand, Merleau-Ponty writes of "the laying down [*l'installation*] of the first co-ordinates, the anchoring [*l'ancrage*] of the active body in an object, the situation of the body in face of its tasks." And elsewhere in this and other chapters (esp. pp. 122, 135, 158, 164, 334, 363 in the French; pp. 105, 116, 136, 140, 288, 314 in the English), he describes the gesture as "gathered" by its anticipatory projection into an "arc" constitutive in advance of the whole of its movement. Thus we see that the connection with Heidegger's discussion of the *legein* is indeed justified—and very much worth pondering. In this regard, see my book *The Body's Recollection of Being* (London: Routledge & Kegan Paul, 1985), pp. 62–68, 72–80, 90–123, and 140–61. Also see my essay "Hermeneutics as Gesture: A Reflection on Heidegger's 'Logos (Heraclitus, Fragment B50)' Study," in Michael Zimmerman, ed., *The Philosophy of Martin Heidegger*, Tulane Studies in Philosophy, vol. 32 (New Orleans: Tulane University Press, 1984), pp. 69–77.

15. Wittgenstein, *Culture and Value*, p. 36.

16. Also see David Sudnow, *Ways of the Hand* (Cambridge, Mass.: MIT Press, 2001).

17. Theodor W. Adorno, *Minima Moralia: Reflexionen aus dem beschädigten Leben*, in *Gesammelte Schriften*, vol. 4 (Frankfurt am Main: Suhrkamp, 1980), aphorism 116, pp. 203–4; translated as *Minima Moralia: Reflections from Damaged Life*, trans. E. F. N. Jephcott (London: Verso, New Left Books, 1984), p. 181.

18. Philip Sydney, *Arcadia*, second version, quoted in Mario Praz, *Mnemosyne: The Parallel Between Literature and the Visual Arts* (Princeton, N.J.: Princeton University Press, 1970), p. 104.

19. This intercorporeality reminds me of a lecture by Emerson: "I remember

460 *Notes to Pages 288–290*

the manifold cord—the thousand or million stranded cord which my being and every man's being is, . . . so that, if everyone should claim his part in me, I should be instantaneously diffused through creation and individually decease." From which he draws a lesson for morality that could have been written by Levinas: "I am an alms of all and live but by the charity of others." See *The Early Lectures of Ralph Waldo Emerson*, ed. Stephen Whicher, Robert Spiller, and Wallace Williams (Cambridge, Mass.: Harvard University Press, 1961), vol. 3, p. 251. I read Merleau-Ponty's phenomenology as setting the stage for a Levinasian ethics grounded in embodied experience. In his *Phenomenology of Perception* (pp. 415–16 in the French; p. 362 in the English), Merleau-Ponty says that the existence of the social is "deeper than any express perception or judgment"; it is "already there when we come to know or judge it." "Prior to the process of becoming aware, the social exists obscurely and as a summons, . . . a buried voice which has never ceased to speak."

20. Concerning our pre-personal, anonymous experience, temporally prior to and structurally underneath the formation of the subject and the object, see Merleau-Ponty, *Phénoménologie de la perception*, pp. 151, 253, 277, 293–94, 309, and 403–8; *Phenomenology of Perception*, pp. 130, 216, 219, 240, 254, 267, and 351–54.

21. Maurice Merleau-Ponty, *La prose du monde* (Paris: Gallimard, 1969), p. 132; translated as *The Prose of the World*, trans. John O'Neill (Evanston, Ill.: Northwestern University Press, 1973), p. 94.

22. Jürgen Habermas, *The Theory of Communicative Action*, trans. Thomas McCarthy (Boston: Beacon, 1984–87), vol. 1, p. 398.

23. Maurice Merleau-Ponty, "Le concept de la nature," in *Résumés de cours, Collège de France, 1952–1960* (Paris: Gallimard, 1968), p. 115; translated as "The Concept of Nature," pt. 1, in *Themes from the Lectures at the Collège de France, 1952–1960*, trans. John O'Neill (Evanston, Ill.: Northwestern University Press, 1970), p. 82.

24. See Adorno, *Minima Moralia*, aphorism 6, p. 28 in the German. Also see Theodor W. Adorno, *Aesthetic Theory*, trans. Robert Hullot-Kentor (Minneapolis: University of Minnesota Press, 1997), pp. 84–85, 118, 331.

25. George Santayana, *Platonism and the Spiritual Life* (New York: Harper & Row, 1957), p. 260.

26. Also see Merleau-Ponty, *Le visible et l'invisible*, p. 195; *The Visible and the Invisible*, p. 148, where there is an allusion to the *corps glorieux*.

27. Maurice Merleau-Ponty, "Le philosophe et son ombre," in *Signes* (Paris: Gallimard, 1960), p. 213; translated as "The Philosopher and His Shadow," in *Signs*, trans. Richard C. McCleary (Evanston, Ill.: Northwestern University Press, 1964), p. 168.

28. Maurice Merleau-Ponty, "Les relations avec autrui chez l'enfant," in *Cours*

de Sorbonne (Paris: Centre de Documentation Universitaire, 1975); translated as "The Child's Relations with Others," trans. William Cobb, in *The Primacy of Perception* (Evanston, Ill.: Northwestern University Press, 1964), pp. 96–155.

29. Merleau-Ponty, *Le visible et l'invisible,* pp. 181, 183, 187–90, 193–94, 203; *The Visible and the Invisible,* pp. 137, 138, 142–44, 147, 155.

30. Merleau-Ponty, "Le philosophe et son ombre," p. 210; "The Philosopher and His Shadow," p. 167.

31. See F. W. J. von Schelling, *Sämtliche Werke,* ed. K. F. A. Schelling (Stuttgart: Cotta, 1856–61), vol. 7, pt. 1, p. 473.

32. See David Michael Levin, *The Listening Self: Personal Growth, Social Change, and the Closure of Metaphysics* (London: Routledge, 1989).

33. Merleau-Ponty, "Le philosophe et son ombre," p. 220; "The Philosopher and His Shadow," p. 174.

34. F. W. J. von Schelling, *Clara; oder, Uber den Zusammenhang der Natur mit der Geisterwelt,* in *Sämtliche Werke,* vol. 9, p. 53; translated as *Clara; or, On Nature's Connection to the Spirit World,* trans. Fiona Steinkamp (Albany: SUNY Press, 2002), p. 39.

35. Ralph Waldo Emerson, "Nature," in *Emerson: Essays and Lectures,* ed. Joel Porte (New York: Library of America, 1983), p. 46. Emerson's remark reminds me of one of Benjamin's vignettes. Recalling experiences from childhood in *One-Way Street,* Benjamin remarks, "The child's hand enjoys a tactile tryst with the comestibles before his mouth savors their sweetness [*so hat der Tastsinn mit ihnen ein Stelldichein*]." This lovely evocation of childhood synesthesia perfectly captures the "messianic" quality of the child's experience: an openness that rewards the child with a foretaste of paradise. Perhaps one should also recognize here the possibility of an "aftertaste" coming through reminiscence, since, for Benjamin, the moment of authentic experience is always "belated," always *nachträglich.* Walter Benjamin, *Einbahnstraße,* in *Gesammelte Schriften,* ed. Rolf Tiedemann and Hermann Schweppenhäuser, vol. 4 (Frankfurt am Main: Suhrkamp, 1991), pt. 1, p. 114; translated as *One-Way Street,* trans. Edmund Jephcott, in *Walter Benjamin: Selected Writings,* ed. Marcus Bullock, Michael W. Jennings, et al., vol. 1, *1913–1926* (Cambridge, Mass.: Belknap Press of Harvard University Press, 1996), p. 464.

36. Adorno, "Subject and Object," p. 500.

37. See my essay "Visions of Narcissism: Intersubjectivity and the Reversals of Reflection," in Martin Dillon, ed., *Merleau-Ponty Vivant* (Albany: SUNY Press, 1991), pp. 47–90. Also see my essay "Justice in the Flesh," in Galen Johnson and Michael Smith, eds., *Ontology and Alterity in Merleau-Ponty* (Evanston, Ill.: Northwestern University Press, 1990), pp. 35–44.

38. Emmanuel Levinas, "De l'intersubjectivité: Notes sur Merleau-Ponty," in

Hors Sujet (Montpellier: Fata Morgana, 1987), p. 148; translated as "On Intersubjectivity: Notes on Merleau-Ponty," in *Outside the Subject*, trans. Michael B. Smith (Stanford, Calif.: Stanford University Press, 1994), p. 99.

39. Ibid., p. 149 in the French; p. 99 in the English.

40. Also see Merleau-Ponty, *Le visible et l'invisible*, pp. 187–90; pp. 142–44. See my book *The Listening Self*, p. 165: "Reversibility teaches us the root meaning of reciprocity." I want to say that reversibility *schematizes* reciprocity: It is a corporeal schema encoded in the flesh, an implicit or implicate order that calls for, and is carried forward to completion by, the *achievement* of reciprocity—by no means inevitable, or even likely—in social and political life. In retrospect, belatedly, as it were, it can of course seem as if that schema anticipated its social and political realization.

41. See Merleau-Ponty, *Le visible et l'invisible*, pp. 163–66, 169; *The Visible and the Invisible*, pp. 122–24, 127. Also see Maurice Merleau-Ponty, *Éloge de la philosophie* (Paris: Librairie Gallimard, 1953), pp. 18, 38; translated as *In Praise of Philosophy*, trans. John Wild and James Edie (Evanston, Ill.: Northwestern University Press, 1963), pp. 12, 30.

42. See Jean-Jacques Rousseau, *Oeuvres complètes*, vol. 4 (Paris: Gallimard, Éditions Pléiade, 1959), pp. 57–58. Autoaffection plays an important role in many philosophical theories, both French and German. Rousseau says: "I exist and I have senses through which I am affected. . . . My sensations take place in myself, for they make me feel my existence." But of course, the extreme subjectivism in his conclusion, viz., that his "sensations" take place in himself, does not follow from the premise(s). Touching may be said to involve sensation and autoaffection, but it should not be reduced to sensation.

43. See my objections to Merleau-Ponty on this point in "Visions of Narcissism." Also see my essay "Justice in the Flesh."

44. Jean-Luc Nancy, *The Muses*, trans. Peggy Kamuf (Stanford, Calif.: Stanford University Press, 1996), p. 17. Also see p. 107 nn. 30 and 31. Jacques Derrida's book on touch, dedicated to Nancy, had not yet appeared when Nancy wrote *The Muses*. But, as always struggling to wrest free of entanglements in the metaphysics of presence, Derrida had already taken up the question of touch in several earlier articles. Unfortunately, it was only after I had already finished formulating the argument presented in this chapter that Jacques Derrida's book *Le toucher: Jean-Luc Nancy* (Paris: Galilée, 2000) appeared. Our points of critique do not significantly differ, although I think one could mount a defense of Merleau-Ponty that would withstand to some extent the Derridean problematizations—if for no other reason than that Merleau-Ponty's phenomenological treatment of the "original ecstasy" of intercorporeality (e.g., in *Signes*, pp. 219–20) is much more ambiguous than Derrida (e.g., *Le toucher*, pp. 219–25) is willing to recognize.

45. For references and allusions to Kant's discussion of the spatial noncoincidence of the right-hand and left-hand gloves, see Merleau-Ponty, *Le visible et l'invisible*, pp. 314 and 317; *The Visible and the Invisible*, pp. 261 and 263. For Derrida's critical remarks on the question of coincidence and noncoincidence in Merleau-Ponty (*Signes*, pp. 231–32), see Derrida, *Le toucher*, esp. pp. 209–40.

46. Maurice Merleau-Ponty, *La nature: Notes, cours du Collège de France*, ed. Domenique Séglard (Paris: Seuil, 1995), p. 285.

47. Also see Merleau-Ponty, "Le philosophe et son ombre," pp. 209–12; "The Philosopher and His Shadow," pp. 166–67.

48. Merleau-Ponty, "Le philosophe et son ombre," p. 212; "The Philosopher and His Shadow," p. 168.

49. Ibid., p. 213 in the French; p. 168 in the English.

50. Levinas, "De l'intersubjectivité," pp. 150–51; "On Intersubjectivity," pp. 100–101.

51. Merleau-Ponty, "Le philosophe et son ombre," p. 215; "The Philosopher and His Shadow," p. 170.

52. Ibid., p. 220 in the French; p. 174 in the English.

53. Adorno, "Subject and Object," pp. 488–89.

54. Theodor W. Adorno, *Negative Dialectics*, trans. E. B. Ashton (New York: Continuum, 1973), p. xx.

55. After finishing my book, I got around to reading *The Being of the Phenomenon*, by Renaud Barbaras. In his Preface, he wrote: "A theory of the motor body, or rather of movement as an originary mode of the perceived body, is still required. As I have tried to show, such movement refers ultimately to desire as the living subject's ultimate ontological sense" (*The Being of the Phenomenon: Merleau-Ponty's Ontology*, trans. Ted Toadvine and Leonard Lawlor [Bloomington: Indiana University Press, 2004], p. xxiii).

Perhaps the present chapter makes a small contribution to such a theory. Here and in the other chapters, I have been working out a hermeneutic phenomenology that reaches beneath the body's ego-logical desire to touch the body's originary ontological sensibility and bring forth its potential for and contribution to a nonrepressive social existence. The phenomenology of gesture proposed in this chapter suggests a process of self-understanding that, as it fulfills the experience of intercorporeality, develops a corresponding acknowledgment of others in their irreducible singularity and difference. This phenomenology puts us in touch with what is essential for ethical life.

Chapter 10

1. Friedrich Schiller, *On the Aesthetic Education of Man: In a Series of Letters*, trans. Reginald Snell (New York: Ungar, 1965), p. 71, note to thirteenth letter.

2. Theodor W. Adorno, *Negative Dialektik,* in *Gesammelte Schriften,* vol. 6 (Frankfurt am Main: Suhrkamp, 1973), p. 192; translated as *Negative Dialectics,* trans. E. B. Ashton (New York: Continuum, 1973), p. 191.

3. Novalis, "Logologische Fragmente," in *Werke und Briefe,* ed. Alfred Kelletat (Munich: Winkler, 1968), §206, p. 447.

4. Henry David Thoreau, *A Writer's Journal,* ed. Laurence Stapleton (New York: Dover, 1960), p. 30.

5. See Emmanuel Levinas, "Reflections on the Philosophy of Hitlerism," *Critical Inquiry,* 17 (Autumn 1990): 62–70. And see Howard Caygill, *Levinas and the Political* (London: Routledge, 2001), a contribution that rises to the highest level of critical thought and that contains, among other things, an admirably lucid exposition of this quite early (1934) text.

6. Emmanuel Levinas, "Transcendence and Intelligibility," trans. Simon Critchley and Tamra Wright, in *Basic Philosophical Writings,* ed. Robert Bernasconi, Simon Critchley, and Adriaan Peperzak (Bloomington: Indiana University Press, 1996), p. 152.

7. Ibid.

8. Emmanuel Levinas, "Le lieu et l'utopie," in *Difficile liberté: Essais sur le judaïsme* (Paris: Éditions Albin Michel, 1976), pp. 144–45; translated as "Place and Utopia," in *Difficult Freedom: Essays on Judaism,* trans. Sean Hand (Baltimore: Johns Hopkins University Press, 1997), p. 100. Is this "usurpation," for which atonement is required, not also implied by Anaximander's fragment—the only one we know of? See Martin Heidegger, "Das Spruch des Anaximander," in *Holzwege* (Frankfurt am Main: Klostermann, 1950), pp. 296–343.

9. See Dieter Henrich's "Ethics of Autonomy," in an edited collection of his essays, *The Unity of Reason: Essays on Kant's Philosophy* (Cambridge, Mass.: Harvard University Press, 1994), p. 102.

10. Franz Rosenzweig, *The Star of Redemption* (Notre Dame: University of Notre Dame Press, 1971), pt. 1, bk. 3, p. 82.

11. Emmanuel Levinas, *Totalité et infini: Essai sur l'extériorité* (The Hague: Nijhoff, 1961), p. 30; translated as *Totality and Infinity: An Essay on Exteriority,* trans. Alphonso Lingis (Pittsburgh: Duquesne University Press, 1969), p. 59. Hereafter, this work will be cited in the text as *TI,* followed by the page numbers, first in the French, then in the English.

12. Walter Benjamin, "Das Kunstwerk im Zeitalter seiner technischen Reproduzierbarkeit," in *Gesammelte Schriften,* ed. Rolf Tiedemann and Hermann Schweppenhäuser (Frankfurt am Main: Suhrkamp, 1972–89), vol. 1, pt. 2, pp. 465–66; translated as "The Work of Art in the Age of Mechanical Reproduction," in *Illuminations,* ed. Hannah Arendt, trans. Harry Zohn (1968; reprint, New York: Schocken, 1969), p. 240. I have modified the translation, replacing

"appropriation" by "reception," in keeping with Benjamin's use of the word *Rezeption.*

13. Emmanuel Levinas, "Langage et proximité," in *En découvrant l'existence avec Husserl et Heidegger* (Paris: J. Vrin, 1967), p. 15; translated as "Language and Proximity," in *Collected Philosophical Papers,* ed. and trans. Alphonso Lingis (Pittsburgh: Duquesne University Press, 1998), p. 116.

14. See Theodor Adorno's critical commentary on Kant's conception of freedom, in *Negative Dialektik,* pp. 211–94; *Negative Dialectics,* pp. 211–99.

15. Emmanuel Levinas, "État d'Israël et religion d'Israël," in *Difficile liberté,* p. 303; translated as "The State of Israel and the Religion of Israel," in *Difficult Freedom,* p. 216.

16. Levinas, "Le lieu et l'utopie," p. 146; "Place and Utopia," p. 101.

17. For a contrasting interpretation of modernity, see Jürgen Habermas, *Die Zukunft der menschlichen Natur* (Frankfurt am Main: Suhrkamp, 2001).

18. John Rawls, *A Theory of Justice* (Cambridge, Mass.: Harvard University Press, 1978), p. 587.

19. Max Horkheimer, *Gesammelte Schriften,* vol. 6 (Frankfurt am Main: Fischer Taschenbuch, 1991), p. 288.

20. Martin Buber, *Tales of the Hasidim,* trans. Olga Marx (New York: Schocken, 1947), p. 130.

21. Rainer Maria Rilke, *Diaries of a Young Poet,* trans. Edward Snow and Michael Winkler (New York: Norton, 1997), p. 37.

22. Alexis de Tocqueville, *Democracy in America,* trans. Henry Reeve (London: Cumberlege, 1952), p. 27.

23. Jean-Jacques Rousseau, *Émile; or, On Education,* trans. Allen Bloom (New York: Basic Books, 1979), p. 1.

24. Emmanuel Levinas, *Autrement qu'être, ou Au-delà de l'essence,* 2nd ed. (The Hague: Nijhoff, 1978), p. 233; translated as *Otherwise Than Being, or Beyond Essence,* trans. Alphonso Lingis (Pittsburgh: Duquesne University Press, 1998), p. 185, italics added. Hereafter, this work will be cited in the text as *AE,* followed by the page numbers, first in the French, then in the English.

25. Emmanuel Levinas, "Diachronie et représentation," in *Entre nous: Essais sur le penser-à-l'autre* (Paris: Éditions Grasset et Fasquelle, 1991), p. 174; translated as "Diachrony and Representation," in *Entre Nous: Thinking-of-the-Other,* trans. Michael B. Smith and Barbara Harshav (New York: Columbia University Press, 1998), p. 168.

26. Emmanuel Levinas, "La philosophie et l'idée de l'infini," in *En découvrant l'existence,* p. 176; translated as "Philosophy and the Idea of Infinity," in *Collected Philosophical Papers,* p. 58. And see Immanuel Kant, *Kritik der Urteilskraft,* in *Gesammelte Schriften,* ed. Königliche Preußische Akademie der Wissenschaften

(Berlin: George Reimer, 1900–), vol. 5, §28, pp. 257 and 262; translated as *Critique of Judgment*, trans. Werner S. Pluhar (Indianapolis: Hackett, 1987), §28, pp. 121, 128

27. Emmanuel Levinas, "Humanisme et an-archie," in *Humanisme de l'autre homme* (Montpellier: Fata Morgana, 1972), p. 82; translated as "Humanism and An-archy," in *Collected Philosophical Papers*, p. 139.

28. Ibid.

29. Emmanuel Levinas, "Freedom and Command," in *Collected Philosophical Papers*, p. 17.

30. Emmanuel Levinas, *L'au-delà du verset: Lectures et discours talmudiques* (Paris: Éditions de Minuit, 1982), avant-propos, p. 12; translated as *Beyond the Verse: Talmudic Lectures and Discussions*, trans. Gary D. Mole (London: Athlone, 1994), preface, p. xv.

31. Emmanuel Levinas, "L'espace n'est pas à une dimension," in *Difficile liberté*, pp. 359–67; translated as "Space Is Not One-Dimensional," in *Difficult Freedom*, pp. 259–64.

32. Ibid., p. 366 in the French; p. 264 in the English.

33. Emmanuel Levinas, "Utopia and Socialism," in *Alterity and Transcendence*, trans. Michael Smith (London: Athlone, 1999), p. 116.

34. Emmanuel Levinas, "L'état de Caesar et l'état de David," in *L'au-delà du verset*, pp. 211, 220; translated as "The State of Caesar and the State of David," in *Beyond the Verse*, pp. 179–83.

35. Emmanuel Levinas, "Textes Messianiques," in *Difficile libérté*, p. 138; translated as "Messianic Texts," in *Difficult Freedom*, p. 96.

36. Ibid., p. 131 in the French; p. 91 in the English.

37. Richard Cohen, ed., *Face to Face with Levinas* (Albany: SUNY Press, 1986), p. 32.

38. Emmanuel Levinas, "Les droits de l'homme et les droits de l'autrui," in *Hors sujet* (Montpellier: Fata Morgana, 1987), pp. 185–86; translated as "The Rights of Man and the Rights of the Other," in *Outside the Subject*, trans. Michael B. Smith (Stanford, Calif.: Stanford University Press, 1994), p. 124.

39. See Levinas, "Textes Messianiques," pp. 129–32; "Messianic Texts," pp. 89–92.

40. Emmanuel Levinas, "Les virtues de la patience," in *Difficile Libérté*, pp. 218–19; translated as "The Virtues of Patience," in *Difficult Freedom*, p. 155.

41. Emmanuel Levinas, "Peace and Proximity," in *Basic Philosophical Writings*, p. 168.

42. Ibid., p. 169.

43. Levinas, "Le lieu et l'utopie," p. 147; "Place and Utopia," p. 102.

44. Emmanuel Levinas, "Ethics as First Philosophy," trans. Sean Hand and Michael Temple, in *The Levinas Reader*, ed. Sean Hand (Oxford: Blackwell, 1989), p. 84.

45. Ralph Waldo Emerson "Experience," in *Emerson: Essays and Lectures*, ed. Joel Porte (New York: Library of America, 1983), pp. 472, 488.

46. See Novalis, *Werke und Briefe* (Munich: Winkler-Verlag, 1962), p. 419. One reads there, standing by itself, without interpretative commentary: "Ich bin Du."

47. Paul Celan, *Poems*, trans. Michael Hamburger (New York: Perseus, 1988), pp. 178–81. This is a bilingual edition. The German reads:

> Schweigen, wie Gold gekocht, in
> verkohlten, verkohlten
> Händen.
> Finger, rauchdünn.
> Wie Kronen
> Luftkronen . . .

48. Primo Levi, *"Se questo è un uomo" e "La tregua"* (Torino: Einaudi, 1989), p. 16; translated as *Survival in Auschwitz*, trans. Stuart Woolf (New York: Simon & Schuster, 1996), pp. 19–21.

49. F. W. J. von Schelling, "Stuttgarter Vorlesungen," in *Sämtliche Werke*, ed. K. F. A. Schelling (Stuttgart: Cotta, 1856–61), vol. 7, p. 476.

50. F. W. J. von Schelling, *Clara; oder, Über den Zusammenhang der Natur mit dem Geisterwelt*, in *Sämtliche Werke*, vol. 9, p. 53; translated as *Clara; or, On Nature's Connection to the Spirit World*, trans. Fiona Steinkamp (Albany: SUNY Press, 2002), p. 39.

51. Ludwig Wittgenstein, *Culture and Value*, ed. G. H. von Wright and Heikki Nyman, trans. Peter Winch (Chicago: University of Chicago Press, 1984), p. 50.

52. George Santayana, *Platonism and the Spiritual Life* (New York: Harper & Row, 1957), p. 260.

53. Emmanuel Levinas, "La révélation dans la tradition juive," in *L'au-delà du verset*, p. 169. Two pages earlier, Levinas refers to "the physiognomy" of the typography in the Talmudic texts, thereby tightening the bond between the Jewish body and the inscriptions of the Law.

54. Buber, *Tales of the Hasidim*, p. 107. Also see my essay "The Living Body of Tradition," in David Michael Levin, *The Body's Recollection of Being* (London: Routledge & Kegan Paul, 1985).

55. Buber, *Tales of the Hasidim*, p. 144. For more on the question of the trace—in particular, its significance as a figure in the ethics of Levinas, see my essay "Tracework: Myself and Others in the Moral Phenomenology of Merleau-Ponty and Levinas," *International Journal of Philosophical Studies*, 6, no. 3 (Oct. 1998): 345–92.

56. G. W. F. Hegel, *Faith and Knowledge*, trans. Walter Cerf and H. S. Harris (Albany: SUNY Press, 1977), p. 117.

57. See my essay "The Embodiment of the Categorical Imperative: Kafka,

Foucault, Benjamin, Adorno, and Levinas," *Philosophy and Social Criticism*, 27, no. 4 (July 2001): 1–20. Also see three very valuable books by Bernhard Waldenfels: *Antwortregister* (Frankfurt am Main: Suhrkamp, 1994), *Das leibliche Selbst* (Frankfurt am Main: Suhrkamp, 2000), and *Bruchlinien der Erfahrung: Phänomenologie, Psychoanalyse, Phänomenotechnik* (Frankfurt am Main: Suhrkamp, 2002). Concerning questions about "human nature," see Habermas, *Die Zukunft der menschlichen Natur*.

58. See the chapter "The Invisible Face of Humanity," published in my book *The Philosopher's Gaze: Modernity in the Shadows of Enlightenment* (Los Angeles: University of California Press, 1999), pp. 234–334.

59. Emmanuel Levinas, "In Memoriam Alphonse de Waelhens: De la sensibilité," in *Hors sujet*, p. 163; translated as "In Memory of Alphonse de Waelhens," in *Outside the Subject*, p. 108.

60. Emmanuel Levinas, "The Youth of Israel," in *Nine Talmudic Readings*, trans. Annette Aronowicz (Bloomington: Indiana University Press, 1990), p. 135. This is a point of great importance, one that he asserts in many different texts and contexts.

61. In *Sensibility and Singularity: The Problem of Phenomenology in Levinas* (Albany: SUNY Press, 2001), John Drabinski says, "To be an ethical subject is to be a body awakened from one's pre-original past and to find oneself unable to account for the history of the very sense constitutive of my unicity." I agree. But after "awakening" to the other's existence, I then have a responsibility and a task: to attempt—though I will fail—to retrieve, belatedly, by the recurrence of recollection, this absent, impoverished sense, already withdrawn from presence, that obligates me to the other. To "be-for-the-other" is to have belatedly felt, or rather to have as a bodily felt sense, the "force of an alterity within me" that already affected me prior to the emergence of egological consciousness.

62. Emmanuel Levinas, "Sans identité," in *Humanisme de l'autre homme*, p. 94; translated as "No Identity," in *Collected Philosophical Papers*, p. 147.

63. See my essay "Persecution: The Self at the Heart of Metaphysics," in Eric Nelson, Kent Still, and Antje Kapust, eds., *Addressing Levinas: Ethics, Phenomenology, and the Judaic Tradition* (forthcoming in 2005 from Northwestern University Press).

64. Also see Levinas, "Humanisme et an-archie," p. 80; "Humanism and Anarchy," p. 137.

65. Levinas, *L'au-delà du verset*, avant-propos, p. 13; *Beyond the Verse*, preface, p. xvi.

66. Caygill, *Levinas and the Political*, p. 187.

67. See my essay "Embodiment of the Categorical Imperative."

68. Levinas, "Humanisme et an-archie," pp. 80–81; "Humanism and Anarchy," p. 137.

69. Ibid.

70. Levinas, "Reflections on the Philosophy of Hitlerism," pp. 68–69.

71. Schelling, *Clara*, p. 53 in the German; p. 39 in the English. Perhaps Schelling was also the inspiration for Emerson's lovely statement "Infancy is the perpetual Messiah, which comes into the arms of fallen men, and pleads with them to return to paradise." See Ralph Waldo Emerson, "Nature," in *Emerson: Essays and Lectures*, p. 46.

72. Concerning this "inscription," see Levinas, *Autrement qu'être*, pp. 191–92; *Otherwise Than Being*, p. 150.

73. Also see ibid., p. 140 in the French; p. 110 in the English. And see a very useful essay by Bernard Casper, "La temporalisation de la chair," in Jean-Luc Marion, ed., *Positivité et transcendence: Études sur Levinas et la phénoménologie* (Paris: Presses Universitaires de France, 2000), pp. 165–80.

74. See Hannah Arendt, *Eichmann in Jerusalem: A Report on the Banality of Evil* (New York: Penguin Books, 1994), p. 126.

75. Also see Emmanuel Levinas, "Dieu et la philosophie," in *De Dieu qui vient à l'idée* (Paris: Vrin, 1982), p. 120; translated as "God and Philosophy," in *Levinas Reader*, p. 182.

76. Jean-Paul Sartre, *Being and Nothingness: An Essay in Phenomenological Ontology*, trans. Hazel E. Barnes (New Jersey: Citadel, 1956), p. 197.

77. There is an important, though brief, discussion of shame in Levinas, *Totalité et infini*, pp. 55–56; *Totality and Infinity*, p. 84.

78. Emmanuel Levinas, "La signification et le sens," in *Humanisme de l'autre homme*, p. 53; translated as "Meaning and Sense," in *Basic Philosophical Writings*, p. 57.

79. F. W. J. von Schelling, *Philosophische Untersuchungen über das Wesen der menschlichen Freiheit und die damit zusammenhängenden Gegenstände*, in *Sämtliche Werke*, vol. 7, pt. 1, *1805–1810*, p. 411; translated as *Of Human Freedom*, trans. James Gutmann (Chicago: Open Court, 1936), p. 92.

80. Walter Benjamin, *Ursprung des deutschen Trauerspiels*, in *Gesammelte Schriften*, vol. 1, pt. 1, p. 299; translated as *The Origin of German Tragic Drama*, trans. John Osborne (London: Verso, New Left Books, 1998), p. 175.

81. Moses Mendelssohn, *Jerusalem; Oder über religiöse Macht und Judentum*, in *Gesammelte Schriften: Jubiläumsausgabe*, vol. 8 (Stuttgart: Frommann-Holzboog, 1974), p. 193; translated as *Jerusalem; or, On Religious Power and Judaism*, trans. Allan Arkush (Hanover, Vt.: Brandeis University Press, 1983), p. 128.

82. Ibid., pp. 158, 169 in the German; pp. 91–92 and 102 in the English.

83. Levinas, *L'au-delà du verset*, avant-propos, p. 9; *Beyond the Verse*, preface, p. xii.

84. In a letter to Walter Benjamin, Gershom Scholem argued that the esoteric communications in the Sacred Scriptures are not lost but merely at present in-

decipherable. See Walter Benjamin and Gershom Scholem, *Briefwechsel 1933– 1940*, ed. Gershom Scholem (Frankfurt am Main: Suhrkamp, 1980), p. 147.

85. Friedrich Hölderlin, "Wie wenn am Feiertage . . . ," in *Sämtliche Werke*, ed. Paul Stapf (Berlin: Tempel-Verlag, 1960), p. 295; translated as "As when on holiday . . . ," trans. Michael Hamburger, in *"Hyperion" and Selected Poems*, ed. Eric Santner, bilingual edition (New York: Continuum, 1990), pp. 192–93. The German reads: "Und was zuvor geschah, doch kaum gefühlt, / Ist offenbar erst jetzt."

86. Levinas, "Diachronie et représentation," p. 178; "Diachrony and Representation," in *Entre Nous: Thinking-of-the-Other*, p. 172.

87. But what about the phrase "forgotten or secret"? Perhaps at least one more comment on this passage is required, since this phrase could also be thought to contradict the reading proposed here. I take Levinas to be rejecting, here, both the representations of memory that figure in psychoanalysis, for which it would be a question of retrieving from the unconscious a traumatism that has been repressed, and those representations that figure in philosophical deployments of psychology and anthropology.

88. Levinas, "Langage et proximité," p. 223; "Language and Proximity," p. 114.

89. Levinas, "In Memoriam Alphonse de Waelhens," p. 166; "In Memory of Alphonse de Waelhens," p. 110.

90. Ibid., p. 163 in the French; p. 108 in the English.

91. Gershom Scholem, *On the Kabbalah and Its Symbolism* (New York: Schocken, 1969), p. 116.

92. Levinas, "La révélation dans la tradition juive," p. 173: "l'homme peut ce qu'il doit, il pourra maîtriser les forces hostiles de l'Histoire et réaliser un règne messianique annoncé par les prophètes; l'attente du Messie est la durée même du temps ou l'attente de Dieu; mais alors l'attente n'atteste plus une absence de Godot qui ne viendra jamais, il atteste la relation avec ce qui ne peut entrer dans le présent, lequel est trop petit pour l'Infini. *Mais c'est peut-être dans un ritualisme réglant tous les gestes de la vie quotidienne*, dans le fameux 'joug de la Loi,' que réside l'aspect le plus caractéristique de la difficile liberté juive: dans le rituel, il n'y a rien de numineux, aucune idolâtrie; c'est une distance *dans* la nature *à l'égard* de la nature, et peut-être ainsi précisément l'attente du Plus-Haut." Italics added.

93. Theodor W. Adorno, *Minima Moralia: Reflexionen aus dem beschädigten Leben*, in *Gesammelte Schriften*, vol. 4 (Frankfurt am Main: Suhrkamp, 1980), §116, p. 205; translated as *Minima Moralia: Reflections from Damaged Life*, trans. E. F. N. Jephcott (London: Verso, New Left Books, 1984), p. 182. And see Manfred Frank, *"Unendliche Annäherung": Die Anfänge der philosophischen Frühromantik* (Frankfurt am Main: Suhrkamp, 1997).

94. Levinas, "La philosophie et l'idée de l'infini," p. 173; "Philosophy and the Idea of Infinity," p. 55. Italics added.

95. Levinas, "Langage et proximité," p. 230; "Language and Proximity," pp. 120–21.

96. Ibid.

97. Levinas "Peace and Proximity," p. 166.

98. Also see *Ancilla to the Pre-Socratic Philosophers,* ed. and trans. Kathleen Freeman (Cambridge, Mass.: Harvard University Press, 1978), p. 33. In fragment 122, attributed to Heracleitus of Ephesos, the philosopher, using the word ἀγχιβασίην—composed of ἄγχι, meaning "near" or "close by," and βαίνω, meaning "to move," "to go," "to advance"—cryptically invokes what seems to be an unending approach or approximation. See also *Die Fragmente der Vorsokratiker,* ed. Walter Kranz, trans. Hermann Diels, a bi-lingual Greek-German edition (Berlin: Weidmann, 1974), vol. 1, p. 178. Also see fragment 26, p. 156, on "rühren," "to touch on," translations of ἅπτομαι.

99. Also see Levinas, "Langage et proximité," pp. 219, 221 and 235; "Language and Proximity," pp. 111, 112, and 125.

100. Ibid., p. 228 in the French; p. 119 in the English.

101. Ibid., p. 229 in the French; p. 120 in the English.

102. Emmanuel Levinas, *À l'heure des nations* (Paris: Éditions de Minuit, 1988), pp. 32–33; translated as *In the Time of Nations,* trans. Michael B. Smith (Bloomington: Indiana University Press, 1994), pp. 24–25. In a few places, I have modified the translation.

103. Emmanuel Levinas, *Of God Who Comes to Mind,* trans. Bettina Bergo (Stanford, Calif.: Stanford University Press, 1998), p. 67.

104. Levinas, "Langage et proximité," pp. 230–31; "Language and Proximity," p. 121.

105. Jacques Derrida, "Violence et metaphysique: Essai sur la pensée d'Emmanuel Lévinas," in *L'écriture et la différance* (Paris: Éditions du Seuil, 1967), pp. 142, 167; translated as "Violence and Metaphysics," in *Writing and Difference,* trans. Alan Bass (Chicago: University of Chicago Press, 1978), pp. 95, 113. In *The Anti-Christ,* trans. R. J. Hollingdale(New York: Penguin Books, 1984), §29, p. 141, Friedrich Nietzsche adverts to the prohibition on touch: "We recognize a condition of morbid sensibility of the sense of touch which makes it shrink back in horror from every contact, every grasping of a firm object. . . . [When translated] into its ultimate logic, [this means] an instinctive hatred of every reality, . . . flight into the 'ungraspable,' into the 'inconceivable.'" This anxiety, along with the cultural taboo it enforces, was perhaps at its most intense in mediaeval and baroque Christianity. See, e.g., Mario Rosa, "The Nun," in Rosario Villari, ed., *Baroque Personae* (Chicago: University of Chicago Press), p. 199: In 1629, in a decision regarding a convent in Lecce, Italy, the Church hierarchy and the Congregation of Religions ordered the bars of the parlatory grate to be made closer together, "so that," as they put it, "the nuns can in no way reach their hands through it to touch the hand, the finger, or any other part of a person from

outside the Convent." Levinas's ethical "prohibition," if that is what it should be called, is very different: for him, it is not an exigency defending against anxieties due to sexual attractions, but rather a demonstration of respect for the other. Also see Waldenfels, *Bruchlinien der Erfahrung*, pp. 64–80, on "Tasten und mehr als Tasten," "Kontakt und Kontiguität," and "Sich-angerührt-fühlen."

106. Concerning touch, contact, and tactility, see Aristotle, *De Anima*, bk. 2, chaps. 6, 10, 11, and bk. 3, chaps. 10–13; Edmund Husserl, *Ideen*, vol. 2, chap. 3, §§635–40; Jacques Derrida, "La main de Heidegger," in *Psyche: Inventions de l'autre* (Paris: Galilée, 1987); Jacques Derrida, *Le toucher: Jean-Luc Nancy* (Paris: Galilée, 2000); Didier Franck, *Chair et corps: Sur la phénoménologie de Husserl* (Paris: Minuit, 1981); Luce Irigaray, "The Fecundity of the Caress," in Cohen, *Face to Face with Levinas*, pp. 254–85; Antje Kapust, *Berührung ohne Berührung: Ethik und Ontologie bei Merleau-Ponty und Levinas* (Munich: Wilhelm Fink, 1999); Jean-Luc Nancy, *Corpus* (Paris: Métaillié, 1992) and *Le sens du monde* (Paris: Galileé, 1993); Waldenfels, *Das leibliche Selbst* and *Bruchlinien der Erfahrung*; and Martin Heidegger, *Die Grundbegriffe der Metaphysik: Welt—Endlichkeit—Einsamkeit*, in *Gesamtausgabe*, vols. 29–30 (Frankfurt am Main: Klostermann, 1983), §47, where he discusses whether and how the rock and the lizard perched on it may be said to be touching one another.

107. Ralph Waldo Emerson, *Emerson in His Journals*, ed. Joel Porte (Cambridge, Mass.: Harvard University Press, 1982), p. 242. The entry is dated "Summer 1840."

108. Walter Benjamin, "Welt und Zeit," in *Gesammelte Schriften*, vol. 6, p. 99; translated as "World and Time," in *Walter Benjamin: Selected Writings*, ed. Marcus Bullock, Michael W. Jennings, et al., trans. Rodney Livingstone (Cambridge, Mass.: Belknap Press of Harvard University Press, 1996–2003), vol. 2, *1927–1934*, pp. 226–27.

109. Levinas, "Langage et proximité," p. 225; "Language and Proximity," p. 116.

110. Levinas, *Hors sujet*, pp. 166–67; *Outside the Subject*, p. 110.

111. Ibid., p. 163 in the French; p. 108 in the English.

112. Levinas, "Langage et proximité," p. 227; "Language and Proximity," pp. 117–18.

113. Levinas, *Hors sujet*, p. 166; *Outside the Subject*, p. 110.

114. Levinas, "Langage et proximité," p. 225; "Language and Proximity," p. 116.

115. Ibid. Also see pp. 230–31 in the French; pp. 120–21 in the English.

116. Ibid., p. 227 in the French; p. 118 in the English.

117. Ibid.

118. Levinas, "Diachronie et représentation," p. 166; "Diachrony and Representation," in Emmanuel Levinas, *Time and the Other*, trans. Richard A. Cohen (Pittsburgh: Duquesne University Press, 1987), p. 99.

119. Levinas, "Langage et proximité," pp. 225–26; "Language and Proximity," pp. 116–17.

120. Henry James, *Selected Letters*, ed. Leon Edel (Cambridge, Mass.: Harvard University Press, 1974), p. 325. Words from a letter to W. Morton Fullerton, September 26, 1890.

121. St. Augustine, *De Beata Vita*, trans. Ludwig Schopp (St. Louis: Herder, 1939), pp. 124–31.

122. Buber, *Tales of the Hasidim*, p. 91.

123. Levinas, *Hors sujet*, p. 170; *Outside the Subject*, p. 114.

124. Emmanuel Levinas, *Le temps et l'autre* (Montpellier: Fata Morgana, 1979), pp. 81–82; translated as *Time and the Other*, p. 89, italics added. For another very important discussion of the caress, see "Langage et proximité," p. 228; "Language and Proximity," pp. 118–19, wherein Levinas briefly reflects on our relation with things and animals and evokes, in exceptionally rhapsodic language, the "poetry" that can be manifested in the tenderness of the caress.

125. See, for example, Walter Benjamin, "The Work of Art in the Age of Mechanical Reproduction," in *Illuminations*, p. 222.

126. See Levinas, "Langage et proximité," p. 230; "Language and Proximity," p. 120.

127. This lovely phrase comes from a letter sent by Rilke to Ilse Jahr, dated February 22, 1923. See *Letters of Rainer Maria Rilke, 1910–1926*, trans. Jane B. Greene and M. D. Herter Norton (New York: Norton, 1972), pp. 323–25.

128. Also see Levinas, "La signification et le sens," p. 19.

129. Jean-Luc Nancy, *The Birth to Presence*, trans. Brian Holmes et al. (Stanford, Calif.: Stanford University Press, 1993), p. 206.

130. Levinas, "Langage et proximité," p. 230; "Language and Proximity," p. 121.

131. Ibid., pp. 230–31 in the French; p. 121 in the English.

132. Derrida, *Le toucher*, p. 94.

133. Ibid., pp. 82, 108, 291.

134. Ibid., p. 94.

135. Levinas, "Diachronie et représentation," pp. 182–83; "Diachrony and Representation," in *Entre Nous: Thinking-of-the-Other*, p. 176.

136. In this regard, see Mary Oliver, "The Swan," in *New and Selected Poems* (Boston: Beacon, 1992):

> the path to heaven
> doesn't lie down in flat miles.
> It's in the imagination
> with which you perceive
> this world,
>
> and the gestures
> with which you honor it.

137. Walter Benjamin, "Theologisch-Politisches Fragment," in *Gesammelte Schriften*, vol. 2, pt. 2, p. 438; translated as "Theologico-Political Fragment," in *Reflections: Essays, Aphorisms, Autobiographical Writings*, ed. Peter Demetz, trans. Edmund Jephcott (New York: Schocken, 1986), p. 313. Italics added.

138. Benjamin, *Ursprung des deutschen Trauerspiels*, p. 373; *Origin of German Tragic Drama*, p. 197. Also see Bernhard Waldenfels, "Pausen und Zäsuren," in *Bruchlinien der Erfahrung*, pp. 215–22.

139. Friedrich Hölderlin, "Anmerkungen zum Ödipus," in *Sämtliche Werke*, ed. Stapf (1960), p. 1056.

140. Walter Benjamin, "Erkenntnistheoretisches, Theorie des Fortschritts," Konvolut N, in *Gesammelte Schriften*, vol. 5, pt. 1, p. 570; translated as "Re: Theory of Knowledge, Theory of Progress," in *The Arcades Project*, trans. Howard Eiland and Kevin McLaughlin (Cambridge, Mass.: Belknap Press of Harvard University Press, 1999), p. 456.

141. Emmanuel Levinas, "La ruine de la représentation," in *En découvrant l'existence*, p. 135.

142. Levinas, "Langage et proximité," p. 229; "Language and Proximity," p. 120.

143. Emmanuel Levinas, "Les nations et la presence d'Israel," in *À l'heure des nations*, pp. 123–24; translated as "Nations and the Presence of Israel," in *In the Time of Nations*, p. 108.

144. *Franz Kafka: Parables and Paradoxes*, ed. Nahum Glatzer, trans. Clement Greenberg, bilingual edition (New York: Schocken, 1946), pp. 8off. Kafka's writing always opens many interpretive possibilities. Without wishing to foreclose any of them, I propose to take this seemingly paradoxical statement to mean this: if only a morally transformed, already redeemed world could recognize the Messiah's coming, then by the time his coming was recognized, the prophetically anticipated time of messianicity that he brought would already have taken place, because only a transformed humanity could recognize the Messiah as Messiah. Thus, if the time of actual arrival is not the same as the time of recognition, not the same as the time of realization, then the arrival that is recognized will be that of a belated, or *nachträglich*, recognition, and, as such, the recognition of an arrival that, in a certain sense, is no longer necessary. The messianic era will have begun "not on the last day, but on the day after," because redemptive transformation is not sufficient; there must also be reflexive awareness and fulfilled understanding. This statement provokes me to wonder whether the "man from the country" in Kafka's parable "Before the Law," a version of which appears in *The Trial*, could perhaps be interpreted as the Messiah, patiently waiting for the defenses constructed to prevent his coming—the innumerable "open" doors, more traps than doors, through which he would have to pass into the world and into our hearts—to be demolished. Or perhaps, at the least, de-

constructed. The doors are all open, seeming to give access to the Law; but in effect, their endless interpretability blocks access, preventing the Messiah's divine justice from reaching and transforming the force of this Law. So he waits—until his hope is finally extinguished. On this reading, the parable would be lamenting the fact that the world is not yet ready for the end of the epoch of positive (legislated) Law that the Messiah's coming announces. Everything depends, of course, on whether the "Law" is understood as divine decree or political legislation.

145. Walter Benjamin, "Geschichtsphilosophische Thesen," in *Schriften*, ed. Theodor W. Adorno and Gretel Adorno (Frankfurt am Main: Suhrkamp, 1955), vol. 1, pp. 495, 506; translated as "Theses on the Philosophy of History," in *Illuminations*, pp. 254, 264. Translation modified.

146. See Jacques Derrida, Round Table held at University of California at Davis, 1997, in Richard Kearney and M. Dooley, eds., *Questioning Ethics* (New York: Routledge, 1998).

147. Levinas, *Le temps et l'autre*, pp. 83–84.

148. Levinas, "Langage et proximité," p. 229; "Language and Proximity," p. 119.

149. Ibid., pp. 229–30 in the French; p. 120 in the English.

150. Benjamin, "Geschichtsphilosophische Thesen," p. 495; "Theses on the Philosophy of History," p. 254.

151. Maurice Blanchot, *The Step Not Beyond*, trans. Lycette Nelson (Albany: SUNY Press, 1992), p. 106.

152. Levinas, "Les nations et la présence d'Israel," p. 123; "Nations and the Presence of Israel," p. 108. On the *Unterbrechung*, see Waldenfels, *Bruchlinien der Erfahrung*, pp. 215–22.

153. Edmund Husserl, *Husserliana*, in *Gesammelte Werke*, ed. Rudolf Boehm and Samuel Ijsseling, vol. 3 (The Hague: Nijhoff, 1976), pt. 1, p. 115.

154. Emmanuel Levinas, "Freibourg, Husserl et la phénoménologie," *Revue d'Allemagne des pays de la lange allemande*, 5, no. 43 (May 1931): 409–10; translated as "Frieburg, Husserl and Phenomenology," in Emmanuel Levinas, *Discovering Existence with Husserl*, ed. and trans. Richard A. Cohen and Michael B. Smith (Evanston, Ill.: Northwestern University Press, 1998), p. 36.

155. See, for example, Emmanuel Levinas, "La conscience non-intentionelle," in *Entre nous: Essais*, pp. 134–36; translated as "Non-intentional Consciousness," in *Entre Nous: Thinking-of-the-Other*, pp. 125–27.

156. Levinas, "Diachronie et représentation," p. 166; "Diachrony and Representation," in *Entre Nous: Thinking-of-the-Other*, p. 160.

157. See Rudolf Bernet, "L'autre du temps," in Marion, *Positivité et transcendence*, p. 149.

158. Maurice Merleau-Ponty, *Phénoménologie de la perception*, 2nd ed. (Paris:

Gallimard, 1945), p. viii; translated as *Phenomenology of Perception*, trans. Colin Smith (London: Routledge & Kegan Paul, 1962), p. xiv.

159. Emmanuel Levinas, "La trace de l'autre," in *En découvrant l'existence*, pp. 194–96.

160. Also see Emmanuel Levinas, "Un Dieu-homme," in *Entre Nous: Essais*, p. 75.

161. Levinas, "Sans identité," p. 95; "No Identity," p. 148. This remark also appears in Levinas, *Autrement qu'être*, p. 10; *Otherwise Than Being*, p. 8.

162. This is also the argument I take away from Levinas, *Autrement qu'être*, pp. 56–57; *Otherwise Than Being*, p. 44.

163. Levinas, *À l'heure des nations*, p. 123; *In the Time of Nations*, p. 108.

164. Ibid.

165. Benjamin and Scholem, *Briefwechsel 1933–1940*, p. 163. In *Origin of German Tragic Drama*, Benjamin refers to a "mode of thought" for which "not only transitoriness but also guilt should seem evidently to have its home in the province of idols and of the flesh." Further illuminating what is at stake, the text continues: "The allegorically significant is prevented by guilt from finding fulfillment of its meaning in itself" (*Origin*, pp. 224–25; and see *Ursprung des deutschen Trauerspiels*, in *Gesammelte Schriften*, vol. 1, pp. 348–49). Levinas also situates guilt in the flesh; and he too regards guilt as aporetic, in the sense that it prevents or evades the moral comportment that its significance implicitly commands. But Levinas would of course have his own way of describing this matter: For him, the experience of guilt that, through preoriginary "substitution," haunts and traumatizes the flesh, compelling it toward the realization of its ethical obligation, also causes us to repress the bodily felt sense of that ethical assignment, which cannot find fulfillment "in itself," but finds it only in an ethical relation to the other. For this reason, one could perhaps argue that the *allegorical* nature of the inscription by grace of which this assignment is registered inevitably imposes a deeply encrypted form of suffering—a suffering entailed by the impossibility of realizing and fulfilling the meaning of the inscription. An allegorical interpretation of the inscription may be, as Benjamin suggests, the only "conceivable salvation."

166. See Levinas in dialogue with Richard Kearney, in Cohen, *Face to Face with Levinas*, p. 23.

167. Levinas, "Humanisme et an-archie," p. 75; "Humanism and An-archy," p. 134.

168. Emmanuel Levinas, "Judaïsme et temps présent," in *Difficile liberté*, pp. 292–99; translated as "Judaism and the Present," in *Difficult Freedom*, pp. 208–15.

169. Levinas, *Le temps et l'autre*, p. 81; *Time and the Other*, p. 88.

170. Walter Benjamin, "Kritik der Gewalt," in *Gesammelte Schriften*, vol. 2,

pt. 1, p. 193; translated as "Critique of Violence," in *Benjamin: Selected Writings*, vol. 1, p. 245.

171. See Levi, *"Se questo è un uomo" e "La tregua."*

172. Rosenzweig, *Star of Redemption*, pp. 296–97.

173. Benjamin, "Geschichtsphilosophische Thesen," p. 506; "Theses on the Philosophy of History," p. 263.

174. Also see Caygill, *Levinas and the Political*, especially his deeply thoughtful chapters "Prophetic Politics" and "Israel in Universal and Holy History," pp. 128–98.

175. Benjamin, "Welt und Zeit," pp. 98–100; "World and Time," pp. 226–27. Also see Walter Benjamin, "Trauerspiel und Tragödie," in *Gesammelte Schriften*, vol. 2, pt. 1, pp. 133–37, where he distinguishes five orders of time: the empirical (concerning natural cause-effect relations), the historical (homogenous, empty time, filled with hope but never bringing fulfillment), tragic time (fulfilling the fate that individuates), the time of the "mourning-play" (time empty and bereft of all hope), and finally, messianic time (the time when the promise of redemption is fulfilled).

176. See Caygill's admirably lucid chapters "Prophetic Politics" and "Israel in Universal and Holy History," in his *Levinas and the Political*, pp. 128–98. Also see Levinas, "Les droits de l'homme et les droits de l'autre," p. 185; "The Rights of Man and the Rights of the Other," p. 123; and Emmanuel Levinas, "Au-delà de l'état dans l'état," in *Nouvelles lectures talmudiques* (Paris: Éditions de Minuit, 1996), pp. 43–76.

177. Levinas, "Textes messianiques," p. 103; "Messianic Texts," p. 69.

178. The no less anguishing question of national forgiveness and reconciliation, which Derrida explores with subtlety and acuity in *On Cosmopolitanism and Forgiveness*, cannot be addressed here. Suffice it to say that I follow Derrida in emphasizing the "aporetic logic" of forgiveness: the paradox that forgiveness can forgive only the unforgivable. For although, as a matter of moral principle, forgiveness must always be unconditional and without measure, nevertheless, pragmatically, forgiveness must always be proportionate to the perpetrator's repentance. See Jacques Derrida, *On Cosmopolitanism and Forgiveness*, trans. Mark Dooley and Michael C. Hughes (New York: Routledge, 2001).

179. Also see Hanna Arendt, *The Human Condition* (Chicago: University of Chicago Press, 1958), pp. 236–43, where she argues that forgiveness is a source of creative renewal, a certain moment of "natality" overcoming cycles of resentment and revenge. And see Jacques Derrida, "Le siècle et le pardon," trans. Michael C. Hughes, in *On Cosmopolitanism and Forgiveness*.

180. Walter Benjamin, "Die Bedeutung der Zeit in der moralischen Welt," in *Gesammelte Schriften*, vol. 6, p. 98; translated as "The Meaning of Time in the Moral Universe," in *Benjamin: Selected Writings*, vol. 1, pp. 286–87. In another

early fragment, Benjamin says: "authentic divine power can manifest itself other than destructively"—but "only in the world to come (the world of fulfillment)." However, "whenever divine power enters into the secular world, it breathes ['a revolutionary force' of] destruction" ("Welt und Zeit," p. 98; "World and Time," pp. 226–27).

181. Emmanuel Levinas, "Four Talmudic Readings," in *Nine Talmudic Readings*, p. 48. See Derrida's critical remarks on Levinas's interpretation of forgiveness, in *Les Cahiers du Grif*, no. 3 (1977): 131–65; reprinted, with alterations, in Thomas Albrecht, Elizabeth Constable, and Georgia Albert, eds., *A Sarah Kofman Reader* (Stanford, Calif.: Stanford University Press, 2004).

182. Levinas, *Difficile liberté*, p. 46; *Difficult Freedom*, p. 26.

183. Simon Wiesenthal, *Die Sonnenblume: Eine Erzählung mit Kommentaren* (Frankfurt am Main: Ullstein, 1984), p. 43; translated as *The Sunflower: On the Possibilities and Limits of Forgiveness*, trans. H. A. Piehler (New York: Schocken, 1990), p. 41.

184. Norman Gobetti, "Il perdono è una cosa che si fa con le mani," *L'indice dei libri del mese*, no. 1 (Jan. 2003): 27.

185. Hayim Nahman Bialik and Yehoshua Hana Ravnitzky, eds., *The Book of Legends: Sefer Ha-Aggadah*, trans. William G. Braude (New York: Schocken, 1992), p. 361.

186. Yehuda Amichai, "Tourists," in *Selected Poetry of Yehuda Amichai*, ed. and trans. Chaim Bloch and Stephen Mitchell (New York: Harper & Row, 1986), pp. 137–38.

187. Paul Auster, *The Book of Illusions* (New York: Holt, Picador, 2002), p. 227. And see Frantz Fanon, *The Wretched of the Earth* (New York: Grove, 1963), p. 71, where he describes the prejudices and hatreds raging in racism and colonialism as a "violence just under the skin." But Levinas also recognizes another "violence under the skin," namely, the trauma of a preoriginary responsibility: "The more I return to myself, the more I divest myself under the traumatic effect of persecution, of my freedom as a constituted, willful, imperial subject, the more I discover myself to be responsible. . . . I am 'in myself' through the others" (*Autrement qu'être*, p. 143; *Otherwise Than Being*, p. 112).

188. Novalis, "Das allgemeine Brouillon," in *Gesammelte Werke*, ed. Carl Seelig (Zürich: Bühl-Verlag, 1945), p. 305; translated as "General Drafts," in *Philosophical Writings*, ed. and trans. Margaret M. Stoljar (Albany: SUNY Press, 1997), p. 128. The German reads: "Der größte Teil unsers Körpers, unsrer Menschheit selbst, schläft noch tiefen Schlummer." In another collection of fragments, Novalis also says: "There is only one temple in the world and that is the human body. Nothing is holier [*heiliger*] than this high form [*Gestalt*]. Bowing to people is an expression of respect [*Huldigung*] for this revelation in the flesh

[*dieser Offenbarung im Fleisch*]." Novalis, *Werke,* ed. Gerhard Schulz (Munich: C. H. Beck, 1969), p. 530.

189. *The Early Lectures of Ralph Waldo Emerson,* ed. Stephen Whicher, Robert Spiller, and Wallace Williams (Cambridge, Mass.: Harvard University Press, 1961), vol. 3, p. 251.

190. Paul Celan, "Die Pole," in *Gesammelte Werke,* ed. Beda Allemann, Stefan Reichert, and Rolf Bücher, vol. 3 (Frankfurt am Main: Suhrkamp, 1983), p. 105.

Index of Names

Achilles, 404n1
Adam, 161
Adeimantus, 9
Adorno, Theodor W., xviii–xxvii
  passim, xxxi, xxxiv, xlii, xlv, 54, 57,
  63, 72–76 *passim*, 80, 94–144 *pas-
  sim*, 162, 196, 200, 202, 207–8,
  231–37, 245, 276, 278, 287, 289,
  293, 305, 311, 316f, 343, 350, 381,
  415n75, 416n91, 427n32, 428–29n43,
  429n53, 431n71, 432n80, 440n105,
  451n58
Agamben, Giorgio, xix–xx, xlv, 33, 45,
  187–94 *passim*, 407n6f, 412n50
Alcmaeon of Croton, 201
Aletheia, 245
Althusser, Louis, xliii
Amichai, Yehuda, 390
Andreas-Salomé, Lou, 1
Apollo, 175
Arendt, Hannah, xx, xxiv–xxviii *passim*,
  6–7, 67, 75f, 343, 427n32, 477n179
Aristotle, xxiii, xxviii f, xxxii, xxxv,
  xxxix f, 5, 9–20 *passim*, 84, 105, 144,
  188, 215, 219, 225, 237, 250, 278–81
  passim, 405n3
Ate, 202
Augustine, Saint, 247, 358
Auster, Paul, 390

Barbaras, Renaud, 463n55
Baudelaire, Charles Pierre, 20, 154–56,
  166, 172, 193, 195, 434n22
Beckett, Samuel, 164
Benjamin, Walter, xvii ff, xxxvii–xl
  passim, 20ff, 33, 40, 56, 80, 96–103
  passim, 126, 132, 134, 138–203 *passim*,
  207–9, 232, 236, 265–66, 315, 325,
  345, 355, 359–69 *passim*, 373–80
  passim, 384–88, 407–8n6, 417nn94–
  95, 418n99, 433n8, 433n9, 434n22,
  435n40, 438n79, 439n100, 440n105,
  442n183, 443n142, 444n153, 445n164,
  446n164, 451n58, 455–56n133, 461n35,
  469n84, 476n165, 477n175, 478n180
Blanchot, Maurice, xvii, xxx f, xxxiii, 7,
  33, 45f, 370, 418n100
Bourdieu, Pierre, 94–95
Brancati, Vitaliano, xv
Brandes, Daniel, 422n25
Brecht, Bertolt, 174, 184, 186
Breton, André, 84
Buber, Martin, 318, 330, 359, 365

Calvino, Italo, xlii
Cavell, Stanley, xxxv
Caygill, Howard, 337, 464n5, 477n176
Celan, Paul, xliii–xliv, 202, 328, 394,
  448n12

M E R I D I A N

Crossing Aesthetics

Neil Hertz, *George Eliot's Pulse*

Maurice Blanchot, *The Book to Come*

Susannah Young-ah Gottlieb, *Regions of Sorrow: Anxiety and Messianism in Hannah Arendt and W. H. Auden*

Jacques Derrida, *Without Alibi*, edited by Peggy Kamuf

Cornelius Castoriadis, *On Plato's 'Statesman'*

Jacques Derrida, *Who's Afraid of Philosophy? Right to Philosophy 1*

Peter Szondi, *An Essay on the Tragic*

Peter Fenves, *Arresting Language: From Leibniz to Benjamin*

Jill Robbins, ed. *Is It Righteous to Be?: Interviews with Emmanuel Levinas*

Louis Marin, *Of Representation*

Daniel Payot, *The Architect and the Philosopher*

J. Hillis Miller, *Speech Acts in Literature*

Maurice Blanchot, *Faux pas*

Jean-Luc Nancy, *Being Singular Plural*

Maurice Blanchot / Jacques Derrida, *The Instant of My Death / Demeure: Fiction and Testimony*

Niklas Luhmann, *Art as a Social System*

Emmanual Levinas, *God, Death, and Time*

Ernst Bloch, *The Spirit of Utopia*

Giorgio Agamben, *Potentialities: Collected Essays in Philosophy*

Ellen S. Burt, *Poetry's Appeal: French Nineteenth-Century Lyric and the Political Space*

Jacques Derrida, *Adieu to Emmanuel Levinas*

Werner Hamacher, *Premises: Essays on Philosophy and Literature from Kant to Celan*

Aris Fioretos, *The Gray Book*

Deborah Esch, *In the Event: Reading Journalism, Reading Theory*

Winfried Menninghaus, *In Praise of Nonsense: Kant and Bluebeard*

David E. Wellbery, *The Specular Moment: Goethe's Early Lyric and the Beginnings of Romanticism*

Edmond Jabès, *The Little Book of Unsuspected Subversion*

Hans-Jost Frey, *Studies in Poetic Discourse: Mallarmé, Baudelaire, Rimbaud, Hölderlin*

Pierre Bourdieu, *The Rules of Art: Genesis and Structure of the Literary Field*

Nicolas Abraham, *Rhythms: On the Work, Translation, and Psychoanalysis*

Jacques Derrida, *On the Name*

David Wills, *Prosthesis*

Maurice Blanchot, *The Work of Fire*

Jacques Derrida, *Points . . . : Interviews, 1974–1994*

J. Hillis Miller, *Topographies*

Philippe Lacoue-Labarthe, *Musica Ficta (Figures of Wagner)*

Jacques Derrida, *Aporias*

Emmanuel Levinas, *Outside the Subject*

Jean-François Lyotard, *Lessons on the Analytic of the Sublime*

Peter Fenves, *"Chatter": Language and History in Kierkegaard*

Jean-Luc Nancy, *The Experience of Freedom*

Jean-Joseph Goux, *Oedipus, Philosopher*

Haun Saussy, *The Problem of a Chinese Aesthetic*

Jean-Luc Nancy, *The Birth to Presence*